IMPLEMEN

GAAS

2007/2008

IMPLEMENTING

GAAS

2007/2008

A Practical Guide
to Auditing and Reporting

Peter Chidgey
Sarah Nendick
BDO Stoy Hayward LLP

Wolters Kluwer (UK) Ltd
145 London Road
Kingston upon Thames
Surrey KT2 6SR
Tel: 0870 777 2906
Fax: 020 8247 1184
E-mail: info@cch.co.uk
www.cch.co.uk

© 2007 Wolters Kluwer (UK) Ltd

Auditing Practices Board material © 2007 Reproduced with the permission of the Auditing Practices Board.

ISBN 978-1-84140-904-7

First edition 1993	Eighth edition 2001
Second edition 1995	Ninth edition 2002
Reprinted 1995	Tenth edition 2003
Third edition 1996	Eleventh edition 2004
Fourth edition 1997	Twelfth edition 2005
Fifth edition 1998	Thirteenth edition 2006
Sixth edition 1999	Fourteenth edition 2007
Seventh edition 2000	

British Library Cataloguing-in-Publication Data
A catalogue record for this book is available from the British Library.

Typeset by YHT Ltd, London
Printed and bound in Italy by Legoprint-Lavis (TN)

SUMMARY OF CHAPTERS

CONTENTS

Contents

Contents

Contents

Contents

Contents

Contents

Contents

Contents

Contents

Contents

PREFACE

In writing the preface to the 14th edition of *Implementing GAAS*, it is interesting to reflect how much things have changed in the intervening years. The main emphasis when the first edition was published was on the newly formed UK Auditing Practices Board and its programme to issue 30 new SASs. Although based on the International Standards of Auditing (ISAs) this was clearly a very national initiative.

Fourteen years later the emphasis is clearly international. The APB have called a halt to new UK standards (unless deemed necessary by a change in law) because of the influence of the EU and the International Audit and Assurance Standards Board (IAASB).

In June 2006 the European Commission issued the Statutory Audit Directive. Amongst other things this enables ISAs to be adopted throughout Europe. This, however, will not happen until the IAASB's 'Clarity Project' has been completed, which is anticipated to be towards the end of 2008.

The purpose of the project is to improve the overall readability and understandability of ISAs through structural and drafting improvements. Part of this involves clarifying levels of obligations imposed on the auditor by substituting 'shall' for 'should' where the expectation is that a requirement is universal and eliminating ambiguity in the existing 'non bold' text as to what is required and what is guidance.

This programme has been made more difficult because some of the standards are being revised as well as clarified. However, progress is being made and the IAASB has now issued 20 'clarity EDs' of which four have been finalised out of a potential 33 standards in the project.

The finalised standards have effective dates for periods beginning on or after 15 December 2008 – so will not take effect until December 2009 year end for most audits. As the APB will not formally adopt these standards in the UK until all the standards have been finalised, the effective date will inevitably end up being later than this.

One area of potential conflict (and future difficulty) is the degree of prescription. The APB favours a more 'principle based' rather than 'detailed' set of standards. The view reflected in their annual review is despite more prescriptive requirements helping with monitoring, this could well be counter productive, as quality may suffer as the incentive and opportunity to exercise professional judgement is restricted, if not discharged.

Whatever the outcome, the new standards based on the revised ISAs will result in some major changes and we have described the effects on the main standards in the relevant chapters.

UK domestic law is also changing. The long-awaited Companies Act 2006 contains a number of changes in relation to auditors' appointments and reporting responsibilities. Amongst the more noteworthy changes are those requiring the 'senior statutory auditor' to sign the audit report in his or her own name for and on behalf of the auditors, the introduction of a criminal offence of knowingly or recklessly issuing a misleading false or deceptive auditors' report and provision allowing the limitation of auditors' liability. These are all expected to apply from April 2008.

There have been a number of other developments in the UK for which we have updated the book, the chief ones being:

- The revised PN15 – *The Audit of Occupational Pension Schemes in the United Kingdom.*
- Updates to PN12 (Revised) – *Money Laundering – Interim Guidance for Auditors in the United Kingdom* and PN16 *Bank Reports for Audit Purposes (Revised) – Interim Guidance.*
- Bulletin 2006/5 *The Combined Code on Corporate Governance – Requirements of Auditors under the Listing Rules of the Financial Services Authority and the Irish Stock Exchange.*
- Bulletin 2006/6 *Auditor's Reports on Financial Statements in the United Kingdom,* which provides updated illustrative examples of audit reports, and 2007/1 *Example Reports by Auditors under Company Legislation in the United Kingdom.*
- The FRC's discussion paper *Promoting Audit Quality.*
- The APB draft guidance on illustrative examples of documentation for the smaller company.
- The ICAEW Audit and Assurance Faculty's papers on *Assurance Reports on Internal Controls of Service Organisations Made Available to Third Parties* and *Management of Risk and Liability.*

As with earlier editions, we have kept for the time being to the following conventions.

- Where there is an existing guideline in an area and a proposed Standard or Practice Note, we have, unless indicated in the text, examined the subject from the point of view of the proposal on the basis that it is a more authoritative and up-to-date indication of GAAS.

- International standards and other overseas guidance is only discussed in detail when they have been exposed by the APB in a national context.
- Where new Standards have been issued but in a number of cases the old guidelines have not been withdrawn, we have ignored the old guidelines except where they have provided helpful insights.

Finally, we would like to acknowledge the contributions of Bob Hymas, Don Bawtree and Philip Rego, who have helped in the drafting of various chapters. Their help has been invaluable.

Peter Chidgey

Sarah Nendick

BDO Stoy Hayward LLP
April 2007

PART 1
INTRODUCTION

1 THE NATURE OF AUDITING STANDARDS

1.1 INTRODUCTION

For the purpose of this book Generally Accepted Auditing Standards (GAAS) are the rules which are acknowledged as those by which auditors can measure their performance and by which others can measure them. These may be formal or informal, written or unwritten. In the widest sense these standards are set by a variety of groups:

- government in the form of legislation;
- professional or standard setting bodies in the form of pronouncements of varying authority;
- courts in judgments on cases involving auditors;
- practitioners whose 'internal' standards may become a generally accepted 'norm' especially in areas where there are no public pronouncements.

In practice it is the professional or standard setting bodies who are the greatest source of authority in this area. Traditionally, government has not become involved in the detail of auditing; UK legislation specifies the matters on which auditors must report but it has been left to the professional bodies to issue detailed standards and guidance covering how auditors collect the evidence to support their opinion and the form that opinion takes in different circumstances. A similar approach has developed in recent years in the area of 'general' standards, for example, independence or maintaining competence, where detailed regulation has again been left to the professional bodies.

For these reasons, this book concentrates mainly on the standards and guidance issued by professional and standard setting bodies as the main source of GAAS, referring where necessary to the decisions of courts or to the practices of firms where these are relevant.

1.2 LIMITATIONS OF STANDARDS

Because of the nature of auditing the development of a framework of Auditing Standards which will provide answers to all the questions and problems faced by auditors is not feasible. There will always be judgements over questions – such as how much evidence is enough in a given case? – to which Auditing Standards will not provide a solution. This is aggravated by the relationship between auditing and accounting. Auditors form opinions on financial statements, the preparation of which involves, amongst other things, appraisals of the likely outcome of uncertain future events. Auditing Standards are also constrained by this uncertainty. Also, methods of producing financial statements adapt to changing circumstances and auditors must be able to adapt their approaches. Because of this GAAS can only be a framework to assist auditors in making judgements and forming opinions, not a rigid system of rules.

1.3 AUTHORITATIVE BODIES

In the main, GAAS emanates from the pronouncements of authoritative bodies which have been established to issue standards and which are accepted by audit practitioners and the bodies which regulate them as having that authority. From the point of view of this book GAAS encompasses not only the standards issued by those bodies but also any guidance on their application.

What constitutes GAAS, in practice, is subject to evolution and change. Auditors in the UK must have regard to a large number of pronouncements issued by various bodies in order to ascertain what actually constitutes GAAS. The main bodies which either issue or have issued standards or related guidance are:

- Auditing Practices Board (APB);
- International Auditing and Assurance Standards Board (IAASB); and
- various other accountancy bodies, for example, The Institute of Chartered Accountants in England and Wales (ICAEW) which issues guidance through its Audit Faculty.

Increasingly auditors have also had to have regard to the pronouncements of the International Auditing and Assurance Standards Board (IAASB). In December 2004 this process took a step forward when the APB issued all of the International Standards of Auditing (ISAs) as ISAs (UK and Ireland) supplemented with additional guidance from a UK and Ireland perspective. Further detail is given below.

1.4 THE AUDITING PRACTICES BOARD

The Auditing Practices Board was established in 1991 by the Consultative Committee of Accountancy Bodies (CCAB). In April 2002, the new APB commenced its activities and adopted the extant guidance previously issued by the old APB. The new APB was at the time a subsidiary of the Accountancy Foundation. Following the publication of the reports of the Consultative Group on Audit and Accounting (CGAA) and the Government 'Review of the Regulatory Regime of the Accountancy Profession' the Auditing Practices Board fell under the remit of the Financial Reporting Council (FRC).

The FRC was established in 1990 to promote good financial reporting through its, then, two subsidiaries, the Accounting Standards Board and the Financial Reporting Review Panel. When the FRC's original remit was enlarged it took a more pro-active role in relation to corporate governance, compliance with company law and accounting standards. It also assumed new responsibilities in relation to overseeing the self-regulation of the professional bodies.

The FRC has five subsidiary boards:

- the Accounting Standards Board;
- the Financial Reporting Review Panel;
- the Auditing Practices Board;
- the Professional Oversight Board for Accountancy; and
- the Accountancy Investigation and Discipline Board.

The FRC and its subsidiaries are funded jointly by the accountancy profession, business and the Government.

In December 2004, and following the announcement of its intention to adopt ISAs, the APB issued a revised Scope and Authority of Pronouncements. The Statement sets outs:

- an overview of the types of document issued by the APB;
- the level of authority associated with each type of document; and
- the regulatory regime supporting APB pronouncements derived from legislation and the rules of the accountancy bodies.

The Statement includes the *Auditors' Code* which sets out the principles that the APB expects to guide the conduct of auditors, as well as underlying its own guidance and the ethical standards of the professional bodies. The code is set out in **Table 1**.

TABLE 1:   *The Auditors' Code*

Accountability

Auditors act in the interests of primary stakeholders, whilst having regard to the wider public interest. The identity of primary stakeholders is determined by reference to the statute or agreement requiring an audit: in the case of companies, the primary stakeholder is the general body of shareholders.

Integrity

Auditors act with integrity, fulfilling their responsibilities with honesty, fairness, candour, courage and confidentiality. Confidential information obtained in the course of the audit is disclosed only when required in the public interest, or by operation of law.

Objectivity and independence

Auditors are objective and provide impartial opinions unaffected by bias, prejudice and compromise and conflicts of interest. Auditors are also independent: this requires them to be free from situations and relationships which would make it probable that a reasonable and informed third party would conclude that the auditors' objectivity either is impaired or could be impaired.

Competence

Auditors act with professional skill, derived from their qualification, training and practical experience. This demands an understanding of financial reporting and business issues, together with expertise in accumulating and assessing the evidence necessary to form an opinion.

Rigour

Auditors approach their work with thoroughness and with an attitude of professional scepticism. They assess critically the information and explanations obtained in the course of their work and such additional evidence as they consider necessary for the purposes of their audit.

Judgement

Auditors apply professional judgement taking account of materiality in the context of the matters on which they are reporting.

Clear complete and effective communication

Auditors' reports contain clear expressions of opinion and set out information necessary for a proper understanding of that opinion. Auditors communicate audit matters of governance interest arising from the audit of financial statements with those charged with governance.

Association

Auditors allow their reports to be included in documents containing other information only if they consider that the additional information is not in conflict with the matters covered by their report and they have no cause to believe it to be misleading.

Providing value

Auditors add to the reliability and quality of financial reporting; they provide to directors and officers constructive observations arising from the audit process; and thereby contribute to the effective operation of business, capital markets and the public sector.

The APB issues four types of pronouncement:

- International Standards of Auditing (UK and Ireland) (ISAs);
- Statements of Auditing Standards (SASs);
- Practice Notes; and
- Bulletins.

1.4.1 International Standards of Auditing (UK and Ireland)

International Standards of Auditing (ISAs) are issued by the International Auditing and Assurance Standards Board (IAASB). In recent years the IAASB has functioned as the independent standard setting body under the auspices of the International Federation of Accountants (IFAC).

In May 2004, the APB announced their intention to adopt the ISAs issued by the IAASB for use in the UK and Ireland, first reviewing all of the SASs to identify instances where they contain higher standards than those contained in the equivalent ISAs, and supplementing the ISAs accordingly. The resultant International Standards of Auditing (UK and Ireland) ('ISAs (UK and Ireland)') were issued, first for consultation, and then in final form in 2004. They are effective for the audit of financial statements for periods commencing on or after 15 December 2004.

The APB believed the change to international-based standards provided the following strategic advantages:

- maintaining the stature of UK and Irish standards internationally, particularly following earlier accounting and auditing failures, and the anticipated requirement from the European Commission for ISAs to be adopted by all Member States; and
- allowing the APB to benefit from future improvements to ISAs.

The ISAs (UK and Ireland) comprise both the standards (which are set out in bold type), which are prescriptive, and explanatory and other material designed to assist auditors in interpreting and applying the standards but which is not prescriptive.

The members of the CCAB undertake to adopt all auditing standards (ISAs (UK and Ireland) and SASs) promulgated by the APB. Failures by auditors to comply with the relevant standards will therefore be enquired into by the appropriate accountancy body.

Only members of a Recognised Supervisory Body (RSB) are eligible for appointment as auditors of limited companies. The ISAs (UK and Ireland) and SASs, as relevant, constitute the technical standards adopted by the RSBs to be applied in company audit work. The RSBs must also monitor and enforce compliance with them.

APB pronouncements, in particular ISAs (UK and Ireland) and SASs, are likely to be taken into account when the adequacy of the work of auditors is being considered in a court of law or in other contested situations.

Like SAS 100 *Objective and General Principles Governing an Audit of Financial Statements* before it, ISA (UK and Ireland) 200 *Objective and General Principles Governing an Audit of Financial Statements* is a 'grandfather standard' and sets out a number of basic principles and assumptions on which all other standards are based.

ISA (UK and Ireland) 200 requires auditors to conduct their audits in accordance with ISAs (UK and Ireland) and with an attitude of professional scepticism. This means that the audit should be approached with a questioning mind, with auditors making critical assessments of the evidence obtained, remaining alert for contradictions or evidence which makes them question the reliability of documents or management representations.

Auditors should also comply with the APB's Ethical Standards (see **Chapter 2**) and other ethical pronouncements issued by their professional body.

ISA (UK and Ireland) 200 requires auditors to plan and perform their work in order to reduce audit risk to an acceptably low level, having regard to the requirements of the ISAs (UK and Ireland), their professional body, legislation and the terms of the engagement. Auditors must make an assessment of the audit risk, but are not responsible for the detection of misstatements that are not material to the financial statements taken as a whole.

1.4.2   Statements of Auditing Standards

Statements of Auditing Standards (SASs) contain basic principles on essential procedures with which auditors are required to comply in any audit of financial statements they carry out. SASs may also apply to other types of audit and related service. They are effective for the audit of financial statements for periods commencing before 15 December 2004.

SASs derive their authority from three sources:

• their adoption by the members of CCAB;
• their role in audit regulation; and
• the courts.

The APB announced in May 1992 that it intended to review and update all existing Auditing Standards and guidelines to take account of:

• their decision to distinguish basic principles and essential procedures (i.e., Auditing Standards) from other explanatory material;

- the need for amendments arising from legislative and other developments since they were originally published; and
- the widespread use of information technology in entities of all sizes.

By April 2004 they had issued 29 SASs. Most of the guidelines dealing with specialised industries have now been issued.

In May 2004 the APB announced its intention to adopt ISAs, having first supplemented them with additional guidance relevant to the UK and Ireland. The ISAs (UK and Ireland) were released in order to be used for the audit of financial statements for periods commencing on or after 15 December 2004, but no further information was provided on when the SASs would be withdrawn or whether those SASs with no international equivalent would be retained.

1.4.3 Practice Notes

The APB also issues Practice Notes to assist auditors in applying audit standards of general application to particular circumstances in specific industries. Practice Notes are persuasive rather than prescriptive although they are indicative of good practice and have similar status to the explanatory material in SASs. To date 20 Practice Notes are in issue and others are at Exposure Draft stage. Some Practice Notes have been updated, or are in the process of being updated following the adoption of ISAs (UK and Ireland).

1.4.4 Bulletins

Bulletins have the same status as Practice Notes and are issued to provide auditors with timely guidance on new and emerging issues. At the date of writing 34 bulletins are in issue. As with Practice Notes, there is an ongoing process of updating Bulletins following the adoption of ISAs (UK and Ireland).

1.5 INTERNATIONAL AUDITING AND ASSURANCE STANDARDS BOARD

As well as the ISAs, the IAASB issues other guidance which is of relevance to UK auditors despite not being adopted directly by the APB.

1.5.1 IAASB's Clarity Project

In October 2005, the IAASB announced a project aimed to improve the clarity of its ISAs. This project would involve:

- setting an overall objective for each ISA;

- improving overall readability and understandability of ISAs by redrafting; and
- replacing the word 'should' with the word 'shall' to emphasise that requirements are relevant to virtually all circumstances.

In response to this announcement, the UK APB issued a consultation paper setting out their proposed approach to the project, and establishing how they would respond to the Exposure Drafts to be issued by the IAASB.

Although the APB welcomes moves by the IAASB to improve readability and understandability of ISAs, they voice concerns about the use of the word 'shall', which they consider will make the standards too prescriptive. Their preference is away from prescriptive standards, favouring a more principles-based approach that relies more heavily on auditor judgement, rather than just following a 'tick box' style of auditing.

The APB are obtaining the views of relevant parties on the 'clarified' ISAs before making their own submissions to the IAASB. They note, however, that this consultation does not form part of the process of introducing UK and Ireland versions of these ISAs. As there is a long proposed lead time on the IAASB revised ISAs, the APB believe it would be preferable to delay exposing UK versions of these until the EU endorses ISAs for use in Europe. This will mean that a complete suite of revised ISAs (UK and Ireland) can be issued at once, minimising confusion over which version to apply.

Where the IAASB have issued clarified ISAs this is discussed in the relevant chapter, together with any APB comment or response.

1.6 OTHER GUIDANCE

Guidance on auditing before the development of the APB (and its predecessor, the APC) came mainly from the statements on auditing of the ICAEW which dealt with particular aspects of auditing practice. Most of the original statements have now been superseded by ISAs (UK and Ireland) or Auditing Standards and guidelines but the few remaining are set out in the **Appendix** to this book.

In addition, the auditing committee of the ICAEW, which was part of their Financial Reporting and Auditing Group, from time to time issues statements (FRAGs) on particular topics, for example, *Reports on Internal Controls of Investment Custodians made available to Third Parties*. This role has now been assumed by the Audit and Assurance Faculty of the ICAEW, which was formed in 1995. These are also listed in the **Appendix**.

1.7 OTHER SOURCES OF AUDITING STANDARDS

This book has taken a narrow definition of GAAS, i.e., based on the pronouncements of standard setting bodies except for those areas where decisions of courts indicate a duty. We have not ignored other sources, and in some areas and where necessary we have drawn on:

- auditing textbooks;
- the published manuals of some of the larger firms; and
- model audit files/methods published by the various institutes.

These have, however, only been used to a limited extent as illustrative material because:

- such information is only a partial indication of the standards applied in practice; and
- such standards will often be higher than GAAS although they may be in the process of becoming generally accepted.

2   AUDIT REGULATION

2.1   INTRODUCTION

Only registered auditors may accept appointment as company auditors in the UK. This has been the case since the relevant provisions of the Companies Act 1989 became effective on 1 October 1991. Audit firms, or in some cases individuals, must be registered with a Recognised Supervisory Body (RSB). In order to qualify as an RSB, an organisation must have rules to ensure that its members, who are therefore qualified to accept appointments as company auditors, are properly regulated and monitored. To date the Institute of Chartered Accountants in England and Wales (ICAEW), the Institute of Chartered Accountants of Scotland (ICAS), the Institute of Chartered Accountants in Ireland (ICAI) and the Association of Chartered Certified Accountants (ACCA) have become RSBs for this purpose.

The RSB's regulations must cover the following areas:

- qualification of auditors;
- control of audit firms by qualified individuals;
- fit and proper persons;
- professional integrity and independence;
- technical standards;
- procedures to maintain competence; and
- meeting claims.

The rules must also provide for monitoring and enforcement, membership eligibility, investigation of complaints and discipline.

The Review of the Regulatory Regime of the Accountancy Profession (the 'DTI Review'), published in January 2003 stated that the APB should take over the professional bodies' responsibilities for setting standards for independence, objectivity and integrity. The APB has commenced this process with the publication of five Ethical Standards and a draft Ethical Standard, *Exemptions Available for Smaller Entities* issued in October 2004. These are discussed in **2.5** and **2.6** below.

In July 2006, the ICAEW issued additional ethical guidance for its members in its Code of Ethics. Further details are given in **2.7** below.

A number of changes were made to the Audit Regulations which were effective from 1 January 2003. These dealt with the need to be registered before accepting an audit appointment, a requirement for registering Institute approval of new Responsible Individuals and a change in the definition of an audit in respect of charities.

The Companies (Audit, Investigations and Community Enterprise) Act 2004 states that RSBs are not able to be directly involved in carrying out standard setting, disciplinary functions and monitoring. They may however, comment on draft auditing standards, provide information for monitoring visits or refer cases to the independent disciplinary body. Typically the APB sets standards and the Professional Oversight Board for Accountancy ('the POBA') has responsibility for disciplinary matters and for monitoring via the Audit Inspections Unit (AIU) (see **2.12** below).

In October 2006, the APB issued the Ethical Standard for Reporting Accountants (ESRA) based on the threats and safeguards approach used in ES 1 to 5 and applicable for all engagements governed by the SIRs, which are covered in **Chapter 50**. The ESRA is discussed in **50.8**.

2.2   QUALIFICATION

The Companies Act states that for a qualification to be recognised it must, among other things, involve:

- a course of theoretical instruction;
- examinations; and
- three years' practical training.

2.3   CONTROL OF AUDIT FIRMS

A firm may not be recognised as a registered auditor unless it is controlled by qualified persons. In simple terms this means that a majority of the members of the firm are qualified persons although certain of the RSBs have in fact imposed more stringent requirements than this.

2.4   FIT AND PROPER PERSON

An RSB must have adequate rules and practices designed to ensure that persons eligible under its rules are fit and proper persons to be so appointed. This will normally involve ensuring that there is a suitable procedure for notification, both to the firm by partners and employees and to the RSB by the firms, of matters relating to partners and employees in respect of:

- financial integrity and reliability;
- convictions or civil liabilities; and
- good reputation or character – including previous disciplinary procedures with professional bodies or other regulatory organisations.

2.5 PROFESSIONAL INTEGRITY AND INDEPENDENCE

In October 2004 the APB issued its *Ethical Standards for Auditors* covering integrity, objectivity and independence. These five APB Ethical Standards replace previous guidance issued by the accounting profession. This is in line with the recommendations of the Review of the Regulatory Regime of the Accountancy Profession (the 'DTI Review') which stated that the APB should take over the professional bodies' responsibilities for setting standards for independence, objectivity and integrity.

This move was also suggested by the final report of the Co-ordinating Group on Audit and Accounting Issues, which recommended that the responsibility for setting standards to uphold auditor independence should be transferred to a body that would be independent of the professional accountancy bodies.

The Ethical Standards also incorporate the requirements set out in:

- the EC Recommendation on 'Statutory auditors' independence in the EU: a set of the fundamental principles'; and
- Section 8 of the International Federation of Accountants ('IFAC') 'Code of Ethics for Professional Accountants',

so that when auditors follow the APB standards they will also have complied with the principles set out in the international guidance.

The Ethical Standards also consider the recommendations of the Combined Code and the Smith Report to develop the role of audit committees.

The APB's aims were to develop standards that:

- are rigorous, complete and likely to be effective in practice in upholding the integrity, objectivity and independence of auditors;
- enhance public confidence in the quality of the audit; and
- are clear to auditors, audit committees and those monitoring audits.

They have set out the fundamental principles which auditors are expected to follow in ES1 and then applied those principles to address particular areas of concern in other standards. A 'threats and safeguards' approach has been used in drafting the Standards, identifying the threats that can arise and giving examples of the safeguards that may be suitable. The Standards have been drafted to be relevant to the audits of both large and small entities, publicly traded or privately owned.

Ethical Standards 1 to 5 are effective for the audits of financial statements for periods beginning on or after 15 December 2004.

Following the public consultation on the Ethical Standards, the APB issued a further draft Ethical Standard, *Exemptions Available for Smaller Entities* ('ES – EASE') alongside the five final Standards. This is discussed in section **2.6**.

2.5.1 Ethical Standard 1: Integrity, Objectivity and Independence

APB Ethical Standard 1 (ES1) states:

> 'Public confidence in the operation of the capital markets and in the conduct of public interest entities depends, in part, upon the credibility of the opinions and reports issued by the auditors in connection with the audit of the financial statements. Such credibility depends on beliefs concerning the integrity, objectivity and independence of the auditors and the quality of audit work they perform.'

It defines each of the terms, integrity, objectivity and independence as follows:

- 'integrity requires not only honesty but a broad range of related qualities such as fairness, candour, courage, intellectual honesty and confidentiality';
- 'objectivity is a state of mind that excludes bias, prejudice and compromise and that gives fair and impartial consideration to all matters that are relevant to the task in hand, disregarding those that are not. Objectivity requires that the auditors' judgement is not affected by conflicts of interests'; and
- 'independence is freedom from situations and relationships which make it probable that a reasonable and informed third party would conclude that objectivity is either impaired or could be impaired'.

The Standard requires firms to establish formal and written policies and procedures to ensure that those in a position to influence the conduct and outcome of an audit act with integrity, objectivity and independence. This should involve the leadership of the firm engendering an environment where ethics are considered more important than commercial considerations, and designating an 'ethics partner' to have overall responsibility for the firm's policies and procedures.

The policies and procedures in place should include those set out in **Table 1**.

TABLE 1:   Ethical policies and procedures

- requirements for partners and staff to report where applicable;
- family and other personal relationships involving an audit client of the firm;
- financial interests in an audit client of the firm;
- decisions to join an audit client;
- monitoring of compliance with the firm's policies and procedures relating to integrity, objectivity and independence. Such monitoring procedures include, on a test basis, periodic review of the audit engagement partners' documentation of their consideration of the auditors' objectivity and independence, addressing, for example:
  - financial interests in audit clients;
  - economic dependency on audit clients;
  - the performance of non-audit services; and
  - audit partner rotation;
- prompt communication of identified breaches of the firm's policies and procedures to the relevant audit engagement partners;
- evaluation by audit engagement partners of the implications of any identified breaches of the firm's policies and procedures that are reported to them;
- reporting by audit engagement partners of particular circumstances or relationships as required by APB Ethical Standards;
- prohibiting members of the audit team from making, or assuming responsibility for, management decisions for the audit client;
- operation of a disciplinary mechanism to promote compliance with policies and procedures; and
- empowerment of staff to communicate to senior levels within the firm any issue of objectivity and independence that concerns them; this includes establishing clear communication channels open to staff, encouraging staff to use these channels and ensuring that staff who use these channels are not subject to disciplinary proceedings as a result.

All firms of more than three partners who are responsible individuals should designate a partner in the firm as 'ethics partner'. The ethics partner will have responsibility for:

- the adequacy of the firm's policies and procedures relating to integrity, objectivity and independence, their compliance with APB Ethical Standards, and the effectiveness of their communications to partners and staff within the firm; and
- providing related guidance to individual partners.

The ethics partner should be suitably experienced and hold sufficient authority within a firm.

Firms with three or less partners where it is not practicable to designate an ethics partner should ensure that the relevant issues are regularly discussed by all partners. Sole practitioners should discuss with the ethics helpline of their professional body any matters where a difficult or objective judgement must be made.

Auditors should identify and assess threats to their objectivity and apply safeguards that will either eliminate or reduce the threat to an acceptable level. The principal types of threat are set out in **Table 2**.

TABLE 2:   Types of threats to objectivity

- Self-interest threat – the auditor has financial or other interest that would affect their decision making.
- Self-review threat – if auditing their own non-audit work.
- Management threat – the firm has made judgements or taken decisions that are the responsibility of management.
- Advocacy threat – the auditor has acted as an advocate and has supported a position taken by management in an adversarial context.
- Familiarity (or trust) threat – the auditor has a close personal relationship with the client.
- Intimidation threat – the auditor is influenced by fear or threats.

The significance of threats should be considered throughout the audit, but at least when:

- considering whether to accept or retain an audit engagement;
- planning the audit;
- forming an opinion on the financial statements;
- considering whether to accept or retain an engagement to provide non-audit services to an audit client; and
- potential threats are reported to the audit engagement partner.

This assessment of threats should be documented, together with details of actions taken as a result of identified threats. The firm should have procedures in place to ensure that any possible threats are reported to the audit engagement partner or the ethics partner. The audit engagement partner should not accept or continue an audit engagement if it is concluded that a threat to objectivity and independence cannot be reduced to an acceptable level.

At the end of the audit process, but prior to issuing the audit report, the audit engagement partner should reach an overall conclusion on whether any threats to objectivity and independence have been properly addressed. If they are unable to conclude that this is the case, the audit report should not be issued, and the firm should resign.

In the case of listed companies and public interest clients the assessment, and documentation of the assessment, should be reviewed by an independent partner and those charged with governance should be informed of any significant facts and matters that bear on the auditors' objectivity and independence on a timely basis.

For all clients, the key elements of the audit engagement partner's consideration of objectivity and independence should be communicated to those charged with governance. These may include:

- the principal threats, if any, to objectivity and independence identified by the auditors, including consideration of all relationships between the audit client, its affiliates and directors and the audit firm;
- any safeguards adopted and the reasons why they are considered to be effective;
- any independent partner review;
- the overall assessment of threats and safeguards; and
- information about the general policies and processes within the audit firm for maintaining objectivity and independence.

The minimum requirements for listed companies are set out in **Table 3**.

TABLE 3: Minimum contents of communications with those charged with governance for listed clients

- disclose in writing:
  - details of all relationships between the auditors and the client, its directors and senior management and its affiliates, including all services provided by the audit firm and its network to the client, its directors and senior management and its affiliates, that the auditors consider may reasonably be thought to bear on their objectivity and independence;
  - the related safeguards that are in place; and
  - the total amount of fees that the auditors and their network firms have charged to the client and its affiliates for the provision of services during the reporting period, analysed into appropriate categories, for example statutory audit services, further audit services, tax advisory services and other non-audit services. For each category, the amount of any future services which have been contracted or where a written proposal has been submitted, are separately disclosed;
- confirm in writing that they comply with APB Ethical Standards and that, in their professional judgement, they are independent and their objectivity is not compromised, or otherwise declare that they have concerns that their objectivity and independence may be compromised (including instances where the group audit engagement partner does not consider the other auditors to be objective); and explaining the actions which necessarily follow from this; and
- seek to discuss these matters with the audit committee.

2.5.2   *Ethical Standard 2: Financial, Business, Employment and Personal Relationships*

ES 2 sets out a number of requirements and prohibitions relating to auditor and client relationships.

Financial relationships

The Standard states that the audit firm, or a person in a position to influence the conduct and outcome of the audit, should not hold:

- any direct financial interest in an audit client or affiliate of an audit client;
- any indirect financial interest in an audit client or an affiliate of an audit client, where the investment is material to the audit firm or the individual and to the intermediary (e.g., an open-ended investment company or a pension scheme); or
- any indirect financial interest in an audit client or an affiliate of an audit client, where the person holding it has both:
  - the ability to influence the investment decisions of the intermediary; and
  - actual knowledge of the existence of the underlying investment in the audit client.

There are no safeguards that can mitigate such threats and the individual involved should either dispose of the whole financial interest, dispose of part of the interest so that the remaining part is not material or the firm or individual concerned should withdraw from the audit. Ethical Standard 2 gives further details of the remedies required.

This requirement also extends to:

- an immediate family member of the person who can influence the conduct and outcome of the audit;
- partners in the same office as the engagement partner; or
- the immediate family of such partners.

Financial interests held by audit firm pension schemes

There are no safeguards that can eliminate or reduce the self-interest threat to an acceptable level where the pension scheme of an audit firm has a financial interest in an audit client and the firm has any influence over the trustees' investment decisions. In such a situation the audit firm would be required to resign from the audit. Where the pension scheme invests in a client through an intermediary such as a collective investment scheme, and the firm cannot influence the investment decisions, the ethics partner must consider whether the position is acceptable, having particular regard to the materiality of the investment to the pension scheme.

Loans and guarantees

There are similar restrictions as those for financial relationships where firms, persons able to influence audits and immediate family members of such persons make loans to, or guarantee the borrowings of, an audit client.

This also extends to accepting a loan from, or having borrowings guaranteed by, an audit client.

The only exemptions for these restrictions are:

- the audit client is a bank or similar institution; and
- the loan or guarantee is made in the ordinary course of business on normal business terms; and
- where the client makes the loan or guarantee to the audit firm, it is neither material to the audit firm or the client, or where the client makes the loan or guarantee to a person able to influence the audit or their immediate family members it is not material to that individual.

Business relationships

Audit firms and persons able to influence audits (and their immediate family members) should not enter into business relationships with audit clients except for the purchase of goods or services in the normal course of business where the transaction is not material to either party.

Examples of business relationships that may create self-interest, advocacy or intimidation threats include:

- joint ventures with the audit client or with a director, officer or other senior management;
- arrangements to combine services or products and market them with reference to both parties;
- acting as a distributor or marketer of any of the audit client's products or services; or
- other commercial transactions such as the audit firm leasing office space from the audit client.

Employment relationships

Audit staff should not:

- be employed by both audit firm and audit client;
- be loaned by the firm to the client, except if the audit client agrees that the member of staff will not hold a management position and will not have responsibility for management decisions or preparing or recording accounting entries; or
- be involved in auditing any work they performed whilst on loan with the client.

If a former partner of the firm joins an audit client, the firm must ensure that all connections with the partner are severed before any further audit work is performed for that client. This includes settling outstanding financial interests and ensuring that the partner does not participate or appear to participate in the firm's business or professional activities.

Firms should have procedures to ensure that partners or senior audit team members are required to notify the firm as soon as there is a potential for them to become employed by an audit client. Other members of the team should notify the firm as soon as their employment by an audit client becomes probable. Any such person must be removed from the audit team immediately and the work they performed on the current and most recent audit should be reviewed.

When a partner becomes a director, including a non-executive director, or enters a key management position with an audit client within two years of acting as an engagement partner, the firm must resign as auditors. Reappointment cannot take place until the two-year period has elapsed. If any other audit team member joins the client within the two-year window, the firm should consider whether the composition of the current audit team remains appropriate.

Similarly, a partner or an employee of an audit firm should not accept a governance role with an audit client. A prohibited governance role would be appointment to the board of directors or any subcommittee of that board or to any position in any entity which holds directly or indirectly, more than 20 per cent of the voting rights of the audit client. Where a governance role is accepted by an immediate or close family member, or another partner or employee in the office, safeguards can usually be put in place to mitigate any threats.

When staff who were involved with the preparation of the financial statements transfer from audit client to audit firm they should not be involved in the audit of that client for a period of two years from leaving the audit client.

Family and other personal relationships
The Standard states that:

> 'a relationship between a person who is in a position to influence the conduct and outcome of the audit and another party does not generally affect the consideration of the auditors' objectivity'.

However, this may not be the case where a family relationship exists and that family member also has a financial, business or employment relationship with the audit client. The significance of any threat will depend on:

- the relevant person's involvement in the audit;
- the nature of the relationship between the relevant person and his or her family member; and
- the family member's relationship with the audit client.

Therefore partners and professional staff should report any immediate family (i.e., spouse and dependents), close family (i.e., parents, non-dependent children and siblings) and other personal relationships involving an audit client, to their firm where they consider it might create a threat to independence or objectivity. Such information should be passed to the engagement partner who will be able to assess the threat to independence and objectivity and apply appropriate safeguards.

The audit engagement partner should also consider whether any external consultant involved in the audit will be objective, and document the rationale for their conclusion.

2.5.3 Ethical Standard 3: Long Association with the Audit Engagement

The Standard states that firms should monitor the length of time that audit engagement partners, key audit partners and staff in senior positions serve as members of the engagement team for each audit.

The Standard suggests rotating the audit partners and senior members of the audit team after a period of time. For listed and public interest entities, the maximum period is determined as five years. A suggested maximum of ten years is given for non-listed clients, although this is not mandatory and alternative safeguards could be applied. Where the individual is not rotated from the audit after ten years the reasons for this should be documented and these facts communicated to those charged with governance.

For listed and public interest entities, the Standard states that partner rotation is the only permissible safeguard. **Table 4** sets out the time limits for rotation.

TABLE 4: Time limits for partner rotation for listed and public interest entities

In the case of listed companies and other public interest entities the audit firm should establish policies and procedures to ensure that:

- no one should act as audit engagement partner or as independent partner for a continuous period longer than five years; [1]
- where an independent partner becomes the audit engagement partner, the combined period of service in these positions should not exceed five years; and
- anyone who has acted as the audit engagement partner or the independent

---

partner, or held a combination of such positions, for a particular audit client for a period of five years should not hold any position of responsibility in relation to the audit engagement until a further period of five years has elapsed.

(1) Where an audit client becomes listed or public interest the period before the listing etc. will be taken into account when calculating the five years elapsed. However, if on listing the partner has served four years or more, they can serve up to two further years.

A seven-year limit is imposed for rotation of key audit partners. A key audit partner is any audit partner of the engagement team (other than the audit engagement partner) who is involved at the group level and is responsible for key decisions or judgements on significant matters, such as on significant subsidiaries or divisions, or on significant risk factors that relate to the audit of that client. Additionally, the seven-year limit applies when the key audit partner becomes the engagement partner. The 'cooling off' period before the key audit partner can assume any responsibility in relation to this client is two years.

The same seven-year limit is relevant to other partners and staff in senior positions after which time a review of the threats and safeguards relevant to objectivity and independence must be made. Where there are threats identified a suitable safeguard may be to remove the member of staff from the audit team.

2.5.4   Ethical Standard 4: Fees, Economic Dependence, Remuneration and Evaluation Policies, Litigation, Gifts and Hospitality

Fees
The Standard sets out the following requirements in relation to fees:

- sufficient partners and staff with appropriate skills must be used on an audit, irrespective of fees charged;
- an audit should not be undertaken on a contingent fee basis;
- audit partners should be informed if other non-audit services are to be provided to the client on a contingent fee basis;
- for listed companies, the audit engagement partner should disclose to the audit committee in writing any contingent fee arrangements for non-audit services;
- fees and payment arrangements should be agreed with the client prior to the audit firm being appointed for the following period; and
- where overdue fees arise, the audit engagement partner, together with the ethics partner, should consider whether it is necessary to resign.

Economic dependence

If the combined fees for audit and non-audit services from any one listed client regularly exceed 10 per cent, or for a non-listed client exceed 15 per cent, of the annual fee income for the firm, the firm should resign as auditors. Where the fees from a listed client will regularly exceed 5 per cent (but not exceed 10 per cent) it should be disclosed to the firm's ethics partner and the client's audit committee or board of directors. In addition, the safeguards in place to ensure the audit firm remains objective should be reviewed. Both the 15, 10 and 5 per cent limits should be calculated by reference to the part of the firm on which the engagement partner's profit share is calculated if profits are not shared on a firm-wide basis.

A new audit firm may find these limits difficult to adhere to, and where this is the case, they should:

- not undertake any audits of listed companies, where fees from such a client would represent 10 per cent or more of the annual fee income of the firm; and
- for a period not exceeding two years, require independent reviews of those audits of unlisted entities that represent more than 10 per cent of the annual fee income by a partner in another audit firm before the audit opinion is issued.

The firm may also develop its practice by accepting work from non-audit clients so as to bring the fees payable by each audit client below 10 per cent.

Remuneration and evaluation policies

The Standard states that the audit team should not include in its objectives the selling of non-audit services to the audit client, and team members should not be evaluated or remunerated based on their success in selling non-audit services.

Litigation

Unless insignificant, the audit firm should not continue or accept an audit engagement where litigation is in progress or is probable.

Gifts and hospitality

The Standard states that the audit firm and those in a position to influence the conduct and outcome of the audit (and their immediate family) should not accept gifts from an audit client other than low-value items of a promotional or commemorative nature. Neither should they accept hospitality unless it is reasonable in terms of its frequency, nature and cost.

The audit firm should establish policies on the nature and value of gifts and hospitality that may be accepted from and offered to audit clients, their directors, officers and employees.

2.5.5   Ethical Standard 5: Non-Audit Services Provided to Audit Clients

ES5 states that a firm must consider whether acceptance of a non-audit service engagement may give rise to threats to objectivity. If this is the case they must either not accept the non-audit service engagement or provide the non-audit service having resigned their positions as auditors. Procedures should be in place to ensure that the possible provision of non-audit services is notified to the audit engagement partner prior to accepting the work.

The audit engagement partner should ensure that those charged with governance of the audit client are informed of all significant facts relating to non-audit services that may have a bearing on the auditors' objectivity and independence. For listed clients they should also be informed where their policy on obtaining non-audit services from their auditor is inconsistent with the requirements of the APB's Ethical Standards, and if their own policy has been breached.

The Standard then details risks to objectivity that may arise from the provision of the following services:

- internal audit;
- information technology;
- valuation;
- actuarial valuation;
- litigation support;
- taxation;
- legal;
- recruitment and remuneration;
- corporate finance;
- transaction-related services; and
- accounting.

It also suggests safeguards which could be put in place, if any, to allow auditors to continue their work in an independent and objective manner.

2.6   ETHICAL STANDARD, PROVISIONS AVAILABLE FOR SMALL ENTITIES

2.6.1   Background

The consultation process for the five ethical standards raised a number of issues where commentators believed the requirements of the standards to be unworkable for smaller entities. One area where there was particular concern was the restrictions on the provision of non-audit services unless 'knowledgeable management' were able to oversee all non-audit services provided by the entity's auditors. It was considered unlikely that smaller entities would have sufficiently knowledgeable management, thus causing accounting and taxation work to be given to a firm other than the auditors. This would have meant the loss of a single, cost-effective source of business advice for such companies. As a result the final version of ES 5 requires 'informed' rather than 'knowledgeable' management, maintaining the need for the client to take responsibility for judgements arising from non-audit services, whilst clarifying the required level of competence.

The APB do not want to reduce the requirements for smaller companies as, if they fall below the audit exemption limits, they may be requesting an audit on the instigation of a third party who would probably expect full ethical standards to apply. Therefore they issued *Provisions Available for Small Entities* (PASE) with a view that the ES – PASE should apply for a period of three years. In this period the APB will consider:

- the extent to which companies have taken advantage of the increased level of audit exemption;
- the reasons for, and main users of, audits that continue to be undertaken of companies below the audit exemption threshold;
- the views of owners of small entities and users of small entity audited accounts on the independence and objectivity of auditors; and
- the feasibility of an alternative assurance service to meet the needs of users of small entity audited accounts.

Other areas where concerns were raised were the 10 per cent economic dependence test in ES 4 and the two-year 'cooling off' period on a partner accepting a management role. These are also addressed in the ES – PASE.

The ES – PASE is effective for the audits of financial statements for periods commencing on or after 15 December 2004.

2.6.2 Non-audit services

The ES – PASE exempts auditors, when working for a Small Entity client, from adhering to the requirement in paragraph 28 of ES 5. A Small Entity client is defined in **Table 5**.

TABLE 5: Definition of a Small Entity client

For the purposes of the ES – PASE, a 'Small Entity' is:

- not a listed company, or an affiliate thereof;
- any company that meets two or more of the following requirements in both the current financial year and the preceding year (the Companies Act 1985 definition):
  - not more than £5.6 million turnover;
  - not more than £2.8 million balance sheet total;

- not more than 50 employees.
- any charity with an income of less than £5.6 million;
- any pension fund with less than 1,000 members (including active, deferred and pensioner members);
- any firm, bank and building society, regulated by the FSA (including any mortgage firm or insurance broker that will be regulated from early 2005), which is not required to appoint an auditor under the FSA Handbook on Supervision;
- any credit union which is a mutually owned financial cooperative established under the Credit Unions Act 1979 and the Industrial and Provident Societies Act 1965 (or equivalent legislation);
- any entity registered under the Industrial and Provident Societies Act 1965, incorporated under the Friendly Societies Act 1992 or registered under the Friendly Societies Act 1974 (or equivalent legislation), which meets the Companies Act 1985 definition of a small company, set out above;
- any registered social landlord with less than 250 homes; and
- any other entity, such as a club, which would be a Small Entity if it were a company.

Where an entity falls into more than one of the above categories, it will only be a Small Entity if it meets the criteria of all relevant categories.

Paragraph 28 requires auditors to assess whether management at the audit client are able to make independent judgements and decisions based on the information provided by the non-audit service. It also states that if management are not suitably able, there are likely to be no other safeguards available to reduce management threat to objectivity and independence to an acceptable level as auditors are increasingly likely to take decisions and make judgements which should be made by management.

Small Entity auditors taking advantage of the exemption from paragraph 28 of ES 5 are not required to apply safeguards provided:

- the audit client has 'informed management'; and
- the audit firm extends the cyclical inspection of completed engagements that is performed for quality control purposes to include a random selection of audit engagements where non-audit services have been provided to ensure that there is documentary evidence that 'informed management' has made relevant judgements and decisions themselves.

The fact that the exemption has been applied should be disclosed in the auditor's report and further disclosure in line with the example in **Table 8** should be made in the financial statements or auditor's report.

In addition, the auditors of a Small Entity will have exemption from the requirements of paragraph 73 of ES 5 which states that:

'the audit firm should not undertake an engagement to provide tax services to an audit client where this would involve acting as an advocate for the audit client, before an appeals tribunal or court in the resolution of an issue:

(a) that is material to the financial statements; or
(b) where the outcome of the tax issue is dependent on a future or contemporary audit judgment.'

Where use is made of the exemption from either paragraph 28 or 73 of ES 5, the working papers should document this fact and the audit report should disclose that advantage has been taken of the exemption. Where a paragraph 28 exemption is used details of the non-audit service should be given in the audit report; when a paragraph 73 exemption is used a description of the relevant circumstances should be included.

2.6.3 Economic dependence

The ES – PASE gives an exemption for Small Audit Firms from paragraphs 23 and 26 of ES 4, the 10 per cent and 15 per cent fee limits, see **2.5.4** above. Small Audit Firms are those with three or less partners that are responsible individuals.

The exemption is available as long as the firm discloses the breaches of the expectation that fees will amount to between 10 and 15 per cent to the ethics partner and to those charged with governance of the client.

2.6.4 Partners joining an audit client

An audit firm of a Small Entity is exempt from the requirement of paragraph 43 of ES 2 as long as the firm takes appropriate steps to ensure that there have been no significant threats to the audit team's integrity, objectivity and independence and discloses the fact that it has taken advantage of the exemption in its audit report. Example steps for a Small Audit Firm to take are set out in **Table 6**.

Paragraph 43 of ES 2 requires an audit firm to resign from an engagement for a two-year 'cooling off' period if a former partner of that firm is appointed as a director or in a key management position at the client, if that partner had acted as audit engagement partner, independent partner, key audit partner or partner in the chain of command at any time in the two years prior to this appointment.

Where this exemption is used, the fact must be disclosed in the auditor's report and further disclosures in line with the example in **Table 8** should be made in the financial statements or the auditor's report.

TABLE 6:   Possible steps for a Small Audit Firm to take to guard against threats to independence relating to paragraph 43 of ES 2

- assess significance of the self-interest, familiarity or intimidation threats having regard to:
    - the position the individual has taken at the audit client;
    - the nature and amount of any involvement the individual will have with the audit team or the audit process;
    - the length of time that has passed since the individual was a member of the audit team or firm; and
    - the former position of the individual within the audit team or firm, and
- if that threat is anything other than clearly insignificant, apply safeguards such as:
    - considering the appropriateness or necessity of modifying the audit plan for the audit engagement;
    - assigning an audit team to the subsequent audit engagement that is of sufficient experience in relation to the individual who has joined the audit client;
    - involving an audit partner or senior staff member with appropriate expertise, who was not a member of the audit team, to review the work done or otherwise advise as necessary; or
    - perform a quality control review of the audit engagement.

2.6.5   Audit report wording

The ES – PASE gives example wording for the disclosure required in the audit report when any exemption given by the ES – PASE is used. The example wording is reproduced in **Table 7**.

TABLE 7:   Example audit report wording where an ES – PASE exemption has been used

"*Basis of audit opinion*

We conducted our audit in accordance with International Standards on Auditing (UK and Ireland) issued by the Auditing Practices Board. An audit includes examination on a test basis, of evidence relevant to the amounts and disclosures in the financial statements. It also includes an assessment of the significant estimates and judgements made by [the directors] in the preparation of the financial statements, and of whether the accounting policies are appropriate to the [company's] circumstances, consistently applied and adequately disclosed.

We planned and performed our audit so as to obtain all the information and explanations which we considered necessary in order to provide us with sufficient evidence to give reasonable assurance that the financial statements are free from material misstatement, whether caused by fraud or other irregularity or error. In forming our opinion we also evaluated the overall adequacy of the presentation of information in the financial statements.

We have undertaken the audit in accordance with the requirements of APB Ethical Standards including APB Ethical Standard – Provisions Available for Small Entities, in the circumstances set out in note [x] to the financial statements.

Opinion

In our opinion..."

Examples of the disclosures required when certain exemptions are applied are also provided by the ES – PASE, as these are reproduced in **Table 8**.

TABLE 8: Example disclosures where exemptions are used

*Management threat in relation to non-audit services (**2.6.2** above)*

In common with many other businesses of our size and nature we use our auditors to prepare and submit returns to the tax authorities and assist with the preparation of the financial statements.

*Advocacy threat – tax services (**2.6.2** above)*

In common with many other businesses of our size and nature we use our auditors to provide tax advice nd to represent us, as necessary, at tax tribunals.

*Partners joining an audit client (**2.6.4** above)*

XYZ, a former partner of [audit firm] joined [audit client] as [a director] on [date].

2.7 ICAEW CODE OF ETHICS

2.7.1 Background

In July 2006, the ICAEW issued its own *Code of Ethics* ('the Code') to assist its members in meeting the highest standards of professional conduct. The Code runs to 174 pages and replaces the previous *Guide to Professional Ethics*. It is effective from 1 September 2006 and applies to all ICAEW members (including students), affiliates, employees of member firms and member firms themselves (together 'professional accountants'). It is applicable to all professional and business activities, whether remunerated or voluntary.

The Code is based on IFAC's *Code of Ethics* and adopts a principles-based approach, with threats to the fundamental principles and related safeguards illustrated by a series of case studies.

The Code is split into four sections dealing with:

- issues of general application to all members; and
- issues of specific interest to:
  - members in practice;
  - members in business; and
  - members undertaking insolvency work.

2.7.2   The fundamental principles

The Code sets out five fundamental principles that must be complied with at all times. These are set out in **Table 9** below.

TABLE 9:   Five fundamental principles in the ICAEW Code of Ethics

Integrity
A professional accountant should be straightforward and honest in all professional and business relationships.

Objectivity
A professional accountant should not allow bias, conflict of interest or undue influence of others to override professional or business judgements.

Professional Competence and Due Care
A professional accountant has a continuing duty to maintain professional knowledge and skill at the level required to ensure that a client or employer receives competent professional service based on current developments in practice, legislation and techniques. A professional accountant should act diligently and in accordance with applicable technical and professional standards when providing professional services.

Confidentiality
A professional accountant should respect the confidentiality of information acquired as a result of professional and business relationships and should not disclose any such information to third parties without proper and specific authority unless there is a legal or professional right or duty to disclose. Confidential information acquired as a result of professional and business relationships should not be used for the personal advantage of the professional accountant or third parties.

Professional Behaviour
A professional accountant should comply with relevant laws and regulations and should avoid any action that discredits the profession.

The environment in which professional accountants operate may lead to specific threats to these fundamental principles. As it is impossible to envisage every possible threat that may occur, the Code sets out a conceptual framework which requires professional accountants to identify, evaluate and address these threats individually rather than just comply with a predetermined set of rules. Where professional accountants identify significant threats they should apply suitable safeguards to eliminate them or reduce them to an acceptable level.

When considering whether a threat is significant, professional accountants should consider both quantitative and qualitative factors. Where suitable safeguards cannot be applied, the professional accountant should not accept, or should resign from, the engagement.

2.7.3   Threats and safeguards

The Code sets out the following types of threats to the fundamental principles:

- self-interest threats, as a result of the financial or other interests of a professional accountant or of an immediate or close family member;
- self-review threats, when a previous judgement needs to be re-evaluated by the professional accountant responsible for that judgement;
- advocacy threats, when a professional accountant promotes a position or opinion to the point that subsequent objectivity may be compromised;
- familiarity threats, when, because of a close relationship, a professional accountant becomes too sympathetic to the interests of others; and
- intimidation threats, when a professional accountant may be deterred from acting objectively by actual or perceived threats.

Each type of threat may arise in relation to the professional accountant themselves or in relation to a connected person such as a close family member, a fellow partner or other professional associate.

There are two main types of safeguard set out in the Code:

- safeguards created by the profession, legislation or regulation; and
- safeguards in the work environment.

The first category includes, but is not restricted to:

- educational, training and experience requirements for entry into the profession;
- continuing professional development requirements;
- corporate governance regulations;
- professional standards;
- professional or regulatory monitoring and disciplinary procedures; and
- external review by a legally empowered third party of the reports, returns, communications or information produced by a professional accountant.

The actual safeguards used will depend on the circumstances. In assessing whether the safeguards are reasonable, professional accountants should consider what a reasonable and informed third party would consider to be acceptable.

2.7.4   *Conflict resolution*

When applying the fundamental principles, conflicts may arise. The Code states that it is preferable for such conflicts to be resolved within the organisation before obtaining advice from the Institute or legal advisors. Where necessary professional accountants should consult with other appropriate persons within the organisation.

When conflicts occur, professional accountants should consider:

- relevant facts;
- relevant parties;
- ethical issues involved;
- fundamental principles related to the matter in question;
- established internal procedures; and
- alternative courses of action.

If, having exhausted all possibilities, the conflict remains unresolved, the professional accountant should refuse to remain associated with the matter creating the conflict. This may involve a firm resignation from an engagement or an individual withdrawing from an engagement team or resigning from a firm.

2.8   TECHNICAL STANDARDS

The body must have rules and practices as to the technical standards to be applied in company audit work and the manner in which they are to be applied. In practice, the UK bodies have adopted the Auditing Standards and guidelines and registered auditors must be able to demonstrate compliance with these. For example, the *Audit Regulations and Guidance* issued in December 1995 by the ICAEW, ICAS and ICAI, state that where the Audit Registration Committee (ARC) has to decide whether registered auditors have complied with Auditing Standards they will consider, in addition to the standards themselves, any relevant guidance in ISAs (UK and Ireland), SASs, Practice Notes and Bulletins.

In practice, to comply with audit regulations firms will normally be expected to have procedures covering, in addition to the areas mentioned above:

- acceptance of appointment and reappointments; and
- quality control.

2.8.1 Acceptance of appointment and reappointment

A firm will normally be expected to have procedures which ensure that before accepting an appointment, and also in considering whether to accept reappointment as auditor of a company, issues of the firm's independence and those of its competence to act are addressed. In addressing competence to act the firm must assess whether or not the partners and employees have the necessary skill and training for the particular type of appointment.

2.8.2 Quality control

There must be an adequate system of quality control, see **Chapter 20**. This will involve not only ensuring adequate review procedures but also some measure of quality assurance procedures, for example, 'hot' review of work by independent partners before the opinion is signed off and also 'cold' review procedures to ensure that work has been properly carried out in accordance with the firm's procedures. Quality control will also ensure that the various procedures necessary to ensure compliance with the regulations of the RSB have been carried out.

2.8.3 Control of confidentiality and independence

A firm must have procedures to ensure that staff are aware of confidentiality and independence issues. Confidentiality applies to the information obtained during the course of professional work and the obligation not to disclose or use it. Firms need to be able to demonstrate that they have procedures to ensure that such issues have been brought to the attention of staff. This can be demonstrated by having staff certify their awareness of the procedures. Additionally, as regards independence, the firm should circulate details of listed companies of which it is the auditors to both partners and employees to enable them to identify any potential conflicts.

2.9 MAINTAINING COMPETENCE

There must be adequate arrangements to ensure that persons eligible for appointment as a company auditor continue to maintain an appropriate level of competence in the conduct of company audits. This is done by ensuring that there are satisfactory arrangements for training and continuing professional education (CPE) for members of bodies – the levels of desired CPE are normally set out in the rules of the various RSBs.

Although an audit firm's ability to audit rests with its partners and staff, these may change over time. As a result, to demonstrate its competence a firm must use audit manuals, audit programmes, checklists and standard procedures.

The amount of formal documentation and procedures will depend on the size of the firm and its clients. Even the smallest firm is likely to need some documentation such as audit programmes, but as it grows in size, or as its clients become more complex in their nature, procedures may need to be developed further to assist staff to carry out audit work in accordance with audit regulations.

2.10   MEETING OF CLAIMS

There must be adequate rules to ensure that any registered auditor has adequate professional indemnity insurance (PII) cover to secure them against claims arising out of company audit work. In order to become a registered auditor a firm must demonstrate that there is sufficient PII cover in place.

2.11   OTHER AREAS

In addition to the above, each RSB must have rules relating to eligibility for membership, disciplinary arrangements, investigation of complaints and keeping a published register of members. It must also take into account the costs of any rules it makes in terms of the benefit to be obtained and be involved in the promotion and maintenance of Auditing Standards.

The changes to audit regulations effective from 1 January 2003 made three main changes to the regulations, namely:

- adding a rule explicitly stating that a firm or member of an Institute must be registered by a RSB before accepting an audit appointment;
- requiring firms to formally apply before appointing a new Responsible Individual (RI), rather than just informing the registering Institute of the new RI; and
- a clarification that the Regulations apply to all charities, not just those registered under the Charities Acts 1992 and 1993 in England and Wales.

2.12   THE PROFESSIONAL OVERSIGHT BOARD FOR ACCOUNTANCY

Following the Government's announcement that the new regulatory regime for financial reporting, auditing and the accounting professions would fall within the remit of the Financial Reporting Council (FRC), the Professional Oversight Board for Accountancy ('the POBA') was set up.

The POBA aims to support investor, market and public confidence in the financial stewardship and governance of listed and other entities by providing:

- independent oversight of the regulation of the auditing profession by the recognised supervisory and qualifying bodies;
- monitoring of the quality of the auditing function in relation to 'economically significant entities'; and
- independent oversight of the regulation of the accounting profession by the professional accountancy bodies.

In relation to audit, the POBA intends to achieve its aims by:

- working for the FRC in discharging the Council's responsibility for authorising professional accountancy bodies to act as supervisory bodies and to offer a recognised professional qualification; and
- monitoring audit quality through an independent Audit Inspections Unit (AIU) which will monitor audit quality by reviewing audit processes and agreeing with audit firms amendments to their procedures where appropriate. In severe cases, the AIU will recommend appropriate regulatory action to the recognised supervisory bodies and refer matters to the Financial Reporting Review Panel (FRRP).

The AIU took over responsibility from the Joint Monitoring Unit (JMU) for monitoring the audit of listed companies and major charities and pension funds, i.e., the entities whose activities have the greatest potential to impact on financial and economic stability.

2.13   THE QUALITY ASSURANCE DIRECTORATE

Since the responsibility for regulatory and disciplinary issues fell to the FRC, the ICAEW have set up their own arrangements for monitoring the audits not covered by the AIU, see **2.12**. The Quality Assurance Directorate (QAD) operates on similar grounds to the old JMU and reports their findings to the ICAEW.

2.14   AUDIT REPORTS

The audit regulations apply to audits of companies, building societies, credit unions, registered charities, friendly and provident societies, and persons authorised under the Financial Services and Markets Act. An audit for this purpose is when an opinion is expressed on the financial statements, or an extract from them under companies' legislation or that governing those other regulated entities.

Where auditors of one of these entities reports on its financial statements, the report must be signed in the name of the firm, together with the phrase 'registered auditor(s)'. Other opinions that are required to be given by registered auditors, for example the report on the transfer of non-cash assets to a public company, are also covered by the regulations and auditors must also sign these as 'registered auditor(s)'.

Occasionally reports are given on entities which are not covered by the regulations but which the auditors sign as registered auditors, either by choice or because of a specific requirement. If an RSB receives a complaint about such a report enquiries may be made into the general standard of the firms' audit work, including non-regulated work.

2.15 WORKING PAPERS

Audit regulations now include specific requirements concerning the retention period of audit working papers and situations where audit work is carried out by another firm.

2.15.1 Retention of working papers

Registered auditors are now required to keep their audit working papers for a period of six years from the balance sheet date to which they relate. Although this regulation only came into force on 1 January 2000, it applies to any papers created before that date. Where a firm previously destroyed its working papers within a shorter period, any papers already destroyed do not have to be recreated. However, the ICAEW indicated in its publication *Audit News* in October 1999, which announced the new regulation, that any firm which continued with a shorter retention period between that date and 1 January 2000 would have to be prepared to justify its actions.

The guidance to the regulation notes that the working papers do not have to be on paper but may be on microfilm or on a computer, in which case there should be adequate methods of retrieving them. Records should be kept of which files have been destroyed.

Firms are advised to exercise caution in deciding whether files should be destroyed as the papers may serve another purpose to which a longer retention period applies.

2.15.2 Work carried out by other auditors

Where auditors subcontract audit work to another firm they should retain a right of access to the working papers if they are not handed over to the auditors at the end of the engagement. Any decision to destroy the papers in question should be made by the registered auditor and not the other firm.

The guidance suggests that where the work is to be performed by another firm which itself is not a registered auditor, it may be appropriate for the engagement letter between the two firms to include the full text of the relevant audit regulations regarding working papers.

PART 2
REPORTING

3 THE AUDIT REPORT

3.1 INTRODUCTION

This Chapter examines the auditor's report on the annual financial statements of a company formed under the Companies Act 1985. Modifications to the auditor's report are discussed in **Chapter 4**. Other Companies Act reports on annual financial statements are considered in **Chapter 5**, while other reports under the Companies Act are considered in **Chapter 6** and reports to the FSA on investment businesses in **Chapter 8**. Reports on accounts prepared by accountants are considered in **Chapter 7**.

3.2 THE STANDARDS

ISA (UK and Ireland) 700 *The Auditor's Report on Financial Statements* was issued in December 2004 and provides standards on reporting covering:

- aim of the audit report;
- contents of the audit report; and
- modified reports.

As with all ISAs (UK and Ireland), the text of the international ISA has been supplemented with additional guidance from a UK and Ireland perspective.

In December 2004, the IAASB issued a revision to ISA 700. The APB issued this revision as an Exposure Draft in summer 2005, with an expected implementation date of audit reports dated on or after 31 December 2006. However, having considered responses to the Exposure Draft, the APB concluded that the revision of ISA (UK and Ireland) 700 should be deferred until progress is made in a number of other areas. Further details are given in **3.14**.

ISA (UK and Ireland) 700 is effective for audits of financial statements for periods commencing on or after 15 December 2004. SAS 600 *Auditor's Reports on Financial Statements* has not yet been officially withdrawn.

Throughout its text, the ISA (UK and Ireland) refers readers to examples of audit reports in 'the most recent version of the APB Bulletin, *Auditor's Reports on Financial Statements*'. The draft Bulletin 2005/4 was issued in May 2005 and the final version in November 2005 following the European Union's consensus on how best to describe the financing reporting framework based on IFRSs as endorsed by the EU. In September 2006, Bulletin 2005/4 was superseded by Bulletin 2006/6 and reports in this chapter and throughout this publication have been updated to reflect this Bulletin. The effective periods of each Bulletin are set out in **3.3** below. Further details of the Bulletin itself are given in **3.3** below.

For all financial statements prepared for periods commencing on or after 1 April 2005, Statutory Instrument 2005/1011 introduced a further change to the audit report in relation to information given in the directors' reports. This is detailed in **3.5.1**.

3.2.1   *Other guidance*

In January 2001 the APB issued two bulletins in response to the changing focus on auditors' reports as a result of the increasing use of the Internet as a medium for publishing financial material. Bulletins 2001/1 *The Electronic Publication of Auditors' Reports* and 2001/2 *Revisions to the Wording of Auditors' Reports on Financial Statements and the Interim Review Report* are considered in section **3.14** below. The example audit reports in this chapter, and throughout the book, take into account these Bulletins. The issue of FRS 18 *Accounting Policies* prompted the APB to issue Bulletin 2000/3 as guidance to auditors on the application of SAS 600 when reporting on financial statements which fall within the scope of a Statement of Recommended Practice (SORP), but contain a departure from the SORP's requirements. This guidance is still relevant following the publication of ISA (UK and Ireland) 700.

The Director's Remuneration Report Regulations 2002 ('the Regulations') came into force on 1 August 2002. The Regulations require certain public companies to produce a Remuneration Report containing detailed information about directors' remuneration for periods ending on or after 31 December 2002. Some of the information specified for inclusion is to be audited, and auditors must state in their report whether the 'auditable part' of the Directors' Remuneration Report has been properly prepared in accordance with the Companies Act 1985. Reports in this Chapter for relevant listed companies have been updated in accordance with the guidance in the related APB Bulletin, 2002/2, *The United Kingdom Directors' Remuneration Report Regulations 2002*, which was published in October 2002. Details of the Bulletin are given in **3.15** below.

In January 2003 the Audit and Assurance Faculty of the ICAEW issued Technical Release Audit 1/03, *The Audit Report and Auditors' Duty of Care to Third Parties* following an earlier judgement in the Scottish courts, *Royal Bank of Scotland* v *Bannerman Johnstone Maclay and others* ('Bannerman'). The aim of 1/03 is to assist auditors in managing the risk of inadvertently assuming a duty of care to third parties in relation to their audit reports. Further details are discussed in **3.18**, and all relevant reports in this publication have been updated to reflect the guidance in the Technical Release.

In April 2006, the Audit and Assurance faculty of the ICAEW issued AAF 02/06, *Identifying and managing certain risks arising from the inclusion of reports from auditors and accountants in prospectuses (and certain other investment circulars)*. This publication develops the principles in 01/03 for reporting accountants. It is detailed in **50.9.**

3.3   BULLETIN 2006/6

Bulletin 2006/6 was issued in September 2006 to provide illustrative examples of:

- unmodified auditor's reports for audits of financial statements:
  - performed in accordance with ISAs (UK and Ireland); and
  - for periods commencing on or after 15 December 2004;
- modified auditor's reports (excluding going concern issues); and
- modified auditor's reports arising from going concern issues.

Modified auditor's reports are considered in **Chapter 4**.

The Bulletin applies to companies incorporated in Great Britain or Northern Ireland which are either:

- 'publicly traded companies' – with securities admitted to or trading on a regulated market in any EU member state; or
- 'non-publicly' traded companies' – with no such securities.

Bulletin 2006/6 superseded Bulletin 2005/4 which contained the previous guidance on audit report wordings. The following changes were incorporated into Bulletin 2005/4, and are retained in Bulletin 2006/6. These are discussed in further detail below:

- changes to the reporting and accounting provisions of the Companies Act 1985;
- the adoption of the IFRSs by the EU for the consolidated financial statements of publicly traded companies; and
- changes to the corporate governance requirements following the publication of the 2003 FRC Combined Code.

Further changes in Bulletin 2006/6 also discussed below are:

- those to the Companies Act 1985 requiring auditors to give a positive opinion as to the consistency of the directors' report with the financial statements;
- revised standard wording for expressing compliance with the financial reporting framework as agreed by the EC; and
- certain conforming changes to some reports.

Bulletin 2005/4 and its examples should be used for audit reports for accounting periods commencing between 15 December 2004 and 31 March 2005. The guidance and examples in Bulletin 2006/6 should be used for the audit reports of accounting periods commencing on or after 1 April 2005.

Bulletin 2006/6 does not incorporate changes which will be required by the enactment of the Companies Act 2006 and further updates are expected in due course.

3.3.1   Changes to the reporting and accounting provisions of the Companies Act 1985

In November 2004, Statutory Instrument 2004/2947 *Companies Act 1985 (International Accounting Standards and Other Accounting Amendments) Regulations 2004* ('SI 2004/2947') introduced a number of changes to the Companies Act which applied to financial years beginning on or after 1 January 2005.

SI 2004/2947 requires auditors to include an introduction to their report to identify the annual accounts audited and the financial framework used to prepare them and to state clearly, in their opinion, whether the annual accounts have been properly prepared in accordance with the requirements of the Companies Act (and where applicable Article 4 of the IAS Regulation which deals with listed companies and the application of IFRSs). In addition the auditor's report must state whether the annual accounts give a true and fair view *in accordance with the relevant financial reporting framework*. Following a meeting of The Accounting Regulatory Committee of the EU in November 2005 the accepted wording was agreed as 'true and fair view, in accordance with IFRSs as adopted by the European Union'. This change is covered by Bulletin 2006/6 and reports in this chapter and elsewhere in this publication have been updated for this amendment.

3.3.2   International Financial Reporting Standards (IFRSs)

The change set out in **3.3.1** above fulfils the requirement in Bulletin 2005/3 for the accounting framework used by companies adopting IFRSs to be referred to in the auditor's opinion. Bulletin 2006/6 states that where auditors are asked to provide an additional opinion that the annual accounts present a true and fair view in accordance with IFRSs issued by the IASB, as well as those adopted by the EU, this should be done in a separate opinion to avoid confusion. An example is given in **Table 8.**

The financial reporting framework used for the group and parent company financial statements may be different, eg IFRSs as adopted for use in the EU for the group and UK GAAP for the parent company. Here, companies may choose to present the financial statements of the group and of the parent company in separate sections of the annual report, and therefore separate auditor's reports would be provided. Examples are given in **Tables 6** and **8**. In such situations, the auditor's responsibilities in relation to the Corporate Governance Statement are given in the auditor's report on the group financial statements and the Directors' Remuneration Report is reported on in the auditor's report on the parent company financial statements.

Where a parent company is taking advantage of the exemption from publishing its profit and loss account and certain related information conferred under section 230 of the Companies Act 1985, the financial reporting framework should be described in the auditor's report as:

> '...true and fair view, in accordance with IFRSs as adopted by the European Union and as applied in accordance with the provisions of the Companies Act 1985...'

In such a situation it is likely that the group and parent company financial statements and audit reports will be presented separately so that it does not appear that a modified opinion has been given on the group financial statements.

3.4 AIM OF THE AUDIT REPORT

The aim of the report is to provide information to the reader on the respective responsibilities of the directors and the auditors and information on what an audit entails.

ISA (UK and Ireland) 700 requires that auditors' reports should contain a clear expression of opinion based on review and assessment of the conclusions drawn from evidence obtained in the course of the audit. The other standards expand this basic principle. An Appendix to the ISA (UK and Ireland) is in the form of a flowchart of the steps involved in forming an opinion (see **Table 10**).

3.5 CONTENTS OF AN AUDIT REPORT

The ISA (UK and Ireland) requires that an audit report should contain the following information:

- a title which identifies to whom the report is addressed;
- an introduction that identifies the financial statements which have been audited;
- the financial reporting framework that has been applied in the preparation of the financial statements;
- the responsibilities of those charged with governance;
- the responsibilities of the auditors;
- a reference to the auditing standards followed;
- the basis of the auditors' opinion;
- the auditors' opinion on the financial statements;
- the manuscript or printed signature of the auditors;
- the auditors' address; and
- the date of the auditors' report.

The standard recommends that using a standard format with appropriate headings will help the user to understand the report. However, it also points out that the report should reflect the particular assignment.

A normal form of unqualified report is shown in **Table 2**.

3.5.1   Statutory Instrument 2005/1011

SI 2005/1011 implemented a requirement for auditors to make a positive statement whether in their opinion the information in the directors' report is consistent with the financial statements. These requirements are effective for all auditor's reports on financial statements prepared for periods commencing on or after 1 April 2005. For earlier periods auditors are required to make a statement only if the information is inconsistent with the accounts.

The changes to the audit report are:

- amendments to the wording in the respective responsibilities paragraph reflecting the changes to the auditor's responsibilities; and
- an additional bullet point in the opinion paragraph.

All example reports in this chapter and throughout the publication have been amended to reflect this change.

The audit report should retain the responsibility for auditors to review the directors' report for misstatements and consider the implications for their report. This is not duplication, as auditors are still required to consider material misstatements that are not covered by the review of consistency with the financial statements, e.g. an error in a disclosure of a post balance sheet event would not necessarily be inconsistent with the financial statements, but could be a material misstatement.

Additional documentation requirements as a result of the SI are detailed in **Chapter 14**.

3.6   ADDRESSEE

Where the auditors are reporting on a company, the report should be addressed to the members as the audit is undertaken on their behalf. For other types of reporting entity the addressee will depend on the terms of the engagement, for example, where the auditors are reporting on a pension fund they will address their report to the trustees.

3.7   IDENTIFICATION

This section should refer to the pages of the report that contain the financial statements and the date of, and period covered by, the financial statements, and is to ensure that there is no confusion over the subject matter of the auditors' report. Bulletin 2001/1 (see **13.4**) outlines the situation where the Annual Report is to be published electronically and the statements covered by the audit report may not be determined from page numbers alone. Here, auditors are required to refer explicitly to the primary statements and notes covered by the audit report.

Technical Release Audit 1/03 was issued in January 2003 to assist auditors in managing the risk of inadvertently assuming a duty of care to third parties in relation to their audit reports. The suggested inclusion in audit reports has been added to all relevant reports in this publication, and the Technical Release is discussed in detail in section **3.18** below.

3.8   UNMODIFIED AUDITOR'S REPORTS EXAMPLES

Bulletin 2006/6 contains a number of examples of unmodified auditor's reports together with a navigation aid to assist auditors in using the correct report. The navigation aid is reproduced in **Table 1**, but with reference to examples in this chapter.

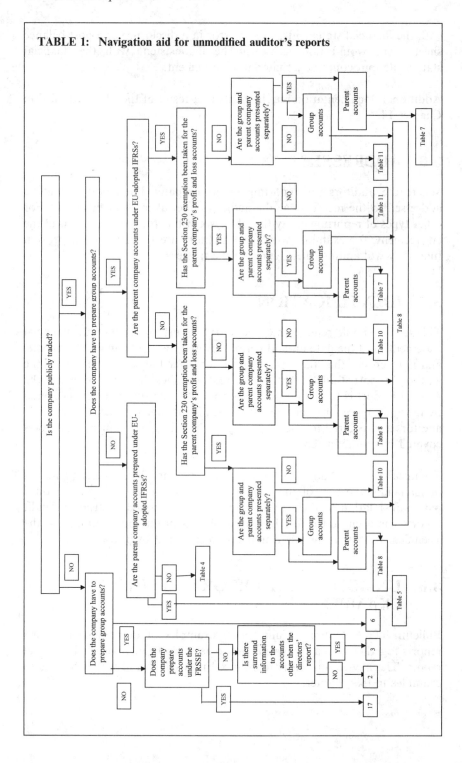

TABLE 1:   Navigation aid for unmodified auditor's reports

TABLE 2: *Unmodified opinion simple example*

- *Company does not prepare group financial statements*
- *Company does not meet the Companies Act definition of a quoted company*
- *UK GAAP used for individual company financial statements*
- *Financial statements contain no surround information other than the directors' report*

Independent auditors' report to the shareholders of XYZ Limited
We have audited the financial statements of [entity name] for the year ended [date] which comprise [state the primary financial statements such as the Profit and Loss Account, the Balance Sheet, the Cash Flow Statement, the Statement of Total Recognised Gains and Losses] and the related notes. These financial statements have been prepared under the accounting policies set out therein.

This report is made solely to the company's members, as a body, in accordance with s235 of the Companies Act 1985. Our audit work has been undertaken so that we might state to the company's members those matters we are required to state to them in an auditors' report and for no other purpose. To the fullest extent permitted by law, we do not accept or assume responsibility to anyone other than the company and the company's members as a body, for our audit work, for this report, or for the opinions we have formed.

Respective responsibilities of directors and auditors
The directors' responsibilities for preparing the financial statements in accordance with applicable law and United Kingdom Accounting Standards (United Kingdom Generally Accepted Accounting Practice) are set out in the Statement of Directors' Responsibilities.

Our responsibility is to audit the financial statements in accordance with relevant legal and regulatory requirements and the International Standards on Auditing (UK and Ireland).

We report to you our opinion as to whether the financial statements give a true and fair view and are properly prepared in accordance with the Companies Act 1985. We also report to you whether in our opinion the information given in the Directors' Report is consistent with the financial statements.

In addition we report to you if, in our opinion, the company has not kept proper accounting records, if we have not received all the information and explanations we require for our audit, or if information specified by law regarding directors' remuneration and other transactions is not disclosed.

We read the Directors' Report and consider the implications for our report if we become aware of any apparent misstatement within it.

Basis of audit opinion
We conducted our audit in accordance with International Standards on Auditing (UK and Ireland) issued by the Auditing Practices Board. An audit includes examination, on a test basis, of evidence relevant to the amounts and

disclosures in the financial statements. It also includes an assessment of the significant estimates and judgements made by the directors in the preparation of the financial statements, and of whether the accounting policies are appropriate to the company's circumstances, consistently applied and adequately disclosed.

We planned and performed our audit so as to obtain all the information and explanations which we considered necessary in order to provide us with sufficient evidence to give reasonable assurance that the financial statements are free from material misstatement, whether caused by fraud or other irregularity or error. In forming our opinion we also evaluated the overall adequacy of the presentation of information in the financial statements.

Opinion
In our opinion:

- the financial statements give a true and fair view, in accordance with United Kingdom Generally Accepted Accounting Practice, of the state of the company's affairs as at [date] and of its profit [loss] for the year then ended;
- the financial statements have been properly prepared in accordance with the Companies Act 1985; and
- the information given in the Directors' Report is consistent with the financial statements.

Registered Auditors
Address
Date

TABLE 3:   Where further surround information is published

This example wording should be substituted when the company publishes additional surround information to the directors' report.
...

Respective responsibilities of directors and auditors
...
We read other information contained in the Annual Report, and consider whether it is consistent with the audited financial statements. This other information comprises only [the Directors' Report, the Chairman's Statement and the Operating and Financial Review]. We consider the implications for our report if we become aware of any apparent misstatements or material inconsistencies with the financial statements. Our responsibilities do not extend to any other information.

TABLE 4: Publicly traded parent company which does not prepare group financial statements

- *Parent company does not prepare group financial statements*
- *Company meets the Companies Act definition of a quoted company*
- *UK GAAP used for parent company financial statements*

Independent auditors' report to the shareholders of XYZ PLC

We have audited the financial statements of [entity name] for the year ended [date] which comprise [state the primary financial statements such as the Profit and Loss Account, the Balance Sheet, the Cash Flow Statement, the Statement of Total Recognised Gains and Losses] and the related notes. These financial statements have been prepared under the accounting policies set out therein. We have also audited the information in the Directors' Remuneration Report that is described as having been audited.

This report is made solely to the company's members, as a body, in accordance with s235 of the Companies Act 1985. Our audit work has been undertaken so that we might state to the company's members those matters we are required to state to them in an auditors' report and for no other purpose. To the fullest extent permitted by law, we do not accept or assume responsibility to anyone other than the company and the company's members as a body, for our audit work, for this report, or for the opinions we have formed.

Respective responsibilities of directors and auditors
The directors' responsibilities for preparing the Annual Report, the Directors' Remuneration Report and the financial statements in accordance with applicable law and United Kingdom Accounting Standards (United Kingdom Generally Accepted Accounting Practices) are set out in the Statement of Directors' Responsibilities.

Our responsibility is to audit the financial statements and the part of the Directors' Remuneration Report to be audited in accordance with relevant legal and regulatory requirements and the International Standards on Auditing (UK and Ireland).

We report to you our opinion as to whether the financial statements give a true and fair view and the financial statements and the part of the Directors' Remuneration Report to be audited have been properly prepared in accordance with the Companies Act 1985. We also report to you whether in our opinion the information given in the Directors' Report is consistent with the financial statements.

In addition we report to you if, in our opinion, the company has not kept proper accounting records, if we have not received all the information and explanations we require for our audit, or if information specified by law regarding directors' remuneration and other transactions is not disclosed.

We review whether the Corporate Governance Statement reflects the company's compliance with the nine provisions of the 2003 FRC Combined Code specified for our review by the Listing Rules of the Financial Services

Authority, and we report if it does not. We are not required to consider whether the board's statements on internal control cover all risks and controls, or form an opinion on the effectiveness of the group's corporate governance procedures or its risk and control procedures.

We read other information contained in the Annual Report, and consider whether it is consistent with the audited parent company financial statements. This other information comprises only [the Directors' Report, the unaudited part of the Directors' Remuneration Report, the Chairman's Statement and the Operating and Financial Review]. We consider the implications for our report if we become aware of any apparent misstatements or material inconsistencies with the financial statements. Our responsibilities do not extend to any other information.

Basis of audit opinion
We conducted our audit in accordance with International Standards on Auditing (UK and Ireland) issued by the Auditing Practices Board. An audit includes examination, on a test basis, of evidence relevant to the amounts and disclosures in the parent company financial statements and the part of the Directors' Remuneration Report to be audited. It also includes an assessment of the significant estimates and judgements made by the directors in the preparation of the parent company financial statements, and of whether the accounting policies are appropriate to the company's circumstances, consistently applied and adequately disclosed.

We planned and performed our audit so as to obtain all the information and explanations which we considered necessary in order to provide us with sufficient evidence to give reasonable assurance that the parent company financial statements and the part of the Directors' Remuneration Report to be audited are free from material misstatement, whether caused by fraud or other irregularity or error. In forming our opinion we also evaluated the overall adequacy of the presentation of information in the parent company financial statements and the part of the Directors' Remuneration Report to be audited.

Opinion
In our opinion:

- the financial statements give a true and fair view, in accordance with United Kingdom Generally Accepted Accounting Practice, of the state of the company's affairs as at [date] and of its profit [loss] for the year then ended;
- the financial statements and the part of the Directors' Remuneration Report to be audited have been properly prepared in accordance with the Companies Act 1985; and
- the information given in the Directors' Report is consistent with the financial statements.

Registered Auditors
Address
Date

TABLE 5: Publicly traded parent company which does not prepare group financial statements and reports under IFRS

- *Parent company does not prepare group financial statements*
- *Company meets the Companies Act definition of a quoted company*
- *IFRSs as adopted for use in the EU used for parent company financial statements*

Independent auditors' report to the shareholders of XYZ PLC
We have audited the financial statements of [entity name] for the year ended [date] which comprise [state the primary financial statements such as the Profit and Loss Account, the Balance Sheet, the Cash Flow Statement, the Statement of Total Recognised Gains and Losses] and the related notes. These financial statements have been prepared under the accounting policies set out therein. We have also audited the information in the Directors' Remuneration Report that is described as having been audited.

This report is made solely to the company's members, as a body, in accordance with s235 of the Companies Act 1985. Our audit work has been undertaken so that we might state to the company's members those matters we are required to state to them in an auditors' report and for no other purpose. To the fullest extent permitted by law, we do not accept or assume responsibility to anyone other than the company and the company's members as a body, for our audit work, for this report, or for the opinions we have formed.

Respective responsibilities of directors and auditors
The directors' responsibilities for preparing the Annual Report, the Directors' Remuneration Report and the financial statements in accordance with applicable law and International Financial Reporting Standards (IFRSs) as adopted by the European Union are set out in the Statement of Directors' Responsibilities.

Our responsibility is to audit the financial statements and the part of the Directors' Remuneration Report to be audited in accordance with relevant legal and regulatory requirements and the International Standards on Auditing (UK and Ireland).

We report to you our opinion as to whether the financial statements give a true and fair view and the financial statements and the part of the Directors' Remuneration Report to be audited have been properly prepared in accordance with the Companies Act 1985. We also report to you whether in our opinion the information given in the Directors' Report is consistent with the financial statements.

In addition we report to you if, in our opinion, the company has not kept proper accounting records, if we have not received all the information and explanations we require for our audit, or if information specified by law regarding directors' remuneration and other transactions is not disclosed.

We review whether the Corporate Governance Statement reflects the company's compliance with the nine provisions of the 2003 FRC Combined Code specified for our review by the Listing Rules of the Financial Services

Authority, and we report if it does not. We are not required to consider whether the board's statements on internal control cover all risks and controls, or form an opinion on the effectiveness of the group's corporate governance procedures or its risk and control procedures.

We read other information contained in the Annual Report, and consider whether it is consistent with the audited parent company financial statements. This other information comprises only [the Directors' Report, the unaudited part of the Directors' Remuneration Report, the Chairman's Statement and the Operating and Financial Review]. We consider the implications for our report if we become aware of any apparent misstatements or material inconsistencies with the financial statements. Our responsibilities do not extend to any other information.

Basis of audit opinion

We conducted our audit in accordance with International Standards on Auditing (UK and Ireland) issued by the Auditing Practices Board. An audit includes examination, on a test basis, of evidence relevant to the amounts and disclosures in the parent company financial statements and the part of the Directors' Remuneration Report to be audited. It also includes an assessment of the significant estimates and judgements made by the directors in the preparation of the parent company financial statements, and of whether the accounting policies are appropriate to the company's circumstances, consistently applied and adequately disclosed.

We planned and performed our audit so as to obtain all the information and explanations which we considered necessary in order to provide us with sufficient evidence to give reasonable assurance that the parent company financial statements and the part of the Directors' Remuneration Report to be audited are free from material misstatement, whether caused by fraud or other irregularity or error. In forming our opinion we also evaluated the overall adequacy of the presentation of information in the parent company financial statements and the part of the Directors' Remuneration Report to be audited.

Opinion

In our opinion:

- the financial statements give a true and fair view, in accordance with International Financial Reporting Standards (IFRSs) as adopted by the European Union, of the state of the company's affairs as at [date] and of its profit [loss] for the year then ended;
- the financial statements and the part of the Directors' Remuneration Report to be audited have been properly prepared in accordance with the Companies Act 1985; and
- the information given in the Directors' Report is consistent with the financial statements.

Registered Auditors
Address
Date

TABLE 6: Group and parent unmodified report

- *Group and parent company financial statements presented together*
- *Company prepares group financial statements*
- *Company does not meet the Companies Act definition of a quoted company*
- *UK GAAP used for group and parent company financial statements*
- *Section 230 exemption taken for parent company's own profit and loss account*

Independent auditors' report to the shareholders of XYZ Limited
We have audited the group and parent financial statements ("the financial statements") of [entity name] for the year ended [date] which comprise [state the primary financial statements such as the Profit and Loss Account, the Balance Sheet, the Cash Flow Statement, the Statement of Total Recognised Gains and Losses] and the related notes. These financial statements have been prepared under the accounting policies set out therein.
...

Respective responsibilities of directors and auditors
...

Basis of audit opinion
...

Opinion
In our opinion:

- the financial statements give a true and fair view, in accordance with United Kingdom Generally Accepted Accounting Practice, of the state of the group's and the parent company's affairs as at [date] and of the group's profit [loss] for the year then ended;
- the financial statements have been properly prepared in accordance with the Companies Act 1985;
- the information given in the Directors' Report is consistent with the financial statements.

Registered Auditors
Address
Date

TABLE 7: Publicly traded parent company unmodified report

- *Group accounts not presented with parent accounts*
- *IFRSs as adopted for use in the EU used for group and parent financial statements*
- *Company is quoted*
- *Corporate governance is reported on in the group audit report*
- *Directors' Remuneration Report reported on in the parent company financial statements*

Independent auditors' report to the shareholders of XYZ PLC
We have audited the parent company financial statements of [entity name] for the year ended [date] which comprise [state the primary financial statements such as [*if section 230 exemption not taken* the Profit and Loss Account,] the Balance Sheet, [the Cash Flow Statement], the Statement of Total Recognised Gains and Losses] and the related notes. These parent company financial statements have been prepared under the accounting policies set out therein. We have also audited the information in the Directors' Remuneration Report that is described as having been audited.

We have reported separately on the group financial statements of [entity name] for the year ended ....

This report is made solely to the company's members, as a body, in accordance with s235 of the Companies Act 1985. Our audit work has been undertaken so that we might state to the company's members those matters we are required to state to them in an auditors' report and for no other purpose. To the fullest extent permitted by law, we do not accept or assume responsibility to anyone other than the company and the company's members as a body, for our audit work, for this report, or for the opinions we have formed.

Respective responsibilities of directors and auditors
The directors' responsibilities for preparing the Annual Report, the Directors' Remuneration Report and the parent company financial statements in accordance with applicable law and International Financial Reporting Standards (IFRSs) as adopted by the European Union are set out in the Statement of Directors' Responsibilities.

Our responsibility is to audit the financial statements and the part of the Directors' Remuneration Report to be audited in accordance with relevant legal and regulatory requirements and the International Standards on Auditing (UK and Ireland).

We report to you our opinion as to whether the parent company financial statements give a true and fair view and the parent company financial statements and the part of the Directors' Remuneration Report to be audited have been properly prepared in accordance with the Companies Act 1985. We also report to you whether in our opinion the information given in the Directors' Report is consistent with the financial statements.

In addition, we report to you if, in our opinion, the company has not kept proper accounting records, if we have not received all the information and explanations we require for our audit, or if information specified by law regarding directors' remuneration and other transactions is not disclosed.

We read other information contained in the Annual Report, and consider whether it is consistent with the audited parent company financial statements. This other information comprises only [the Directors' Report, the unaudited part of the Directors' Remuneration Report, the Chairman's Statement and the Operating and Financial Review]. We consider the implications for our report if we become aware of any apparent misstatements or material inconsistencies with the financial statements. Our responsibilities do not extend to any other information.

Basis of audit opinion
We conducted our audit in accordance with International Standards on Auditing (UK and Ireland) issued by the Auditing Practices Board. An audit includes examination, on a test basis, of evidence relevant to the amounts and disclosures in the parent company financial statements and the part of the Directors' Remuneration Report to be audited. It also includes an assessment of the significant estimates and judgements made by the directors in the preparation of the parent company financial statements, and of whether the accounting policies are appropriate to the company's circumstances, consistently applied and adequately disclosed.

We planned and performed our audit so as to obtain all the information and explanations which we considered necessary in order to provide us with sufficient evidence to give reasonable assurance that the parent company financial statements and the part of the Directors' Remuneration Report to be audited are free from material misstatement, whether caused by fraud or other irregularity or error. In forming our opinion we also evaluated the overall adequacy of the presentation of information in the parent company financial statements and the part of the Directors' Remuneration Report to be audited.

Opinion
In our opinion:

- the parent company financial statements give a true and fair view, in accordance with International Financial Reporting Standards (IFRSs) as adopted by the European Union, of the state of the company's affairs as at [date] [*if section 230 exemption not taken* and of its profit [loss] for the year then ended];
- the parent company financial statements and the part of the Directors' Remuneration Report to be audited have been properly prepared in accordance with the Companies Act 1985 and Article 4 of the IAS Regulation; and
- the information given in the Directors' Report is consistent with the parent company financial statements.

Registered Auditors
Address
Date

TABLE 8: **Amendments to Table 7 example for a publicly traded parent company where UK GAAP is used by parent, with IFRS used by group**

Independent auditors' report to the shareholders of XYZ PLC
...

Respective responsibilities of directors and auditors
The directors' responsibilities for preparing the Annual Report, the Directors' Remuneration Report and the parent company financial statements in accordance with applicable law and United Kingdom Accounting Standards (United Kingdom Generally Accepted Accounting Practice) are set out in the Statement of Directors' Responsibilities.

Our responsibility is to audit the parent company financial statements and the part of the Directors' Remuneration Report to be audited in accordance with relevant legal and regulatory requirements and the International Standards on Auditing (UK and Ireland).

We report to you our opinion as to whether the parent company financial statements give a true and fair view and whether the parent company financial statements and the part of the Directors' Remuneration Report to be audited have been properly prepared in accordance with the Companies Act 1985. We also report to you whether in our opinion the information given in the Directors' Report is consistent with the parent company financial statements.

In addition we report to you if, in our opinion, the company has not kept proper accounting records, if we have not received all the information and explanations we require for our audit, or if information specified by law regarding directors' remuneration and other transactions is not disclosed.

We read other information contained in the Annual Report, and consider whether it is consistent with the audited parent company financial statements. This other information comprises only [the Directors' Report, the unaudited part of the Directors' Remuneration Report, the Chairman's Statement and the Operating and Financial Review]. We consider the implications for our report if we become aware of any apparent misstatements or material inconsistencies with the financial statements. Our responsibilities do not extend to any other information.

Basis of audit opinion
...

Opinion
In our opinion:

- the parent company financial statements give a true and fair view, in accordance with United Kingdom Generally Accepted Accounting Practice, of the state of the company's affairs as at [date] [*if section 230 exemption not taken* and of its profit [loss] for the year then ended];
- the parent company financial statements and the part of the Directors'

Remuneration Report to be audited have been properly prepared in accordance with the Companies Act 1985; and

- the information given in the Directors' Report is consistent with the financial statements.

Registered Auditors
Address
Date

TABLE 9: Unmodified report on publicly traded group financial statements (not including parent company)

- *Parent company accounts not presented with group accounts*
- *IFRSs as adopted for use in the EU used for group financial statements (either IFRS or UK GAAP used for parent company)*
- *Group is quoted*
- *Corporate governance is reported on in the group audit report*
- *Directors' Remuneration Report reported on in the parent company financial statements*

Independent auditors' report to the shareholders of XYZ PLC
We have audited the group financial statements of [entity name] for the year ended [date] which comprise [state the primary financial statements such as the Profit and Loss Account, the Balance Sheet, the Cash Flow Statement, the Statement of Total Recognised Gains and Losses] and the related notes. These group financial statements have been prepared under the accounting policies set out therein.

We have reported separately on the parent company financial statements of [entity name] for the year ended ... and on the information in the Directors' Remuneration Report that is described as being audited.

This report is made solely to the group's members, as a body, in accordance with s235 of the Companies Act 1985. Our audit work has been undertaken so that we might state to the company's members those matters we are required to state to them in an auditors' report and for no other purpose. To the fullest extent permitted by law, we do not accept or assume responsibility to anyone other than the group and their members as a body, for our audit work, for this report, or for the opinions we have formed.

Respective responsibilities of directors and auditors
The directors' responsibilities for preparing the Annual Report and the group financial statements in accordance with applicable law and International Financial Reporting Standards (IFRSs) as adopted by the European Union are set out in the Statement of Directors' Responsibilities.

Our responsibility is to audit the group financial statements in accordance with relevant legal and regulatory requirements and the International Standards on Auditing (UK and Ireland).

We report to you our opinion as to whether the group financial statements give a true and fair view and whether the group financial statements have been properly prepared in accordance with the Companies Act 1985 and Article 4 of the IAS Regulation. We also report to you whether in our opinion the information given in the Directors' Report is consistent with the group financial statements.

In addition we report to you if, in our opinion, we have not received all the information and explanations we require for our audit, or if information specified by law regarding directors' remuneration and other transactions is not disclosed.

We review whether the Corporate Governance Statement reflects the company's compliance with the nine provisions of the 2003 FRC Combined Code specified for our review by the Listing Rules of the Financial Services Authority, and we report if it does not. We are not required to consider whether the board's statements on internal control cover all risks and controls, or form an opinion on the effectiveness of the group's corporate governance procedures or its risk and control procedures.

We read other information contained in the Annual Report, and consider whether it is consistent with the audited group financial statements. This other information comprises only [the Directors' Report, the Chairman's Statement, the Operating and Financial Review and the Corporate Governance Statement]. We consider the implications for our report if we become aware of any apparent misstatements or material inconsistencies with the group financial statements. Our responsibilities do not extend to any other information.

Basis of audit opinion
We conducted our audit in accordance with International Standards on Auditing (UK and Ireland) issued by the Auditing Practices Board. An audit includes examination, on a test basis, of evidence relevant to the amounts and disclosures in the group financial statements. It also includes an assessment of the significant estimates and judgements made by the directors in the preparation of the group financial statements, and of whether the accounting policies are appropriate to the group's circumstances, consistently applied and adequately disclosed.

We planned and performed our audit so as to obtain all the information and explanations which we considered necessary in order to provide us with sufficient evidence to give reasonable assurance that the group financial statements are free from material misstatement, whether caused by fraud or other irregularity or error. In forming our opinion we also evaluated the overall adequacy of the presentation of information in the group financial statements.

Opinion
In our opinion:

- the group financial statements give a true and fair view, in accordance with International Financial Reporting Standards (IFRSs) as adopted by the

European Union, of the state of the group's affairs as at [date] and of its profit [loss] for the year then ended;
- the group financial statements have been properly prepared in accordance with the Companies Act 1985 and Article 4 of the IAS Regulation; and
- the information given in the Directors' Report is consistent with the financial statements.

[*Separate opinion where group has also complied with IFRS (non EU version)*
As explained in Note x to the group financial statements, the group in addition to complying with its legal obligation to comply with IFRSs as adopted by the European Union, has also complied with the IFRSs as issued by the International Accounting Standards Board.

In our opinion the group financial statements give a true and fair view, in accordance with IFRSs, of the state of the group's affairs as at ... and of its profit [loss] for the year then ended.]

Registered Auditors
Address
Date

TABLE 10: Unmodified report on publicly traded group and parent company

- *Parent company and group accounts presented together*
- *IFRSs as adopted for use in the EU used for group financial statements, UK GAAP used for parent company*
- *Publicly traded*

Independent auditors' report to the shareholders of XYZ PLC
We have audited the group and parent company financial statements ("the financial statements") of [entity name] for the year ended [date] which comprise [state the primary financial statements such as the Group Income Statement, [*if section 230 exemption not taken* the Parent Company Profit and Loss Account,] the Group and Parent Company Balance Sheets, the Group Cash Flow Statement, the Group Statement of change in Shareholders' Equity] and the related notes. These financial statements have been prepared under the accounting policies set out therein. We have also audited the information in the Directors' Remuneration Report that is described as having been audited.

This report is made solely to the members, as a body, in accordance with s235 of the Companies Act 1985. Our audit work has been undertaken so that we might state to the members those matters we are required to state to them in an auditors' report and for no other purpose. To the fullest extent permitted by law, we do not accept or assume responsibility to anyone other than the parent company, the group and their members as a body, for our audit work, for this report, or for the opinions we have formed.

Respective responsibilities of directors and auditors
The directors' responsibilities for preparing the Annual Report and the group

financial statements in accordance with applicable law and International Financial Reporting Standards (IFRSs) as adopted by the European Union, and for preparing the parent company financial statements and the Directors' Remuneration Report in accordance with applicable law and United Kingdom Accounting Standards (United Kingdom Generally Accepted Accounting Practice) are set out in the Statement of Directors' Responsibilities.

Our responsibility is to audit the financial statements and the part of the Directors' Remuneration Report to be audited in accordance with relevant legal and regulatory requirements and the International Standards on Auditing (UK and Ireland).

We report to you our opinion as to whether the financial statements give a true and fair view, the financial statements and the part of the Directors' Remuneration Report to be audited have been properly prepared in accordance with the Companies Act 1985 and whether in addition, the group financial statements have been properly prepared in accordance with Article 4 of the IAS Regulation. We also report to you whether in our opinion the information given in the Directors' Report is consistent with the financial statements.

In addition we report to you if, in our opinion, the company has not kept proper accounting records, if we have not received all the information and explanations we require for our audit, or if information specified by law regarding directors' remuneration and other transactions is not disclosed.

We review whether the Corporate Governance Statement reflects the company's compliance with the nine provisions of the 2003 FRC Combined Code specified for our review by the Listing Rules of the Financial Services Authority, and we report if it does not. We are not required to consider whether the board's statements on internal control cover all risks and controls, or form an opinion the effectiveness of the group's corporate governance procedures or its risk and control procedures.

We read other information contained in the Annual Report, and consider whether it is consistent with the audited financial statements. This other information comprises only [the Directors' Report, the unaudited part of the Directors' Remuneration Report, the Chairman's Statement, the Operating and Financial Review and the Corporate Governance Statement]. We consider the implications for our report if we become aware of any apparent misstatements or material inconsistencies with the financial statements. Our responsibilities do not extend to any other information.

Basis of audit opinion
We conducted our audit in accordance with International Standards on Auditing (UK and Ireland) issued by the Auditing Practices Board. An audit includes examination, on a test basis, of evidence relevant to the amounts and disclosures in the financial statements and the part of the Directors' Remuneration Report to be audited. It also includes an assessment of the significant estimates and judgements made by the directors in the preparation of the financial statements, and of whether the accounting policies are appropriate to the group's and company's circumstances, consistently applied and adequately disclosed.

We planned and performed our audit so as to obtain all the information and explanations which we considered necessary in order to provide us with sufficient evidence to give reasonable assurance that the financial statements and the part of the Directors' Remuneration Report to be audited are free from material misstatement, whether caused by fraud or other irregularity or error. In forming our opinion we also evaluated the overall adequacy of the presentation of information in the financial statements and the part of the Directors' Remuneration Report to be audited.

Opinion
In our opinion:

- the group financial statements give a true and fair view, in accordance with International Financial Reporting Standards (IFRSs) as adopted by the European Union, of the state of the group's affairs as at [date] and of its profit [loss] for the year then ended;
- the group financial statements have been properly prepared in accordance with the Companies Act 1985 and Article 4 of the IAS Regulation;
- the parent company financial statements give a true and fair view, in accordance with United Kingdom Generally Accepted Accounting Practice, of the state of the parent company's affairs as at [date] [*if section 230 exemption not taken* and of its profit [loss] for the year then ended];
- the parent company financial statements and the part of the Directors' Remuneration Report to be audited have been properly prepared in accordance with the Companies Act 1985; and
- the information given in the Directors' Report is consistent with the financial statements.

Registered Auditors
Address
Date

TABLE 11: Unmodified report on group and parent company accounts prepared under International Financial Reporting Standards (IFRSs) as adopted for use in the European Union

- *Group and parent company financial statements presented together*
- *International Financial Reporting Standards (IFRSs) as adopted for use in the European Union used for both parent company and group financial statements*
- *Publicly traded*

Independent auditors' report to the shareholders of XYZ PLC
We have audited the group and parent company financial statements ("the financial statements") of [entity name] for the year ended [date] which comprise [state the primary financial statements such as the Group Income Statement, [*if section 230 exemption not taken* the Parent Company Profit and Loss Account,] the Group and Parent Company Balance Sheets, the Group and Parent Company Cash Flow Statement, the Group and Parent Company Statement of

Change in Shareholders' Equity] and the related notes. These financial statements have been prepared under the accounting policies set out therein. We have also audited the information in the Directors' Remuneration Report that is described as having been audited.

This report is made solely to the members, as a body, in accordance with s235 of the Companies Act 1985. Our audit work has been undertaken so that we might state to the members those matters we are required to state to them in an auditors' report and for no other purpose. To the fullest extent permitted by law, we do not accept or assume responsibility to anyone other than the parent company, the group and their members as a body, for our audit work, for this report, or for the opinions we have formed.

Respective responsibilities of directors and auditors
The directors' responsibilities for preparing the Annual Report and the group financial statements in accordance with applicable law and International Financial Reporting Standards (IFRSs) as adopted by the European Union are set out in the Statement of Directors' Responsibilities.

Our responsibility is to audit the financial statements and the part of the Directors' Remuneration Report to be audited in accordance with relevant legal and regulatory requirements and the International Standards on Auditing (UK and Ireland).

We report to you our opinion as to whether the financial statements give a true and fair view and whether the financial statements and the part of the Directors' Remuneration Report to be audited have been properly prepared in accordance with the Companies Act 1985 and, as regards the group financial statements, Article 4 of the IAS Regulation. We also report to you whether in our opinion the information given in the Directors' Report is consistent with the financial statements.

In addition we report to you if, in our opinion, the company has not kept proper accounting records, if we have not received all the information and explanations we require for our audit, or if information specified by law regarding directors' remuneration and other transactions is not disclosed.

We review whether the Corporate Governance Statement reflects the company's compliance with the nine provisions of the 2003 FRC Combined Code specified for our review by the Listing Rules of the Financial Services Authority, and we report if it does not. We are not required to consider whether the board's statements on internal control cover all risks and controls, or form an opinion the effectiveness of the group's corporate governance procedures or its risk and control procedures.

We read other information contained in the Annual Report, and consider whether it is consistent with the audited financial statements. This other information comprises only [the Directors' Report, the unaudited part of the Directors' Remuneration Report, the Chairman's Statement, the Operating and Financial Review and the Corporate Governance Statement]. We consider the implications for our report if we become aware of any apparent misstatements or material inconsistencies with the financial statements. Our responsibilities do not extend to any other information.

Basis of audit opinion
We conducted our audit in accordance with International Standards on Auditing (UK and Ireland) issued by the Auditing Practices Board. An audit includes examination, on a test basis, of evidence relevant to the amounts and disclosures in the financial statements and the part of the Directors' Remuneration Report to be audited. It also includes an assessment of the significant estimates and judgements made by the directors in the preparation of the financial statements, and of whether the accounting policies are appropriate to the group's and company's circumstances, consistently applied and adequately disclosed.

We planned and performed our audit so as to obtain all the information and explanations which we considered necessary in order to provide us with sufficient evidence to give reasonable assurance that the financial statements and the part of the Directors' Remuneration Report to be audited are free from material misstatement, whether caused by fraud or other irregularity or error. In forming our opinion we also evaluated the overall adequacy of the presentation of information in the financial statements and the part of the Directors' Remuneration Report to be audited.

Opinion
In our opinion:

- the group financial statements give a true and fair view, in accordance with International Financial Reporting Standards (IFRSs) as adopted by the European Union, of the state of the group's affairs as at [date] and of its profit [loss] for the year then ended;
- the parent company financial statements give a true and fair view, in accordance with International Financial Reporting Standards (IFRSs) as adopted by the European Union and as applied in accordance with the provisions of the Companies Act 1985 (*see* **3.3.2**), of the state of the parent company's affairs as at [date] [*if section 230 exemption not taken* and of its profit [loss] for the year then ended];
- the financial statements and the part of the Directors' Remuneration Report to be audited have been properly prepared in accordance with the Companies Act 1985 and Article 4 of the IAS Regulation; and
- the information given in the Directors' Report is consistent with the financial statements.

Registered Auditors
Address
Date

3.9 RESPONSIBILITY STATEMENTS

ISA (UK and Ireland) 700 requires that auditors should distinguish between their responsibilities and those of the directors. This can be achieved by:

- a full statement of directors' responsibilities in the audit report; or
- reference to a statement contained elsewhere in the financial statements or accompanying information (**Table 2**).

As part of the section relating to directors' responsibilities, the auditor's report should set out the framework used for the preparation of the financial statements.

Example Statement of Directors' Responsibilities are set out in **Tables 12** to **16**. Bulletin 2006/6 suggests that legal advice on the exact wording of the statement may be sought in complex situations and that the wording applicable to publicly traded companies will vary depending on the rules of the market on which its securities are traded.

The statement of auditors' responsibilities should be included in the audit report following the guidance in Bulletin 2000/2 (see **3.5**) which extended this requirement to the audit reports of both listed and unlisted companies.

3.10 BASIS OF AUDIT OPINION

The ISA (UK and Ireland) requires auditors to explain the basis of their opinion. This should include:

- a statement of compliance or otherwise with relevant auditing standards, together with reasons for any departure;
- a description of the audit process; and
- a statement that the auditors planned and performed their work to give reasonable assurance that the financial statements are free from material misstatement and that they also evaluated the overall adequacy of the presentation of information in the financial statements.

It is necessary to include a statement concerning compliance with auditing standards to provide the reader with assurance that the audit has been carried out in accordance with generally accepted standards. Where there is a justifiable departure from auditing standards, for example, where it is necessary to fulfil the specific objectives of an audit more effectively, this should be disclosed, together with the reasons for this departure. Where it is necessary to use other standards, such as the Code of Audit Practice for Local Authorities and the National Health Service, these standards should be referred to. Where there has been departure which is not justifiable this constitutes a limitation of scope (see **4.2.3** below) and the auditors should assess whether there should be a qualified opinion, or a disclaimer.

TABLE 12: *Example wording of a description of the directors' responsibilities for inclusion in a non-publicly traded company's financial statements, reporting under UK GAAP*

The directors are responsible for preparing the Annual Report and the financial statements in accordance with applicable law and United Kingdom Generally Accepted Accounting Practice.

Company law requires the directors to prepare financial statements for each financial year which give a true and fair view of the state of affairs of the company and of the profit or loss of the company for that period. In preparing these financial statements, the directors are required to:

- select suitable accounting policies and then apply them consistently;
- make judgements and estimates that are reasonable and prudent;
- state whether applicable accounting standards have been followed, subject to any material departures disclosed and explained in the financial statements [except for small or medium-sized companies as defined by the Companies Act];
- prepare the financial statements on the going concern basis unless it is inappropriate to presume that the company will continue in business.

The directors are responsible for keeping proper accounting records which disclose with reasonable accuracy at any time the financial position of the company and to enable them to ensure that the financial statements comply with the Companies Act 1985. They are also responsible for safeguarding the assets of the company and hence for taking reasonable steps for the prevention and detection of fraud and other irregularities.

TABLE 13: *Example wording of a description of the directors' responsibilities for inclusion in a publicly traded company's financial statements*

- *Group accounts prepared under IFRS*
- *Parent company accounts prepared under UK GAAP*

The directors are responsible for keeping proper accounting records which disclose with reasonable accuracy at any time the financial position of the company, for safeguarding the assets of the company, for taking reasonable steps for the prevention and detection of fraud and other irregularities and for the preparation of a Directors' Report and Directors' Remuneration Report which comply with the requirements of the Companies Act 1985.

The directors are responsible for preparing the Annual Report and the financial statements in accordance with the Companies Act 1985. The directors are also required to prepare financial statements for the group in accordance with

---

International Financial Reporting Standards (IFRSs) as adopted by the European Union and Article 4 of the IAS Regulation. The directors have chosen to prepare financial statements for the company in accordance with United Kingdom Generally Accepted Accounting Practice.

Group financial statements
International Accounting Standard 1 requires that financial statements present fairly for each financial year the company's financial position, financial performance and cash flows. This requires the faithful representation of the effects of transactions, other events and conditions in accordance with the definitions and recognition criteria for assets, liabilities, income and expenses set out in the International Accounting Standards Board's 'Framework for the preparation and presentation of financial statements'. In virtually all circumstances, a fair presentation will be achieved by compliance with all applicable IFRSs. A fair presentation also requires the directors to:

- consistently select and apply appropriate accounting policies;
- present information, including accounting policies, in a manner that provides relevant, reliable, comparable and understandable information; and
- provide additional disclosures when compliance with the specific requirements in IFRSs is insufficient to enable users to understand the impact of particular transactions, other events and conditions on the entity's financial position and financial performance.

Parent company financial statements
Company law requires the directors to prepare financial statements for each financial year which give a true and fair view of the state of affairs of the company and of the profit or loss of the company for that period. In preparing these financial statements, the directors are required to:

- select suitable accounting policies and then apply them consistently;
- make judgements and estimates that are reasonable and prudent;
- state whether applicable accounting standards have been followed, subject to any material departures disclosed and explained in the financial statements;
- prepare the financial statements on the going concern basis unless it is inappropriate to presume that the company will continue in business.

The directors are responsible for keeping proper accounting records which disclose with reasonable accuracy at any time the financial position of the company and to enable them to ensure that the financial statements comply with the Companies Act 1985. They are also responsible for safeguarding the assets of the company and hence for taking reasonable steps for the prevention and detection of fraud and other irregularities.

[*Where financial statements are published on a website, see* **3.16.2**]

Financial statements are published on the group's website in accordance with legislation in the United Kingdom governing the preparation and dissemination of financial statements, which may vary from legislation in other jurisdictions. The maintenance and integrity of the group's website is the responsibility of the directors. The directors' responsibility also extends to the ongoing integrity of the financial statements contained therein.

TABLE 14: *Example wording of a description of the directors' responsibilities for inclusion in a publicly traded company's financial statements*

- *Group accounts prepared under IFRS*
- *Parent company accounts prepared under IFRS*

The directors are responsible for keeping proper accounting records which disclose with reasonable accuracy at any time the financial position of the company, for safeguarding the assets of the company, for taking reasonable steps for the prevention and detection of fraud and other irregularities and for the preparation of a Directors' Report and Directors' Remuneration Report which comply with the requirements of the Companies Act 1985.

The directors are responsible for preparing the Annual Report and the financial statements in accordance with the Companies Act 1985. The directors are also required to prepare financial statements for the group in accordance with International Financial Reporting Standards (IFRSs) as adopted by the European Union and Article 4 of the IAS Regulation. The directors have chosen to prepare financial statements for the group and the company in accordance with IFRSs.

International Accounting Standard 1 requires that financial statements present fairly for each financial year the company's financial position, financial performance and cash flows. This requires the faithful representation of the effects of transactions, other events and conditions in accordance with the definitions and recognition criteria for assets, liabilities, income and expenses set out in the International Accounting Standards Board's 'Framework for the preparation and presentation of financial statements'. In virtually all circumstances, a fair presentation will be achieved by compliance with all applicable IFRSs. A fair presentation also requires the directors to:

- consistently select and apply appropriate accounting policies;
- present information, including accounting policies, in a manner that provides relevant, reliable, comparable and understandable information; and
- provide additional disclosures when compliance with the specific requirements in IFRSs is insufficient to enable users to understand the impact of particular transactions, other events and conditions on the entity's financial position and financial performance.

TABLE 15:   *Example wording of a description of the directors' responsibilities for inclusion in a non-listed company's financial statements (including AIM listed companies)*

- *Group voluntarily prepares accounts under IFRS*
- *Parent company voluntarily prepares accounts under IFRS*

The directors are responsible for keeping proper accounting records which disclose with reasonable accuracy at any time the financial position of the company, for safeguarding the assets of the company, for taking reasonable steps for the prevention and detection of fraud and other irregularities and for the preparation of a Directors' Report and Directors' Remuneration Report which comply with the requirements of the Companies Act 1985.

The directors are responsible for preparing the Annual Report and the financial statements in accordance with the Companies Act 1985. The directors have chosen to prepare financial statements for the group and the company in accordance with International Financial Reporting Standards (IFRSs) as adopted by the European Union.

International Accounting Standard 1 requires that financial statements present fairly for each financial year the company's financial position, financial performance and cash flows. This requires the faithful representation of the effects of transactions, other events and conditions in accordance with the definitions and recognition criteria for assets, liabilities, income and expenses set out in the International Accounting Standards Board's 'Framework for the preparation and presentation of financial statements'. In virtually all circumstances, a fair presentation will be achieved by compliance with all applicable IFRSs. A fair presentation also requires the directors to:

- consistently select and apply appropriate accounting policies;
- present information, including accounting policies, in a manner that provides relevant, reliable, comparable and understandable information; and
- provide additional disclosures when compliance with the specific requirements in IFRSs is insufficient to enable users to understand the impact of particular transactions, other events and conditions on the entity's financial position and financial performance.

TABLE 16:   *Example wording of a description of the directors' responsibilities for inclusion in an unlisted company's financial statements (including AIM listed companies)*

- *Group voluntarily prepares accounts under IFRS*
- *Parent company accounts prepared under UK GAAP*

The directors are responsible for keeping proper accounting records which disclose with reasonable accuracy at any time the financial position of the company, for safeguarding the assets of the company, for taking reasonable steps for the prevention and detection of fraud and other irregularities and for the preparation of a Directors' Report and Directors' Remuneration Report which comply with the requirements of the Companies Act 1985.

The directors are responsible for preparing the Annual Report and the financial statements in accordance with the Companies Act 1985. The directors have chosen to prepare financial statements for the group in accordance with International Financial Reporting Standards (IFRSs) as adopted by the European Union and have chosen to prepare the parent company accounts in accordance with United Kingdom Generally Accepted Accounting Practice.

Group financial statements
International Accounting Standard 1 requires that financial statements present fairly for each financial year the company's financial position, financial performance and cash flows. This requires the faithful representation of the effects of transactions, other events and conditions in accordance with the definitions and recognition criteria for assets, liabilities, income and expenses set out in the International Accounting Standards Board's 'Framework for the preparation and presentation of financial statements'. In virtually all circumstances, a fair presentation will be achieved by compliance with all applicable IFRSs. A fair presentation also requires the directors to:

- consistently select and apply appropriate accounting policies;
- present information, including accounting policies, in a manner that provides relevant, reliable, comparable and understandable information; and
- provide additional disclosures when compliance with the specific requirements in IFRSs is insufficient to enable users to understand the impact of particular transactions, other events and conditions on the entity's financial position and financial performance.

Parent company financial statements
Company law requires the directors to prepare financial statements for each financial year which give a true and fair view of the state of affairs of the company and of the profit or loss of the company for that period. In preparing these financial statements, the directors are required to:

- select suitable accounting policies and then apply them consistently;
- make judgements and estimates that are reasonable and prudent;
- state whether applicable accounting standards have been followed, subject to any material departures disclosed and explained in the financial statements;
- prepare the financial statements on the going concern basis unless it is inappropriate to presume that the company will continue in business.

When describing the audit process, the auditors should mention that it includes:

- examining, on a test basis, evidence which supports the amounts and disclosures in the financial statements;

- assessing the significant estimates and judgements made by the directors in preparing the financial statements; and
- considering the appropriateness of the accounting policies given the nature of the entity's activities, the consistency of their application and the adequacy of their disclosure.

3.11   EXPRESSION OF OPINION

ISA (UK and Ireland) 700 requires that the report should contain a clear expression of the auditors' opinion on the financial statements and on any further requirements of statute or the particular assignment.

The opinion may be unqualified or qualified. Qualifications are considered in detail in **3.13** below.

Where the opinion is unqualified, this means that, in the auditors' opinion, the financial statements give a true and fair view and have been properly prepared in accordance with the relevant accounting framework. The judgements that the auditors should make to reach this conclusion concern whether:

- the financial statements have been prepared within the relevant accounting framework, using appropriate accounting policies and these have been consistently applied;
- the financial statements are prepared in accordance with relevant legislation, regulations, or applicable accounting standards and any departures from these are adequately explained and disclosed; and
- there is adequate disclosure of all information relevant to the proper understanding of the financial statements.

3.12   RELEVANT ACCOUNTING REQUIREMENTS

3.12.1   *The role of Accounting Standards*

The auditors have to express their opinion in the context of relevant accounting requirements. Where the reporting entity is a company this will be the Companies Act 1985 and auditors must include in their report a statement that financial statements 'have been properly prepared in accordance with the Companies Act 1985'.

There is no specific legal requirement to comply with accounting standards, either UK Financial Reporting Standards or International Accounting Standards. The Companies Act 1989, however, defines accounting standards and requires larger companies to state that their financial statements have been prepared in accordance with applicable accounting standards and to give particulars of, and reasons for, any material departure from them. This implies that compliance with accounting standards is generally necessary to give a true and fair view.

This view is supported by an opinion from Mrs Justice Arden obtained by the Accounting Standards Board and which is contained in the appendix to its *Foreword to Accounting Standards* (June 1993). She examines the relationship between accounting standards and the Companies Act arguing that it is the courts who decide whether a true and fair view is given. They will generally look to accounting standards to provide a set of principles which must be applied to each case, expecting any departures from them to be justified.

Auditors must apply similar principles in forming their opinion. One practical effect of this is that it is less likely that auditors will concur with a company's non-compliance with accounting standards.

The opinion also considers the abstracts of the Urgent Issues Task Force (UITF) and expresses the view that the court is likely to treat them as being of considerable standing. This 'will lead to a readiness on the part of the court to accept that compliance with abstracts of the UITF is also necessary to meet the true and fair requirement'.

Where financial statements do not comply with accounting standards the auditors should assess whether:

- there are sound reasons for the departure;
- adequate disclosure has been made; and
- as a result the financial statements do not give a true and fair view of the state of affairs and profit or loss.

A departure will normally result in the issue of a qualified or adverse opinion (see **4.2.2** below).

Inadequate disclosure of a departure from accounting standards may itself prevent the financial statements from giving a true and fair view and as a result lead to a qualified opinion, even when the departure is justifiable.

In 2005, after the introduction of the requirement for listed companies to adopt International Accounting Standards (IASs) and the replacement of the SASs by ISAs (UK and Ireland), the Financial Reporting Council (FRC) issued a comment paper to allay fears that the new regime amounted to a weakening of the safeguards against corporate scandals.

With the implementation of IASs and ISAs, the concept of 'fair presentation' was introduced, which resulted in changes to the format and content of both company accounts and audit reports. In response to the suggestions that the 'true and fair view' was in jeopardy, the FRC stated:

- 'the concept of the "true and fair view" remains a cornerstone of financial reporting and auditing in the UK;
- there has been no substantive change in the objectives of an audit and the nature of auditors' responsibilities; and
- the need for professional judgement remains central to the work of preparers of accounts and auditors in the UK.'

3.12.2 Primary statements

As well as the profit and loss account and balance sheet, Financial Reporting Standards (FRSs) and International Financial Reporting Standards (IFRSs) require other primary statements to be provided in certain circumstances. For example, the cash flow statement and the statement of total recognised gains and losses are required by UK accounting standards but are not statements which the directors have a strict legal obligation to prepare. By contrast, the only primary statements required by the Companies Act are the profit and loss account and the balance sheet.

The ISA (UK and Ireland) is silent about which primary statements are referred to. The previous standard contained guidance that there was no requirement to refer to primary statements beyond the profit and loss account and the balance sheet.

Omission of primary statements, if material, will usually be a departure from the relevant accounting standard and as such the auditors should consider if the departure is justified and explained adequately. In most cases omission will result in a qualified or adverse opinion. Where the report is qualified in this respect the opinion paragraph would read as shown in **Table 17**.

TABLE 17: *Omission of primary statement*

Extract from a qualified opinion arising from omission of cash flow statement
As explained in note ... the financial statements do not contain a statement of cash flows as required by Financial Reporting Standard 1. Net cash flows for the year ended 31 December 20.. amounted to £ ... and in our opinion information about the company's cash flows is necessary for a proper understanding of the company's state of affairs and profit.

Except for the failure to provide information about the company's cash flows, in our opinion:

- the financial statements give a true and fair view, in accordance with United Kingdom Generally Accepted Accounting Practice, of the state of the company's affairs as at 31 December 20.. and of its profit for the year then ended;

- the financial statements have been properly prepared in accordance with the Companies Act 1985; and
- the information given in the Directors' Report is consistent with the financial statements.

There may be occasions when auditors are asked to report separately on one or more primary statements. Where this is the case they should ensure that they do not give the impression that the primary statement is other than integral to the financial statements as a whole.

3.12.3 Small companies

The Financial Reporting Standard for Smaller Entities

The introduction of the Financial Reporting Standard for Smaller Entities (FRSSE) led the APB to issue guidance for auditors of companies adopting this all-embracing accounting standard. Bulletin 1997/3 *The FRSSE: Guidance for Auditors* covers four areas of concern:

- whether auditors consider other accounting pronouncements when assessing the truth and fairness of the financial statements;
- the responsibility of auditors with regard to voluntary disclosures made in such financial statements;
- the effect of the FRSSE on ISAs (UK and Ireland); and
- the effect of the FRSSE on the auditors' report on the financial statements.

The FRSSE notes that, where it does not address a particular matter, reference may be made to other pronouncements to establish best practice and hence the Bulletin advises that in such cases auditors would also need to refer to them.

Voluntary disclosures made in financial statements prepared under the FRSSE are subject to audit. Where such disclosures are outside the financial statements but elsewhere in the annual report the requirements of ISA (UK and Ireland) 720 should be followed (see **Chapter 13**).

Only ISA (UK and Ireland) 550 *Related Parties* is directly affected by the FRSSE. FRS 8 requires materiality to be considered from the point of view of 'individual' related parties as well as the reporting entity. The FRSSE, on the other hand, like IAS 24, only requires materiality to be considered from the point of view of the reporting entity. The guidance in the ISA (UK and Ireland) on this is therefore not relevant (see **30.5**).

Where financial statements apply the FRSSE, the introductory section of the auditors' report has to be amended. Example wording for an unmodified audit report for a company preparing financial statements under the FRSSE is given in **Table 18**.

TABLE 18: Example unmodified auditor's report for a company preparing financial statements under the FRSSE

Independent auditors' report to the shareholders of XYZ Limited
We have audited the financial statements of [entity name] for the year ended [date] which comprise [state the primary financial statements such as the Profit and Loss Account, the Balance Sheet, [the Cash Flow Statement,] the Statement of Total Recognised Gains and Losses] and the related notes. These financial statements have been prepared under the accounting policies set out therein and the requirements of the Financial Reporting Standard for Smaller Entities.

This report is made solely to the company's members, as a body, in accordance with s235 of the Companies Act 1985. Our audit work has been undertaken so that we might state to the company's members those matters we are required to state to them in an auditors' report and for no other purpose. To the fullest extent permitted by law, we do not accept or assume responsibility to anyone other than the company and the company's members as a body, for our audit work, for this report, or for the opinions we have formed.

Respective responsibilities of directors and auditors
The directors' responsibilities for preparing the financial statements in accordance with applicable law and United Kingdom Accounting Standards (United Kingdom Generally Accepted Accounting Practice) are set out in the Statement of Directors' Responsibilities.

Our responsibility is to audit the financial statements in accordance with relevant legal and regulatory requirements and the International Standards on Auditing (UK and Ireland).

We report to you our opinion as to whether the financial statements give a true and fair view, are properly prepared in accordance with the Companies Act 1985. We also report to you whether in our opinion the information given in the Directors' Report is consistent with the financial statements.

In addition we report to you if, in our opinion, the company has not kept proper accounting records, if we have not received all the information and explanations we require for our audit, or if information specified by law regarding directors' remuneration and other transactions is not disclosed.

We read the Directors' Report and consider the implications for our report if we become aware of any apparent misstatement within it.

Basis of audit opinion
We conducted our audit in accordance with International Standards on Auditing (UK and Ireland) issued by the Auditing Practices Board. An audit includes examination, on a test basis, of evidence relevant to the amounts and

---

disclosures in the financial statements. It also includes an assessment of the significant estimates and judgements made by the directors in the preparation of the financial statements, and of whether the accounting policies are appropriate to the company's circumstances, consistently applied and adequately disclosed.

We planned and performed our audit so as to obtain all the information and explanations which we considered necessary in order to provide us with sufficient evidence to give reasonable assurance that the financial statements are free from material misstatement, whether caused by fraud or other irregularity or error. In forming our opinion we also evaluated the overall adequacy of the presentation of information in the financial statements.

Opinion
In our opinion:

- the financial statements give a true and fair view, in accordance with United Kingdom Generally Accepted Accounting Practice applicable to Smaller Entities, of the state of the company's affairs as at [date] and of its profit [loss] for the year then ended;
- the financial statements have been properly prepared in accordance with the Companies Act 1985; and
- the information given in the Directors' Report is consistent with the financial statements.

Registered Auditors
Address
Date

Companies Act 1985 Schedule 8

Unlike its predecessor, SAS 600, ISA (UK and Ireland) 700 gives no guidance on cases where a small company takes advantage of the exemptions set out in Schedule 8 Companies Act 1985. This Schedule was amended by Statutory Instrument 1997 No 220 and sets out the reduced requirements for small companies, rather than the exemptions.

Although the disclosure requirements are limited, the financial statements should still show a true and fair view. The auditors of a company which prepares its accounts under Schedule 8 are still therefore required to form an opinion on whether the financial statements give a true and fair view. The normal wording for an unqualified opinion should now be used.

Prior to the amendments there was an implication in the Act, which was reflected in the practice note, that the audit report should refer to the financial statements being properly prepared in accordance with the provisions applicable to small companies. This no longer appears to be necessary.

Similarly, if the financial statements do not show a true and fair view because of compliance with the requirements, the auditors' report should say so rather than reporting that they 'have been properly prepared in accordance with the provisions of the Companies Act 1985 applicable to small companies', which was required in such cases under the previous rules.

3.13   DATING ISSUES

ISA (UK and Ireland) 700 requires that:

- before the auditors can give an opinion on the financial statements they must have been approved by the directors and the auditors must have considered all of the available evidence; and
- the auditors' report has to be dated as at the date the opinion is expressed.

The significance of the date of the auditors' report is that they are informing the reader that they are aware of events up to that date and have considered the effect of these on the financial statements.

Before they sign the audit report the following must have occurred:

- receipt of the approved financial statements, together with any accompanying information, from the directors;
- review of all the documents which the auditors are required to consider in addition to the financial statements, for example, the directors' report; and
- completion of all the procedures thought necessary by the auditor to be able to form an opinion, including a post balance sheet event review.

The auditors must sign in manuscript and date their report expressing an opinion on the financial statements for distribution with the financial statements. Firms must therefore have procedures to ensure reports are not signed before the above events have occurred.

The report should also state the location of the auditors' offices, typically the city in which the office that has responsibility is based.

Although the date of the auditors' report has to be after the directors have approved the financial statements, it does not mean that the auditors cannot commence their work until the directors have approved the financial statements. Rather, they cannot conclude it until this has happened. In many cases the preparation of the financial statements will take place at the same time as the auditors are gathering evidence.

Although they will normally be in a position to give their opinion at the same date as the financial statements are approved, it does not have to be on the same day. Unless the auditors have gathered all their evidence and completed their work at that time (including a post balance sheet events review) they are unable to sign their report despite the directors approving the financial statements.

Where the date the opinion is expressed is before the final printing of the financial statements, the auditors will have to ensure the drafts on which they form their opinion are sufficiently clear for them to assess the overall presentation. One area to be especially aware of is where the directors have approved the profit and loss account and the balance sheet, but the notes have yet to be finally completed. In such cases the auditors will have to delay giving their opinion until they are finished.

Where the date the auditors sign their report is later than the date of approval they may need to obtain additional assurances from the directors that there have been no events in the intervening period that would affect the financial statements. They will also need to have their own procedures for reviewing subsequent events and assessing their impact on the financial statements.

3.14 PROPOSED REVISION TO ISA (UK AND IRELAND) 700

In December 2004 the IAASB issued a proposed revision to ISA 700, which, in turn, the APB exposed for comment in the UK and Ireland in the summer of 2005. In November 2005, and following a review of the comments received, the APB issued a press notice stating that the expected implementation of a revision to ISA (UK and Ireland) 700 was to be deferred.

The APB stated that a number of issues needed resolution before an amendment could be published, and identified the following as significant outstanding matters:

- forthcoming changes to the UK Companies Act;
- revision of the European 8th Directive; and
- standards on Modifications to the Auditor's Report.

The APB stated that it would be unnecessarily complicated to issue a revision to ISA (UK and Ireland) 700 until conclusions were reached on these issues, as each one could require further amendment to ISA 700.

3.14.1 UK Companies Act

The Companies Act 2006 received Royal Assent in November 2006. Provisions on directors and auditors are contained in Parts 10 and 16 respectively.

3.14.2   European 8th Directive

The revision of the European 8th Directive on Company Law was approved at the end of September 2005. This Directive addresses audit requirements and provides for the adoption of ISAs in the European Union. However, it does not set out the process by which adoption is to be achieved, or whether the form and content of the auditor's report set out in ISA 700 will be approved for adoption in the EU. As one of the aims of the revision of ISA 700 by the IAASB was to set out auditor's report wording which would be applied consistently in all jurisdictions, the APB believe it is prudent to await the decision whether the EU will accept the current wording in ISA 700 or whether amendment is required.

3.14.3   Standards on Modifications to the Auditor's Report

When the Exposure Drafts of ISA 705 and 706 were issued by the IAASB (see **Chapter 4),** it was intended that the definitive version of these ISAs would be finalised in time to have the same effective date as the amended ISA 700, ie audit reports issued on or after 15 December 2006. However, the Exposure Drafts of ISAs 705 and 706 have now been included in the IAASB's *Clarity Project*, see **1.5.1**, and their finalisation has been delayed.

3.15   APB BULLETIN 2002/2, THE UNITED KINGDOM DIRECTORS' REMUNERATION REPORT REGULATIONS

3.15.1   Introduction

With effect from 1 August 2002 the UK Government brought into force Regulations that require quoted companies to prepare a Directors' Remuneration Report for each financial year. This report contains specified information, some of which is subject to audit.

An amendment to s235 of the Companies Act 1985 requires auditors of quoted companies to include within their report on the annual accounts their opinion as to whether the 'auditable part' of the Directors' Remuneration Report has been properly prepared in accordance with the Companies Act.

In October 2002, the APB issued Bulletin 2002/2, *The United Kingdom Directors' Remuneration Report Regulations 2002*, to provide auditors with guidance about their responsibilities with respect to the unaudited part of the Directors' Remuneration Report and illustrations of the revised audit report and statement on Summary Financial Statements.

The guidance in **Chapter 5** on Summary Financial Statements reflects this.

3.15.2 Companies affected by the rules

The regulations apply to 'quoted' companies. A quoted company is defined as a company incorporated under the Companies Act 1985:

- whose equity share capital has been included in the official list; or
- is officially listed in an European Economic Area (EEA) state; or
- is admitted to dealing on either the New York Stock Exchange of the exchange known as Nasdaq.

The definition does not include companies traded on the Alternative Investment Market (AIM).

3.15.3 The 'auditable part' of the Directors' Remuneration Report

Auditors are required to report on the disclosures in the 'auditable part' of the Directors' Remuneration Report. The 'auditable part' is the part which contains the information required by Part 3 of Schedule 7A, as demonstrated in **Table 19**.

TABLE 19: Directors' remuneration disclosure and auditing requirements

Requirement	Quoted companies	Unquoted companies	Required to be audited
Schedule 6 to the Companies Act 1985 Disclosure of Information: Emoluments and other Benefits of Directors and others (These disclosures are required to be made in the notes to the financial statements)			
Information about the aggregate amounts of emoluments paid to directors, plus information about gains made, benefits received under long-term incentives plans, contributions to pension schemes, the number of directors in pension schemes, share options (Part I, paragraph 1)	✓	✓	✓

Information about the highest paid directors' emoluments, excess retirement benefits of directors and past directors, compensation to directors for loss of office, sums paid to third parties for directors' services, (Part I, paragraphs 2–14)		✓	✓
Information about loans, quasi loans and other dealings in favour of directors (Part II)	✓	✓	✓
Information about other transactions, arrangements and agreements (Part III)	✓	✓	✓
Schedule 7A to the Companies Act 1985 Directors' Remuneration Report (These disclosures are required to be made in the Directors' Remuneration Report)			
Information about remuneration committees, performance related remuneration and liabilities in respect of directors' contracts (Part 2)	✓		
Information about directors' remuneration (Part 3)	✓		✓

3.15.4   Reporting on the Directors' Remuneration Report

Auditors report on the Directors' Remuneration Report as part of their report on the financial statements. As they are not required to audit all of the information in the Directors' Remuneration Report, they must clearly identify the elements that have been audited. If this cannot be done by cross-reference, auditors should set out the particulars that have been audited within the auditors' report. It is not satisfactory for auditors to describe what they have audited as 'the disclosures required by Part 3 of Schedule 7A to the Companies Act'.

An example report for a quoted company is set out in **Table 7**.

3.15.5   The Directors' Remuneration Report as a separate document

If a quoted company issues its Directors' Remuneration Report as a separate document, the scope of the auditors' report in the Annual Report will still be required to include the parts of this separately published report which are to be audited.

When the Directors' Remuneration Report is issued as a separate document, auditors should:

- when their report is unqualified, encourage the directors to indicate in the Directors' Remuneration Report where the report can be found; or
- when their report contains a qualification, adverse opinion or disclaimer which is relevant to the Directors' Remuneration Report, encourage directors to reproduce the relevant parts of the auditors' report as part of the Directors' Remuneration Report. If the directors refuse to comply with this request, the Bulletin suggests that auditors should consider whether to resign.

3.16   CHANGES TO AUDIT REPORTS RESULTING FROM ELECTRONIC PUBLICATION

3.16.1   Background

In January 2001, the APB published two Bulletins covering changes required to audit reports as a result of a number of developments in the Listing Rules and the way financial statements are circulated to members.

Bulletin 2001/1 *The Electronic Publication of Auditors' Reports* was published in response to the enactment of the Companies Act 1985 (Electronic Communications) Order 2000 ('the Order'). The Order enables companies, subject to certain conditions, to meet their statutory reporting obligations to shareholders by distributing financial statements and certain other reports (including summary financial statements) electronically, or to post their financial statements on their website and advise shareholders of this.

Published at the same time, Bulletin 2001/2 *Revisions to the Wording of Auditors' Reports on Financial Statements and the Interim Review Report* includes revisions to standard audit reports as a result of the Order and its implications for the readers of audit reports, as well as changes to responsibility for the Listing Rules in the United Kingdom.

The Companies Act 2006 set out additional requirements to facilitate electronic communication with shareholders. This was one of the first areas of the new Companies Act to be implemented and is effective from 20 January 2007. It is discussed in **3.16.3** below.

3.16.2   *Electronic publication of audit reports*

As stated above, following the enactment of the Order, companies may either send their members copies of the annual financial statements by electronic means or post the annual financial statements on their website and advise their members of this, rather than post hard copies to them. The purpose of the Bulletin is to provide guidance to auditors in each of these circumstances, and also in the more common current situation where annual financial statements, accompanied by the auditors' report, are published on an entity's website.

For auditors of entities which publish their Annual Report by taking advantage of the provisions of the Order, the guidance in Bulletin 2001/1 is effective immediately. Where financial statements are more generally available on a company's website but hard copies are still circulated to members, the guidance is effective for periods beginning after 22 December 2000.

The main aim of the guidance is to ensure that auditors' duty of care is not extended solely as a result of their report being published in electronic rather than hard-copy form. In addition, as information published on websites is available in many countries with different legal requirements, it must be clear which legislation governs the preparation and dissemination of financial statements.

Additional work to provide assurance on the integrity of an entity's website is considered a separate engagement and is not covered in the Bulletin.

Directors' responsibilities
The fact that financial statements are reproduced or published electronically does not change the responsibilities of the directors concerning preparation, dissemination and signing of financial statements. The APB's view is in order to comply with their responsibilities, directors will still produce paper-based versions of their financial statements.

At the request of the Department of Trade and Industry, the Institute of Chartered Secretaries and Administrators (ICSA) has issued guidance on information published on corporate websites. If a company wishes to publish its financial statements on its website, auditors should enquire whether the directors have obtained a copy of this guidance and are following its recommendations relating to the presentation of the annual report and accounts.

The main ICSA recommendations are set out in **Table 20**. Auditors should be aware of these, as non-compliance of any of these by an entity may mean auditors are unable to agree to the electronic publication of their audit report.

TABLE 20: *Summary of ICSA recommendations for electronic publication of the annual report and accounts*

- inclusion of a 'watermark' or 'banner' on each page containing statutory or audited information to ensure that the status of that information is clear;
- add a warning message each time a user moves from or to a statutory or audited part of a website;
- not mixing statutory and non-statutory or audited and unaudited information on any one page;
- including a link to the statutory part of the website on the homepage;
- at any early stage ask auditors for clearance for the publication of audited information on the website;
- ask auditors to confirm that they agree with the way information is being presented, including the exact format of their audit report;
- listed companies should have procedures in place to ensure that no price sensitive information is published prior to notification of the relevant authorities; and
- ensure they comply with s240 of the Companies Act, which states that statutory accounts must be published with the relevant auditors' report and that non-statutory accounts must be accompanied by a statement that they are not statutory accounts.

The directors' responsibility statement should include reference to the fact that legislation in the United Kingdom governing the preparation and dissemination of financial statements may differ from legislation in other jurisdictions.

Hard-copy reports cannot be amended unless a revised printed version is issued to shareholders. However, it is easy for all or part of an electronic report to be amended without it being apparent that a revision has occurred. Inaccurate information may be placed on a website by a company employee (either accidentally or maliciously) or by a person outside the organisation who is able to gain access to the website.

Directors should therefore establish a regular procedure for checking that statutory or audited information has not been tampered with. Auditors will have no further responsibility for either the controls in place or the integrity of the information on a website once it is issued in electronic form. The APB recommends that directors state clearly in their statement of responsibilities that the maintenance and integrity of the website is their responsibility alone. If the directors' statement does not make this clear such as in **Table 13** above, or if the auditors otherwise consider it appropriate, they should add a note to the bottom of their audit report. The example wording from the Bulletin is given in **Table 21** below.

Where auditors are aware that the financial statements no longer agree to the set the directors have approved, they should inform the directors and request that they be amended immediately. If the necessary amendments are not made, auditors should obtain legal advice and consider resignation.

Auditors' considerations
When companies publish their annual report on their website or distribute it electronically, auditors should:

- review the process used to derive the electronically published financial statements from the manually signed version;
- check the electronic version is identical to the manual accounts; and
- check that conversion to the electronic version has not distorted the overall presentation (e.g., by use of different fonts or colour to highlight certain information).

In addition, for future reference, auditors should obtain a printed copy of the electronic version that they have reviewed.

Auditors are not expected to perform the above procedures on any prior period information. Prior period information should be clearly identified as such, or the auditors should request management to delete it.

Auditors' report
Three main issues should be considered in relation to the wording of the audit report:

- identification of the nationality of the accounting and auditing standards applied;
- identifying the financial statements that have been audited and the information that has only been reviewed or read by the auditors; and
- limiting the auditors' association with any other information distributed with the annual report.

The revised wording in Bulletin 2001/2 deals with the first issue, by stating that the standards used are those relevant in the United Kingdom. This means that the relevant jurisdiction is clear to readers in other countries. In addition, auditors should ensure that their report gives sufficient of their address to enable readers to understand in which country the auditors are located.

Where the directors' responsibility statement does not include the statement relating to different legislation requirements in different jurisdictions referred to above, the auditors should include a statement at the foot of their report. The example wording from the Bulletin is given in **Table 21** below.

TABLE 21: *Possible notes for inclusion at the foot of audit reports presented on a website*

1. The maintenance and integrity of the [name of entity] website is the responsibility of the directors; the work carried out by the auditors does not involve consideration of these matters and, accordingly, the auditors accept no responsibility for the changes that may have occurred to the financial statements since they were initially presented on the website.
2. Legislation in the United Kingdom governing the preparation and dissemination of financial statements may differ from legislation in other jurisdictions.

Hard-copy annual reports will have page numbers by which auditors can identify the financial statements that have been audited in their report. Where Hypertext Mark-up Language (HTML) has been used to publish annual reports on a website, page numbers are often no longer included and thus identification of audited information is difficult. Where a Portable Document Format (PDF) file is used, page numbers generally continue to be effective.

Therefore, where page numbers are no longer an effective way of identifying audited information the APB recommends that the auditors' report describes, by name, the primary statements that comprise the financial statements. The same technique can be used to identify information that has been reviewed, or read, by the auditors.

The problem of identifying other information in the annual report, which the auditor has neither audited, reviewed nor read, is exacerbated by the use of hyperlinks that allow the user to move easily from one area of the website to another. To reduce misunderstandings, auditors should request that readers are warned when they move from an audited to an unaudited part of the website. An additional safeguard is for auditors to request that all audited information, such as disclosures relating to directors' emoluments, are included within the financial statements. If the scope of the audit report is not clear because of the use of hyperlinks, the report itself should list in detail all the areas within its scope.

Where auditors are not satisfied with the proposed presentation of the audited financial statements and their report, they should request that the presentation is amended. If the presentation is not amended, the auditors should refuse to give their consent for the electronic release of their audit report. If the report is used without their consent, the auditors should seek legal advice and consider resigning from the engagement.

The electronic report should have the same date as the manually signed version. Amending the manual report for electronic publication (such as the substitution of the names of primary statements for page numbers) does not constitute a new audit opinion. The auditor is not required to perform any further subsequent events work, as the date of the opinion has not changed.

Engagement letters

The responsibilities of directors and auditors in relation to the electronic publication of financial statements should be clarified in the engagement letter. The engagement letter should also state that directors must seek the consent of their auditors for the electronic publication of their audit report. This will ensure that auditors have a right to request amendments to the wording or presentation of an electronic audit report.

The engagement letter should note that:

- the auditors recognise that the company may wish to publish its financial statements and the auditors' report on its website or distribute them electronically;
- the presentation of the financial information and auditors' report is the responsibility of the directors;
- the directors should advise the auditors in advance of the intended electronic publication;
- the auditors reserve the right to withhold consent to the electronic publication of their report if the audited financial statements or the audit report itself are presented in an inappropriate way;
- the directors are responsible for controls over the maintenance and security of the website;
- examination of the controls over maintenance and integrity are outside the scope of the audit; and
- where applicable, directors are responsible for establishing and controlling the process for electronically distributing the Annual Report to shareholders and the Registrar of Companies.

3.16.3   The Companies Act 2006

One of the first parts of the Companies Act 2006 to be implemented was that relating to the electronic communication by companies with shareholders, debenture holders and others with an effective date of 20 January 2007.

The 2006 Act considers the use of electronic means for all communications, whereas the 1985 Act only considered it in certain areas. Subject to the individual's right to continue to receive information in paper format, companies should, under the new Act, be able to default to electronic communication.

A key change is to allow publication of documents on a website as a default where:

- the company's articles of association or a shareholder resolution permit those documents which should be supplied to a shareholder to be published on a website; and
- a person has not objected to receiving information via a website within 28 days of being 'individually' asked.

For communication via email rather than a website, an individual is still required to provide positive consent to receiving communications in this way.

However, even if a member or debenture holder has agreed to receive communications electronically, they still retain the right to request a hard copy under the 2006 Act.

3.17 DEPARTURE FROM SORPS

The Auditing Practices Board issued Bulletin 2000/3 to provide guidance to auditors on the application of SAS 600 when reporting on financial statements that fall within the scope of, but contain a departure from, a Statement of Recommended Practice (SORP). Its guidance remains relevant in relation to ISA (UK and Ireland) 700.

The Bulletin *Departure from Statements of Recommended Practice for the Preparation of Financial Statements: Guidance for Auditors* is effective for accounting periods beginning on or after 24 December 2000, or for any financial statements where FRS 18 *Accounting Policies* has been applied before that date.

3.17.1 Requirements of FRS 18

FRS 18 requires an entity to select accounting policies that are most appropriate to its particular circumstances and give a true and fair view. This selection includes consideration of whether accepted industry practices, such as those detailed in a SORP, are suitable.

Paragraph 58 of FRS 18 states that where an entity falls within the scope of a SORP it should state:

- the title of the SORP; and
- whether the financial statements have been prepared in accordance with the current requirements of that SORP.

If there is a departure from the requirements of the SORP, the entity should give a brief description of how the financial statements depart from the recommended practice. However, the effect of the departure need not be quantified unless this is required to give a true and fair view.

3.17.2   Audit considerations

When an entity's financial statements fall within the scope of, but depart from, an SORP, the auditors should assess whether:

- the departure is reasonable and that the treatment adopted is more appropriate to give a true and fair view;
- the requirements of FRS 18 to disclose the departure have been complied with.

In making their assessments, auditors should consider:

- consistency with accounting policies used in prior periods;
- directors' justification for changes to accounting policies;
- if the alternative accounting policies comply with applicable accounting standards, UITF Abstracts, legislation and industry-specific rules and regulations;
- impact on the financial statements; and
- level of compliance with the SORP by other entities in the industry.

3.17.3   Audit opinion

If, as a result of their assessment, the auditors are of the opinion that the financial statements do not give a true and fair view, they should issue a qualified or adverse opinion. Non-compliance with the disclosure requirements outlined above will usually result in a qualified opinion.

Reporting options are detailed in the flowchart in **Table 22.**

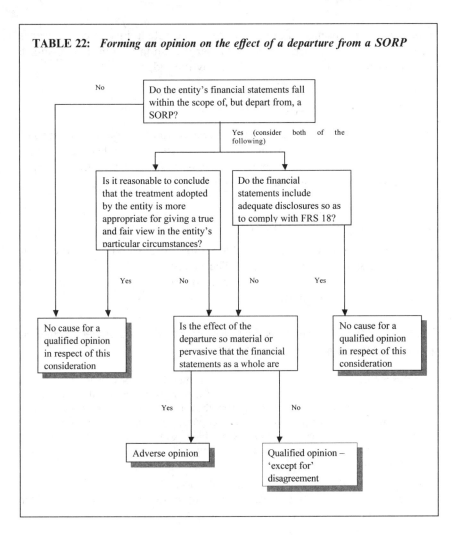

TABLE 22: *Forming an opinion on the effect of a departure from a SORP*

3.18   THE BANNERMAN CASE

3.18.1   Introduction

As a result of the legal judgement in the Scottish Court of Session in the *Bannerman* case, auditors have considered whether they should include additional wording in their audit reports to protect against exposure to third party claims. The ICAEW issued Technical Release 1/03 in January 2003, and this guidance contains a suitable wording for inclusion in audit reports. They have discussed the format and inclusion of such wording with Leading Counsel.

In the *Bannerman* case the judge held that, although there was no direct contact between Bannerman (the auditors) and the third party, knowledge gained by Bannerman through the course of their normal audit work was sufficient, in the absence of any disclaimer, to create a duty of care towards the third party. The absence of a disclaimer was an important circumstance supporting the finding of a duty of care by the judge.

3.18.2   Auditors' responsibilities

The Technical Release is clear that the responsibilities of auditors are not changed as a result either of the *Bannerman* case or the release of 1/03. It states that 'the best risk management policy is for firms to take the steps that are necessary to carry out quality audits'.

3.18.3   Recommended wording

It is clear that auditors automatically assume responsibility for the audit report to the shareholders as a body. The *Bannerman* case indicates that the absence of a disclaimer may, depending on the facts of the case, make auditors liable to third parties.

The ICAEW therefore suggests the following wording is included in the first or second paragraph of all audit reports.

> 'This report is made solely to the company's members, as a body, in accordance with Section 235 of the Companies Act 1985. Our audit work has been undertaken so that we might state to the company's members those matters we are required to state to them in an auditor's report and for no other purpose. To the fullest extent permitted by law, we do not accept or assume responsibility to anyone other than the company and the company's members as a body, for our audit work, for this report, or for the opinions we have formed.'

The wording, or a variation of it, may also be suitable for inclusion in other reports issued by auditors.

It is important to note that the inclusion of this paragraph in audit reports does not means that auditors can never agree to take on responsibilities to third parties, or that they may inadvertently assume a duty of care through subsequent comments or actions inconsistent with the wording of this paragraph. Where auditors are aware of circumstances which may give rise to a duty of care, they should disclaim this responsibility by writing a letter to the third party in line with guidance in Technical Release Audit 4/00, see **Chapter 42**.

3.18.4   Engagement letters

The Technical Release also contains suggested wording for inclusion in an engagement letter, to inform clients about the clarification paragraph in the audit report. This is not mandatory, and is set out in **Chapter 21**.

3.19   READING AUDIT REPORTS

When SAS 600 was first issued, there was some concern that there would be problems at annual general meetings where auditors were asked to read their report to the members present. In response to this the ICAEW issued FRAG 1/94 *Reading of auditors' reports at annual general meetings*. This suggested that there were two options, either:

- to read out the full report; or
- to read out 'highlights' of the report.

Where highlights were read out it should be made clear that this was not the full report and where there were any modifications to the normal wording of the report these were noted.

In March 2000, the Technical & Practical Auditing Committee of the ICAEW's Audit Faculty reviewed the FRAG in the light of the changes in corporate governance. It decided that the 'short' form of the audit report contained in the FRAG could be misleading, as it did not:

- cover the current 'read' and 'review' responsibilities of the expanded version of the report made on listed companies; nor
- highlight some of the restrictions of the audit report as shown in the full accounts, particularly with regard to not considering risks and controls.

The Committee therefore concluded that the use of the short form of audit report should be discontinued, noting that if auditors were asked to read their report at AGMs, they should consider whether it was appropriate to abbreviate it at all.

4 MODIFIED AUDITOR'S REPORTS

4.1 INTRODUCTION

In **Chapter 3** the content and format of unmodified auditor's reports was considered. Where auditors are unable to issue an unmodified report, their report may follow a number of formats, which are discussed below.

As with unmodified reports, guidance on modified auditor's reports is provided by ISA (UK and Ireland) 700, *The Auditor's Report on Financial Statements* and Bulletin 2006/6, *Auditor's Reports on Financial Statements in the United Kingdom* which replaced Bulletin 2005/4 in September 2006.

In April 2005, the APB issued two exposure drafts of ISAs (UK and Ireland):

- ISA (UK and Ireland) 705 *Modifications to the Independent Auditor's Report*; and
- ISA (UK and Ireland) 706 *Emphasis of Matter Paragraphs and Other Matters Paragraphs in the Independent Auditor's Report.*

These UK exposure drafts are based on the exposure drafts of proposed standards issued by the IAASB in March 2005. They are covered in **4.3** and **4.4** below.

4.2 TYPES OF MODIFICATION

An auditor's report is considered to be modified in the following situations:

- matters that do not affect the auditor's opinion:
  - emphasis of matter;
- matters that do affect the auditor's opinion:
  - disclaimer of opinion;
  - adverse opinion;
  - qualified opinion.

4   Modified auditor's reports

Bulletin 2006/6 contains a navigation aid to help auditors select the correct type of report. This is reproduced in **Table 1**.

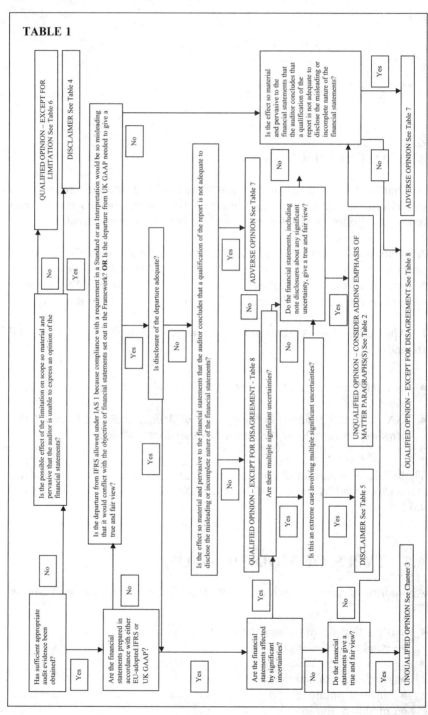

4.2.1   Emphasis of matter

In some circumstances, the audit report may be modified by adding an emphasis of matter paragraph to highlight a matter which is included in a note to the financial statements. Typical examples are where there is a going concern problem (see **Chapter 13**) or where a significant uncertainty exists, the resolution of which depends on future events and which may affect the financial statements.

A significant uncertainty is one which, if it is not fully disclosed in the financial statements, would be seriously misleading, for example the outcome of major litigation. The nature of an uncertainty is that it can be expected to be resolved in the future when there will be sufficient evidence available to assess its outcome. In other circumstances where such evidence is available, or could reasonably be expected to be available, but it is not made available to the auditors, there is a limitation of scope which may lead to a qualification or disclaimer of opinion (see **4.2.2** below).

When assessing whether an uncertainty is significant, auditors should consider:

- the risk that the estimate associated with the uncertainty is likely to change;
- the range of possible outcomes of the uncertainty; and
- the consequences of those outcomes on the view given by the financial statements.

Where auditors decide that the uncertainty is significant they must include in their report an explanatory paragraph (**Table 2**) which describes the matter, the effect on the financial statements and, where practicable, quantifies it. Where quantification is not possible, this should be stated. A reference to the notes to the financial statements alone is not sufficient. The explanation in the audit report must be such that a reader can appreciate the principal points at issue and their implications.

TABLE 2:   *Unqualified with explanatory paragraph on fundamental uncertainty*

Independent auditor's report to the shareholders of ABC Limited
....

Basis of audit opinion
We conducted our audit in accordance with International Standards on Auditing (United Kingdom and Ireland) issued by the Auditing Practices Board. An audit includes examination, on a test basis, of evidence relevant to the amounts and disclosures in the financial statements. It also includes an assessment of the significant estimates and judgements made by the directors in the preparation of the financial statements, and of whether the accounting policies are appropriate to the company's circumstances, consistently applied and adequately disclosed.

We planned and performed our audit so as to obtain all the information and explanations which we considered necessary in order to provide us with sufficient evidence to give reasonable assurance that the financial statements are free from material misstatement, whether caused by fraud or other irregularity or error. In forming our opinion we also evaluated the overall adequacy of the presentation of information in the financial statements.

Opinion
In our opinion:

- the financial statements give a true and fair view, in accordance with United Kingdom Generally Accepted Accounting Practice, of the state of the company's affairs as at 31 December 20.. and of its profit for the year then ended;
- the financial statements have been properly prepared in accordance with the Companies Act 1985; and
- the information given in the Directors' Report is consistent with the financial statements.

Emphasis of matter – possible outcome of a lawsuit
In forming our opinion, which is not qualified, we have considered the adequacy of the disclosures made in the financial statements concerning the possible outcome of litigation against B Limited, a subsidiary of the company, for an alleged breach of environmental regulations. The future settlement of this litigation could result in additional liabilities and the closure of B Limited's business, whose net assets included in the consolidated balance sheet total £ ... and whose profit before tax for the year is £ .... Details of the circumstances relating to this significant uncertainty are described in note.... .

Registered Auditors
Address
Date

As with any inherent uncertainty, where the disclosure of a fundamental uncertainty in the financial statements is insufficient, or its outcome is materially misstated, the auditors should qualify their report on the grounds of disagreement.

4.2.2 Qualified opinions

Qualified opinions arise from either a limitation of scope or a disagreement over an accounting treatment or disclosure. There are three possible outcomes, as illustrated in **Table 3**:

- *'disclaimer' of opinion*, where there is a limitation of scope which is so material or pervasive that the auditors are unable to form an opinion;
- *'adverse' opinion*, where the effect of the disagreement is so material or pervasive as to lead the auditors to conclude that the financial statements are seriously misleading; and

- *'except for'* or *qualified opinion*, which is given when the limitation of scope or disagreement is not so material or pervasive as to require either an adverse opinion or disclaimer of opinion.

The decision whether an 'except for' qualification is sufficient has to be made based on the available information.

Whenever any opinion other than an unqualified one is given, auditors should include a clear description of all the substantive reasons for the report and a quantification of the likely effects on the financial statements, if possible.

TABLE 3: Types of qualification		
Effect	*Limitation of scope*	*Disagreement*
Not material or pervasive	Except for	
So material or pervasive	Disclaimer	Adverse

4.2.3   Limitation of audit scope

Where there is a limitation of scope which prevents the auditors from obtaining sufficient evidence they should:

- describe the factors leading to the limitation in the opinion section of their report; and
- issue a disclaimer where the possible effect is so material or pervasive that they are unable to express an opinion; or
- in other cases issue an opinion qualified as to the possible adjustments that might have been necessary had the limitation not existed.

The ISA (UK and Ireland) does not define the term 'limitation of scope' but it is generally understood to be where the auditors are unable to express an unqualified opinion because their work has been restricted, they have not been able to carry out alternative procedures and as a result have had insufficient evidence on which to conclude on either the statements as a whole or a particular area. An example of this is an entity with a significant amount of cash sales over which there is no system of control upon which the auditors can rely and where no alternative procedures are possible.

Examples of disclaimers of opinion ('unable to' form an opinion, **Table 4 and 5**) and a report which is qualified on an 'except for' basis (**Table 6**) are provided below.

In assessing whether there is a limitation of scope, auditors must have regard to the evidence that they would reasonably expect to be available to support a particular figure or disclosure. The expectation of reasonable availability of evidence is critical to the decision on the limitation of scope. In all cases where there is a lack of evidence leading to a limitation of scope the auditors should take all possible steps to obtain alternative evidence to support an unqualified opinion. Inherent uncertainties are not in themselves a limitation of scope as, because of their nature, the auditors would not expect to find a great deal of information.

The details given about the nature of the limitation should distinguish between those which are imposed on the auditors and those which are outside their control or the control of the directors. Examples of these are:

- lack of a system of control over cash sales or refusal of directors to allow the auditors to contact a third party who holds stock on behalf of the entity (limitations imposed on the auditors);
- the auditor was not appointed until after the year end and so could not attend the stock take and there is no alternative evidence of existence (limitations outside the control of the auditors and the directors).

TABLE 4:   Extract from an example 'disclaimer' of opinion

Basis of audit opinion
We conducted our audit in accordance with International Standards on Auditing (UK and Ireland) issued by the Auditing Practices Board, except that the scope of our work was limited as explained below.

An audit includes examination, on a test basis, of evidence relevant to the amounts and disclosures in the financial statements. It also includes an assessment of the significant estimates and judgements made by the directors in the preparation of the financial statements, and of whether the accounting policies are appropriate to the company's circumstances, consistently applied and adequately disclosed.

We planned our audit so as to obtain all the information and explanations which we considered necessary in order to provide us with sufficient evidence to give reasonable assurance that the financial statements are free from material misstatement, whether caused by fraud or other irregularity or error. However, the evidence available to us was limited because we were unable to observe the counting of physical stock having a carrying amount of £X and send confirmation letters to trade debtors having a carrying amount of £Y due to limitations placed on the scope of our work by the company. As a result of this we have been unable to obtain sufficient appropriate audit evidence concerning both stock and trade debtors. Because of the significance of these items, we have been unable to form a view on the financial statements.

In forming our opinion we also evaluated the overall adequacy of the presentation of information in the financial statements.

Opinion: disclaimer on the view given by the financial statements
Because of the possible effect of the limitation in evidence available to us, we are unable to form an opinion as to whether the financial statements:

- give a true and fair view, in accordance with United Kingdom Generally Accepted Accounting Practice, of the state of the company's affairs as at [date] and of its profit [loss] for the year then ended; and
- have been properly prepared in accordance with the Companies Act 1985.

In respect solely of the limitation of our work referred to above:

- we have not obtained all the information and explanations that we considered necessary for the purpose of our audit; and
- we were unable to determine whether proper accounting records had been maintained.

Notwithstanding our disclaimer on the view given by the financial statements, in our opinion the information given in the Directors' Report is consistent with the financial statements.

Registered Auditors
Address
Date

TABLE 5: Extract from an example of multiple disclaimers

Opinion: disclaimer on the view given by the financial statements
In forming our opinion we have considered the adequacy of the disclosures made in the financial statements concerning the following matters:

- [significant uncertainty 1]
- [significant uncertainty 2]
- [significant uncertainty 3]

Because of the potential significance, to the financial statements, of the combined effect of the three matters referred to in the paragraph above, we are unable to form an opinion as to whether the financial statements:

- give a true and fair view, in accordance with United Kingdom Generally Accepted Accounting Practice, of the state of the company's affairs as at [date] and of its profit [loss] for the year then ended; and
- have been properly prepared in accordance with the Companies Act 1985.

Notwithstanding our disclaimer on the view given by the financial statements, in our opinion the information given in the Directors' Report is consistent with the financial statements.

Registered Auditors
Address
Date

TABLE 6: *Extract from an 'except for' report*

Basis of audit opinion
We conducted our audit in accordance with International Standards on Auditing (UK and Ireland) issued by the Auditing Practices Board, except that the scope of our work was limited as explained below.

An audit includes examination, on a test basis, of evidence relevant to the amounts and disclosures in the financial statements. It also includes an assessment of the significant estimates and judgements made by the directors in the preparation of the financial statements, and of whether the accounting policies are appropriate to the company's circumstances, consistently applied and adequately disclosed.

We planned our audit so as to obtain all the information and explanations which we considered necessary in order to provide us with sufficient evidence to give reasonable assurance that the financial statements are free from material misstatement, whether caused by fraud or other irregularity or error. However, with respect to stock having a carrying amount of £X the evidence available to us was limited because we did not observe the counting of the physical stock as of 31 December 20X1, since that date was prior to our appointment as auditors of the company. Owing to the nature of the company's records, we were unable to obtain sufficient appropriate audit evidence regarding the stock quantities by using other audit procedures.

In forming our opinion we also evaluated the overall adequacy of the presentation of information in the financial statements.

Qualified opinion arising from limitation in audit scope
Except for the financial effects of such adjustments, if any as might have been determined to be necessary had we been able to satisfy ourselves as to physical stock quantities, in our opinion the financial statements:

- give a true and fair view, in accordance with United Kingdom Generally Accepted Accounting Practice, of the state of the company's affairs as at [date] and of its profit [loss] for the year then ended; and
- have been properly prepared in accordance with the Companies Act 1985.

In respect solely of the limitation on our work relating to stocks:

- we have not obtained all the information and explanations that we considered necessary for the purpose of our audit; and
- we were unable to determine whether proper accounting records had been maintained.

In our opinion the information given in the Directors' Report is consistent with the financial statements.

Registered Auditors
Address
Date

In the example in the Bulletin, reference to both the failure to obtain all information and explanations considered necessary and to determine whether proper records have been maintained are included in the opinion paragraph. These follow the main opinion and are restricted to the area in which the lack of scope has occurred.

Imposed limitation of scope

ISA (UK and Ireland) 700 refers to cases where directors or management restrict access to sensitive information such that an effective audit cannot be carried out. This may occur where there is a statutory requirement for an audit but the owners are indifferent to the requirement, for example:

- an owner-managed business; or
- an overseas controlled entity which requires an on-shore report.

In these cases the owners or directors may be prepared to accept a disclaimed opinion for a nominal fee so long as they have a set of accounts that may be filed at Companies House.

The ISA (UK and Ireland) sets out the opinion of the APB that acceptance of such an engagement would not be compatible with auditors' obligations from the point of view of their legislative duties, auditing standards and the ethical guidance issued by their Professional Bodies.

Therefore, if auditors are aware, before accepting an audit engagement that the directors of the entity, or those who appoint its auditors, will impose a limitation on the scope of their work which they consider likely to result in the need to issue a disclaimer of opinion on the financial statements, they should not accept that engagement.

Where auditors become aware after accepting an engagement of such a restriction, the ISA (UK and Ireland) requires that they should consider whether to resign if the limitation is not removed. Alternatively they may decide to continue the engagement and then not seek reappointment. Factors they would take into account in deciding on the most appropriate course of action are the extent to which any work is complete and what is in the best public interest. The guidance suggests that the imposition of such a limitation may be a matter for any statement on the circumstances of ceasing to hold the office of auditor or for professional clearance letters to possible successor auditors.

4.2.4 Disagreement

ISA (UK and Ireland) 700 requires that where the auditors either disagree with the accounting treatment or the disclosure of a matter in the financial statements and the effect is material to the financial statements they should:

- describe the substantive factors giving rise to the disagreement, the implications for, and, where practicable, a quantification of the effect on, the financial statements; and either
- issue an adverse opinion where the possible effect is so material or pervasive that the financial statements are seriously misleading; or
- issue a qualified opinion indicating that it is expressed except for the effects of the matter giving rise to the disagreement.

The examples given in Bulletin 2006/6 include an adverse (**Table 7**) and a qualified 'except for' opinion (**Table 8**). It should be noted that in the example of the qualified opinion the opinion paragraph is clearly titled indicating the reason for the qualification, i.e., disagreement about accounting treatment to distinguish it from a qualification due to a limitation of scope which should also be clearly titled.

TABLE 7: *Extract from an adverse report*

Adverse opinion
As more fully explained in note ... no provision has been made for losses expected to arise on certain long-term contracts currently in progress, as the directors consider that such losses should be off-set against amounts recoverable on other long-term contracts. In our opinion, provision should be made for foreseeable losses on individual contracts as required by [*specify accounting standard*]. If losses had been so recognised the effect would have been to reduce the profit before and after tax for the year and the contract work in progress at 31 December 20.. by £... .

In view of the effect of the failure to provide for the losses referred to above, in our opinion the financial statements do not give a true and fair view, in accordance with United Kingdom Generally Accepted Accounting Practice, of the state of the company's affairs as at 31 December 20.. and of its profit for the year then ended.

In all other respects, in our opinion the financial statements have been properly prepared in accordance with the Companies Act 1985.

Notwithstanding our opinion on the financial statements, in our opinion the information given in the Directors' Report is consistent with the financial statements.

Registered Auditors
Address
Date

TABLE 8: *Extract from an 'except for' disagreement report*

Qualified opinion arising from disagreement about accounting treatment
Included in the debtors shown on the balance sheet is an amount of £ ... due
from a company which has ceased trading. XYZ plc has no security for this
debt. In our opinion the company is unlikely to receive any payment and full
provision of £ ... should have been made, reducing profit before tax and net
assets by that amount.

Except for the financial effect of not making the provision referred to in the
preceding paragraph, in our opinion the financial statements:

- give a true and fair view, in accordance with United Kingdom Generally
  Accepted Accounting Practice, of the state of the company's affairs as at 31
  December 20.. and of its profit for the year then ended; and
- have been properly prepared in accordance with the Companies Act 1985.

In our opinion the information given in the Directors' Report is consistent with
the financial statements.

Registered Auditors
Address
Date

When referring to the disagreement, it is not sufficient for the auditors
merely to refer to the relevant note in the financial statements without giving
further details. The reader must be able to judge the facts to understand
their impact on the financial statements from the audit report alone.

4.3   ISA (UK AND IRELAND) 705 EXPOSURE DRAFT

4.3.1   Background

The scope of the revised ISA 700 issued by the IAASB in December 2004, is
restricted to unmodified auditor's reports and issues relating to modifications are to be contained in separate ISAs, such as ISA 705 *Modifications to
the Independent Auditor's Report*. The APB issued a UK and Ireland specific
version of ISA 705 for comment in April 2005, as a temporary measure until
a revised version of ISA (UK and Ireland) 700 was published. However, the
Exposure Draft of ISA 705 has been included in the IAASB's Clarity Project
(see **1.5.1**) and therefore finalisation of the International version has been
delayed, with a UK and Ireland version expected once all the ISAs are
adopted by the European Union.

4.3.2 Form of reports

ED ISA (UK and Ireland) 705 provides guidance on the circumstances that may result in a modification to an audit report, the appropriate type of opinion in the circumstances and the correct form and content of modified reports.

The Exposure Draft provides example wordings which have been superseded by examples in Bulletin 2006/6 (see examples in this chapter).

4.3.3 Multiple uncertainties

ED ISA (UK and Ireland) 705 permits auditors to issue a disclaimer of opinion in the case of multiple uncertainties where 'the cumulative nature and possible effect of the multiple uncertainties are such that it is not possible to form an opinion'. This may cause difficulties for auditors who are also required to comply with the guidance in ISA (UK and Ireland) 706 that requires auditors to include an emphasis of matter paragraph in their report when a significant uncertainty is both unusual and of fundamental importance to the user's understanding of the financial statements. Through the consultation on the Exposure Draft the APB were particularly keen to ascertain whether auditors are likely to be confused about which guidance to follow.

4.4 ISA (UK AND IRELAND) 706 EXPOSURE DRAFT

4.4.1 Background

At the same time as issuing ED ISA (UK and Ireland) 705 (see **4.3**) the APB issued ED ISA (UK and Ireland) 706 *Emphasis of Matter Paragraphs and Other Matter Paragraphs in the Independent Auditor's Report* to give guidance on other types of modification in the audit report.

4.4.2 'Emphasis of matter' and 'other matters'

ED ISA (UK and Ireland) 706 gives guidance on the circumstances where such paragraphs should be inserted in an audit report and their positioning. The Exposure Draft provides example wordings which have been superseded by examples in Bulletin 2006/6 (see examples in this chapter). As in ISA (UK and Ireland) 700, the definition of an item that should be the subject of an emphasis of matter paragraph in the audit report is one which is both unusual and of fundamental importance to the user's understanding of the financial statements. The inclusion of an emphasis of matter paragraph in a report is not a qualification.

The Exposure Draft describes 'other matters' as those that auditors may find necessary to communicate to the readers of the report but that are not required to be presented or disclosed in the financial statements. This may include information to avoid auditors being associated with misleading information in the document containing financial information or matters that provide further explanation of auditors' responsibilities. Again this is not a qualification and details of such matters should be given under the heading 'Other Matters' in the opinion section, following both the opinion and any emphasis of matter.

5 OTHER REPORTS ON FINANCIAL STATEMENTS

5.1 INTRODUCTION

This Chapter considers other reports that auditors may be required to make on a company's financial statements. It covers the reports on:

- summary financial statements;
- abbreviated accounts;
- exemptions for small and medium-sized groups;
- revised financial statements; and
- preliminary announcements.

The main source of guidance on reporting on small and medium-sized groups and revised financial statements comes from Practice Note 8 *Reports by Auditors under Company Legislation in the United Kingdom*. The examples in the appendix to Practice Note 8 were updated in Bulletin 2007/1 issued in January 2007. At the same time the APB announced its intention to review the body of Practice Note 8 prior to the Companies Act 2006 coming into force.

On summary financial statements guidance is taken from Bulletin 1999/6 *The Auditors' Statement on the Summary Financial Statement* and for preliminary announcements it comes from Bulletin 2004/1 *The Auditors' Association with Preliminary Announcements*. Abbreviated accounts guidance is found in Bulletin 2006/3 *The Special Auditor's Report on Abbreviated Accounts in the United Kingdom*. For some reports there is additional guidance on the procedures necessary to support such reports and the source of this has been noted below.

In July 2005, the APB requested comments on an Exposure Draft of ISA 800, *The Independent Auditor's Report on Summary Audited Financial Statements* issued by the IAASB. The comments received will assist the APB in deciding whether to issue an ISA (UK and Ireland) version. This is discussed in **5.2.5** below.

At the same time as the ED of ISA 800 was released, the APB issued an Exposure Draft of ISA (UK and Ireland) 701, *The Independent Auditor's Report on Other Historical Information*. Taken together these two publications represent a revision of standards and guidance in the extant ISA 800, *The Auditor's Report on Special Purpose Audit Engagements*. This Exposure Draft is covered in **5.3** below.

5.2   SUMMARY FINANCIAL STATEMENTS

5.2.1   Legal background

Under s251 of the Companies Act 1985, companies in the United Kingdom may send summary financial statements (SFSs) to their shareholders instead of the full report and accounts. There are strict requirements as to the contents of the summary financial statements which are set out in the Companies (Summary Financial Statements) Regulations 1995.

Previously an option for listed companies only, the possibility of preparing summary financial statements was extended to all companies from 1 January 2005.

These financial statements must be accompanied by a statement from the company's auditors that the summary statement is consistent with the full accounts and that it complies with s251 and the Regulations. There is no need to include the auditors' report on the full financial statements unless this is either qualified or contains a statement concerning proper accounting records or inadequate returns under s237(2), or failure to obtain certain necessary information and explanations under s237(3).

5.2.2   Auditing Standards and Guidelines

The guidance in relation to summary financial statements comes from Bulletin 1999/6 *The Auditors' Statement on the Summary Financial Statement*. This Bulletin supersedes the guidance in Practice Note 8 and in the *Note on Legal Requirements Applicable to Companies* attached to SAS 600 Auditors' Reports on Financial Statements, although Bulletin 2007/1, which updates the appendices to Practice Note 8, includes an up to date auditors' statement on summary financial statements.

Where quoted companies prepare a Summary Financial Statement they are required to include either the whole, or a summary, of certain information concerning directors' remuneration contained in the notes to the financial statements and in the Directors' Remuneration Report. The relevant information is

• the aggregate amount of directors' emoluments;

- a statement of the company's policy on directors' remuneration for the next following financial year; and
- the performance graph.

The last two items are not required to be audited, but should be read as required by ISA (UK and Ireland) 720.

5.2.3 Audit procedures

As with any assignment, auditors should ensure that their responsibilities and terms of engagement with reference to the SFS are included in an engagement letter.

Auditors should plan to carry out their work on the SFS at the same time as completing the audit so that their statement under s251 and their audit report can be issued at the same time.

They should plan their work so that they can report:

- on the consistency of the SFSs with the full financial statements; and
- whether the SFSs comply with s251 and the Regulations.

These are not independent of each other as consistency is required by the Regulations. The Regulations require that where additional information is necessary to achieve consistency with the full financial statements this is included in the SFS. The auditors are not required to state whether the SFSs give a true and fair view and it is unlikely that this will be the case.

Consistency

It is the issue of consistency that concerns the auditors the most. There is no guidance on the definition of consistency. The most simplistic interpretation is that the information should be taken directly from the full statements.

The other extreme is that users should be able to reach the same conclusion as they would from studying the full accounts. If the latter view is taken then the amount of information required would be so great that there would be no advantage to providing summary financial statements. Accordingly, the former view is invariably taken. This is supported by the Bulletin, which comments that users of SFS do not have the same expectations of SFS as they do of the full financial statements.

The Bulletin gives four instances when inconsistency may occur:

- where information has been incorrectly extracted from the full financial statements, which should generally be easy to identify and correct;
- where headings that are used in a summary primary statement are incompatible with the statutory headings in the full financial statements;

- where the information given has been summarised too much or too selectively; or
- where, in the opinion of the auditors, the summary needs to give more information than is required by the Regulations to achieve consistency. For example, details of an exceptional item are not specified by the Regulations but may be necessary if the summary is to be consistent with the full financial statements and the user is to gain a reasonable understanding of them.

Where inconsistencies have been identified, the auditors should discuss the matter with the directors so that corrections can be made to whichever set of financial statements is incorrect. If no agreement is reached the auditors should modify their statement under s251(4)(b) to include a description of the inconsistency. The inconsistency will also mean that the accounts do not comply with the Regulations and should also be qualified in this respect.

Compliance with s251 and the Regulations
The auditors should include all matters required by the Regulations and s251 within the scope of their examination. This includes the summarised directors' report, the aggregate figure required in respect of directors' emoluments and any statements specifically required by the legislation.

Where there are items in the SFS which, although not inconsistent with the full financial statements, are not properly derived from them, then a modification of the report may be necessary.

If the report on the full financial statements has been qualified, then it will be necessary for the auditors to decide whether or not there is sufficient disclosure of the matter in the SFSs for the user to understand the qualification. This will be in addition to the reproduction of the report itself. They may consider that to achieve this, extra notes would have to be included in the SFSs that are not specifically required by the Regulations.

Although not addressed in the legislation, the Bulletin suggests that where there was an explanatory paragraph referring to a fundamental uncertainty in the auditors' report in the full financial statements, this should also be referred to in their report on the SFS. Where the explanatory paragraph in the report on the full financial statements includes a reference to a note accompanying the full financial statements, but does not reproduce the information in that note, that information should be reproduced in the SFS.

Other information
If the SFSs are being sent out with other information the auditors should ensure that it is clear that their report relates to the summary only and not to any other information. The Bulletin suggests that the auditors read the other information before it is sent out to ensure that they are not aware of any apparent misstatements or material inconsistencies. If there is any

disagreement this should be discussed and changes made as appropriate. Where changes are not made, the Bulletin suggests that the auditors may need to take legal advice.

5.2.4 *Reporting*

The auditors' statement should include the following elements:

- addressee – normally the shareholders;
- introductory paragraph – identifying the SFS by reference to page numbers;
- a paragraph in accordance with the Bannerman judgement and Technical Release 1/03 (see **3.18**);
- respective responsibilities of the auditors and the directors;
- basis of opinion – indicating that the work was carried out in accordance with the Bulletin;
- opinion – regarding the consistency with the full financial statements and the compliance with the legislation; and
- other information – for example, a qualification in the auditors' report on the full financial statements would require the reproduction of that audit report.

The report should be dated when the auditors sign the report in manuscript, which must be after the directors have approved the SFS. Bulletin 1999/6 recommends that this is the same day as the audit report on the full financial statements in order to avoid the impression that the report on the SFS updates that on the full financial statements. If the SFS report is signed at a later date, the report should state that the auditors have not considered the effect of any events between the two dates.

An example of an unmodified report is shown in **Table 1** below.

TABLE 1: Report on summary financial statements

Independent auditors' statement to the shareholders of ABC Plc
We have examined the summary financial statements of ABC Plc [which comprises the Summary Consolidated Profit and Loss Account, Summary Consolidated Balance Sheet, Summary Consolidated Statement of Total Recognised Gains and Losses, [Summary Consolidated Cash Flow Statement] [and the Summary Directors' Remuneration Report] [set out on pages ... to ...].

This statement is made solely to the company's members, as a body, in accordance with section251 of the Companies Act 1985. Our work has been undertaken so that we might state to the company's members those matters we are required to state to them in this statement and for no other purpose. To the fullest extent permitted by law, we do not accept or assume responsibility to anyone other than the company and the company's members as a body, for our work, for this statement, or for the opinions we have formed.

Respective responsibilities of directors and auditors
The directors are responsible for preparing the [*summarised annual report*] in accordance with United Kingdom law.

Our responsibility is to report to you our opinion on the consistency of the summary financial statement within the [*summarised annual report*] with the full annual financial statements [, the Directors' Report] [and the Directors' Remuneration Report], and its compliance with the relevant requirements of section 251 of the Companies Act 1985 and the regulations made thereunder.

We also read the other information contained in the [*summarised annual report*] and consider the implications for our report if we become aware of any apparent misstatements or material inconsistencies with the summary financial statement.

Basis of opinion
We conducted our work in accordance with Bulletin 1999/6 *The Auditors' Statement on the Summary Financial Statement* issued by the Auditing Practices Board. Our report on the company's full financial statements describes the basis of our audit opinion[s] on those financial statements [and the Directors' Remuneration Report].

Opinion
In our opinion the summary financial statement is consistent with the full annual financial statements [, the Directors' Report] [and the Directors' Remuneration Report] of ABC Plc for the year ended 31 December 20.. and complies with the applicable requirements of section 251 of the Companies Act 1985, and the regulations made thereunder.

Registered Auditors
Address
Date

Where the date is after the date of the auditors' report on the full financial statements the following words should be added:

'We have not considered the effects of any events between the date on which we signed our report on the annual financial statements [insert date] and the date of this statement.'

5.2.5   ED ISA 800, The Independent Auditor's Report on Summary Audited Financial Statements

In July 2005, ISA 800 Exposure Draft was issued by the APB for comment in the UK. Based on the comments received the APB will decide whether to issue a UK and Ireland version of the ISA.

The IAASB issued the proposed ISA 800 together with ISA 701, *The Independent Auditor's Report on Other Historical Information*, see **5.3** below, and together they will replace the extant ISA 800. Some commentators have expressed concern that the guidance surrounding the review of summary financial statements is contained in an ISA, as the work performed is not an audit. These commentators would prefer the guidance to be contained in an International Standard on Assurance Engagements (ISAE), and the APB has made its sympathy with these views known.

In introducing the draft, the APB states that adoption of a UK and Ireland version of ISA 800 would require amendment to the IAASB version to bring it in line with domestic legislative requirements. For example, UK legislation requires auditors to report on the 'consistency' of the summary financial statements with the annual accounts, rather than giving an opinion that the summary financial statements are 'an appropriate summary' as required by the ISA. This is in contrast to other ISAs (UK and Ireland) where the full IAASB text has been supplemented, but not replaced, by UK specific paragraphs.

5.3   ED ISA (UK AND IRELAND) 701

As noted above, ED ISA 701 and ED ISA 800 will together replace the extant ISA 800. Unlike ED ISA 800, ED ISA 701, *The Independent Auditor's Report on Other Historical Financial Information*, has been published by the APB in a UK and Ireland specific version. This is a prospective change in approach for the APB which has previously only adopted those ISAs which are relevant to a complete set of general purpose financial statements. An exception has been made as the APB believes that its introduction may have a positive impact on the rigour and consistency of reporting on special purpose engagements.

The Exposure Draft states that its aim is to 'establish standards and provide guidance for the independent auditor's report issued as a result of an audit of historical financial information other than a complete set of general purpose financial statements prepared in accordance with a financial reporting framework designed to achieve fair presentation'.

Other historical information includes:

- a complete set of financial statements prepared in accordance with a financial reporting framework designed for a general purpose, but not designed to achieve fair presentation;
- a complete set of financial statements prepared in accordance with a financial reporting framework designed for a special purpose;
- a single financial statement, or statements, that would otherwise be part of a set of financial statements; and
- one or more specific elements, accounts or items of a financial statement.

The financial reporting frameworks that could be used include:

- a tax basis of accounting;
- the financial reporting provisions set out by a Regulator; and
- the financial reporting provisions of a contract, such as a bond or loan agreement.

The Exposure Draft relates only to situations where unmodified opinions are given, and guidance on the form of the opinion and example reports are provided. Where a modified opinion is given, auditors should refer to the proposed ISA (UK and Ireland) 705, *Modifications to the Opinion in the Independent Auditor's Report* (see **Chapter 4**).

The Exposure Draft also provides guidance on:

- areas to consider when forming an opinion;
- unaudited supplementary information provided with other historical information which is audited; and
- specific reporting considerations when reporting on a single financial statement, element, account or item.

5.4   ABBREVIATED ACCOUNTS

5.4.1   Legal background

Companies which meet the criteria set out in the Companies Act 1985 for small and medium-sized companies are entitled to file abbreviated or modified financial statements with the Registrar of Companies. These have to be prepared in accordance with Schedule 8 to the Act but are not required to give a true and fair view. There is no provision for group accounts to be prepared on an abbreviated basis.

Those companies who have elected to prepare their individual accounts using IFRSs cannot prepare abbreviated accounts.

5.4.2   Guidance

Bulletin 2006/3 *The Special Auditor's Report on Abbreviated Accounts in the United Kingdom*, which superseded Bulletin 1997/1, provides guidance on the special report to be provided by auditors. The updated Bulletin was issued following changes to:

- legislation, in particular, *The Companies Act 1985 (International Accounting Standrds and Other Accounting Amendments) Regulations 2004*; and
- terminology, following the replacement of SAS 600 with ISA (UK and Ireland) 700.

Its scope was also extended to include Northern Ireland.

5.4.3 Audit procedures

Where abbreviated accounts are prepared to be delivered to the Registrar, they must be accompanied by a copy of a special report of the auditor. The Companies Act does not state to whom the report should be addressed, but in absence of guidance, the Bulletin states that the report should be addressed to the company. Despite the fact that abbreviated accounts must be properly prepared in accordance with the relevant provisions, the auditor's opinion cannot be in terms of 'true and fair'. Instead it is limited to whether:

- the directors are entitled to the exemptions claimed; and
- the abbreviated accounts have been properly prepared under Schedule 8 to the Act.

The report should be dated as close as possible to the date of the report on the full financial statements, and preferably on the same day. If there is a significant delay in reporting on the abbreviated accounts it may give the impression that the report on the full accounts is being 'updated'. In practical terms, this means that auditors may be required by the directors to confirm informally in advance of the preparation of abbreviated accounts that the exemptions are available. Where the report on the abbreviated accounts is dated later than that on the full financial statements, the abbreviated report should state that auditors have not considered the effect of any events between the two dates.

If the auditors cannot confirm that the directors are entitled to the exemptions, they should report this to the directors and full accounts will have to be filed with the Registrar.

If the report on the full financial statements is qualified, abbreviated accounts may be prepared so long as they are an accurate extract. If the qualification relates to one of the criteria for exemption, the auditors should consider the maximum possible misstatement that this would give rise to. Where this means that the company would exceed the limits full accounts will have to be filed with the Registrar. If the auditors have disclaimed on the financial statements then this will normally prevent them from assessing the criteria at all.

A reproduction of the report given on the full financial statements is not required unless the report on the full financial statements has been qualified. Where this is the case, the Act requires that the report given on that full financial statements is reproduced together with sufficient material either in the accounts or following the auditors' report, to ensure that the reader is able to understand the qualification fully.

TABLE 2: Report on abbreviated accounts

Independent auditors' report to XYZ Limited under section 247B of the Companies Act 1985
We have examined the abbreviated accounts of XYZ Limited set out on pages ... to ... , together with the financial statements of the company for the year ended ... prepared under section 226 of the Companies Act 1985.

This report is made solely to the company, in accordance with section 247B of the Companies Act 1985. Our audit work has been undertaken so that we might state to the company those matters we are required to state to them in an auditors' report and for no other purpose. To the fullest extent permitted by law, we do not accept or assume responsibility to anyone other than the company and the company's members as a body, for our audit work, for this report, or for the opinions we have formed.

Respective responsibilities of directors and auditors
The directors are responsible for preparing the abbreviated accounts in accordance with section 246 [section 246A if medium-sized] of the Companies Act 1985. It is our responsibility to form an independent opinion as to whether the company is entitled to deliver abbreviated accounts prepared in accordance with sections 246(5) and (6) [section 246A(3)] of the Act to the Registrar of Companies and whether the abbreviated accounts have been properly prepared in accordance with those provisions and to report our opinion to you.

Basis of opinion
We conducted our work in accordance with Bulletin 2006/3 *The special auditor's report on abbreviated accounts in the United Kingdom* issued by the Auditing Practices Board. In accordance with that Bulletin we have carried out the procedures we consider necessary to confirm, by reference to the financial statements, that the company is entitled to deliver abbreviated accounts and that the abbreviated accounts to be delivered are properly prepared. [The scope of our work for the purpose of this report did not include examining or dealing with events after the date of our report on the financial statements.]

Opinion
In our opinion the company is entitled to deliver abbreviated accounts prepared in accordance with sections 246(5) and (6) [section 246A(3)] of the Companies Act 1985, and the abbreviated accounts have been properly prepared in accordance with those provisions.

Other information
[*This section is only to be included where there is such information*]

Registered Auditors   Address
Date

In addition, if the report on the full financial statements contains a statement under s237(2) (accounts, records or returns inadequate or accounts not agreeing with records and returns) or s237(3) (failure to obtain necessary information and explanations), the special report should set out that statement in full under the heading 'other information'.

There is no legal requirement to reproduce the report on the full financial statements where this contains a reference to a fundamental uncertainty or some other explanatory paragraph. The Bulletin notes that the legislation only sets out minimum requirements and does not preclude other information being provided where the auditors consider it to be important.

Hence, the APB recommends that both the explanatory paragraph, and sufficient information for it to be properly understood, are included in the special report under the heading 'other information'.

It is preferable for the same auditors to report on both full and abbreviated sets of accounts. If there is to be a change of auditors and the new auditors are to report on the abbreviated accounts they only need to perform additional work if they have grounds to doubt the accuracy of their predecessor. Where such a change occurs it should be indicated in the report.

5.5 EXEMPTIONS FOR SMALL AND MEDIUM-SIZED GROUPS

5.5.1 Legal background

Under Companies Act 1985 small and medium-sized groups of companies may choose not to prepare group accounts. Where the directors have taken advantage of the exemptions under s248 and in the auditors' opinion they are not entitled to do so, s235(4)(A) requires that this be stated in the auditors' report on the parent company's financial statements. A suitable wording for the additional opinion paragraph is given in **Table 3**.

If the auditors do not believe that the directors are entitled to the exemption they should initially discuss the matter with them. Directors should be made aware that where they file parent company accounts with such a qualification the Registrar of Companies may decide to investigate the matter.

5.5.2 Audit procedures

Although there is no specific guidance on the procedures to be carried out it is reasonable to assume that similar considerations to those described under abbreviated accounts (see above) would apply to the exercise auditors must carry out to assess whether the limits which allow the directors to claim the exemption have been complied with.

TABLE 3:   Additional opinion paragraph where not eligible for group accounts exemption

Other matters
As detailed in note .. to the financial statements, the directors have taken advantage of the exemptions in s248 of the Companies Act 1985 from preparing group accounts. In our opinion, they are not entitled to do so because the group does not qualify as a small/medium-sized group.

5.6   REVISED FINANCIAL STATEMENTS

5.6.1   Legal background

The Companies Act 1985 allows directors to withdraw financial statements which have been found to be defective after they had been filed with the Registrar of Companies. In addition, the court has powers to make directors revise defective accounts.

5.6.2   Auditing Guideline

In addition to the reporting guidance in Practice Note 8, an exposure draft of an auditing guideline was published in May 1991 by the APC entitled *Auditors' Reports on Revised Annual Accounts and Directors' Reports*, which covers the procedures necessary to give such a report. There is no indication of when or if the APB intend to revisit this and it does not form part of their current programme.

5.6.3   Types of revision

Revision of accounts may be by:

- issue of replacement financial statements;
- supplementary note, to be appended to the existing financial statements; or
- revision to the directors' report.

In each case the auditors have to report on the revision and the directors' statement of the reason why the original financial statements are now considered incorrect. They must consider if the statement by the directors of the reason for the revision is sufficient for the reader to obtain a clear picture of the relevant facts. It is also necessary to consider if the method of revision is appropriate and whether any further adjustments are necessary.

Where the only revision is to the directors' report, the auditors have to make a positive statement that it is consistent with the information in the financial statements, unlike normal reports where they need only report on any inconsistency.

Examples of the recommended reports are given in **Table 4** (directors' report only) and **Table 5** (full revision or supplementary note).

It is possible to revise abbreviated financial statements where these alone prove to be defective. In these instances, auditors are only required to report on the preparation of the abbreviated financial statements, rather than the revision.

Where either the full revision or supplementary note option is chosen, there should be a statement of directors' responsibilities under the Regulations. As with the annual financial statements this may be either in the auditors' report or elsewhere in the financial statements or accompanying information. The responsibilities that should be noted are shown in **Table 6**.

Where it is necessary to qualify such a report, the considerations are the same as for reports on other financial statements. For example, if the auditors consider that the reasons for the revision given by the directors are inadequate they should qualify and give further details in their report.

TABLE 4: Revised directors' report

Independent auditors' report to the shareholders of XYZ Limited
We have considered the information given in the revised directors' report for the year ended ... , on pages ... to ... The revised directors' report replaces the original directors' report approved by the directors on . . [and consists of the attached supplementary note together with the original report which was circulated to the members on ...]. The revised directors' report has been prepared under the Companies (Revision of Defective Accounts and Report) Regulations 1990 and accordingly does not take account of events which have taken place after the date on which the original report was approved.

This report is made solely to the company's members, as a body, in accordance with section 235 of the Companies Act 1985 and under the Companies (Revision of Defective Accounts and Report) Regulations 1990. Our audit work has been undertaken so that we might state to the company's members those matters we are required to state to them in an auditors' report and for no other purpose. To the fullest extent permitted by law, we do not accept or assume responsibility to anyone other than the company and the company's members as a body, for our audit work, for this report, or for the opinions we have formed.

Respective responsibilities of directors and auditors
The directors are responsible for the preparation of the revised directors' report.

Our responsibility is to report to you whether the revised directors' report is consistent with the annual financial statements.

Basis of audit opinion
Our consideration has been directed towards matters of consistency alone and not to whether the revised report complies with the requirements of the Companies Act 1985.

Opinion
In our opinion the information given in the revised directors' report is consistent with the annual financial statements for the year ended ... which were circulated to members on ... .

Registered Auditors   Address
Date

TABLE 5: Revised financial statements

Independent auditors' report to the shareholders of XYZ Limited
We have audited the revised accounts of XYZ Limited for the year ended ... which comprise [state the primary financial statements such as the Profit and Loss Account, the Balance Sheet, the Cash Flow Statement, the Statement of Total Recognised Gains and Losses] and the related notes. These revised financial statements have been prepared under the accounting policies set out therein and replace the original financial statements approved by the directors on ... (*and consist of the attached supplementary note together with the original financial statements which were circulated to members on ...*).

The revised financial statements have been prepared under the Companies (Revision of Defective Accounts and Report) Regulations 1990 and accordingly do not take account of events which have taken place after the date on which the original financial statements were approved.

This report is made solely to the company's members, as a body, in accordance with section 235 of the Companies Act 1985 and under the Companies (Revision of Defective Accounts and Report) Regulations 1990. Our audit work has been undertaken so that we might state to the company's members those matters we are required to state to them in an auditors' report and for no other purpose. To the fullest extent permitted by law, we do not accept or assume responsibility to anyone other than the company and the company's members as a body, for our audit work, for this report, or for the opinions we have formed.

Respective responsibilities of directors and auditors
As described in the Statement of Directors' Responsibilities the directors are responsible for the preparation of financial statements in accordance with applicable law and United Kingdom Accounting Standards (United Kingdom Generally Accepted Accounting Practice).

Our responsibility is to audit the financial statements in accordance with relevant legal and regulatory requirements and International Standards on Auditing (UK and Ireland).

We report to you our opinion as to whether the revised financial statements give a true and fair view and are properly prepared in accordance with the Companies Act 1985 as they have effect under the Companies (Revision of Defective Accounts and Report) Regulations 1990. We also report to you whether in our opinion the information given in the [revised] Directors' Report is not consistent with the revised financial statements.

In addition we report to you if, in our opinion, the company has not kept proper accounting records, if we have not received all the information and explanations we require for our audit, or if information specified by law regarding directors' remuneration and transactions is not disclosed.

We read the [revised] Directors' Report and consider the implications for our report if we become aware of any apparent misstatements within it.

We are also required to report whether in our opinion the original financial statements failed to comply with the requirements of the Companies Act 1985 in the respects identified by the directors.

Basis of opinion
We conducted our audit in accordance with International Standards on Auditing (UK and Ireland) issued by the Auditing Practices Board. An audit includes examination, on a test basis, of evidence relevant to the amounts and disclosures in the revised financial statements. It also includes an assessment of the significant estimates and judgements made by the directors in the preparation of the revised financial statements, and of whether the accounting policies are appropriate to the company's circumstances, consistently applied and adequately disclosed.

The audit of revised financial statements includes the performance of additional procedures to assess whether the revisions made by the directors are appropriate and have been properly made.

We planned and performed our audit so as to obtain all the information and explanations which we considered necessary in order to provide us with sufficient evidence to give us reasonable assurance that the revised financial statements are free from material misstatement, whether caused by fraud or other irregularity or error. In forming our opinion we also evaluated the overall adequacy of the presentation of information in the revised financial statements.

Opinions
In our opinion

- the revised financial statements give a true and fair view, in accordance with United Kingdom Generally Accepted Accounting Practice, seen as at the date the original financial statements were approved, of the state of the company's affairs as at ... and of its profit for the year then ended;

- the revised financial statements have been properly prepared in accordance with the provisions of the Companies Act 1985 as they have effect under the Companies (Revision of Defective Accounts and Report) Regulations 1990;
- the original financial statements for the year ended ... failed to comply with the requirements of the Companies Act 1985 in the respects identified by the directors in (*statement contained in note .. to these revised financial statements*)/(*supplementary note*); and
- the information given in the [revised] Directors' Report is consistent with the revised financial statements.

Registered Auditors   Address
Date

TABLE 6:   Directors' responsibilities with regard to revised financial statements

Under s245 of the Companies Act 1985 the directors have the authority to revise financial statements or a directors' report if they do not comply with the Act. The revised financial statements must be amended in accordance with the Companies (Revision of Defective Account and Report) Regulations 1990 and in accordance therewith do not take account of events which have taken place after the date on which the original financial statements were approved. The Regulations require that revised financial statements show a true and fair view as if they were prepared and approved by the directors, as at the date of the original financial statements.

There is no specific guidance on what the auditors should do if they do not agree that there are grounds for revision but the directors decide to go ahead with the revision. However, as the auditors must give an opinion on whether the revision is in accordance with the Regulations and these only permit revision in certain circumstances, where they disagree with it, they will have to give an adverse opinion. This is because the revised financial statements have not been prepared in accordance with the Regulations and may also be on the grounds that in their opinion the original financial statements did comply with the requirements of the Companies Act.

The auditors will need to assess whether the discovery that leads to the revision indicates that proper accounting records have not been kept and the effect this has on their report.

There is no duty on auditors to search for further evidence after they have signed their report, but if they do become aware of anything that they should have known at the original date of signing they should inform the directors immediately and consider whether revision is necessary.

When deciding on the best course of action once an error is discovered, various factors should be taken into consideration, including the proximity to the next set of financial statements. It may be better to make a prior year adjustment rather than carry out a revision, if the error is discovered during the course of the next year's audit due to the costs and value of the information that will result from a revision. This is not precluded by the Regulations and will often be the best course of action if a significant amount of time has elapsed since the incorrect financial statements were produced.

5.6.4   Procedures

In determining the extent of audit procedures necessary, auditors should analyse the matter giving rise to the revision and consider:

- whether the nature of the matter suggests that errors in the financial statements may be pervasive, for example the discovery of fraud;
- whether the facts discovered since the approval of the financial statements affect past assumptions in areas of judgement, for example provisions;
- the extent of any consequential changes to the form of financial statements which arise from the matter. For example, group financial statements may be required for the first time; and
- any steps taken by the directors to investigate and correct the defect.

Where the auditors have changed since the date of the original financial statements which have subsequently been found to be defective, the new auditors should make the required reports, unless the previous auditors have been specifically engaged by management and they are still eligible to report as 'registered auditors'.

Where the auditors reporting on the original and revised financial statements are the same, it is unlikely that a re-performance of the original audit will be required. However, in determining the extent of their examination, the auditors should assess the risk of other misstatements in the original accounts. Where different auditors are reviewing the revised accounts the amount of work that is necessary will depend on the reason for the revision and their assessment of risk.

Based on their assessment of this, they should determine appropriate review procedures to identify any significant events in the period since the approval of the original financial statements. Such a review must be sufficient to:

- ensure that the factors which have led the directors to determine that the original financial statements were defective have been properly reflected in the proposed adjustments; and
- identify any further adjustments which should be made to the revised accounts.

Auditors would therefore normally undertake the following specific procedures:

- review of the original audit plans (and programmes) in the light of the analysis of the matter leading to revision and the extent to which additional audit evidence is required should be considered;
- reassessment of the various matters of judgement involved in the preparation of the original financial statements;
- obtaining evidence specific to the adjustments made to the original financial statements;
- review of the period after the date on which the original financial statements were approved;
- review of the revised financial statements to the extent that, in conjunction with the conclusions drawn from the other audit evidence obtained, there is a reasonable basis for the opinion on the financial statements; and
- consideration of any legal and regulatory consequences of the revision.

Each of these steps may in turn indicate a need for further procedures.

Engagements to report on revised directors' reports should be conducted following the principles outlined above.

5.7   PRELIMINARY ANNOUNCEMENTS

5.7.1   *Background*

It is a requirement of the Listing Rules of the Financial Services Authority (12.40) that a company's preliminary statement of annual results 'must have been agreed with the company's auditors', 'show the figures in the form of a table, consistent with the presentation to be adopted in the annual accounts for that financial year', if the audit report is likely to be qualified, give 'details of the nature of the qualification' and 'include any significant additional information necessary for the purpose of assessing the results being announced'.

The required figures to be included in preliminary statement are set out by Listing Rule 12.40(a)(ii) through a cross reference to Listing Rule 12.52.

In July 1998 the Accounting Standards Board issued a non-mandatory Statement containing guidance on the content of preliminary announcements.

5.7.2   *Guidance*

Main guidance on this issue is in APB Bulletin 2004/1 *The Auditors' Association with Preliminary Announcements*. This supersedes Bulletin 1998/

7 of the same name that provided guidance on the 'legitimate and important role [auditors of listed companies] play in the process leading to the orderly release of preliminary announcements'. The updated Bulletin reflects changes to the Listing Rules and emphasises the need for auditors to consider the way in which non-statutory information is presented in preliminary announcements before agreeing to their release.

In February 2003, the APB wrote to all auditors of listed companies to alert them to the possibility that shareholders may sometimes be misinformed by the way in which 'pro forma' financial information is included in unaudited preliminary announcements, and to emphasise the need for auditors to consider the way in which pro forma information is presented before agreeing to the release of preliminary announcements. A further letter was issued in December 2003 reminding auditors of the February 2003 letter.

5.7.3 Terms of engagement

From the auditors' point of view, the objective of the engagement is to report that the preliminary figures are consistent with the financial statements which are being or have been audited.

The scope of any engagement to review a preliminary announcement should be clearly established with the client and any public statements must also make this clear. The terms of the engagement should be set out either in a separate engagement letter or by incorporating them within the standard engagement letter.

In particular, auditors are required to agree the contents of the preliminary statement, whether or not its contents exceed the minimum laid down by the Listing Rules.

The Bulletin contains example paragraphs for inclusion in an engagement letter where a preliminary announcement is being made. These are shown in **Table 7** (audit complete) and **Table 8** (audit not yet complete).

Bulletin 2004/1 removed from the preliminary announcement engagement letter paragraphs the section concerning reference to the auditors in the announcement and copying the auditors' letter to third parties which was included in Bulletin 1998/7. It was removed on the basis that their inclusion in any engagement letter is a risk management issue and therefore was for consideration by each firm. The paragraph is provided for information as follows:

> 'You agree not to refer to us in the preliminary announcement or make available copies of our letter indicating our agreement to any other party without our prior written consent.'

5.7.4   Procedures

A preliminary announcement may be based on financial statements where the audit report has been finalised, or on financial statements whose audit is at an advanced stage. Whilst there is the expectation that the figures in the preliminary announcement will be consistent with those in the final audited financial statements, this cannot be guaranteed where the full financial statements are yet to be approved.

The Bulletin defines an 'advanced stage' as being where the audit has been completed, including appropriate reviews by personnel not otherwise involved in the audit, subject only to the following:

- clearing outstanding audit matters which the auditors are satisfied are unlikely to have a material impact on the financial statements or disclosures in the preliminary announcement;
- completing audit procedures on the detail of note disclosures to the financial statements that will not have a material impact on the primary financial statements and completing their reading of the other information in the annual report in accordance with ISA (UK and Ireland) 720, *Other information in documents containing audited financial statements*;
- updating the subsequent events review to cover the period between the issue of the preliminary announcement and the date of the auditors' report on the financial statements; and
- obtaining written representations, where relevant, from management and establishing that the financial statements have been reviewed and approved by the directors.

TABLE 7:   Example paragraphs for engagement letter where audit is complete

Review of preliminary announcement
The Listing Rules state that 'a preliminary statement of the annual results ... must have been agreed with the company's auditors'. As directors of the company, you are responsible for preparing and issuing the preliminary statement of annual results and ensuring that we agree with its release.

We undertake to review the preliminary announcement having regard to Bulletin 2004/1 *The Auditors' Association with Preliminary Announcements*, issued by the Auditing Practices Board. Accordingly, our review will be limited to checking the accuracy of extraction of the financial information in the preliminary announcement from the audited financial statements of the company for that year, considering whether any non-statutory financial information and associated narrative explanations may be misleading and reading the management commentary, including any comments on, or separate presentation of, the final interim period figures, and considering whether it is in conflict with the information that we obtained in the course of our audit.

You will provide us with such information and explanations as we consider

---

necessary for the purposes of our work. We request sight of the preliminary announcement in sufficient time to enable us to complete our work. The Board/ Committee of the Board will formally approve the preliminary announcement before we agree to it.

TABLE 8: Example paragraphs for engagement letter where audit is not yet complete

Review of preliminary announcement
The Listing Rules state that 'a preliminary statement of the annual results ... must have been agreed with the company's auditors'. As directors of the company, you are responsible for preparing and issuing the preliminary statement of annual results and ensuring that we agree with its release.

We undertake to review the preliminary announcement having regard to Bulletin 2004/1 *The Auditors' Association with Preliminary Announcements* issued by the Auditing Practices Board. Accordingly, our review will be limited to checking the accuracy of extraction of the financial information in the preliminary announcement from the audited financial statements of the company for that year, considering whether any non-statutory financial information and associated narrative explanations may be misleading and reading the management commentary, including any comments on, or separate presentation of, the final interim period figures, and considering whether it is in conflict with the information that we have obtained in the course of our audit.

You will provide us with such information and explanations as we consider necessary for the purposes of our work. We shall request sight of the preliminary announcement in sufficient time to enable us to complete our work. The Board/Committee of the Board will formally approve the preliminary announcement before we agree to it. You will also make available to us the proposed text of the company's annual report.

We will not agree to the release of the preliminary announcement until the audit is complete subject only to the following:

- clearing outstanding audit matters which we are satisfied are unlikely to have a material impact on the financial statements or disclosures in the preliminary announcement;
- completing audit procedures on the detail of note disclosures to the financial statements and completing our reading of the other information in the annual report;
- updating the subsequent events review to cover the period between the date of the preliminary announcement and the date of the auditors' report on the financial statements; and
- obtaining written representations, where relevant, from management and establishing that the financial statements have been reviewed and approved by the directors.

The scope of our work will be necessarily limited in that we will only be able to check the consistency of the preliminary announcement with draft financial statements on which our audit is incomplete. Accordingly, we shall not, at that stage, know whether further adjustments may be required to those draft financial statements. Consequently, there is an unavoidable risk that the company may wish to revise its preliminary announcement in the light of audit findings or other developments occurring between the preliminary announcement being notified to a regulatory information service and the completion of the audit.

In the event that we disagree with the release of the preliminary announcement we will send you a letter setting out the reasons why.

The Bulletin provides a list of audit procedures which will normally be carried out by the auditors in relation to the preliminary announcement, regardless of whether that announcement is based on a draft statement or extracted from audited financial statements. These procedures will ensure that there are no material differences expected between the preliminary and final figures:

- checking that the figures in the preliminary announcement covering the full year have been accurately extracted from the audited or draft financial statements and reflect the presentation to be adopted in the audited financial statements. For example, any summarisation should not change the order in which items are presented where this is specified by law or accounting standards;
- considering whether the information (including the management commentary) is consistent with other expected contents of the annual report of which the auditors are aware; and
- considering whether the financial information in the preliminary announcement is misstated. A misstatement exists when the information is stated incorrectly or presented in a misleading manner. A misstatement may arise, for example, as a result of an omission of a significant change of accounting policy disclosed or due to be disclosed in the audited financial statements.

Auditors should also consider whether the preliminary announcement includes:

- the directors' statements required by s240 of the Companies Act 1985; and
- the minimum information required in interim reports under Listing Rule 12.52, subject to any omissions authorised by the Stock Exchange (Listing Rule 12.59), and any significant additional information necessary for the purpose of assessing the results under Listing Rule 12.40(a)(iv).

5.7.5   Pro forma information

The APB's alert to auditors of listed companies in February 2003 (reiterated in December 2003) regarding misleading pro forma information included in preliminary announcements states that, whilst much pro forma information is of use to shareholders, it has the greatest potential to be misleading when:

- it is given greater prominence than the statutory numbers;
- there is no explanation of its purpose; or
- adjusted numbers are not reconciled to the statutory numbers.

Pro forma information will typically include adjustments of statutory results to exclude certain items to give alternative earnings figures, such as EBITDA, to exclude certain business segments or to reflect significant non-adjusting post balance sheet events, such as disposals or acquisitions.

Therefore Bulletin 2004/1 recommends that prior to auditors agreeing the release of a preliminary announcement, they should consider whether:

- appropriate prominence has been given to the statutory numbers;
- any pro forma information clearly and accurately described, stating the purpose for which it has been prepared;
- any pro forma information is reconciled to the statutory numbers; and,
- any pro forma information is not misleading in the form or context in which it is given.

5.7.6   Management commentary

Auditors should read any management commentary in the preliminary statement, together with any other narrative disclosures and any final interim period figures, and consider whether they are in conflict with the information that they have obtained in the course of their work. If it is available, auditors should also read the text of any Chairman's Statement, operating and financial review or similar document to be included in the annual report to ensure no discrepancies with the preliminary statement.

5.7.7   Directors' approval

The preliminary statement should state the date on which it was approved by the directors. Auditors do not agree the preliminary announcement until the Board has formally approved its entire content.

5.7.8   Reporting

Auditors are not required to prepare an audit report on the preliminary announcement. However, the Bulletin recommends that, to avoid possible misunderstanding and to make explicit their agreement to the preliminary announcement, they should issue a letter to the company to signify their agreement. An example of this letter is shown in **Table 9**.

TABLE 9:   Example report on preliminary announcement

Dear Sirs

In accordance with the terms of our engagement letter dated [ ], we have reviewed the attached proposed preliminary announcement of XYZ plc for the year ended [ ]. Our work was conducted having regard to Bulletin 2004/1 issued by the United Kingdom Auditing Practices Board. As directors you are responsible for preparing and issuing the preliminary announcement.

Our responsibility is solely to give our agreement to the preliminary announcement having carried out the procedures specified in the Bulletin as providing a basis for such agreement. In this regard we agree to the preliminary announcement being notified to a Regulatory Information Service.

[*Insert paragraph* below only where the preliminary announcement is made before the audit is complete.*]

Yours faithfully
Registered auditors
Address
Date

* As you are aware we are not in a position to sign our report on the annual financial statements as they have not yet been approved by the directors and we have not yet [*insert significant procedures that are yet to be completed, for example completing the subsequent events review and obtaining final representations from directors*]. Consequently there can be no absolute certainty that we will be in a position to issue an unmodified audit opinion on financial statements consistent with the results and financial position reported in the preliminary announcement. However, at the present time, we are not aware of any matters that may give rise to a modification to our report. In the event that such matters do come to our attention we will inform you immediately.

The Listing Rules state that where the final auditors' report on the financial statements is likely to be qualified, details of the nature of the qualification should also be given. Section 240 of the Companies Act extends this requirement so that details of qualifications which have already been approved (i.e., where the preliminary announcement is based on audited financial statements) should also be provided. Care must be taken in this situation, however, not to breach the requirement of section 240(3) of the Companies Act, which states that an auditors' report on the statutory accounts may not be published with non-statutory accounts.

Fundamental uncertainty

The Bulletin also states that where the final audit report does, or will, contain an explanatory paragraph dealing with a fundamental uncertainty, the auditors must not agree to the preliminary announcement unless the directors have made mention of the fundamental uncertainty. It is the directors' responsibility to make this disclosure and the preliminary announcement need not refer to the auditors in this respect.

Disclosure of the fundamental uncertainty must also be made where such conditions exist at the time of clearance of the preliminary announcement, even if it is likely that this uncertainty will be resolved by the time the final audit report is signed. If the matter is cleared before the final audit opinion is given, the change in circumstances since the preliminary announcement should be disclosed in a note to the financial statements.

Unresolved matters

If the precise details of a matter giving rise to a qualification or explanatory paragraph are critical to the full understanding of the auditors' report, and this matter is still to be resolved, the Bulletin strongly recommends that the auditors should not agree to the release of the preliminary announcement containing information about a qualification until the matter is resolved.

5.7.9 *Announcements not agreed*

Where the auditors are not in agreement with the content of the preliminary announcement, they should communicate this to the directors in a letter setting out the reasons for this disagreement and advising the directors not to release the announcement to a Regulatory Information Service.

Where they become aware that the company has released the announcement, without first obtaining their consent, they should first ascertain the reasons for this. If the announcement was released inadvertently, the Bulletin advises auditors to remind the directors of their obligations under the Listing Rules to obtain the auditors' agreement. However, where an announcement with which they disagree has been released, the Bulletin advises taking legal advice with a view to notifying the Listing Authority of the fact that the announcement had not been agreed.

6 OTHER STATUTORY AUDIT REPORTS

6.1 INTRODUCTION

This Chapter considers the other types of reports that auditors may be required to make under the Companies Act. It covers the reports on:

- distributions;
- financial assistance;
- purchase and redemption of own shares;
- re-registration of companies;
- allotment of shares otherwise than for cash; and
- transfer of non cash assets.

The guidance on the form of these is contained in Practice Note 8 *Reports by Auditors under Company Legislation in the United Kingdom*. For some reports there is additional guidance on the procedures necessary to support such reports and the source of this has been noted below.

Example reports in this chapter have been modified to include suggested disclaimer wording based on Technical Release 1/03 following the Bannerman case (see **3.18**). In order to protect those giving reports, the logic of including disclaimer paragraphs in audit reports would seem to apply also to these other reports. It is recommended that legal advice is sought in relation to specific client circumstances to ensure that the wording is suitable.

6.2 DISTRIBUTIONS: QUALIFIED REPORTS

6.2.1 Legal background

Sections 270 and 271 of the Companies Act 1985 require that where the auditors' report on a company's financial statements contains a qualification, before those statements may be used to justify a distribution, it is necessary for the company's auditors to make a further statement. This must be laid before the members in general meeting, and cover the effect of the qualification on the company's ability to make a distribution.

6.2.2   *Guidance*

The statement may be issued as a separate report to the members and sent to the company secretary, or as an additional paragraph in the normal report to the members. This will depend upon the individual circumstances.

The report is restricted to the consideration of the effect of the last qualification on the company's distributable profits. The auditors are required to state whether the subject matter of the qualification is material for determining whether the proposed distributions, and any which have not yet been proposed, are permitted. Some qualifications will not be material because of their nature, for example, if the qualification related to the misclassification of creditors due within one year, there would be no effect on distributable profits.

Other qualifications will by their nature be potentially material. For example, a qualification for failure to make a provision in respect of the carrying value of properties could have an adverse effect on the distributable reserves of the company. Here the auditors would have to assess the maximum potential write down, if known, before they could say whether the proposed distribution was permitted.

It should be noted that fundamental uncertainties do not give rise to a qualification and as a consequence will not result in the need for a report under s271(4).

If they are unable to quantify the effect of the qualification, its effect would have to be assessed as material for the purposes of determining the distributable reserves, unless the only possible impact was favourable. In this case the auditors would have to state either that the qualification is material or that they are unable to form an opinion whether it is material. Whatever opinion is given, legally the company could pay a dividend so long as a statement, irrespective of its conclusion, is laid before the members. It is only when the auditors do not provide such a statement that the distribution is illegal.

The following tables provide suitable wordings for these reports. **Table 1** is where a separate report is given and the amount of the proposed distribution is known. If the proposed dividend is as yet unquantified, the wording in **Table 2** should be used. If a separate report is not required, the additional paragraph should be based on **Table 3**.

TABLE 1:   Report required on company's ability to make a distribution

Independent Auditors' statement to the shareholders of XYZ Limited pursuant to s271(4) of the Companies Act 1985
We have audited the financial statements of XYZ Limited for the year ended ...
. in accordance with International Standards on Auditing (United Kingdom and Ireland) issued by the Auditing Practices Board and have expressed a qualified opinion thereon in our report dated .....

This statement is made solely to the company's members, as a body, in accordance with section 271(4) of the Companies Act 1985. Our audit work has been undertaken so that we might state to the company's members those matters we are required to state to them in this opinion and for no other purpose. To the fullest extent permitted by law, we do not accept or assume responsibility to anyone other than the company and the company's members as a body, for our audit work, for this report, or for the opinions we have formed.

Respective responsibilities of directors and auditors
As set out in the Statement of Directors' Responsibilities in the financial statements for the year ended ..., the directors are responsible for the preparation of the financial statements in accordance with applicable law and United Kingdom Accounting Standards. They are also responsible for considering whether the company, subsequent to the balance sheet date, has sufficient distributable profits to make a distribution at the time the distribution is made.

Our responsibility is to report whether, in our opinion the subject matter of our qualification of our auditors' report on the financial statements for the year ended ... is material for determining, by reference to those financial statements, whether the distribution proposed by the company is permitted under section 263 [section 264/265[1]] of the Companies Act 1985. We are not responsible for giving an opinion on whether the company has sufficient distributable reserves to make the distribution proposed at the time it is made.

Basis of audit opinion
We have carried out such procedures as we considered necessary to evaluate the effect of the qualified opinion on the determination of profit available for distribution.

Opinion
In our opinion the subject matter of that qualification is not material for determining, by reference to those financial statements, whether the distribution/interim dividend for the year ended ... of £ ... proposed by the company is permitted under section 263 (*section 264/265*) of the Companies Act 1985.

Registered Auditors
Address
Date

---

[1] Section 264 should be used for public companies and Section 265 for investment companies.

TABLE 2:   Alternative opinion paragraph where amount of distribution not known

In our opinion the subject matter of that qualification is not material for determining, by reference to those financial statements, whether a distribution of not more than £ ... by the company would be permitted under section 263 (*section 264/265*) of the Companies Act 1985.

TABLE 3:   Additional paragraph concerning ability to make a distribution for audit report on annual accounts

In our opinion the subject matter of the above qualification is not material for determining, by reference to those financial statements, whether the distribution of £ ... proposed by the company is permitted under section 263 (*section 264/265*) of the Companies Act 1985.

6.3   DISTRIBUTIONS: INITIAL DISTRIBUTIONS

6.3.1   Legal background

Where a company wishes to make a distribution during its first accounting period, or after its end but before the accounts have been laid before the members in general meeting, initial accounts have to be prepared. These accounts should be prepared under the accounting provisions of the Companies Act, although in the case of a parent company group accounts are not required. Where the company concerned is a public company, the auditors are required to issue an audit report on these accounts.

6.3.2   Guidance

This report may be addressed to the directors, as there is no statutory requirement for it to be sent to anyone else, and should identify the period covered by the initial accounts. As with any report, the audit should be carried out in accordance with Auditing Standards (or ISAs (UK and Ireland) for periods ending commencing on or after 15 December 2005) and this should be stated in the report.

The auditors are required to comment on whether the accounts have been properly prepared, that is, the accounts give a true and fair view and are in accordance with the accounting provisions of the Act. This, in effect, means that the procedures necessary to support such an opinion could be almost as extensive as those necessary to support the opinion on annual financial statements. If the report is qualified then a paragraph on whether the matter is material to the distribution must be included (see **Table 3** above).

An example report is shown in **Table 4**.

TABLE 4: Report on initial accounts of a public company wishing to make a distribution

Independent auditors' report to the directors of XYZ Plc pursuant to s273(4) of the Companies Act 1985
We have audited the initial accounts of XYZ Plc on pages ... to ... which comprise [state the primary financial statements such as the Profit and Loss Account, the Balance Sheet, the Cash Flow Statement, the Statement of Total Recognised Gains and Losses] and the related notes. The initial accounts have been prepared under the accounting policies set out therein.

This report is made solely to the company's directors, as a body, in accordance with section 273(4) of the Companies Act 1985. Our audit work has been undertaken so that we might state to the company's directors those matters we are required to state to them in this opinion and for no other purpose. To the fullest extent permitted by law, we do not accept or assume responsibility to anyone other than the company and the company's directors as a body, for our audit work, for this report, or for the opinions we have formed.

Respective responsibilities of directors and auditors
As described on page ... the directors are responsible for the preparation of the initial accounts in accordance with applicable law and United Kingdom Accounting Standards.

Our responsibility is to audit the initial accounts in accordance with relevant legal and regulatory requirements and the International Standards on Auditing (UK and Ireland). We report to you our opinion as to whether the initial accounts have been properly prepared within the meaning of s273 of the Companies Act 1985.

Basis of audit opinion
We conducted our audit in accordance with International Standards on Auditing (UK and Ireland) issued by the Auditing Practices Board. An audit includes examination, on a test basis, of evidence relevant to the amounts and disclosures in the initial accounts. It also includes an assessment of the significant estimates and judgements made by the directors in the preparation of the initial accounts, and of whether the accounting policies are appropriate to the company's circumstances, consistently applied and adequately disclosed.

We planned and performed our audit so as to obtain all the information and explanations which we considered necessary in order to provide us with sufficient evidence to give reasonable assurance that the initial accounts are free from material misstatement, whether caused by fraud or other irregularity or error. In forming our opinion we also evaluated the overall adequacy of the presentation of information in the initial accounts.

Opinion
In our opinion the initial accounts for the period from ... to ... have been properly prepared within the meaning of s273 of the Companies Act 1985.

Registered Auditors
Address
Date

6.4   FINANCIAL ASSISTANCE

6.4.1   Legal background

'Financial assistance' includes assistance given by way of:

- gift;
- guarantee, security, release or waiver;
- loan or agreement in which the assisting company's obligations are to be fulfilled before those of the other parties;
- the replacement or assignment of rights under any loan or other agreement; or
- any other financial assistance given by a company whose net assets are thereby reduced or which has no net assets. Net assets in this context means the aggregate of assets less the aggregate of liabilities.

In general, a company may only give financial assistance for the purchase of its shares or those of its holding company if it meets certain conditions, which are set out in s153 of the Companies Act 1985. For private companies these restrictions are relaxed, but the financial assistance must be approved by special resolution of the company. As part of this process, the directors must make a statutory declaration concerning the assistance and the solvency of the company. This declaration has to be accompanied by a report from the auditors to the directors stating that the auditors have inquired into the state of affairs of the company and whether this has led them to believe that anything said in the declaration is unreasonable.

Both the report and the declaration have to be made in the week before the approval of the special resolution.

It should be noted that:

- the auditors' report should not be dated earlier than the declaration;
- the report cannot be qualified and should not be issued unless unqualified.

An example of the report is shown in **Table 5**.

TABLE 5:   Report for private company wishing to provide financial assistance

Independent auditors' report to the directors of XYZ Limited pursuant to s156(4) of the Companies Act 1985
We report on the attached [statutory declaration]/[statement] of the directors dated ... prepared pursuant to the Companies Act 1985, in connection with the proposal that the company should give financial assistance for the purchase of ... (number) of the company's ordinary shares.

This report is made solely to the company's directors, as a body, in accordance with section 156(4) of the Companies Act 1985. Our audit work has been undertaken so that we might state to the company's directors those matters we are required to state to them in this opinion and for no other purpose. To the fullest extent permitted by law, we do not accept or assume responsibility to anyone other than the company and the company's directors as a body, for our audit work, for this report, or for the opinions we have formed.

Basis of opinion
We have enquired into the state of the company's affairs in order to review the bases for the [statutory declaration]/[statement].

Opinion
We are not aware of anything to indicate that the opinion expressed by the directors in their [statutory declaration]/[statement] as to any of the matters mentioned in s156(2) of the Companies Act 1985 is unreasonable in all the circumstances.

Registered Auditors
Address
Date

6.4.2   Guidance

There is no published guidance on the procedures that are necessary to support such a report. However, in general, the auditors' work should cover the following areas:

- consideration of the validity of the assumptions on which the directors' declaration is based;
- a review of up-to-date management accounts to cover the period since the last audited accounts. Where particular risks exist or the net asset position is not clear, interim audited accounts may be required;
- a review of projected cash flows, ensuring they are consistent with the stated assumptions and the auditors' knowledge of the business;
- determining whether the transaction is legal in terms of the distributable reserves of the company. In the light of events since the last audited accounts, the auditors should consider whether there are sufficient distributable profits at the time of the assistance;
- the consideration of asset and liability values, future commitments, expected changes in levels of activity or problems affecting profitability or gearing; and
- the consideration of whether the assistance would reduce net assets in contravention of s154. The auditors must ensure that the financial assistance does not reduce net assets, or if it does, that the reduction is covered by distributable profits. This is not a reporting requirement, but the auditors should not give a report on a declaration of solvency where the assistance would be illegal under s154.

This latter point may also be an issue on which the company's bankers would want assurance in the form of a comfort letter from the auditors. Recent guidance issued by the ICAEW (FRAG 26/94 *Financial Assistance for Acquisition of a Company's Own Shares: Non-Statutory Reports to Banks by Auditors*) suggests that auditors obtain a memorandum from the Board regarding the net asset position and containing a similar statement to the statutory declaration under s156(4). This memorandum together with the auditors' other procedures will usually enable them to provide a comfort letter to the bank. Where the company is close to breaching the net assets rule it may be necessary to continuously review the position until the day the declaration is signed. An example of the letter to the bank is shown in **Table 6**.

TABLE 6:   Comfort letter to bank regarding financial assistance

Report by the independent auditors of XYZ Limited (The Company) to Anybank Plc (The Bank)
This report is given in connection with the proposed arrangement whereby the company will give financial assistance for the purchase of its own shares, particulars of which are given in the statutory declaration made this day by the directors pursuant to s155(6) of the Companies Act 1985 (the Act).

The purpose of this report is to assist the bank in considering whether the proposed arrangement is permitted under s155(2) of the Act and it is not intended to be used, quoted or referred to for any other purpose.

We have examined the Board Memorandum dated ... (a copy of which is attached, initialled by us for identification) for which the directors are solely responsible and have enquired into the company's state of affairs so far as it is necessary for us to review the bases for the Board Memorandum. Our enquiry did not constitute an audit under the provisions of the Companies Act 1985.

We confirm that as at the close of business on ... [the same date as in the Board Memorandum] the aggregate of the company's assets as stated in its accounting records exceeded the aggregate of its liabilities as so stated.

We are not aware of anything to indicate that the opinion expressed in the Board Memorandum (*concerning the effect of giving the financial assistance*) is unreasonable in all the circumstances.

Registered Auditors
Address
Date

6.5 PURCHASE AND REDEMPTION OF OWN SHARES

6.5.1 *Legal background*

Where a private company decides to redeem or purchase its own shares wholly or partly out of capital, this has to be approved by a special resolution of the company. A directors' declaration is required concerning the amount by which the purchase price exceeds any available profits (the permissible capital payment) and the solvency of the company. This statement has to be accompanied by an auditors' report.

The auditors' report should be addressed to the directors and states that the amount specified as the permissible capital payment has been properly determined and that the solvency statement is reasonable. The report should be made and dated in the week prior to the meeting which passes the special resolution.

6.5.2 *Guidance*

As with the report on financial assistance:

- the auditors' report should not be dated earlier than the declaration;
- the report cannot be qualified and should not be issued unless unqualified.

An example of the report is shown in **Table 7**.

There is no published guidance on the procedures that are necessary to support such a report, although there are similarities in the procedures necessary to give the report for financial assistance. In general, before giving the report the auditors must:

- be satisfied that the directors' assumptions are realistic and consistently applied;
- review the cash flow forecasts;
- review asset and liability values, including provisions and future commitments;
- confirm that any support being received from lenders or group companies will be continued; and
- ensure that the permissible capital payment calculation is correct, taking into account any movements since the relevant accounts were prepared. These relevant accounts need not be audited but must be sufficient to enable a reasonable judgement to be made as to the financial position of the company.

TABLE 7:   Report for private company redeeming or purchasing shares out of capital

Independent auditors' report to the Directors of XYZ Limited pursuant to s173(5) of the Companies Act 1985

We report on the attached statutory declaration of the directors dated ..., prepared pursuant to the Companies Act 1985, in connection with the company's proposed [purchase]/[redemption] of ... (*number*) [ordinary]/ [preferred] shares by a payment out of capital and reserves.

This report is made solely to the company's directors, as a body, in accordance with section 173(5) of the Companies Act 1985. Our audit work has been undertaken so that we might state to the company's directors those matters we are required to state to them in this opinion and for no other purpose. To the fullest extent permitted by law, we do not accept or assume responsibility to anyone other than the company and the company's directors as a body, for our audit work, for this report, or for the opinions we have formed.

Basis of opinion
We have enquired into the state of the company's state of affairs in order to review the bases for the statutory declaration.

Opinion
In our opinion, the amount of £ ... specified in the statutory declaration of the directors as the permissible capital payment for the shares to be [purchased]/ [redeemed] is properly determined in accordance with ss171 and 172 of the Companies Act 1985.

We are not aware of anything to indicate that the opinion expressed by the directors in their statutory declaration as to any of the matters mentioned in s173(3) of the Companies Act 1985 is unreasonable in all the circumstances.

Registered Auditors
Address
Date

6.6   RE-REGISTRATION OF COMPANIES

6.6.1   *Legal background*

When a private company wishes to re-register as a public company, it has to deliver certain documents to the Registrar of Companies before it will be issued with a new certificate of incorporation. These include a copy of the company's balance sheet, at a date not more than seven months before the application, together with an auditors' report on that balance sheet without material qualification, and a further written statement from the auditors. If the last financial statements are at a date more than seven months before, an up-to-date balance sheet will be need to be prepared and audited.

This statement should confirm that the company's net assets are not less than the total of its share capital and non-distributable reserves. An example of a statement where the previous financial statements are used is shown in **Table 8**. **Table 9** gives the auditors' report where a new balance sheet is prepared.

6.6.2 Guidance

The procedures to support such a report may be restricted to a simple examination of the amounts in the relevant financial statements. The report should indicate that the work is limited to such an examination.

If the balance sheet is qualified, the auditors will have to state that this is not material for the purposes of determining whether at the balance sheet date the net assets of the company were not less than the aggregate of its called-up share capital and non-distributable reserves. The considerations required for this are similar to those for the effect of qualifications on distributions. Where this is the case an extra paragraph will need to be inserted in the auditors' statement as illustrated in **Table 8**.

The auditors' report should not be dated earlier than the date of the audit report on the relevant balance sheet.

If there has been a change of auditors, the new auditors can accept the balance sheet audited by their predecessors unless the audit report thereon has been qualified. The new auditors should refer in their report to the firm that has carried out the audit of the relevant balance sheet.

TABLE 8: Statement required when a private company wishes to re-register as a public company

Independent auditors' statement to the directors of XYZ Limited pursuant to s43(3)(b) of the Companies Act 1985
We have examined the balance sheet and related notes of XYZ Limited as at . . . which formed part of the financial statements for the year then ended audited by us.

This report is made solely to the company's directors, as a body, in accordance with section 43(3)(b) of the Companies Act 1985. Our audit work has been undertaken so that we might state to the company's directors those matters we are required to state to them in this opinion and for no other purpose. To the fullest extent permitted by law, we do not accept or assume responsibility to anyone other than the company and the company's directors as a body, for our audit work, for this report, or for the opinions we have formed.

Respective responsibilities of directors and auditors
As described on page ... the company's directors are responsible for the preparation of the balance sheet and related notes. It is our responsibility to

---

form an independent opinion based on our examination and to report our opinion to you.

Basis of opinion
The scope of our work for the purpose of this statement, was limited to an examination of the relationship between the company's net assets and its called up share capital and undistributable reserves as stated in the audited balance sheet.

Opinion
In our opinion the audited balance sheet as at ...shows that the amount of the company's net assets (within the meaning given to that expression by section 264(2) of the Companies Act 1985) was not less than the aggregate of its called-up share capital and undistributable reserves.

[(*Where appropriate*) We audited the financial statements of XYZ Limited for the year ended ... in accordance with International Standards on Auditing (UK and Ireland) issued by the Auditing Practices Board and expressed a qualified opinion thereon.

[Description of qualified opinion
In our opinion the matter giving rise to our qualification is not material for determining, by reference to the balance sheet at ... , whether, at that date, the company's net assets (within the meaning given to that expression by section 264(2) of the Companies Act 1985) was not less than the aggregate of its called-up share capital and undistributable reserves.]

Registered Auditors
Address
Date

TABLE 9:   Report for re-registration where new balance sheet prepared

Independent auditors' report to XYZ Limited
We have examined the balance sheet and related notes of XYZ Limited as at ... which were prepared for the purpose of the proposed re-registration of XYZ Limited as a public company and audited by us.

This report is made solely to the company, in accordance with section 43(3)(c) of the Companies Act 1985. Our audit work has been undertaken so that we might state to the company those matters we are required to state to them in an auditor's report and for no other purpose. To the fullest extent permitted by law, we do not accept or assume responsibility to anyone other than the company as a body, for our audit work, for this report, or for the opinions we have formed.

Respective responsibilities of directors and auditors
As described on page ... the company's directors are responsible for the preparation of the balance sheet and related notes. It is our responsibility to

form an independent opinion, based on our examination, and to report our opinion to you.

Basis of opinion
The scope of our work for the purpose of this statement, was limited to an examination of the relationship between the company's net assets and its called up share capital and undistributable reserves as stated in the audited balance sheet.

Opinion
In our opinion the audited balance sheet as at ...shows that the amount of the company's net assets (within the meaning given to that expression by section 264(2) of the Companies Act 1985) was not less than the aggregate of its called-up share capital and undistributable reserves.

Registered Auditors
Address
Date

6.7 ALLOTMENT OF SHARES OTHERWISE THAN FOR CASH

6.7.1 Legal background

All companies may allot shares and receive payment for them in something other than cash. However, where the company concerned is a public company, during the six months prior to the allotment, it is necessary to obtain a report on the value of the asset to be received instead of cash.

This report should be prepared by independent accountants. This is either the company's auditors, or a firm suitably qualified to be the company's auditors, i.e., a registered auditor. The accountants are entitled to rely on an expert, who is not connected with the company, to make a valuation of part or all of the asset.

The report should be addressed to the company and sent to the company secretary for distribution to the allottees. It should include the following information:

- the nominal value of the shares in question;
- any premium payable on them;
- a description of the consideration;
- a description of the part of the consideration valued by the independent accountants, the method used and the date of the valuation; and
- the extent to which the nominal value of the shares and any premium are to be treated as paid up by the consideration and in cash.

If the valuation was carried out by someone else, the independent accountants should give their opinion on whether that valuation is reasonable and provide details on the expert's qualifications, the method used, and the amount and the date of the valuation. The expert must be independent of the company.

Where the allotment of shares represents only part of the consideration for the asset, the report should apply to as much of the value as is attributable to the shares. It must state what valuations have been made to determine the proportion of the consideration and the reasons for and methods of that valuation.

6.7.2   Guidance

The accountants' work will consist of:

- either valuing the consideration themselves or assessing whether it is reasonable to accept an external valuation;
- confirming that the value of the consideration is not less than the total amount to be treated as being paid up on the shares, together with any premium; and
- considering whether there has been any change in the value of the asset since the valuation and confirming that it has not diminished. Where they have used an expert to provide the valuation it may be necessary to obtain written confirmation that there has been no diminution since the original valuation exercise.

The report, which must not be qualified, is shown in **Table 10**. If it were qualified the company registrars would be unable to issue the share certificates.

TABLE 10:   Report where shares allotted other than for cash

Independent accountants' report to XYZ Plc for the purposes of s103(1) of the Companies Act 1985
We report on the value of the consideration for the allotment to ... (*name of allottee*) of ... shares, having a nominal value of [...] each, to be issued at a premium of ... pence per share. The shares and share premium are to be treated as fully paid up.

The consideration for the allotment to ... (*name*) is the freehold building situated at ... (*address*) and ... [number] shares, having a nominal value of [...] each in Blue Chip plc.

This report is made solely to the company, in accordance with section 103(1) of the Companies Act 1985. Our work has been undertaken so that we might state to the company those matters we are required to state to them in this opinion

---

and for no other purpose. To the fullest extent permitted by law, we do not accept or assume responsibility to anyone other than the company, for our work, for this report, or for the opinions we have formed.

Basis of opinion
The freehold building was valued on the basis of open market value by ... , a Fellow of the Royal Institution of Chartered Surveyors, on ... and in our opinion it is reasonable to accept such a valuation.

The shares in Blue Chip Plc were valued by us on ... on the basis of the price shown in The Stock Exchange Daily Official List at ...

Opinion
In our opinion, the methods of valuation of the freehold building and of the shares in Blue Chip Plc were reasonable in all the circumstances. There appears to have been no material change in the value of either part of the consideration since the date(s) at which the valuations were made.

On the basis of the valuations, in our opinion, the value of the total consideration is not less than £ ... (being the total amount to be treated as paid up on the shares allotted together with the share premium).

Registered Auditors/Independent Accountants
Address
Date

6.8 TRANSFER OF NON-CASH ASSETS TO A PUBLIC COMPANY BY ONE OF ITS MEMBERS

6.8.1 Legal background

A similar report to that described in **6.7** above is required when a public company, in the first two years following its registration, purchases a non-cash asset from one of its members for a consideration of at least one-tenth of the nominal value of its issued share capital. The Act does not allow such a purchase without approval by an ordinary resolution of the company and the submission of a report by independent accountants.

This report must be prepared by independent accountants and must be made to the company in the six months preceding the allotment of shares.

Instead of being sent to the allottees it will be addressed to the company and sent to the members and will detail the asset to be purchased by the company, together with details of the valuation. Again this report must not be qualified.

7 REPORTS ON ACCOUNTS PREPARED BY ACCOUNTANTS

7.1 INTRODUCTION

For accounting periods ending on or after 30 March 2004 companies with a turnover of less than £5.6 million are exempt from the Companies Act requirement for an audit. Small groups whose total turnover falls below the £5.6 million threshold are also eligible for the exemption.

This limit has been steadily raised over recent years from £90,000 prior to August 1994, through £350,000 and most recently £1 million for periods ending between 26 July 2000 and 30 March 2004.

Charitable companies are excluded from making use of the increased exemptions until a full consultation has taken place. Audit exemption reports for small charities are covered in **Chapter 43**.

As a result of the increase in the audit exemption threshold there are a number of issues with which auditing practitioners have had to deal. Some of the considerations arising from the removal of many companies from the audit requirement are detailed in section **7.5**.

7.2 GUIDANCE

The original guidance on the form and content of reports issued by accountants who prepare accounts on behalf of clients was contained in Technical Release Audit 1/95 issued by the Audit Faculty of the ICAEW.

In April 2004, the Audit and Assurance Faculty of the ICAEW issued Audit 02/04, *Chartered Accountants' Reports on the Compilation of Financial Statements of Incorporated Entities* to supersede Audit 1/95 in relation to incorporated entities only. It was issued in response to the increasing number of companies that, since the increase in the audit threshold, no longer require statutory audit, but still require chartered accountants to compile their financial statements. In February 2005, Audit 01/05 *Chartered*

Accountants' Reports on the Compilation of Historical Financial Information of Unincorporated Entities was published to supersede the remainder of Audit 1/95. However, where accountants of unincorporated entities are asked to compile a set of financial statements in full compliance with the provisions of UK GAAP they should follow the guidance in Audit 02/04.

The statement reminds accountants that the five fundamental ethical principles of integrity, objectivity, competence, performance and courtesy apply to compilation engagements as they do to audits. It also reminds them that no tests are required on the assertions underlying the information they are presented with and therefore reporting accountants can express no assurance on the financial statements.

7.3   INCORPORATED ENTITIES

7.3.1   Terms of engagement

Audit 02/04 states that there must be clear understanding between the client and the accountants regarding the terms of the engagement. An example engagement letter extract is provided, which is reproduced in **Table 1**.

In addition, accountants should consider whether it is appropriate to include a section on the limitation of the accountants' liability.

TABLE 1:   Engagement letter extracts for the compilation of unaudited financial statements

Responsibilities of directors
As directors of the company, you are responsible for maintaining proper accounting records and for preparing financial statements which give a true and fair view and which have been prepared in accordance with the Companies Act 1985 ('the Act').

In preparing financial statements, you are required to:

- select suitable accounting policies and then apply them consistently;
- make judgements and estimates that are reasonable and prudent; and
- prepare financial statements on a going concern basis unless it is inappropriate to presume that the company will continue in business.

You are responsible for keeping proper accounting records which disclose with reasonable accuracy at any time the financial position of the company and for ensuring that the financial statements comply with the Act. You are also responsible for safeguarding the assets of the company and hence for taking reasonable steps for the prevention and detection of fraud and other irregularities.

You are also responsible for determining whether in respect of each financial

---

year, the company meets the conditions for exemption from audit, as set out in Section 249A [or 249AA] of the Act and for determining whether, in respect of that year, the exemption is not available for any of the reasons set out in Section 249B.

You have undertaken to make available to us, as and when required, all the company's accounting records and related financial information, including minutes of management and shareholders' meetings, necessary to carry out our work. You will make full disclosure to us of all relevant information.

Scope of the accountants' work
You have asked us to assist you in the preparation of the financial statements. We will compile the annual financial statements for your approval based on the accounting records maintained by you and the information and explanations given to us by you. We shall plan our work on the basis that no report is required by statute or regulation for the year, unless you inform us in writing to the contrary. In carrying out our engagement we will make enquiries of management and undertake any procedures that we judge appropriate but are under no obligation to perform procedures that may be required for assurance engagements such as audits or reviews.

You have advised us that the company is exempt from an audit of the financial statements. We will not carry out any work to determine whether or not the company is entitled to audit exemption, However, should our work indicate that the company is not entitled to the exemption, we will inform you of this.

Our work will not be an audit of the financial statements in accordance with Auditing Standards. Consequently, our work will not provide any assurance that the accounting records or the financial statements are free from material misstatement, whether caused by fraud, other irregularities or error and cannot be relied on to identify weaknesses in internal controls.

Since we have not carried out an audit, nor confirmed in any way the accuracy or reasonableness of the accounting records maintained by the company, we are unable to provide any assurance as to whether the financial statements that we prepare from those records present a true and fair view.

We have a professional duty to compile financial statements that conform with generally accepted accounting principles from the accounting records and information and explanations given to us. Furthermore, as directors, you have a duty to prepare financial statements that comply with the Act and applicable accounting standards. Where we identify that the financial statements do not conform to accepted accounting principles or if the accounting policies adopted are not immediately apparent this will need to be disclosed in the financial statements.

We have a professional responsibility not to allow our name to be associated with financial statements which may be misleading. Therefore, although we are not required to search for such matters, should we become aware, for any reason, that the financial statements may be misleading, we will discuss the matter with you with a view to agreeing appropriate adjustments and/or disclosures in the financial statements. In such circumstances where adjustments and/or disclosures that we consider appropriate are not made or where we are not provided with appropriate information, and as a result we consider that the financial statements are misleading, we will withdraw from the engagement.

As part of our normal procedures, we may request you to provide written confirmation of any information or explanations given by you orally during the course of our work.

Form of the accountants' report
We shall report to the Board of Directors, with any modifications that we consider may be necessary, that in accordance with this engagement letter and in order to assist you to fulfil your responsibilities, we have compiled, without carrying out an audit, the financial statements from the accounting records of the company and from the information and explanation supplied to us.

Liability provisions
We will perform the engagement with reasonable skill and care. The total aggregate liability to the Company and the Board of Directors, as a body, of whatever nature, whether in contract, tort or otherwise, of [name of accountants] for any losses whatsoever and howsoever caused arising from or in any way connected with this engagement shall not exceed [amount].

7.3.2   Directors' responsibilities

Although they have asked their accountants to compile the financial statements, directors are ultimately responsible for ensuring that the company maintains proper accounting records and for preparing financial statements which give a true and fair view and have been prepared in accordance with the Companies Act 1985. In addition directors are required to:

● select suitable accounting policies and then apply them consistently;
● make judgements and estimates that are reasonable and prudent; and
● prepare financial statements on a going concern basis unless it is inappropriate to presume that the company will continue in business.

They are also responsible for safeguarding the assets of the company and for taking steps for the prevention and detection of fraud and other irregularities.

7.3.3   Accountants' procedures

Accountants will plan their work, and this includes obtaining a general understanding of the business and operations of the company and the accounting principles and practices of the industry in which the company operates.

Accountants also consider whether the financial statements are consistent with their understanding of the company, but are under no obligation to perform procedures that may be required for an audit or review.

There is no mandatory requirement to document the work that has been carried out; however, adequate documentation will demonstrate that the work performed is of the requisite quality and has been performed in accordance with the terms of engagement. Accountants may use a disclosure checklist or software package to check that all relevant disclosures have been made.

Accountants will also consider obtaining written confirmation of oral representations made by management.

7.3.4   Misleading financial statements

Although accountants are not reviewing or auditing the financial statements, they may become aware that the financial statements are misleading. If this is the case, the matter should be discussed with management with a view to making adjustments or giving additional disclosures. If such amendments are not made, accountants should withdraw from the engagement.

If there are departures from accounting standards, but these have been adequately disclosed, the accountants may wish to highlight this in their compilation report.

7.3.5   Approving financial statements

The financial statements should be approved and signed by the directors before the accountants' report is signed.

The directors are statutorily responsible for their company's accounts. They are required to approve the accounts and the balance sheet should state the name of the directors signing the accounts on behalf of the board. Under s249B(4) of the Companies Act 1985, introduced by the audit exemption regulations, directors acknowledge, on the face of the balance sheet, their responsibilities for keeping accounting records and for preparing true and fair accounts as well as entitlement to exemption.

7.3.6   Accountants' reports

The aim of the accountants' report is for readers to draw comfort from the fact that the accounts have been compiled by a chartered accountant who is subject to the ethical and other guidance issued by the Institute. An example report is given in **Table 2**.

The financial statements must contain a reference to the fact that they are unaudited, either on the front cover or on each page of the financial statements.

TABLE 2:   Example accountants' report

Chartered Accountants'/Accountant's Report to the Board of Directors on the Unaudited Financial Statements of XYZ Ltd

In accordance with the engagement letter dated [date], and in order to assist you to fulfil your duties under the Companies Act 1985, we have compiled the financial statements of the company which comprise [the Profit and Loss Account, the Balance Sheet, the Cash Flow Statement, the Statement of Total Recognised Gains and Losses] and the related notes from the accounting records and information and explanations you have given to us.

This report is made to the Company's Board of Directors, as a body, in accordance with the terms of our engagement. Our work has been undertaken so that we might compile the financial statements that we have been engaged to compile, report to the Company's Board of Directors that we have done so, and state those matters that we have agreed to state to them in this report and for no other purpose. To the fullest extent permitted by law, we do not accept or assume responsibility to anyone other than the Company and the Company's Board of Directors, as a body, for our work or for this report.

We have carried out this engagement in accordance with technical guidance issued by the Institute of Chartered Accountants in England and Wales and have complied with the ethical guidance laid down by the Institute relating to members undertaking the compilation of financial statements.

You have acknowledged on the balance sheet for the year ended [date] your duty to ensure that the company has kept proper accounting records and to prepare financial statements that give a true and fair view under the Companies Act 1985. You consider that the company is exempt from the statutory requirement for an audit for the year.

We have not been instructed to carry out an audit of the financial statements. For this reason, we have not verified the accuracy or completeness of the accounting records or information and explanations you have given to us and we do not, therefore, express any opinion on the financial statements.

[We draw your attention to note x in the financial statements which discloses and explains a departure from applicable accounting standards. The company has not depreciated its goodwill held in the financial statements in the year and this is a departure from the Financial Reporting Standard for Smaller Entities and from the Companies Act 1985.]

Accountants
Address
Date

Abbreviated accounts

Where the company wishes to take advantage of the ability to file abbreviated accounts and the turnover of the company is such as to require no statutory report (below £5.6 million), the same wording as used in the report for the full accounts compiled for directors should be used in the abbreviated accounts that are filed (see **Table 2**). There is no other report to which reference needs to be made.

7.4 UNINCORPORATED ENTITIES

7.4.1 Scope of guidance

Technical Release Audit 01/05 is intended to give general guidance to accountants when they compile historical financial information for their clients, and covers situations where the request is by unincorporated entities for a specific purpose, such as for tax purposes, partnership accounts or for grant claims.

However, where a set of financial statements which comply fully with the provisions of UK GAAP for an unincorporated entity are requested, the guidance in Audit 02/04 should be followed (see **7.3**).

Audit 01/05 may be of use, however, when accountants compile historical financial information, other than financial statements, for incorporated entities.

7.4.2 Professional ethics

When compiling historical financial information for unincorporated entities, accountants are bound by all ethical and other guidance laid down by the ICAEW. They should not, therefore compile, or allow their names to be associated with, financial information which they consider to be misleading.

7.4.3 Accounting basis

Accountants are not required to test assertions underlying the information which they are compiling and therefore are not able to express any assurance on the financial information being compiled.

There is no statutory requirement for the financial information of unincorporated entities to give a true and fair view and it is acceptable to compile the information on an accounting basis other than full UK GAAP. The appropriate accounting basis should be discussed with the clients and clearly defined so that the accountants can compile the information.

The accounting basis, purpose and limitations of the information presented should be fully disclosed in a note to the financial information and referred to in the accountants' report.

7.4.4   Terms of engagement

As with compilations performed under Audit 02/04 there must be clear understanding between the client and the accountants regarding the terms of the engagement. An example engagement letter extract for the compilation of historical financial information under Audit 01/05 is provided in **Table 3**.

In addition, accountants should consider whether it is appropriate to include a section on the limitation of the accountants' liability.

TABLE 3:   Engagement letter extracts for the compilation of historical financial information for unincorporated entities

Client's responsibilities
You will be responsible for the reliability, accuracy and completeness of the accounting records.

You have undertaken to make available to us, as and when required, all your accounting records and related financial information, including minutes of management meetings, necessary to carry out our work. You will provide us with all the information and explanations relevant to the purpose and compilation of the financial information.

Scope of the accountants' work
You have asked us to assist you in the preparation of [insert type of information required] for [insert purpose]. We will compile the financial information for your approval based on the accounting records maintained by you and the information and explanations given to us by you.

We shall plan our work on the basis that no report is required by statute or regulation, unless you inform us in writing to the contrary. In carrying out our engagement we will make enquiries of [management] and undertake any procedures that we judge appropriate but are under no obligation to perform procedures that may be required for assurance engagements such as audits or reviews.

Our work will not be an audit of the financial information in accordance with Auditing Standards. Consequently, our work will not provide any assurance that the accounting records or the financial information are free from material misstatement, whether caused by fraud, other irregularities or error and cannot be relied on to identify weaknesses in internal controls.

Since we have not carried out an audit, nor confirmed in any way the accuracy or reasonableness of the accounting records maintained by the company, we are unable to provide any assurance as to whether the financial information that we prepare from those records presents a true and fair view.

We have a professional duty to compile financial information that conforms with generally accepted accounting principles selected by management as being appropriate for the purpose for which the information is prepared. The accounting basis on which the information has been compiled, its purpose and limitations will be disclosed in an accounting policy note to the financial information and will be referred to in our accountants' report.

We also have a professional responsibility not to allow our name to be associated with financial information which we believe may be misleading. Therefore, although we are not required to search for such matters, should we become aware, for any reason, that the financial information may be misleading, we will discuss the matter with you with a view to agreeing appropriate adjustments and/or disclosures in the financial information. In circumstances where adjustments and/or disclosures that we consider appropriate are not made or where we are not provided with appropriate information, and as a result we consider that the financial information is misleading, we will withdraw from the engagement.

As part of our normal procedures, we may request you to provide written confirmation of any information or explanations given by you orally during the course of our work.

You will approve and sign the financial information thereby acknowledging responsibility for it, including the appropriateness of the accounting basis on which it has been compiled, and for providing us with all information and explanations necessary for its compilation.

Form of the accountants' report
We shall report to you that in accordance with this engagement letter we have compiled, without carrying out an audit, the financial information from the accounting records of the entity and from the information and explanation supplied to us. The report should not be used for any purpose other than as set out in this engagement letter.

Liability provisions
We will perform the engagement with reasonable skill and care. The total aggregate liability to you, of whatever nature, whether in contract, tort or otherwise, of [name of accountants] for any losses whatsoever and howsoever caused arising from or in any way connected with this engagement shall not exceed [amount].

7.4.5 Client's responsibilities

The client is responsible for the reliability, accuracy and completeness of the accounting records of the entity and for disclosing all relevant information to the accountant.

7.4.6 Planning

Having agreed a basis and format for the financial information, the accountant will plan the engagement. The level of planning will vary depending on the complexity and completeness of the client's accounting records and the reporting accountant's experience of the business.

7.4.7 Procedures

As in **7.3.3** above, reporting accountants will obtain a general understanding of the operations of the entity, consider whether the financial information is consistent with their understanding of the business and check whether relevant disclosures have been made. In addition they will obtain written representations from management, particularly in relation to estimates and the reliability, accuracy and completeness of information provided to them.

The accountants are under no obligation to perform procedures that would be necessary to enable them to give assurance on the financial information.

There is no mandatory requirement to document the work carried out, although full documentation will assist with performing a good quality engagement.

7.4.8 Misleading financial information

Accountants compiling financial information for unincorporated entities have the same responsibilities towards misleading financial information as accountants working for incorporated entities (see **7.3.4**).

7.4.9 Approval of financial information

Although there is no statutory duty for the financial information of unincorporated entities to be signed or approved by the client, it is recommended that the client does sign the information to acknowledge their responsibility for it. An example wording is given in **Table 4**.

TABLE 4: Example wording for approval of financial information

In accordance with the engagement letter dated [...], I/we approve the financial information which comprises [state the financial information compiled]. I/we acknowledge my/our responsibility for the financial information, including the appropriateness of the accounting basis as set out in note [x], and for providing [the accountants] with all information and explanations necessary for its compilation.

7.4.10 Accountants' reports

As stated in **7.3.6** above, the aim of the accountants' report is to help users derive comfort from the fact that the financial information has been compiled by an accountant who is subject to the ethical and other guidance issued by the ICAEW. It also clarifies that an audit has not taken place. An example report wording for the compilation of financial information for unincorporated entities is given in **Table 5**.

TABLE 5: Example accountants' report for the compilation of financial information for unincorporated entities

Chartered Accountants'/Accountant's Report to [Entity] on Unaudited Financial Information

In accordance with the engagement letter dated [date] we have compiled the financial information of [the entity] which comprises [the Profit and Loss Account, the Balance Sheet, the Cash Flow Statement and, where relevant, the related notes] from the accounting records and information and explanations you have given to us.

The [financial information] has been compiled on the basis set out in note [x] to the [financial information]. The financial information is not intended to achieve full compliance with the provisions of UK Generally Accepted Accounting Principles.

This report is made to you in accordance with the terms of our engagement. Our work has been undertaken so that we might compile the [financial information] that we have been engaged to compile, report to you that we have done so, and state those matters that we have agreed to state to you in this report and for no other purpose. To the fullest extent permitted by law, we do not accept or assume responsibility to anyone other than the [addressee of this report], for our work or for this report.

We have carried out this engagement in accordance with technical guidance issued by the Institute of Chartered Accountants in England and Wales and have complied with the ethical guidance laid down by the Institute.

You have approved the [financial information] [where appropriate, insert period to which the financial information relates] and have acknowledged your responsibility for it, for the appropriateness of the accounting basis and for providing all information and explanations necessary for its compilation.

We have not verified the accuracy or completeness of the accounting records or information and explanations you have given to us and we do not, therefore, express any opinion on the financial information.

Accountants
Address
Date

7.5 CONSIDERATIONS FOLLOWING THE INCREASE IN THE AUDIT EXEMPTION LIMIT

Introduction

Many companies who fulfil the size criteria for audit exemption (profit and loss, balance sheet or number of employees) are still required to have an audit. This may be because they are 'ineligible' under the legislation, such as public, banking and insurance companies, trade unions, employers' associations, certain companies that are members of groups and companies regulated under the Financial Services Act. An audit may also be required where the company's constitution requires it or where it is requested by the provider of finance.

Registered auditor status

It is an offence under s41 of the Companies Act 1989 for anyone to describe themselves as, or hold themselves out to be, a registered auditor when they are not. If an audit report is published with the financial statements, or otherwise made available to the public, the auditor who signed that report must be registered to avoid committing an offence. Practitioners should bear this is mind when deciding whether to renew their registered status.

Requirements when a company becomes exempt

Where clients become audit exempt, either as a result of changing exemption limits, or due to changes in their results and employee count, auditors should not continue to perform an audit without telling the client about the options open to them. Discussing these options will allow the auditor to sell the advantages of continuing with the annual audit process.

Engagement letters

Where there is a significant change in the nature of the services provided, a new engagement letter will be required. Therefore, when a client becomes audit exempt and takes advantage of that exemption a new engagement letter will be required, assuming the practitioner continues to act in some other capacity for that client. Where the client becomes exempt, but elects to continue with the audit process the ICAEW have stated that it is also desirable to issue a new engagement letter, regardless of whether the audit report is filed with the financial statements.

Resignation procedures

Where a client becomes audit exempt and an audit is no longer requested for non-statutory reasons, auditors do not, in theory, have to resign from office. There is a lack of clarity within the Companies Act 1985 as to whether an audit firm still engaged to an audit exempt client is required to issue an annual report even if the client is exempted from the requirement to have an audit.

Commentators' views on this matter have varied and therefore in order to avoid unnecessary risk auditors should resign from office when a client becomes audit exempt.

The Department of Trade and Industry have advised that audit exemption is not, in itself, an issue that should be brought to the attention of members or creditors. However, when an auditor ceases to hold office a section 394 statement should still be made and deposited at the company's registered office in the normal way. An example wording is set out in **Table 6**.

TABLE 6: Example section 394 statement for use when client becomes audit exempt

To the Directors of XYZ Limited

Dear Sirs

We hereby give notice, under s392 of the Companies Act, of our resignation as auditors to XYZ Limited as of .. [date]. In accordance with s394 of the Companies Act 1985, we confirm that there are no circumstances connected with our ceasing to hold office that we consider should be brought to members' or creditors' attention.

Yours faithfully

...

---

8 REPORTS TO THE FSA ON INVESTMENT BUSINESSES

8.1 LEGAL BACKGROUND

This Chapter covers the reporting requirements for auditors of investment business regulated by the Financial Services Authority (FSA).

Where companies are registered under the Financial Services and Markets Act 2000 (FSMA) (and previously the Financial Services Act 1986) their auditors are obliged to report to the FSA as regulator under the FSA's Handbook of Rules and Guidance (the FSA Rules). This is in addition to reporting on annual financial statements to the members.

The FSA took over the regulation of investment businesses previously regulated by the Securities and Futures Authority (SFA), the Investment Management Regulatory Organisation (IMRO) and the Personal Investment Authority (PIA) on 1 December 2001 (known as 'N2'). SFA, IMRO and PIA were previously Self Regulatory Organisations (SROs) under the Financial Services Act.

The FSA has High Level Standards, Regulator Processes and Redress Sourcebooks that apply to all FSA regulated firms. Investment businesses must also comply with the FSA's Interim Prudential Sourcebook for Investment Businesses. This chapter describes the auditor's role in ensuring compliance with those rules.

There are similar sourcebooks for banks, building societies, insurers and friendly societies. Due to the specialist nature of these types of business, we do not cover these in detail in this chapter and auditors of these types of business should refer to the relevant APB guidance and FSA Rules.

The FSA is planning to harmonise prudential standards across the financial services sector in an Integrated Prudential Sourcebook. In addition, auditors have a duty in certain circumstances to communicate directly with the FSA. This is discussed in detail in **8.10** below.

8.2 AUDITING STANDARDS AND GUIDANCE

The standards and guidance on reporting for this type of engagement are included in:

- Section B of ISA (UK and Ireland) 250 *The Auditor's Right and Duty to Report to Regulators in the Financial Sector* (see **8.10** below);
- Practice Note 21 *The Audit of Investment Businesses in the United Kingdom*; and
- APB Bulletin 2001/7 *Guidance for Auditors of Investment Businesses.*

During the process of issuing the ISAs (UK and Ireland), the APB appended Section B to ISA 250, as there was no equivalent guidance in the existing ISAs. Section B is effective for audits of financial statements for periods commencing on or after 15 December 2004. SAS 620 *The Auditor's Right and Duty to Report to Regulators in the Financial Sector* which was applied to all audits commencing before this date and has not yet been officially withdrawn.

Practice Note 21 was issued in June 2000 and updated earlier guidance to reflect the changes in regulatory arrangements and changes to Auditing Standards to that date. Practice Note 21 was supplementd in December 2001 by APB Bulletin 2001/7, which deals with the changes that occurred at N2. This chapter considers only the reports of auditors of investment businesses. Other aspects of the audits of investment businesses are covered in **Chapter 46**.

In March 2006, the APB issued a consultation draft of a revision to Practice Note 21. When it is issued in its final form, it will replace the existing Practice Note 21 and Bulletin 2001/7. The areas of the consultation draft relating to reporting to the FSA are considered in **8.11** below. The rest of the draft is detailed in **Chapter 46**.

8.3 AUDITORS' ANNUAL REPORTING RESPONSIBILITIES

A regulated investment business's management are required to:

- prepare financial statements which give a true and fair view of the state of affairs and the profit or loss for the period;
- prepare statements of financial resources, both actual and required, as detailed by the appropriate FSA Rules;
- establish and maintain adequate accounting and other records and systems of control; and
- ensure clients' assets are protected and the rules on clients' assets are followed.

In general, the report covers the following:

- confirmation that they have received all the information and explanations considered necessary for their audit;
- whether the financial statements give a true and fair view and have been properly prepared in accordance with the relevant FSA Rules;
- whether the statements of the actual and required financial resources have been properly prepared and whether the requirements have been met at the balance sheet date;
- whether the accounting records and systems are adequate throughout the period; and
- whether the business complied with the FSA Rules concerning client assets (including client money) at the relevant dates.

The auditors should always be aware of any changes to the FSA Rules during the period and the impact this will have on their report.

Details of the FSA Rules applicable to auditors are contained within section 3 of the *FSA Supervision Handbook*, available on *www.fsa.gov.uk*.

8.4 PLANNING

The amount of work planned by auditors to support their report depends on the risk associated with the particular investment business. The main factors to consider are:

- the scope of authorisation in relation to the holding of client assets;
- the extent of investment management discretion permitted;
- the introduction of new rules;
- changes to existing legislation or rules; and
- rule waivers granted or special conditions imposed by the FSA.

The auditors' assessment of risk would involve meeting senior management and the Compliance Officer, but they would also consider:

- operational and compliance manuals;
- documentation of systems and controls;
- compliance monitoring programmes and results;
- the records of any rule breaches and notifications to the FSA;
- correspondence with the FSA;
- results of FSA's inspections; and
- the register of client complaints.

8.5 PROCEDURES

Auditors' work will normally comprise procedures designed to confirm the business's compliance with its controls, and procedures and substantive tests to verify the amounts shown in the accounting records and to check the reconciliations performed. The auditors of smaller businesses are likely to concentrate more heavily on substantive, rather than compliance, testing.

Compliance with the FSA Rules on client assets is stipulated by the *FSA Handbook of Rules and Guidance* and the auditors must report on the adequacy of the business's systems and controls in this regard. In order to ascertain whether the systems are adequate for the size and complexity of the business, the auditors will perform their tests at specific dates, and then rely on the evidence collected to conclude on adequacy throughout the period.

If a change has been made to systems and controls during the year, the periods before and after the change should be tested individually, and separate conclusions drawn.

8.6 EVIDENCE

In planning and performing their work, auditors should consider materiality based on the nature and scale of the business's operations. Their procedures should be planned to give them reasonable expectation of detecting fraud, errors and other irregularities, which would be of material interest to the clients of the business, taken as a whole.

8.7 REPORTING

The exact form of the auditors' report depends on the type of investment business. Under the FSA Rules, there are three types of investment businesses:

- Securities and Futures Firms (previously regulated by SFA);
- Investment Management Firms (previously regulated by IMRO); and
- Personal Investment Firms (previously regulated by PIA).

The FSA has agreed to a common form of report, which is modified for the specific reporting requirements of the type of business. The standard unqualified report for Securities and Futures Firms, Investment Management Firms and Personal Investment Firms is shown below and should be used wherever possible.

For less complex entities (such as corporate finance advisory firms, locals,

OPS firms or non-ISD investment management firms subject only to an own funds requirement) the report should be tailored to reflect the reduced requirements.

It should be noted that this report is regarded by the APB as a private report to informed persons (the FSA) and consequently does not fall within the provisions of ISA (UK and Ireland) 700, even though it includes a true and fair opinion.

The Practice Note considers the reports under the following headings:

- the addressee;
- the financial statements and other information audited;
- the Auditing Standards followed;
- the audit opinion on the financial statements;
- any other information;
- the identity of the auditors; and
- the date of their report.

TABLE 1: **Independent Auditors' report to the Financial Services Authority ('the FSA') in respect of ABC Limited for the [year/period] ended [year end date]**

We report in respect of ABC Limited ('the firm'), a Securities and Futures Firm/an investment management firm/a personal investment firm, on:

- the attached annual financial statements;
- the following information set out in the attached
  - the balance sheet and profit and loss account;
  - the statements of financial resources and financial resources requirement;
- the statement of the firm's expenditure requirement for the forthcoming year [if applicable];
- [for securities and future firms only] the attached reconciliation between the balance sheets in the annual financial statements, the Annual Reporting Statement and the [monthly/quarterly] financial return;
- [for Personal Investment Firms only] the attached reconciliation between the balance sheets in the annual financial statements and the [monthly/ quarterly] reporting statement;
- the attached consolidated reporting statement [if applicable];

and on the further matters set out below. Our report is provided to the FSA in its capacity as a regulator under the Financial Services and Markets Act 2000. Our report should not be disclosed to any third party or otherwise quoted or referred to without our prior written consent.

We have audited the annual financial statements in accordance with International Standards on Auditing (UK and Ireland) issued by the Auditing

---

Practices Board, and have carried out such other procedures, as we considered necessary for the purposes of this report having regard to Practice Note 21, 'The audit of investment businesses in the United Kingdom'. We have obtained all the information and explanations which, to the best of our knowledge and belief, are necessary for the purposes of our report to the FSA.

Financial statements

In our opinion:

- the annual financial statements give a true and fair view of the firm's state of affairs as at [year end date] and of its [profit/loss] for the year then ended;
- the [see Note] has been properly prepared in accordance with the FSA's rules;
- the balance sheet and profit and loss account in the [see Note] are in agreement with the firm's accounting records and returns;
- [Securities and Futures Firms only] the balance sheet in the Annual Reporting Statement has been properly reconciled to the balance sheet of the annual financial statements and to the balance sheet in the [monthly/ quarterly] reporting statement prepared by the firm as at [year end date].
- [Personal Investment Firms only] the balance sheet in the Annual Financial Statement has been properly reconciled to the balance sheet in the [monthly/quarterly] reporting statement prepared by the firm as at [year end date].

Financial resources

In our opinion:

- the firm's statement of financial resources and financial resources requirement as at [year end date] have been properly prepared in accordance with the FSA's rules;
- the firm's financial resources as at [year end date] are sufficient to meet the firm's financial resources requirement at that date;
- the statement of the firm's expenditure requirement for the forthcoming year has been prepared in accordance with the FSA's rules [if applicable].

Accounting records

In our opinion the firm has kept proper accounting records:

- in accordance with the rules of its previous regulator for the period from [start of year] to 30 November 2001; and
- in accordance with the FSA's rules for the period from 1 December 2001 to [year end date].

Consolidated reporting statement [if applicable]

In our opinion, the firm's consolidated reporting statement as at [year end date] has been prepared in accordance with the FSA's rules.

Client Assets

Either

In our opinion:

- the firm maintained systems adequate to enable it to comply with the rules of its previous regulator in respect of client money and custody assets for the period from [start of year] to 30 November 2001 and the rules in COB 9.1 to 9.4 (Client Assets) for the period from 1 December 2001 to [year end date];
- the firm was in compliance with rules in COB 9.1 to 9.4 (Client Assets) as at [year end date].
- [if applicable] in relation to the secondary pooling event during the period, the firm complied with the rules in COB 9.5 (Client money distribution).

Or

The scope of the firm's permission does not allow it to hold client money or custody assets.

The directors have stated that the firm did not hold client money or custody assets during the year. Based on review procedures performed, nothing has come to our attention that causes us to believe that the firm held client money or custody assets during the year.

Nominee companies

In our opinion, [name of nominee companies], subsidiaries of the firm which are nominee companies in whose name custody assets are registered, maintained throughout the year systems for the custody, identification and control of custody assets which are adequate to enable the firm to comply with rules of its previous regulator for the period from [start of year] to 30 November 2001 and the rules in COB 9.1 to 9.4 (Client Assets) for the period from 1 December 2001 to [year end date], which included reconciliations between the records maintained (whether by the firm or the nominee company) and statements or confirmations from custodians or from the person who maintains the record of legal entitlement at appropriate intervals.

Registered Auditors   *Address*
Date

Note:

For Securities and Futures Firms, insert 'Annual Reporting Statement'. This is the statement in SUP 16 Ann 10R, section 1.

For Investment Management Firms, insert 'Annual Financial Return'. This is the form referred to as the Annual Financial Return in SUP 16 Ann5R.

For Personal Investment Firms, insert 'Annual Financial Statement'. This is the statement referred to in SUP 16 Ann 7R as the 'Financial Reporting forms for Category A Personal Investment Firms' or the 'Financial Reporting forms for Category B Personal Investment Firms' as appropriate.

8.7.1   The addressee

The report should be addressed to the FSA. The FSA may disclose it to others for regulatory, legal or other public purposes but it should not be shown to other third parties, including the customers or shareholders of the business. As well as in their audit report, the auditors should also include a term in their engagement letter restricting the directors/management from passing the report to anyone other than the FSA.

8.7.2   The financial statements and other information audited

As with Companies Act reports, the auditors should clearly identify the financial statements and any other information on which they are reporting. Auditors should ensure that sufficient information is included within the prescribed form for a true and fair view to be given.

8.7.3   The auditing standards followed

The report should state that the audit of the financial statements has been carried out in accordance with ISAs (UK and Ireland) and that the other procedures have been carried out with regard to Practice Note 21.

8.7.4   The audit opinion

The opinion on the financial statements should be expressed in terms of the 'true and fair view' and should cover any matters specially required by the regulator in addition to the financial statements. The other main headings are:

- financial resources;
- accounting records; and
- clients' assets.

Each type of firm is subject to slightly different requirements concerning other specific reporting requirements as can be seen from the example report above.

8.8 SIGNING AND DATING

As with other audit reports, the name of the auditors and the date of their report should be given. Such reports are required to be made by registered auditors.

The date of the report should ideally be the same as the date of the opinion on the statutory financial statements. If the report to the regulator is dated later than the date of the report on the financial statements, the auditors will need to ensure that they have carried out procedures to identify any material events between the two dates and, if there are any, to have assessed their impact on their report to the regulator.

It is also possible under the FSA Rules to prepare the report on client money and custody assets as at a different date to the firm's accounting reference date. The deadline for submission would be four months after the end of the period under report. Subsequent client assets reports may be submitted covering any period of up to 53 weeks commencing at the end of the previous period under report.

There are time limits for submitting these reports and the auditors should endeavour to meet these deadlines, as failure may result in the FSA acting against the audit firm. The timing of submissions is as follows:

Type of firm	Opinion on financial resources, accounting records and accounting policies	Opinion on client money and custody assets
Securities and futures firms	3 months after the period end	4 months after the period end
Investment management firms	4 months after the period end	4 months after the period end
Personal investment firms	4 months after the period end	4 months after the period end

In addition, auditors are required to notify the FSA in writing before the deadline where they anticipate that the reports and accompanying documents will not be delivered on time and stating the reason for this.

The FSA has made specific rules which apply to all reports submitted to it; these are set out in section 16 of the *FSA Supervision Manual*. Key provisions are:

- the report must contain the firm's FSA reference number and be marked for the attention of its normal supervisory contact;
- the FSA coversheet contained in section 16 of the FSA's Supervision

Manual must be used;

- the audit report and accompanying documents may be faxed to the FSA by the deadline but an original version must be submitted within five business days;
- if the deadline is not a normal business day, then the report can be submitted by the next business day after the due date.

8.9   QUALIFIED REPORTS

Qualifications will arise in two situations. The first comes from the requirement to give a true and fair view, and the judgements that have to be made are similar to those for other audits. The other types of qualifications that may arise are where there is non-compliance with the FSA Rules.

In all cases where there are breaches, it is necessary to understand what the FSA Rules are trying to achieve. In the case of regulated investment business this is not only numerical accuracy. An overriding objective is to ensure that clients' assets are safeguarded.

Where there is doubt whether particular FSA Rules have been complied with it may be necessary to refer the matter to one of the technical advisory services of the professional bodies or to a member of the FSA supervision team who deals with the audit client.

The FSA allows auditors to classify some FSA Client Asset Rule breaches as 'trivial' and not report them. In order to classify breaches of the FSA Rules as trivial, auditors must carry out extra work and decide that:

- the breaches were minor in nature and would not cause concern to the FSA;
- no loss to the client has been incurred or would be caused by the breach; and
- the firm has immediately corrected the breach on discovery.

Even where breaches are reported, auditors may also wish to inform the FSA that the breaches have been put right and that they appeared not to cause, or were not likely to cause, any loss to a client. It is usual for auditors to inform the FSA of such matters by way of an accompanying letter.

Where auditors find evidence of breaches and have informed their client, the responsibility for corrective action lies with the management. The fact that corrective action has been taken will not remove the necessity for the auditors to consider qualifying their report on the matter where the breach is not trivial.

Where there is a breach of the FSA Rules the auditors' report should clearly indicate the specific requirement and how it has not been met so that it can be easily understood and evaluated by the FSA.

Once the auditors have informed their client that they intend to qualify their audit report, the client will immediately need to inform the FSA. Where the client does not inform the FSA the auditors should consider whether to do so themselves in a special report.

If auditors identify a breach which existed for a period both before and after N2, they need only report the breach once, but refer to the period during which the breach existed and to both the old (SRO) and the new (FSA) rule reference in order to clarify that the breach existed in both periods.

8.10 SPECIAL REPORTS

Since 1 May 1994 (1 July 1994 for insurance companies) the auditors of banks, building societies, insurance companies, friendly societies and investment businesses previously registered under the Financial Services Act, and now under the Financial Services and Markets Act 2000, have special reporting duties. They have a duty to report to the FSA certain information, relevant to the FSA's functions, which has come to their attention 'in the capacity of auditor' during their audit work.

Further regulations within the Financial Services and Markets Act 2000 clarify the matters to be reported and extend the application of the statutory duty to information to which auditors of a financial institution become aware in their capacity as auditors of other entities with close links to the financial institution.

8.10.1 Guidance

Guidance on the implications of and the procedures necessary under these regulations is contained in Section B of ISA (UK and Ireland) 250 *The Auditors' Right and Duty to Report to Regulators in the Financial Sector*. This includes guidance covering:

- the right and duty to report to regulators;
- material significance;
- procedures;
- reporting;
- communication with the regulator; and
- relationship with other reporting responsibilities.

Practice Notes have also been developed for each type of entity – for example, Practice Note 18 covers Building Societies, Practice Note 19 covers

Banks and Practice Note 20 covers Insurers. These have all been supplemented by APB Bulletins 2001/4 to 2001/6 to take into account the introduction of FSA as a single regulator. Where entities are governed by more than one regulator, auditors should ensure that they follow the guidance in each relevant Practice Note.

8.10.2   Right and duty to report

Section B of ISA (UK and Ireland) 250 requires auditors to bring to the attention of the regulator information of which they become aware in the course of the work required to fulfil their audit responsibilities, which in their opinion is:

- relevant to the FSA's functions (such as breaches of FSA Rules or concerns about the fit and proper status of management); and
- of material significance to the FSA.

Other than their reports on the financial statements, auditors will typically be required to provide a regular, usually annual, report to the regulator on items specified by the regulator or by legislation. To make this report, the auditor will be required to perform additional procedures.

In addition, auditors may have a statutory duty to report certain other information, typically breaches of regulations which may come to their attention during their work. Auditors are not required to perform any additional procedures to search out these matters. This statutory duty applies only to information which comes to the auditor in their capacity as auditor. Guidance on what constitutes information gained in their capacity as auditor is given in the ISA (UK and Ireland).

The statutory duty to report to a regulator applies to information which comes to the attention of auditors in their capacity as auditors. If the information is discovered by someone not involved in the audit, but it is of relevance to the audit, and the work that it related to, it should be taken into account as if it were audit evidence. If the work is not relevant to the audit then it is unlikely that it will give rise to a duty to report.

Where information is discovered in the course of work performed for another client the auditors have no right to breach their duty of confidentiality in respect of it. However, they may choose to make enquiries during the audit of the regulated entity to establish whether the information can be substantiated from that source.

The guidance stresses that firms should ensure that they have suitable lines of communication so that any information which may give rise to a duty to report is brought to the attention of the partner responsible for the audit, usually by enquiries of other members of the firm as part of the audit planning and completion.

The statutory right to report to the FSA is not affected if the auditors cease to hold office. Hence, if they are aware of information, this may be reported either before or after ceasing to hold office.

Auditors may have a right to report certain matters direct to the regulator in addition to those which they have a duty to report. This right will usually be exercised where the auditors consider that doing so is necessary to protect the interests of those for whose benefit the regulator is required to act.

8.10.3 'material significance'

This is defined in the ISA (UK and Ireland) as being where the FSA is likely to investigate a matter because of its nature or potential financial impact. Material significance does not mean the same as materiality in the context of the audit of financial statements. Whilst an event may be trivial in its financial impact, it may be of a nature or type likely to change the perception of the FSA. Further guidance concerning each type of regulated entity is contained in the Practice Notes and supplementary APB Bulletins.

Under the Financial Services and Markets Act new statutory definitions are provided for matters giving rise to a duty to report. They are generally matters which the auditor has a reasonable cause to believe will, or may be, of material significance in determining whether:

- a person is a fit and proper person to carry on investment business; or
- disciplinary action or powers of intervention should be used to stop investors suffering loss.

Although the particular nature of the various sectors are considered in the legislation, in general the definitions incorporate the following terms:

- circumstances indicating that the regulated entity's authorisation could be revoked;
- there is, has been, or may have been, either:
  (i) a failure to fulfil specified requirements; or
  (ii) a contravention of other provisions of the Rules which is likely to be of material significance to the FSA concerned for the exercise of its functions;
- there is no doubt as to the entity's status as a going concern; and
- the auditors conclude that their report on the entity's financial statements should include a qualified opinion.

Practice Note 21 gives additional guidance on the meaning of material significance in relation to investment businesses. It states that any breach of the FSA Rules may be reportable, whether an isolated or recurring breach, depending on size or significance, and auditors must use their judgement in determining whether a breach will be of material significance to the FSA. In doing so, auditors must consider both the facts of the matter and their implication.

The Practice Note gives examples of items which may fall into each of these categories.

Status of regulated entities, directors and senior management as fit and proper persons
When planning the audit, auditors must familiarise themselves with any guidance issued by the FSA on the information that the FSA takes into consideration when deciding whether the fit and proper requirement has been met.

Generally, the FSA assesses entities against three broad measures:

- honesty;
- competence; and
- solvency.

Although auditors cannot be expected to make judgements on competence, soundness of judgement and diligence, there may be persuasive evidence which calls the appropriateness of some of the entity's actions into question. Therefore, auditors should be alert for any indication of shortfalls in any of the following areas:

- probity, honesty, skill, care and integrity;
- attention to establishing satisfactory compliance arrangements;
- attention to compliance with notification requirements;
- observing appropriate standards of market practice; and
- openness with the FSA.

Any report on the fitness and propriety of the entity, or any of its directors or management, should be made to the FSA without prior reference to the directors of the entity.

Risk of loss – client assets
The auditor should report any identified deficiency in client assets which cannot be explained or accounted for, as well as any suspicions that misappropriation of assets may occur. Immediate action is required to ensure that the FSA can take appropriate action to protect client assets from future loss.

Risk of loss – financial position
Areas of material significance to the FSA will be those that indicate:

- the occurrence or possibility of a material loss to the regulated entity; or
- the breach, or likelihood of breach, by the entity of the requirements concerning the adequacy of its financial resource or solvency requirements.

A material loss to the business will include an event leading to a loss which is material in meeting the entity's solvency or capital adequacy requirements, or the requirement of a subsidiary, related or nominee company. This may include litigation against the entity, which may give rise to contingent liabilities and costs in defending the action.

An entity may be required to notify the FSA if its financial resources fall below a multiple of the financial requirement (e.g., 110 per cent). Failure to make this notification will also be regarded by the FSA as having material significance.

Compliance with requirements for the management of its affairs
Areas that auditors are likely to be aware of as a result of their work include:

- significant concerns over the internal control environment;
- disagreements or lack of evidence about amounts in the financial statements which cannot be resolved;
- material breaches of client asset rules and the rules requiring suitable systems in relation to client assets;
- evidence of business being conducted outside the entity's authorised scope; and
- significant matters affecting the regulated businesses' appointed representatives.

Doubt as to the entity's status as a going concern
Any doubt as to the entity's ability to continue to undertake investment business should be reported to the FSA.

8.10.4 Procedures

The ISA (UK and Ireland) stresses that neither the legislation nor the ISA (UK and Ireland) require auditors to perform any extra work to discover information that may give rise to a duty to report. The duty relates only to work performed to fulfil other reporting responsibilities where auditors must be alert to instances which would give rise to a duty to report.

Although there is no obligation to perform additional procedures, time must still be spent complying with the FSA Rules. When planning, time must be allocated to understanding the FSA Rules. Additionally, if matters which may give rise to the duty have been found, further procedures are necessary to assess whether the matter should be reported, and if so, how.

In addition to information of which the auditors become aware in their capacity as auditors of the regulated entity, the FSA Rules have extended the application of the duty to the information of which auditors become aware in the context of their work as auditors of a body which is closely linked by control to the regulated entity. An entity is closely linked with its parent, subsidiary and fellow subsidiary undertakings, or persons who would be so if they were undertakings, and also any person in accordance with whose directions its directors are accustomed to act. Hence, where auditors audit both the regulated entity and the closely linked entity they have a duty to report any information relevant to the regulated entity discovered in their capacity as auditor of that closely linked entity.

The duty does not only cover matters which are in the financial statements or are covered by the requirements of the auditors' standard report to the FSA, as there may be implications for the FSA's functions in any information discovered during the audit. For example, where information comes to light which could cast doubt on the fit and proper status of the management, this should be investigated and reported if appropriate, even though it is not a matter that the annual report to the FSA covers.

Planning
Section B of ISA (UK and Ireland) 250 extends ISA (UK and Ireland) 315 concerning the knowledge of the business, to cover the statutory provisions and the Rules.

As part of their assessment of the accounting systems and internal controls, auditors should consider the control environment, including the attitude of management to compliance with the relevant FSA Rules. Auditors should also assess whether the business is being conducted outside its authorisation as this could result in a need to report.

Supervision and control
ISA (UK and Ireland) 250 requires staff involved in regulated business audits to obtain a sufficient knowledge of what constitutes reportable matters to be able to identify them. Practice Note 21 states that as a basic minimum, the knowledge of all staff involved in the audit of a regulated business will extend to:

- the provisions of the Regulations concerning the auditors' duty to report to the regulators (FSMA 2000 (Communication by Auditors Regulations 2001));
- Part B of ISA (UK and Ireland) 250;
- Practice Note 21 and APB Bulletin 2001/7;
- the *FSA Principles for Business*; and
- the types of business which require authorisation by other regulatory authorities.

In addition, and depending on the individual's role in the engagement, understanding will be required of the *FSA Rules and guidance* relating to matters on which auditors are routinely required to report, in particular section 3 of the *FSA Supervision Manual.*

Other staff who are only involved in non-audit work for a regulated entity are not required to have a detailed knowledge of the FSA Rules nor to bring any information to the attention of the audit partner. However, there should be procedures in firms to ensure that any relevant relationship is notified to the partner responsible for the audit by other departments of the firm.

Identifying matters requiring a report
When auditors become aware of matters that they suspect may give rise to a report to the FSA, they should:

- obtain evidence to assess the implications for reporting;
- determine whether the matter is of material significance to the FSA; and
- consider whether the breach is criminal conduct that gives rise to criminal property, and therefore should be reported to the relevant authority.

It is necessary to perform these procedures in this order because not all matters may be of material significance and this may only be apparent once the matter has been investigated further. Minor breaches may be reportable if they indicate a general lack of compliance which calls into question the fit and proper status. Breaches which have been rectified and reported by the entity itself do not normally need to be reported by the auditors, but if they have not been rectified or reported then a report may be required.

It is not necessary to collect sufficient evidence to determine the full implications of the matter before deciding to report. It is only necessary that there are reasonable grounds. What constitutes reasonable grounds is a matter for professional judgement. Such a judgement will be based on:

- discussions with management and staff; and
- a review of correspondence and documents relating to the matter.

Certain matters, such as a loss of client money, may be so serious as to necessitate an immediate report to the FSA to prevent further losses being sustained.

The evidence obtained by the auditors should be documented so that their decision whether to proceed with a report can be clearly demonstrated should the need arise in the future.

Reliance on other auditors
The same principles apply as in a statutory audit and these are discussed in

35.3. Group auditors would have a responsibility to report matters arising from the regulated entity's own and the consolidated financial statements. If they do not audit one of the regulated subsidiaries, they are not responsible for reporting on that company, but they must assess the effect of any matter on the group. Where there are joint auditors each has a responsibility and there should be an exchange of information.

8.10.5   Reporting

The ISA (UK and Ireland) does not suggest a format for the report, only that it should be 'in a form and manner which will facilitate appropriate action'. The report should be made without delay and may be made orally, so long as it is followed up in writing. Normally, auditors should agree the report to the FSA with the directors before it is made and a copy of the report should be sent to the directors.

Where a statutory duty to report arises, auditors must report the matter, even if it has already been reported by another party, including the directors.

ISA (UK and Ireland) 250 notes that there may be occasions where it is not appropriate for the directors to be involved – for example, where the integrity of the directors is questioned. In such extreme cases, the guidance notes that speed is of the essence and that the auditors may wish to take legal advice.

Any evidence indicating money laundering with links to the proceeds of any crime that auditors discover must be reported to the appropriate authority. Under the Money Laundering Regulations 2003 and the Proceeds of Crime Act 2002 it is an offence not to do so. This is an extension of the requirements under the old Criminal Justice Act to report the proceeds of suspected terrorist or drug trafficking activities. It is also an offence to report suspicions to any other party. The FSA may require that such information is disclosed to them, but if the directors are implicated, the auditors must not inform them of the matter as this would amount to 'tipping off' (see **Chapter 12)**. It will often be the case that matters that are required to be reported to the regulator will also lead to a report under the Money Laundering Regulations 2003 and the Proceeds of Crime Act 2002.

Auditors' right to report directly to regulators
Under the FSMA 2000, auditors are not held to breach any duty by communicating in good faith to the FSA, information or an opinion on a matter that they reasonably believe is relevant to any functions of the FSA. This only applies to information obtained as auditors. Auditors should ensure compliance with legislation relating to 'tipping off' (see **Chapter 12)**.

In addition to the statutory duty to report directly, auditors have a right to do so where they believe the matter to be relevant to the regulator's function and the directors have not informed the regulator themselves. On discovery of such a matter, the auditors should inform the directors in writing that, in their opinion, it should be reported, and if they do not obtain evidence within a reasonable period that the directors have reported it, they should do so themselves. No examples are given in the ISA (UK and Ireland).

Auditors may wish to take legal advice before deciding on what, and in what form, to report. However, it is important to balance this against the need for prompt reporting to protect the interests of investors.

8.10.6 Form of report

Section B of ISA (UK and Ireland) 250 states that the report should include the following:

- the name of the regulated entity;
- the statutory power under which the report was made;
- a statement that it has been prepared in accordance with ISA (UK and Ireland) 250, Section B;
- a description of the context in which the report is given;
- a description of matters giving rise to the report;
- a request that the FSA confirms receipt of the report; and
- the name of the auditors making the report, the date of the written report and, if appropriate, the date of the oral report and the name of the person to whom it was made.

The description of the matter should give an indication of the extent of any discussions with the directors on the matter.

The context of the report will depend on several matters such as:

- the nature of the appointment from which the report derives;
- the interpretation of the relevant legislation;
- the extent to which the auditors have investigated the matter;
- whether the matter has been discussed with the directors; and
- whether steps have been taken to rectify the matter.

No example of the report is given in the ISA (UK and Ireland).

8.10.7 Communication by the regulator

The FSA may pass on to auditors any information which it considers relevant to their function. Auditors are bound by the confidentiality provisions set out in Part XXIII of the Financial Services and Markets Act 2000 (Public record, disclosures of information and co-operation). Communications of this nature must be treated as confidential by auditors and must not be disclosed to their client or any other party. The FSA will indicate if anyone at the client has been informed of the matter.

The FSA has confirmed that it will take the initiative in communicating with auditors. The most likely matters are those which may affect the opinion that the auditors give on the financial statements. However, auditors should not assume that no communication from the FSA means that there is nothing that may be materially significant.

Where information has been brought to their attention, the auditors may need to amend their approach, but there is no requirement to change the scope of their work or actively investigate the matter further, unless specifically requested to do so by the FSA.

8.10.8   *Relationship with other reporting responsibilities*

Where matters have been reported directly to regulators, auditors should consider the implications for their report on the financial statements. These are most likely to give rise to contingencies or other uncertainties which should be disclosed in the financial statements.

8.11   CONSULTATION DRAFT: PRACTICE NOTE 21 (REVISED)

A proposed revision to Practice Note 21 was issued for comment in March 2006. The aim of the revision was to incorporate the requirements of the ISAs (UK and Ireland) which were issued in 2005. The majority of the revision is discussed in **Chapter 46**, but the following areas are the main additions in relation to reporting to the FSA.

8.11.1   *Closely linked entities*

The draft revised Practice Note, like the previous version, does not require auditors to perform any additional audit work as a result of the statutory duty to report or to specifically seek out breaches of the requirements. Information to be communicated is that which has been identified:

- in their capacity as auditors of the authorised person; and
- if they are also auditors of a person who has close links with the authorised person, in their capacity as auditors of that person.

The draft proposals give further information about closely linked entities.

During planning, auditors should establish whether any closely linked entities exist, of which they are also auditor. A closely linked entity is a:

- parent undertaking;
- subsidiary undertaking;
- parent undertaking of a subsidiary undertaking; or
- subsidiary undertaking of a parent undertaking.

Where such entities exist and are commonly audited, auditors consider the significance of the entities and the nature of the issues that might arise which may be of material significance to the regulator. The audit engagement partner should contact the audit engagement partner of the closely linked entity to inform them of the audit firm's responsibility to report to the FSA and notify them of circumstances which might be of material significance to the regulator. Prior to completion of the audit, auditors of the regulated entity obtain written confirmation that such circumstances do not exist from the other audit team. If circumstances do exist, further information may need to be obtained from the other auditors and the closely linked entity itself.

There is no duty for the auditors of the closely linked entity to report.

8.11.2 Items reportable on an ad hoc basis

Appendix 8 to the draft revision to Practice Note 21 sets out a number of 'themes' within which 'relevant requirements' or matters of concern which may give rise to a statutory duty to report are likely to fall. These are reproduced in **Table 2**.

TABLE 2: Examples of items reportable on an ad hoc basis

- controllers, directors and senior management who may not be 'fit and proper';
- serious breaches of law/regulations;
- potential disciplinary action against the firm or directors;
- undertaking activities outside the scope of their permission;
- failure to comply with limitations or restriction on permission or individual requirements;
- false or misleading information given to the FSA or matters concealed;
- problems with another 'regulator', e.g. Office of Fair Trading (i.e. regards the Consumer Credit Act) or overseas regulators;
- breaches of prudential limits and/or any financial limits;
- significant actual or potential loss by investors e.g. loss of customer assets or breach of client money rules; where there appear to be conflicts of interest; where there appears to be systemic abuse of advice or discretionary decisions; or as identified by complaints or by cases where a customer sues under s150 FSMA;
- failure to clearly allocate responsibilities between senior managers or to implement clear reporting lines;
- major systems and control weaknesses (including major reconciliation failures and backlogs);

- possible going concern issues; and
- adverse skilled person's report or qualified auditor's report.

8.11.3   Cumulative minor breaches

Minor breaches would not normally be of material significance to the FSA and give rise to an ad hoc report. However ISA (UK and Ireland) 250 requires auditors of regulated entities to review whether the cumulative effect of a number of minor breaches is such as to give rise to a duty to report to the regulator. Auditors may wish to seek legal advice on whether such a report would be necessary.

The facts and circumstances of their decision to report or not should be clearly documented in the audit work papers.

8.11.4   General principles for annual reports to the FSA

Auditors making annual reports to the FSA are usually the same auditors who have worked on the financial statements of the entity. Therefore, the work performed to enable auditors to issue their annual report will not constitute a second audit carried out in accordance with ISAs (UK and Ireland).

Where procedures additional to the work related to the audit of the financial statements is performed, auditors should have regard to the general principles set out in the draft revision to Practice Note 21. These are set out in **Table 3** below.

TABLE 3:   General principles applicable to performing additional procedures for the purposes of reporting to the FSA

- Auditors plan the work to be undertaken in relation to the regulatory report so as to perform that work in an effective manner, taking into account their other reporting responsibilities;
- Auditors familiarise themselves with the relevant rules contained in the FSA Handbook;
- Auditors comply with ethical guidance issued by their relevant professional bodies;
- Auditors agree the terms of the engagement with the investment business and record them in writing;
- Auditors undertake their work with an attitude of professional scepticism and carry out procedures designed to obtain sufficient appropriate evidence on which to base their opinions;
- When using the work of others, auditors assess their objectivity and competence and obtain sufficient appropriate evidence that such work is adequate for the purposes of the report;
- Auditors obtain written confirmation of appropriate representations from management before their report is issued;

- Auditors record in their working papers:
  - Details of the engagement planning;
  - The nature, timing and extent of the procedures performed in relation to their auditors' report to the regulator, and the conclusions drawn; and
  - Their reasoning and conclusions on all significant matters which require the exercise of judgement;
- Auditors consider the matters which have come to their attention while performing their procedures and whether they should be included in a report to directors or management;
- If the auditors become aware of matters of material significance to the FSA, they make a report direct to the FSA. In addition, when issuing their auditors' report to the FSA, auditors:
  - Consider whether there are consequential reporting issues affecting their opinion which arise from any report previously made direct to the FSA in the course of their appointment; and
  - Assess whether any matters encountered in the course of their work indicate a need for a further direct report;
- Auditors take steps to ensure that any delegated work is directed, supervised and reviewed in a manner which provides reasonable assurance that such work is performed competently;
- Auditors consider materiality and its relationship with the risk of material misstatement in the report to the FSA in planning their work and in determining the effect of their findings on their report; and
- Auditors perform procedures designed to obtain sufficient appropriate evidence that all material subsequent events up to the date of their report to the FSA which require adjustment or disclosure have been identified and properly reflected in the report.

8.11.5 Reconciliation of periodic financial statements to annual financial statements

The draft Practice Note states that where quarterly or monthly financial statements are required to be submitted to the FSA a reconciliation may be required between these statements and the annual financial statements.

Where such a reconciliation is required, auditors are then required to report on whether the reconciliation has been properly prepared. They should agree the reconciliation back to source and confirm that any reconciling items are reasonable.

8.11.6 The auditors' report

The proposed revision to the Practice Note contains an example auditors' annual report suitable for all firms to which, under rule 3.1.2R of the Supervision Manual, sections 3.9 and 3.10 of the Manual apply. This essentially incorporates all investment management firms, UCITs management companies, securities and futures firms and personal investment firms except small personal investment firms and certain oil and energy market participants. It is not designed to take account of the specific reporting requirements of Category D corporate finance advisory firms, locals, OPS firms or non-ISD investment management firms subject only to an own funds requirement.

As the report varies in some respects from that in the current Practice Note, it is reproduced in **Table 4**.

The report includes explicit statements required by the FSA that auditors have received all the information and explanations considered necessary for the purposes of the audit, and on the adequacy of books and records. This second area is in contrast to the requirements of the Companies Act 1985 which only requires reporting by exception in this area.

TABLE 4: Standard auditors' report to the FSA

Independent Auditors' report to the Financial Services Authority ('the FSA') pursuant to Chapters 3.9 and 3.10 of SUP, in respect of ABC Limited, FSA reference [number], for the year/period ended [date]

We report in respect of ABC Limited ('the firm'), a securities and futures firm/ investment management firm/UCITs management company/personal investment firm, on:

- the attached annual financial statements;
- the following information set out in the attached [Annual Reporting Statement/Annual Financial Return/Annual Retail Mediation Activities Return]
  - the balance sheet and profit and loss account;
  - the statements of financial resources and financial resources requirement;
- the statement of the firm's expenditure requirement for the forthcoming year [if applicable];
- [for securities and future firms only] the attached reconciliation between the balance sheets in the annual financial statements, the Annual Reporting Statement and the [monthly/quarterly] financial return;
- [for Personal Investment Firms only] the attached reconciliation between the balance sheets in the annual financial statements and the [half yearly/ quarterly] reporting statement;
- the attached consolidated reporting statement [if applicable];

and on the further matters set out below. Our report has been prepared in accordance with SUP 3.9.4 and 3.10.4 and is addressed to the FSA in its capacity as a regulator under the Financial Services and Markets Act 2000. Our report should not be disclosed to any third party or otherwise quoted or referred to without our prior written consent.

Respective responsibilities of directors and auditors

The detailed responsibilities of the directors and auditors with respect to the annual financial statements are set out within these annual financial statements. The directors are responsible for the preparation of the [Annual Reporting Statement/Annual Financial Return/Annual Retail Mediation Activities Return] and the consolidated reporting statement [if applicable] under the provisions of the FSA's rules. The [Annual Reporting Statement/Annual Financial Return/Annual Retail Mediation Activities Return] and the consolidated reporting statement [if applicable] are required to be prepared in the manner specified by the rules. It is our responsibility to form an independent opinion as to whether the [Annual Reporting Statement/Annual Financial Return/Annual Retail Mediation Activities Return] and the consolidated reporting statement [if applicable] meet those requirements and to report our opinions to you.

The directors are responsible for establishing and maintaining adequate accounting and other records and systems and controls procedures which are appropriate to the business and adequate for them to comply with the applicable provisions of the FSA's Client Assets Sourcebook. It is our responsibility to form an independent opinion, based on our procedures as set out below, and to report our opinion to you.

Basis of opinion

We have audited the annual financial statements in accordance with International Standards on Auditing (UK and Ireland). The basis of our audit opinion with respect to the annual financial statements is set out within those annual financial statements.

With respect to the [Annual Reporting Statement/Annual Financial Return/ Annual Retail Mediation Activities Return] and the consolidated reporting statement [if applicable], our work included examination, on a test basis, of evidence relevant to the amounts and disclosures in the [Annual Reporting Statement/Annual Financial Return/Annual Retail Mediation Activities Return] and the consolidated reporting statement [if applicable]. The evidence included that previously obtained by us relating to the audit of the annual financial statements for the financial year. It also included an assessment of the significant estimates and judgements made by the company in the preparation of the [Annual Reporting Statement/Annual Financial Return/Annual Retail Mediation Activities Return] and the consolidated reporting statement [if applicable].

We have carried out such other procedures as we considered necessary for the purposes of this report having regard to Practice Note 21, 'The audit of investment business in the United Kingdom (Revised)'. We have obtained all the information and explanations which to the best of our knowledge and belief, are necessary for the purposes of our report to the FSA.

Systems and controls procedures relating to client assets are subject to inherent limitations and, accordingly, errors or irregularities may occur and not be detected. Such procedures cannot be proof against fraudulent collusion, especially on the part of those holding positions of authority or trust. Furthermore, this opinion relates only to the year ended on [date] and should not be seen as providing assurance as to any further position, as changes to systems or controls procedures may alter the validity of our opinion.

Financial statements

In our opinion:

- the annual financial statements give a true and fair view in accordance with [UK Generally Accepted Accounting Practice/IFRSs as adopted by the EU] of the firm's state of affairs as at [year end date] and of its [profit/loss] for the year then ended;
- the [Annual Reporting Statement/Annual Financial Return/sections A, B and relevant parts of section D of the Annual Retail Mediation Activities Return] [has/have] been properly prepared in accordance with the FSA's rules;
- the balance sheet and profit and loss account in the [Annual Reporting Statement/Annual Financial Return/Annual Retail Mediation Activities Return] are in agreement with the firm's accounting records and returns;
- [Securities and Futures Firms only] the balance sheet in the Annual Reporting Statement has been properly reconciled to the balance sheet of the annual financial statements and to the balance sheet in the [monthly/ quarterly] reporting statement prepared by the firm as at [year end date].
- [Personal Investment Firms only] the balance sheet in the Annual Retail Mediation Activities Return has been properly reconciled to the balance sheet in the [half yearly/quarterly] Retail Mediation Activities Return prepared by the firm as at [year end date].

Financial resources

In our opinion:

- the firm's statement of financial resources and financial resources requirement as at [year end date] have been properly prepared in accordance with the FSA's rules;
- the firm's financial resources as at [year end date] are sufficient to meet the firm's financial resources requirement at that date;
- the statement of the firm's expenditure requirement for the forthcoming year has been prepared in accordance with the FSA's rules [if applicable].

Accounting records

In our opinion the firm has kept proper accounting records in accordance with the FSA's rules for the year ended [year end date].

Consolidated reporting statement [if applicable]

In our opinion, the firm's consolidated reporting statement as at [year end date] has been prepared in accordance with the FSA's rules.

Client Assets

Either

In our opinion:

- the firm maintained throughout the year systems adequate to enable it to comply with the rules in [*depending on whether the firm holds both client money and assets or only one of these* CASS 2, CASS 3, CASS 4.1 to 4.3 and CASS 4.5/ CASS 2, CASS 3, and CASS 4.5/ CASS 3, CASS 4.1 to 4.3 and CASS 4.5]
- the firm was in compliance with rules in [*depending on whether the firm holds both client money and assets or only one of these* CASS 2, CASS 3, CASS 4.1 to 4.3 and CASS 4.5/ CASS 2, CASS 3, and CASS 4.5/ CASS 3, CASS 4.1 to 4.3 and CASS 4.5]as at [year end date].
- [if applicable] in relation to the secondary pooling event during the period, the firm complied with the rules in CASS 4.4 (Client money distribution) in relation to that pooling event.

Or

The scope of the firm's permission does not allow it to hold [client money] [or] [custody assets].

The directors have stated that the firm did not hold [client money] [or] [custody assets] during the year. Based on review procedures performed, nothing has come to our attention that causes us to believe that the firm held [client money] [or] [custody assets] during the year.

Nominee companies

In our opinion, [name of nominee companies], subsidiaries of the firm which are nominee companies in whose name custody assets are registered, maintained throughout the year systems for the custody, identification and control of custody assets which are adequate to enable the firm to comply with the rules in CASS 2, CASS 3 and CASS 4.5 and which included reconciliations between the records maintained (whether by the firm or the nominee company) and statements or confirmations from custodians or from the person who maintains the record of legal entitlement at appropriate intervals.

Registered Auditors
Address
Date

8.11.7 Accounting records

As stated above, auditors are required to report explicitly on the adequacy of a firm's books and records. The FSA rules require that adequate accounting records should be kept to show and explain the investment business's transactions and that these records must:

- be up to date and disclose, with reasonable accuracy, at any time, the financial position of the investment business at that time;
- enable the investment business to demonstrate its continuing compliance with the FSA's requirements for financial resources;
- provide the information which the investment business needs to prepare annual financial statements and to produce reports required by the FSA;
- provide the information which the auditors need to form an opinion on any statements of the investment business on which they are required to report; and
- provide a proper record of transactions undertaken for clients and of assets held for clients.

Where a third party is appointed to maintain any accounting records, they must be maintained in accordance with these rules.

8.11.8   Client assets

There are three elements to auditors' reporting requirements in relation to client assets, whether the investment business:

- has kept adequate accounting records throughout the period and performed the required reconciliations;
- has maintained adequate systems to allow it to comply with the relevant rules; and
- was in compliance with the relevant rules at certain dates.

The extent and nature of auditors' work will be a matter for judgement, but should fulfil the following general requirements. Auditors should:

- understand the business and the environment in which it operates;
- review the business's systems and consider whether they are adequate for control and accounting purposes; and
- test those systems and controls to establish that they are operating effectively.

Appendix 4 to the draft Practice Note revision gives detailed guidance on the significant control objectives which should be in place and the audit evidence which may be gathered in relation to them.

Even when investment businesses do not hold client money or custody assets, either by choice or by a limitation in their scope of permission, the FSA may still require a report from the auditors stating that neither client money or custody assets are held.

9   REPORTS TO MANAGEMENT

9.1   INTRODUCTION

In addition to reporting under the Companies Act 1985, auditors may also report to management – for example, on the adequacy of the company's system of internal control and on possible improvements to the financial and accounting efficiency of the business. The timing, form and content of such reports should be covered in the engagement letter between the auditors and their client.

This Chapter considers such reports, particularly in the context of ISA (UK and Ireland) 260, *Communication of Audit Matters to those Charged with Governance*. ISA 260 was issued in December 2004 and replaces SAS 610 (revised).

In April 2005, the APB issued an Exposure Draft of a revision to ISA (UK and Ireland) 260 for comment. The revision is based on the exposure drafts of proposed revised ISAs issued by the IAASB in March 2005. The IAASB Exposure Draft has now been included in its Clarity Project and as a result the UK update is not expected until after the conclusion of the IAASB project and the expected adoption of ISAs for use in the European Union. The Exposure Drafts are covered in **9.13** below.

In September 2002 the APB issued a briefing paper, *Effective Communication between Audit Committees and External Auditors*, to assist audit committees' understanding of the changes introduced in the updated SAS 610. The briefing paper supersedes the 1998 Briefing Paper, *Communication between External Auditors and Audit Committees*.

9.2   AUDITING STANDARDS

ISA (UK and Ireland) 260 provides guidance on:

- the purpose of the report;
- format of the report;

- report contents; and
- requirements for listed companies.

9.3   THOSE CHARGED WITH GOVERNANCE

ISA (UK and Ireland) 260 defines those charged with governance as including 'the directors (executive and non-executive) of a company or other body, the members of an audit committee where one exists, the partners, proprietors, committee of management or trustees of other forms of entity, or equivalent persons responsible for directing the entity's affairs and preparing its financial statements'.

Depending on the nature and circumstances of the entity, management, i.e., those persons who perform senior management functions, may include some or all of those charged with governance. These individuals are executive directors. Non-executive directors are not usually part of management.

9.4   AIMS OF REPORTS TO THOSE CHARGED WITH GOVERNANCE

ISA (UK and Ireland) 260 requires auditors to 'communicate audit matters of governance interest arising from the audit of the financial statements with those charged with governance'. These reports must be made on a sufficiently prompt basis to enable those charged with governance to take appropriate action.

The main purposes of such reports are to:

- ensure there is a mutual understanding of the scope of the audit and the respective responsibilities of the auditors and the client;
- share information to enable the parties to fulfil their responsibilities; and
- provide constructive observations to those charged with governance.

Those charged with governance are ultimately responsible for the financial statements, and although the ISA (UK and Ireland) concentrates on the form and content of auditors' communications with the client, there must be an effective two-way process for the audit of the financial statements to be concluded satisfactorily.

All reports should be relevant to the particular client, and auditors should consider the extent, form and frequency of their reports in accordance with the size and nature of the client. The attitude of those charged with governance and the importance of the issues to be raised will also affect the format and timing of the report. For example, reports of relatively minor matters to a small client may be best handled orally via a meeting or telephone conversation rather than with a formal written report. These considerations are considered further in **9.6** below.

All reports should be made promptly to allow those charged with governance to take appropriate action. The speed with which auditors report will depend on the nature of the issue arising, but matters relating to the qualitative aspects of the entity's accounting and financial reporting will usually be communicated prior to the approval of the financial statements.

9.5   ESTABLISHING EXPECTATIONS

At an early stage in their relationship auditors should agree the level of detail and timing of communication between themselves and those charged with governance. This will vary depending on the circumstances of the client. Auditors should also clarify that they will only report matters which they consider relevant to those charged with governance as a result of their normal audit procedures, and will not perform additional procedures specifically to determine other matters to report.

9.6   FORM OF COMMUNICATION

The auditors' report should be made in writing. The format of the report will depend on factors such as:

*   the size, operating structure, legal structure and communication process of the entity being audited;
*   the nature, sensitivity and significance of the matters being communicated;
*   statutory and regulatory requirements; and
*   the arrangements made with the client at the outset of the engagement.

A written report should be produced even if its content is limited to an explanation of why there are no significant matters that the auditor wishes to report.

Typically auditors will discuss their findings with management or those with direct responsibility for an area before reporting them to those charged with governance. This should ensure that all facts are clarified as well as providing management with an opportunity to provide further explanations. Where it will aid the understanding of those charged with governance, the auditors will include details of comments made by management in their final communication.

9.7 EFFECTIVENESS OF COMMUNICATIONS

The responsiveness of those charged with governance to communications from auditors may be considered when assessing the effectiveness of the entity's control environment. This may also affect the auditor's assessment of the risks of material misstatements. Auditors may consider:

- the appropriateness and timeliness of actions taken by those charged with governance following the auditors' recommendations;
- how open those charged with governance appear to be when communicating with the auditors;
- the willingness of those charged with governance to meet with the auditors; and
- the ability of those charged with governance to comprehend the recommendations made by the auditor.

9.8 MATTERS TO BE COMMUNICATED

9.8.1 Definition

Auditors will communicate 'audit matters of governance interest' to those charged with governance. These are matters arising from the audit of financial statements and which, in the opinion of auditors, are both important and relevant to those charged with governance in their role of overseeing the financial statements and disclosure process. Only matters which have come to auditors' attention as a result of the audit will be reportable, and auditors are not required to perform additional procedures to identify matters of governance interest.

9.8.2 Listed companies

ISA (UK and Ireland) 260 states that for listed companies the auditors should, at least annually:

- disclose in writing and discuss as appropriate:
    - all relationships between the audit firm and its related entities and the client entity and its related entities that may reasonably be thought to bear on the firm's independence and the objectivity of the audit engagement partner and audit staff;
    - the related safeguards that are in place; and
    - the total amount of fees charged by the auditor and the auditors' network firms to the client and its affiliates for the provision of services during the reporting period. This should be analysed into suitable categories such as statutory audit, tax and other non-audit services. The amount of future contracted services should also be given by category;

- where this is the case, confirm in writing to the audit committee that, in their professional judgement, the firm is independent within the meaning of regulatory and professional requirements and the objectivity of the audit engagement partner and audit staff is not impaired.

9.8.3 Integrity, independence and objectivity

For all companies, listed and unlisted, Ethical Standard 1 requires that those charged with governance should be told of any significant facts and matters which may impact the auditors' objectivity and independence.

The communication should include the key issues considered by the engagement partner such as:

- the principal threats, if any, to objectivity and independence identified by the auditor;
- any safeguards implemented with an explanation of why they were thought to be effective;
- any independent partner review;
- the overall assessment of threats and safeguards;
- information about the general policies and processes employed by the audit firm to maintain independence and objectivity.

9.8.4 Planning information

The ISA (UK and Ireland) states that auditors of all entities, listed or unlisted, should inform those charged with governance of the nature, scope and limitations, if any, of the work they plan to perform. Matters that might be communicated in outline include:

- the concept of materiality and its application to the audit;
- the approach the auditors will use in relation to assessing and relying on internal controls;
- the extent, if any, that reliance can be placed on internal audit; and
- where relevant, the work to be performed by other auditors and how auditors intend to ensure the adequacy of the work of those other auditors.

These matters may be dealt with in the engagement letter, and where the audit team consider that there has been no change in this information from one year to the next there is no requirement to reproduce it. Instead the auditors need only to make those charged with governance aware that no change has taken place. In all cases auditors should ensure that those charged with governance are provided with a copy of the engagement letter.

9.8.5 Findings from the audit

ISA (UK and Ireland) 260 lists the following areas as those that auditors should communicate to those charged with governance:

- the auditors' views on the qualitative aspects of the entity's accounting practices and financial report – this will include the auditors' opinions on the accounting policies used, the appropriateness of accounting estimates, the potential impact of uncertainties and apparent misstatements in other material issued with the financial statements;
- the final draft of the management letter for signature;
- uncorrected misstatements (see below);
- expected modifications to the auditor's report – to ensure that those charged with governance are aware of the proposed modification, that there are no disputed facts and that those charged with governance have an opportunity to provide further information so that a modification is no longer required;
- material weakness in internal control identified during the audit;
- matters specifically required by other ISAs (UK and Ireland) to be communicated to those charged with governance; and
- any other matters of governance interest.

Unadjusted misstatements

Where auditors find uncorrected misstatements, they should report them to the entity's management to request that they be corrected. These misstatements should be clearly distinguished as either errors of fact or matters of judgement. There is no requirement to report those misstatements which are 'clearly trivial' or inconsequential whether taken individually or in aggregate.

Where any of these misstatements are not corrected by management they are reported to those charged with governance. If those charged with governance refuse to make any of the adjustments, auditors should discuss the matter with them and consider the implications for their report. Auditors should also obtain written representations from those charged with governance that explains why they have not been corrected.

Even where management have corrected the misstatements auditors may consider that including the details of the misstatement in their communications may assist those charged with governance with their role, including considering the effectiveness of the system of internal control.

Where matters previously reported have not been rectified by those charged with governance, auditors consider repeating the point. Failing to do so may lead to the auditor giving the impression that they are satisfied that the matter has been addressed.

9.9 ADDRESSEES

Auditors should use judgement to determine to whom they communicate certain matters. This may be contrary to the arrangement agreed at the start of the audit if the matter is sufficiently important to require reporting directly to the board or governing body.

For listed companies and other entities where they have been constituted, reports will often be made to the audit committee. However, auditors and boards should understand that a report to the audit committee will only form part of the auditors' overall obligation to report to those charged with governance and additional reports to other parts of the client's organisation may also be required, such as reports direct to the remuneration or to individual departments. In any case it is important that the report is seen by those who have the authority to implement the recommendations included therein. If the report is presented in sections of varying importance, it may be appropriate for the more detailed matters to be referred directly to the division or branch to which they relate.

9.10 GROUPS

Where a parent undertaking is preparing group financial statements, auditors bring to the attention of those charged with governance any matters arising through the audit of the subsidiary entities which they judge to be of significance in the context of the group.

There is a statutory requirement for auditors of corporate subsidiaries in the UK to supply this information to parent company auditors. Where no statutory obligation exists (for example for non-corporate or overseas entities) permission may be needed from those charged with governance in the subsidiary entity before the auditors can release this information to the parent company auditors.

9.11 THIRD PARTIES

The report is solely for the use of the addressee. If the auditors wish to disclose its contents to a third party they should obtain permission from the client before releasing it. In practical terms, once the report has been sent, auditors have little control over it and it may be given to third parties without the knowledge of the auditors. The auditors should ensure that their report therefore contains the appropriate disclaimer, as shown in **Table 1**, so that any third parties who see the report understand it was not prepared for their benefit.

In the public or regulated sectors auditors may have a duty to submit a copy of their report to the relevant regulatory or funding bodies and therefore the disclaimer will not be appropriate. However, any communication with those charged with governance is confidential and the auditor will require prior consent from those charged with governance before sending a copy to the regulator or funding body.

Where reports are required by such third parties, auditors should show due consideration for the requirements of those bodies when compiling their reports. For example public sector bodies may be particularly interested in:

- misconduct, fraud or other irregularity;
- failure to maintain the requisite high standard of financial integrity by a member of the board; and
- expenditure which is considered to be extravagant or wasteful.

9.12   FORM OF REPORTS

The form of the report will depend on the type of organisation concerned. It may be appropriate to divide the report into sections, which cover significant and general points for senior management first, and then proceed to more specific, divisional points in subsequent sections. The ISA (UK and Ireland) does not include example wordings, but the report covering findings from the audit may typically be formed of a covering letter (see **Table 1**) and a schedule of points raised.

TABLE 1:   Reports to management covering letter

Private & Confidential

The Directors
XYZ Plc
1 High Street
London W1

24 June 20XX

Dear Sirs

XYZ Plc

Following our recent audit of your company, we are writing to advise you of various matters which came to our attention.

We set out on the attached schedule the major areas of weakness which we noted, together with our recommendations. These recommendations have already been discussed with ... and their comments have been included.

As the purpose of the audit is to form an opinion on the company's financial statements, you will appreciate that our examination cannot necessarily be expected to disclose all shortcomings of the system and for this reason, the matters raised may not be the only ones which exist.

We should appreciate your comments as to how you propose to deal with the matters raised in this letter. If you require any further information or advice, please contact us.

We have prepared this letter for your use only. It should not be disclosed to a third party and we can assume no responsibility to any person to whom it is disclosed without our written consent.

We would like to take this opportunity to thank you and your staff for your help and co-operation during the course of our audit.

Yours faithfully

ABC & Co

9.13   EXPOSURE DRAFTS

9.13.1   Background

In April 2005, the APB issued an Exposure Draft of a revision to ISA (UK and Ireland) 260, based on the draft ISA revision issued by the IAASB in March 2005. Subsequently the IAASB included ISA 260 in their Clarity Project and reissued the Exposure Draft in November 2006 it having been redrafted under the new conventions. The IAASB asked for comments on the revised and redrafted ISA, but limited those only to changes resulting from applying the clarity drafting conventions as other issues had been addressed in the earlier consultation period.

In line with their stated intentions, the APB have reissued the IAASB's Exposure Draft in the UK and requested comments for inclusion in their submission letter on the international ISA.

9.13.2   UK Exposure Draft

As a result of the inclusion of ISA 260 in the IAASB's Clarity Project and the resulting reissue of the international Exposure Draft, the publication of the revised ISA (UK and Ireland) is expected to be delayed until after the completion of that project and the expected adoption of ISAs for use in the European Union. This is in order to ensure that all revisions are issued by the APB in one batch and to reduce confusion about which version of ISAs (UK and Ireland) to use.

In their Exposure Draft the APB comment that the March 2005 IAASB revision had incorporated as core text much of the UK and Ireland specific guidance that had previously been added to the ISA (UK and Ireland) as additional (shaded) paragraphs. However some additional UK and Ireland paragraphs remain in the proposed revision, covering requirements:

- to ensure that those charged with governance are provided with a copy of the audit engagement letter on a timely basis; and
- for auditors to seek to obtain written representation from those charged with governance explaining their reasons for not correcting misstatements brought to their attention by auditors.

In addition references have been added to the requirements for auditors in the UK and Ireland to comply with the APB's Ethical Standard 1 (see **Chapter 2**) and to clarify relevant legal and regulatory matters in the UK and Ireland.

9.13.3   Definitions

In the original ISA, the IAASB assumed that 'management' and 'those charged with governance' were different people; however for smaller entities this will not always be the case. In addition, there was the assumption that management is responsible for the financial statements, whereas those charged with governance have an oversight role only. This was a particular problem in the UK where the APB had to tailor this definition by inclusion of footnotes in each ISA (UK and Ireland) to clarify that those charged with governance had responsibility for the financial statements.

In their revision, the IAASB have adopted the following definitions for developing new documents and revising existing ones:

- *those charged with governance*: 'the person or persons with responsibility for overseeing the strategic direction of the entity and obligations related to the accountability of the entity. This includes overseeing the financial reporting and disclosure process. In some cases, those charged with governance are responsible for approving the financial statements';
- *management*: 'the person or persons who have executive responsibility for the conduct of the entity's operations. In some entities, management include some or all of those charged with governance, e.g., executive directors, or owner-managers. Management is responsible for preparing the financial statements, overseen by those charged with governance.'

9.13.4   Small entities

The Exposure Draft also seeks to make the guidance more relevant for small entities, particularly where those charged with governance are involved in the management of the entity. Specifically, the Exposure Draft recognises that:

- if matters are communicated to management and those persons in management have responsibilities for governance, the matters do not need to be communicated again to those charged with governance; and
- where matters are relevant only to the oversight function of those charged with governance, they do not need to be reported by auditors as there is no oversight separate from management.

10 FRAUD AND ERROR

10.1 INTRODUCTION

This Chapter covers the responsibility of auditors in relation to fraud. In recent years, well-publicised cases of major company fraud have focused the public attention on the auditors' responsibility in relation to fraud and illegal acts. This has in turn raised the question of the auditors' responsibility in terms of discovering and reporting them.

It is widely believed by the general public that the auditors' principal duty is to detect fraud. This is one of the components of the so-called 'gap' between the expectations of users of audit reports and the auditors' perception of their responsibilities.

This chapter does not cover non-compliance with law and regulations, which is covered in **Chapter 11**.

10.2 AUDITING STANDARDS

ISA (UK and Ireland) 240 *The Auditor's Responsibility to Consider Fraud in an Audit of Financial Statements* was issued in December 2004 and provides standards on auditing fraud covering:

- the definition of fraud and error;
- the responsibilities of those charged with governance;
- auditors' responsibilities;
- evaluating audit evidence;
- reports to management;
- communication with those charged with governance;
- communication with the authorities; and
- documentation.

As with all ISAs (UK and Ireland), the text of the international ISA has been supplemented with additional guidance from a UK and Ireland perspective. SAS 110 *Fraud and Error* has not yet been officially withdrawn.

ISA (UK and Ireland) 240 is effective for audits of financial statements for periods commencing on or after 15 December 2004.

In December 2006, the IAASB issued a final version of their revision to the international version of ISA 240. This is discussed in **10.11** below.

In November 2003, the Audit and Assurance Faculty of the ICAEW issued a paper entitled, *Fraud: Meeting the Challenge Through Internal Audit*. The document is part of the Faculty's ongoing *Audit Quality* programme and develops a ten-point action plan for audit firms to take to respond to fraud risk in the light of increasing public expectation. The paper is covered in **10.12** below.

10.3   DEFINITIONS

Auditors plan and perform audit procedures to reduce audit risk to an acceptably low level. As part of this process, the ISA (UK and Ireland) requires them to consider the risk of material misstatement in the financial statements due to fraud.

Misstatements can arise from either fraud or error. The main difference between fraud and error is whether the action that resulted in the misstatement was intentional or unintentional.

10.3.1   Fraud

ISA (UK and Ireland) 240 defines fraud as:

> 'an intentional act by one or more individuals among management, those charged with governance, employees, or third parties, involving the use of deception to obtain an unjust or illegal advantage'.

Although fraud has a wide legal definition, for the purpose of the ISA (UK and Ireland), auditors are only concerned with fraud that causes a material misstatement in the financial statements.

Fraudulent financial reporting involves intentional misstatements in financial statements to deceive the users of those financial statements. It may be a result of:

- falsification or alteration of records and documents;
- misappropriation of assets or theft;
- suppression or omission of the effects of transactions from records or documents;
- recording fictitious transactions;
- wilful misrepresentation of transactions or of an entity's state of affairs; or

- intentional misapplication of accounting policies.

Fraud often involves management override of controls using such techniques as:

- recording fictitious journal entries, particularly close to the end of the accounting period;
- adjusting assumptions and changing judgements used when performing accounting estimates;
- omitting, advancing or delaying recognition of items in the financial statements;
- concealing facts that could affect the amounts recorded in the financial statements;
- engaging in complex transactions which aim to misrepresent the financial position or performance of the entity; or
- altering records and terms related to significant and unusual transactions.

10.3.2 Error

Error is distinguished from fraud and is defined as unintentional mistakes in the financial statements. It may arise from:

- mathematical or clerical mistakes in the underlying records and accounting data;
- oversight or misinterpretation of facts; or
- unintentional misapplication of accounting policies.

As part of their assessment of an error, auditors should decide its cause and whether it was intentional or unintentional.

10.4 RESPONSIBILITIES OF THOSE CHARGED WITH GOVERNANCE

As stewards of the company, both those charged with governance and management have a fiduciary duty towards the owners of the company. Those charged with governance also have a statutory duty to maintain proper accounting records and prepare financial statements that give a 'true and fair view'. Those charged with governance are responsible for the prevention and detection of fraud and error. It is not possible to achieve absolute assurance against fraud and error, but the implementation and continued operation of adequate accounting and internal control systems may reduce the likelihood of such occurrences.

An additional responsibility is that, under s389A of the Companies Act

1985, it is a criminal offence to give auditors information or explanations which are misleading, false or deceptive.

The guidance to the standard suggests that those charged with governance take steps to prevent and detect fraud, among which they may:

- create a culture of honesty and ethical behaviour, including setting a proper tone;
- develop an appropriate control environment;
- hire, train and promote appropriate employees; and
- require periodic confirmation by employees of their responsibilities and taking appropriate action in response to actual, suspected or alleged fraud.

10.5   AUDITORS' RESPONSIBILITIES

The position has not altered since the pronouncement of Lord Justice Lopes in *Re Kingston Cotton Mill Company (1896)* that an auditor 'is a watchdog ... not a bloodhound'. The auditors' responsibilities are thus very much tied in with the duty to report on financial statements and are restricted by the concept of 'reasonable assurance'.

ISA (UK and Ireland) 240 expects auditors to recognise that fraud or error may materially affect the financial statements when planning their work and when evaluating and reporting their findings.

Compliance with Auditing Standards will not guarantee that the financial statements are free from material misstatement. The risk of undetected misstatement will be higher with regard to those resulting from fraud or error due to:

- the inherent limitations of the accounting and internal control systems and the use of audit sampling to test them;
- the persuasive, rather than conclusive, nature of the evidence generally obtained by auditors;
- frauds sometimes taking place over a number of years but only being discovered when they become material;
- audit procedures which are planned to detect error may not be appropriate to detect fraud which does not immediately affect the financial statements; and
- frauds often involving collusion or intentional misrepresentations to auditors.

Often auditors are less likely to detect fraud perpetrated by management than fraud perpetrated by employees. This is because management are frequently in a position to directly or indirectly manipulate accounting records or override control procedures.

Because fraud or errors are subsequently discovered which were not detected by the audit it does not mean that the audit was defective. The guidance stresses that although auditors cannot prevent fraud and error the very fact that an annual audit is carried out may act as a deterrent.

10.5.1 Professional scepticism

Auditors should maintain an attitude of professional scepticism throughout the audit. Professional scepticism requires an enquiring mind and a critical questioning of the audit evidence, and is particularly important when considering the risks of material misstatement due to fraud. Even when management and those charged with governance have been found previously to be honest and trustworthy, a sceptical view should be maintained. However, as auditors are not trained to be experts in the authentication of documents, they will accept records and documents as genuine as long as there is no evidence to the contrary.

10.5.2 Engagement team discussion

The ISA (UK and Ireland) introduces a new requirement for the audit team to discuss the susceptibility of the entity's financial statements to material misstatement due to fraud. ISA (UK and Ireland) 315 requires auditors to discuss any susceptibilities of the financial statements to material misstate-ment (see **21.3.3**), and ISA (UK and Ireland) 240 requires this discussion to include particular emphasis on those risks arising from fraud.

The discussion should include the engagement partner and key staff, and the engagement partner has a responsibility to ensure that those engagement team members not present at the discussion are informed of matters relevant to their work. Areas that the discussion would normally consider are set out in **Table 1**.

TABLE 1: Considerations for the engagement team discussion

- how and where they believe the financial statements may be susceptible to material misstatement due to fraud, how management could perpetrate and conceal fraudulent financial reporting and how assets of the entity could be misappropriated;
- circumstances that might be indicative of earnings management and how earnings may be managed fraudulently;
- the known external and internal factors affecting the entity that may create an incentive for management or others to commit fraud;
- management's involvement in overseeing employees with access to cash or other assets susceptible to misappropriation;

- the important of maintaining an air of professional scepticism;
- types of circumstances that might be indicative of fraud;
- how an element of unpredictability will be incorporated into the nature, timing and extent of the audit procedures to be performed;
- the audit procedures selected to respond to the risk of fraud and whether some types of procedures are more effective than others;
- any allegations of fraud that have come to the auditors' attention; and
- the risk of management override of controls.

After the initial discussion it is important that the engagement team members continue to communicate and discuss their findings.

Where a small audit is being carried out entirely by the engagement partner, that partner must consider the susceptibility of the entity to fraud during the planning and execution of the work.

10.5.3   Risk assessment

ISA (UK and Ireland) 240 requires an assessment of the risk that fraud or error may lead to misstatement. It sets out four stages that auditors should complete in their identification of any risks of material misstatement due to fraud:

- make enquiries about the entity's processes for identifying and responding to the risk of fraud;
- consider whether fraud risks are present;
- consider any unusual or unexpected relationships that have been identified through analytical procedures; and
- consider other information that may be helpful in identifying the risks of material misstatement due to fraud.

Enquiries about the entity's processes
As those charged with governance are responsible for the preparation of the financial statements and for the entity's internal control, there should be a procedure in place whereby they also assess the risk of fraud. The nature and extent of this assessment will vary from entity to entity, but auditors should understand the work done by the entity and the results arising from it. If those charged with governance do not assess the risk of fraud it may be indicative of the lack of importance they place on internal control.

Auditors should enquire about the entity's:

- assessment of the risk that the financial statements may be materially misstated by fraud;
- process for identifying and responding to the risks of fraud in the entity including any specific risks of fraud that have been identified or account

212

balances, classes of transactions or disclosures for which a risk of fraud is likely to exist;

- communication, if any, with those charged with governance regarding its fraud risk identification procedures; and
- communication, if any, to employees regarding its views on business practices and ethical behaviour.

Auditors should also ask those charged with governance, management and internal audit about any actual, suspected or alleged fraud affecting the entity. Where there is an internal audit department auditors should ask about the department's view of the risk of fraud, whether internal auditors have performed any procedures to detect fraud in the period and whether management and those charged with governance have responded satisfactorily to any findings resulting from those procedures.

Others to whom auditors may direct enquiries about fraud include:

- operating personnel not directly involved in the financial reporting process;
- employees with different levels of authority;
- employees involved in initiating, processing or recoding complex or unusual transactions and those who supervise or monitor such employees;
- in-house legal counsel;
- chief ethics officer or equivalent; and
- the person or persons who deal with allegations of fraud.

Those charged with governance have a duty to oversee the systems for monitoring risk, financial control and compliance with the law and this will include the entity's assessment of the risks of fraud and controls put in place to mitigate specific risks of fraud that have been identified. Auditors should understand how those charged with governance fulfil this responsibility, and this may give insight into the susceptibility of the entity to fraud, the adequacy of internal control and the competence and integrity of management.

Fraud risks

After their work on understanding the entity and its environment is complete, auditors should consider whether it indicates that one or more fraud risk factor is present. Examples include the:

- need to meet expectations of third parties to obtain additional financing; or
- granting of significant bonuses if unrealistic profit targets are met.

Fraud risk factors may not necessarily indicate that a fraud has occurred or is likely to occur and auditors use their judgement to assess whether the existence of a fraud risk factor does actually affect the risk of material misstatement of the financial statements.

Fraud risk factors are generally classified as:

- an incentive or pressure to commit fraud, e.g., profitability being threatened by changes in the market;
- a perceived opportunity to commit fraud, e.g., the handling of large amounts of cash; and
- an ability to rationalise the fraudulent action, e.g., a known history of violations against laws and regulations.

Unusual or unexpected relationships
Any unusual results from analytical review work should make auditors consider the possibility of fraudulent financial reporting.

Other information
Any other information that comes to auditors' attention should be considered as a possible indicator of fraudulent financial reporting. The engagement team member discussion (see **10.5.2)** may be particularly useful in this respect. In addition, work performed as part of acceptance or reacceptance procedures, and work done for the entity in other capacities may be of use.

10.5.4   Identification and assessment of fraud risk

As part of their work of identifying and assessing the risk of material misstatement at the financial statements and assertion level, auditors should assess the risks of material misstatement due to fraud. Fraud risks will automatically be significant risks (see **22.3.6)** and therefore auditors should evaluate the design of the related controls and determine whether they have been implemented.

The assessment of fraud risk is a three-stage process. Auditors use their professional judgement to:

- identify risks of fraud through risk assessment procedures;
- relate the risks of fraud to the assertions; and
- consider the likely size of the potential misstatement and the likelihood of the risk occurring.

Not all fraud risks will have related controls, as the entity's management and those charged with governance may believe that some risks are so remote that the implementation of controls to mitigate them is not necessary.

Revenue recognition

As material misstatement due to fraud often results in an understatement or overstatement of revenue, the ISA (UK and Ireland) states that auditors ordinarily assume that there are risks of fraud in revenue recognition. This means that these risks will be significant risks and the three-stage assessment noted above should be followed, together with consideration of associated controls.

10.5.5 Responses to fraud risk

Overall responses

Where the risk of material misstatement in the financial statements due to fraud has been identified, auditors will respond in ways that have an overall effect on how the audit is conducted. This means that professional scepticism will be increased in all areas which may lead to an increased need to corroborate explanations and representations, and take greater care when examining documentation in relation to material matters.

In their overall response to the risk of material misstatement due to fraud, auditors are required by ISA (UK and Ireland) 240 to pay particular attention to:

- the assignment and supervision of suitably experienced personnel and experts;
- the accounting policies used by the entity, particularly those related to subjective and complex areas; and
- the selection, nature and timing of audit procedures, including incorporating an element of unpredictability in their audit plan.

Responses at the assertion level

Auditors' responses to the risk of material misstatement from fraud at the assertion level may include changing the nature, extent and timing of tests planned. They will aim to obtain more relevant and reliable audit evidence and additional corroborative evidence. This may include a greater reliance on observation and inspection procedures or, where relevant, CAATs. Auditors may conclude that better quality evidence will be obtained by performing more, or all, of their procedures at the period end, rather than during an interim visit, unless the fraud risk has arisen from improper revenue recognition during an interim period, which may be best investigated earlier in the audit process. More extensive testing may also be suitable in response to the increased risk assessment.

Table 2 sets out possible audit procedures to address the assessed risks of material misstatement due to fraud.

TABLE 2:   Example audit procedures to address the assessed risks of material misstatement due to fraud

- visiting locations or performing certain tests on a surprise or unannounced basis. For example, observing stock at locations where auditor attendance has not been previously announced or counting cash at a particular date on a surprise basis;
- requesting that stocks be counted at the end of the reporting period or on a date closer to period end to minimise the risk of manipulation of balances in the period between the date of completion of the count and the end of the reporting period;
- altering the audit approach in the current year. For example, contacting major customers and suppliers orally in addition to sending written confirmations, sending confirmation requests to a specific party within an organisation, or seeking more or different information;
- performing a detailed review of the entity's year end adjusting entries and investigating any that appear unusual as to nature or amount;
- for significant and unusual transactions, particularly those occurring at or near year end, investigating the possibility of related parties and the sources of financial resources supporting the transactions;
- performing substantive analytical procedures using disaggregated data. For example, comparing sales and costs of sales by location, line of business or month to expectations developed by the auditors;
- conducting interviews of personnel involved in areas where a risk of material misstatement due to fraud has been identified, to obtain their insights about the risk and whether, or how, controls address the risk;
- when other independent auditors are auditing the financial statements of one or more subsidiaries, division or branches, discussing with them the extent of work necessary to be performed to address the risk of material misstatement due to fraud resulting from transactions and activities among these components;
- if the work of an expert becomes particularly significant with respect to a financial statement item for which the risk of misstatement due to fraud is high, performing additional procedures relating to some or all of the expert's assumptions, methods or findings to determine that the findings are not unreasonable, or engaging another expert for that purpose;
- performing audit procedures to analyse selected opening balance sheet accounts of previously audited financial statements to assess how certain issues involving accounting estimates and judgements, for example a provision for sales returns, were resolved with the benefit of hindsight;
- performing procedures on account or other reconciliations prepared by the entity, including considering reconciliations performed at interim periods;
- performing computer-assisted techniques to test for anomalies in a population;
- testing the integrity of computer-produced records and transactions;
- seeking additional audit evidence from sources outside of the entity being audited.

Responses to management override of controls

The extent of the risk that management may use their position to override controls to manipulate accounting records and prepare fraudulent financial statements will vary from entity to entity. However, there will be some risk in all entities, and the ISA (UK and Ireland) deems this to be a significant risk (see **22.3.6**). Therefore, in accordance with ISA (UK and Ireland) 315 specific procedures should be planned and performed to address this risk. ISA (UK and Ireland) 240 requires auditors to:

- test the appropriateness of journal entries recorded in the general ledger and other adjustments made in the preparation of financial statements;
- review accounting estimates for biases that could result in material misstatement due to fraud; and
- obtain an understanding of the business rationale of significant transactions that the auditors become aware of that are outside the normal course of business for the entity, or that otherwise appear to be unusual given the auditors' understanding of the entity and its environment.

Auditors' assessment of the risk of material misstatement due to fraud may lead them to perform additional procedures to those set out above.

Journal entries

The financial reporting process is often manipulated by the recording of inappropriate or unauthorised journal entries or other adjustments. When considering which journals or adjustments to test, auditors consider:

- their assessment of the risks of material misstatement, which may indicate a type of class or adjustments for testing;
- whether there are effective controls over journal entries and adjustments;
- the nature of evidence that can be obtained, particularly when journal entries are made electronically;
- the typical characteristics of fraudulent journal entries, including entries:
  - made to unrelated, unusual or seldom-used accounts;
  - made by individuals who do not usually make journal entries;
  - recorded at the end of the period or as post-closing entries that have little or no explanation or description;
  - made either before or during the preparation of the financial statements; or
  - containing round numbers or consistent ending numbers;
- the nature and complexity of the accounts involved, as fraudulent entries may be made to accounts that:
  - contain transactions that are complex or unusual in nature;
  - contain significant estimates and period end adjustments;
  - have been prone to misstatements in the past;
  - have not been reconciled on a timely basis or contain unreconciled differences;

- contain intercompany transactions; or
- are otherwise associated with an identified risk of material misstatement due to fraud; and
- those journals processed outside the normal course of business.

Accounting estimates

Fraudulent financial reporting is often performed through intentional misstatement of accounting estimates. Therefore, the ISA (UK and Ireland) suggests that, when auditors are reviewing accounting estimates, they should consider whether the estimates indicate a bias on the part of the entity's management. Auditors may also perform a retrospective review of management judgements and assumptions in the prior year to see if any bias is indicated in the current period.

If a bias is indicated, auditors should consider whether the circumstances represent a risk of material misstatement due to fraud.

Business rationale of transactions

Auditors aim to understand the rationale of unusual business transactions in order to consider whether the transactions have been entered into to conceal fraudulent financial reporting or misappropriation of assets. Auditors should consider whether:

- the transaction appears overly complex;
- management has discussed the nature of, and accounting for, the transaction with those charged with governance;
- management is placing emphasis on the need for a particular accounting treatment;
- transactions involving related parties have been properly reviewed and approved by those charged with governance; and
- the transaction involves previously unidentified related parties or parties that do not have the substance to support the transaction without the assistance of the entity being audited.

10.6   EVALUATING AUDIT EVIDENCE

In accordance with ISA (UK and Ireland) 330, once audit evidence has been obtained, auditors should revisit their assessment of the risk of material misstatement and consider whether it remains valid or needs amendment. This includes the risk of material misstatement due to fraud. If the risk assessment requires amendment, further audit procedures may be required.

Auditors' overall analytical review procedures at the end of the audit should include consideration of whether there is an indication of material misstatement due to fraud. For example, uncharacteristically large amounts of income being reported in the last few weeks of the accounting period may indicate fraudulent activity.

Any misstatements discovered during the audit process should be considered as possible indicators of fraud. If fraud is indicated, auditors should reconsider the reliability of management representations.

Auditors must consider the severity of the fraud and its impact on their report. Where a suspected fraud has caused a misstatement that is not material to the financial statements, auditors consider its implications to the rest of their evidence. For example, a petty cash fraud perpetrated by a clerk is not likely to impact auditors' opinions. However, if the same fraud was perpetrated by management, auditors may consider that it is indicative of a more pervasive problem with the integrity of management.

10.7   MANAGEMENT REPRESENTATIONS

ISA (UK and Ireland) 240 requires auditors to obtain written representations from management 'that:

- it acknowledges its responsibility for the design and implementation of internal controls to prevent and detect fraud;
- it has disclosed to the auditor the results of its assessment of the risk that the financial statements may be material misstated as a result of fraud;
- it has disclosed to the auditor its knowledge of fraud or suspected fraud affecting the entity involving:
  - management;
  - employees who have significant roles in internal control; or
  - others where the fraud could have a material effect on the financial statements; and
- it has disclosed to the auditor its knowledge of any allegations of fraud, or suspected fraud, affecting the entity's financial statements, communicated by employees, former employees, analysts, regulators or others.'

10.8   COMMUNICATION WITH THOSE CHARGED WITH GOVERNANCE

Where auditors have identified a fraud, or has indications that a fraud may exist, this should be communicated to an appropriate body as soon as possible.

Where the fraud involves an employee, notification should be made to an appropriate level of management given the magnitude of the fraud and the likelihood of collusion. If fraud is identified involving:

- management;
- employees who have significant roles in internal control; or
- others where the fraud could have a material effect on the financial statements,

auditors should communicate with those charged with governance as soon as practicable. Communication may be oral or in writing, having regard to the factors set out in section **8.5**.

If the integrity or honesty of management or those charged with governance is doubted, auditors consider seeking legal advice before continuing with their work.

In addition, auditors should inform those charged with governance about any material weaknesses in the design and implementation of internal controls to prevent and detect fraud, or other matters related to fraud which may have come to their attention.

10.9   COMMUNICATION WITH THE AUTHORITIES

The auditors' duty of confidentiality will be overridden by the requirements of the anti-money laundering regulations and the Proceeds of Crime Act 2002, which impose a duty on auditors to report all suspicions that a criminal offence giving rise to any direct or indirect benefit from criminal conduct has been committed. Further details are given in **Chapter 12**.

10.10   DOCUMENTATION

As part of their understanding of the entity as required by ISA (UK and Ireland) 315, auditors should document:

- the significant decisions reached during the engagement team discussion about the susceptibility of the entity's financial statements to material misstatement due to fraud (see **10.5.2** above); and
- the identified and assessed risks of material misstatement due to fraud at the financial statements level and at the assertion level.

Auditors should also document:

- their planned responses to the assessed risk of material misstatement due to fraud;
- the results from the procedures planned;
- communications about fraud made to management and those charged with governance; and

- if they have assessed that there is no risk of material misstatement due to fraud related to revenue recognition, their reasons for this conclusion.

10.11   ISA 240 REVISED

In December 2006, the IAASB issued the final version of its revision to the international version of ISA 240. The revision is one of the first ISAs to be issued as part of the IAASB's Clarity Project, the aim of which is to make the standards clearer and easier to understand. The revision process also ensured that the guidance was more easily applied to smaller entities.

The provisional effective date is 15 December 2008, although the actual date will not be any earlier than this. The long lead-in time allows the IAASB to reissue all extant ISAs so that they conform to the principles of the Clarity Project and they all share the same effective date. The APB are expected to await a decision from the EU to adopt the revised international standards before it undertakes a wholesale revision of the ISAs (UK and Ireland).

10.12   FRAUD: MEETING THE CHALLENGE THROUGH EXTERNAL AUDIT

10.12.1   Background

In November 2003, the Audit and Assurance Faculty of the ICAEW issued their paper *Fraud: Meeting the Challenge Through External Audit* as part of their ongoing *Audit Quality* programme. The document develops a ten-point action plan for audit firms, their partners and staff to take the initiative in developing audit procedures to respond to fraud risk in the light of increasing public expectation. It will enable firms to benchmark their current practices and assess them for effectiveness. The Faculty expects the review to cover both engagement level and whole firm procedures.

The action plan approach was seen to be the most practical solution in an area where many pages of guidance already exist, and where ISA (UK and Ireland) 240 contains extensive, detailed guidance. This paper reminds auditors that whilst they are not responsible for finding all fraud, increasing their detection rate is desirable in light of recent auditing scandals.

A ten-point plan was proposed in anticipation of the publication of ISA (UK and Ireland) 240, and it is detailed below to identify where procedures under SAS 110 should be further improved, and where practices need to move forward to meet the requirements in ISA (UK and Ireland) 240.

Although some of the points have been overtaken by the ISA (UK and

Ireland), the plan provides a useful summary of steps that can be taken in this area.

10.12.2   The ten-point plan

The ten-point plan is set out in **Table 1**.

TABLE 1:   The Ten-Point Plan

1 Perform an in depth review of the effectiveness of your 'whole firm' procedures and engagement level procedures to combat fraud risk at your client's firm

Firms need to keep their anti-fraud audit procedures under regular review to ensure that they are as effective as possible. They should have methodologies that address current good practices in terms of identifying and responding to fraud risk, and which all partners, managers and staff understand and can practically implement.

2 Cover fraud risk in client acceptance and continuance procedures

Dealing with difficult clients can be both challenging and very time consuming so it is worth investing in rigorous acceptance procedures for new clients to avoid later regrets. Continuous procedures are important to ensure action is taken when knowledge of audit problems is available and up to date. Firms need to pay attention to acceptance and continuance procedures where there are concerns about management integrity. Procedures for sharing critical information between predecessor and successor audit firms should be followed.

3 Reinforce professional rigour, scepticism and judgement from the top, especially when there is heightened fraud risk

Leaders of audit practices should ensure everyone understands the importance to the firm's reputation of focusing on fraud risk. The involvement of an experienced and senior review partner or 'adviser' outside the main audit team (either from within the firm or externally) will reinforce the audit partner's judgement, particularly if difficult decisions have to be taken. Audit firms need to develop quality control procedures that promote and reinforce professional scepticism.

4 Deliver fraud risk training and best practices to all

Firms should look at how to improve the effectiveness of all their people in relation to fraud risk. This includes recruitment, development and reward (for quality work). It can also include making more effective use of specialists and more effective use of knowledge within the firm about fraud risks, for example, in particular industries. A combination of on-the-job and classroom training, together with regular sharing of experiences and work on case studies will help develop skills and foster a sceptical state of mind that takes nothing for granted.

---

5 Make a specific, separate assessment of fraud risk to help focus on the key issues

The ISA 240 puts greater emphasis on the specific consideration of fraud risk on every audit. Although auditors must currently assess fraud risk in accordance with SAS 110, adopting the new ISA approach is likely to improve performance.

The fraud risk assessment is based on consideration of the three conditions that are normally present when fraud occurs (incentive/pressure, opportunity and attitude/rationalisation, meaning the ability to justify, or an ethos that allows, the intentional commission of a fraudulent act) in relation to every client. There is a higher risk of fraud where two, or all three conditions, are present, but even one factor being present may be enough to warrant the auditor taking further steps. A variety of approaches to fraud risk assessment may be effective, the key ones being the specific focus on fraud risk factors separate from considering error, the interpretation of information collected and the link to audit procedures.

6 Keep the fraud risk assessment under review and tailor audit procedures to respond to fraud risk factors identified

Unless the firm's basic approach for all audits already assumes a high risk of fraud, audit effectiveness will usually be increased if procedures on individual engagements are tailored to address fraud risks identified. Emphasis on more targeted procedures and the application of individual judgement (depending on the nature of the risk) is likely to be more effective than merely increasing the extent of work on 'routine' audit procedures.

7 Consider the risk of management fraud as being more likely to result in material misstatement of the financial statements and harder to detect

While the risk of 'employee fraud' is still important, experience shows that the most material frauds involve management, and the auditor therefore benefits from a specific assessment of management fraud risk and related responses.

8 Give risks relating to aggressive earnings management as much weight as those associated with other types of fraud

The audit considerations and procedures relating to the risk of aggressive earnings management can be different from those of other frauds, so specific consideration within overall fraud risk assessment will increase audit effectiveness. The same risk can exist in an owner-managed company where, for example, there is pressure to comply with bank loan conditions or to make the business attractive for takeover. Auditors should pay attention to accounting estimates, particularly if revenue or profit manipulation could be involved, in order to assess whether there is management bias.

9 Discuss with senior management and others charged with governance, how they discharge their fraud risk responsibilities

These discussions are crucial. They enable auditors to find out about management's knowledge of any fraud (whether actual, suspected or alleged) in the entity, and about anti-fraud measures. This in turn gives auditors a better understanding of fraud risk factors and the risk that the financial statements could be materially affected by fraud. Discussions can also help to ensure management and those charged with governance in entities understand that it is their responsibility to prevent fraud, through effective internal control and diligence, and to detect it, if it occurs, in a timely fashion.

10 Put fraud risk on the agenda of audit team meetings that include experienced team members

Knowing the client, sharing that knowledge, and applying independent judgement and scepticism, are crucial to effective auditing. Team discussions on the nature and level of any fraud risk help to ensure that all members of the team think about fraud risk and enable them to identify patterns of unusual activity from discussing individual members' audit findings. Team meetings reinforce professional scepticism and stimulate a fresh look at the risk of fraud, combating over-familiarity with the audit approach.

11 CONSIDERATION OF LAW AND REGULATIONS

11.1 INTRODUCTION

This Chapter covers the responsibility of auditors in relation to illegal acts or non-compliance with laws and regulations. In recent years, well-publicised cases where major companies have not acted in accordance with the laws and regulations which apply to them have focused public attention on the auditors' responsibility for discovering and reporting upon such acts.

This chapter does not cover fraud and error, which are covered in **Chapter 10** or money laundering and the Money Laundering Regulations 2003 which is covered in **Chapter 12.**

11.2 AUDITING STANDARDS

ISA (UK and Ireland) 250 was issued in December 2004. The ISA (UK and Ireland) has two parts: Part A covers *Consideration of Laws and Regulations in an Audit of Financial Statements* and Part B covers *The Auditor's Right and Duty to Report to Regulators in the Financial Sector.*

Part A of the ISA (UK and Ireland) contains guidance covering:

- management's responsibilities;
- auditor's consideration of compliance;
- reporting non-compliance; and
- withdrawal from the engagement.

Part B of the ISA (UK and Ireland) is detailed in **Chapter 8**.

As with all ISAs (UK and Ireland), the text of the international ISA has been supplemented with additional guidance from a UK and Ireland perspective. SAS 120 *Consideration of Law and Regulations* has not yet been officially withdrawn.

ISA (UK and Ireland) 250 is effective for audits of financial statements for periods commencing on or after 15 December 2004.

11.3   DEFINITION

The guidance to the ISA (UK and Ireland) defines non-compliance as 'acts of omission or commission by the entity, either intentional or unintentional which are contrary to the prevailing laws or regulations. Such acts include transactions entered into by, or in the name of, the entity or on its behalf by its [directors] or employees'. Personal misconduct unrelated to the business activities of the entity is not covered by the ISA (UK and Ireland).

Examples of non-compliance might be:

- dividends paid when reserves available for the dividends do not exist;
- a casino operating in breach of the Gaming Act, which could cause it to lose its licence and place its whole operation in jeopardy; and
- a waste disposal company depositing dangerous chemicals in a landfill site instead of incinerating them as required by its operating licence.

The guidance recognises that auditors may not have the 'professional competence' to determine what constitutes non-compliance, but that they may be able to recognise possible non-compliance.

The amount of law and regulation that an entity is governed by will depend on the industry it operates in and its constitution. For example, some sectors are heavily regulated, such as banks or pharmaceutical companies, whilst others are only subject to 'general' laws such as health and safety regulations. The further removed the non-compliance is from what is reflected in the financial statements, the less likely the auditor is to recognise it.

11.4   MANAGEMENT RESPONSIBILITY

It is management's responsibility to ensure that the entity complies with law and regulations and that they establish procedures to prevent and detect non-compliance. To do this they would normally set up procedures whereby they:

- maintain a register of significant laws and regulations as they affect the entity;
- monitor relevant legal requirements and ensure operating procedures and conditions meet them;
- institute and operate an appropriate system of internal control;
- develop and publish within the entity relevant codes of conduct;

- ensure employees are properly trained and understand the relevant codes of conduct;
- monitor compliance with the code;
- engage legal advisers to assist in monitoring; and
- maintain a record of complaints.

In larger entities, these methods may be supplemented by the establishment of:

- a wide-ranging internal audit function;
- a legal department;
- a compliance department; and/or
- an audit committee.

In certain industries these compliance procedures may be imposed by regulations, such as the financial services sector.

Non-compliance with law and regulations may lead to financial penalties being imposed on an entity or a loss of its business. Therefore, the implications of any non-compliance, either suspected or actual, should be assessed using SSAP 18 Accounting for Contingencies now replaced by FRS 12, Provisions, Contingent Liabilities and Contingent Assets, with regard to the inclusion and/or disclosure in the financial statements of such liabilities. In serious cases this may also affect the directors' consideration of going concern.

11.5   RESPONSIBILITY OF THE AUDITORS

The auditors have no responsibility for the prevention of illegal acts or duty to report them except in certain restricted circumstances. However, the annual audit and the auditors' right to report in the public interest may act as a deterrent. Auditors may also highlight areas where illegal acts could occur, and suggest practical solutions in their reports to management (see **Chapter 9**).

Under ISA (UK and Ireland) 200 auditors 'should plan and perform the audit with an attitude of professional scepticism recognising that the audit may reveal conditions or events that would lead to questioning whether an entity is complying with laws and regulations'.

The guidance goes on to stress that an audit cannot be expected to detect all possible non-compliance. There is always a risk that material misstatement arising from non-compliance will not be detected, but the level of risk will be affected by:

- whether the non-compliance can be captured by the system of internal controls and accounting system;

227

- the inherent limitations of the internal control system and the use of audit testing;
- the fact that auditors obtain evidence which is persuasive rather than conclusive; and
- non-compliance may involve concealment.

The risk will also be affected by management's ethos as regards compliance as well as consideration of any relevant codes of conduct. A review of management's procedures and controls together with relevant correspondence with those authorities responsible for regulation in industries where specific laws and regulations may be expected to have such a fundamental effect may be useful.

As part of their planning process, auditors should obtain a general understanding of the legal and regulatory framework applicable to the client and its industry. Auditors should also consider the procedures the entity follows to ensure that it complies with this framework. Procedures would include:

- using and updating existing knowledge of the entity's industry, regulatory and other external factors;
- enquiring of those charged with governance about the entity's policies and procedures for complying with laws and regulations;
- enquiring of those charged with governance as to the regulations that may be expected to have a fundamental effect on the operations of the entity;
- discussing the policies for identifying, evaluation and accounting for litigation claims with those charged with governance; and
- discussing the legal and regulatory framework with auditors of subsidiaries in other countries.

11.6   CONSIDERATION OF COMPLIANCE

11.6.1   *Laws with a direct effect on the financial statements*

Evidence should be obtained by the auditors of compliance with laws and regulations which have a direct effect on the financial statements under ISA (UK and Ireland) 250. Examples of such laws are:

- those which determine the form and content of an entity's financial statements – for example, Schedule 4A of the Companies Act 1985;
- those which determine when a company is prohibited from making a distribution – for example, s263 of the Companies Act 1985;
- those which oblige auditors to report in accordance with specific statutory requirements – for example, failure of a company to maintain proper accounting records, or disclosure of directors' remuneration; and

- financial reporting requirements for specific industries – for example, the Friendly and Industrial and Provident Societies Act 1968.

The Taxes Acts are a special case and the extent to which they need to be considered by auditors depends on whether that firm also acts as tax advisors. If they do not, their only consideration will be the material misstatement of the tax liability. Where auditors are also tax advisors, even though different people may be involved in each service, those responsible for the audit should inform the partner responsible for tax advice of any non-compliance they come across during the course of their work, in addition to assessing the effect of the matter on the financial statements.

Where laws determine the form and content of an entity's financial statements or, alternatively, are reportable on by auditors, the auditors have a responsibility to properly plan, perform and evaluate their audit with these in mind. In doing this, auditors must aim to give themselves a reasonable expectation of identifying non-compliance and any resulting misstatements in the financial statements which would be important to the user, although not necessarily material in quantitative terms. Auditors therefore must have regard to these laws when planning their audit, by understanding them and then testing compliance with them.

To identify instances of non-compliance with laws which have a direct effect on the financial statements, the ISA (UK and Ireland) requires auditors to:

- review correspondence with relevant authorities;
- make enquiries of those charged with governance to ascertain whether they are aware of any non-compliance; and
- obtain written confirmation from the directors that they have disclosed to the auditors all possible non-compliance, together with the consequences that may arise.

11.6.2 Laws affecting the operations of the entity

In addition, in the UK and Ireland, the auditor should plan and perform procedures which are designed to identify possible or actual instances of non-compliance with the laws and regulations within which the entity conducts its business and which are central to the entity's ability to continue operating. These may include environmental restrictions or non-compliance with terms of an operating licence.

11.7 MONEY LAUNDERING

Following the introduction of the Money Laundering Regulations 2003 and the Proceeds of Crime Act 2002, the scope of offences reportable by auditors to the relevant authorities has been considerably increased. Auditors should, therefore, be aware that instances of possible or actual non-compliance with laws and regulations discovered during the audit may incur obligations for partners and staff to report money laundering offences to the authorities. Further guidance is given in **Chapter 12**.

11.8   NON-COMPLIANCE

Auditors may receive specific information from testing which may alert them to the possibility that illegal acts have occurred. For example:

- investigation by government department;
- payment of fines or penalties;
- large payments for unspecified services or loans to consultants;
- excessive sales commissions;
- purchasing at prices significantly above or below market price;
- unusual payments in cash, cheques payable to bearer or transfers to numbered bank accounts;
- unusual transactions with companies registered in tax havens;
- payments for goods or services made to a country other than that where goods originated;
- existence of an accounting system or part of one which fails, whether by design or accident, to give an adequate audit trail;
- unauthorised or improperly recorded transactions; or
- media comment.

When auditors become aware of possible non-compliance, they should obtain an understanding of the nature of the act and the circumstances in which it has occurred, and sufficient other information to evaluate the possible effect in the financial statements.

Evaluating the effect on the financial statements involves considering:

- any contingent liabilities, such as fines;
- whether the going concern assumption is still appropriate; and
- the extent of required disclosure.

The consideration may involve matters outside the knowledge of the auditors and in these cases expert advice should be sought on the effect on the financial statements. ISA (UK and Ireland) 620 *Using the Work of an Expert* sets out the procedures that auditors should follow in such circumstances (see **37.4**).

Once auditors believe there is non-compliance, ISA (UK and Ireland) 520 requires them to:

- document their findings, including taking copies of original records which give rise to suspicions and make full notes of minutes of

conversations with management on the subject if appropriate;
- report them direct to a third party if necessary; and
- discuss them with the directors, subject to consideration of the risk of 'tipping off', see **Chapter 12**.

The guidance suggests that where management does not provide sufficient information about the suspected non-compliance to demonstrate that the entity is in fact complying, auditors should consider taking legal advice. In normal circumstances they would consult the entity's lawyers, but if they believe that it is not appropriate or they are unable to consult them, the auditors may obtain their own legal advice. If there is still insufficient information concerning the non-compliance then auditors should consider the implications for their report, and whether there is any obligation to report to third parties.

However, it is not just the effect on the audit report that should be considered. The ISA (UK and Ireland) stresses that auditors need to assess the reliability of management representations they have received in the light of the suspected non-compliance. This may be particularly important where the non-compliance includes:

- an apparent failure of specific control procedures;
- involvement of management; and
- any concealment of the act.

The guidance cites the example of a series of instances which, although financially immaterial, are 'symptomatic of management's probity' and cast doubt on the integrity of the financial statements.

11.9 REPORTING

11.9.1 *Reporting to management*

The discovery of non-compliance should normally be reported to senior management as soon as is practicable. If they do not do this directly, auditors should obtain evidence that management have been appropriately informed. Where the suspected non-compliance is material or intentional a report should be made immediately on discovery.

The non-compliance should be reported to the next level of management who are not suspected of being involved. Where it is suspected senior management are involved it may be necessary to report the matter to the audit committee, or in the case of money laundering directly to the appropriate authority. Legal advice may be required if auditors believe that no higher authority exists or that their report may not be acted on. If money laundering or some other reportable event is suspected it may be appropriate to report suspicions directly to the relevant authority.

11.9.2   Reporting to owners/members

Where a non-compliance has a material effect on the financial statements, and it has not been adequately reflected in those financial statements, auditors should issue a qualified audit report.

If management have not given sufficient evidence for the auditor to conclude that the entity is free from non-compliance a limitation of scope opinion should be given. This will be either a disclaimer of opinion or a qualified opinion depending on the severity of the limitation.

If the auditor is unable to determine whether a non-compliance has occurred as a result of circumstances rather than management intervention, a limitation of scope opinion will also be suitable.

In all the above situations, and where there is the suspicion of money laundering, auditors must consider whether issuing their audit report would be considered to be 'tipping off' (see **Chapter 12)**. In such a situation, auditors should obtain specialist legal advice.

Auditors should not refrain from qualifying their report or omitting an explanatory paragraph because the matter has since been corrected. They should base their assessment on the adequacy of the view given by the financial statements.

The consideration of the disclosure of the non-compliance will focus on going concern issues and contingencies. In particular:

- whether shareholders require the information to assess the performance of the directors;
- any potential consequences for the operational future of the company; and
- any contingencies such as fines or litigation costs.

The disclosure should be sufficient to provide a true and fair view enabling users to 'appreciate the significance of the information disclosed'. Normally full disclosure of the potential consequences will be necessary to give a true and fair view.

Where there is no specific disclosure requirement, auditors must assess the potential financial consequences and, in particular, have regard to whether non-compliance or its consequences are material to the financial statements and the probability of the act or its consequences recurring.

11.9.3 *Reporting to third parties*

Where auditors become aware of an actual or suspected non-compliance which gives rise to a statutory duty to report they should do so to the appropriate authority without delay. The guidance in Section B of ISA (UK and Ireland) 250, which covers reporting to regulators in such circumstances, should be adapted for non-regulated entities whose auditors are under a statutory duty to report, for example where they suspect money laundering.

ISA (UK and Ireland) 250 requires auditors who become aware of suspected or actual non-compliance to:

- consider if the matter should be reported to 'a proper authority in the public interest'; and where this is the case
- discuss the matter with the board and the audit committee, except in cases where they no longer have confidence in the integrity of the directors (see below).

Once they have reached a decision, auditors should then notify the directors in writing that they are of the opinion that the matter is reportable. If the directors do not report the matter themselves, or do not provide evidence that they have already reported the matter, the auditors should report directly. Auditors may take legal advice before making a decision on whether the matter needs to be reported.

Where auditors have lost confidence in the integrity of the directors as a result of the suspected or actual non-compliance, they may report extreme cases directly to the proper authority in the public interest, without discussing the matter with the board.

Reporting to third parties may lead to some concerns regarding the apparent breach of confidentiality and what is meant by the public interest. The guidance in the ISA (UK and Ireland) considers both in detail.

11.10 RESIGNATION

The guidance suggests that as a last resort, where auditors cannot obtain the necessary information, or have no opportunity to inform the shareholders, or where management refuse to issue financial statements, they should withdraw from the engagement.

12 MONEY LAUNDERING

12.1 BACKGROUND

Chapter 11 deals with laws and regulations and the need for auditors to take them into account in the course of their audits. One area which is of great concern to auditors in relation to this is money laundering. Until 1 March 2004 the specific duties of auditors in the UK to report money laundering suspicions extended only to the suspected proceeds of drug trafficking or terrorist funds. From that date new regulations, the Money Laundering Regulations 2003, were introduced which extended the Proceeds of Crime Act 2002 to accountants. This new legislation has extended money laundering reporting to include possessing or any way dealing with, or concealing, the proceeds of any criminal conduct, where criminal conduct is defined as conduct which constitutes an offence in any part of the United Kingdom, or is an indictable offence in the Republic of Ireland.

The Serious Organised Crime and Police Act 2005, which was passed by Parliament in April 2005, made some changes to the Anti-Money Laundering reporting requirements. These are detailed below.

12.2 CONSEQUENCES FOR ACCOUNTANTS IN PRACTICE

In February 2004, the Consultative Committee of Accounting Bodies (CCAB) issued guidance for all accountants on meeting their obligations under the new Money Laundering Regulations entitled *Anti-Money Laundering (Proceeds of Crime and Terrorism), Second Interim Guidance for Accountants*. Under this guidance, accountants in practice must report any suspicions or grounds for suspicion to the Serious Organised Crime Agency (SOCA) into which the previous responsible body, the National Crime Intelligence Squad (NCIS) has been subsumed. Firms must:

- appoint a nominated officer (a money laundering reporting officer (MLRO)) to receive reports of suspicions from colleagues and pass them on to the SOCA;

- train partners and staff on the requirements of the legislation, and how to recognise and report money laundering suspicions;
- verify the identity of new clients and keep records of the evidence obtained; and
- establish appropriate internal procedures to prevent or halt money laundering.

Sole practitioners are not required to appoint a MLRO, but in other respects are recommended to follow the CCAB guidance.

In assessing whether an individual had knowledge or suspicion of money laundering which they should have reported, the courts are likely to take into account the level of skill and experience held by that individual, including any professional qualification. Wilful blindness will also be seen as having knowledge.

12.3   AUDITORS' RESPONSIBILITIES

The Money Laundering Regulations 2003 extended to the Proceeds of Crime Act to all accountants. This chapter is concerned with how these regulations impact on the responsibilities of auditors specifically and outlines various sources of guidance which have been published.

Whilst the main guidance for auditors is set out in Practice Note 12 (see **12.4**), further guidance is also available in Section B of ISA (UK and Ireland) 250, and this is covered in **12.5** below. In addition, **12.6** includes details of ICAEW guidance notes and useful information which was published in the original Practice Note 12, but which has not been reproduced in the revised version.

12.4   PRACTICE NOTE 12

12.4.1   Introduction

Practice Note 12, *Money Laundering – Interim Guidance for Auditors in the United Kingdom* was originally issued in May 1997. It has undergone a continued programme of updates to ensure that it addresses new legislation as it is published. The most recent update, issued in January 2007, reflects the legislation effective at 31 December 2006. Recent legislation has a major impact on auditors' responsibilities to report money laundering suspicions. The Practice Note concentrates on the impact of the new legislation on auditors' responsibilities when auditing and reporting on financial statements; it does not provide general guidance on the legislation.

12.4.2   What is money laundering?

The widening of the definition of money laundering is illustrated by examples of offences set out in Appendix 1 to the Practice Note, an example of which is set out below.

Example

A subsidiary of a public company has guaranteed a £20,000 loan made by the bank to one of its directors. Such provision of guarantees for loans to directors are prohibited by s330 of the Companies Act 1985, and for subsidiaries of public companies such loans can give rise to criminal offences under s342(2) of the Act. If none of the exemptions set out in the Act apply and the company could not claim that it did not know the relevant circumstances at the time of the loan, the auditors would conclude that the director is in possession of the proceeds of the company's crime and make a report to their MLRO.

The appendix contains a number of situations where suspicions of money laundering may be reportable. With the frequently changing legislation surrounding money laundering, the Practice Note suggests that each case is assessed individually in relation to the current rules and independent advice obtained as necessary.

The Serious Organised Crime and Police Act 2005 states that it is no longer necessary for auditors to report money laundering suspicions where the suspect cannot be identified and the whereabouts of the proceeds are unknown. Commentators are assuming that this change also includes situations where an auditor knows that their client keeps records of suspected shoplifters or other minor criminals, but does not need to access those records for the purposes of the audit.

As stated above, the definition of money laundering has been widened, but the scope of the audit has not been extended. Auditors are required to make a report when information comes to their attention in the normal course of their audit work. All incidences should be reported, not just those which are material to the financial statements. Failure to make a report is a criminal offence and auditors, both partners and staff, face criminal penalties if they breach the requirements. Auditors are not required to undertake any further work to determine whether an offence has been committed; the suspicion alone is reportable.

Auditors must report offences committed in the United Kingdom and conduct overseas which would have been an offence if it had been committed in the United Kingdom. Therefore when considering non-UK parts of a group audit, the UK parent company auditors will need to consider whether information obtained as part of the group audit procedures, such as discussions with subsidiary auditors or discussions with UK or non-UK directors, gives rise to a reportable offence.

The Serious Organised Crime and Police Act 2005 takes steps to remove the possession of proceeds of foreign actions which would be illegal in the UK, from the definition of money laundering. However, implementation of these changes are being delayed until further procedures are in place to ensure that reports of suspicious activities such as terrorism and organised crime are still received, wherever the underlying behaviour took place.

12.4.3   Changes to procedures

Firms are required to implement training programmes to ensure that their partners and staff are aware of the Proceeds of Crime Act 2002, the Money Laundering Regulations 2003, the Terrorism Act 2000 and the Serious Organised Crime and Police Act 2005. In addition, firms are required to review their client acceptance procedures to ensure that they fulfil all the requirements set out in the CCAB guidance – see **Table 1** for examples.

TABLE 1:   Example client identification procedures suggested by the CCAB guidance

- establish the identity of the entity itself and its business activity, e.g., on a certificate of incorporation
- obtain evidence of the company's registered address;
- establish the current list of shareholders and directors; and
- where there is a perceived high risk, view, and take copies of, evidence establishing the full names and permanent addresses of owners, partners, sole traders or principal directors for clients, e.g., on a driving licence or a passport.

For new clients, a form of pre-engagement communication may be of use in explaining the procedures being undertaken. The requirement for obtaining additional evidence of clients' identities may also be explained in the engagement letter for ongoing clients. The example in **Table 2** could be used for both purposes.

Annual reappointment of the auditor does not automatically require the client identification procedures to be reperformed. However, if there has been a change of circumstances, such as a change of beneficial owner or change of directors, then the procedures may need to be reperformed and documented.

TABLE 2:   Example client identification wording

Client identification
As with other professional services firms, we are under stringent requirements to identify our clients for the purposes of the anti-money laundering legislation. We are likely to request from you, and retain, some information and documentation for these purposes and/or to make searches of appropriate databases. If satisfactory evidence of your identity is not provided within a reasonable time, there may be circumstances in which we are not able to proceed with the audit appointment.

It may also be useful to include a paragraph similar to the example in **Table 3** to inform clients of auditors' responsibility to report suspicions or knowledge that a money laundering offence has taken place.

TABLE 3: Example money laundering reporting wording for engagement letter

Money laundering reporting
The provision of audit services is a business in the regulated sector under the Proceeds of Crime Act 2002 and, as such, partners and staff in audit firms are required to report all knowledge or suspicion, or reasonable grounds to know or suspect, that a criminal offence giving rise to any direct or indirect benefit from criminal conduct has been committed, regardless of whether that offence has been committed by their client or by a third party. If as part of our normal audit work we have knowledge or suspicion, or have reasonable grounds to know or suspect, that such offences have been committed we are required to make a report to the National Criminal Intelligence Service. It is not our practice to discuss such reports with you because of the restrictions imposed by the tipping off provisions of the UK anti-money laundering legislation.

Where a decision is taken to include paragraphs such as those in **Tables 2** and **3** in engagement letters, this should be done for all clients. Where the paragraphs are included in only some of the auditor's engagement letters, the inclusion of these paragraphs may be seen as 'tipping off'.

12.4.4 *Tipping off*

Once the auditor has knowledge or suspicion that a money laundering offence has occurred, they must be aware that various actions may mean that they breach the 'tipping off' requirements, that is disclosing information to any person or individual if doing so is likely to prejudice an investigation. Therefore auditors should:

* ensure that any further investigation consists only of steps that the auditor would have performed as part of their normal audit work;
* obtain clearance from their MLRO before any further investigation is performed;
* consider whether the wording of a qualified audit report will fall foul of the tipping off regulations, consulting with the law enforcement agency for agreement as necessary;
* issue their report on a timely basis, as an unnecessary delay may be construed as tipping off; and
* take advice on the precise dating of the s394 statement if they decide to resign from the engagement in order to avoid tipping off.

12.4.5 *Reporting to the MLRO and SOCA*

All suspicions or knowledge of money laundering offences must be reported to the firm's MLRO or, for sole practitioners, direct to the Serious Organised Crime Agency (SOCA). The MLRO must then report the matter 'as soon as is practicable' to the SOCA, and at the latest up to one month after the audit report is signed. There is no de minimis limit for reporting, or provision for a report not to be made where the auditors consider that the SOCA is already aware of the matter, so all incidences, however small, will warrant a report. The Serious Organised Crime and Police Act paved the way for the introduction of mandatory reporting forms, and the SOCA is currently reviewing its system for reporting including the use of 'standard' and 'limited intelligence value' reports. For sole practitioners making reports directly to the SOCA, the SOCA disclosure forms are available on its website *www.soca.gov.uk* and these can be submitted electronically.

Reporting to the SOCA does not relieve auditors from other statutory duties such as reporting to the FSA for entities in the financial sector or other regulators for entities such as pension schemes and charities. The need to report to the SOCA is likely to be a matter of 'material significance' to a regulator, and therefore will require to be reported to them. Again auditors should ensure that they do not breach tipping off regulations in making reports to regulators.

12.4.6 *Auditors' report on the financial statements*

Where it is suspected that money laundering has occurred auditors should be wary about breaching the regulations relating to 'tipping off' when issuing their audit report. When considering the nature of their audit report, auditors should apply the concept of materiality, considering whether the disclosure of the:

- crime itself;
- consequences of the crime; or
- outcome of any subsequent investigation by police or other investigatory body

may have a material effect on the financial statements.

12.5 CONSIDERATION OF LAWS AND REGULATIONS

ISA (UK and Ireland) 250 requires auditors to gain an understanding of the legal and regulatory framework within which an entity operates and to plan and perform procedures designed to help identify possible or actual instances of non-compliance with those laws and regulations. As a result of this work, auditors may uncover evidence which creates a duty to report money laundering offences.

The Money Laundering Regulations 2003 have widened the scope of reportable offences to include the concealing, disguising, converting, transferring, removing, using, acquiring or possessing of property which constitutes or represents a benefit from any criminal conduct. Criminal conduct is defined as 'conduct which constitutes an offence in any part of the UK or would constitute such an offence if it occurred in any part of the UK'. As a result auditors are more likely to come into contact with matters that should be reported.

As the number of reportable incidences increase, so does the likelihood of auditors falling foul of the offence of 'tipping off'. Many of the procedures set out in ISA (UK and Ireland) 250 may constitute 'tipping off' if actioned where an incidence of money laundering is discovered or suspected. Examples include:

- discussing non-compliances with management or those charged with governance;
- issuing a qualified audit report;
- issuing a report to a regulatory authority; or
- resigning their position as auditors.

In such situations, auditors should discuss their actions with experts in the SOCA.

12.6 OTHER GUIDANCE

In December 1999, the Institute of Chartered Accountants in England and Wales issued a set of guidance notes for auditors. They deal with the statute law, regulations and professional requirements in relation to the avoidance, recognition and reporting of money laundering. Although the guidance notes are based on the law and conditions existing in England and Wales prior to 1 March 2004, they outline a number of useful procedures which should be followed by every entity, covering:

- identification: obtaining evidence of the identity of prospective clients;
- records: keeping records of identity documents and of transactions;
- reporting: ensuring that all suspicions of money laundering are reported to the appropriate authorities; and
- training: training partners and staff, particularly in how to recognise suspicious transactions.

In order to ensure that a firm has sufficient knowledge of their new and existing clients, auditors should ask and document the answers to the questions in **Table 4**.

TABLE 4:   Questions to ensure that the identity of a client is known

- is the prospective client who they claim to be?
- is enough known about their personal or business and financial background to be able to provide an effective service?
- if the client's premises are not visited, what is being taken on trust?
- are changes in the continuing clients' circumstances notified to the firm?

The guidance also indicates potential danger signals, which may point to underlying money laundering, and these are set out in **Table 5**.

TABLE 5:   Money laundering danger signals

- the client is reluctant to provide details of identity and background, or is over-plausible. This may be of greater importance where the client is never met in person, or the client's premises are never visited;
- the client has no obvious reason for using a particular auditor. Other auditors may be available nearer the client's base or the client is asking for services which are outside the normal remit of the firm;
- the client's transactions lack, or include steps which lack, apparent commercial purpose – for example, the structure of transactions appears unnecessarily complex, or there is no obvious commercial requirement for the number of subsidiaries, branches, trusts or nominees included in the client's structure;
- there is an inability to obtain convincing evidence as to the origins of the funds behind the financial and legal structure;
- the client asks its auditors to hold or transmit money or other assets, without giving a convincing reason for the auditor's involvement;
- the client comes from, or is introduced by a third party in, a country where drug production and trafficking may be prevalent. Similar caution should be exercised where the client has links with a country with an ineffective anti-money laundering system.

Where the laws on money laundering are considered to be central to the entity's operations auditors must assess compliance with them. Where the legislation is not central to the operations of the entity, auditors should consider whether the business is one of those which is more prone to involvement, either knowingly or unknowingly, in money laundering. Businesses which are conducted mainly in cash, such as auction houses and garages, may have a higher risk of being used by criminals to launder the proceeds of their activities.

The old Practice Note provided illustrative lists of factors which may give rise to an increased risk of involvement in money laundering, shown in **Table 6** and **Table 7**. The guidance stressed that the existence of one of these factors does not give rise to a suspicion that money laundering is occurring, but that auditors should be alert to circumstances in which a combination of factors may give rise to a suspicion. These factors remain relevant under the new regulations.

TABLE 6: Factors arising from action by the entity or its directors which may indicate an increased risk of money laundering

- complex corporate structure where complexity does not seem to be warranted;
- complex or unusual transactions, possibly with related parties;
- transactions with little commercial logic taking place in the normal course of business;
- transactions not in the normal course of business;
- transactions where there is a lack of information or explanations, or where explanations are unsatisfactory;
- transactions at an undervalue;
- transactions with companies whose identity is difficult to establish as they are registered in countries known for their commercial secrecy;
- extensive or unusual related party transactions;
- many large cash transactions when not expected;
- payments for unspecified services, or payments for services that appear excessive in relation to the services provided;
- the forming of companies or trusts with no apparent commercial or other purpose;
- long delays in the production of company or trust accounts;
- foreign travel which is apparently unnecessary and extensive.

TABLE 7: Factors arising from action by a third party which may indicate an increased risk of money laundering

- a customer establishing a pattern of small transactions and then having one or two substantially larger ones;
- unusual transactions or a pattern of trading with one customer that is different from the norm;
- unusual requests for settlement of sales in cash;
- taking out of single premium life assurance policies, with subsequent early cancellation and encashment;
- a customer setting up a transaction that appears to be of no commercial advantage or logic;
- a customer requesting special arrangements for vague purposes;
- unusual transactions with companies registered overseas;
- requests for settlement in bank accounts or jurisdictions which would be unusual for a normal commercial transaction.

---

13 GOING CONCERN

13.1 INTRODUCTION

Auditors' consideration of the going concern basis is an area that has recently been the subject of much debate. High profile cases where companies have collapsed with apparently inadequate warning in financial statements and audit reports have concentrated attention in this area. This is, however, a difficult area in which to set standards for auditors, being one involving more judgements than most others which auditors face.

Directors have a responsibility to prepare financial statements on the going concern basis unless it is inappropriate to do so. This involves an assessment of, and judgements about, the future. If they decide the basis is inappropriate, assets may need to be written down to recoverable amounts or reclassified, and liabilities restated to reflect changes in amount or date of maturity. Auditors must assess how directors have carried out this assessment on a realistic basis and that the consequences, where relevant, are reflected in the financial statements.

13.2 AUDITING STANDARDS

ISA (UK and Ireland) 570 *Going Concern* was issued in December 2004 and provides in relating to the going concern basis covering:

- general requirements;
- the entity's responsibilities;
- the auditors' responsibilities; and
- audit conclusions and reporting.

As with all ISAs (UK and Ireland), the text of the international ISA has been supplemented with additional guidance from a UK and Ireland perspective. SAS 130 *Going Concern* has not yet been officially withdrawn.

ISA (UK and Ireland) 570 is effective for audits of financial statements for periods commencing on or after 15 December 2004.

In March 2007, the IAASB issued an Exposure Draft of a revision to the international version of ISA 570 which incorporates the drafting conventions of its Clarity Project (see **Chapter 1**). Changes are limited to those required by that project and no substantive revisions have been made. The comment period ended on 31 May 2007.

Bulletin 2006/6, *Auditor's Reports on Financial Statements in the United Kingdom* (see **Chapters 3** and **4**), provides additional guidance on modified auditor's reports arising from going concern issues. It is considered further in **13.6** below.

13.3   GENERAL REQUIREMENT

ISA (UK and Ireland) 570 requires auditors to consider, when forming an opinion on whether the financial statements present a true and fair view:

- the entity's ability to continue as a going concern; and
- any disclosures in the financial statements.

The guidance focuses on the auditors' responsibility to assess how the directors have satisfied themselves that the financial statements have been prepared on an appropriate basis.

It is implied therefore that the directors must make their assessment and, on the basis of this, decide what disclosure is necessary.

13.4   THE ENTITY'S RESPONSIBILITIES

Those charged with governance have the responsibility of determining whether the entity is a going concern and for preparing the financial statements on a going concern basis. Under the going concern assumption an entity will be assumed to continue in business for the foreseeable future without the intention or need to liquidate, cease trading or seek protection from its creditors. Assets and liabilities will, therefore, be recorded assuming that they will be traded or settled in the normal course of business.

Those charged with governance may be preparing their financial statements under either IFRS or UK accounting standards. The requirements governing going concern are the same under the two frameworks, except that if the period considered by the directors is less than one year from the date of approval of the financial statements disclosure of that fact must be made in the financial statements under FRS 18. There is no such requirement under IAS 1, where the relevant 12-month period runs from the balance sheet date.

When making their assessment, those charged with governance should be aware that:

- the outcome of an event is less certain the further it is likely to occur from the date the assessment is made;
- judgements can only be made on the basis of information available at the time. Subsequent events can contradict a decision which was reasonable at the time it was made; and
- any judgement will be affected by the size and complexity of the entity, its type of business and how susceptible its activities are to outside influences.

Auditors should also consider these factors when forming an opinion on the assessment made by those charged with governance.

Examples of events or circumstances which may cause doubt about the suitability of using the going concern assumption are given in **Table 1**. However, such circumstances may be mitigated, for example, the loss of a principal supplier may be mitigated by the availability of a suitable alternative supplier.

TABLE 1: Events or circumstances which may cause doubt over use of the going concern assumption

Financial

- net liability or net current liability position;
- necessary borrowing facilities have not been agreed;
- fixed-term borrowing approaching maturity without realistic prospects of renewal or repayments; or excessive reliance on short-term borrowings to finance long-term assets;
- major debt repayment falling due where refinancing is necessary to the entity's continued existence;
- major restructuring of debt;
- indications of withdrawal of financial support by debtors and other creditors;
- negative operating cash flows indicated by historical or prospective financial statements;
- adverse key financial ratios;
- substantial operating losses or significant deterioration in the value of assets used to generate cash flows;
- major losses or cash flow problems which have arisen since the balance sheet date;
- arrears or discontinuance of dividends;
- inability to pay creditors on due dates;
- inability to comply with the terms of loan agreements;
- reduction in normal terms of trade credit;
- change from credit to cash-on-delivery transactions with suppliers;

- inability to obtain financing for essential new product development or other essential investments;
- substantial sales of fixed assets not intended to be replaced.

Operating

- loss of key management without replacement;
- loss of key staff without replacement;
- loss of a major market, franchise, licence or principal supplier;
- labour difficulties or shortages of important suppliers;
- fundamental changes in the market or technology to which the entity is unable to adapt adequately;
- excessive dependence on a few product lines where the market is depressed;
- technical developments which render a key product obsolete.

Other

- non-compliance with capital or other statutory requirements;
- pending legal or regulatory proceedings against the entity that may, if successful, result in claims that are unlikely to be satisfied;
- changes in legislation or government policy expected to adversely affect the entity;
- issues which involve a range of possible outcomes so wide that an unfavourable result could affect the appropriateness of the going concern basis.

13.5   THE AUDITORS' RESPONSIBILITIES

Auditors are responsible for considering the decision to use the going concern assumption made by those charged with governance. They are also required to consider whether there is a need for additional disclosure about going concern in the financial statements so that those statements give a true and fair view.

13.5.1   *Planning the audit*

As part of their gathering of knowledge of the business, auditors should remain alert for indications that the use of the going concern assumption may not be appropriate. They should continue to be mindful of any such circumstances throughout the audit and if they become aware of any events and related business risks which may indicate that the entity is not a going concern, they should perform the procedures set out in **Table 2.**

If such events or risks are identified, auditors should also consider their impact on the assessment of the risk of material misstatement (see **Chapter 22).**

TABLE 2: **Audit work to be performed if events or circumstances are identified which indicate that the entity may not be a going concern**

- review the entity's plan for future actions based on the going concern assessment, e.g. the use of the financial statements to secure funding;
- gather evidence to support or dispel the material uncertainty, including considering the plans of management and any mitigating factors; and
- obtain written representations from those charged with governance concerning:
  - their future plans;
  - their belief that the entity is a going concern; and
  - any relevant disclosures in the financial statements.

At the planning stage auditors may be able to review any preliminary assessment of going concern made by those charged with governance. If no preliminary assessment has been made, auditors should discuss going concern with the entity at this early stage to enable any further reviews and resolution of issues to be completed.

13.5.2 Evaluating the entity's assessment of going concern

ISA (UK and Ireland) 570 requires that:

'the auditor should assess the adequacy of the means by which those charged with governance have satisfied themselves that:

(a) it is appropriate for them to adopt the going concern basis in preparing the financial statements; and

(b) the financial statements include such disclosures, if any, relating to going concern as are necessary for them to give a true and fair view.'

Auditors' procedures will involve:

- holding discussions with those charged with governance;
- examining appropriate supporting documentation; and
- planning and performing procedures designed to identify any material matters which could impact on the entity's ability to continue as a going concern, including considering the process followed to make the assessment, the assumptions on which the assessment is based and plans for the future.

The issues auditors should consider may include the:

- period assessed by those charged with governance;
- system for identifying future risks;
- existence/quality of budgets or forecasts;
- appropriateness of assumptions;

- sensitivity of budgets;
- adequacy of borrowing facilities; and
- the entity's plans for resolving going concern problems.

The extent of the procedures carried out will depend on the headroom between financial resources and the facilities available. The more demonstrably healthy the company, the less elaborate the procedures need to be.

Borrowing facilities

The assessment of the going concern assumption also involves comparing available cash with requirements and assessing the 'headroom' available. For companies financed by debt, the assessment involves deciding what level of borrowing facilities may reasonably be expected to be available.

The ISA (UK and Ireland) highlights the need for auditors to make their own assessment of ongoing facilities. It notes that auditors may need to make an assessment of the intentions of the company's bankers, the most common provider of finance, where:

- there is a low margin of financial resources available;
- the company's facilities are shortly due for renewal;
- they are aware of previous difficulties in agreeing facilities and the bankers have imposed further conditions for continued lending;
- the directors have projected a significant deterioration in the cash position; or
- the company has recently breached or is likely to breach its borrowing covenants.

Such an assessment may include:

- reviewing correspondence between directors and their bankers; and
- meeting with the directors and bankers to clarify the latter's intentions.

The auditors may, despite the above, decide it is necessary to obtain confirmation from bankers of the existence and terms of facilities.

If they are neither able to satisfy themselves about the existence and terms of facilities or about the bankers' future intentions, auditors need to consider whether:

- there is sufficient disclosure of the uncertainty in respect of the facilities in the financial statements to give a true and fair view; and
- to refer to the matter in their audit report (see below).

Some possible procedures that auditors may consider where the situation is complex and headroom is tight are shown in **Table 3**.

TABLE 3: Possible audit procedures

Forecasts and budgets
Review cash flow forecasts and budgets, where available, from the expected date of approval of the financial statements. Perform sensitivity analysis on the key components of forecasts and budgets.

Consider the assumptions used in preparing the forecasts, for example:

- anticipated levels of sales;
- projected winning of new customers;
- expected cash collection performance;
- capital expenditure programme;
- timing of anticipated payments to Inland Revenue or Customs; and
- basis of payment terms to existing suppliers.

Assess reliability of directors' previous forecasting.

Borrowing facilities
Confirm the existence and terms of facilities.
Establish the date for renewal of facilities.
Assess the future intentions of lenders via discussion or correspondence.
Assess possible breaches of any borrowing covenants imposed by lenders.
Check for any arrears of interest on current borrowings.
Review the value of any assets granted as security for borrowings.
Review correspondence between directors and lenders.

Contingent liabilities
Consider possible exposure to contingent liabilities arising, for example, from:

- legal proceedings;
- guarantees or warranties; and
- retentions.

Assess potential intra-group guarantees (e.g., unlimited multilateral guarantees).
Review possible breaches of grant conditions leading to repayment of grants.

Financial risk
Review directors' assumptions about projected foreign currency exchange rates.
Consider exposure to major fixed-price contracts.

Financial adaptability
Assess entity's ability to adapt to unexpected events, for example:
- disposal of fixed assets;
- leasing;
- debt restructuring;
- share capital issue;
- financial support from group companies; and
- new sources of finance.

13.5.3 *Period covered by auditors' review*

Auditors should ensure that their procedures cover the same period of time considered by those charged with governance when they made their initial assessment of going concern. The ISA (UK and Ireland) states that where those charged with governance have considered a period shorter than 12 months from the balance sheet date, the auditor should ask management to extend their assessment period to cover the full 12 months. This is then supplemented by a somewhat contradictory UK and Ireland specific paragraph which states that 'it is not possible to specify a minimum length for this period'. Instead the UK and Ireland specific guidance goes on to stress that the period considered will depend on:

- the entity's reporting and budgeting systems; and
- the nature of the entity, including its size and complexity.

Under ISA (UK and Ireland) 570, where the period considered by those charged with governance is less than 12 months from the date of approval of the financial statements disclosure of this fact should normally be made in the financial statements. Where those charged with governance do not make this disclosure in the financial statements, the auditors are required to do so within their report. **Table 5** gives an extract from a report where the financial statements have been prepared under UK GAAP. As the period considered by those charged with governance has not extended to 12 months from the date of approval of the financial statements there is a qualification arising from the failure to disclose this under FRS 18.

In this example there is no emphasis of matter paragraph required because no disclosure has been made about the 12-month period in the financial statements and all references to the elapsed period have been made in the qualified opinion.

When the entity is preparing financial statements under IFRS, there is an anomaly between the period those charged with governance are required to consider under IAS 1 (twelve months from the balance sheet date) and the period specified by ISA (UK and Ireland) 570 (twelve months from the date of approval of the financial statements). Therefore, the situation may arise where the requirements of IAS 1 are fulfilled, but those in ISA (UK and Ireland) 570 are not. In such circumstances the financial statements are unqualified as the accounting requirements have been met, but an emphasis of matter paragraph should be added to the auditor's report to draw attention to the fact that the requirements of ISA (UK and Ireland) 570 have not been fulfilled (see **Table 6**).

Where financial statements have been prepared under IFRS, and those charged with governance have refused to extend their assessment period to a period of more than 12 months from the balance sheet date (to comply with

IAS 1) or 12 months from the date of approval of the financial statements (to comply with ISA (UK and Ireland) 570), the auditor should follow the example in **Table 7** which includes both a qualification and an emphasis of matter paragraph.

In contrast to **Table 5**, **Table 7** includes a case under IAS 1, where the qualification results from the fact that the correct period has not been considered, and here, an emphasis of matter refers to the inadequate disclosure which is not considered to be a matter for qualification under these rules.

The period under consideration may not have formal cash flow forecasts and budgets prepared for it, but this does not necessarily mean that the going concern assumption cannot be used.

One of the examples in an appendix to the ISA (UK and Ireland) illustrates this with the case of a small software design company where cash flows are prepared on a rolling six-month basis but beyond which there is no formal assessment by the directors. However, despite the absence of cash budgets beyond six months, the directors' assessment is considered to be sufficient as they have considered a number of additional factors that go beyond the six months in making their assessment, in particular:

- the state of the company's order book and its tendering activities;
- its relationship with its bankers (the company has renewed its arrangements with its bankers for a further year in this example);
- the stability of the work force; and
- the ability to reduce cash needs if work is not obtained.

13.5.4 Events after the period considered by those charged with governance

Auditors should enquire of those charged with governance if they are aware of any events or circumstances which may occur after their period of assessment has elapsed (i.e., after 12 months from the date of approval of the financial statements) which may impact the use of the going concern assumption. Events this far in the future are unlikely to be certain, but auditors should consider the impact of any such event which is made known to them up until the date of their audit report. However, auditors have no responsibility to design audit procedures to discover such events.

13.6 AUDIT CONCLUSIONS AND REPORTING

13.6.1 Entity considered not to be a going concern

ISA (UK and Ireland) 570 requires that auditors should document any concerns they have about the entity's ability to continue in operational existence. Concerns may arise not only from their evaluation of the entity's assessment, but also from other evidence or knowledge of the business obtained during the audit, together with any other information of which they may have become aware.

If there is a significant level of concern about the entity's ability to continue as a going concern auditors could disagree with the use of the going concern assumption in preparing the financial statements. If this is the case, auditors would draw the attention of those charged with governance to the need to obtain specialist advice.

Where the financial statements have been incorrectly prepared assuming the entity is a going concern, auditors would give an adverse opinion in their report, as shown in **Table 8**.

However, if those charged with governance have correctly prepared the financial statements using an alternative appropriate basis of preparation, and this has been adequately disclosed, the audit report can be unqualified. An emphasis of matter paragraph may be required in the audit report to draw readers' attention to the alternative basis.

If the alternative basis of preparation has not been adequately disclosed an adverse or disagreement opinion may been given, see examples in **Tables 8** and **9**. In extreme circumstances, where there are multiple significant uncertainties, a disclaimer of opinion may be suitable.

13.6.2   Inadequate disclosures

Auditors are required to consider whether the financial statements are required to include disclosures about going concern and whether those disclosures are adequate. For example if the period considered by those charged with governance is less than 12 months from the date of approval of the financial statements, this should be disclosed. Where it is not disclosed in the financial statements, auditors should make reference to it in the basis of audit opinion section of their report, as in the example extract in **Table 6**.

13.6.3   Those charged with governance not taking adequate steps

Where auditors are of the opinion that those charged with governance have not taken adequate steps to assess the reasonableness of the going concern assumption, they would give a qualified opinion. Such a qualification would be a limitation on the scope of the auditors' work as they are unable to obtain all the information and explanations which they consider necessary for the purpose of their audit. Depending on the severity of the limitation, the extract examples in **Tables 10** and **11** could be used.

13.6.4   Material uncertainty

If auditors consider that the use of the going concern assumption is correct but that there remains a material uncertainty, they should assess whether the financial statements:

- describe adequately the principal events or conditions that give rise to the uncertainty that the entity can continue in operation and the entity's plans to deal with these events or conditions; and
- state that the material uncertainty exists and that it may cast significant doubt on the entity's ability to continue as a going concern and, therefore, that it may not be unable to realise its assets and discharge its liabilities in the normal course of business.

If these disclosures are made, the audit report would be unqualified, but would contain an emphasis of matter paragraph to bring readers' attention to the matter. **Table 12** sets out an example emphasis of matter paragraph. To be content with the disclosures made in the financial statements, auditors should ensure that the financial statements include:

- a statement that the going concern basis has been used;
- a statement of relevant facts;
- the nature of the concern;
- the assumptions adopted by the entity;
- the entity's plans, where practicable, to resolve the concern; and
- details of any relevant actions taken by the entity.

Where the relevant disclosures are not made or are inadequate, the example in **Table 9** should be followed.

13.6.5   Example report extracts

Bulletin 2006/6 (see **Chapter 3**) sets out a number of extracts from example reports together with a navigation aid to assist auditors in using the correct form of report. The navigation aid is reproduced in **Table 4** below, together with reference to the example reports which follow.

TABLE 4: Navigation aid for modified auditor's reports arising from going concern issues

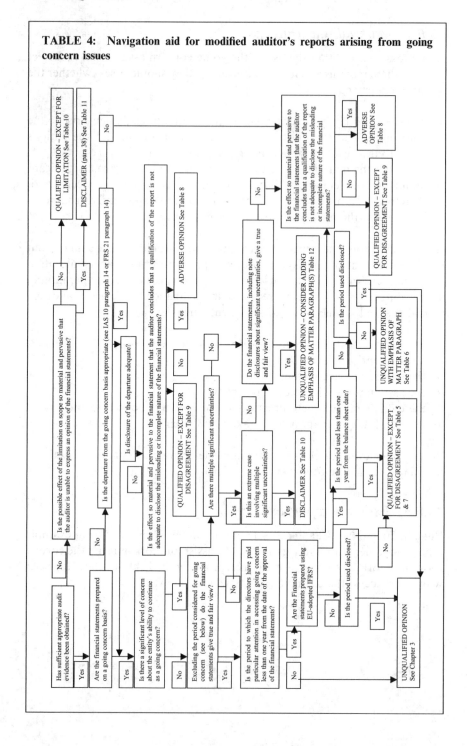

TABLE 5: Example of disagreement under UK GAAP where the requirements of FRS 18 have not been fulfilled and no disclosure of this fact is made

Qualified opinion arising from departure from FRS 18 'Accounting Policies'
In assessing whether it is appropriate to prepare the financial statements on a going concern basis the directors have paid particular attention to a period ending on 30 September 20X3 which is less than twelve months from the date of approval of the financial statements. This fact has not been disclosed in the financial statements, contrary to the requirements of Financial Reporting Standard 18 'Accounting Policies'.

Except for the absence of the disclosure referred to above in our opinion the financial statements:

- give a true and fair view, in accordance with United Kingdom Generally Accepted Accounting Practice, of the state of the company's affairs as at 31 December 20X1 and of its profit [loss] for the year then ended; and
- have been properly prepared in accordance with the Companies Act 1985;

In our opinion the information given in the Directors' Report is consistent with the financial statements.

Registered Auditors
Address
[Date]

TABLE 6: Example of emphasis of matter where entity has complied with IAS 1, but not ISA (UK and Ireland) 570

Emphasis of matter – Going concern
In forming our opinion, which is not qualified, we have considered the adequacy of the disclosures made in note x to the financial statements concerning the period used by the directors in assessing whether the going concern assumption is appropriate. In making their assessment the directors have considered the period up to 31 March 20X3 which is less than 12 months from the date of the approval of the financial statements and the directors have not disclosed this fact. International Standards on Auditing (UK and Ireland) required the auditors to draw this fact to the attention of readers of the financial statements.

TABLE 7: Example of disagreement under IFRS where the financial statements do not comply with the requirements of IAS 1 and inadequate disclosure of this fact is made

Qualified opinion arising from departure from IAS 1 'Presentation of financial statements'
In assessing whether it is appropriate to prepare the financial statements on a going concern basis the directors have paid particular attention to a period

ending on 30 November 20X2 which is less than 12 months from the balance sheet date. This is contrary to the requirements of International Accounting Standard 1 'Presentation of financial statements'.

Except for the non-compliance with IAS 1 referred to above in our opinion:

- the financial statements give a true and fair view, in accordance with International Financial Reporting Standards (IFRSs) as adopted by the European Union, of the state of the company's affairs as at 31 December 20X1 and of its profit [loss] for the year then ended; and
- the financial statements and the part of the Directors' Remuneration Report to be audited have been properly prepared in accordance with the Companies Act 1985 and, as regards the group financial statements, Article 4 of the IAS Regulation.

In our opinion the information given in the Directors' Report is consistent with the financial statements.

Emphasis of matter – Going concern

In forming our opinion, we have considered the adequacy of the disclosures made in note x to the financial statements concerning the period used by the directors in assessing whether the going concern assumption is appropriate. In making their assessment the directors have considered the period up to 30 November 20X2 which is less than 12 months from the date of the approval of the financial statements and the directors have not disclosed this fact. International Standards on Auditing (UK and Ireland) required the auditors to draw this fact to the attention of readers of the financial statements. Our opinion is not further qualified in respect of this matter.

Registered Auditors
Address
[Date]

TABLE 8:   Example adverse opinion

Adverse opinion

As explained in note x to the financial statements the company's financing arrangements expired and the amount outstanding was payable on 31 December 20X1. The company has been unable to re-negotiate or obtain replacement financing and is considering entering insolvency proceedings. These events indicate a material uncertainty which may cast significant doubt on the company's ability to continue as a going concern and therefore it may be unable to realise its assets and discharge its liabilities in the normal course of business. The financial statements (and notes thereto) do not disclose this fact and have been prepared on the going concern basis.

In our opinion, because of the omission of the information referred to above, the financial statements do not give a true and fair view, in accordance with United Kingdom Generally Accepted Accounting Practice, of the state of the company's affairs as at 31 December 20X1 and or its profit [loss] for the year then ended.

In all other respects, in our opinion the financial statements have been properly prepared in accordance with the Companies Act 1985.

Notwithstanding our adverse opinion on the financial statements, in our opinion the information given in the Directors' Report is consistent with the financial statements.

Registered Auditors
Address
[Date]

TABLE 9: **Example of disagreement over non-disclosure of going concern problems**

Qualified opinion arising from omission of information concerning going concern
The company's financing arrangements expire and amounts outstanding are payable on 19 July 20X2. The company has been unable to re-negotiate or obtain replacement financing. This situation indicates the existence of a material uncertainty which may cast significant doubt on the company's ability to continue as a going concern and therefore it may be unable to realise its assets and discharge its liabilities in the normal course of business. The financial statements (and notes thereto) do not disclose this fact.

Except for the omission of the information included in the preceding paragraph, in our opinion the financial statements:

- give a true and fair view, in accordance with United Kingdom Generally Accepted Accounting Practice, of the state of the company's affairs as at 31 December 20X1 and of its profit [loss] for the year then ended; and
- have been properly prepared in accordance with the Companies Act 1985.

In our opinion the information given in the Directors' Report is consistent with the financial statements.

Registered Auditors
Address
[Date]

TABLE 10: **Example of limitation of scope**

Basis of audit opinion
We conducted our audit in accordance with International Standards on Auditing (UK and Ireland) issued by the Auditing Practices Board, except that the scope of our work was limited as explained below.

An audit includes examination, on a test basis, of evidence relevant to the amounts and disclosures in the financial statements. It also includes an assessment of the significant estimates and judgements made by the directors in the preparation of the financial statements and of whether the accounting policies are appropriate to the company's circumstances, consistently applied and adequately disclosed.

We planned our audit so as to obtain all the information and explanations which we considered necessary in order to provide us with sufficient evidence to give reasonable assurance that the financial statements are free from material misstatement whether caused by fraud or other irregularity or error. However, the evidence available to us was limited because the company has prepared cash flow forecasts and other information needed for the assessment of the appropriateness of the going concern basis of preparation of the financial statements for a period of only nine months from the date of approval of these financial statements. We consider that the directors have not taken adequate steps to satisfy themselves that it is appropriate for them to adopt the going concern basis because the circumstances of the company and the nature of the business require that such information be prepared, and reviewed by the directors and ourselves, for a period of at least 12 months from the date of the approval of the financial statements. Had this information been available to us we might have formed a different opinion.

In forming our opinion we also evaluated the overall adequacy of the presentation of information in the financial statements.

Qualified opinion arising from limitation in audit scope
Except for any adjustments that might have been found to be necessary had we been able to obtain sufficient evidence concerning the appropriateness of the going concern basis of preparation of the financial statements, in our opinion the financial statements:

- give a true and fair view, in accordance with United Kingdom Generally Accepted Accounting Practice, of the state of the company's affairs as at 31 December 20X1 and of its profit [loss] for the year then ended; and
- have been properly prepared in accordance with the Companies Act 1985.

In respect solely of the limitation on our work relating to the assessment of the appropriateness of the going concern basis of preparation of the financial statements we have not obtained all the information and explanations that we considered necessary for the purpose of our audit.

In our opinion the information given in the Directors' Report is consistent with the financial statements.

Registered Auditors
Address
[Date]

TABLE 11: Disclaimer of opinion

Basis of audit opinion
We conducted our audit in accordance with International Standards on Auditing (UK and Ireland) issued by the Auditing Practices Board, except that the scope of our work was limited as explained below.

An audit includes examination, on a test basis, of evidence relevant to the amounts and disclosures in the financial statements. It also includes an assessment of the significant estimates and judgements made by the directors in the preparation of the financial statements and of whether the accounting policies are appropriate to the company's circumstances, consistently applied and adequately disclosed.

We planned our audit so as to obtain all the information and explanations which we considered necessary in order to provide us with sufficient evidence to give reasonable assurance that the financial statements are free from material misstatement whether caused by fraud or other irregularity or error. However, the evidence available to us to confirm the appropriateness of preparing the financial statements on the going concern basis was limited because the company has not prepared any profit or cash flow projections for an appropriate period subsequent to the balance sheet date. As a result, and in the absence of any alternative evidence available to us, we have been unable to form a view as to the applicability of the going concern basis, the circumstances of which, together with the effect on the financial statements should this basis be inappropriate, are set out in note x to the financial statements.

In forming our opinion we also evaluated the overall adequacy of the presentation of information in the financial statements.

Opinion: disclaimer on view given by financial statements
Because of the possible effect of the limitation in evidence available to us, we are unable to form an opinion as to whether the financial statements:

- give a true and fair view, in accordance with United Kingdom Generally Accepted Accounting Practice, of the state of the company's affairs as at 31 December 20X1 and of its profit [loss] for the year then ended; and
- have been properly prepared in accordance with the Companies Act 1985.

In respect solely of the limitation on our work referred to above we have not obtained all the information and explanations that we considered necessary for the purpose of our audit.

Notwithstanding our disclaimer on the view given by the financial statements, in our opinion the information given in the Directors' Report is consistent with the financial statements.

Registered Auditors
Address
[Date]

TABLE 12:   Example emphasis of matter paragraph

Emphasis of matter – Going concern

In forming our opinion, which is not qualified, we have considered the adequacy of the disclosures made in Note 1 of the financial statements concerning the company's ability to continue as a going concern. The company incurred a net loss of £x during the year ended ... and, at that date, the company's current liabilities exceeded its total assets by £y. These conditions, along with the other matters explained in note 2 to the financial statements, indicate the existence of a material uncertainty which may cast significant doubt about the company's ability to continue as a going concern. The financial statements do not include the adjustments that would result if the company was unable to continue as a going concern.

13.7   REGULATED ENTITIES

Where the entity is regulated it may be necessary to inform the regulator at an early stage of the intention to use an explanatory paragraph or qualify the audit report. This may lead to corrective action being requested by the regulator, which may serve to reduce the concerns that led to the proposal to include the explanatory paragraph or qualify the audit report.

13.8   GROUPS

The provisions of ISA (UK and Ireland) 570 apply to group financial statements as well as individual company ones. However, the going concern basis may be appropriate for a group, even though it may not be for one or more of the group companies on the grounds of materiality. Where this is the case auditors should ensure that they document their considerations, and those of the directors, fully.

13.9   PRELIMINARY ANNOUNCEMENTS

The Listing Rules of the Financial Services Authority require that the preliminary announcement of full year results include a reference to any qualification on those financial statements. The announcement should also be agreed with the auditors. Although there is no reference in these requirements to going concern, best practice suggests that auditors would not agree a preliminary statement that made no reference to significant concerns where these existed.

14 OTHER INFORMATION IN DOCUMENTS CONTAINING AUDITED FINANCIAL STATEMENTS

14.1 INTRODUCTION

Companies issue, because of legal requirement, custom or investor demand, other information as part of the annual report, which contains the audited financial statements. Some of this is interrelated to audited information while other parts of it are new. There is often confusion over the auditors' role in respect of this information.

14.2 AUDITING STANDARDS

ISA (UK and Ireland) 720 *Other information in documents containing audited financial statements* provides guidance on the auditor's consideration of other information, on which the auditor has no obligation to report, in documents containing audited financial statements. It contains standards covering:

- identification of inconsistencies;
- resolution of inconsistencies; and
- material misstatements of fact.

As with all ISAs (UK and Ireland), the text of the international ISA has been supplemented with additional guidance from a UK and Ireland perspective. The ISA (UK and Ireland) supersedes SAS 160 *Other information in documents containing audited financial statements (revised)*.

ISA (UK and Ireland) 720 is effective for audits of financial statements for periods commencing on or after 15 December 2004.

In October 2005, the APB issued an Exposure Draft of a revision to ISA (UK and Ireland) 720. The purpose of the revision was to introduce standards for the auditor's new statutory reporting responsibilities in relation to directors' reports and operating and financial reviews (OFR), taking account of changes to the UK Companies Act applicable to financial years starting on or after 1 April 2005. The ED was in three sections:

- Section A – The Auditor's Statutory Reporting Responsibility in Relation to Directors' Reports;
- Section B – The Auditor's Reporting Responsibility in Relation to Operating and Financial Reviews; and
- Section C – Other Information in Documents Containing Audited Financial Statements.

However, following an announcement by the Chancellor of the Exchequer in November 2005 that the Government was to repeal the requirement for quoted companies to publish an OFR, the APB withdrew Section B of the Exposure Draft. Sections A and C of the Exposure Draft, together with the cost assessment paper issued at the same time as the draft are discussed in **14.8** below.

The issue of a final revision to ISA (UK and Ireland) 720 is likely to be delayed following the IAASB's inclusion of the international version of ISA 720 in their clarity project (see **Chapter 1**). The APB have stated their intention to await the outcome of this project before reissuing any ISAs (UK and Ireland). The IAASB Exposure Draft issued as part of the Clarity Project in December 2006 is detailed in **14.9** below.

'Other information' is defined as the other financial and non-financial information, apart from the audited financial statements, that is contained in an entity's 'annual report' (for example, the chairman's statement, the operating and financial review, or any other financial summaries). However, it does not include other information which is released in conjunction with financial statements either of which the auditors have no knowledge or which has been issued without their consent. It does not address issues that may arise where financial information is extracted from the annual report and issued separately, or published in a different format (for example, on the Internet).

14.3   ISA (UK AND IRELAND) 720

The revised version of ISA (UK and Ireland) 720, which was published in April 2006, contains two sections:

- *Section A* 'Other Information in Documents Containing Audited Financial Statements' which applies to all 'other information' including the directors' report, and remains largely unchanged from the earlier version of the standard; and

- *Section B* 'The Auditor's Statutory Reporting Responsibility in Relation to Directors' Reports' which gives additional guidance on the requirement for auditors to report whether the information given in the directors' report is consistent with the financial statements. This requirement arose from changes to the Companies Act applicable to financial years beginning on or after 1 April 2005.

14.4 AUDITORS' RESPONSIBILITY

Auditors have a statutory responsibility to review the directors' report and, following the enactment of The Companies Act 1985 (Operating and Financial Review and Directors' Report etc) Regulations 2005, they are required to state in their report whether, in their opinion, the information given in the directors' report for the financial year for which the annual accounts are prepared is consistent with the financial statements. For periods beginning before 1 April 2005, auditors were only required to make a comment in their report if any inconsistencies existed.

To support this additional statement in their report, auditors must ensure that the documentation of their review of the directors' report includes:

- where the information in the directors' report is a direct extraction from the financial statements, agreement of the information to the financial statements;
- where the information is more detailed than that contained in the financial statements, agreement of the information to specific audit working papers or the client's financial records as appropriate;
- where the information in the directors' report has been prepared on a different basis from that in the financial statements, the documentation should include:
  - a consideration of whether there is adequate disclosure to enable an understanding of the differences between the information in the directors' report and that in the financial statements; and
  - substantive testing of the reconciliation of the information to that contained in the financial statements.

ISA (UK and Ireland) 720 goes further and requires them to read the other information to make themselves aware of any apparent misstatement and identify any material inconsistencies with the audited financial statements. Where there are material inconsistencies or misstatements the auditors should seek to resolve them as the credibility of the audited financial statements and the related auditors' report may be undermined by such inconsistencies.

It is pointed out that when auditors read the other information they should do this in the light of their knowledge acquired during the audit and it stresses that they are not required to verify any of this information but to identify any inconsistencies or significant misstatements contained in it.

The other information should be read by a senior member of the audit team who can reasonably be expected to be aware of the more important matters arising during the audit and to have a general understanding of the entity's affairs.

In certain circumstances auditors may have a statutory or contractual obligation to report on aspects of this other information. For listed companies, this would include the auditors' review of the directors' statement of compliance with the Combined Code.

14.5   AUDITORS' CONSIDERATION OF OTHER INFORMATION

ISA (UK and Ireland) 720 requires that if as a result of their consideration of any 'other information', including the director's report, they identify inconsistencies or misstatements, the auditors should consider whether an amendment should be made to either the financial statements or the other information, and aim to resolve the matter through discussions with those charged with governance.

Misstatements and inconsistencies are defined as:

- *misstatement*: when the other information is stated incorrectly or presented in a misleading manner;
- *inconsistency:* when the other information contradicts, or appears to contradict, information contained in the financial statements.

An inconsistency may give rise to doubts over the conclusions drawn from evidence previously obtained and, in turn, over the audit opinion given.

14.5.1   Misstatements

If the material misstatement of fact concerns only the other information and does not affect the financial statements themselves, the audit report will not be qualified in this respect.

If auditors become aware that a material misstatement of fact exists, they should discuss the matter with management. If management refuse to amend the other information, the auditor should consider including an emphasis of matter paragraph in their audit report, describing the material misstatement.

14.5.2 Inconsistencies

If an inconsistency is found, the auditor should determine whether the financial statements or the other information require amendment.

If the directors' report is inconsistent with the financial statements the auditors have a statutory responsibility to comment on this in their report. Matters that may require resolution or reference within the auditors' report include:

- amounts or narrative appearing in the financial statements and the directors' report;
- the bases of preparation of related items appearing in the financial statements and the directors' report, where the figures themselves are not directly comparable and the different bases are not disclosed; and
- figures contained in the financial statements and a narrative interpretation of the effect of those figures in the directors' report.

An example of the wording where the directors' report is inconsistent with the financial statements is shown in **Table 1**.

TABLE 1: Extract from auditors' report where inconsistency between financial statements and directors' report

Opinion

In our opinion the financial statements:

- give a true and fair view, in accordance with United Kingdom Generally Accepted Accounting Practice, of the state of the company's affairs as at ... and of its profit for the year then ended; and
- have been properly prepared in accordance with the Companies Act 1985.

Inconsistency between the financial statements and the directors' report

In our opinion, the information given in the seventh paragraph of the directors' report is not consistent with the financial statements. That paragraph states without amplification that 'the company's trading for the period resulted in a 10% increase in profit over the previous period's profit'. The profit and loss account, however, shows that the company's profit for the period includes a profit of £Z which did not arise from trading but arose from the disposal of assets of a discontinued operation. Without this profit on the disposal of assets, the company would have reported a profit for the year of £Y, representing a reduction in profit of 25% over the previous period's profit on a like for like basis. Except for this matter, in our opinion, the information given in the directors' report is consistent with the financial statements.

Where there are inconsistencies between other information that is not in the directors' report and the financial statements, and these misstatements or inconsistencies have not been resolved through discussion with the directors, the auditors should consider requesting the directors to consult with a qualified third party, such as the entity's lawyers.

If, subsequently, the auditors still consider an amendment is necessary to the other information and the directors refuse to make it, the auditors should consider including in the audit report an explanatory paragraph describing the apparent misstatement or material inconsistency. If the amendment is necessary in the financial statements, the auditor should express a qualified or adverse opinion.

14.5.3   Matters of fact and judgement

Auditors should consider the nature of the inconsistency or misstatement that they consider exists. A distinction may be drawn between a matter of fact and one of judgement. It is more difficult for auditors to take issue with a qualitative statement, such as the directors' view of the likely out-turn for the following year, than a factual error. However, even here there may be circumstances in which auditors are aware that the expressed view of the directors is 'significantly at variance with the entity's internal assessment or is so unreasonable as not to be credible to someone with the auditors' knowledge'. In these circumstances, the guidance suggests that auditors may need to take legal advice, including advice on whether they would be protected by qualified privilege from a defamation claim if they were to refer to the matters in their report or subsequently in a resignation statement or at the annual general meeting.

This reflects an unsatisfactory legal position in that auditors may be aware of misleading information but are unable to disclose this in public.

Auditors may also choose to make use of their entitlement to be heard at a general meeting of the company as the business of the meeting would concern them as auditors.

Where they decide to resign from the assignment, under the Companies Act 1985 they should make a statement concerning their ceasing to hold office. Even in these cases legal advice must be taken about any intended comments.

14.6   ACCESS TO INFORMATION

ISA (UK and Ireland) 720 requires that all of the other information to be approved by the entity is present before an audit opinion is expressed, and that the auditors consider all the necessary evidence. This means that timely access to the information is required and that the auditors must see all the information that is to be included in the annual report, for example, the chairman's statement before they sign and date their report.

14.7 ELECTRONIC PUBLICATION

The Companies Act 1985 (Electronic Communications) Order 2000 allows companies to meet, subject to certain conditions, their statutory reporting obligations to shareholders by distributing their annual financial statements and certain other reports electronically, or to post their financial statements on their website and advise shareholders of this. The implications for the auditor's work and report are set out in section **3.15**.

14.8 ED ISA (UK AND IRELAND) 720 (REVISED)

As noted above, the Exposure Draft of a revision to ISA (UK and Ireland) 720 was issued in three sections in October 2005. Following the Government's decision to withdraw requirements for quoted companies to publish an Operating and Financial Review, Section B of the ED was withdrawn by the APB. Sections A and C cover:

- auditors' responsibilities in relation to directors' reports; and
- other information in financial statements.

Part C, on other information, contains the text in the original version of ISA (UK and Ireland) 720.

As noted above, the publication of a final version of a revision to ISA (UK and Ireland) 720 is likely to be delayed until the completion of the IAASB's Clarity Project, of which ISA 720 is part. Further details of the IAASB's Exposure Draft are given in **14.9** below.

14.8.1 *Auditors' responsibilities in relation to directors' reports*

The Companies Act 1985 (Operating and Financial Review and Directors' Report etc) Regulations 2005 require auditors to state in their report whether, in their opinion, the information given in the directors' report for the financial year for which the annual accounts are prepared is consistent with the financial statements. Section A of the Exposure Draft deals with this requirement as well as providing guidance which is relevant to other information for which auditors are required by law or regulation to report on consistency with the financial statements.

The procedures outlined by the ED mirror those already covered in the extant ISA (UK and Ireland), which now forms Section C of the proposed revision. Auditors should:

- read the information in the directors' report and assess whether it is consistent with the financial statements;
- seek to resolve any inconsistencies;
- where inconsistencies cannot be resolved, state that fact in their audit report and give details of the inconsistency; and
- express a qualified or adverse opinion, if, in their opinion, a change is required to the financial statements and those charged with governance refuse to make this amendment.

Auditors should document the work performed in assessing consistency between the financial statements and the directors' report, and the conclusion reached.

An example wording for an auditor's report with a modified opinion on the directors' report is given in **Table 2**.

TABLE 2:   Proposed example wording for an auditor's report with a modified opinion on the directors' report

Respective responsibilities of directors and auditors
...
We report to you whether in our opinion the information given in the directors' report is consistent with the financial statements.
...
Opinion
In our opinion:
...
Material inconsistency between financial statements and the directors' report
In our opinion, the information given in the seventh paragraph of the directors' report is not consistent with the financial statements. That paragraph states without amplification that 'the company's trading for the period resulted in a 10% increase in profit over the previous period's profit'. The profit and loss account, however, shows that the company's profit for the period includes a profit of £Z which did not arise from trading but arose from the disposal of assets of a discontinued operation. Without this profit on the disposal of assets, the company would have reported a profit for the year of £Y, representing a reduction in profit of 25% over the previous period's profit on a like for like basis. Except for this matter, in our opinion, the information given in the directors' report is consistent with the financial statements.

14.8.2   Cost implications

In issuing the Exposure Draft of the revision to ISA (UK and Ireland) 720, the APB have taken the unusual step of providing an estimate of the increase in annual ongoing audit costs of the new requirements, and by supporting this estimate by the publication of a separate cost assessment paper.

Their estimate is that, for an audit usually costing £25,000, the additional requirements relating to the enhanced directors' report will cost a further £400, or 1.6% of the audit fee. This unusual move appears to be due to the fact that the DTI performed a Regulatory Impact Assessment during the development of the changes to the legislation, and the APB have extended this to consider the audit cost. Their estimates are limited, however, because of the number of variables which are included, such as:

- the amount of information in the directors' report, and the proportion of that which would be relevant to matters which have come to auditors' attention;
- the amount of disclosures which have already been substantiated by auditors;
- whether material inconsistencies are found; and
- auditor charge out rates.

Given the withdrawal of the OFR requirements, which would have made up the largest percentage of additional audit time, the value of such an estimate of cost implications is now open to question.

14.9   IAASB CLARITY PROJECT REVISION TO ISA 720

In December 2006 the IAASB issued an Exposure Draft of a revision to ISA 720 as part of its Clarity Project. There have been no major amendments to the requirements of ISA 720 other than redrafting to bring it in line with the new clarity drafting conventions and to bring any factors relevant to the audit of small entities within the text of the ISA itself rather than in International Auditing Practice Statement 1005, *The Special Considerations in the Audit of Small Entities.*

The APB has requested that interested parties in the UK submit their comments to them for inclusion in the APB response to the IAASB.

14.10   STATUTORY INSTRUMENT 2005/1101

Statutory Instrument 2005/1101 implemented a requirement for auditors to make a positive statement that the information given in the directors' report is consistent with the financial statements. This requirement applies to all financial statements for periods commencing on or after 1 April 2005.

The change in the SI necessitated amendments to the auditor's report, and these are detailed in **3.5.1**.

To support this additional statement in their report, auditors must ensure that the documentation of their review of the directors' report includes:

- where the information in the directors' report is a direct extraction from the financial statements, agreement of the information to the financial statements;
- where the information is more detailed than that contained in the financial statements, agreement of the information to specific audit working papers or the client's financial records as appropriate;
- where the information in the directors' report has been prepared on a different basis from that in the financial statements, the documentation should include:
  - a consideration of whether there is adequate disclosure to enable an understanding of the differences between the information in the directors' report and that in the financial statements; and
  - substantive testing of the reconciliation of the information to that contained in the financial statements.

Where auditors are unable to give this statement, the details of the inconsistency should be given in the opinion paragraph, see **Tables 1** and **2**.

15 CORPORATE GOVERNANCE

15.1 BACKGROUND

Corporate governance arrangements for listed companies have been subject to formal external scrutiny since the Cadbury Committee reported in 1992. Since then the Greenbury Committee focused on directors' remuneration and, subsequently, in June 1998, the Hampel Committee published its 'Combined Code'. This was derived from its own final report and those of the Cadbury and Greenbury Committees. At the same time the Stock Exchange issued an amendment to its Listing Rules regarding statements of compliance with the Combined Code.

The Stock Exchange then appended the Combined Code to the Listing Rules, although it does not form part of those Rules. From 1 May 2000, responsibility for the Listing Rules themselves, and the Combined Code, has fallen under the auspices of the Financial Services Authority. Under the Listing Rules, companies have to disclose in their Annual Report how they have applied the principles of the Code and whether or not they have complied throughout the accounting period with the best practice provisions.

Most recently, in January 2003, the Higgs and Smith reports on the role of non-executive directors and audit committees were published which proposed revisions to the Combined Code based on best practice that had developed since Hampel. This code ('the 2003 FRC Code') was published in July 2003 and is effective for reporting years beginning on or after 1 November 2003. Listed companies with year ends prior to 31 October 2004 are required to report under the 'old' Combined Code.

A review of the Turnbull Guidance was published in October 2005. *Internal Control: Revised Guidance for Directors on the Combined Code* ('Turnbull Guidance') made only a small number of changes to the original issued in 1999. The Listing Rules were amended to take account of the changes in the 2003 FRC Code, and require that the auditors review compliance with 9 out of the 45 provisions of the 2003 FRC Code. The relevant provisions of the current code on which auditors must report are set out in **Table 1**.

TABLE 1:   Provisions of the Combined Code which auditors are required to review

C1.1

The directors should explain in the annual report their responsibility for preparing the accounts and there should be a statement by the auditors about their reporting responsibilities.

C2.1

The Board should, at least annually, conduct a review of the effectiveness of the group's system of internal controls and should report to shareholders that they have done so. The review should cover all material controls, including financial, operational and compliance controls and risk management systems.

C3.1

The Board should establish an audit committee of at least three, or in the case of smaller companies two, members, who should all be independent non-executive directors. The Board should satisfy itself that at least one member of the audit committee has recent and relevant financial experience.

C3.2

The main role and responsibilities of the audit committee should be set out in written terms of reference and should include:

- to monitor the integrity of the financial statements of the company, and any formal announcements relating to the company's financial performance, reviewing significant financial reporting judgements contained in them;
- to review the company's internal financial control and, unless expressly addressed by a separate Board risk committee composed of independent directors, or by the Board itself, to review the company's internal control and risk management systems;
- to monitor and review the effectiveness of the company's internal audit function;
- to make recommendations to the Board, for it to put to the shareholders for their approval in general meeting, in relation to the appointment, reappointment and removal of the external auditors and to approve the remuneration and terms of engagement of the external auditor;
- to review and monitor the external auditor's independence and objectivity and the effectiveness of the audit process, taking into consideration relevant UK professional and regulatory requirements;
- to develop and implement policy on the engagement of the external auditor to supply non-audit services, taking into account relevant ethical guidance regarding the provision of non-audit services by the external audit firm; and to report to the Board, identifying any matters in respect of which it considers that action or improvement is needed and making recommendations as to the steps to be taken.

C3.3

The terms of reference of the audit committee, including its role and the authority delegated to it by the Board, should be made available. A separate section of the annual report should describe the work of the committee in discharging those responsibilities.

C3.4
The audit committee should review arrangements by which staff of the company may, in confidence, raise concerns about possible improprieties in matters of financial reporting or other matters. The audit committee's objective should be to ensure that arrangements are in place for the proportionate and independent investigation of such matters and for appropriate follow-up action.

C3.5
The audit committee should monitor and review the effectiveness of the internal audit activities. Where there is no internal audit function, the audit committee should consider annually whether there is a need for an internal audit function and make a recommendation to the Board, and the reasons for the absence of such a function should be explained in the relevant section of the annual report.

C3.6
The audit committee should have primary responsibility for making a recommendation on the appointment, reappointment and removal of the external auditors. If the Board does not accept the audit committee's recommendation, it should include in the annual report, and in any papers recommending appointment or reappointment, a statement from the audit committee explaining the recommendation and should set out reasons why the Board has taken a different position.

C3.7
The annual report should explain to shareholders how, if the auditors provides non-audit services, auditors' objectivity and independence is safeguarded.

The tenth verifiable 2003 FRC Code provision, C1.2 on going concern, is covered by Listing Rule (LR) 9.8.6R(3) which separately states that the going concern statement made by the directors should undergo auditor review.

The other 39 Code provisions not included in the Listing Rule 9.8.10R Requirement for review must be read by auditors to ensure that any apparent misstatements or material inconsistencies with the audited financial statements are identified and resolved. This is in line with the requirements of ISA (UK and Ireland) 720.

The Listing Rules do not specifically require auditors to report on their review of the directors' statement. In the APB's view the statement of auditors' responsibilities avoids the need for a separate report dealing with the review of corporate governance matters.

15.2 GUIDANCE

In September 2006, the APB issued Bulletin 2006/5, *The Combined Code on Corporate Governance: Requirements of Auditors Under the Listing Rules of the Financial Services Authority and the Irish Stock Exchange* to provide guidance for auditors when reviewing a company's statement made in relation to the Combined Code.

The Bulletin replaces guidance in:

- APB Bulletin 2004/3, *The Combined Code on Corporate Governance: Requirements of Auditors Under the Listing Rules of the Financial Services Authority*; and
- APB Bulletin 2004/4, *The Combined Code on Corporate Governance: Requirements of Auditors Under the Listing Rules of the Irish Stock Exchange*.

This updated guidance reflects:

- The publication of *Internal Control: Revised Guidance for Directors on the Combined Code* ('Turnbull Guidance') by the Financial Reporting Council in October 2005. However, this revised Turnbull Guidance made only a small number of changes to the original issued in 1999 and these are discussed in **15.6.3** below under the guidance on specific procedures relating to section 2.1 of the Combined Code;
- Revised listing rules published in July 2005, which changed the text of the rules, but not the substance of the requirements.

Further guidance for auditors is given in Bulletin 2002/2, *The United Kingdom Directors' Remuneration Report Regulations 2002*, which was issued following the publication of the publication of the Directors' Remuneration Report Regulations 2002 **(see 15.6.2)**.

There is additional guidance issued by the APB in July 2001 for situations where auditors are requested to perform further work on internal control procedures to issue an opinion on their effectiveness. The Briefing Paper, *Providing Assurance on the Effectiveness of Internal Control* is covered in section **15.6.1**.

In September 2002 the APB issued a briefing paper, *Effective Communication between Audit Committees and External Auditors*, to assist audit committees' understanding of the changes introduced in the updated SAS 610. The briefing paper supersedes the 1998 Briefing Paper, *Communication between External Auditors and Audit Committees*. It is considered in **15.7**.

The guidance in the briefing paper has been written primarily with regard to the audit committees of listed companies but is also of relevance to other board members of listed companies, and directors of non-listed entities. It does not cover communications between external and internal auditors.

Guidance in this area was also supplemented in 2003 and 2004 with the publication of:

- an Audit and Assurance Faculty document *The Power of Three: Understanding the roles and relationships of internal and external audits and audit committees*; and
- seven ICAEW booklets containing guidance for audit committees.

These are considered in **15.10** and **15.11** below.

15.3   TERMS OF ENGAGEMENT

Bulletin 2006/5 contains an example of suitable paragraphs to include in an engagement letter with respect to the company's compliance with the Listing Rule (LR) 9.8.10R. This is reproduced in **Table 2** below. The example terms of engagement also include the paragraphs required following the publication of the Directors' Remuneration Report Regulations 2002 and the subsequent APB Bulletin 2002/2, *The United Kingdom Directors' Remuneration Report Regulations 2002*.

TABLE 2:   Example terms of engagement

Review of the company's disclosures relating to corporate governance and going concern

Responsibilities of directors
As directors of the company you are responsible for ensuring that the company complies with the Listing Rules of the Financial Services Authority including rules LR 9.8.6R (3), (5) and (6) 'Additional information' and LR 9.8.10R 'Auditors report'.

Responsibilities of auditors
Listing Rule 9.8.10R states that a 'A listed company must ensure that the auditors review each of the following before the annual report is published:

(1) LR 9.8.6R (3) (statement by the directors that the business is a going concern); and
(2) the parts of the statement required by LR 9.8.6R (6) (corporate governance) that relate to the following provisions of the Combined Code:
  (a) C1.1;
  (b) C2.1; and
  (c) C3.1 to C3.7'

As we have agreed, we will carry out the review required of us by the Listing

---

Rules having regard to the guidance published in APB Bulletin 2006/5. We are not required to form an opinion on the company's corporate governance procedures.

Having finalised our review we expect to communicate and discuss with you the factual findings of our review.

Scope of reviews
You will provide us with such information and explanations as we consider necessary. We may request you to provide written confirmation of oral representation which you make to us during the course of our reviews. We shall request sight of all documents or statements which are due to be issued with either the statement of compliance or the going concern statement and all documentation prepared by or for the Board in support of the company's statements.

As we have agreed we will attend the meeting of the audit committee [full Board] at which the Annual Report and Accounts, including the statement of compliance, are considered and approved for submission to the Board of directors.

Internal control
With respect to Code Provision C.2.1, our work will be restricted to:

(a) assessing, based on enquiry of the directors, the supporting documentation prepared by or for the directors and our knowledge obtained during the audit of the financial statements, whether the company's summary of the process the Board (and where applicable its committees) has adopted in reviewing the effectiveness of internal control appropriately reflects that process; and

(b) assessing whether the company's disclosures of the processes it has applied to deal with material internal control aspects of any significant problems disclosed in the Annual Report and Accounts appropriately reflects those processes.

As our work is not designed to:

- consider whether the Board's statements on internal control cover all risks and controls; or
- form an opinion on the effectiveness of the company's risk and control procedures; or
- assess whether the directors' decision as to what constitutes a significant failing or weakness, or whether the actions, taken or to be taken, will in fact remedy the significant failings or weaknesses identified by the directors,

our work on internal control will not be sufficient to enable us to express any assurance as to whether or not your internal controls are effective. In addition, our financial statement audit should not be relied upon to draw to your attention matters that may be relevant to your consideration as to whether or not your system of internal control is effective.

Going concern

With respect to the company's going concern statement our work will be restricted to a consideration of whether the statement provides the disclosures required by LR 9.8.6R (3) and is not inconsistent with the information of which we are aware from our audit work on the financial statements. We will not carry out the additional work necessary to give an opinion that the company has adequate resources to continue in operational existence.

Statement of auditors' responsibilities

Code provision C.1.1 requires among other things that there should be a statement in the Annual Report about the auditors' reporting responsibilities. As we have agreed we will incorporate a full description of our reporting responsibilities in our audit report on the financial statements.

Audit of directors' remuneration disclosures

The disclosures that quoted companies are required to make with respect to directors' remuneration are specified in:

- Paragraph 1 in Part I of Schedule 6 to the Companies Act 1985; and
- Schedule 7A to the Companies Act 1985.

The disclosures specified by paragraph 1 of Part I of Schedule 6 are required to be given in notes to the annual accounts whereas the disclosures specified by Schedule 7A are required to be given in the Directors' Remuneration Report.

With respect to the disclosures specified by Schedule 7A we are only required to report on that part of the Directors' Remuneration Report which contains the information required by Part 3 of that Schedule. You have agreed that the disclosures in the Directors' Remuneration Report that are required to be audited will be clearly and unambiguously identified as such. If the disclosures are not capable of being clearly described to our satisfaction we will need to set out all the particulars that we have audited within the auditors' report.

The Companies Act requires that we include in our report any required particulars omitted by the directors if we are reasonably able to do so.

The APB does recommend that, in order to clarify auditors' responsibilities, the:

- engagement letter explains the scope of the auditors' review; and
- auditors discuss the findings of their review with those charged with governance, prior to the publication of their report.

15.4 STATEMENT OF AUDITORS' RESPONSIBILITIES

Auditors have different responsibilities for different parts of the annual report. They are required to audit the financial statements, review the company's compliance with some aspects of the Combined Code and read all information in the annual report that is not subject to any other requirement. Code provision C1.1 requires auditors to include a statement about their reporting responsibilities within the annual report. This statement may either be within their audit report or be a separate statement within the annual report. The inclusion of such a statement of reporting responsibilities aims to reduce misunderstanding about the varying level of work undertaken on different elements of an annual report (i.e., auditing, reviewing or reading).

Table 3 sets out an example responsibility statement.

TABLE 3:   Example auditors' responsibility statement

...

Respective responsibilities of directors and auditors
The directors' responsibilities ...

Our responsibility is to ...

We report to you our opinion ...

We review whether the Corporate Governance Statement reflects the company's compliance with the nine provisions of the 2003 FRC Code specified for our review by the Listing Rules of the Financial Service Authority, and we report if it does not. We are not required to consider whether the Boards' statements on internal control cover all risks and controls, or form an opinion on the effectiveness of the [company's][group's] corporate governance procedures or its risk and control procedures.

We read the other information ...

Basis of audit opinion
We conducted our audit in accordance with ...

15.5   AUDITORS' RESPONSIBILITIES FOR THE 'COMPLY OR EXPLAIN' STATEMENT

The Listing Rules require listed companies to include a two-part statement in their annual report relating to the 2003 FRC Code:

- *Part one*: explaining how the company has applied the main and supporting principles of the 2003 FRC Code;
- *Part two*: Either:
  - *Comply* – include 'a statement as to whether or not it has complied throughout the accounting period with the Code provisions set out in Section 1 of the Combined Code'; or

- *Explain* – 'A company that has not complied with the Code provisions, or complied with only some of the Code provisions or (in the case of provisions whose requirements are of a continuing nature) complied for only part of an accounting period, must specify the Code provisions with which it has not complied, and (where relevant) for what part of the period such non-compliance continued, and give reasons for any non-compliance'.

Auditors have no responsibility to assess and comment upon a company's decision to depart from the provisions of the Code. The auditor is, however, required by LR 9.8.10R(2), to review nine of the ten objectively verifiable 2003 FRC Code provisions relating to accountability and audit as set out in **Table 1**.

15.6 PROCEDURES

Bulletin 2006/5 sets out a number of general procedures relating to the auditors' review of the statement of compliance, and specific procedures relating to each 2003 FRC Code provision that is to be reviewed.

15.6.1 *General procedures*

For the code provisions within the scope of their review, auditors should obtain appropriate evidence to support the compliance statement made by the company. Procedures they may undertake include:

- reviewing Board and relevant committee meeting minutes (e.g., audit or risk management committees);
- review of supporting documents prepared for the Board or committees;
- making enquiries of the directors or company secretary about the procedures used by the company to implement the Code provisions;
- attending meetings of the audit committee at which the annual report and accounts, including the statement of compliance, are considered and approved for submission to the Board of directors; and
- requesting written confirmation of representations made by directors during the review.

15.6.2 *Non-compliance with the Code*

Where auditors discover a non-compliance with a Code provision that is within the scope of their review, they should ascertain whether adequate disclosure of the failure has been made in the directors' statement of compliance. They need not perform any additional procedures in this respect, and as long as the non-compliance has been adequately disclosed, they need not refer to it in their audit report.

If the non-compliance is not adequately disclosed, the auditors should report this in the opinion section of their report. This does not, however, give rise to a qualified audit report. An example wording is given in **Table 4**.

TABLE 4:   Example opinion paragraph where non-compliance is not adequately disclosed

Opinion
In our opinion:

- the financial statements give a true and fair view, in accordance with International Financial Reporting Standards (IFRSs) as adopted by the European Union, of the state of the company's affairs as at [date] and of its profit [loss] for the year then ended;
- the financial statements have been properly prepared in accordance with the Companies Act 1985 and Article 4 of the IAS Regulations;
- the information given in the Directors' Report is consistent with the financial statements.

Other matter
We have reviewed the Board's statement of compliance with the Combined Code set out on page [x] of the annual report. In our opinion, the Board's comments concerning [...] do not appropriately reflect our understanding of the process undertaken by the Board because [...].

15.6.3   Specific procedures – the nine verifiable code provisions

Responsibilities of directors and auditors (2003 FRC Code provision C1.1)
Changes from old Hampel Code
2003 FRC Code provision C1.1 is the same as old code provision D.1.1 except for the addition of the words 'in the annual report'. The change is for clarification alone and has no impact on the auditors' responsibilities.

Directors' responsibilities
Auditors should ensure that the directors' responsibility for preparing the accounts is explained in the annual report.

Auditors' responsibilities
Auditors have responsibilities to audit, review or read different parts of the annual report. These should be clarified by inclusion of a statement of auditors' responsibilities in the audit report or as a separate statement (see **Table 3**) and by inclusion of a paragraph in the engagement letter (see **Table 2**).

Internal Control (2003 FRC Code provision C2.1)
Changes from old Hampel Code
Provision C2.1 is substantially the same as old provision D.2.1, except for the clarification that the review should cover all 'material' controls.

Under the revision to the Turnbull Guidance issued in October 2005 boards were additionally recommended to 'confirm that necessary actions have been or are being taken to remedy any significant failings or weaknesses identified from [their review of the effectiveness of the system of internal control]' in their statement on internal control.

Auditors' responsibilities with respect to the directors' narrative statement
The annual report will contain a narrative statement about how the company has applied Code principle C2.1. This should, as a minimum, disclose that there is an ongoing process for identifying, evaluating and managing the significant risks faced by the company that is regularly reviewed by the Board. This statement is likely to vary significantly from company to company.

Auditors have no responsibility to review this narrative statement, but are expected to read it in line with the requirements of ISA (UK and Ireland) 720 to ensure that there are no apparent misstatements or inconsistencies with the audited financial statements.

However, in relation to the additional recommendation that the Board should confirm that actions have been or are being taken to remedy significant weaknesses, Bulletin 2006/5 recommends that auditors:

- review the documentation prepared to support the Board's statement in relation to any significant failings or weaknesses and consider whether or not this documentation provides sound support for the Board's statement;
- discuss actions already taken or about to be taken with directors; and
- consider the statement made in relation to their knowledge of the company obtained during the audit of the financial statements. This would include whether the directors have considered any material weaknesses in internal control reported to those charged with governance in accordance with ISA (UK and Ireland) 260 (see **Chapter 9**).

Auditors are not required, however, to assess the Board's decision as to what constitutes a 'significant' failing or weakness or whether the actions taken or planned will actually remedy the failure identified.

Auditors' review of compliance
Auditors are, as part of their review, required to assess whether the summary of the process given by the Board is supported by documentation

and reflects the actual process that took place. Auditors' procedures will include:

- discussing the process used with the directors and comparing the understanding this provides with the statement made in the annual report;
- reviewing the documentation connected with the process and considering whether it supports the statement; and
- considering whether the statement is reasonable given the knowledge gained about the company during the audit of the financial statements.

Auditors should also consider whether the directors' statement covers the year under review and the period to the date of approval of the annual report and accounts, as recommended by the Turnbull guidance.

As their knowledge of the client is narrower than the directors', auditors are not expected to assess whether all risks and controls have been addressed or that risks are satisfactorily addressed by internal controls. However, if auditors discover a material weakness in internal control as part of their audit work, they should report it to those charged with governance as soon as possible so that it can be considered as part of the statement on internal control.

Significant problems in the annual report

The Turnbull guidance recommends that the internal control aspects of any 'significant problems' disclosed in the annual report and accounts are discussed in the Board's statement. Unfortunately, the term 'significant problem' is not defined, and in practice this is likely to be highly subjective and include both financial and non-financial items.

Auditors have a responsibility to:

- discuss the steps the directors have taken to identify 'significant problems' disclosed in the annual report and accounts; and
- assess whether the narrative disclosure of the process applied to deal with any internal control aspects of these problems is an appropriate reflection of the actual process undertaken.

If auditors are aware of a significant problem in the annual report and accounts which has not been considered in the statement this should be brought to the attention of the directors. If the matter cannot be resolved, auditors should consider whether there is an impact on their report.

Failure to conduct a review

LR 9.8.6R (6)(b) requires the company to disclose if the Board has failed to conduct a review of the effectiveness of internal control. Auditors should consider whether this recommendation is met and whether the explanation given for the failure is consistent with their understanding.

Groups of companies

The review of effectiveness of internal control should be from a group perspective and where material joint ventures and associated companies have been excluded this fact should be disclosed. Using their knowledge of the client, auditors should assess whether any material joint ventures or associated companies have been excluded.

Non-executive Directors (2003 FRC Code provision C3.1)

Changes from old Hampel Code

The main changes from old Code provision D.3.1 are:

- the reference to an audit committee of at least two members for smaller companies. A smaller company is one that is below the FTSE 350 throughout the year immediately prior to the reporting year;
- that all of the members of the audit committee should be independent and not just that a majority of the members should be independent; and that
- the Board should satisfy itself that at least one member of the audit committee has recent and relevant financial experience.

Auditors' procedures

The Bulletin recommends that auditors should:

- check the number of members of the audit committee complies with the Code requirements (at least three members, or two for smaller companies);
- obtain an understanding of the process used by the Board to determine:
  - if the audit committee are all independent non-executive directors; and
  - that at least one member of the audit committee has recent and relevant financial experience; and
- review evidence, such as minutes and other documentation, to support the above.

Auditors are not responsible for determining whether the directors are independent or whether a particular audit committee member has the relevant financial experience. However, if they have doubts over either of these areas, they should be communicated to the audit committee and Board.

Audit Committee (2003 FRC Code provision C3.2)

Changes from old Hampel Code

2003 FRC Code C3.2 provides additional detail to that in the old Code provision D.3.2 on the main role and responsibilities of the audit committee.

Auditors' procedure
The Bulletin recommends that auditors should obtain a copy of the terms of reference of the audit committee and review whether the roles and responsibilities described therein reflect the recommendations of 2003 FRC Code provision C3.2.

Auditors are not responsible for considering whether the audit committee has fulfilled its roles and responsibilities.

Audit Committee Terms of Reference (2003 FRC Code provision C3.3)
Changes from old Hampel Code
This is an additional review responsibility for auditors.

Auditors' procedures
Auditors should review whether:

- the terms of reference for the audit committee are posted on the company's website or otherwise made readily available; and
- a description of the work performed by the audit committee is included in a separate section of the annual report, and is not materially inconsistent with the information that the auditor has obtained in the course of their audit work.

Raising Staff Concerns (2003 FRC Code provision C3.4)
Changes from old Hampel Code
This is an additional review responsibility for auditors.

Auditors' procedures
Auditors should review:

- supporting documentation to determine whether there is evidence that the audit committee has reviewed the arrangements and discuss the review with staff as necessary; and
- documentation supporting the company's arrangements for 'proportionate and independent' investigations.

Auditors are not responsible for considering whether the arrangements do allow 'proportionate and independent' investigations or whether follow-up action is appropriate, but rather should review the process undertaken to assure the audit committee that this is the case.

Internal Audit (2003 FRC Code provision C3.5)
Changes from old Hampel Code
This is an additional review responsibility for auditors.

Auditors' procedures
The Bulletin states that auditors should perform the following procedures:

- hold discussions with the audit committee chairman and review supporting documentation to establish that the effectiveness of any internal audit function has been monitored and reviewed;
- where no internal audit function exists, review whether:
  - the audit committee has considered the need for an internal audit function;
  - there is documentation that this recommendation has been made to the Board; and
  - the reasons for not having an internal audit function are included in the relevant section of the annual report.

The auditor is not responsible for considering whether the internal audit function is effective or whether the reasons disclosed in the annual report for not having an internal audit function are reasonable.

Appointment, Reappointment and Removal of the External Auditor (2003 FRC Code provision C3.6)
Changes from old Hampel Code
This is an additional review responsibility for auditors.

Auditors' procedures
Auditors should:

- review the terms of reference of the audit committee, or other documentation, to ensure that the audit committee has primary responsibility for making a recommendation on the appointment, reappointment and removal of auditors;
- review documentation of the audit committee's recommendation to the Board;
- where the Board has not accepted the audit committee's recommendation, review the annual report and any papers recommending appointment or reappointment of the auditors, to ensure inclusion of:
  - a statement from the audit committee explaining its recommendation; and
  - a statement from the Board setting out reasons why they have taken a different position from that recommended by the audit committee.

Non-audit activities (2003 FRC Code provision C3.7)
Changes from old Hampel Code
This is an additional review responsibility for auditors.

Auditors' procedures
The Bulletin recommends that auditors should review whether the annual report includes a statement explaining how the objectivity and independence of the auditor is safeguarded if they provide non-audit services. Auditors should consider this statement and:

- notify the audit committee and Board if the audit committee has not fulfilled its responsibilities to review and monitor the independence and objectivity of the external auditor and to develop and implement policy on the engagement of the external auditors to supply non-audit services; and
- consider the requirements of ISA (UK and Ireland) 720 in relation to other information issued with audited financial statements if they believe the explanation is misleading. This will involve attempting to resolve differences with the Board, and considering the implications for their report if they are not able to do so.

15.6.4   *Going concern*

The requirement for directors to report that the business is a going concern is set out in 2003 FRC Code provision C1.2. This provision is identical to the corresponding one in the old Hampel Code. This provision is not included in the list of nine verifiable code provisions because LR 9.8.6R(3) requires the directors of all companies incorporated in the United Kingdom to include in the annual report and accounts a statement that:

> 'the business is a going concern with supporting assumptions or qualification as necessary, as interpreted by the Guidance on Going Concern and Financial Reporting for directors of listed companies..., published in November 1994; such statement to be reviewed by the auditors before publication'.

Auditors' procedures
The Bulletin recommends that auditors assess:

- the consistency of the directors' going concern statement with their knowledge of the client obtained during the course of the audit; and
- whether the directors' statement meets the disclosure requirements of the guidance for directors referred to in LR 9.8.6R(3) (see above).

Paragraph 49 of that guidance for directors dealing with going concern suggests the following wording where the going concern assumption is appropriate:

> 'After making enquiries, the directors have a reasonable expectation that the company has adequate resources to continue in operational existence for the foreseeable future. For this reason, they continue to adopt the going concern basis in preparing the accounts'.

Auditors do not review this statement to express an opinion on the ability of the company to continue in operational existence and do not undertake any procedures to support such an opinion. In addition, they do not assess or report on any of the other requirements of the guidance for directors mentioned in the Listing Rule.

15.7 OTHER DISCLOSURES

ISA (UK and Ireland) 720 sets out the auditors' responsibilities in relation to other information in documents containing audited financial statements. This other information will include the 2003 FRC Code disclosures.

These Auditing Standards require that where there is an inconsistency between the audited financial statements and the 2003 FRC Code disclosures, the auditors determine which needs to be amended and seek to resolve the matter with those charged with governance.

If an amendment is needed to the audited financial statements and the entity refuses to make the amendment, auditors express a qualified or adverse opinion on the financial statements.

If an amendment is needed to the 2003 FRC Code disclosures and the entity refuses to make the amendment, the auditors consider including an emphasis of matter paragraph describing the material inconsistency in their report.

If, rather than an inconsistency, the auditors identify a material misstatement of fact in the 2003 FRC Code disclosures they discuss the matter with those charged with governance. The auditors may request that the advice of a qualified third party, such as the entity's legal counsel, is consulted. If the auditors conclude that the disclosures should be amended, but the entity refuses to make that amendment, auditors should include in their report an emphasis of matter paragraph describing the material misstatement.

15.8 OTHER MATTERS

15.8.1 *Assurance on internal control*

In March 1998 the APB issued a consultative document *Providing Assurance on Internal Control*, which proposes a framework for auditors to report privately to directors on internal controls. This follows a recommendation of the Hampel Committee that reports on internal controls should be private, rather than public, as this 'allows for an effective dialogue to take place and for best practice to evolve'.

The paper proposes eight 'basic principles', which the APB believes 'are applicable to all engagements involving the provision of assurance on internal control matters by reporting accountants'. These are shown in **Table 5** below.

The paper continues by providing example reports for both limited scope controls opinion engagements, such as those made by custodians' auditors (see **42.14.1**) and controls opinion engagements. Where the latter is performed, five 'additional basic principles' are proposed as shown in **Table 6**.

One of the examples given in the paper of a 'controls opinion' engagement is where reporting accountants report on the process undertaken by management in making an assertion regarding the adequacy of internal control. Such a report may be requested by audit committees to support their corporate governance disclosures concerning internal controls. The suggested report is shown in **Table 7**. It highlights that the reporting accountants are commenting on the process rather than the design, adequacy or effectiveness of the underlying internal controls.

TABLE 5:   Basic principles for engagements providing assurance on internal control

The reporting accountants should:

- together with the appointing party, agree on the objective of the engagement and the nature of the assurance to be provided (i.e., issue an engagement letter);
- ensure that staff used on the engagement possess the necessary skills and experience;
- only allow reports that provide assurance on internal control to be included in documents containing other information when such other information is not in conflict with the matters covered by their report and they have no cause to believe it to be misleading;
- plan and conduct an engagement to provide assurance on internal control with an attitude of professional scepticism;
- obtain sufficient appropriate evidence on which to base the opinions expressed in their report;
- express a clear opinion about the subject matter in their report;
- include in their report:
  - the addressee;
  - a description of the engagement including identification of the subject matter;
  - an identification of the party responsible for the subject matter and a statement setting out the respective responsibilities of the responsible party and the reporting accountants;
  - identification of the standards under which the engagement was conducted;
  - their opinion;
  - the date;
  - their name;
- express a clear reservation or denial of opinion when they are unable to obtain sufficient appropriate evidence to support the assurance that the appointing party is seeking.

TABLE 6:   Additional basic principles for controls opinion engagements

- reporting accountants should make a preliminary assessment to establish whether there is a reasonable basis for believing that assurance based on criteria can be established;
- the engagement letter should refer to the criteria or control objectives to be used for evaluating the subject matter;
- in conducting the engagement the reporting accountants should confirm their preliminary assessment that the criteria are suitable for evaluating the subject matter;
- reporting accountants should assess what would constitute a reportable deficiency when both planning and conducting an engagement in order to reduce the risk of expressing an inappropriate opinion;
- the reporting accountants' report should identify the suitable criteria or control objectives used by the reporting accountants.

TABLE 7:   Report concerning management process

To the Audit Committee of XYZ plc
The objective of this engagement is to report on whether the process followed by the directors in making their assertion (included on page ... of the XYZ plc Annual Report) concerning the system of internal control for the year ended 31 December 20... constitutes due and careful enquiry. The directors of the company are responsible for maintaining an adequate system of internal control.

Our responsibility is to express an opinion as to whether the directors' process constitutes due and careful enquiry sufficient for them to make the statement set out on page ... under the 'criteria for effectiveness' described in 'Internal control and financial reporting' issued by the Internal Control Working Group. This opinion is based on the evidence we obtained, that evidence being persuasive rather than conclusive in nature. In accordance with the terms of our engagement we have not examined either the design of the system of internal control or its operational adequacy. Accordingly we neither express nor imply opinions on any aspect of the company's system of internal control, other than the evaluation process undertaken by the directors.

This engagement has been undertaken in accordance with the United Kingdom Auditing Practices Board's [insert title of guidance yet to be decided] and accordingly included such procedures as we considered necessary in the circumstances.

In our opinion the directors have made their assertion concerning the system of internal control, referred to above, after due and careful enquiry.

Reporting Accountants
Address
Date

15.8.2   *Directors' remuneration*

Specific disclosure requirements were added to the Listing Rules regarding directors' remuneration as a result of the Greenbury Report and these have been incorporated into the Combined Code. The board of directors should report on:

- a statement of the company's policy on executive remuneration;
- the amount of each element in the remuneration package of each director by name, including basic salary, bonuses and benefits in kind;
- information on share options for each director;
- details of other long-term incentive schemes;
- details of elements of remuneration which are pensionable, other than basic salary; and
- information on directors' service contracts with notice periods in excess of one year and the unexpired term of any service contract of a director who is seeking re-election at the forthcoming annual general meeting.

The second, third, fourth and fifth points are to be audited and if the company has not provided the information the auditors should provide it, so far as they are able, in their report on the annual financial statements.

Most recently, in August 2002, The Directors Remuneration Report Regulations (SI 2002 No. 1986) received royal assent. These require directors to publish an annual Remuneration Report containing detailed narrative and numerical disclosures on directors' remuneration. The numerical disclosures must be audited. This applies for financial years ending on or after 31 December 2002.

Scope of auditors' work

Bulletins 2002/2 and 2004/3 note that auditors' work is limited to examining the specified disclosures of individual directors' remuneration contained within the Listing Rule and the corresponding Companies Act disclosures. In general, there should be little difficulty in carrying out appropriate procedures but the auditors may need to liaise with the company's pension advisers with regard to the disclosures concerning the valuation of pension benefits.

Where companies choose to disclose 'sufficient information to enable a reasonable assessment to be made of the values of the increase in accrued pension', auditors will need to assess whether there is any relevant information which will significantly affect the value of the benefits. When both considering the need for, and the audit of, such disclosures the APB recommend that auditors only take into account information of which they are aware from:

- their normal audit work on the financial statements; and
- reasonable enquiry of the directors and the company's pension advisers.

There is no statutory requirement to audit or review the narrative disclosures. However, Bulletin 2002/2 notes the requirement for auditors to read such 'other information' and if they become aware of any apparent misstatements or identify material inconsistencies with the financial statements to seek to resolve them with the directors.

Auditors' report
Bulletin 2002/2 stresses the importance of making sure that the information that forms the auditable part of the Remuneration Report is clearly distinguished from the unaudited part. It suggests that this be communicated to directors in the letter of engagement (see **15.3** above).

The Bulletin suggests that directors should be encouraged to clearly mark the disclosures that have been audited. If this is not done to their satisfaction, auditors should set out the particulars that have been audited within their audit report. **Table 12** in **Chapter 3** provides an example of an audit report for a quoted company where the auditable part of the remuneration report has been adequately distinguished from the unaudited part.

There is no requirement to report positively on the disclosures required by the Listing Rules or Schedule 7A. Where the disclosures do not comply with the Listing Rules, the auditors must state this in their report and provide the disclosures where they are reasonably able Although the disclosures required by Schedule 7A are very similar to those required by the Listing Rules, they are not identical. Therefore it is possible for a company to comply with the Act, but not the Listing Rules. However, all of the disclosures in the Listing Rules that the auditors must review are also disclosable and auditable under Schedule 7A. Unlike under the previous regime, a situation should not arise where the accounts give a true and fair view but do not give the disclosures required by the Listing Rules.

As set out in APB Bulletin 2001/2 (see **Chapter 3**) reference in any audit report to 'the Listing Rules of the Financial Services Authority' may be replaced by 'the Listing Rules of the United Kingdom Listing Authority'.

15.8.3 Independent non-executives

As there is no precise definition of independence in respect of a non-executive director in the Combined Code, the Bulletin recommends that auditors should only establish that:

- an audit committee has been formed;
- the audit committee has written terms of reference; and
- the majority of members of the committee are independent non-executives as identified in the Annual Report.

The Bulletin notes that it is not for the auditors to consider whether directors are properly described as 'independent' non-executives.

The Code proposed by Higgs states that it is the responsibility of the Board as a whole to determine who is and who is not independent. It lists circumstances and relationships which could affect, or appear to affect, the directors' judgement.

15.8.4   Other matters

In addition to the specific audit procedures, auditors should read the entire statement of compliance (not just the specific paragraphs upon which they report) to ensure that the statement is consistent with their knowledge of the company. This should not involve actively searching for other matters that have not been properly disclosed in the compliance statement. However, if as a result of their review or as a result of their audit of the financial statements they have identified a non-compliance that has not been properly disclosed, they should request the directors to amend the compliance statement accordingly.

15.9   COMMUNICATION BETWEEN EXTERNAL AUDITORS AND AUDIT COMMITTEES

The Auditing Practices Board sees communication between external auditors and audit committees as an important element of corporate governance and in June 1998 issued an Audit Briefing Paper on the subject. The paper covers:

- understanding the audit committee role;
- designing communication to complement the audit committee role;
- communicating plans for conducting the audit;
- private communication between the auditor and audit committee; and
- communicating audit findings.

15.9.1   Understanding the audit committee role

The scope of these will differ depending on the terms of reference. The role will normally include:

- challenging management in respect of the financial reporting process;
- monitoring management's commitment to a sound control environment and a satisfactory system of internal control; and
- considering the arrangements for external audit and supporting the external auditors.

15.9.2 Designing communication to complement the audit committee role

Auditors should be frank and unambiguous in their communication with the audit committee. They should not play down sensitive issues and should ensure that all relevant and significant issues are brought to the committee and openly discussed. Reports to the committee should enable its members to assess management's response to issues raised.

Sometimes it may be necessary to bypass the management when direct contact with the audit committee may be a means of 'anticipating and facilitating the resolution of potentially contentious situations'. However, auditors should also beware treating communicating with the audit committee as satisfying their obligation to communicate certain matters to the full Board.

15.9.3 Communicating plans for conducting the audit

Auditors should discuss with the audit committee prior to the audit matters such as the nature and scope of the audit, the planned methods for carrying it out (covering such matters as the role of internal audit), the fees and the extent of other services provided.

15.9.4 Private communication between the auditors and audit committee

This may be required to discuss:

- observations on the overall control consciousness and operating style of management;
- the state of relationships between the auditors and management; and
- observations on the extent to which the spirit of good corporate governance is followed.

15.9.5 Communicating audit findings

At the completion of the audit, the auditors' discussion with the audit committee should cover:

- all matters on which they are required by regulation or standard to report, for example, actual instances of non-compliance with law or regulation discovered in their audit;
- the control environment;
- any differences between the auditors and management and how these have been resolved;
- significant adjustments made to the financial statements and any unadjusted amounts; and

- observations on other information to be published with the statements.

The auditors may also wish to discuss other matters such as presentation issues in respect of the Annual Report, operational and business risks and, in the public sector, findings in respect of regularity, value for money and probity.

15.10 PROVIDING ASSURANCE ON INTERNAL CONTROL

15.10.1 Background

As discussed in **15.5**, auditors of fully listed companies are required to review their clients' compliance with provision C2.1 of the combined code. The procedures that auditors perform to support the review required by the Listing Rules are considerably narrower in scope than those that would be required to provide assurance on the effectiveness of internal control. Indeed, audit reports of fully listed companies make it clear that the auditors' responsibilities do not extend to considering whether the Board's statements on internal control cover all risks and controls, or to forming an opinion on the effectiveness of corporate governance or risk and control procedures.

However, auditors may be engaged, separately from the statutory audit, to report on such matters. There is increasing interest, not only from capital markets but also from regulators, in the effectiveness of companies' systems of internal control. There is therefore an expectation that greater demand will develop for either external or internal auditors to provide assurance on internal control. To contribute to developing a model of how practitioners might be able to express assurance on the reliability of internal control systems the APB published a Briefing Paper in July 2001 entitled *Providing Assurance on the Effectiveness of Internal Control*.

15.10.2 Framework

The paper sets out a framework for forming an opinion on the effectiveness of internal control, identifying the following three key processes that management undertakes in order to establish an effective system of internal control:

- risk identification and assessment, which is based on an understanding of the entity's business objectives;
- the design of the system of internal control, based on a knowledge of the applicable risks;
- system evaluation, to determine that the system actually operates in accordance with the system description.

The framework is reproduced in **Table 8**.

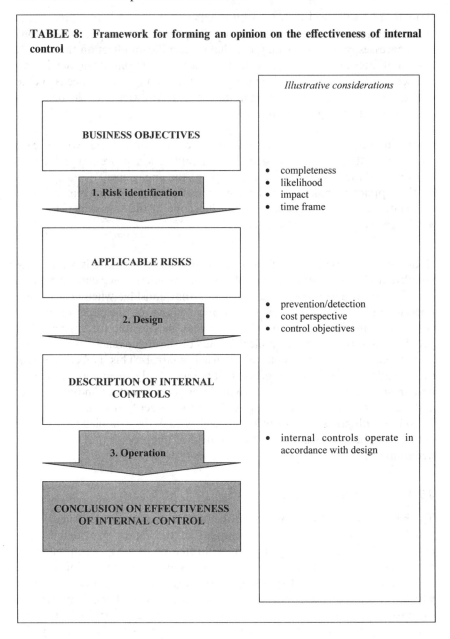

TABLE 8: Framework for forming an opinion on the effectiveness of internal control

Illustrative considerations

BUSINESS OBJECTIVES

1. Risk identification

- completeness
- likelihood
- impact
- time frame

APPLICABLE RISKS

2. Design

- prevention/detection
- cost perspective
- control objectives

DESCRIPTION OF INTERNAL CONTROLS

3. Operation

- internal controls operate in accordance with design

CONCLUSION ON EFFECTIVENESS OF INTERNAL CONTROL

The framework illustrates the management processes which practitioners will assess when engaged to provide assurance on the effectiveness of internal control.

15.10.3   Providing assurance

Practitioners will need to have a knowledge of the entity's business that is sufficient to enable them to identify and understand the events, transactions and processes that may, or ought to, have a significant effect on the entity's system of internal control. The extent of knowledge required will depend on the scope of each individual engagement. Depending on the needs of the entity, the starting point (other than the requisite knowledge of the business) of a particular engagement may be:

- the description of the system of internal control (in which case consideration of management's risk identification process and internal control design is not within the scope of the engagement);
- the 'applicable risks' (in which case consideration of management's risk identification process is not within the scope of the engagement); or
- the entity's business objectives.

If the entity's description of its system of internal control is sufficiently detailed, auditors are likely to be able to gather sufficient evidence to express a high level of assurance on engagements that consider whether a system operated in accordance with that description. However, the paper recognises that only a moderate level of assurance may be possible for engagements providing assurance on the applicable risks or the effectiveness of the design and operation of the system of internal control. This is because risk identification and assessment processes are highly judgemental as companies and their internal control needs will differ as a result of industry, size, culture and management philosophy. Therefore practitioners are unlikely to be able to obtain sufficient evidence concerning the completeness of the entity's 'applicable risks' or the effectiveness of the process that was used to determine them.

15.10.4   Narrative reports

The paper makes it clear that the scope of a control assurance engagement will have a large impact on the content of the report provided by the auditor. It is anticipated that reports will often be lengthy to communicate accurately to the addressee the various judgements the practitioners have made, the reasoning underpinning those judgements, and the context in which the opinion is given. There is a danger that short form reports expressing an assurance opinion that internal controls are 'effective' or 'adequate' will lead to misunderstandings and are not advocated by the paper.

An example of a narrative report providing assurance on the effectiveness of internal control is set out in **Table 9**. The example should be carefully tailored depending on the requirements of the engaging party and is not intended to be authoritative.

TABLE 9: **Illustration of a narrative report providing assurance on the effectiveness of internal control**

Date
The Audit Committee
XYZ Limited

Dear Sirs

Effectiveness of internal controls relating to the advertising revenues of XYZ Limited
In accordance with the arrangements set out in our letter dated ..., we are writing to summarise the outcome of our work in assessing the effectiveness of internal controls relating to the advertising revenues of XYZ Limited during the period ... to .... A separate report submitted to senior management contains a full description of the design of the system of internal control which, in the interests of brevity, has been excluded from this report.

Scope of the Engagement
Included in the scope of our engagement were the processes relating to:

• maintaining XYZ's competitiveness by keeping current with the advertisement presentation styles of its competitors;
• the booking in and recording of advertisements;
• the accuracy and timeliness of the inclusion of advertisements in the newspapers published by XYZ Limited;
• adherence of the advertisements to XYZ's 'Code of publication values';
• the processing of the related advertising revenues to the general ledger and the management accounts; and
• the collection and banking of cash and the recording of cash receipts.

As agreed we have not assessed the systems that control bank payments or the onward reporting and summarisation of general ledger information into either the management or statutory accounts.

Inherent Limitations of the Engagement
There are inherent limitations as to what can be achieved by internal control and consequently limitations to the conclusions that can be drawn from this engagement. These limitations include the possibility of faulty judgement in decision making, of breakdowns because of human error, of control activities being circumvented by the collusion of two or more people and of management overriding controls. Also there is no certainty that internal controls will continue to operate effectively in future periods or that the controls will be adequate to mitigate all significant risks which may arise in future. Accordingly we express no opinion about the adequacy of the system of internal control to mitigate future risk.

Companies and their internal control needs differ by industry, size, culture and management philosophy. When designing a system of internal control there are many options as to the nature and extent of controls that may be implemented. Internal controls, for example, may be preventive or detective in nature and may be performed by people or by information technology systems. There is a balance to be achieved between the cost of implementation of controls and the identified benefits derived from the controls. Consequently one company's internal controls system may be very different from another's in relation to similar business processes.

Decisions made in designing internal controls inevitably involve the acceptance of some degree of risk. As the outcome of the operation of internal controls cannot be predicted with absolute assurance any assessment of internal control is very judgemental.

Business Objectives
We discussed the business and control objectives of XYZ Limited relating to advertising revenues with the executive directors and senior management and understand them to be:

- to maximise revenues from advertisements placed in XYZ Limited newspapers by ensuring that the presentation of advertisements keeps pace with developments at its competitors, but without incurring the expense of being the brand leader;
- to ensure that all advertisements booked by customers are published accurately in accordance with each advertiser's requirements;
- to ensure that all advertisements placed in newspapers are invoiced in accordance with the appropriate rate card;
- to accept that a proportion of revenues may not be collectible as a result of credit risk, but given the low marginal cost of advertisements being published, to accept a level of uncollectible revenue of up to 2.5% of total revenue as a feature of the business;
- to ensure that the textual and pictorial content of advertisements adhere to XYZ's 'Code of publication values';
- to ensure that XYZ Limited is able to receive and process advertisements even when its computer systems are unavailable.

Work Performed
We performed our work during the period [date] to [date].

Our assessment of the effectiveness of internal controls was divided into four phases:

- understanding the business and management's business objectives in controlling advertising revenues;
- reviewing management's embedded risk identification processes and observing management's risk screening process that is intended to identify those risks (the 'applicable risks') that represent both a significant and likely risk to the business;
- assessing the effectiveness of the design of controls intended to control the applicable risks;
- testing the effectiveness of the operation of those controls during the period [date] to [date].

Understanding the business
To provide the necessary background information to carry out the engagement we obtained an understanding of the following:

- the trends in the financial results of the business, and the key performance measures used by management, together with comparisons to similar businesses;
- the systems used to process transactions and produce management information.

We also obtained an understanding of the background to the business, including its people, customers, suppliers and competitors, the key business processes and the current business environment.

Risk identification
We assessed both the effectiveness and results of management's ongoing processes for identifying and managing risks. This included obtaining an understanding of the overall control environment, the key performance measures used by management and management's processes designed to identify emerging risks.

Using these assessments and this background information about the business, we reviewed the adequacy of the listing of potential risks identified by management. The potential risks identified are set out in an appendix to this letter.

Risk screening
Risk screening is a process whereby all of the potential risks are evaluated by management, based on their assessment of the likelihood of the risk occurring and the potential impact of the risk. Risks meeting certain criteria are deemed to be applicable risks. The screening process was organised and facilitated by consultants skilled in this field. We observed and participated in risk screening meetings held at each division.

The process of risk screening involves a significant degree of judgement and the culmination of the process was the final screening meeting with the executive directors, which the audit committee also attended, on [date]. This meeting considered:

- the potential risks previously identified by line management and the executive directors;
- whether there were other risks requiring consideration;
- the likelihood and significance of each potential risk.

Risks were screened out from further consideration if they met one of the following three criteria:

- if the effect of the risk is capable of being quantified and its direct financial effect was less than a materiality level of £x;
- if an appropriate risk management strategy such as insurance effectively mitigates the risk;
- based on judgemental assessments of the likelihood and possible

significance of the risk, if it was judged to be either unlikely to occur or not of high significance.

The detailed results of this screening process are set out in the appendix to this letter. This shows the risks identified, the results of the screening process and the reasons why risks were screened out from further consideration.

This resulted in the following list of applicable risks:

- the risk that advertising revenue may not be maximised because of a failure to monitor developments by competitors in the presentation of advertisements;
- the risk that advertisements may be published that do not meet XYZ's 'Code of publication values';
- the risk of inaccurate transfer of data between the editorial and billing system, and hence of incomplete billings;
- the risk that cheque receipts are not properly banked or are misappropriated;
- the risk that cash received at the front desk is not passed to the cashiers or is misappropriated;
- the risk that the editorial and billing systems are not available.

The risk screening processes were initially undertaken in [date]. During the period to [date] we updated our understanding of the business and its processes for any indications that there may be changes which would indicate that risks previously screened required more consideration, or for indications of new risks.

We have not considered the impact on the risks to the business arising from the changes in sales ledger and general ledger systems implemented in [date] and the associated personnel changes.

Controls designed to mitigate applicable risks
We assessed the design of the internal controls relating to each applicable risk. These controls comprise:

- specific controls – relating to the processing of individual transactions;
- pervasive controls – relating to the processing environment, access to systems, quality and training of personnel, physical safeguards etc.;
- monitoring controls – relating to performance of key reconciliations of account balances, management oversight of the key performance measures and other monitoring procedures.

For each individual applicable risk we assessed the effectiveness of the design of the specific, pervasive and monitoring controls. Apart from the exceptions described below, in all cases, we concluded that the controls were effectively designed. Details of the design of the internal controls relating to the applicable risks are set out in the report that we have previously sent to senior management.

Operation of controls
We tested whether the controls operated in accordance with their design during

the period [date] to [date]. These tests consisted of reviewing evidence of the application of the controls, discussion with key personnel and evaluating the integrity of the information used to perform the controls. We did not test those specific controls where we found that both the related pervasive and monitoring controls were operating effectively.

Exceptions arising
Our work indicated that there were adequate controls over five of the six applicable risks. In the case of the risk relating to the availability of the editorial and billing systems we found that XYZ Limited does not have an appropriate plan in place to enable it to continue operating if these systems are not available. Whilst there have been no incidences of any problems arising in the period [date] to [date], we strongly recommend that management should develop and test a detailed plan for continuing operations in the event of a failure of these computer systems.

Conclusions
Our conclusions in relation to the internal controls over advertising revenue processing at XYZ Limited in the period [date] to [date] are as follows:

During the course of our work, as described above, nothing came to our attention to indicate that there are any risks, other than the applicable risks detailed in the section on risk screening above, that we consider should have been assessed as both likely to arise and having high impact.

In our opinion:

- except for the risk of non-availability of the editorial and billing systems, the design of the controls related to the applicable risks were in all cases effective to mitigate the applicable risks to an acceptable level;
- the monitoring and pervasive controls identified which related to the applicable risks (and which are described in the detailed report sent to management) were in all cases operating effectively during the period [date] to [date].

Limitation of use
This report is for the internal use of XYZ Limited only. It should not be made available to any third party without our prior written consent. We accept no responsibility to any other party who may gain access to this report.

Yours faithfully

15.11 EFFECTIVE COMMUNICATION BETWEEN AUDIT COMMITTEES AND EXTERNAL AUDITORS

In September 2002 the APB issued a briefing paper, *Effective Communication between Audit Committees and External Auditors*, to assist audit committees' understanding of the changes introduced in the updated SAS 610.

The guidance in the briefing paper has been written primarily with regard to the audit committees of listed companies but is also of relevance to other board members of listed companies, and directors of non-listed entities. It does not cover communications between external and internal auditors.

15.11.1   Introduction

The aim of the APB briefing paper is to assist audit committees understand the changes introduced in the update to SAS 610, *Communication of audit matters to those charged with governance*. It supersedes the 1998 Briefing Paper issued by the APB, *Communication between external auditors and audit committees*.

Although SAS 610 has itself been superseded, the guidance in the briefing paper is still relevant.

The Briefing Paper describes matters that are often covered in communications between auditors and audit committees and focuses on:

- establishing expectations of both parties;
- the scope of the audit;
- findings from the audit; and
- the independence of the auditors.

15.11.2   Establishing the expectations of both parties

The audit committee and auditors must have a clear understanding of each other's expectations. The auditors should understand how the audit committee operates and the committee's role in relation to identifying and managing business risks.

Auditors should agree with the committee the extent, format and frequency of the communications they will make at an early stage. Communication may be oral or in writing. The form of communication used will depend on a number of factors, but these will include:

- the size and activities of the company;
- the responsibilities of the audit committee;
- how the committee operates;
- legal and regulatory requirements; and
- how important the issues are.

Issues reported to the audit committee will normally be discussed with management in advance, and the audit committee should be given copies of management's comments to enable them to form a view about the adequacy of the response.

In some situations a private meeting may be the most appropriate way to communicate sensitive matters.

All communication should be made on a prompt basis to ensure that it remains relevant to the audit committee and to allow the committee to take appropriate action.

15.11.3   The scope of the audit

Ultimate responsibility for determining the nature and scope of work needed to express an opinion on the financial statements rests with the auditors. However, to gain an understanding of the scope of the audit work performed the audit committee may benefit from knowledge of:

- management's views on risk;
- the way auditors intend to address the risk of misstatement;
- the process for monitoring the effectiveness of the internal control system;
- the auditors' approach to assessing and relying on internal control;
- if the auditors will rely on internal audit;
- what work is to be undertaken by other firms of auditors;
- relevant developments in law, accounting standards, the Listing Rules, etc; and
- whether auditors review or audit interim financial statements.

15.11.4   Findings from the audit

Information provided by auditors may help the audit committee to:

- appraise the actions and judgements of management;
- monitor management's commitment to a satisfactory control environment;
- consider the adequacy and cost effectiveness of internal audit; and
- assess whether the directors have discharged their responsibility for the financial statements.

Auditors must comment on the following in communicating with those charged with governance to satisfy Auditing Standards:

- misstatements identified by the audit that have not been adjusted by management;
- material weaknesses in the accounting and internal control system;
- their views on the quality of the company's accounting practices and financial reporting; and
- expected modifications to the audit report.

Unadjusted misstatements

Other than those that are 'clearly trifling', auditors should ask management to adjust all misstatements identified. Where management have not made all the adjustments requested, the audit committee should be informed of the reasons why the adjustments have not been made and implications for the audit report. This may assist the committee in appraising the actions and judgements of management.

Material weaknesses in the accounting and internal control system

Information from auditors about material weaknesses in the accounting and internal control systems can help the audit committee perform aspects of its role such as:

- monitoring management's commitment to a sound system of internal control; and
- reviewing the scope and results of the audit and its cost effectiveness.

The directors are required by the Combined Code to review all controls and therefore their review will be broader in scope than the review undertaken by the auditors, who do not have to conclude on the effectiveness of internal controls. The auditors work will tend to focus on those controls that relate to amounts in the financial statements.

Quality of accounting practices and financial reporting

The auditors' observations in relation to the quality of the company's financial reporting may help the audit committee come to an assessment of the financial reporting process. The benefit is likely to be greater when discussions are held face to face, to avoid 'boilerplate' wording in written reports.

Discussions are likely to include:

- the appropriateness of the accounting policies applied;
- the timing of transactions and period in which they are recorded;
- the appropriateness of accounting estimates and judgements;
- effects of unusual transactions;
- effects of uncertainties;
- doubts over going concern;
- apparent misstatements in 'other information'; and
- overall clarity of information in the annual report.

Expected modifications to the audit report

Any anticipated modification to the audit report, such as a qualification or fundamental uncertainty should be discussed with the committee before the report is finalised. The audit committee may be able to assist with any disagreements between auditors and management.

15.11.5   The independence of the auditors

Audit committees have a duty to keep under review the independence and objectivity of auditors. At least annually listed company auditors must make a written statement of independence to the audit committee outlining any potential conflicts of interest and the safeguards that are in place to ensure that independence is maintained.

Audit committees should be informed of any possible difficulties in maintaining independence and objectivity prior to the proposed appointment or reappointment of auditors, and the committee may wish to establish its own safeguards in addition to those maintained by the auditors. Actions taken may include:

* ensuring a written confirmation is received from the auditors and understanding the impact of the information included therein;
* monitoring the quality and nature of the relationship with the auditor;
* considering whether the audit fee is reasonable for a high quality audit; and
* consider whether it is appropriate to obtain other services from the audit firm.

15.12   THE POWER OF THREE

In May 2003, the Audit and Assurance Faculty of the ICAEW published *The Power of Three: Understanding the roles and relationships of internal and external auditors and audit committees*. This guidance develops a number of principles that members of audit committees may wish to consider in order to help them gain a better understanding of the roles that both internal and external auditors play within an organisation and how their respective responsibilities can contribute to its overall governance. This is in line with the recommendation of the Smith report, for audit committees to play an active role in relationships with both internal and external auditors.

In order to assist with these relationships the paper provides a number of principles around the need:

* to understand the roles that both sets of auditors play in relation to those charged with governance;
* for an overall assurance framework to help organisations and audit committees make the best use of the total resources that are available from both the internal and external auditors; and
* for continuous evaluation and improvement to ensure that the relationships are working effectively.

The Faculty believes their publication is relevant to both listed companies and to other types of entity.

The guidance complements the seven booklets for audit committees published by the ICAEW, in May 2003 and March 2004, see **15.13** below.

15.13   ICAEW GUIDANCE BOOKLETS

In May 2003, the ICAEW published the first four booklets in a series of publications aimed at assisting non-executive directors on audit committees to gain an understanding of the proposals set out in the Smith report. Three further publications were issued in March 2004. The seven booklets are:

- *Working with your auditors*;
- *Company reporting and audit requirements*;
- *Reviewing auditor independence;*
- *Evaluating your auditors;*
- *Monitoring the integrity of financial statements*;
- *The internal audit function, and*
- *Whistleblowing arrangements.*

15.13.1   *Working with your auditors*

The Smith report requires that the audit committee acts as a 'body responsible for overseeing the company's relations with the external auditor'. The booklet outlines two aspects of this relationship:

- the audit committee ensures that appropriate plans are in place for the audit at the start of each audit cycle; and
- the audit committee reviews, with the external auditors, the findings of their work.

The booklet looks at how these aspects work in practice and how they relate to the requirements made of auditors by Auditing Standards.

15.13.2   *Company reporting and audit requirements*

This booklet provides a high level overview of reporting by listed companies and audit requirements, covering:

- the legal requirements and accounting and auditing standards;
- recommendations of codes and guidance; and
- the sources and authorities of those requirements and recommendations.

It does not, however, provide guidance on how to deal with specific situations and recommends making reference to the underlying guidance for detailed information.

15.13.3   Reviewing auditor independence

One of the elements of the audit committee's role laid down by the Smith report was the overseeing of auditor independence. Whilst the prime responsibility for remaining independent is the auditors', it may assist members of the audit committee to be familiar with the key elements of the applicable guidance.

This booklet is written in relation to audit engagements (although much of its contents may be relevant to the provision of other services), and contains:

- a summary of the key requirements for audit committees in respect of auditor independence that the Smith report sets out;
- an outline of the approach taken by auditors to achieving independence;
- appendices giving more information on the approach and setting out some of the general considerations for key areas referred to in the Smith report:
  1. Analysis of threats to independence and available safeguards to be adopted.
  2. Advantages of a threats and safeguards approach.
  3. Non-audit services by auditors to their clients.
  4. Rotation of audit partners.
  5. Fee dependence on the client by the auditor.
  6. Employment by the client of former audit partners and staff.

15.13.4   Evaluating your auditors

This booklet explains how proposals in the Smith report relating to the evaluation of auditors might be addressed by audit committees and how they relate to legal requirements and Auditing Standards. Practically, this will involve a structure for an annual appraisal and recommendation of external auditors, which is agreed by all concerned. Suggestions for this structure are set out in this booklet.

15.13.5   Monitoring the integrity of financial statements

One of the roles of the audit committee set out in the Combined Code is to monitor the integrity of the financial statements and any other formal announcements relating to the financial performance of the company. This booklet gives a high level overview of these provisions and the issues to consider, including the content of the financial statements and areas where judgement are required. However, it does not deal with individual situations.

15.13.6   *The internal audit function*

This publication sets out a brief background to internal audit and explains how an internal audit function may operate and how it may interact with the audit committee. This booklet is aimed at assisting audit committee members with the requirements set out in the Combined Code to assess the effectiveness of their internal audit function or determine whether an internal audit department is required.

15.13.7   *Whistle-blowing arrangements*

The Combined Code requires audit committees to ensure arrangements are in place whereby members of staff can raise any concerns about inappropriate activities or work practices ('whistle-blowing'). This publication provides background information on whistleblowing and examples of how an audit committee can meet the requirements set out in the Combined Code.

16 REVIEW OF INTERIM REPORTS

16.1 INTRODUCTION

The Listing Rules require that listed companies produce a half yearly report which includes, as a minimum:

- a summarised profit and loss account;
- a balance sheet;
- a cash flow statement; and
- an explanatory statement.

In addition, the Accounting Standards Board's non-mandatory statement, *Interim reports*, recommends presentation of:

- a statement of total recognised gains and losses;
- associated notes; and
- a management commentary.

Companies may choose to have this statement reviewed by their auditors, and the Listing Rules state that where such a review has taken place it must be published with the interim report.

16.2 GUIDANCE FOR AUDITORS

The APB has issued guidance on these engagements in Bulletin 1999/4 *Review of Interim Financial Information.*

The Bulletin covers:

- assurance provided;
- agreeing the terms of the engagement;
- planning;
- procedures and evidence;
- changes in auditor appointment;
- documentation;

- subsequent events;
- going concern;
- management representations;
- other information;
- discussion of findings with the board and the audit committee;
  - reporting; and
  - requests to discontinue an interim review engagement.

The APB urges auditors to encourage directors to describe financial information as 'neither audited nor reviewed' where the scope of the review is less than that specified in the Bulletin.

In January 2007, the APB issued an Exposure Draft of International Standard on Review Engagements (UK and Ireland) (ISRE (UK and Ireland)) 2410 *Review of Interim Financial Information Performed by the Independent Auditor of the Entity*. The proposals adopt the text of the international ISRE 2410 with additional supplementary guidance relevant to users in the UK and Ireland given in shaded text. Once comments have been received a final version of the ISRE (UK and Ireland) is expected to be effective for reviews of interim periods commencing on or after 20 January 2007. The ISRE (UK and Ireland) will replace Bulletin 1999/4 and is discussed in **16.16** below.

16.3   ASSURANCE PROVIDED

The interim financial information will be significantly less in scope than that included in the annual financial statements and will not usually include sufficient information to give a true and fair view. Similarly, the review by the auditors will involve less work than a full audit and will provide a lower level of assurance than an audit. The review will not include:

- inspection, observation or confirmation of accounting records;
- obtaining corroborative evidence in response to enquiries; or
- other typical audit tests such as tests of controls or verification of assets and liabilities.

Where auditors have not audited the latest annual financial statements or have not reviewed the corresponding financial information in the preceding year, additional review procedures are likely to be necessary.

Additional guidance on cases where there are changes of auditor is given in **16.7** below.

16.4 ENGAGEMENT LETTERS

An engagement letter for the review, or a separate section in the main audit engagement letter, confirms the auditors' acceptance of the appointment and helps to avoid misunderstandings about the level of assurance provided by the review. It also clarifies the extent of the auditors' responsibilities for the review.

An illustrative engagement letter is shown in **Table** 1 below.

TABLE 1: Example engagement letter for interim review report

Board of Directors XYZ PLC

Date

Dear Sirs

XYZ Plc Financial information for the six months ended 30 June 20..
1 This letter sets out our understanding of the terms of our engagement to review the financial information to be included in the interim report of XYZ PLC for the six months ended 30 June 20. It explains the scope of the work which we will undertake, and the form of our proposed review report, and draws attention to the inherent limitations of a review.

Directors' responsibilities
2 As directors of XYZ PLC you are responsible under the Companies Act 1985 for keeping proper accounting records. You are also responsible for presenting an interim report complying as a minimum with the requirements of the continuing obligations for companies listed on the London Stock Exchange.

3 For the purpose of our review you will make available to us all of the company's accounting records and all other related information, including minutes of directors', shareholders', and audit committee meetings and of all relevant management meetings, that we consider necessary.

Scope and limitations of our review
4 We will review the financial information of XYZ PLC for the six months ending 30 June 20... This financial information will comprise *[specify the financial information, for example: summarised profit and loss account, statement of total gains and losses, summarised balance sheet information as at 30 June 20.., summarised cash flow statement, comparative figures and associated notes]*.

5 Our work will be substantially less in scope than an audit in accordance with Auditing Standards and therefore provides a lower level of assurance than an audit. It will consist principally of making enquiries of [group] management and applying analytical procedures to financial data, assessing whether accounting policies and presentation have been consistently applied. It will not include audit procedures such as tests of controls and verification of assets

---

and liabilities. Our review will have regard to the guidance contained in the Bulletin 1999/4 *Review of Interim Financial Information* issued by the Auditing Practices Board.

[If appropriate, for example to avoid any subsequent misunderstanding, provide a more detailed explanation of the procedures including the consequences of any proposed limitation in scope.]

6 If, in the course of our review, we find increased risk of potential misstatement in the financial information we may decide that further more detailed enquiries or examinations are necessary for us to reach conclusions. We will discuss the nature and extent of these procedures with you before undertaking any such procedures.

7 Our review is not designed to, and therefore cannot not be relied upon to, disclose any irregularities, including fraud, which may exist.

8 Our review is not designed to, and therefore will not necessarily, reveal weaknesses in internal controls, errors in the accounting records, misstatements of management estimates, or other matters which might be revealed if we were to conduct an audit in accordance with Auditing Standards.

9 There is no assurance that our review will reveal all matters of significance related to the interim report. However, we shall report to you and to the audit committee, any significant findings from our work which we consider should be brought to your attention.

Reporting
10 We will not carry out an audit of the financial information in accordance with Auditing Standards and we will not therefore, express an audit opinion thereon. We will issue a review report in accordance with Bulletin 1999/4 Review of Interim Financial Information addressed to XYZ PLC (as amended by Bulletin 2001/2 *Revisions to the Wording of Auditors' Reports on Financial Statements and Interim Review Reports*), for publication in the interim report. Our review report will be prepared to assist the company in meeting Stock Exchange requirements and in the proper control of its affairs; our review will be performed and our report will be issued for these purposes only. Our report will not be prepared for any purpose connected with any specific transactions and should not be relied upon for any such purpose.

11 We expect to report on the financial information as follows:

*[Insert proposed text of report — see **Table 3**]*

Representations by management
12 As part of our procedures, we may request you to provide written confirmation of oral representations that we have received from you during the course of the review engagement.

The interim report: documents issued with financial information
13 To assist us with our work, we shall request sight of all documents or

statements which are due to be issued with the financial information, including any that form part of XYZ PLC's published interim report.

Other auditors
14 [*A paragraph should be included where material divisional, subsidiary and associated or joint undertakings are audited by other auditors.*]
In carrying out the engagement it may be necessary to arrange for auditors of divisions, subsidiary and associated or joint undertakings to perform such work as we consider necessary. As part of this process, we may request you to communicate with directors of divisions, subsidiary and associated or joint undertakings, particularly where they are resident or operate outside the United Kingdom, in order to explain and expedite the necessary review procedures.

Fees
15 Our fees are computed on the basis of the time spent on the review of the financial information by the partners and our staff, and on the levels of skill and responsibility involved. Our fees will be billed [on completion of/at intervals during] the engagement.

Agreement of terms
16 We shall be grateful if you could confirm in writing your agreement to the terms of this letter by signing and returning the enclosed copy. If you wish to discuss the terms of this engagement letter further before replying, please let us know.

Yours faithfully

16.5 PLANNING

As with any other engagement, auditors should plan their review so that it is carried out effectively. The planning process, which should focus on areas of potential risk of material misstatement, will include:

- updating the auditors' knowledge of the business;
- consideration of the company's organisation, accounting and control systems and operating characteristics;
- consideration of the nature of its assets, liabilities, revenues and expenses;
- familiarisation with the Listing Rules and the ASB Statement.

The planning exercise should determine the extent of the review work required, if any, for the different parts of the business, such as divisions, subsidiaries and associates or joint ventures. The following factors will influence this decision:

- the materiality of, and risk of misstatement in, the financial information associated with each part of the business;

- the extent to which management control is centralised within the group, and therefore the degree to which central management have a detailed understanding of operations and financial information in those parts of the business; and
- the strength of the control environment including the group accounting and reporting processes.

Where other auditors are involved, the principal auditors should ensure that the work of the other auditors is adequate for the purposes of the review.

16.6 PROCEDURES AND EVIDENCE

The auditors' evidence will be obtained primarily through enquiry and analytical review procedures. In the context of the review of interim financial information, analytical procedures are:

- comparison with comparable information for the prior period – both interim and full;
- evaluation of the information by consideration of plausible relationships between financial data and also between non-financial and financial data elements; and
- comparison of amounts and ratios with the auditors' expectations, based on their knowledge of the business.

The extent of the procedures necessary will be based on the auditors' assessment of the risk of material misstatement. In determining the procedures necessary, auditors should consider:

- the financial position and trading conditions of the company;
- their knowledge of the business derived through previous audits;
- their knowledge of the company's accounting systems;
- the extent to which an item is affected by management judgement;
- management's own assessment of risks and the controls in place; and
- the materiality of transactions and account balances.

An appendix to the Bulletin suggests various procedures that auditors may use as part of their review. These include:

- reviewing prior year matters which may have a material effect on the financial information;
- considering whether the financial information is prepared on a basis which is consistent with the previous period and with the stated accounting policies;
- reviewing significant consolidation adjustments for consistency with the previous period;
- reading the financial information and considering it in the light of

matters which have come to their attention during the course of their review work, and reading the rest of the interim report to ensure there are no inconsistencies or misstatements;
- considering the disclosures;
- considering the going concern status of the entity and the disclosures of any significant uncertainties;
- obtaining a management letter; and
- ascertaining whether the financial information has been approved by the directors and the audit committee.

Where auditors consider that there is a high risk of material misstatement they should carry out additional procedures in order to be able to issue an unmodified review report.

16.7   CHANGES IN AUDITOR APPOINTMENT

If the current auditors did not perform the audit of the most recent full financial statements additional work will be required on which they can base their conclusion. Areas in which additional work is required are:

- knowledge of the business;
- assessment of inherent risk;
- understanding the accounting systems; and
- verification of opening balances.

Such work can, of course, be utilised as part of the following year end audit.

In addition, extra review procedures are required where the auditors did not review the corresponding prior year interim financial information. The Listing Rules require comparatives to be given and readers will have expectations that these comparatives have been reviewed on the same basis as the prior period figures. If auditors are unable to perform additional procedures on the comparatives, they should modify their report to indicate that the comparative figures have not been reviewed (see **16.14**).

16.8   DOCUMENTATION

The auditors should record in their working papers:

- details of the planning of the engagement;
- the nature, timing and extent of the procedures performed and their conclusions; and
- their reasoning and conclusions on all significant matters which require the exercise of judgement.

16.9 SUBSEQUENT EVENTS

To ensure that any relevant subsequent events are properly dealt with in the financial information, auditors should make enquiries about events up to the date of the approval of the financial information.

16.10 GOING CONCERN

At the interim period end, directors should undertake a review of the going concern assessment they made at the previous full year end. In the light of the directors' review, auditors should consider whether any significant factors identified at the previous audit have changed to such an extent as to affect the appropriateness of the going concern presumption. Particular attention should be paid to the period since the sign off of the full financial statements.

Where auditors do not have significant concerns they should limit their enquiries to discussions with management about changes to cash flow and banking arrangements.

Where there are significant concerns the Bulletin notes that additional procedures will be necessary.

16.11 MANAGEMENT REPRESENTATIONS

As with the year end audit, auditors may obtain from directors written representations to confirm matters arising throughout the review. The confirmation should include an acknowledgement of the limited scope of the review and of the directors' responsibilities for the interim report and the completeness of the financial records and minutes.

An example representation letter is included in the Bulletin and this is shown in **Table 2** below, which should be tailored to suit the circumstances of the review engagement.

16.12 OTHER INFORMATION

The other information in the interim report will often include:

- the management commentary;
- prospective information; and
- a chairman's statement.

TABLE 2: Illustrative management representation letter for review of interim financial information

ABC & Co 1 High Street London

Date

Dear Sirs

We confirm to the best of our knowledge and belief and having made appropriate enquiries of other directors and officials of the company, the following representations given to you in connection with your review of the financial information of the company for the six months ended 30 June 20.. in accordance with Bulletin 1999/4.

We acknowledge that your review was substantially less in scope than an audit performed in accordance with International Standards on Auditing (United Kingdom and Ireland) issued by the Auditing Practices Board and that accordingly you do not express an audit opinion on the financial information.

We acknowledge our responsibility as directors for the interim report and the consistency of accounting policies and presentation with those applied in the preceding annual financial statements [other than to reflect the change in accounting policy referred to in note x – *if appropriate*].

We acknowledge our responsibility for the completeness of the financial records and minutes, and that all minutes of meetings of shareholders, directors, audit committee and other committees of directors (and summaries of meetings for which minutes have not been prepared) have been made available for your review.

We confirm that we have reviewed our assessment of going concern made by us for the purposes of preparing the annual financial statements dated [insert date of preceding annual financial statements]. No significant factors identified at that date have changed so as to affect the appropriateness of the going concern assumption in the preparation of the financial information.

We are not aware of any material amounts, transactions, agreements or contingencies not fairly described and properly recorded in the accounting records underlying the financial information.

Events since 30 June 20..:

(a) have been fully taken into account in so far as they have a bearing on the amounts attributable to assets and/or liabilities at that date; and
(b) have not made the present financial position substantially different from that shown in the financial information.

Should any material matter come to our attention that might require adjustment to, or disclosure in, the interim report, we will inform you.

Yours faithfully

Director on behalf of the Board of XYZ PLC

The auditors should only allow their review report to be included where they consider that the additional information is not in conflict with their report and that it is not misleading.

Where there is an apparent misstatement or a material inconsistency between the other information and the financial information which cannot be resolved through discussion with the directors, the Bulletin suggests that the auditors should consider taking legal advice and that they are likely to make reference to the matter in their review report.

16.13   DISCUSSIONS WITH THE BOARD AND THE AUDIT COMMITTEE

In addition to issuing their review report, the auditors should communicate their findings to the Board and the Audit Committee, Matters that may require discussion and reporting include:

- the scope and the results of the procedures carried out;
- the process used by management to prepare the financial information;
- changes to accounting policies; and
- issues which have been discussed with management.

16.14   REPORTING

The report of the auditors on their review of interim financial information contains the following:

- a title giving the addressee – in this case the company – and highlighting that it is a review report;
- an introductory paragraph identifying the financial information involved;
- a statement of directors' responsibility for the interim financial information;
- a statement that the review has been carried out in accordance with the Bulletin;
- a description of the work performed;
- a review conclusion;
- the name, signature and designation of the auditors – only the name and designation are required on the copies sent to shareholders and others; and
- the date of the review report.

TABLE 3: Unmodified review report

Independent review report to XYZ plc

Introduction
We have been instructed by the company to review the financial information set out for the [number] months ended [date] on pages .. to ... We have read the other information contained in the interim report and considered whether it contains any apparent misstatements or material inconsistencies with the financial information.

Directors' responsibilities
The interim report, including the financial information contained therein, is the responsibility of, and has been approved by the directors. The Listing Rules of the Financial Services Authority require that the accounting policies and presentation applied to the interim figures should be consistent with those applied in preparing the preceding annual accounts except where any changes, and the reasons for them, are disclosed.

Review work performed
We conducted our review in accordance with guidance contained in Bulletin 1999/4 issued by the Auditing Practices Board for use in the United Kingdom. A review consists principally of making enquiries of [group] management and applying analytical procedures to the financial information and underlying financial data and based thereon, assessing whether the accounting policies and presentation have been consistently applied unless otherwise disclosed. A review excludes audit procedures such as tests of controls and verification of assets, liabilities and transactions. It is substantially less in scope than an audit performed in accordance with International Standards on Auditing (United Kingdom and Ireland) and therefore provides a lower level of assurance than an audit. Accordingly we do not express an audit opinion on the financial information.

Review conclusion
On the basis of our review we are not aware of any material modifications that should be made to the financial information as presented for the [number] months ended 30 June 20.. .

Chartered Accountants
Address
Date

16.14.1 Work performed

The review report should make clear that the scope of the review is significantly less than that of a full audit and that, accordingly, an audit opinion is not expressed.

16.14.2 Changes in accounting policy

Where changes to accounting policies have been made and both current and prior periods are stated on the basis of the new policy, the auditors must review both the adjustments to the prior period and disclosure of the nature of the change and its effect on opening reserves. If they consider that the policy changes have not been properly reflected in the financial information they should consider the impact on their review report.

16.14.3 Modification of the review report

The auditors' review report will be modified if they consider that:

- a material amendment is required to the financial information; or
- the other information contains an apparent misstatement or material inconsistency with the financial information.

Examples of where a material modification is required may include where:

- an accounting policy is inconsistent with that used in a prior period and the changes and reason for the changes are not properly disclosed;
- the financial information has not been adjusted for a change in accounting policy which is to be effective for the first time in the next full financial statements; or
- there is inadequate disclosure of a fundamental uncertainty.

In addition, auditors may have to modify their review report if an 'integral' method of accounting has been adopted, rather than a 'discrete' method. The discrete method will treat the interim period as distinct from the full annual reporting and any incomplete transactions are treated according to the same principles applied at the year end. The Accounting Standards Board recommends the use of the discrete method. Where the integral approach is used, auditors should consider whether the disclosure of any material differences between the two methods are adequate and if they are not, modification of the review report should be considered.

Any modification to the review report should describe the matter identified and, if practicable, state the effect on the financial information. **Table 4** shows an extract from a modified review report.

TABLE 4:   Extract from modified review report

...

Review conclusion
Included in debtors shown on the balance sheet is an amount of £X due from a company which has ceased trading. XYZ PLC has no security for this debt. In our view the company is unlikely to receive any payment and full provision of £X should have been made, reducing profit before tax by that amount and net assets by £Y.

On the basis of our review, with the exception of the matter described in the preceding paragraph, we are not aware of any material modifications that should be made to the financial information as presented for the six months ended 30 June 20...

Limitation of scope

Where there has been a limitation in the scope of the auditors' review work that prevents them from obtaining sufficient evidence to give an unmodified report, the review report should:

- describe the limitation; and
- indicate that the report is modified as to the possible adjustments to the financial information that may have been determined to be necessary had the limitation not existed.

If the limitation is so significant that the auditors conclude that no assurance can be given, their report should contain a denial of review conclusion and the Bulletin advises them to consider their appointment.

Fundamental uncertainty

Any fundamental uncertainty that exists should be referred to in an additional paragraph in the auditors' review report provided that the matter is properly disclosed in the interim report, as shown in **Table 5**. If the disclosure is inadequate, a modification to the review report would be necessary.

16.14.4   *Prior period modifications*

Where the prior period review report was modified or the audit report on the most recent financial statements was qualified and the matter has not been resolved, the review report should refer to the earlier modification or qualification and discuss the current status of the matter.

TABLE 5:   Extract from review report with fundamental uncertainty

Review work performed

....

Fundamental uncertainty
In arriving at our review conclusion, we have considered the adequacy of disclosures made in the financial information concerning the possible outcome of litigation against B Limited, a subsidiary undertaking of the company, for an alleged breach of environmental regulations. The future settlement of this litigation could result in additional liabilities and the closure of B's business, whose net assets included in the summarised balance sheet total £Y and whose profit before tax for the year is £Z. Details of the circumstances relating to this fundamental uncertainty are described in note X.

Review conclusion
On the basis of our review we are not aware of any material modifications that should be made to the financial information as presented for the six months ended 30 June 20.. .

16.14.5   Designation of auditors

While auditors can include their professional qualification when signing off the review report (for example 'Chartered Accountants'), they should not use the term 'Registered Auditors' as this may give a misleading impression of the extent of work performed.

16.14.6   Date of review report

The date the auditors sign their report should be the same date as the directors approve the financial information.

16.15   REQUESTS TO DISCONTINUE AN INTERIM REVIEW ENGAGEMENT

As a review of the interim statement is not mandatory, directors may request auditors to discontinue their review engagement if it becomes clear that a modified review report will be given.

If this is the case the auditors must inform the Audit Committee of this in writing. If, in the auditors' opinion, the company does not take appropriate action to address their concerns about the interim financial information, the auditors may request the directors discuss the issue with the company's brokers. The directors and brokers should then consider whether the matter should be reported to the Stock Exchange.

In such a case, the auditors should also consider whether as a result they should resign as the company's auditors. The Bulletin suggests that they may consider taking legal advice in these circumstances. If they decide to resign the details of the issue should be included, after taking appropriate legal advice, in their s394 statement.

16.16   ED ISRE (UK AND IRELAND) 2410

An exposure draft of ISRE (UK and Ireland) 2410 *Review of Interim Financial Information Performed by the Independent Auditor of the Entity* was issued for comment in January 2007. When it is finalised it will replace Bulletin 1999/6 and is expected to be effective for interim periods commencing on or after 20 January 2007. This is in line with revised FSA rules under the European Transparency Directive for half-yearly financial reporting prepared by listed entities which also become effective from that date.

The adoption of the ISRE (UK and Ireland) in preference to the existing Bulletin will bring the APB's guidance in line with that issued by the IAASB. However, with the addition of the UK and Ireland specific guidance to the international version of the ISRE, the proposals are broadly consistent with those of the extant Bulletin.

The main area where auditors' work may be increased is by the ISRE's requirement that the interim financial information agrees or reconciles with the underlying accounting records, a requirement not included in Bulletin 1999/6. The APB has proposed supplementary guidance in this area in respect of the interim reports of groups, namely that interim financial information should be agreed or reconciled to the consolidation schedules and journals of the group rather than directly to the underlying financial records of each group component. The APB's opinion is that the original ISRE required clarification in this area, and that by confirming this interpretation the increase in auditors' costs will be limited.

In addition, the requirements of the ISRE (UK and Ireland) may require auditors to perform some of their procedures, such as updating their understanding of the entity including its internal control, earlier in the financial year. However, this will be a matter of timing rather than an increase in workload and cost.

17 PLANNING

17.1 AUDITING STANDARDS

ISA (UK and Ireland) 300 *Planning an Audit of Financial Statements* was issued in December 2004 and provides standards on the planning process covering:

- overview of planning;
- preliminary planning activities;
- the overall audit strategy;
- the audit plan;
- changes to planning decisions during the course of the audit;
- direction, supervision and review;
- documentation;
- communication with those charged with governance; and
- initial audit engagements.

As with all ISAs (UK and Ireland), the text of the international ISA has been supplemented with additional guidance from a UK and Ireland perspective. SAS 200 *Planning* has not yet been officially withdrawn.

ISA (UK and Ireland) 300 is effective for audits of financial statements for periods commencing on or after 15 December 2004.

In December 2006, the IAASB issued a revision to ISA 300. This is discussed in **17.11** below.

17.2 PLANNING THE WORK

'The auditor should plan the audit so that the engagement will be performed in an effective manner'.

Planning is discussed in the context of recurring audits and is described as 'not a discrete phase of an audit, but rather a continual and iterative process that often begins shortly after (or in connection with) the completion of the previous audit and continues until the completion of the current audit engagement'. However, some planning activities will, by necessity, have to be completed at the beginning of the audit, such as understanding the legal and regulatory framework within which the entity operates and briefing the audit team.

The objectives of planning include:

- ensuring that appropriate attention is directed to important areas of the audit;
- ensuring that potential problems are identified;
- organising and managing the engagement properly;
- assisting with proper allocation of work to engagement team members;
- where appropriate, assisting with the coordination of work performed by other auditors or specialists;
- facilitating review; and
- enabling the audit to be performed in an effective and timely manner.

The guidance stresses that planning varies according to the size of the entity and complexity of the audit. In the case of a smaller audit where accountancy assistance is provided by the auditors, the audit plan should take account of any areas of audit risk identified, and evidence obtained, during that exercise.

17.3 PRELIMINARY ENGAGEMENT ACTIVITIES

In order to ensure that auditors have considered any events or circumstances which may affect their ability to plan to reduce the risk of material misstatement to an acceptable level, they should:

- perform client and audit engagement acceptance procedures in accordance with ISA (UK and Ireland) 220 *Quality Control for Audits of Historical Financial Information* (see **Chapter 20**);
- evaluate compliance with ethical and independence requirements (see **Chapters 2 and 20**); and
- establish the terms of the engagement, in accordance with ISA (UK and Ireland) 210 *Terms of Audit Engagements* (see **Chapter 21**).

The factors affecting client acceptance and ethical and independence issues should be continually re-evaluated during the audit as circumstances may change. However, the main element of this work should be performed before any other audit procedures are started and, for continuing engagements, this may be at the end of the prior year's audit.

17.4   THE OVERALL AUDIT STRATEGY

Auditors should set an overall strategy for the audit which assists with the development of the more detailed audit plan. This will involve:

- considering the scope of the engagement, i.e., what reporting requirements are there, what financial reporting framework is the client using, what group companies are covered;
- understanding reporting deadlines and key dates for communications with those charged with governance; and
- making initial assessments in relation to, for example:
  - appropriate materiality levels;
  - areas where there may be a higher risk of material misstatement;
  - the identification of material components and account balances;
  - possible reliance on the effectiveness of internal control; and
  - identification of recent significant events in terms of the business and its industry.

Table 1 sets out a list of matters auditors may consider when determining their overall audit strategy.

TABLE 1:   Matters to consider when determining the overall audit strategy

Scope of the audit engagement

- the financial reporting framework on which the financial information to be audited has been prepared, including any need for reconciliations to another financial reporting framework;
- industry specific reporting requirements such as reports mandated by industry regulators;
- the expected audit coverage, including the number of locations of components to be included;
- the nature of the control relationships between a parent and its components that determine how the group is to be consolidated;
- the extent to which components are audited by other auditors;
- the nature of the business segments to be audited, including the need for specialised knowledge;
- the reporting currency to be used including any need for currency translation for the financial information audited;
- the need for a statutory audit of standalone financial statements in addition to an audit for consolidation purposes;
- the availability of the work of internal auditors and the extent of the auditor's potential reliance on such work;
- the entity's use of service organisations and how the auditors may obtain evidence concerning the design or operation of controls performed by them;
- the expected use of audit evidence obtained in prior audits, for example, audit evidence related to risk assessment procedures and tests of controls;
- the effect of information technology on the audit procedures, including the

---

availability of data and the expected use of computer-assisted audit techniques;

- the coordination of the expected coverage and timing of the audit work with any reviews of interim financial information and the effect on the audit of the information obtained during such reviews;
- the discussion of matters that may affect the audit with firm personnel responsible for performing other services to the entity; and
- the availability of client personnel and data.

Reporting objectives, timing of the audit and communications required

- the entity's timetable for reporting, such as at interim and final stages;
- the organisation of meetings with management and those charged with governance to discuss the nature, extent and timing of the audit work;
- the discussion with management and those charged with governance regarding the expected type and timing of reports to be issued and other communications, both written and oral, including the auditor's report, management letters and communications to those charged with governance;
- the discussion with management regarding the expected communications on the status of audit work throughout the engagement and the expected deliverables resulting from the audit procedures;
- communication with auditors of components regarding the expected types and timing of reports to be issued and other communications in connection with the audit of components;
- the expected nature and timing of communications among engagement team members, including the nature and timing of team meetings and timing of the review of work performed; and
- whether there are any other expected communications with third parties, including any statutory or contractual reporting responsibilities arising from the audit.

Direction of the audit

- with respect to materiality:
  - setting materiality for planning purposes;
  - setting and communicating materiality for auditors of components;
  - reconsidering materiality as audit procedures are performed during the course of the audit;
  - identifying the material components and account balances;
- audit areas where there is a higher risk of material misstatement;
- the impact of the assessed risk of material misstatement at the overall financial statement level on direction, supervision and review;
- the selection of the engagement team (including, where necessary, the engagement quality control reviewer) and the assignment of audit work to the team members including the assignment of appropriately experienced team members to areas where there may be higher risks of material misstatement;
- engagement budgeting, including considering the appropriate amount of time to set aside for areas where there may be higher risks of material misstatement;
- the manner in which the auditor emphasises to engagement team members

the need to maintain a questioning mind and to exercise professional scepticism in gathering and evaluating audit evidence;

- results of previous audits that involved evaluating the operating effectiveness of internal control including the nature of identified weaknesses and action taken to address them;
- evidence of the commitment of those charged with governance to the design and operation of sound internal control including evidence of appropriate documentation of such internal control;
- volume of transactions which may determine whether it is more efficient for the auditors to rely on internal control;
- importance attached to internal control throughout the entity to the successful operation of the business;
- significant business developments affecting the entity, including changes to information technology and business process, changes in key management and acquisitions, mergers and divestments;
- significant industry developments such as changes in industry regulations and new reporting requirements;
- significant changes in the financial reporting framework such as changes in accounting standards; and
- other significant relevant developments such as changes in the legal environment affecting the entity.

The completed audit strategy should clearly set out:

- the resources to deploy;
- the amount of resources to allocate to different audit areas;
- the timing of the deployment; and
- how the resources are managed, supervised and directed.

A smaller audit team is likely to be involved in the audits of small entities and this makes coordination and communication easier. Developing an audit strategy for small entities need not be a time-consuming or complex exercise, and a brief memorandum prepared at the completion of the previous audit and based on a review of the working papers may suffice.

17.5 THE AUDIT PLAN

Once the audit strategy has been formulated, the audit plan can be prepared to address the various matters identified in the overall audit strategy in detail. Documentation of the audit plan also acts as a record that the planning has been properly completed, which can be reviewed and approved before further work is undertaken.

The audit plan should contain:

- a description of the nature, timing and extent of planned risk assessment procedures sufficient to assess the risks of material misstatement in accordance with ISA (UK and Ireland) 315 (see **Chapter 22**);

- a description of the nature, timing and extent of audit procedures planned at assertion level for each material class of transactions, account balance and disclosure in accordance with ISA (UK and Ireland) 330 (see **Chapter 22**); and
- details of other audit procedures required by ISAs (UK and Ireland).

17.6 CHANGES TO PLANNING DECISIONS DURING THE COURSE OF THE AUDIT

The ISA (UK and Ireland) explains that the planning decisions should be reviewed and, if necessary, revised as necessary during the course of the audit. The results of the audit tests or new information may lead to changes in the approach adopted or the assessment of risks and materiality and these should be formally documented.

17.7 DIRECTION, SUPERVISION AND REVIEW

The amount of time spent directing and supervising audit team members will depend on a number of factors including their experience and the complexity of the areas in which they are working. ISA (UK and Ireland) 220 gives further details on the direction, supervision and review of audit work (see **Chapter 20**). For areas of higher risk of material misstatement, the extent of direction and supervision may be increased.

Direction, supervision and review is not relevant where the audit work is carried out by the audit engagement partner who is sole practitioner. However, that individual must be content that the audit has been performed in accordance with ISAs (UK and Ireland), and a sole practitioner may plan to consult with an outside source on particularly difficult or complex areas.

17.8 DOCUMENTATION

Auditors are required to document the overall audit strategy and the audit plan, including any significant changes made during the course of the audit. The ISA (UK and Ireland) does not stipulate a format, as this will vary depending on the size and complexity of the engagement, but it must be sufficient to demonstrate the nature, timing and extent of risk assessment procedures and further audit procedures in response to the assessed risks. Where standard programmes and checklists are used, the ISA (UK and Ireland) encourages auditors to tailor them to reflect the circumstances of the engagement.

17.9 COMMUNICATIONS WITH THOSE CHARGED WITH GOVERNANCE

Auditors may discuss elements of the planning with those charged with governance to improve the efficiency and effectiveness of the audit. However, the overall audit strategy and the audit plan remain the auditors' responsibility.

17.10 INITIAL AUDIT ENGAGEMENTS

ISA (UK and Ireland) 300 states that prior to starting an initial audit, auditors should:

- perform client and audit engagement acceptance procedures in accordance with ISA (UK and Ireland) 220 *Quality Control for Audits of Historical Financial Information* (see **Chapter 20**);
- communicate with the previous auditor to determine if there are any matters of which they should be aware.

Much of the planning for ongoing or initial engagements will be identical, however, first time auditors will not be able to draw on their knowledge of the client from earlier work. Therefore, additional matters that auditors may consider when developing their overall audit strategy and audit plan include:

- as far as allowed by law, arrangements to review the previous auditors' working papers;
- following up any matters discussed with management or those charged with governance as part of the process followed to select them as auditors;
- procedures planned to give assurance about opening balances in accordance with ISA (UK and Ireland) 510, see **Chapter 31**;
- the assignment of appropriately experienced audit firm personnel; and
- other procedures required by the firm's quality control systems, such as appointment of a technical or concurring partner.

17.11 ISA 300 REVISED

In December 2006, the IAASB issued the final version of its revision to the international version of ISA 300. The revision was one of the first ISAs to be issued as part of the IAASB's Clarity Project, the aim of which is to make the standards clearer and easier to understand. The revision process also ensured that the guidance was more easily applied to smaller entities.

The provisional effective date is 15 December 2008, although the actual date will not be any earlier than this. The long lead-in time allows the IAASB to reissue all extant ISAs so that they conform to the principles of the Clarity Project and they all share the same effective date. The APB are expected to revise all of its ISAs (UK and Ireland) once the revised ISAs are adopted by the EU.

18   MATERIALITY AND THE AUDIT

18.1   AUDITING STANDARDS

ISA (UK and Ireland) 320 *Audit Materiality* was issued in December 2004 and provides guidance on the use of materiality by auditors. The ISA contains standards covering:

- the need to consider materiality;
- materiality and audit risk;
- determining audit work;
- evaluating misstatements;
- adjusting financial statements for aggregate uncorrected misstatements; and
- communication of errors.

As with all ISAs (UK and Ireland), the text of the international ISA has been supplemented with additional guidance from a UK and Ireland perspective. SAS 220 *Materiality and the Audit* has not yet been officially withdrawn.

ISA (UK and Ireland) 320 is effective for audits of financial statements for periods commencing on or after 15 December 2004.

In December 2004, the IAASB issued an Exposure Draft of a revision to ISA 320. The draft, entitled *Materiality in the Identification and Evaluation of Misstatements,* was developed in connection with the UK APB, conforms the original ISA to the revised risk and fraud standards released by the IAASB. As a result of the responses received, it was agreed that the guidance would be enhanced by addressing materiality and misstatements in separate ISAs. The two ISAs, ISA 320 (Revised and Redrafted), *Materiality in Planning and Performing an Audit* and ISA 450 (Redrafted), *Evaluation of Misstatements Identified During the Audit* were reissued in a single document in November 2006 following redrafting in line with the requirements of the IAASB's Clarity Project. They are discussed further in section **18.8** below.

18.2   DEFINITION

The guidance in the ISA (UK and Ireland) uses the definition of materiality from the International Accounting Standard Board's 'Framework for the Preparation and Presentation of Financial Statements':

> 'Information is material if its omission or misstatement could influence the economic decisions of users taken on the basis of the financial statements. Materiality depends on the size of the item or error judged in the particular circumstances of its omission or misstatement. Thus, materiality provides a threshold or cut-off point rather than being a primary qualitative characteristic which information must have if it is to be useful.'

Materiality may also be considered in relation to individual items in the financial statements or for each primary statement. There is no mathematical definition of materiality, as it has both qualitative and quantitative aspects.

18.3   THE NEED TO CONSIDER MATERIALITY

Auditors plan and perform their audits so as to obtain reasonable assurance that the financial statements are free from material misstatement. However, whether an item is to be considered as material is a matter of professional judgement. The relationship of materiality to audit risk should also be considered.

The consideration of materiality should not simply be a matter of amount, the nature of the error should also be assessed. For example, if the auditors find an illegal payment of an otherwise immaterial amount this may lead to a material contingent liability, a material loss of assets or a material loss of revenue, and the effects on the audit report should be considered. Similarly, a failure to disclose a breach of regulatory requirements may result in the imposition of restrictions, which could impair a company's ability to operate.

Auditors also need to be aware of qualitative misstatements. For example, an inadequate description of an accounting policy which would mislead users of accounts is material to those users.

The level of materiality may be influenced by:

- legal and regulatory requirements;
- the level of exposure of the financial statements;
- whether the company is using the financial statements to negotiate additional finance or a listing on the Stock Exchange; and
- the auditors' previous experience of the company.

The expected degree of accuracy of certain statutory disclosures, such as directors' emoluments, may make normal materiality considerations irrelevant.

Auditors will consider materiality at both the overall financial statements level and in relation to classes of transactions, account balances and disclosures. Because of the different factors that may affect materiality, different materiality may be applied to different areas of the financial statements.

18.4   MATERIALITY AND AUDIT RISK

When planning the audit, auditors will assess the risk of material misstatement of the financial statements and plan how to respond to those risks throughout the audit. This risk assessment also helps auditors to establish materiality and continually assess whether the materiality assessment remains valid throughout the course of the audit.

The assessment of materiality helps auditors to determine the type and extent of testing required to reduce audit risk to an acceptably low level.

Materiality is used specifically in:

- *Planning the audit*. At this stage materiality assists the auditors in deciding what areas need to be addressed and particularly where material misstatement is likely to occur, so that their approach is efficient and effective.
- *Planning individual audit procedures*. Materiality is used to determine what items to examine and whether to use sampling and the extent of testing to be carried out on the particular transaction class or account balance. This enables specific audit procedures to be selected to support the opinion whilst reducing to a low level the risk of giving an inappropriate opinion.

18.5   EVALUATION OF AUDIT EVIDENCE

It is possible for the assessment of materiality (and audit risk) to change during the course of the audit. This may be because of a change in circumstances or knowledge as a result of the audit, for example, the actual results and financial position may be substantially different from that initially anticipated. In addition, auditors may set the level of error that will be acceptable at a level lower than materiality in order to reduce the likelihood of undiscovered material misstatement and to provide a margin of safety.

If factors are identified which result in the revision of their preliminary materiality assessment, the auditors should consider the implications for their audit approach and, if necessary, modify the nature, timing and extent of planned audit procedures. If their revised assessment results in a lower level of materiality, auditors may find it necessary to carry out more audit work.

18.6   THE EFFECT OF MISSTATEMENTS

In evaluating whether the financial statements give a true and fair view auditors are required to assess the materiality of the aggregate of uncorrected misstatements. Uncorrected misstatements arise from:

- specific misstatements identified by the auditors, including those from a previous financial period to the extent that they impact on the current financial statements; and
- the auditors' best estimate of other misstatements which cannot be quantified specifically, i.e., projected errors.

The various errors found during the audit should be assessed in aggregate to ensure that there is no material misstatement in the financial statements. If the auditors are of the opinion that these may be material, they will need to consider reducing audit risk by extending audit procedures or requesting management to adjust the financial statements.

If no adjustment is made after such a request, they will need to consider the effect on their report.

If the aggregate of uncorrected errors approaches materiality, auditors should consider whether undetected errors could make this total material. In such a situation they may perform additional procedures or request that the identified errors are adjusted.

Auditors should also be aware of areas where errors are likely to be material by their nature and without aggregation. An example would be the disclosure of directors' emoluments, where any error should be amended. US guidance, in the form of SEC Staff Accounting Bulletin 99, reiterates the importance of not discounting errors simply because they fall below the materiality threshold.

18.7   COMMUNICATION OF ERRORS

Where a material misstatement has been found, auditors should provide details to the appropriate level of management on a timely basis. Depending on the circumstances, auditors may also consider it necessary to bring the error to the attention of those charged with governance, in accordance with ISA (UK and Ireland) 260 (see **Chapter 9**).

18.8   EXPOSURE DRAFT OF ISAS 320 AND 450

In December 2004, an Exposure Draft of a revision to ISA 320 was issued by the IAASB. The Exposure Draft was written in conjunction with the UK APB and defined materiality in terms of the size and nature of an item judged in the surrounding circumstances.

It stated that materiality must reflect the needs of users of the financial statements and the users of general purpose financial statements should be considered as a group by auditors assessing their needs. Guidance was given on the use of percentages to determine materiality, but the Exposure Draft was not intending to set formulaic rules.

Following receipt of comments from users, the IAASB decided to split the contents of the Exposure Draft into two ISAs:

- ISA 320 (Revised and Redrafted), *Materiality in Planning and Performing an Audit*; and
- ISA 450 (Redrafted) *Evaluation of Misstatements Identified During the Audit*.

When creating the two ISAs, the IAASB drafted the revisions in line with the requirements of their Clarity Project (see **Chapter 1**).

In November 2006 the IAASB reissued Exposure Drafts of the ISAs for public comment. However, as the content of the ISAs had been subject to a comment period following its issue in December 2004, they limited comments required to those arising from redrafting in line with the Clarity Project.

In the UK the APB subsequently reissued the IAASB's Exposure Drafts requesting comments from UK users which would assist with their response to the IAASB.

19 DOCUMENTATION

19.1 AUDITING STANDARDS

ISA (UK and Ireland) 230 (Revised) *Documentation* was issued in January 2006. The original ISA (UK and Ireland) 230 was revised following amendments by the IAASB to the international version. The revised ISA (UK and Ireland) provides standards on documentation covering:

- form of working papers;
- content of working papers;
- changes to audit documentation after the date of the auditor's report; and
- confidentiality, safe custody and retention of audit documentation.

As with all ISAs (UK and Ireland), in publishing ISA (UK and Ireland) 230 (Revised), the APB has supplemented the text of the international ISA with additional guidance from a UK and Ireland perspective. SAS 230 *Working Papers* has not yet been officially withdrawn.

ISA (UK and Ireland) 230 (Revised) is effective for audits of financial statements for periods commencing on or after 15 June 2006.

In December 2006, the IAASB issued an Exposure Draft of a revision to the international version of ISA 230 as part of its clarity project. Details are given in **19.7** below.

19.2 PURPOSE OF DOCUMENTATION

ISA (UK and Ireland) 230 (Revised) requires that auditors should document matters which are important in providing audit evidence to support their opinion and evidence that the audit was carried out in accordance with ISAs (UK and Ireland).

Working papers are defined as any material the auditors obtain, prepare or retain in the course of their audit. This may be in paper form but may also include, for example, film, scanned documents, computer discs or electronic files, including e-mail.

Working papers provide a record of supervision and review, the planning and performance of the audit by the staff and the evidence to support the audit opinion. They provide the individuals responsible for approving the audit report with the means to satisfy themselves that the work delegated has been properly performed. Other advantages of working papers are that they are seen as providing a source of reference that may be used in subsequent years and that they encourage a methodical approach.

19.3   FORM AND CONTENT

Working papers should be sufficiently complete and detailed so as to provide an overall understanding of the audit. They should contain information on planning the audit, the nature, timing and extent of the audit procedures performed and the results and conclusions from the procedures.

The previous definition and guidance on the extent of working papers has been expanded in the revised ISA (UK and Ireland). The requirement is for an 'experienced auditor, having no previous connection with the audit' to be able to understand:

- the nature, timing, extent and results of the audit procedures;
- the results of the audit procedures; and
- significant matters arising during the audit and conclusions reached thereon.

Whilst the Exposure Draft of the revised ISA (UK and Ireland) provided a definition of an 'experienced auditor', this has not been retained in the final revision. The revised ISA (UK and Ireland) states that it may be necessary for that experienced auditor to hold discussions with the auditors to obtain a detailed understanding.

Because of a wide variety of circumstances in which working papers have to be prepared and the many types of business transactions to which they relate, it is not practicable to lay down a standard form for their preparation suitable for each and every situation. How the relevant information can best be shown, what audit procedures need to be applied and how their results can best be summarised is a matter for the particular circumstances. They should, however, be set out in such a fashion that the salient facts are readily apparent.

Working papers should be designed for each assignment and the factors set out in **Table 1** will determine their extent.

TABLE 1: Factors affecting form and content and extent of working papers

- the nature of the engagement;
- the identified risks of material misstatement;
- the extent of judgement required in performing the work and evaluating the results;
- the significance of the audit evidence obtained;
- the nature and extent of exceptions identified;
- the need to document a conclusion or the basis for a conclusion not readily determinable from the documentation of the work performed or audit evidence obtained; and
- the specific methodology and technology the auditors use.

The use of standardised working papers, such as checklists, specimen letters and a standard index may aid efficiency and control, but auditors should be aware of the dangers of following a standard approach mechanically. Professional judgement should be exercised when such aids are used.

If schedules have been drawn up by the client, auditors require evidence that they have been properly prepared before relying on them.

As indicated above the term 'working papers' refers to the record of all of the evidence that auditors consider necessary to collect in order to support an opinion. This may relate to the current year or be of a permanent nature, i.e., of continuing importance and as a result be filed separately. The specific nature will depend on the assignment. Examples of the content of working papers are shown in **Table 2**.

TABLE 2: Contents of working papers

- information on the legal nature of the client, including copies of important documents;
- information concerning the industry and the economic and legislative environments within which the entity operates;
- evidence of the planning process, including any changes;
- notes on the accounting and internal control systems including extracts from the entity's internal control manual;
- assessment of inherent and control risks at the financial statements and assertion level;
- consideration of and conclusions on the work of internal audit;
- analyses of transactions and balances, including significant ratios and trends;
- audit programmes showing the nature, timing and extent of the audit procedures performed in response to risks at the assertion level, and the conclusions thereon;
- evidence that the work performed by assistants was supervised and reviewed;
- an indication as to who performed the audit procedures and when they were performed;

- correspondence with other auditors, experts and third parties;
- details of audit procedures applied where components of the financial statements are audited by another auditor;
- correspondence with the entity, including reports to management and notes of discussions with management concerning audit matters;
- letters of representation from management;
- a summary of the significant aspects of the audit, the conclusions reached and how matters have been resolved and the views of those charged with governance; and
- copies of the approved financial statements and auditors' reports.

19.3.1   Documenting characteristics of items tested

The revised ISA (UK and Ireland) requires auditors to include in their documentation details of the identifying characteristics of the items or matters tested. The characteristics recorded will vary depending on the items being tested, but may specifically identify the actual items testing, e.g., for a detailed test of entity-generated purchase orders, auditors may identify the actual documents tested by providing their purchase order number, or alternatively, indicate the population as a whole, e.g., for a review of credit notes over a certain amount, auditors may document the scope of the procedure and the threshold value above which items were reviewed.

Recording the items tested at this level of detail allows the subsequent investigation of exceptions or inconsistencies as well as enabling the audit team to be accountable for its work.

Typically, however, copies of the entity's records will only be required when they are necessary for an experienced auditor to understand the work performed and the conclusions reached.

19.3.2   Judgement areas

ISA 230 (Revised) requires that working papers should include the auditors' reasoning on all significant matters which require the exercise of judgement, together with the auditors' conclusions thereon.

The revised ISA (UK and Ireland) provides examples of items which would be deemed to be 'significant matters':

- matters that give rise to significant risks;
- results of audit procedures which indicate either that financial information could be materially misstated or that there is a need to revise auditors' previous assessment of the risks of material misstatement;
- circumstances where auditors have significant difficulty in performing their procedures; and
- findings that could result in a modification to the auditor's report.

The working papers should note the relevant facts at the time the judgement was reached. This is particularly important where it concerns a difficult area which may be questioned later with the benefit of hindsight. The ISA (UK and Ireland) suggests that use of a summary of significant matters cross-referenced to detailed working papers may aid consideration of these matters together with assisting with review of the work performed and conclusions reached. This may form part of a 'completion memorandum'.

The revised ISA (UK and Ireland) also requires auditors to document any discussion held with management and others, including those charged with governance, about significant matters.

Where auditors have found information that contradicts their final conclusion on a significant matter the inconsistency should be documented on file, together with an explanation of how the final conclusion was reached. This does not mean, however, that incorrect or superseded documentation should be retained on file.

19.3.3 Documentation of departures from ISAs (UK and Ireland)

Where it is necessary to depart from the requirements of the basic or essential procedures in an ISA (UK and Ireland), auditors are required to document the alternative procedures followed and the reasons for the departure. This does not apply to procedures that are not relevant to the engagement, e.g., auditors need not apply the standards in ISA (UK and Ireland) 510 regarding initial engagements for ongoing audits.

19.3.4 Identification of the preparer and reviewer of documentation

The performer of audit work should be clearly identified on each piece of documentation, including the date on which their work was performed. There is no requirement to provide on each piece of documentation evidence of who reviewed the audit work. The documentation should indicate, however, who reviewed each element of the audit work and when. This may be on a control sheet rather than by, for example, initialling and dating each sheet of documentation itself.

19.4 ASSEMBLY OF THE FINAL AUDIT FILE

ISA (UK and Ireland) 230 (Revised) requires the final audit file to be assembled on a timely basis. The requirements of ISQC (UK and Ireland) 1, in an amendment published with ISA (UK and Ireland) 230 (Revised), suggest this should be within 60 days of the date of the auditor's report (see **19.3.8**).

The final assembly of the audit file is an administrative process and should not involve any further audit work or the drawing of new conclusions. Only administrative changes can be made to the audit documentation, such as:

- deleting or discarding superseded documentation;
- sorting, collating or cross-referencing working papers;
- signing off completion checklists relating to the file assembly process; or
- documenting audit evidence that auditors have obtained, discussed and agreed with the relevant members of the audit team before the date of their report.

Other audit documentation must not be deleted or discarded before the end of the retention period.

19.5 CHANGES TO AUDIT DOCUMENTATION

ISA (UK and Ireland) 230 (Revised) states that exceptional circumstances may arise which require auditors to perform new procedures after the date of the audit report or modify existing documentation. The ISA (UK and Ireland) requires auditors to record who made the changes and when, the consequential changes to documentation, the reasons for the changes and the effect on their previous conclusions.

19.6 CONFIDENTIALITY, CUSTODY AND OWNERSHIP OF WORKING PAPERS

Although the revised ISA (UK and Ireland) 230 no longer contains specific requirements that auditors should adopt appropriate procedures for maintaining the confidentiality and safe custody of their working papers, these have been added to ISQC (UK and Ireland) 1 (see **20.3.8**), and so such procedures should still be in place. It is the auditors' responsibility to ensure that the audit working papers are kept safely. They should bear in mind that their work is strictly confidential.

The audit working papers are the property of the auditors. Papers relating to accountancy work will normally be the property of the client although this will depend on the particular circumstances. Certain papers may be made available to clients but care should be taken not to undermine the independence or validity of the audit process. Because of their confidential nature they should not be divulged to third parties without the client's permission, although some third parties, for example the Inland Revenue, may have a right of access in certain circumstances. However, whatever the circumstances, they should not be seen as a substitute for the client's accounting records.

Audit Regulation 3.08b states that 'A Registered Auditor must keep all audit working papers which auditing standards require for a period of at least six years. The period starts with the end of the accounting period to which the papers relate.' The actual length of time they are kept for will be a matter of judgement based on auditors' own needs, those of the client and any regulatory requirements. However, it suggests that prior to their destruction a review is carried out to ensure that there is no need to refer to them again.

In addition to maintaining the confidentiality and safe custody of their audit documentation and retaining their documents for the minimum period required by law, auditors should also have appropriate procedures for audit documentation that:

- protects its integrity; and
- enables its accessibility and retrievability.

This is particularly relevant for any audit evidence held electronically and means that audit firms should ensure that they retain at least one version of any, otherwise superseded, information technology applications required to access old audit documentation. This may include both proprietary word-processing or spreadsheet tools which may have been upgraded, or any internally developed audit tools which have become obsolete or have been replaced or revised. The ability to retrieve work papers and other documentation is also an issue if it was originally prepared on paper and has later been scanned or microfiched for storage.

It is important that auditors have procedures in place to ensure that the integrity of data is maintained when it is stored electronically such as introducing appropriate back-up routines and use of restricted passwords. When original paper documentation is scanned or fiched, auditors should ensure that the scanned copy is identical to the original, properly integrated in the audit file and able to be retrieved and printed.

19.7 IAASB CLARITY PROJECT REVISION TO ISA 230

As part of their clarity project (see **Chapter 1**), the IAASB issued an Exposure Draft of ISA 230 (Redrafted) in December 2006. In addition to the amendments required to bring the ISA in line with the clarity drafting conventions, proposed amendments were made to reflect changes required as a result of an amendment to the *Preface to the International Standards on Quality Control, Auditing, Review, Other Assurance and Related Services* which was approved by the IAASB in September 2006. These changes provide further clarification on the documentation of significant judgements made by the auditor and how to document a departure from the requirements of an ISA.

The APB have requested that interested parties in the UK submit their comments to them for inclusion in the APB response to the IAASB.

19.8 ACCESS TO WORKING PAPERS

When a company becomes a target for potential purchasers, the purchaser's investigating accountants will frequently want access to the audit working papers to assist in their investigations. The granting of access to working papers in these circumstances involves issues of confidentiality and also the possibility that auditors may be alleged to have accepted an additional duty of care.

The Audit Faculty of the Institute of Chartered Accountants issued Audit *4/ 2003: Access to Working Papers by Investigating Accountants,* to attempt to facilitate the agreement of access to working papers in these situations. This supersedes Audit *3/95* of the same title. It recommends that access to papers is granted on the basis of client authorisation and 'release' letters. These seek to deal with confidentiality issues and limit as far as possible additional risks. The guidance has been updated due to the complexity of transaction funding, coupled with the emergence of different approaches such as vendor due diligence, which has resulted in an increase in the number and diversity of parties seeking to gain access to work papers.

The main area of change in the release letter is in relation to the indemnity sought by the auditors, which is now narrowed to an indemnity against loss caused by the breach by the purchasers or the investigating accountants of the terms of the letter, rather than any claims arising from any breach of the provisions of the access to the working papers. In many cases this amounts to the same thing because the purchaser and the investigating accountants agree that the auditors do not assume a duty of care, and agree not to disclose the contents of the working papers to anyone else. If they do disclose the working paper contents, they are in breach of the terms of the letter and the indemnity applies.

In addition, it is recommended that auditors include a disclaimer notice with the working papers and require such a notice to be attached to the investigating accountants' due diligence report.

19.8.1 *Work paper ownership and access*

The working papers of auditors are their legal property and they have the right to restrict or decline access to them. They would not provide access to their work papers or provide explanations on those papers until they have received:

- an authorisation letter signed by the vendor and the target company permitting the auditor to give access (**Table 3**); and
- a release letter signed by the prospective purchaser and its investigating accountant in which they agree that the auditors do not assume any duties or liabilities as a result of granting access (**Table 4**).

The release letter also requires the purchaser to indemnify the auditor for any loss suffered in the event of the purchaser or investigating accountant failing to comply with their obligations in the release letter.

In addition, to assist in excluding any other duty of care which may arise, and to reinforce the importance and purpose of audit working papers, the guidance suggests:

- attaching a 'notice' to the working papers when access is provided which summarises the characteristics, and records the exclusion of, liability (see Attachment 1 in the example letter in **Table 4**); and
- obtaining an undertaking from the purchaser and investigating accountants to include such a standard notice in the text of their due diligence report.

This assumes that the purchaser and investigating accountant will not allow the working papers to be viewed by another third party without written consent from the auditor. Whether this will be granted depends on the circumstances, and will usually be dependent on the signing of a formal release letter. In many cases the auditor controls access to the files by requiring the investigating accountants to view them on the auditors' premises.

Auditors would normally give access to all working papers. If some are withdrawn, they should inform the investigating accountants and purchaser that this is the case.

TABLE 3:   Client authorisation letter

Private and Confidential

The Directors

[Vendor]

[Address]

The Directors

[The Company]

[Address]

[Date]

Dear Sirs

Proposed sales of [Company Limited ('the Company') by [XYZ plc] ('the Vendor') to [ABC plc] ('the Purchaser')

In relation to the proposed sale by the Vendor [of the ordinary shares of the Company] to the Purchaser ('the Proposed Transaction') in which you requested this firm to allow [the Purchaser and/or] the Purchaser's accountants [PQR & Co] ('the Investigating Accountants') access to this firm's working papers relating to the statutory audit[s] of the Company's [and its subsidiaries'] financial statements for the year ended 31 December 20XX ('the Audit Working Papers').]

[As you are aware, this firm has not yet completed this year's statutory audit[s] of the Company's [and its subsidiaries'] financial statements, and therefore, the Audit Working Papers for this year are incomplete. Further this firm is not able to give any opinion on those financial statements and has not done so. Nevertheless, I understand that the Purchaser and the Investigating Accountants still wish the Investigating Accountants to review such Audit Working Papers as are available to date.]

[In addition, you requested this firm to allow the Investigating Accountants to review the taxation returns and computations of the Company [and its subsidiaries], so far as in the possession of this firm, as submitted to and/or agreed with the UK Inland Revenue for each of the last [insert number] years[, working papers relating to those returns and computations] and copies of the correspondence and related documents passing between this firm and the UK Inland Revenue in respect of those returns and computations (together, 'the tax papers').

This firm's general policy is not to allow third parties to have access to the working papers in the possession of this firm. However, this firm is content to allow such access to the Audit Working Papers [and the Tax Papers] ([together] 'the Papers'), but only on the basis of the guidance contained in Technical Release 04/03 issued by the Institute of Chartered Accountants in England and Wales. In accordance with that guidance I am now writing to confirm your agreement to the terms set out in this letter and to secure the authorisation of the Company [and its subsidiaries] for that access.

As a condition of providing access to the Investigating Accountants and responding to any requests for information and explanations in relation to the Papers in the course of or in connection with their review of the Papers, this firm requires that the Purchaser and the Investigating Accountants agree to the terms of the letter enclosed.

As you will appreciate, the Audit Working Papers were created for the sole purpose of the statutory audit[s] of the Company's [and its subsidiaries'] financial statements [and the Tax Papers were prepared and/or obtained for the purpose of calculating and agreeing the Company's [and its subsidiaries'] UK tax liabilities]. The Papers were not created for the purpose of the Proposed Transaction. Consequently, the information in the Papers should not be treated as suitable for the purposes of the Proposed Transaction. Furthermore, it is not this firm's function or responsibility to provide to the Purchaser or the Investigating Accountants any Papers that may come into existence, or information that may come to this firm's attention, after [date].

Accordingly, this firm requires the Vendor and its directors and the Company [(and its subsidiaries)] and [its] [their] directors to agree to the following conditions:

(a) They each accept the risk, and do not and will not hold this firm responsible, if the Investigating Accountant's review of the Papers or any information or explanations that this firm gives to them in relation to the Papers or in connection with their review of the Papers:

    (i) results in or contributes to the termination or reduction of the interest of the Purchaser in, or to the alternation to the proposed terms of, the Proposed Transaction, or otherwise affects the Proposed Transaction or the prospects of its maturing into a binding transaction; or

    (ii) causes an action or proceeding to be brought at any time against the Vendor or its directors or the company [(or any of its subsidiaries)] or [its] [their] directors [respectively]; or

    (iii) results in the Purchaser, the Investigating Accountants or any other person or entity using or misusing any confidential information obtained from a review of the Papers or from any information or explanations given by this firm.

(b) They each accept that, to the fullest extent permitted by law, this firm owes them no duty of care or other obligation and has no liability to them, in relation to or in connection with the Proposed Transaction as a result of granting the Investigating Accountants access to the Papers or any information or explanations that this firm gives in relation to the Papers or in connection with the review by the Investigating Accountants of the Papers.

The audit of the financial statements of the [Company/Companies] was undertaken by and is the sole responsibility of this firm, that is [insert full, exact name of UK firm carrying out the audit]. In paragraph (a) and (b) above references to 'this firm', where appropriate in the context, shall have an extended meaning so that they include, in addition to [insert full, exact name of the UK firm carrying out the audit], [partners/directors/members], employees and agents of this firm [and any person or organisation associated with this firm through membership of the international association of professional service firms to which this firm belongs and their [partners/directors/members], employees and agents]. This letter is for the benefit of all those included within the reference to this firm and each of them may enforce in their own right all of the terms of this letter.

Please confirm that the Company [and its subsidiaries] authorise[s] this firm to allow access to the Papers and to give information or explanations on the terms described above by signing the enclosed copy of this letter on behalf of the Vendor and its directors and the Company and its directors [and its subsidiaries and their directors] and returning it to this firm marked for the attention of...........

Yours faithfully

....

ACKNOWLEDGEMENT

Acknowledged and agreed, for and on behalf of [Vendor] and the directors of [Vendor].

....
Director   Date

Acknowledged and agreed, for and on behalf of [the Company] and the directors of [the Company].

....
Director   Date

[Acknowledged and agreed, for and on behalf of [subsidiaries] and the directors of [subsidiaries].

....
Director   Date]

TABLE 4:   Release letter to prospective purchaser and investigating accountants

(The Release Letter assumes a proposed purchase of a company and that both Audit Working Papers and Tax Papers are to be made available. It must be amended as appropriate for the circumstances of each transaction.)

Private and Confidential

[Purchaser]

[Address]

[Investigating Accountants]

[Address]

[Date]

Dear Sirs

Proposed Acquisition of [Company] Limited

1   In connection with the proposed acquisition by [ABC plc] ('the Purchaser') of [Company] Limited ('the Company') ('the Proposed Transaction') the Company [(and the subsidiary undertakings identified in Attachment 2)] [(together 'the Companies')] [has/have] requested this firm to allow [the Purchaser and/or] [name of Firm of Accountants] (the 'Investigating Accountants') access to this firm's working papers relating to the statutory audit[s] [(including the audits currently in progress)] of the financial statements of the [Company/Companies] for the year[s] ended [date] ('the Audit Working Papers') [and the taxation returns and computation of the [Company/Companies], so far as in this firm's possession, as submitted to and/or agreed with the UK Inland Revenue for each of the last [number] years[, working papers relating to those returns and computations] and copies of the correspondence and related documents passing between this firm and the UK Inland Revenue in respect of those returns and computations (together 'the Tax Papers')].[[The Company/Companies] [has/have] authorised this firm at this firm's discretion to give information or explanations in relation to the Audit Working Papers [and the Tax Papers]]. The Audit Working Papers [and the Tax Papers together] are also referred to below as 'the Papers'.

2   The Purchaser and the Investigating Accountants should note that this firm has not reported on the [Company's/Companies'] financial statements for any period subsequent to [date] [nor have any tax liabilities of the [Company/Companies] been agreed for any subsequent period to [date]] and significant events may well have occurred since [that date/those dates]. It is not this firm's function or responsibility to provide to the Purchaser or the Investigating Accountants any Audit Working Papers [or Tax Papers] that may come into existence, or information that may come to this firm's attention, at any point after [date].

3   This firm does not accept or assume responsibility to anyone other than the [Company/Companies] and the [Company's/Companies' respective] members as a body, for its audit work, for its audit report(s) or for the opinions it has formed. The statutory audit is undertaken in order that this firm might report to the [Company's/Companies' respective] members, as a body, in accordance with Section 235 of the Companies Act 1985. The audit procedures and the Audit Working Papers were designed and created solely for the purpose of enabling this firm to form and state an opinion to the [Company's/Companies' respective] members as a body, in accordance with the statutory requirements for audit, on whether the financial statements of [the Company/the Companies], which are the responsibility of the directors of the [the Company/the Companies], give a true and fair view of the state of affairs of [the Company/the Companies] as at the end of the relevant financial year and of the profit and loss for the period then ended. This firm's auditing procedures were designed to enable this firm to express an opinion on [the Company's/the Companies' respective] financial statements as a whole or not, for example and save where otherwise

expressly stated, on individual account balances, financial amounts, financial information or the adequacy of financial, accounting or management systems. [The Tax Papers were prepared and/or obtained solely for the purpose of calculating and/or agreeing [the Company's/the Companies'] tax liabilities.]

4   This firm's audit(s) of the [Company's/Companies'] financial statements, and the Audit Working Papers prepared or obtained in connection therewith, [was/were] not planned or conducted in contemplation, or for the purpose, of the Proposed Transaction. [Nor were the Tax Papers.] Further, the scope of an audit is normally substantially narrower than an investigation on behalf of a potential purchaser. Moreover, there are a number of inherent limitations in audited financial statements [and the calculation or agreement of tax liabilities] as the Investigating Accountants will be able to advise.

5   Therefore, items of possible interest to the Purchaser may not have been specifically addressed for the purposes of the audit [or of calculating and agreeing [the Company's/the Companies'] tax liabilities]. The user of professional judgement and assessment of materiality for the purpose of this firm's audit [or of calculating and agreeing [the Company's/the Companies'] tax liabilities] means that matters may have existed that would have been assessed differently by the Purchaser or the Investigating Accountants for the purposes of the Proposed Transaction. This firm does not warrant or represent that the information in the Papers, or that information or explanations given by this firm in relation to the Papers or in connection with the review by the Investigating Accountants of the Papers, is appropriate for the purposes of the Purchaser or the Investigating Accountants. The Audit Working Papers were not created for, and should not be treated as suitable for, any purpose other than the Statutory Audit. [The Tax Papers were not created for, and should not be treated as suitable for, any purpose other than [calculating and agreeing [the Company's/the Companies'] tax liabilities.]

6   For the foregoing reasons, neither the Papers nor the information or explanations given by this firm in relation to the Papers or in connection with the review by the Investigating Accountants of the Papers can in any way serve as a substitute for other enquiries and procedures that the Purchaser and Investigating Accountants would (or should) otherwise undertake and judgements they must make for the purpose of satisfying themselves regarding [the Company's/the Companies' respective] financial condition or for any other purpose in connection with the Proposed Transaction. No one should rely for any purpose whatsoever upon the Papers or any information or explanations that this firm may give in relation to them or in connection with the review by the Investigating Accountants of them.

7   This firm is prepared to grant the [Purchaser and/or the] Investigating Accountants access to the papers and at this firm's discretion to give information and explanations in relation to the Papers or in connection with the review by the Investigating Accountants of the Papers, on

condition that the Purchaser and the Investigating Accountants acknowledge and accept the foregoing paragraphs (including that the position in respect of this firm's audit reports on the [Company's /Companies'] financial statements will remain as stated in paragraph 3 above following the grant of access to the Papers and giving of information and explanations in relation to the Papers) and agree to the following conditions upon which access to the Papers is granted and the explanations and information referred to are given:

(1) The Purchaser and the Investigating Accountants accept, agree and acknowledge:

    (a) For the purposes of this letter, the expression 'the information' shall mean the Papers and any information and explanations given by this firm in relation to the Papers or in connection with the review by the Investigating Accountants of the papers;

    (b) Where any information or explanation is given by this firm the onus shall be upon the Purchaser and the Investigating Accountants to verify any such information or explanation direct with [the Company/the Companies] rather than seek to rely on this firm;

    (c) to the fullest extent permitted by law, this firm owes no duty to them, whether in contract or in tort or under statute or otherwise (including in negligence) with respect to or in connection with the information or its provision or in relation to the audit reports on the [Company's/Companies'] financial statements;

    (d) if, notwithstanding the terms of this letter, they do rely upon any of the information or the audit reports on the [Company's / Companies] financial statements for any purpose, they will do so entirely at their own risk;

    (e) they will not bring any actions, proceedings, or claims against this firm where the action, proceeding or claim in any way relates to or concerns or is connected with the use of or reliance on the information or the audit reports on the [Company's/Companies'] financial statements;

    (f) to the fullest extent permitted by law, this firm has no liability to them for any loss or damage suffered or costs incurred by them, arising out of or in connection with the information or its use or the audit reports on the [Company's/Companies'] financial statements, however such loss or damage is caused;

    (g) they will not refer to the information nor allow access to it or any report derived therefrom to any person or entity without this firm's prior written consent. (However the Investigating Accountants will not need to obtain such consent in order to disclose and discuss the same (i) with [the Company/the Companies] for the purpose of obtaining information or verification from [the Company/the Companies] in respect of any report to be prepared by the Investigating Accountants in connection with the Proposed Transaction; (ii) with the Purchaser's legal advisers but then only on the basis that the firm will have no duty or liability to them; or (iii) otherwise as required by a Court or by statute.) Where this firm is willing to give written consent, this firm will require as a condition of such consent that the other person or entity agrees in writing to be bound by and to observe the terms set out in this letter, as if references to the Purchaser were a reference to the other person or entity.

(2) To the fullest extent permitted by law, the Purchaser agrees to indemnify and hold harmless this firm against all actions, proceedings and claims brought or threatened against this firm, and all loss, damage and expense (including legal expenses) relating thereto where such action, proceeding or claim has arisen out of or results from or is connected with the failure of the Purchaser, or any of its professional advisers or the Investigating Accountants to comply with the terms of this letter.

(3) Without limiting the obligation in paragraph 7(1)(g) above, the Purchaser and the Investigating Accountants agree to ensure that the notice attached as Attachment 1 to this letter is attached to any document obtained as a result of the Investigating Accountants' access to the Papers and is included in any note or report or other document in which they make reference to the information.

8 The audit of the financial statements of the [Company/Companies] was undertaken by and is the sole responsibility of this firm, that is [insert full, exact name of UK firm carrying out the audit]. In paragraph 7(1)(c) to (g) and 7(2) of this letter all references to 'this firm' (except for the first and the last two references in the paragraph 7(1)(g) shall have an extended meaning so that they include, in addition to [insert full, exact name of the UK firm carrying out the audit], [partners/directors/members], employees and agents of this firm [and any person or organisation associated with this firm through membership of the international association of professional service firms to which this firm belongs and their [partners/directors/members], employees and agents. This letter is for the benefit of all of those referred to in the previous sentence and each of them may enforce in their own right all of the terms of this letter.

9 This letter sets out the entire agreement as between the Purchaser and the Investigating Accountants and this firm in relation to the conditions upon which access to the Papers is given by this firm and upon which information and explanations in relation to the Papers or in connection with the review by the Investigating Accountants are given by this firm to the Purchaser and the Investigating Accountants. It replaces all prior agreements or understandings (if any) between or amongst the Purchaser, the Investigating Accountants and this firm in that regard.

10 The terms of the agreement shall be governed solely by English law, and the Courts of England and Wales shall have exclusive jurisdiction in respect of any dispute arising out of it or in connection with it. [The Purchaser, the Investigating Accountants, and this firm irrevocably waive any right to object to proceedings being brought in those Courts, to claim that the proceedings have been brought in an inappropriate forum, or to claim that those Courts do not have jurisdiction.]

11 Please confirm the agreement of the Purchaser and the Investigating Accountants to, and acceptance of, the provisions of this letter by signing,

dating and returning to us a copy of this letter.

Yours faithfully

[Firm]

The Purchaser hereby acknowledges that it agrees to and accepts the provisions of this letter.

_____   [Date]
Director

The Investigating Accountants hereby acknowledge that they agree to and accept the provisions of this letter.

_____   [Date]
Director

Attachment 1 to Release Letter

Notice of the Auditor

1   [Firm name] ('the Auditor'), the auditor of [Company name] ('the Company'), has, on certain conditions, allowed [name of Investigating Accountants] ('the Investigating Accountants') to have access to the Auditor's working papers relating to the statutory audit of the Company's financial statements for the [year/period] ended [date] ('the Audit Working Papers').

2   The Auditor does not accept or assume responsibility to anyone other than the Company and the Company's members as a body, for its audit work, for its audit report or for the opinions it has formed. To the fullest extent permitted by law, the Auditor does not accept or assume responsibility to anyone as a result of the access given to the Audit Working Papers or for any information or explanation given to the Investigating Accountants in relation to the Audit Working Papers or in connection with the review by the Investigating Accountants of the Audit Working Papers.

3   The Audit Working Papers were not created for, and should not be treated as suitable for, any purpose other than the statutory audit. The statutory audit is undertaken in order that the Auditor might report to the Company's members, as a body, in accordance with Section 235 of the Companies Act 1985. The audit work of the Auditor is undertaken so that the Auditors might state to the Company's members those matters it is required to state to them in auditor's report and for no other purpose.

Attachment 2 to Release Letter

List of companies referred to in paragraph 1 for which access to the Audit Working Papers [and the Tax Papers] is to be provided.

19.8.2 Further explanations

If an auditor provides further explanation which extends to matters beyond the content of their work papers, they increase the risk of assuming a duty of care. In particular, auditors should take care not to give oral representations about matters arising after the date of the audit report.

If further explanations are sought, auditors are advised to re-emphasise the matters in the Notice in Attachment 1 to **Table 4** at the time, perhaps by reading this out, or circulating a copy of the Notice at the beginning of the meeting.

If matters outside the auditors' working papers are to be discussed, the auditors consider whether this is appropriate. If the risks can be managed they may wish to structure this as a separate engagement with appropriate liability protection in a separate engagement letter.

Auditors are recommended not to agree to any request by the investigating accountants to review or approve their due diligence report. Such requests do not give auditors any added protection and may serve to confuse auditors' roles in transactions.

19.8.3 Access for other parties

The example release letter in **Table 4** assumes a simple investment transaction where an existing corporate entity purchases a subsidiary of the vendor. There are other situations where the release letter may require amendment.

Syndicated financings
In syndicated financings the investigating accountants may be requested to provide copies of their investigation report, incorporating information derived from the audit working papers, to other parties who were not identified at the time the release letter was signed, and therefore could not be party to it. Providing this information without the auditors' consent would be in breach of paragraph 7(1)(g) of the release letter.

It might be appropriate for the lead bank or equity provider to sign a modified release letter containing the following paragraph:

> 'This letter is addressed to [Lead Bank/Lead Equity Provider] for itself and on behalf of all [Banks/Equity Providers] listed in the [Loan/Equity Agreement] (together "the [Banks/Equity Providers"). By signing and accepting the terms of this letter, [Lead Bank/Equity Provider] warrants and represents that it has authority to accept the same on its own behalf and as agent for the [Banks/Equity Providers]'.

The lead bank or equity provider may seek to amend paragraph 7(2) of the letter to seek to provide an indemnity for its own breaches only. If this is agreed, auditors should be aware of the risks of another bank or equity provider passing information on to another party.

Alternatively, each bank or equity provider should sign a release letter in its own right. This may be difficult where the draft investigating accountants' report is circulated to potential finance parties as a basis for their decision whether or not to go ahead with the finance. Technical Release Audit 4/2003 contains detailed guidance on this situation.

Flotations

Where access is provided in connection with a flotation, the auditors are advised to obtain a release letter signed by the:

- firm acting as reporting accountants;
- new company incorporated for the purpose of the float; and
- sponsor.

Auditors should obtain legal advice about limiting liability where no new company has been incorporated.

Where the reporting accountants are preparing an accountants' report (a short form report) there is no need to attach or refer to the Notice. Paragraph 7(3) of the Notice should be amended accordingly.

Vendor due diligence

Where a vendor has instructed a firm of accountants to prepare a due diligence report that will eventually be addressed to a purchaser, the auditors will require the vendor and the target company to sign an authorisation letter. The wording of that letter will be extended to include an indemnity from the vendor, as it is the vendor, rather than the purchaser, who will control the distribution of the due diligence report.

The auditors will also require a release letter signed by the investigating accountants, based on **Table 4**, but without the indemnity paragraph 7(2). Risks to unknown potential purchasers will be managed in much the same way as for financing syndicates above.

Alternatively auditors may be prepared to acknowledge that the investigating accountants will require permission to circulate their report to prospective purchasers, and replace paragraphs 7(1)(g) and 7(2) with **Table 5**.

TABLE 5:   Alternative paragraph 7(1)(g) and 7(2) for use in vendor due diligence situations

'they will not refer to the Information nor allow access to it or any report derived therefrom to any person or entity without this firm's prior written consent. The Investigating Accountants may allow access to the Information or any part thereof, in the form of a report of Investigating Accountants incorporating or referring to any part of the Information, to any prospective purchaser of the Company ("Prospective Purchaser") provided that the Investigating Accountants obtain the express prior agreement and acknowledgement of each Prospective Purchaser, addressed to this firm, that (a) this firm has, to the fullest extent permitted by law, no duty or liability and assumes no responsibility to the Prospective Purchaser or its professional advisers, whether in contract or tort or under statue or otherwise (including in negligence), with respect to or in connection with the Information or any part thereof the report and that (b) Prospective Purchaser will not disclose (including by reference or by copy, in whole or in part) any Information, including without limitation the report, to any other person or entity. Prior to the Investigating Accountants addressing to any party acquiring interest in the Company ("Purchaser") any report incorporating or referring to any part of the Information, the Investigating Accountants shall procure that Purchaser binds itself to this firm and accepts all the provisions of a letter in the terms of this letter (but adjusted to refer to Purchaser), together with an obligation in the following terms:

To the fullest extent permitted by law, Purchaser agrees to indemnify and hold harmless this firm against all actions, proceedings and claims brought or threatened against this firm and all loss, damage and expense (including legal expenses) relating thereto, where such action, proceedings or claim has arisen out of or results from or is connected with the failure of Purchaser, or any of its professional advisers or Investigating Accountants to comply with the terms of this letter.'

Where the vendor due diligence report is prepared by the same firm as the auditors, the firm may manage its risk relating to the purchaser or prospective purchaser by:

- requiring the purchaser to agree the terms of the release letter before agreeing to address the vendor due diligence report to them; or
- placing an obligation on the vendor to ensure that the purchaser signs the release letter.

Business refinancing where there is no acquisition
Where a firm of accountants are instructed to report to funders in respect of a proposed refinancing of the entity, it is recommended that auditors obtain a signed release letter from the funders and investigating accountants prior to releasing the audit working papers.

19.8.4   Investigating accountants from the same firm as the auditors

Where auditors and investigating accountants are from the same firm, there still remains a risk from releasing audit working papers to a purchaser.

In this situation, some firms will wish to amend the release letter so that it is addressed only to the purchaser. The indemnity may also be restricted to breaches by the purchaser only.

20 QUALITY CONTROL FOR AUDIT WORK

20.1 INTRODUCTION

This Chapter examines the area of quality control relating both to audit firms and to individual audits.

Under audit regulation, each RSB must ensure that its members have an adequate system of quality control (see **Chapter 2**).

20.2 GUIDANCE

International Standard on Quality Control (ISQC) (UK and Ireland) 1, *Quality Control for Firms that Perform Audits and Reviews of Historical Financial Information, and Other Assurance and Related Services Engagements*, was in December 2004 to provide guidance on quality control for all audits and review work on historical information.

ISA (UK and Ireland) 220 *Quality Control for Audits of Historical Financial Information* was issued at the same time and provides guidance on quality control specifically for audits.

As with other ISAs (UK and Ireland), the texts of the international ISA and ISQC have been supplemented with additional guidance from a UK and Ireland perspective. SAS 240 *Quality Control for Audit Work* has not yet been officially withdrawn.

ISA (UK and Ireland) 220 is effective for audits of financial statements and other reviews of historical information for periods commencing on or after 15 December 2004. Firms are required to have systems of quality control in place to comply with ISQC (UK and Ireland) 1 by 15 June 2005.

In November 2002, the Audit and Assurance Faculty of the ICAEW issued *Audit Quality*, a publication which examines the components that make up a quality audit. This document is discussed in **20.6.** This was followed in

November 2006 by a discussion paper issued by the FRC entitled *Promoting Audit Quality*. Details of this paper are given in **20.7**.

20.3   ISQC (UK AND IRELAND) 1: QUALITY CONTROL FOR FIRMS THAT PERFORM AUDITS AND REVIEWS OF HISTORICAL FINANCIAL INFORMATION, AND OTHER ASSURANCE AND RELATED SERVICES ENGAGEMENTS

20.3.1   *Basic requirement*

ISQC (UK and Ireland) 1 requires firms to establish a system of quality control which is designed to provide reasonable assurance that the firm and its personnel comply with professional standards and regulatory and legal requirements, and that reports issued by the firm or engagement partners are appropriate in the circumstances. The relevant ethical pronouncements with which auditors must comply are the APB's *Ethical Standards* (**Chapter 2**) and *Scope and Authority of Pronouncements* (**Chapter 1**).

The ISQC (UK and Ireland) is an overall quality standard from which the requirements for audits in ISA (UK and Ireland) 220 are derived. The APB's *Ethical Standards* share many requirements with the ISQC (UK and Ireland).

In January 2006, the APB issued a revision to ISA (UK and Ireland) 230, *Documentation* (see **Chapter 19**). In the appendices to this revision was a significant amendment to ISQC (UK and Ireland) 1 relating to engagement documentation. Firms are required to have the policies and procedures required by this amendment in place by 15 June 2006. The amendment is detailed in **20.3.8** below.

20.3.2   *Elements of a system of quality control*

The ISQC (UK and Ireland) sets out six areas which should be addressed by a firm's quality control policies and procedures, documented and communicated to the firm's personnel:

- leadership responsibilities for quality within the firm;
- ethical requirements;
- acceptance and continuance of client relationships and specific engagements;
- human resources;
- engagement performance; and
- monitoring.

These are discussed in greater detail below.

20.3.3   Leadership

From the very top of the organisation, the firm should establish policies which promote a culture of quality. The ISQC (UK and Ireland) states that this should be demonstrated practically, with actions and messages from all levels of the firm's management emphasising their commitment to quality. This should also be demonstrated in the firm's overall business strategy, which should promote the need for quality.

The firm's managing board of partners, or equivalent, will maintain ultimate responsibility for the quality of the work performed, but operational responsibility may be delegated to someone with sufficient and appropriate experience, ability and authority.

20.3.4   Ethical requirements

The firm should have procedures in place to provide it with assurance that its personnel comply with the APB's *Scope and Authority of Pronouncements* and *Ethical Standards* (see **Chapters 1** and **2**).

In relation to independence, the firm should ensure that it is able to:

- communicate its independence requirements to personnel and any others bound by them; and
- identify and evaluate threats to its independence and apply safeguards as necessary.

To adhere to these requirements, sufficient information must be held about the engagements undertaken by the firm, including the scope of the services provided to each client. Changes to the information should be notified to the person responsible for maintaining it on a timely basis.

Firms should also ensure that they have policies and procedures for informing the relevant individual when breaches of independence take place. The engagement partner and others who need to take action should be informed of the breach promptly.

In addition, the firm should obtain annual declarations of independence from all personnel who are required to do so by the Ethical Standards. Firms should set out criteria for rotation of senior personnel to ensure that no familiarity threat is created, and this should be in accordance with the requirements of the APB's Ethical Standards for audit engagements.

20.3.5   *Client acceptance and continuance*

The firm's policies should ensure that it:

- considers the integrity of each client;
- is competent and has the resources to provide the service; and
- can comply with ethical requirements.

The information should be gathered or reviewed at the commencement of the relationship with the client, when accepting recurring work in second or subsequent years or when accepting a new engagement from an existing client. Matters to be considered are set out in **Table 1**.

Where issues are discovered that cause concern, but the engagement continues, the issues, and their resolution should be fully documented.

TABLE 1:   Matters to consider when accepting or reaccepting a client

Client integrity

- the identity and business reputation of the client's principal owners, key management, related parties and those charged with governance;
- the nature of the client's operations, including its business practices;
- information concerning the attitude of the client's principal owners, key management and those charged with governance towards such matters as aggressive interpretation of accounting standards and the internal control environment;
- whether the client is aggressively concerned with keeping the firm's fees as low as possible;
- indication of an inappropriate limitation in the scope of work;
- indications that the client might be involved in money laundering or other criminal activities; and
- the reasons for the proposed appointment of the firm and non-reappointment of the previous firm (if relevant).

Firm resources and capabilities

- whether firm personnel have knowledge of relevant industries or subject matters;
- if firm personnel have experience with relevant regulatory or reporting requirements or the ability to gain the necessary skills and knowledge effectively;
- whether the firm has sufficient personnel with the necessary capabilities and competence;
- the availability of experts, if needed;
- whether individuals meeting the criteria and eligibility requirements to perform engagement quality control reviews are available, where applicable; and
- whether the firm can complete the engagement within the reporting deadline.

If the firm later discovers something that would have lead it to declining the engagement, they should take legal advice and consider resigning.

20.3.6 Human resources

Firms should have policies and procedures to ensure that they have sufficient capable, competent and committed staff. Policies should cover:

- recruitment;
- performance evaluation;
- capabilities;
- competence;
- career developments;
- promotion;
- compensation; and
- the number of staff needed.

Firms should allocate appropriately experienced and qualified staff to each engagement, together with an engagement partner whose responsibilities will be clearly defined and understood. The identity and role of the engagement partner should be communicated to key members of the client's management team and those charged with governance.

20.3.7 Engagement performance

ISQC (UK and Ireland) 1 requires firms to implement policies and procedures to provide it with assurance that its engagements are performed in accordance with professional and legal standards. The aim is to ensure consistently high quality engagements, and this can be accomplished through the use of manuals, software tools and standardised documentation as applicable.

The engagement team should be sufficiently briefed prior to commencing their work, adequately supervised throughout the engagement and their work reviewed by a more experienced team member.

Consultation
Policies should be in place which set out the requirement for consultation to take place on difficult or contentious matters and for that consultation, together with its conclusions, to be fully documented in order to enable an understanding of the matter and the results of the consultation.

Differences of opinion
There should be firm policies about resolution and documentation of differences of opinion within the engagement team. The firm's report should never be issued until any such differences have been resolved.

Engagement quality control review
For certain engagements, the firm should implement engagement quality
control reviews to ensure that significant judgements made by the
engagement team undergo an objective evaluation. The policies for such
reviews should:

- require reviews for audits of listed companies; and
- set out criteria against which all other work should be assessed to see if it
  requires a review.

When setting these criteria firms would consider the nature of the
engagement, including the extent to which it involves a matter of public
interest, any unusual circumstances surrounding the work and whether a
review is required by law.

The review should be completed before any report is issued.

Policies should also be developed to set out:

- the nature, extent and timing of the engagement quality control review;
- eligibility criteria for reviewers; and
- documentation requirements.

Nature, timing and extent of review
An engagement quality control review will usually involve discussions with
the engagement partner, a review of the financial statements, consideration
of the audit report and review of selected working papers. Reviews of audits
of listed clients include considering:

- the engagement team's evaluation of the firm's independence in relation
  to the specific engagement;
- significant risks identified during the engagement and the responses to
  those risks;
- judgements made, particularly with respect to materiality and significant
  risks;
- whether appropriate consultation has taken place on matters involving
  differences of opinion or other difficult or contentious matters, and the
  conclusions arising from those consultations;
- the significance of corrected and uncorrected misstatements identified
  during the engagement and the actions taken in relation to them;
- the matters to be communicated to those charged with governance and
  other parties such as regulatory bodies;
- whether working papers selected for review reflect the work performed in
  relation to the significant judgements and support the conclusions
  reached; and
- the appropriateness of the report to be issued.

Where the review is for an engagement other than the audit of a listed company, some or all of the above considerations will be relevant.

Eligibility of reviewers
The firm's policies should set out the technical qualifications, experience and authority required of quality control reviewers together with the extent to which the quality control reviewer can be consulted by the engagement partner during the audit without compromising the reviewer's objectivity.

For the audit of the financial statements of listed companies, the reviewer should be sufficiently experienced to act as an engagement partner on listed audits.

For sole practitioners or small firms, suitably qualified external persons may be contracted to perform quality control reviews.

Review documentation
There should be documentation on file that the review occurred, that it was completed before the report was issued and that the reviewer is not aware of any unresolved matters that suggest that the conclusions of the engagement team were not appropriate.

20.3.8 Engagement documentation

As part of the process of revising ISA (UK and Ireland) 230, *Documentation*, changes to ISQC (UK and Ireland) 1 were published in January 2006.

The revision sets out the requirement for firms to establish policies and procedures for engagement teams to complete the assembly of final engagement files on a timely basis after the engagement reports have been finalised. For audits this is 'ordinarily not more than 60 days after the date of the auditor's report'.

The revision also requires firms to establish policies and procedures designed to maintain the confidentiality, safe custody, integrity, accessibility and retrievability of engagement documentation. For audits, these areas are detailed in the APB's Ethical Standards.

ISQC (UK and Ireland) is also amended to state that policies and procedures should be implemented to ensure that firms retain engagement documentation for the period required by law or regulation. Requirements for audit work papers are set out in section **19.6**.

20.3.9 Monitoring

Each firm should have procedures to monitor their quality control policies and to ensure that they are complied with in practice. Evaluation of the system of quality control will include:

- analysis of:
  - changes in professional standards and regulatory and legal requirements;
  - written confirmation by staff of compliance with policies and procedures on independence;
  - continuing professional development and training; and
  - decisions related to acceptance and continuance of engagements;
- suggestions for corrective actions and improvements to the system;
- communication of weaknesses in the system to those in authority; and
- follow-up procedures to ensure that modifications are made as suggested.

Monitoring should also include a periodic review of completed engagements on a cyclical basis, typically with at least one engagement for each engagement partner in an inspection cycle (which should be no longer than three years). The monitoring inspector will be separate from the engagement partner or the quality control reviewer and may select engagements without prior notification. For small firms or sole practitioners, an external person may be engaged, or arrangements established with another small firm to provide personnel on a reciprocal basis.

The reviewer should consider whether any deficiencies found are:

- systemic, repetitive or significant which require prompt corrective action; or
- not indicative of failings in the firm's quality control system,

and an appropriate report should be given at the end of the work.

Where deficiencies are found, they should be communicated to the engagement partner and recommendations made for remedial action. Recommendations may include one or more of the following:

- taking action in relation to an individual engagement or member of personnel;
- informing those in charge of training and professional development;
- changing quality control policies and procedures; and
- disciplinary action against offenders.

Where an incorrect report is found to have been issued, firms should seek legal advice.

At least annually, a summary of the findings of the quality control review process should be provided to the managing board of partners, or equivalent. This should include details of the process undertaken, its conclusions and information about any systemic failures. Where the firm is part of a network of firms, this summary should also be sent to appropriate individuals in the network.

20.3.10 Complaints

ISQC (UK and Ireland) 1 also requires firms to have procedures for handling complaints or allegations that work performed does not comply with professional standards, or with the firm's own system of quality control, whether these arise from inside or outside the firm.

20.3.11 Documentation of quality control system

Firms are required to have sufficient documentation to provide evidence that their quality control system is operating effectively. The ISQC (UK and Ireland) does not set a standard form for this documentation, but points out that the content of documentation will vary depending on the size of the firm, the number of offices, and the nature and complexity of the firm's practice and organisation.

20.4 ISA (UK AND IRELAND) 220, QUALITY CONTROL FOR AUDITS OF HISTORICAL FINANCIAL INFORMATION

20.4.1 General requirement

ISA (UK and Ireland) 220 requires auditors to implement quality control procedures for the individual audit engagement. ISQC (UK and Ireland) 1 (see **20.3** above) sets out the detailed requirements for quality control systems for all reports on historical information, and ISA (UK and Ireland) 220 sets out the details of how those systems should be applied to audit engagements. The additional guidance concerns engagement partner responsibilities and is covered in **20.4.2**.

20.4.2 Engagement partner responsibilities

Where ISQC (UK and Ireland) 1 sets out the need for policies and procedures in relation to engagement partners, ISA (UK and Ireland) 220 gives more details of what these policies should cover:

- the direction, supervision and performance of the audit;
- ensuring the audit evidence supports the opinion given in the audit report;
- ensuring the team consults with experts on any contentious or difficult issues;
- determining that a quality control reviewer has been appointed as required;

- discussing significant matters with the quality control reviewer; and
- not issuing their report until the quality control review has been completed.

20.5   CONFLICTS OF INTEREST

The ICAEW's Business Law Committee has issued guidance on conflicts of interest and confidentiality. This follows from the decision in the case of *Prince Jefri Bolkiah* v *KPMG*.

The judgement stresses that where an accountant is acting as a fiduciary, he cannot act for clients with conflicting interests without their informed consent. Since the law is unclear about when accountants act as fiduciaries, consent should be obtained whenever where there is potential conflict. Such conflicts of interest could be wide ranging and could extend to audit clients who are competitors with one another in a particular market. This requirement does not apply to former clients, although duties of confidentiality will continue.

The guidance suggests additional paragraphs to be included in the engagement letter to deal with these issues. The paragraphs are set out in **Table 2**.

TABLE 2:   Paragraphs to be included in an engagement letter where potential conflict of interest exists

Conflict and Confidentiality

You agree that we may reserve the right to act during this engagement for other clients whose interests are or may be adverse to yours, subject to the confidentiality requirements detailed here.

We confirm that where you give us confidential information we shall at all times keep it confidential, except as required by law or as provided for in regulatory, ethical or other professional pronouncements applicable to our engagement.

You agree that it will be sufficient compliance with our duty of confidence for us to take such steps as we in good faith think fit to preserve confidential information both during and after termination of this engagement.

Although these paragraphs leave accountants potentially liable for any actual breach of confidence, this is only where they do not take appropriate steps to keep confidential information secure. This means that the erection of 'Chinese Walls' may be avoided.

20.5.1 Chinese Walls

Where an accountant is not able to obtain consent from their client in line with the paragraphs in **Table 2**, it is possible for a Chinese Wall to be effective within a firm. The Prince Jefri ruling states that the Chinese Wall must have the characteristics noted in **Table 3** to be effective.

TABLE 3: Characteristics of an effective Chinese Wall

- the physical separation of the various departments in order to insulate them from each other (this may include details such as separate dining arrangements);
- training to emphasise the importance of not divulging confidential information;
- strict and defined procedures for when it is felt that the wall should be crossed and the maintaining of proper records where this occurs;
- monitoring of the effectiveness of the wall by compliance officers; and
- disciplinary sanctions where there has been a breach of the wall.

In addition, an effective Chinese Wall needs to be an established part of an organisation, not created on an ad hoc basis. Physical segregation would not create an effective barrier within a single department.

20.6 AUDIT QUALITY

In November 2002, the Audit and Assurance Faculty of the ICAEW published *Audit Quality* to provide detailed discussion and illustrations of good practice to facilitate audit quality.

The publication has a general introduction which considers the role of audit within the modern economy and business world, followed by detailed chapters covering:

- the need for strong leadership to champion audit quality throughout a firm;
- requirements for staff to have technical competence, professionalism and judgement underpinned by a clear ethical framework. The chapter also considers the need for continued training and the development and retention of professional scepticism;
- managing client relationships to enable clear communications and an effective and efficient audit process;
- the need for a strong audit team, coupled with good communication and knowledge sharing amongst the team; and
- internal and external monitoring, on both formal and informal bases.

In addition, the publication examines the limitations of the audit, particularly in relation to fraud, whilst at the same time acknowledging that auditing must adapt to continue to meet the requirements of a changing business environment.

20.7   FRC DISCUSSION PAPER: PROMOTING AUDIT QUALITY

20.7.1   *Background*

The FRC issued the first of a series of discussion papers in November 2006, as part of a discussion of its objectives. By issuing this series of papers, the FRC wants to invite comments on whether it is correctly identifying the key issues on which to focus its attention and whether it is taking the correct steps to address those issues.

This first discussion paper, *Promoting Audit Quality*, addresses the FRC's objective of 'promoting and maintaining confidence in the audit process and the resulting audit report as a key component of the corporate reporting and governance regime and the effective operation of capital markets'. In order for this objective to be met, users of the financial statements must be able to rely on the audit report.

At a more fundamental level, the FRC is aware of concerns that the financial reporting regime in its entirety is not capable of meeting users' needs. However, given the widespread changes in recent years, they are keen to give users time to operate within the new environment before considering more wholesale changes. Therefore this discussion paper seeks opinions as to whether all appropriate steps are being taken within the existing legal and regulatory framework, and only after responses to this paper have been received by the FRC will they consider whether a discussion paper should be issued to consider the wider financial reporting regime.

This paper identifies the 'drivers' that are central to achieving a high quality audit and considers any threats to them.

20.7.2   *Audit quality*

Despite the recent changes aimed at improving audit quality, the discussion paper identifies the following concerns about audit quality which are still felt by commentators:

- changing business environment and increasing complexity of financial reporting, particularly in relation to the increasing requirement for estimates and valuations;
- audits possibly not detecting management fraud;
- relationships between executive management and auditors;

- lack of transparency in auditors' work and judgements; and
- an increasingly prescriptive approach to audit.

Against this background, the FRC have identified four main drivers of audit quality in the discussion paper. These are the:

- culture within the audit firm;
- skills and personal qualities of the audit partners and staff;
- quality of the audit process; and
- reliability and usefulness of audit reporting.

Audit firm culture

The discussion paper states that audit quality 'can be driven by audit firms creating an environment where achieving high quality is valued, invested in and rewarded'. It identifies a number of indicators that enhance audit quality, including respect for underlying auditing and ethical standards, partner and staff development systems and the promotion of consultation on difficult issues. Threats to quality oriented cultures include over-emphasis on winning and retaining audits or on non-audit services and excessive cost cutting in times of economic downturn.

Skills of partners and staff

The key drivers of audit quality in this area are subdivided into the skills required of partners and staff, the training provided to them and the appraisal process they undergo. Threats that may undermine quality in this area include failure to retain experienced staff, insufficient or ineffective training and lack of effective mentoring to develop the necessary personal characteristics.

Audit process

The discussion paper sets out the following characteristics of an effective audit process:

- an audit team appropriately structured for the engagement with relevant experience and knowledge;
- availability of high quality technical support;
- a well structured audit methodology which provides a good framework to obtain sufficient appropriate audit evidence, ensures compliance with auditing standards, requires appropriate documentation and ensures effective review;
- objectives under ethical standards being achieved; and
- effective quality control procedures.

The paper identifies possible threats, including the increased use of computerised audit methodologies which may be over-prescriptive and reduce the importance of auditor judgement and a focus on producing documentation to the detriment of performing procedures properly.

Reliability of audit reporting

The discussion paper recognises that the structure of the audit report is specified by law and auditing standards and as such acts as 'a signal rather than a source of new information'. This means that confidence in the report is inextricably linked to the presumed quality of the audit process. This quality is best clarified through clear communication between the auditors and audit committees, as it is in this forum that auditors can provide further information about the process followed, key risks identified and issues found.

The FRC are aware that confidence in the audit report may be undermined by the concerns of some users and commentators. These concerns include whether auditors are fulfilling their responsibilities in relation to the adequacy of a company's accounting records and whether audit reports should contain more information about key issues.

20.7.3   *Factors outside auditors' control*

In addition, the discussion paper warns that some factors which affect audit quality will remain outside the control of auditors. It lists these as:

- the approach taken by management;
- contributions made by audit committees;
- the role of shareholders and commentators;
- litigation as a driver of audit quality;
- the approach of regulators; and
- pressures caused by tight reporting deadlines.

21 ENGAGEMENT LETTERS

21.1 AUDITING STANDARDS

ISA (UK and Ireland) 210 *Terms of Audit Engagements* was issued in December 2004 and provides guidance on engagement letters issued by auditors. The ISA contains standards covering:

- agreeing terms of engagement in writing;
- respective responsibilities of auditors and those charged with governance;
- recurring audits; and
- changes in engagements.

As with all ISAs (UK and Ireland), the text of the international ISA has been supplemented with additional guidance from a UK and Ireland perspective. SAS 140 *Engagement Letters* has not yet been officially withdrawn.

ISA (UK and Ireland) 210 is effective for audits of financial statements for periods commencing on or after 15 December 2004.

21.2 PURPOSE

ISA (UK and Ireland) 210 requires that 'the auditor and the client should agree on the terms of the engagement' and these terms should be recorded in writing.

The purpose of an engagement letter is to:

- define clearly the extent of the auditors' responsibilities;
- minimise the possibility of any misunderstanding between the client and the auditors; and
- provide written confirmation of the auditors' acceptance of appointment, the scope of the audit and the form of the report.

There may be occasions when an engagement letter is not appropriate, but the terms should still be agreed in some other form of contract.

It is important that the letter takes account of the relevant legislative requirements and should be tailored for each assignment.

The ISA (UK and Ireland) is primarily concerned with the audit of annual financial statements but the guidance to it notes that its principles can be applied to other audit related assignments, such as reporting on interim financial information or Combined Code compliance statements (see **Chapter 15** and **Chapter 16** for examples of appropriate engagement letters).

It is made clear in the ISA (UK and Ireland) that it does not encompass other services such as tax and accounting and suggests that separate letters may be required for each such service. However, such services may be included in the audit engagement letter, but if so, the paragraphs must be clearly distinguished from those relating to the audit.

21.3   CONTENTS

An engagement letter should be sent to each new client as soon after the acceptance of the appointment as possible and certainly before the commencement of any audit work.

The principal contents of an audit engagement letter may vary for each client, but reference would generally be made to:

- the objective of the audit of the financial statements;
- those charged with governance's responsibility for the financial statements;
- the scope of the audit, including reference to applicable legislation, regulations or pronouncements of professional bodies to which the auditor adheres;
- the form of any reports or other communication of results of the engagement;
- the fact that because of the test nature and other inherent limitations of an audit, together with the inherent limitations of internal control, there is an unavoidable risk that even some material misstatement may remain undiscovered; and
- the need for unrestricted access to whatever records, documentation and other information requested in connection with the audit.

Auditors may also include:

- arrangements regarding the planning and performance of the audit;
- expectation of receiving written confirmation of oral representations made by management;

- a request for the client to confirm acceptance of the terms of engagement;
- descriptions of any other letters or reports auditors expect to issue to the client;
- any confidentiality of other letters and reports to be issued and, where appropriate, the conditions, if any, on which permission might be given to make those reports available to others;
- basis on which fees are computed and any billing arrangements;
- complaint procedures;
- arrangements concerning the involvement of other auditors, experts or internal audit;
- for an initial audit, arrangements to be made with the predecessor auditor;
- a restriction of audit liability, where this is possible; and
- a reference to any further agreements between auditor and client.

An example engagement letter is shown in **Table 1**.

TABLE 1: Example terms of engagement for a non-listed company

Responsibilities of directors and auditors

1.1 As directors of the [company name], you are responsible for ensuring that the company maintains proper accounting records and for preparing financial statements which give a true and fair view and have been prepared in accordance with the Companies Act 1985 (**or other relevant legislation**). You are also responsible for making available to us, as and when required, all the company's accounting records and all other relevant records and related information, including minutes of all management and shareholders' meetings. We are entitled to require from the company's officers such other information and explanations as we think necessary for the performance of our duties as auditors.

1.2 We have a statutory responsibility to report to the members whether in our opinion the financial statements give a true and fair view and whether they have been properly prepared in accordance with the Companies Act 1985 (**or other relevant legislation**). In arriving at our opinion, we are required to consider the following matters, and to report on any in respect of which we are not satisfied:

(a) whether proper accounting records have been kept by the company and proper returns adequate for our audit have been received from branches not visited by us;
(b) whether the company's balance sheet and profit and loss account are in agreement with the accounting records and returns;
(c) whether we have obtained all the information and explanations which we consider necessary for the purposes of our audit; and
(d) whether the information in the directors' report is consistent with the financial statements.

In addition, there are certain other matters which, according to the circumstances, may need to be dealt with in our report. For example, where

---

the financial statements do not give details of directors' remuneration or of their transactions with the company, the Companies Act 1985 requires us to disclose such matters in our report.

1.3 We have a professional responsibility to report if the financial statements do not comply in any material respect with applicable accounting standards, unless in our opinion the non-compliance is justified in the circumstances. In determining whether or not the departure is justified we consider:

(a) whether the departure is required in order for the financial statements to give a true and fair view; and
(b) whether adequate disclosure has been made concerning the departure.

1.4 Our professional responsibilities also include:

- a description in our report of the directors' responsibilities for the financial statements where the financial statements or accompanying information do not include such a description; and
- considering whether other information in documents containing audited financial statements is consistent with those financial statements.

Scope of Audit

2.1 Our audit will be conducted in accordance with the International Auditing Standards (UK and Ireland) issued by the Auditing Practices Board, and will include such tests of transactions and of the existence, ownership and valuation of assets and liabilities as we consider necessary. We shall obtain an understanding of the accounting and internal control systems in order to assess their adequacy as a basis for the preparation of the financial statements and to establish whether proper accounting records have been maintained by the company. We shall expect to obtain such appropriate evidence as we consider sufficient to enable us to draw reasonable conclusions therefrom.

2.2 The nature and extent of our procedures will vary according to our assessment of the company's accounting system and, where we wish to place reliance on it, the internal control system, and may cover any aspect of the business's operations that we consider appropriate. Our audit is not designed to identify all significant weaknesses in the company's systems but, if such weaknesses come to our notice during the course of our audit which we think should be brought to your attention, we shall report them to you. Any such report may not be provided to third parties without our prior written consent. Such consent will be granted only on the basis that such reports are not prepared with the interests of anyone other than the company in mind and that we accept no duty or responsibility to any other party as concerns the reports.

2.3 As part of our normal audit procedures, we may request you to provide written confirmation of certain oral representations which we have received from you during the course of the audit on matters having a material effect on the financial statements. In connection with representations and the supply of information to us generally, we draw your attention to s389A of the Companies Act 1985 under which it is an offence for an officer of the company to mislead the auditors.

2.4 In order to assist us with the examination of your financial statements, we shall request sight of all documents or statements, including the chairman's statement, operating and financial review and the directors' report, which are due to be issued with the financial statements. We are also entitled to attend all general meetings of the company and to receive notice of all such meetings.

2.5 The responsibility for safeguarding the assets of the company and for the prevention and detection of fraud, error and non-compliance with law or regulations rests with yourselves. However, we shall endeavour to plan our audit so that we have a reasonable expectation of detecting material misstatements in the financial statements or accounting records (including those resulting from fraud, error and non-compliance with law or regulations), but our examination should not be relied upon to disclose all such material misstatements or frauds, errors or instances of non-compliance as may exist.

2.6 (**Where appropriate**) We shall not be treated as having notice, for the purposes of our audit responsibilities, of information provided to members of our firm other than those engaged on the audit (e.g., information provided in connection with accounting, taxation and other services).

2.7 Once we have issued our report we have no further direct responsibility in relation to the financial statements for that financial year. However, we expect that you will inform us of any material event occurring between the date of our report and that of the Annual General Meeting which may affect the financial statements.

Other Services

3 You have requested that we provide other services in respect of ... The terms under which we provide these other services are dealt with in a separate letter. We will also agree in a separate letter of engagement the provision of any services relating to investment business advice as defined by the Financial Services Act 1986.

Fees

4 Our fees are computed on the basis of the time spent on your affairs by the partners and our staff, and on the levels of skill and responsibility involved. Unless otherwise agreed, our fees will be billed at appropriate intervals during the course of the year and will be due on presentation.

Applicable law

5 This [engagement letter] shall be governed by, and construed in accordance with [English] law. The Courts of [England] shall have exclusive jurisdiction in relation to any claim, dispute or difference concerning the [engagement letter] and any matter arising from it. Each party irrevocably waives any right it may have to object to an action being brought in those Courts, to claim that the action has been brought in an inconvenient forum, or to claim that those Courts do not have jurisdiction.

Complaints

6 We aim to provide you with a fully satisfactory service and [name] as engagement partner will seek to ensure that this is so. If, however, you are unable to deal with any difficulty through [him][her] then please contact [name]. We undertake to look into any complaints promptly and to do what we can to resolve the position. If you are still not satisfied you may of course take up the matter with [professional body] by whom we are regulated for audit purposes.

Agreement of terms

7 Once it has been agreed, this letter will remain effective, from one audit appointment to another, until it is replaced. We shall be grateful if you could confirm in writing your agreement to these terms by signing and returning the enclosed copy of this letter, or let us know if they are not in accordance with your understanding of our terms of appointment.

Yours faithfully

21.3.1   Recurring audits

Once agreed the letter will remain in force until it is replaced, but should be reviewed annually to ensure that it is appropriate to the client's circumstances. If a change has taken place then a new letter may need to be sent.

A new engagement letter may be appropriate when there is:

- any indication that the client misunderstands the objective and scope of the audit;
- a recent change of management;
- a significant change in ownership;
- a significant change in the client's business; or
- a change in legal or professional requirements.

The guidance suggests that it may be appropriate to remind the client of the original letter when in the context of one of the above it is decided that a new letter is unnecessary.

21.3.2   Groups of companies

The ISA (UK and Ireland) does not deal with group or joint audits. However, accepted practice suggests that where the same firm of auditors is appointed for several companies within a group, they should consider whether separate letters should be sent to each Board. The decision will be influenced by:

- who appoints the auditors of the component;
- whether a separate audit report is to be issued on the component;

- whether the terms are the same for each component;
- legal requirements;
- the extent of any work performed by other auditors; and
- the degree of ownership by the parent.

Where a group letter is sent it should clearly identify the companies concerned and confirmation should be obtained from each Board.

Where joint auditors are appointed the audit engagement should be described in similar terms by each firm and that a joint letter be sent if there are no additional services provided by either party.

21.3.3 Changes in terms

ISA (UK and Ireland) 210 requires that where auditors are requested to change the terms of the engagement before the audit has been completed, to one which 'provides a lower level of assurance, [they] should consider the appropriateness of doing so'. If they consider the changes appropriate, the auditors obtain written agreement to them.

Such situations arise from:

- changes in circumstances affecting the need for the service;
- misunderstandings as to the nature of the audit originally requested; or
- restrictions of the scope of the engagement.

Where they consider the changes inappropriate, normally because it may lead to the recipients of their report being misled in some way, they should consider their position and, if necessary, take legal advice. If they decide to withdraw from the engagement they should consider whether the reasons for this have to be notified to any party. For example, under the Companies Act 1985, outgoing auditors must send a notice of any circumstances which they consider should be brought to the attention of the members or creditors of the company. Auditors should not agree to a change of engagement where there is no reasonable justification for doing so.

PART 3
ACCOUNTING SYSTEMS AND INTERNAL CONTROLS

22 AUDIT RISK ASSESSMENT

22.1 GUIDANCE

Three ISAs (UK and Ireland) provide guidance on the process involved in assessing the risk of material misstatement in an entity. These are:

- ISA (UK and Ireland) 200 *Objective and General Principles Governing an Audit of Financial Statements*, which provides a general overview of the process;
- ISA (UK and Ireland) 315 *Understanding the Entity and its Environment and Assessing The Risks of Material Misstatement*; and
- ISA (UK and Ireland) 330 *The Auditor's Procedures in Response to Assessed Risks*.

All three ISAs (UK and Ireland) were issued in December 2004 and are effective for audits of financial statements for periods commencing on or after 15 December 2004.

As with all ISAs (UK and Ireland), the text of the international ISAs have been supplemented with additional guidance from a UK and Ireland perspective. SAS 210 *Knowledge of the Business* and SAS 300 *Accounting and Internal Control Systems and Audit Risk Assessment* have not yet been officially withdrawn.

In June 2001, the APB published a Consultation Paper on Aggressive Earnings Management. The paper aimed to alert directors, auditors and users of financial statements to the potential threat that increasing commercial and economic pressures may cause 'aggressive earnings management' and consequently increase audit risk.

In the United States, in January 2002 the American Institute of Certified Public Accountants (AICPA), released a detailed list of 'risk factors' that might also be helpful in planning the audit of a client's financial statements. These background considerations are covered in **22.5** below.

As part of their Clarity Project (see **Chapter 1**), the IAASB issued revised versions of ISA 315 and 330 in December 2006. These are discussed in **22.6** below.

22.2   GENERAL OVERVIEW

ISA (UK and Ireland) 200 *Objective and General Principles Governing an Audit of Financial Statements*, provides a general overview of the audit risk assessment process.

Auditors are required to 'plan and perform the audit to reduce audit risk to an acceptably low level that is consistent with the objective of an audit' (ISA (UK and Ireland) 200). Audit risk is a function of the risk of material misstatement of the financial statements (i.e., the risk that the financial statements are materially misstated prior to audit) and the risk that auditors will not detect such misstatements ('detection risk').

Auditors determine what the risk of material misstatement is and seek to reduce their detection risk by performing audit tests based on that assessment. This involves focusing on what could lead to a misstatement at the assertion level and planning tests to address these areas.

Auditors also consider the risk of material misstatement at the overall financial statements level which may affect many assertions. This type of risk often relates to a failing in the control environment, such as management override of certain internal controls, and may be particularly indicative of a risk of fraud.

In addition, the risk of material misstatement at class of transaction, account balance and disclosure level should also be considered as this often determines the extent, nature and timing of audit tests at assertion level.

The components of audit risk
As stated above, audit risk is a function of the risk of material misstatement and detection risk. The risk of material misstatement is the entity's risk, and can be further broken down into:

- inherent risk; and
- control risk.

Inherent risk is the susceptibility of an assertion to misstatement that could be material, either individually or when aggregated with other misstatements, assuming that there are no related controls. This will vary depending on the nature of the assertion, transaction or account balance being considered. For example, items subject to complex calculations or accounting estimates are likely to have a higher inherent risk than others. External circumstances may create business risks which increase the inherent risk of some assertions, e.g., technological developments may render some stock obsolete, increasing the inherent risk of stock valuation.

Control risk is the risk that a misstatement that could occur in an assertion and that could be material, either individually or when aggregated with other misstatements, will not be prevented, or detected and corrected by the entity's internal control. There will always be some control risk as no internal control system is infallible.

Inherent and control risks may be assessed individually or using a combined assessment depending on the auditors' preferred methods and practical considerations.

Detection risk is the risk that the auditor will not detect a misstatement that exists in an assertion that could be material, either individually or when aggregated with other misstatements. Detection risk cannot be eliminated completely as auditors do not usually examine all of a class of transactions, account balance or disclosure. In addition, auditors may select the wrong audit procedure or misinterpret the results of a procedure.

For a given level of audit risk the level of detection risk bears an inverse relationship to the assessment of the risk of material misstatement. That is, the higher the risk of material misstatement, the less detection risk can be accepted and therefore more assurance is required from audit procedures, which are inevitably increased both in number and quality as a result.

22.3   ISA (UK AND IRELAND) 315

22.3.1   Guidance

ISA (UK and Ireland) 315 *Understanding the Entity and its Environment and Assessing the Risks of Material Misstatement* provides guidance on understanding the entity, including its internal control and using this understanding to assess the risks of material misstatement in the financial statements. The ISA contains guidance covering:

- risk assessment procedures and information about the entity and its internal control;
- understanding the entity;
- assessing the risks of material misstatement;
- communicating with those charged with governance; and
- documentation.

22.3.2   Background

ISA (UK and Ireland) 315 requires auditors to:

'obtain an understanding of the entity and its environment, including its internal control, sufficient to identify and assess the risks of material misstatement of the financial statements whether due to fraud or error, and sufficient to design and perform further audit procedures.'

The risk assessment should be made at the financial statement and assertion levels, and ISA (UK and Ireland) 330 *The Auditor's Procedures in Response to Assessed Risks* (see below) sets out the auditors' responsibility to plan and perform audit procedures relating to these identified risks.

Further guidance in relation to the risk of material misstatement arising from fraud and error is set out in ISA (UK and Ireland) 240 *The Auditor's Responsibility to Consider Fraud and Error in an Audit of Financial Statements* (see **Chapter 10**).

22.3.3   Risk assessment procedures

Procedures

Although concentrated at the early stages of the audit, procedures to obtain an understanding of the entity, its environment and internal control, will be performed throughout the audit. Audit procedures designed and performed to obtain such an understanding are defined by the ISA (UK and Ireland) as 'risk assessment procedures'. Such procedures may also provide evidence about transactions, balances, disclosures or the operation of controls, although they were not specifically designed to.

The ISA (UK and Ireland) requires auditors to perform the following risk assessment procedures to obtain an understanding of different aspects of the entity and its environment:

- enquiries of management and others within the entity;
- analytical procedures; and
- observation and inspection.

Much information may come from management, but other directors or staff may be able to provide different perspectives which highlight the risk of material misstatement. For example, talking to sales personnel may uncover a change in sales trends or contractual arrangements with customers, or meeting with internal audit may highlight potential problems with the design or effectiveness of the internal control system.

Analytical procedures may identify unusual transactions or trends which may indicate material misstatements. At the risk assessment stage such analytical procedures tend to be at a high level and are therefore likely only to provide a broad initial indication of a misstatement which will require further investigation.

Observation and inspection may support management representations or may provide information directly. Procedures will normally include:

- observation of entity activities and operations;
- inspection of documents (such as business plans and strategies), records and internal control manuals;
- reading reports (such as quarterly management reports and minutes of directors' meetings);
- visits to the entity's premises; and
- tracing transactions through the information systems relating to financing reporting, i.e., walkthroughs.

Prior year information

For ongoing audits, information gained at the prior year's audit will be of use when performing risk assessment procedures in the current year. However, the ISA (UK and Ireland) requires auditors to 'determine whether changes have occurred that may affect the relevance of such information in the current year'. The continuing relevance of such information can be determined by performing system walkthroughs.

Information gathered during any interim review may also be relevant to the year end risk assessment procedures, but its ongoing accuracy should also be verified.

Engagement team discussion

ISA (UK and Ireland) 315 introduces a requirement for members of the engagement team to discuss the susceptibility of the entity's financial statements to material misstatement. This meeting is often combined with the fraud discussion outlined in **10.5.2**. The meeting should include all key members of the engagement team, but the exact participants, timing and extent of the meeting are matters of professional judgement. Typically such a discussion would include the engagement partner, audit manager and senior and tax manager, where such services are provided. More junior members of the engagement team may be included to enable them to gain a better understanding of how the results of the work assigned to them affect other aspects of the audit.

The engagement team must also consider whether experts assigned to the team, such as IT or valuation specialists, are including in the meeting.

The discussion should emphasise the need for professional scepticism and, in accordance with the requirements of ISA (UK and Ireland) 240 *The Auditor's Responsibility to Consider Fraud and Error in an Audit of Financial Statements* particular importance should be given to the susceptibility of the entity's financial statements to material misstatement due to fraud.

Further meetings may be held during the course of the engagement to allow team members to communicate and share information gained during the audit which may affect the assessment of risk or the audit procedures performed.

22.3.4   *Understanding the entity, its environment and internal control*

Detailed areas

The following areas should be included in auditors' understanding of the entity and its environment:

- industry, regulatory and other external factors, including the applicable financial reporting framework;
- nature of the entity, including the entity's selection and application of accounting policies;
- objectives and strategies and the related business risks that may result in a material misstatement of the financial statements;
- measurement and review of the entity's financial performance; and
- internal control.

Table 1 sets out examples of items that the auditor may consider in relation to the first four items above. Internal control is considered in **22.3.5** below.

Industry, regulatory and other external factors

ISA (UK and Ireland) 315 requires auditors to 'obtain an understanding of relevant industry, regulatory, and other external factors including the applicable financial reporting framework'. Details of the areas to consider are set out in **Table 1**.

The industry in which the entity operates may give rise to certain risks of material misstatement, for example as a result of the level of regulation within the industry.

Nature of the entity

ISA (UK and Ireland) 315 states 'the auditor should obtain an understanding of the nature of the entity'. An entity's nature is its operations, ownership and governance, the way it is structured, the investments it makes and how it is financed.

A full understanding is required to ensure that any risks relating to group structures or the need for consolidation are identified. Such knowledge will also assist with identifying related party transactions.

The ISA (UK and Ireland) also requires auditors to consider whether the accounting policies selected and applied by the entity are suitable given the business and its industry. Auditors should consider new financial reporting standards that may be relevant to the entity and situations where the entity has changed its accounting policies.

Objectives, strategies and related business risks

Auditors are required by the ISA (UK and Ireland) to 'obtain an understanding of the entity's objectives and strategies, and the related business risks that may result in material misstatement of the financial statements'.

A business will define overall plans, or 'objectives' to respond to a variety of internal and external factors. To implement these objectives, practical 'strategies' are used. The risk that events or circumstances will mean that strategies cannot be implemented and objectives are not achieved is 'business risk'.

Business risk is a wider concept than the risk of material misstatement of the financial statements, but understanding business risk will increase the likelihood of identifying such risk. Whether a business risk will result in a risk of material misstatement will depend on the entity's circumstances. Examples of conditions that may indicate a risk of material misstatement are given in **Table 2**.

Smaller entities may not have formal, documented objectives and strategies. Therefore, to understand the business risk for such entities, auditors must make enquiries and observations of management.

TABLE 1: Example items to consider when gaining an understanding of the entity and its environment

Industry, regulatory and other external factors

- Industry conditions
  - the market and competition, including demand, capacity and price competition;
  - cyclical or seasonal activity;
  - product technology relating to the entity's products; and
  - energy supply and cost.
- Regulatory environment
  - accounting principles and industry-specific practices;
  - regulatory framework for a regulated industry;
  - legislation and regulation that significantly affect the entity's operations;
    - regulatory requirements;
    - direct supervisory activities;
  - taxation (corporation tax and other);
  - government policies currently affecting the conduct of the entity's business
    - monetary including foreign exchange controls;
    - fiscal;

- financial incentives (e.g., grant programmes);
- tariffs and trade restrictions; and
- environmental requirements affecting the industry and the entity's business.
- Other external factors
  - general level of economic activity (e.g., recession or growth);
  - interest rates and availability of financing; and
  - inflation, currency revaluation.

Nature of the entity

- Business operations
  - nature of revenue sources (e.g., manufacture, wholesale, banking, insurance or other financial services, import/export trading, utilities, transportation and technology products and services);
  - products or services and markets (e.g., major customers and contracts, terms of payment, profit margins, market share, competitors, experts, pricing policies, reputation of products, warranties, order book, trends, marketing strategy and objectives, manufacturing processes);
  - conduct of operations (e.g., stages and methods of production, business segments, delivery or products and services, details of declining or expanding operations);
  - alliances, joint ventures and outsourcing activities;
  - involvement in electronic commerce including Internet sales and marketing activities;
  - geographic dispersion and industry segmentation;
  - location of production facilities, warehouses and offices;
  - key customers;
  - important suppliers of goods and services (e.g., long-term contracts, stability of supply, terms of payment, imports. methods of delivery such as 'just in time');
  - employment (e.g., by location, supply, wage levels, union contracts, pension benefits, share option or incentive bonus arrangements and government regulation related to employment matters);
  - research and development activities and expenditure; and
  - transactions with related parties.
- Investments
  - acquisitions, mergers or disposals of business activities (planned or recently executed);
  - investment and dispositions of securities and loans;
  - capital investment activities, including investments in plant and equipment and technology and any recent or planned changes; and
  - investments in non-consolidated entities, including partnerships, joint ventures and special-purpose entities.
- Financing
  - group structure – major subsidiaries and associated entities, including consolidated and non-consolidated structures;
  - debt structure, including covenants, restrictions, guarantees and off-balance sheet financing arrangements;
  - leasing of property, plant or equipment for use in the business;
  - parent companies (local, foreign, business reputation and experience);

- related parties; and
- use of derivate financial instruments.
- Financial reporting
  - accounting principles and industry specific practices;
  - revenue recognition practices;
  - accounting for fair values;
  - stock (e.g., locations and quantities);
  - foreign currency assets, liabilities and transactions;
  - industry specific significant categories (eg loans and investments for banks, trade debtors and stock for manufacturers, research and development for pharmaceuticals);
  - accounting for unusual or complex transactions including those in controversial or emerging areas; and
  - financial statements presentation and disclosure.

Objectives and strategies and related business risks

- Existence of objectives relating to:
  - industry developments (a potential business risk might be that the entity does not have the personnel or expertise to deal with the changes in the industry);
  - new products and services (a potential related business risk might be that there is increased product liability);
  - expansion of the business (a potential business risk might be that the demand has not been accurately estimated);
  - new accounting requirements (a potential business risk might be incomplete or improper implementation or increased costs);
  - regulatory requirements (a potential business risk might be increased legal exposure);
  - current and prospective financing requirements (a potential business risk might be the loss of financing due to the entity's inability to meet requirements); and
  - use of IT (a potential business risk might be that systems and processes are incompatible).
- Effects of implementing a strategy, particularly any effects that will lead to new accounting requirements (a potential business risk might be incomplete or improper implementation).

Measurement and review of the entity's financial performance
- Key ratios and operating statistics
- Key performance indicators
- Employee performance measures and incentive compensation policies
- Trends
- Use of forecasts, budgets and variance analyses
- Analyst reports and credit rating reports
- Competitor analyses
- Period-on-period financial performance (revenue growth, profitability, leverage)

TABLE 2:   Example of conditions that may indicate a risk of material misstatement

- operations in regions that are economically unstable, e.g., countries with significant currency devaluation or highly inflationary economies;
- operations exposed to volatile markets, e.g., futures trading;
- high degree of complex regulation;
- going concern and liquidity issues including loss of significant customers;
- constraints on the availability of capital and credit;
- changes in the industry in which the entity operates;
- changes in the supply chain:
- developing or offering new products or services, or moving into new lines of business;
- expanding into new locations;
- changes in the entity such as large acquisitions or reorganisations or other unusual events;
- entities or business segments likely to be sold;
- complex alliances and joint ventures;
- use of off-balance sheet finance, special purpose entities and other complex financing arrangements;
- significant transactions with related parties;
- lack of personnel with appropriate accounting and financial reporting skills;
- changes in key personnel including departure of key executives;
- weaknesses in internal control, especially those not addressed by management;
- inconsistencies between the entity's IT strategy and its business strategies;
- changes in the IT environment;
- installation of significant new IT systems related to financial statements;
- enquiries into the entities' operations or financial results by regulatory or Government bodies;
- past misstatements, history of errors or a significant amount of adjustments at period end;
- significant amount of non-routine or non-systematic transactions including intercompany transactions and large revenue transactions at period end;
- transactions that are recorded based on management's intent, eg debt refinancing, assets to be sold and classification of marketable securities;
- application of new accounting pronouncements;
- accounting measurements that involve complex processes;
- events or transactions that involve significant measurement uncertainty, including accounting estimates;
- pending litigation and contingent liabilities, e.g., sales warranties, financial guarantees and environmental remediation.

Measurement and review of financial performance

ISA (UK and Ireland) 315 states 'the auditor should obtain an understanding of the measurement and review of the entity's financial performance'. By understanding which areas management are keen to monitor and review, auditors can make assumptions about the areas which management perceive to be of relatively high risk. In turn, the existence of such performance measures may create a pressure on management, which may lead to motivation to misstate the financial statements.

Information used by management to monitor performance may include key performance indicators (both financial and non-financial), budgets, variance analysis, segment information and divisional, departmental or other level performance reports, and comparison of an entity's performance with that of competitors. Much of this information is likely to be internally generated and auditors must consider whether it is likely to be accurate and precise enough to detect material misstatement.

Although smaller entities may not have formal performance review procedures, management are still likely to focus on a number of performance indicators. Auditors can observe these in the same way as for larger entities.

22.3.5 Internal control

Components of internal control
ISA (UK and Ireland) 315 requires auditors to obtain an understanding of internal control relevant to the audit in order to identify types of misstatement and design audit procedures. It defines internal control as:

> 'the process designed and effected ... to provide reasonable assurance about the achievement of the entity's objectives with regard to reliability of financial reporting, effectiveness and efficiency of operations and compliance with applicable laws and regulations. It follows that internal control is designed and implemented to address identified business risks that threaten the achievement of any of these objectives'.

Internal control consists of five components:

* the control environment;
* the entity's risk assessment process;
* the information system, including the related business processes, relevant to financial reporting and communication;
* control activities; and
* monitoring of controls.

Each of these is considered in detail below.

The design and implementation of internal control will vary from entity to entity and will differ depending on the entity's size and complexity. For smaller entities, the five components above may be blurred with an owner-manager taking sole responsibility for elements of each of them. Although the components of internal control may not be clearly distinguished in a smaller entity, their purpose will still stand.

Ordinarily, auditors will be concerned with those controls relevant to the preparation of financial statements. Controls over information not directly relevant to the financial statements may also be of concern to auditors if that information is used in the design or performance of an audit procedure, for example production statistics or controls, or pertains to the detection of non-compliance with laws and regulations. Therefore in assessing whether a control is relevant to the audit, auditors consider:

- materiality;
- the size of the entity;
- the nature of the entity's business;
- the diversity and complexity of the entity's operations;
- applicable legal and regulatory requirements; and
- the nature and complexity of the systems that are part of the entity's internal control.

Once auditors have determined which controls are relevant to the audit they should evaluate the design of each control and determine whether it has been properly implemented. When evaluating the design of the control, auditors consider whether it is capable of preventing, detecting or correcting material misstatements. If a control is poorly designed it may lead to a weakness which should be reported to those charged with governance.

Obtaining an understanding of a control is not the same as testing its operating effectiveness. In order to obtain assurance that a control is mitigating the risk of material misstatement the control must be found to be operating effectively throughout the period. This is further explained in **Chapter 17**.

Control environment
ISA (UK and Ireland) 315 states 'the auditor should obtain an understanding of the control environment' and defines control environment as including:

> 'the governance and management functions and the attitudes, awareness, and actions of those charged with governance and management concerning the entity's internal control and its importance in the entity. The control environment sets the tone of an organisation, influencing the control consciousness of its people. It is the foundation for effective internal control, providing discipline and structure'.

When evaluating the design of the entity's control environment, auditors consider how the following elements have been incorporated:

- communication and enforcement of integrity and ethical values;
- commitment to competence;
- participation of those charged with governance, including their independence from management;

- management's philosophy and operating style, their approach to taking risk and attitude to financial reporting and financial reporting staff;
- organisational structure and how activities are planned, executed, controlled and reviewed;
- assignment of authority and responsibility; and
- human resources policies and practices, such as recruitment, training and evaluating.

In understanding the control environment, auditors must also consider whether the policies have actually been implemented. This will involve enquiries and corroboration using observation techniques or review of documents. For some controls documentary evidence may be limited. For example a commitment to ethical values is often demonstrated rather than documented. In smaller entities communication between management and other personnel may be particularly informal. In such situations auditors' observations will be important.

An entity's control environment has a pervasive effect on assessing the risk of material misstatement. Even the best documented and implemented internal control system will be rendered useless by a poor management attitude which allows control environment weaknesses and thinks little of overriding controls. However, the existence of a satisfactory control environment can be a positive factor when assessing the risk of material misstatement, and may allow auditors to have more confidence in the reliability of internally generated audit evidence.

The risk assessment process

The entity's risk assessment process is the way in which they identify the business risks that are relevant to financial reporting and determine actions to address those risks. Auditors are required to obtain an understanding of this process. This will involve considering how management identifies business risks, estimates their significance, assesses the likelihood of them occurring and determines actions to manage them.

The entity's process can assist the auditor in identifying risks of material misstatement, however, if auditors discover material risks which were not identified by the entity's process they consider whether there is a weakness which should be reported to those charged with governance.

The information system

Auditors are required to obtain an understanding of the information system insofar as it relates to financial reporting objectives. This will include gaining an understanding of the accounting system. The ISA (UK and Ireland) sets out the following areas that auditors should consider:

- the classes of transactions which are significant to the financial statements;

- the procedures by which transactions are initiated, recorded, processed and reported in the financial statements (these may be IT based or manual);
- the records supporting the above processes, held either electronically or manually;
- how other events are captured, i.e., those that are not normal transactions for the entity; and
- the process used to prepare the financial statements from the accounting records.

Whilst gaining their understanding of the information system, auditors should be particularly aware of how non-standard and non-recurrent transactions or events are recorded as these are likely to fall outside existing controls. Auditors should also be aware of whether and how controls are overridden and how incorrect processing of transactions is dealt with once it has been discovered. In addition, auditors should consider how information is transferred from the processing system to the general ledger or the financial reporting systems.

Auditors should also consider whether the entity's information system is suitable for its circumstances. This will involve gaining an understanding of the entity's business processes and how transactions originate during these processes.

As part of understanding the information system, auditors should also consider how the roles and responsibilities within the system are communicated to the individuals involved in the day-to-day running of that system. A risk of material misstatement may be reduced by the entity ensuring that all roles are set out in suitably detailed policy or financial reporting manuals.

Control activities
Auditors' risk assessment procedures performed to date will have provided a good indication of the areas where a risk of material misstatement exists. When assessing an entity's control activities, auditors will concentrate on those areas where material misstatements are more likely to occur.

In order to understand an entity's control activities auditors consider how a particular activity, individually or in conjunction with others, prevents, detects or corrects a material misstatement. Specific control activities may include:

- authorisation of payments;
- performance reviews;
- physical controls over assets; or
- segregation of duties.

Specifically, the ISA (UK and Ireland) requires auditors to consider how the entity has responded to risks arising from IT. Auditors should consider how control activities have responded to different risks posed by the advent of IT systems, and consider whether the integrity of the information and security of the data has been maintained.

IT controls can be categorised as 'general IT controls' or 'application controls'. General IT controls are policies and procedures that relate to many applications and assist with ensuring that the information system operates properly. Examples are controls over access to IT systems or development of new systems. Application controls typically operate at a more detailed level, can be preventative or detective in nature and aim to ensure the integrity of the accounting records. Examples include numerical sequence checks or checks to ensure that items are suitably authorised.

Monitoring of controls
ISA (UK and Ireland) 315 requires auditors to gain an understanding of what the entity does to monitor its own controls. This monitoring should encompass both the day-to-day operation of the controls and the overall design of the control system. Where the information used to monitor the controls is taken from the information system itself, auditors consider how the entity ensures it is reliable.

Manual and automated elements of internal control
An entity's system of internal control is likely to include both manual and automated elements. For smaller companies there is likely to be a greater emphasis on manual procedures, but even for some large entities, elements of their internal control system may still rely heavily on manual intervention. The benefits and risks of using automated controls are set out in **Table 3**.

TABLE 3: Benefits and risks of using automated controls

Benefits – an entity is able to:

- consistently apply predefined business rules and perform complex calculations in processing large volumes of transactions or data;
- enhance the timeliness, availability and accuracy of information;
- facilitate the additional analysis of information;
- enhance the ability to monitor the performance of the entity's activities and its policies and procedures;
- reduce the risk that controls will be circumvented; and
- enhance the ability to achieve effective segregation of duties by implementing security controls in applications, databases and operating systems.

Risks

- reliance on systems or programmes that are inaccurately processing data, processing inaccurate data, or both;

- unauthorised access to data that may result in destruction of data or changes to data, including the recording of unauthorised or non-existent transactions or inaccurate recording of transactions. Particular risks occur where multiple users access a common database;
- the possibility of IT personnel gaining access privileges beyond those necessary to perform their assigned duties thereby breaking down segregation of duties;
- unauthorised changes to data in master files;
- unauthorised changes to systems or programmes;
- failure to make necessary changes to systems or programmes;
- inappropriate manual interventions; and
- potential loss of data or inability to access data as required.

Manual systems or elements of systems may be more suitable when judgement and discretion are required, such as for:

- large, unusual or non-recurring transactions;
- circumstances where errors are difficult to define, anticipate or predict;
- changing circumstances that require a control response outside the scope of an existing automated control; or
- monitoring the effectiveness of automated controls.

However, manual controls are generally less reliable than automated controls as they rely on people to perform them. Therefore, it cannot be assumed that a manual control has been applied consistently.

Limitations of internal control

Internal control, however well designed and implemented, can at best only provide reasonable assurance about achieving an entity's financial reporting objectives. Even automated controls are subject to some human involvement and, therefore, human error. There may have been errors at the programming stage, operatives may input data incorrectly and individuals receiving reports from the system may not understand the purpose of such reports.

In addition all controls are subject to override by collusion of one or more individuals. In smaller entities formal segregation of duties may be impossible, and the potential for override of controls by an owner-manager may be great.

22.3.6 Assessing the risks of material misstatement

Relating risks to assertions

Having gained an understanding of the entity, its environment and relevant controls, auditors relate the risks identified to the financial statements assertions. Further details of assertions are given in **24.2.2**. This means that each risk is considered in terms of the financial statements balance or balances it may affect and what that effect might be. For example a risk that goods may have been incorrectly invoiced to customers without being despatched may impact the existence and valuation of turnover and trade debtors.

Auditors then consider whether the risk is such that the effect on the financial statements would be material and then how likely it is that this will occur.

Auditors will next consider whether controls have been identified which are likely to prevent or detect and correct material misstatement arising from each risk. Often individual controls do not completely address a risk, but the controls within a particular process or system may together address an assertion. However, the less directly a control relates to an assertion, the less effective that control may be in preventing or detecting and correcting risks related to the assertion.

Once risks have been allocated to assertions and matched with controls, auditors can plan tests of control and substantive tests to gain their audit evidence.

Pervasive risks
Although many risks can be related to specific assertions, some risks may affect the financial statements as a whole, typically as a result of a weak control environment. Examples would be concerns about the integrity of the entity's management or untrained or inexperienced staff in a key accounting role.

In severe situations, the weakness of internal control may raise doubts about the auditability of the financial statements, for example unscrupulous management may lead to a very high risk of management misrepresentation in the financial statements or very poor accounting records may mean that insufficient audit evidence is available to support an unqualified audit opinion. In such cases auditors may issue a qualification or disclaimer of opinion, but if the situation is severe the only action available to the auditor is to resign.

Significant risks
As part of their risk assessment, auditors may decide that certain risks are 'significant risks'. Significant risks require special audit consideration as a result of the nature of the risk or the magnitude or likelihood of the error which may result. Significant risks often arise from non-routine transactions or judgemental matters as a result of:

● greater management intervention to specify the accounting treatment;
● greater manual intervention during data collection and processing;
● complex calculations or accounting principles, which may also be unfamiliar; and

- the difficulty of planning and implementing effective controls over non-routine transactions.

Having identified significant risks, auditors consider the controls, if any, in place to mitigate those risks. As such risks are often as a result of non-routine transactions there may not be controls specific to each risk, but rather general procedures for responding to such risks such as approval processes for any transaction falling outside of the standard accounting process.

If auditors wish to rely on the operating effectiveness of controls to mitigate a significant risk they will plan and perform tests of control. In addition, substantive procedures should be planned to address the significant risk. This is covered further in ISA (UK and Ireland) 330, which is discussed below.

Risks that cannot be mitigated by substantive procedures alone
At the risk assessment stage auditors should be aware of any risks which may not be mitigated by planning and performing substantive tests alone. Such risks are likely to arise in an environment where much of the entity's information is initiated, recorded, processed or reported electronically with little or no manual intervention. In such an integrated system, audit evidence may only be available electronically and its sufficiency and appropriateness will depend on the effectiveness of the controls over its accuracy and completeness. If such controls are not operating properly the potential for fictitious transactions to be created or existing transactions to be amended without detection may be large.

In such a situation auditors should plan and perform tests of control to satisfy themselves that controls are working to eliminate any risk of material misstatement. Due to the nature of such systems, the use of CAATs will be required (see **Chapter 23**).

22.3.7   *Communicating with those charged with governance*

Where auditors find material weaknesses in the design or implementation of internal control, or a risk of material misstatement which has not been addressed by one or more control, they should inform those charged with governance as soon as practical.

22.3.8   *Documentation*

ISA (UK and Ireland) 315 requires auditors to document:

- the engagement team's discussion about the likelihood of material misstatement arising from fraud or error and the significant decisions reached;

- their understanding of the entity and its environment, assessment of the component parts of internal control, risk assessment procedures and sources of their information;
- risks of material misstatement by financial statement area and assertion;
- significant risks; and
- risks that cannot be mitigated by substantive tests alone.

There are many techniques that may be used to document these areas:

- narrative descriptions;
- questionnaires;
- checklists; and
- flow charts.

These may be used in isolation or in combination. The extent and form of the documentation to support the assessment will depend on the complexity of the systems and the extent of the auditors' procedures required to assess them.

22.4   ISA (UK AND IRELAND) 330

ISA (UK and Ireland) 330 *The Auditor's Procedures in Response to Assessed Risks* provides guidance covering:

- overall responses;
- audit procedures responsive to risks of material misstatement at the assertion level;
- evaluating the sufficiency and appropriateness of audit evidence obtained; and
- documentation.

22.4.1   Overall responses

The first stage is for auditors to respond to any risks of material misstatement at the overall financial statements level. Responses may include:

- emphasising the need for professional scepticism;
- assigning more experienced audit staff;
- using specialists or experts;
- providing additional supervision; and
- incorporating further elements of unpredictability in the selection of audit tests.

Auditors may also decide to perform all audit procedures at the period end date rather than during any interim visit. Only if auditors have confidence in the effectiveness of the control environment may some audit procedures be performed at an interim date.

Where there are concerns about the control environment auditors are likely to use a substantive approach, rather than a combined approach which also relies on tests of control.

22.4.2   *Responses at the assertion level*

Procedures planned by auditors should link directly to their risk assessment. Auditors should consider:

- the significance of the risk;
- the likelihood that a material misstatement will occur;
- the characteristics of the class of transactions, account balance or disclosure involved;
- the nature of the specific controls used by the entity and in particular whether they are manual or automated; and
- whether the auditors expect to obtain audit evidence about related controls.

Auditors may plan to perform tests of controls alone, tests of controls combined with substantive procedures or follow a purely substantive testing route. The latter approach may be used where the risk assessment procedures have not identified any effective controls relevant to the assertion or because testing the operating effectiveness of controls would be inefficient. For smaller entities a fully substantive approach would probably be used as the number of control activities are likely to be limited.

Nature of procedures

The higher the auditors' assessment of risk, the more reliable and relevant the audit evidence must be. This will affect both the types of audit procedures performed and their mix. Where auditors have considered related controls in their assessment of material misstatement, they should test the effective operation of those controls. Where auditors use information produced by the entity's information system in their testing, the accuracy and completeness of that information should be verified. For example if analytical procedures include comparisons to budget data, the accuracy and completeness of the budget data should be considered.

Timing of procedures

The higher the assessed risk of material misstatement, the more likely auditors are to consider that performing substantive procedures at period end rather than at an interim date would be most effective. A disadvantage of performing all procedures at the period end is that auditors may lose the ability to identify and address significant matters at an early stage. Another strategy might be to perform procedures unannounced or at unpredictable times.

In considering when to perform their procedures, auditors consider:

- the control environment;
- when information is available;
- the nature of the risk, for example risks relating to the state of work in progress would be performed at the period end; and
- the period or date to which the audit evidence relates.

Extent of procedures

The extent of any audit procedure is a matter of judgement based on the materiality, the assessed risk and the degree of assurance the auditor plans to obtain. The use of CAATs may allow more extensive testing of electronic transactions and account files (see **Chapter 23**).

Tests of controls

Auditors should perform tests of control when:

- substantive procedures alone do not provide sufficient evidence; or
- the auditors' risk assessment includes the expectation that controls are operating effectively.

Typically, an enquiry will form part of auditors' testing of controls, but an enquiry will not be sufficient in itself and should be combined with other procedures such as observation, inspection or reperformance. The type of testing will be determined by the details of the control itself. For example some controls are documented and review of this documentation may provide evidence about the effective operation of the control. Others may not be documented, such as control activities performed by a computer, where the use of CAATs may be required.

Controls are generally tested throughout the period. Testing at one point in time only may be effective for some areas such as for controls over the entity's physical stock count at the period end. When testing has only covered part of the period, alternative audit procedures should normally be used for the remainder.

Relying on prior periods' assessments

If auditors plan to rely on evidence about the operating effectiveness of controls obtained in prior periods they should ensure, through observation or inspection, that the controls have not changed. If controls have changed, they must test the operating effectiveness of those controls in the current audit. Even if they have not changed, the ISA (UK and Ireland) requires that the operating effectiveness should be retested at least once every third audit. When there are a number of controls which are not being retested each year, a proportion of them should be tested at each audit.

In considering whether it is acceptable to rely on the testing carried out in prior periods, auditors consider:

- the effectiveness of other elements of internal control, including the control environment, the entity's monitoring of controls and risk assessment process;
- the characteristics of the control, including whether it is manual or automated;
- the effectiveness of general IT controls;
- the effectiveness of the control and its application by the entity, including the nature and extent of failures of the control in prior audits;
- whether the lack of change in a control is itself a risk, given changing circumstances elsewhere; and
- the risk of material misstatement and the extent of reliance placed on the control.

Where the operation of one or more controls is intended to mitigate a significant risk (see **22.3.6** above) evidence about the operating effectiveness of the control must be made in the current period.

Extent of tests of controls
Matters that auditors consider when deciding on the extent of tests of controls include:

- how frequently the control is performed during the period;
- the length of time during the audit period that auditors are relying on the operating effectiveness of the control;
- the quality of the audit evidence likely to be obtained;
- the extent to which other controls related to the assertion will provide audit evidence;
- the extent to which the control is relevant to the assessment of risk; and
- expected deviations in the control (although if this is too high, no reliance may be placed on the control).

The more auditors rely on the operating effectiveness of controls, the greater the extent of testing required.

Where controls are automated, auditors will not gain additional assurance from increasing the extent of testing of the control. The control should function consistently throughout the period unless the application is changed. Once auditors are content that the control is operating as intended, usually by testing it once only, testing should concentrate on ensuring that the application is not changed without appropriate change controls and testing.

Substantive procedures

Auditors should plan and perform substantive procedures for each material class of transactions, account balance and disclosure, regardless of their risk. In addition auditors are required by the ISA (UK and Ireland) to:

- agree the financial statements to the underlying accounting records; and
- examine material journal entries and other adjustments made during the course of preparing the financial statements.

Where the risk assessment process has identified a significant risk (see **22.3.6**) substantive procedures should be planned and performed in response to that risk. The example provided by the ISA (UK and Ireland) is of a company which is under pressure to meet earnings expectations and where auditors have determined that a risk exists that sales may be inflated by invoicing before delivery. In this situation, auditors may use external confirmations to confirm outstanding amounts and details of sale agreements. The confirmations may be supplemented with enquiries of non-financial personnel regarding any changes in sales agreements and delivery terms.

Substantive procedures may be analytical procedures or tests of detail. Substantive analytical procedures are generally more applicable to large volumes of transactions that tend to be predictable over time and suit gathering evidence about existence and valuation assertions. When designing substantive analytical procedures, auditors should consider:

- the suitability of using substantive analytical procedures given the assertions;
- the reliability of the data, whether internal or external, used to generate ratios and comparisons;
- whether the expected results are sufficiently precise to identify and material misstatement at the desired level of assurance; and
- the amount of any difference in recorded amounts from expected values that is acceptable.

If substantive procedures are performed at an interim date, auditors should perform further tests (either tests of control, substantive tests or a combination of both) to cover the remaining time to the period end. The decision whether it is worthwhile performing substantive procedures at an interim date will depend on the:

- control environment and other relevant controls;
- availability of information at the date of the interim procedure;
- the objective of the test;
- the assessed risk of material misstatement;
- the nature of the class of transactions or account balance and related assertions being tested; and

- the ability of the auditor to perform additional tests to cover the period between the interim testing and the period end.

If testing has occurred at an interim date and has detected misstatements, auditors would usually modify the assessment of risk and the nature, timing or extent of further audit procedures to be performed at the period end.

Relying on prior periods' work

Unlike for tests of control, it is not sufficient to rely on substantive procedures performed in prior periods to obtain evidence to address a risk of material misstatement in the current period. If any assurance is to be taken from work performed in prior periods, the audit evidence and related subject matter must not change fundamentally. An example would be where legal opinion was obtained about the structure of a securitisation in the prior period, and that securitisation has not changed.

Extent of substantive procedures

The greater the risk of material misstatement, the greater the extent of substantive procedures. Substantive procedures may also be extended if there are unsatisfactory results from the work performed on tests of control.

For tests of detail, the extent of testing is often thought of in terms of the sample size. ISA (UK and Ireland) 530 contains details on the use of sampling and other methods to select items for testing (see **Chapter 29**).

Presentation and disclosure

The ISA (UK and Ireland) requires auditors to plan and perform procedures to determine that the presentation of, and disclosure within, the financial statements is in line with accounting standards and the requirements of the Companies Act 1985.

22.4.3   *Evaluating audit evidence*

Throughout the audit, auditors are required to evaluate whether their original assessment of the risk of material misstatement requires amending. For example, auditors may be required to amend their assessment as a result of:

- a higher level of misstatements being discovered than planned during the performance of substantive procedures;
- failures of the entity's controls during the period; or
- discrepancies coming to light as a result of the overall analytical review of the financial statements at the completion stage of the audit.

Changes to the assessment may require changes to the nature, timing and extent of the audit procedures.

At the completion of the audit procedures, auditors are required to conclude whether sufficient appropriate audit evidence has been obtained to reduce the risk of material misstatement in the financial statements to an acceptably low level. The factors influencing what constitutes sufficient appropriate audit evidence are set out at **24.2.1**. Where they conclude that the evidence obtained is not sufficient, auditors should attempt to gather further information. Where this is not possible, they should issue a qualified or disclaimer of opinion audit report.

22.4.4 Documentation

Auditors should ensure that the following are fully documented:

- overall responses to address the assessed risks of material misstatement at the financial statements level;
- nature, timing and extent of further audit procedures;
- linkage of those procedures with assessed risks at the assertion level;
- results of audit procedures; and
- where using evidence about the operating effectiveness of controls obtained in prior audits, the justification for relying on that work.

22.5 AUDITING IN AN ECONOMIC DOWNTURN

22.5.1 Introduction

In the United States there have been a number of high profile cases where companies have adopted aggressive accounting practices in an attempt to satisfy commercial demands. This may include selecting inappropriate accounting policies or stretching judgements about acceptable actions.

Such practices result in the misleading of stakeholders and may, at the extreme, constitute a criminal offence. The publication of the APB Consultation Draft, Aggressive Earnings Management and the AICPA's assessment of risk factors set out a number of issues of which auditors should be aware when planning and carrying out their work anywhere in the world.

22.5.2 The use of judgement

Whilst accounting standards attempt to narrow the opportunities for manipulating reported profits, it is unrealistic to expect standards to eliminate the need for judgement to be made in the preparation and audit of financial statements. Auditors are required to determine whether the judgements made by management are reasonable in the client's circumstances and, where necessary, these judgements and estimations are adequately disclosed.

411

In addition, when a difference is identified between the auditors' estimate and the amount included in the financial statements, auditors consider whether an adjustment will be required. This will be assessed on the grounds of materiality, which itself is a judgement influenced by a number of quantitative and qualitative factors which should be assessed in relation to the individual circumstances of the client.

22.5.3 Factors affecting financial reporting

The AICPA paper sets out a number of environmental factors which will affect financial reporting, and therefore may be the cause of increased use of aggressive or misleading accounting policies. Although these are written from a US perspective they are also relevant to the UK reporting environment. Auditors might consider each of the following when assessing risk and deciding the extent of audit procedures:

- difficult economic times such as the downturn in profitability of high tech, telecommunications and media;
- pressure from markets and investors to perform;
- complexity and sophistication of business structures and transactions formulated to meet specific reporting or economic objectives; and
- complex and voluminous accounting standards.

The other areas which the AICPA list as being worthy of additional auditor attention are:

- liquidity and viability issues where the changing business environment and market conditions can cause doubt about the going concern position of the client;
- changes in internal control if reduction in staff numbers reduces the effectiveness of separation of duties or other control procedures;
- unusual transactions outside of the entity's normal activities which may not be accounted for correctly;
- transactions with related parties which may increase in an attempt to achieve financial targets;
- transactions involving off balance sheet arrangements, such as those with Special Purpose Entities intended to shift assets or liabilities off balance sheet; and
- adequacy of disclosure to ensure that readers of financial statements are clearly informed of the range of possible effects of applying the accounting policies selected by management.

22.5.4 Warning signs

As they usually relate to areas of judgement, aggressive accounting methods are often difficult to discover. There are, however, a number of warning signs of which auditors should be aware during their work. Examples of these include:

- directors or management deciding many of the amounts for provisions rather than amounts being determined by others as part of the routine processing of the entity's accounting system;
- the final draft figure for earnings being significantly changed by journal entries generated at head office or non-standard journal entries being made close to the year end;
- contracts or transactions, especially undertaken close to the year end, the commercial rationale for which is unclear;
- earnings which are different from industry trends;
- directors or management unreasonably seeking to bring forward the reporting date, making it difficult for the auditors to obtain the required quantity and quality of audit evidence;
- a pattern whereby accounting policies or judgements and estimates made in the preparation of the financial statements are all biased in the direction that directors or management desire, or that are pushing the boundaries of acceptability; and
- delays in providing the auditors with the necessary information and explanations that they require to complete the audit by the due reporting date.

22.5.5 *Auditors' actions*

Whilst auditors should always maintain a high level of professional scepticism, in times of economic uncertainty their alertness to unusual or questionable circumstances should be increased. They can ensure that they are well placed to identify instances of aggressive earnings management by:

- understanding how the company is affected by changes in the current business environment;
- understanding the stresses on the company's internal control over financial reporting, and how they may impact its effectiveness;
- identify key risk areas, particularly those involving significant estimates and judgements;
- approach the audit with objectivity and scepticism, notwithstanding prior experiences with, or belief in, management's integrity;
- pay special attention to complex transactions, especially those involving potential substance over form issues;
- consider whether additional specialised knowledge is needed within the audit team;
- make management aware of identified audit differences on a timely basis;
- question the unusual and challenge anything that fails to make sense;
- foster open, ongoing communications with management and any audit committee, including discussions about the quality of financial reporting and any pressures to compromise on financial reporting issues; and

- when faced with grey areas, ensure that adequate corroboration of management's representations are obtained.

22.6   ISAS 315 AND 330 REVISED

In December 2006, the IAASB issued the final version of its revision to the international versions of ISAs 315 and 330. The revisions are amongst the first ISAs to be issued as part of the IAASB's Clarity Project, the aim of which is to make the standards clearer and easier to understand. The revision process also ensured that the guidance was more easily applied to smaller entities.

The provisional effective date is 15 December 2008, although the actual date will not be any earlier than this. The long lead-in time allows the IAASB to reissue all extant ISAs so that they conform to the principles of the Clarity Project and they all share the same effective date. The APB are expected to await a decision from the EC to adopt the revised international standards before it undertakes a wholesale revision of the ISAs (UK and Ireland).

23 AUDITING IN AN INFORMATION SYSTEMS ENVIRONMENT

23.1 EXISTING GUIDANCE

Until December 1999, Auditing Guideline 407 *Auditing in a Computer Environment* provided guidance in this area. It was then withdrawn because, in the view of the APB, it was out of date but the guidance has not yet been replaced.

As there is now no extant guidance in the UK this chapter is based on ISA 401 *Auditing in a Computer Information Systems Environment*. This contains eight statements of 'basic principles and essential procedures', equivalent to the standards in an APB ISA (UK and Ireland), covering:

- consideration of the effect of the Information Systems (IS) environment on the audit;
- skills and competence;
- planning;
- risk assessment; and
- audit procedures.

23.2 BACKGROUND

The first requirement of the ISA is that the auditors should consider how an IS environment affects the audit. It notes the overall objective or scope does not change, but that the use of a computer may impact on:

- the procedures used to obtain a sufficient understanding of the accounting and internal control systems;
- the consideration of risk; and
- the design and performance of both tests of control and substantive procedures.

23.3   SKILLS AND COMPETENCE

ISA 401 requires that auditors have sufficient knowledge of IS to enable them to plan, direct, supervise and review the work performed. In some cases, it notes, specialist skills may be required to:

- obtain sufficient understanding of the effect of the IS on the accounting and internal controls system;
- determine the effect of the IS on the assessment of risk; and
- design and perform appropriate tests of control and substantive procedures.

Where an expert is used the auditors should consider the guidance in the relevant auditing standard – in the UK the appropriate guidance would be ISA (UK and Ireland) 620 *Using the Work of an Expert* (see **Chapter 38**).

23.4   PLANNING

It is essential that auditors obtain an understanding of the accounting and internal control system, which is sufficient to plan the audit and an effective audit approach (see **Chapter 22**). When planning parts of the audit which are affected by the IS environment, the ISA requires auditors to obtain an understanding of the significance and complexity of the IS activity and the availability of data for use in the audit.

This would include considering:

- materiality of the financial statement areas affected by the computerisation;
- complexity of the computer operation;
- organisation of the IS activities, in particular whether there is still adequate segregation of duties; and
- availability of data required by the auditors.

Auditors should also consider the impact of the IS on the assessment of inherent and control risk where there is significant computerisation within the entity. The areas where risk may differ from that associated with a manual system include:

- lack of transaction trails;
- uniform processing of transactions – clerical error is less of a risk in an IS environment but there is a risk of a programming error resulting in large numbers of similar transactions being incorrectly processed;
- lack of segregation of duties;
- potential to alter data without visible signs of this being done;
- lack of human involvement may mean that errors are not detected as quickly;

- automatic transactions carried out by the IS;
- potential for increased management supervision using analytical tools available via the IS; and
- potential for using computer assisted audit techniques.

23.5 ASSESSMENT OF RISK

ISA (UK and Ireland) 315 *Understanding the Entity and its Environment and Assessing the Risks of Material Misstatement*, requires that auditors consider the risk of material misstatement for the various assertions in the financial statements. Where there is an IS environment any pervasive or account-specific risks should be assessed.

23.6 AUDIT PROCEDURES

When auditors consider the procedures that are necessary to reduce risk to an acceptable level, in accordance with ISA (UK and Ireland) 315, the IS environment should be considered. Although its existence will not alter the auditors' specific objectives, the manner in which the evidence is obtained may alter, for example where computer-assisted audit techniques are required.

23.7 COMPUTER-ASSISTED AUDIT TECHNIQUES

ISA 401 does not provide any detailed guidance on computer-assisted audit techniques (CAATs), but we provide some background on them below.

Auditors may use CAATs to:

- examine the entity's computer files (audit software); and
- check the processing of data (test data).

CAATs may in some cases be the only way to obtain some of the required audit evidence or may improve the efficiency of the audit.

The main type of CAAT is an audit enquiry package. These may take various forms, including separate software packages or audit functions embedded in the client's software. This can be used to perform substantive tests, compliance tests and analytical review procedures including:

- reperforming calculations and casts, such as payroll calculations, calculations of royalties payable, casts of debtor balances, etc;
- selecting samples and checking the population for unusual conditions, such as duplicated items;

- testing items for certain conditions and printing out exceptions;
- comparing files at two points in time to detect records that have been added or deleted so that the reason and authority for these can be examined;
- creating information not otherwise available from or reported by the client's system; and
- proving certain figures in total by matching standing data with transaction data.

The choice between CAATs and manual audit techniques will depend on:

- whether there is any evidence of performance, as computers may not leave visible audit evidence, making manual testing impracticable;
- the cost-effectiveness of the CAAT and whether it can be used for other audit tests;
- whether the use of CAATs will be quicker and, if so, whether this is important;
- whether the relevant computer files are available, as some CAATs need to be carried out before ledgers for the relevant period are closed down;
- where CAATs are used by internal auditors, the extent that the external auditors are able to rely on them; and
- whether the data can be made available in a form capable of being interpreted by the computer auditors.

PART 4
EVIDENCE

24 AUDIT EVIDENCE

24.1 AUDITING STANDARDS

There are three ISAs (UK and Ireland) covering various elements of the subject of audit evidence. These are:

- ISA (UK and Ireland) 500 *Audit Evidence*;
- ISA (UK and Ireland) 501 *Audit Evidence – Additional Considerations for Specific Items*; and
- ISA (UK and Ireland) 505 *External Confirmations*.

As with all ISAs (UK and Ireland), the text of the international ISAs have been supplemented with additional guidance from a UK and Ireland perspective. SAS 400 *Audit Evidence* has not yet been officially withdrawn.

The three ISAs (UK and Ireland) are effective for audits of financial statements for periods commencing on or after 15 December 2004.

24.2 ISA (UK AND IRELAND) 500

24.2.1 *Concept of audit evidence*

ISA (UK and Ireland) 500, *Audit Evidence* requires auditors to 'obtain sufficient appropriate audit evidence to be able to draw reasonable conclusions on which to base the audit opinion'.

Audit evidence is obtained from a combination of tests of control and substantive procedures.

Audit evidence is defined as 'all the information used by the auditor in arriving at the conclusions on which the audit opinion is based'. It may comprise:

- source documents and accounting records underlying the financial statement assertions; and
- corroborative information from other sources.

'Tests of control' are tests that test the suitability of design and effective operation of the accounting and internal control systems.

'Substantive procedures' are tests designed to detect material misstatement in the financial statements, and are of two types:

- tests of detail of transactions and balances; and
- analytical procedures.

24.2.2 Sufficient appropriate evidence

The ISA (UK and Ireland) contains a discussion on what 'sufficient appropriate evidence' means. Sufficiency is seen as a measure of the quantity of audit evidence, and appropriateness is a measure of its quality, including its relevance and its reliability.

Auditors are rarely able to rely on conclusive evidence, but use persuasive evidence which is supported by information from different sources. They seek reasonable, but not absolute, assurance that there are no material misstatements and may choose to rely on sample data, extracted either statistically or judgementally, in order to form their opinion on a particular balance or class of transaction.

The decision on whether there is sufficient appropriate evidence is a matter for the auditors' judgement and is influenced by:

- the assessment of the nature and degree of risk of material misstatement at both the financial statement level and at the account balance or transaction level;
- the nature of the accounting and internal control systems and the assessment of the control environment;
- the materiality of the item being examined;
- previous experience of the client and the auditors' knowledge of the business;
- the results of auditing procedures and work on preparing the financial statements; and
- the source and reliability of information available.

The reliability of audit evidence can be judged using the following general criteria:

- external evidence, for example, confirmation obtained from third parties, is generally more reliable than internal evidence;
- evidence from the entity's records and systems is generally more reliable when the related accounting and internal control system is satisfactory;
- evidence obtained directly by the auditors is generally more reliable than that obtained from the entity;

- evidence in the form of documents and written representations is generally more reliable than oral representations; and
- original documents are generally more reliable than photocopies, telexes or facsimiles.

Where auditors perform procedures on information produced by the entity, they should first satisfy themselves as to the accuracy and completeness of the information. For example, if auditors are verifying provisions against debtors outstanding at the year end, using an aged debts list prepared by the entity, they should first satisfy themselves that the listing is complete and correctly aged by checking invoices raised in the period for inclusion on the listing where appropriate and amounts on the listing back to dated invoices.

Consistency is obviously important in deciding the sufficiency and appropriateness of the evidence obtained. Where evidence is inconsistent, for example, one piece of evidence leads auditors to believe a company owns an asset whilst another piece of evidence throws doubt on this, the auditors will need to consider what other procedures are necessary to resolve the inconsistency and ultimately what effect it has on their opinion. They also need to consider the relationship between the cost of obtaining evidence and its usefulness bearing in mind that the difficulty and expense of obtaining evidence is not a valid reason for not obtaining it.

24.2.3 Using assertions to gather audit evidence

ISA (UK and Ireland) 315 requires that auditors consider the risk of material misstatement is made at assertion level (see **Chapter 21**). ISA (UK and Ireland) 500 states that when seeking to obtain audit evidence from audit procedures auditors should consider the extent to which the evidence supports the relevant financial statement assertions.

The term 'assertions' refers to the individual representations made by management and which make up the financial statements. The assertions considered by auditors are set out in **Table 1,** although the audit approaches of different firms may use different terminologies.

TABLE 1: Audit assertions

Assertions about classes of transactions and events for the period under audit

- Occurrence – transactions and events that have been recorded have occurred and pertain to the entity;
- Completeness – all transactions and events that should have been recorded have been recorded;
- Accuracy – amounts and other data relating to recorded transactions and events have been recorded appropriately;

- Cut-off – transactions and events have been recorded in the correct accounting period;
- Classification – transactions and events have been recorded in the proper accounts.

Assertions about account balances at the period end

- Existence – assets, liabilities and equity interests exist;
- Rights and obligations – the entity holds or controls the right to assets, and liabilities are the obligations of the entity;
- Completeness – all assets, liabilities and equity interests that should have been recorded have been recorded;
- Valuation and allocation – assets, liabilities and equity interests are included in the financial statements at appropriate amounts and any resulting valuation or allocation adjustments are appropriately recorded.

Assertions about presentation and disclosure

- Occurrence and right and obligations – disclosed events, transactions and other matters have occurred and pertain to the entity;
- Completeness – all disclosures that should have been included in the financial statements have been included;
- Classification and understandability – financial information is appropriately presented and described and disclosures are clearly expressed;
- Accuracy and valuation – financial and other information is disclosed fairly and at appropriate amounts.

24.2.4   *Audit procedures*

Auditors use audit procedures to:

- obtain an understanding of the entity and its environment;
- test the operating effectiveness of controls; and
- detect material misstatements at the assertion level.

The objectives of testing the operating effectiveness of controls is to test the design of control systems by aiming to establish whether the system is capable of preventing and detecting material misstatement. When testing the operation of controls, auditors seek to establish whether the controls have operated for the whole of the period under review.

Substantive procedures are planned and performed in response to the risk of material misstatement assessed at the planning stage. Auditors use one or more of the types of audit procedure listed below.

The nature and timing of audit procedures will depend on the information available to auditors. Where information is held in electronic form, auditors may carry out Computer Assisted Audit Techniques (CAATs) (see **Chapter 23**).

Inspection of records or documents

This consists of examining records or documents whether internal or external, in paper form, electronic form or other media. It provides evidence of different degrees of persuasiveness depending on the nature and source of the documentation. The criteria used in assessing the reliability of evidence in general are noted at **24.2.1** above, and they should be applied to the type of evidence that can be obtained by inspection. For example, depending on the case, different degrees of reliability will apply to documentary evidence:

- created and provided by third parties;
- created by third parties and held by the entity; and
- created and held by the entity.

Some documentation will give direct evidence about existence, but may not provide evidence of ownership or value, for example share or bond certificates.

Inspection of tangible assets

This consists of physical examination of the assets. Again, the inspection of tangible assets provides evidence of their existence but alone is not sufficient to provide evidence of their ownership or value.

Observation

This consists of inspecting a particular process or procedure being performed by others. It is particularly useful where an internal control procedure does not leave an audit trail or for 'one off' procedures such as stocktakes. It is normally used in combination with other procedures.

Enquiry

This consists of seeking information from knowledgeable persons both inside and/or outside the entity. This may either be written or oral. Its reliability will vary depending on its source in a similar way to the evidence resulting from inspection.

An important part of the enquiry process is evaluation of the responses received, which may lead to amending the audit plan or performing additional audit procedures.

Enquiry alone is not sufficient to provide evidence of material misstatement or to confirm the effectiveness of controls. For example in relation to management intentions, in addition auditors should consider management's past history of carrying out is stated intentions and obtain written representation of oral responses.

Confirmation

Confirmation is a type of enquiry and involves obtaining information directly from a third party. For example a debtors' circularisation obtains confirmation of outstanding balances directly from the entity's debtors. Further information is provided in ISA (UK and Ireland) 505, *External Confirmations* (see **24.4**).

Recalculation
Recalculation involves checking the mathematical accuracy of documents or records, and may be done through the use of CAATs (see **Chapter 23**).

Reperformance
This describes the independent reperformance of calculations, for example, the calculations on a sales invoice or on a debtors' listing. Again, CAATs may be used to perform this task.

Analytical procedures
These involve the analysis of relationships between items of financial data both within the financial statements and between the financial statements and other internally and externally produced data. These are discussed in greater detail in **Chapter 25**.

24.3   ISA (UK AND IRELAND) 501

ISA (UK and Ireland) 501 *Audit Evidence – Additional Considerations for Specific Items* provides guidance on:

- attendance at stocktaking;
- enquiries about litigation and claims;
- valuation and disclosure of long-term investments; and
- segment information.

24.3.1   Attendance at stocktaking

Further guidance on the audit of stocktakes in the United Kingdom is given by Practice Note 25, *Attendance at Stocktaking* (see **Chapter 37**).

ISA (UK and Ireland) 501 requires auditors to attend stock counts to obtain evidence about the existence and condition of the entity's stock, unless this is 'impracticable'. If they are unable to attend on the count date they should take or observe physical counts on another date and perform audit procedures on the transactions between the two counts. If auditors cannot attend, for example, due to the nature and location of the stock they should consider whether alternative audit evidence is available to support the existence and condition of stock at the period end date. If there is no suitable and adequate alternative, auditors would be required to give a limitation of scope opinion in their audit report.

24.3.2 Enquiries about litigation and claims

The ICAEW statement on auditors' problems concerning contingencies arising from pending litigation against the entity upon which they are reporting is discussed in **37.3**. ISA (UK and Ireland) 501 provides some additional guidance about the audit procedures to be performed.

Auditors should perform audit procedures to determine whether a risk of material misstatement may arise from any litigation or claims made against the entity. This may involve reviewing board minutes, examining legal expense accounts or making enquiries of those charged with governance.

If a risk of material misstatement is discovered or suspected, auditors should seek to confirm the nature and estimated financial implications of the risk directly with the entity's legal advisors. Procedures for doing this, and an example pro forma letter are set out in section **37.3**.

If those charged with governance refuse to give permission for auditors to communicate with the entity's lawyers a limitation of scope opinion will be relevant.

24.3.3 Valuation and disclosure of long-term investments

If long-term investments are material to the financial statements, auditors should obtain sufficient audit evidence concerning:

- the entity's ability to hold the investments on a long-term basis;
- management's intentions whether to hold the investments long term;
- market quotations for valuation;
- comparison of market values to carrying values in the financial statements; and
- recoverability of the carrying value.

24.3.4 Segment information

When segmental information is material to the financial statements, auditors should plan and perform procedures to confirm the presentation and disclosure of the information. This will usually involve analytical techniques and discussion with those charged with governance about the techniques used to determine the segmental information.

24.4 ISA (UK AND IRELAND) 505

As stated above, audit evidence is more reliable when it is obtained from independent sources outside the entity. ISA (UK and Ireland) 505 *External*

Confirmations provides guidance on using external confirmations to provide sufficient appropriate audit evidence at assertion level.

External confirmations are frequently used in connection with account balances and their components, such as debtors' circularisations, which are discussed in detail in section **37.2**. However, they need not be limited to this and may be used to confirm the terms of agreements or transactions an entity has with third parties. Examples of where external confirmations may be used are:

- bank balances and other information with bankers (see **Chapter 36**);
- stocks held by third parties at bonded warehouses for processing or on consignment;
- property title deeds held by lawyers or financiers for safe custody or as security;
- investments purchased from stockbrokers but not delivered at the balance sheet date;
- loans from lenders; and
- accounts payable and receivable balances.

The assertions covered by external confirmations will vary. For example in the case of goods held on consignment evidence will be obtained about existence and rights and obligations assertions, but not about the value. Confirmation about the completeness assertion can be obtained by contacting certain parties. For example, evidence about completeness of accounts payable balances can be obtained by circularising suppliers with a nil balance at the year end to determine whether all liabilities to them have been recorded. This means that external confirmation requests must be tailored to the specific audit objective.

All confirmation requests are usually sent on the entity's headed paper and contain the management's authorisation to disclose the information requested. In order to have control over the process, all responses should be sent directly to the auditors, not to the entity.

Auditors may use positive or negative confirmations, or a combination of both. Positive confirmations ask respondents to reply and either confirm information or provide data themselves. Negative confirmations ask for responses only in the event of a disagreement with the information provided in the request. There is an additional risk with negative confirmations that auditors will assume that information was correct when the respondent simply chooses not to respond. With positive confirmations the response rate tends to be lower the more information auditors request. However, by requesting information from respondents, the value of audit evidence is greater than where they are asked only to confirm a balance included in the request. In order to obtain good quality responses auditors should consider to whom the confirmation request is addressed.

If those charged with governance refuse to allow auditors to obtain direct confirmations auditors should consider whether this is reasonable, whether alternative suitable audit evidence is available and whether a limitation of audit scope has arisen. Similarly where no response is obtained from a positive confirmation or where the response has not provided sufficient reliable evidence, auditors should perform alternative procedures. Where no response has been obtained they should first attempt to contact the recipient of the confirmation to elicit a response.

Once any alternative procedures have been performed, auditors evaluate whether the results in total have provided sufficient appropriate audit evidence, and where this is not the case, they consider the implications for their report.

25 ANALYTICAL PROCEDURES

25.1 AUDITING STANDARDS

ISA (UK and Ireland) 520 *Analytical Procedures* was issued in December 2004 and provides guidance on the use of analytical procedures covering:

- the nature and purpose of analytical procedures;
- use of analytical procedures in risk assessment;
- analytical procedures as substantive procedures;
- overall review at the end of the audit; and
- investigating unusual items.

As with all ISAs (UK and Ireland), the text of the ISA has been supplemented with additional guidance from a UK and Ireland perspective. SAS 410 *Analytical Procedures* has not yet been officially withdrawn.

ISA (UK and Ireland) 520 is effective for audits of financial statements for periods commencing on or after 15 December 2004.

25.2 WHAT IS MEANT BY ANALYTICAL PROCEDURES?

The ISA (UK and Ireland) requires that auditors should apply analytical procedures at the planning and overall review stages of an audit. Analytical procedures are the examination and comparison of the financial and non-financial information of a business with internal and external information, for both the current and different periods. This is usually achieved by calculating ratios and trends and investigating fluctuations and inconsistencies. It may be described as the process of reviewing the figures to see if they make sense. Methods used range from simple comparisons to complex analyses using advanced statistical techniques. Analytical procedures may be applied to consolidated financial statements, financial statements of components, such as subsidiaries or divisions, and individual elements of financial information.

As well as comparing the current year information with that of prior periods, analytical review also includes comparisons with:

- budgets;
- estimates prepared by the auditors, such as depreciation; and
- similar industry information.

It also includes the consideration of various relationships among elements of financial information that are expected to conform to a predictable pattern based on the entity's experience, such as gross profit margin percentages, and between financial information and relevant non-financial information, such as payroll costs to number of employees. An example of this is shown in **Table 1**.

TABLE 1:   Variable relationships

A company had 50 employees last year with total wages of £420,000 and 50 employees this year with a wage bill of £525,000, an increase of 25%. It is known that the annual pay rise was 12% and the level of business has remained approximately constant.

At first sight, the figures do not appear to make sense because the increase is substantially greater than expected. There may, however, be satisfactory explanations. For example, there may have been a change in sales mix with previously bought-in goods being replaced by goods manufactured in-house, resulting in substantial authorised overtime. This could be verified by looking at the sales figures for different products as well as the payroll. Alternatively, there could have been a switch to more skilled, and hence more expensive, labour; this could be verified from payroll and production records.

If no such explanation is available, it is possible that the payroll has been inflated by, for example:

(a) misposting in the general ledger;
(b) 'dummy' employees on the payroll;
(c) unauthorised overtime being paid; or
(d) employees being paid at higher rates of pay than authorised.

The auditors may direct their substantive testing towards finding any errors of this nature.

Comparisons should also be made with other branches or divisions in the same line of business, which are part of the same company or group or with other companies within the same industry. It is often helpful to make comparisons on a monthly or quarterly basis where such figures are available. This can eliminate any distorting effects of seasonal trade and may enable auditors to distinguish genuine seasonal fluctuations from window dressing around the year end.

25.3 PROBLEMS IN PRACTICE

Although analytical procedures are a useful source of evidence there are certain pitfalls in relying on conclusions drawn from such comparisons. In particular, care must be taken that:

- *they are computed on a consistent basis for each period or location under review.* Where there is a change in the basis of the calculation of a ratio or in the relationships which make up the ratio, comparability may be lost. The ratio for the prior year may be restated to obtain a meaningful comparison. For example, if stock turnover is calculated using average stocks for the previous period, there is little point trying to make a comparison with a ratio for this year using year end stocks. Major changes in pricing policy and product lines may also render past relationships inconsistent with current results;
- *there ought to be a meaningful relationship between the items being compared.* For example, there is little point in comparing head office overheads with sales since there is unlikely to be any connection between them. Similarly there is little point in examining the relationship between sales and gross profit if stocks are valued by reference to a fixed gross profit ratio;
- *results and balance sheet values are not distorted by the effects of changing price levels.* For example, under historical cost accounting, assets acquired at different times are stated at different price levels. This means that any ratio involving fixed assets is affected by when the assets were purchased. Hence ratios such as return on capital employed and fixed asset turnover can be distorted and comparisons between different companies made meaningless unless they are carried out on a current cost basis;
- *they are not distorted by unusual items.* Such items are often first detected by means of analytical review procedures and once detected, they should be investigated separately and their effects removed from any ratios and trends;
- *they are not distorted by changes in accounting policy or accounting estimates.* It is necessary to adjust the figures for the prior year in order that comparisons can be made. It may also be useful to calculate the figures or ratios using the old accounting policy or estimate; this is not always possible but, if it is, it may give some indication of the effect, if any, of the change.

25.4 USE OF ANALYTICAL PROCEDURES IN RISK ASSESSMENT

The ISA (UK and Ireland) requires that auditors 'apply analytical procedures to assist in planning the nature, timing and extent of other audit procedures', including obtaining 'an understanding of the entity and its environment'.

The use of analytical procedures at the planning stage may also indicate aspects of the business of which the auditors are unaware but which they should take into account in planning their audit.

Analytical procedures at the planning stage are usually based on interim financial information, budgets and management accounts. For smaller entities such management information is often not extensive, and performance is monitored and controlled by less formal means. In such cases it is suggested that auditors extract information from the existing accounting records, such as VAT returns and bank statements, as well as any draft financial statements and then discuss variations with management.

25.5   ANALYTICAL PROCEDURES AS A SUBSTANTIVE PROCEDURE

There is no requirement for analytical procedures to be used as substantive procedures, and the decision whether to use them, and the extent of such use is a matter for auditors' professional judgement.

Auditors should consider whether sufficient reliable information is available to apply analytical procedures and the results of any similar procedures already performed by the entity. In addition, when designing and performing analytical procedures, auditors should consider:

- the suitability of using substantive analytical procedures;
- the reliability of the data, whether internal or external, from which the expectation of recorded amounts or ratios is developed;
- whether the expected results are precise enough to show when a material misstatement has occurred; and
- the difference between expected and actual results which would be acceptable to the auditor.

Each item is considered in more detail below.

25.5.1   *Suitability of using analytical procedures*

Substantive analytical procedures are most effective when directed at high volumes of transactions that tend to be predictable over time. Where a financial statements amount is a result of few transactions, year-on-year comparisons are unlikely to be a useful source of evidence, as the components of the balance are likely to be different year on year.

In addition, if auditors note weak controls over an area, analytical procedures may be less conclusive than extensive detailed substantive tests.

Similarly, an area with a historical problem of high error levels may be best tested using tests of detail as analytical procedures may show little or no trends for comparison purposes.

The ISA (UK and Ireland) notes that where material balances occur auditors would not rely on analytical procedures alone, instead coupling them with tests of detail. Tests of detail will also be required if a significant risk has been identified over a financial statements area or assertion at the planning stage.

25.5.2 Reliability of data

The reliability of data will depend on its nature, source and how it was obtained, i.e., direct from a third party or via the client. Auditors should consider:

- the source of the information available: information is normally more reliable when it is obtained from a source outside the entity;
- comparability of the information available: general industry data may need to be supplemented when the particular client deals only in a specialised area within the industry;
- nature and relevance of the information available: does the entity set attainable budgets, therefore making them a good benchmark for analytical procedures;
- controls over the preparation of the information: are budgets amended during the period to bring them closer in line to actual results? If so, this will lessen their use for comparative purposes;
- prior year knowledge and understanding: what data has been previously reliable and useful;
- whether the information has been produced internally: as noted above this will be less reliable than external information, but its reliability is enhanced if it is produced independently of the accounting system or there are adequate controls over its preparation; and
- whether controls over the preparation of the data are reliable.

25.5.3 Precision of expected results

Auditors must consider whether they can determine what the expected results of the analytical procedure will be with suitable precision before the test is performed. Precise expectations are required to allow auditors to determine when results indicate that a material misstatement has occurred. Auditors should consider:

- the accuracy with which the expected result can be determined. Some results can be more easily predicted than others, such as gross margins compared to discretionary expense payments;

- the degree to which information can be disaggregated. Results may be more easily predicted for individual sections of an operation;
- the availability of information; and
- the frequency with which a relationship is observed.

25.5.4   Acceptable differences

The amount of difference from expectation that auditors may accept without further investigation depends on the materiality of the item and the level of assurance they wish to derive from the procedure.

25.6   ANALYTICAL PROCEDURES IN THE OVERALL REVIEW AT THE END OF THE AUDIT

The ISA (UK and Ireland) requires that the auditors should also apply analytical procedures at or near the end of the audit when forming an overall conclusion as to whether the financial statements as a whole are consistent with the auditors' knowledge of the entity's business.

The results from this review should corroborate the results of the detailed audit testing, both in individual areas and in forming the final conclusion. They may also indicate areas where further work needs to be carried out.

Auditors should consider the following when carrying out such procedures:

- whether the financial statements adequately reflect the information and explanations previously obtained and conclusions previously reached during the course of the audit;
- whether the procedures reveal any new factors that may affect the presentation of, or disclosures in, the financial statements;
- whether analytical procedures applied when completing the audit, such as comparing the information in the financial statements with other pertinent data, produce results which support the overall conclusion that the financial statements as a whole are consistent with their knowledge of the entity's business;
- whether the presentation adopted in the financial statements may have been unduly influenced by the desire of those charged with governance to present matters in a favourable or unfavourable light; and
- the potential impact on the financial statements of the aggregate of uncorrected misstatements (including those arising from bias in making accounting estimates) identified during the course of the audit and the preceding period's audit, if any.

25.7 INVESTIGATING UNUSUAL ITEMS

The ISA (UK and Ireland) requires that, when analytical procedures identify 'significant fluctuations or relationships that are inconsistent with other relevant information or that deviate from predicted amounts, the auditors should investigate and obtain adequate explanations and appropriate corroborative audit evidence'.

Unexpected results may occur as a result of:

- actions of the client of which the auditors are unaware when they perform the review;
- external factors not controllable by the client of which the auditors are unaware when they carry out their review; or
- errors or omissions.

The investigation of unusual fluctuations will usually involve discussion between the client and the auditors. The auditors will then corroborate management's explanations by:

- comparing them with their existing knowledge of the business, either from previous years or obtained during the audit; or
- performing extra audit procedures to confirm the explanations received.

Where management are unable to offer any explanation the auditors should carry out additional work to identify the cause of the inconsistency.

Not all explanations are capable of verification; nevertheless the auditors may be able to decide on the reasonableness of those offered. For example, if a decrease in sales is attributed to a fall in demand, it may not be possible to verify this explanation directly nor quantify its effect (unless there are total market figures published and available in time for the audit). If the decrease is in line with the auditors' knowledge of the industry and prevailing market conditions, they may accept it as being reasonable. If the explanation cannot be verified, they must rely on other sources of evidence to satisfy themselves in this area.

25.8 RECORDING

Although the ISA (UK and Ireland) does not cover this area, there was a section in the APC Guideline 417 *Analytical Review*. This provides useful guidance on how analytical procedures should be recorded.

The recording of analytical procedures will normally contain:

- the information examined, the sources thereof and the factors considered in establishing its reliability;

- the extent and nature of material variations found;
- the sources and level of management from which explanations for material unexpected variations have been obtained;
- the verification of those explanations;
- any further action taken; and
- the conclusions drawn by the auditors.

It may also be helpful to compile a client profile in permanent working papers detailing key ratios and trends from year to year. This allows the auditors to establish a base of financial and non-financial information for use in subsequent years.

26 THE AUDIT OF FRS 17

26.1 BACKGROUND

FRS 17 *Retirement Benefits,* which was issued in 2000, deals with accounting by companies for the defined benefit and defined contribution schemes which provide pensions for their employees.

FRS 17 requires that for defined benefit schemes:

- scheme assets and liabilities are valued using specified methods;
- the surplus or deficit is recognised by the reporting entity as an asset or liability;
- the change in the defined benefit asset or liability (other than that arising from contributions to the scheme) to be analysed into specified components and recognised in the profit and loss account or the statement of total recognised gains and losses ('the STRGL'); and
- certain additional disclosures in the reporting entity's financial statements.

The full requirements of FRS 17 should be applied for accounting periods ending on or after 22 June 2003.

The recognition of pension fund assets and liabilities in companies' balance sheets or even in the notes to the balance sheet presents auditors with a number of problems. These include, for example, access to records and how far to rely on Actuaries valuations.

Guidance in this chapter is also relevant to IAS 19 which, in many ways, gives the auditor similar issues to FRS 17.

26.2 GUIDANCE

To deal with these new problems, in November 2001 The APB issued Practice Note 22 *The Auditors' consideration of FRS 17 Retirement Benefits - Defined Benefit Schemes* ('the Practice Note').

This was followed in February 2002 by the issue of Technical Release Audit 1/02 in, *Practical Points for Auditors in Connection with the Implementation of FRS 17 'Retirement Benefits' – Defined Benefit Schemes* ('the Technical Release') by the Audit and Assurance Faculty of the ICAEW. This is designed to supplement the Practice Note in certain areas and also to help auditors deal with practical issues they may encounter.

Although the Practice Note and Bulletin were issued prior to the APB adopting the ISAs (UK and Ireland) for the audit of periods beginning on or after 15 December 2004, the guidance within them remains relevant under the new regime. Where the guidance refers to the old SASs, this commentary also includes references to the relevant ISA (UK and Ireland).

26.3   RESPECTIVE RESPONSIBILITIES

The Practice Note makes clear that it is the directors' responsibility to develop procedures to enable the entity to comply with FRS 17 requirements. As directors may not have immediate access to the records of scheme assets, and are unlikely to possess the expertise to value the scheme liabilities, they may need to involve others in the process:

- the scheme trustees to value the scheme assets; and
- a qualified actuary to value the scheme liabilities.

Auditors' objectives are to consider the appropriateness of the steps taken by directors to satisfy themselves that the amounts and disclosures made in the financial statements are sufficiently reliable. Auditors are especially concerned whether directors have devoted sufficient resources to this process.

The Practice Note emphasises that it is not the auditors' role to 'second guess' actuaries' work in valuing scheme liabilities. Auditors should, however, assess whether the procedures taken by directors are appropriate and whether the FRS 17 accounting entries and disclosures are consistent with their knowledge of the reporting entity.

The Practice Note stresses the need for auditors to satisfy themselves that they are independent and objective when the audit firm provides other services to a client. This is especially important when such services directly affect the client's financial statements. Where an audit firm provides actuarial services to a client for FRS 17 purposes, this could constitute a threat to auditors' objectivity and independence. Where the audit firm concludes that it cannot adopt safeguards to address this problem, the firm would be unable to accept both engagements.

26.4 PLANNING

When planning, auditors should assess the process by which directors intend to comply with FRS 17 in preparing their financial statements. Auditors' discussions with directors are likely to cover:

- who is responsible for the process;
- the arrangements to identify the schemes where FRS 17 is significant;
- who is valuing the scheme assets;
- the arrangements to identify significant matters affecting the actuarial valuation;
- who is valuing the scheme liabilities;
- how the actuarial assumptions are to be developed and approved;
- whether there is a realistic co-ordinated timetable (allowing time for auditors to complete their work on retirement benefits); and
- whether procedures exist to enable effective communication between all parties.

The Technical Release highlights the potential problem where auditors discover at the planning stage that directors have taken no steps to comply with FRS 17 requirements. In these circumstances auditors should consider whether the necessary information can be obtained at short notice (for example, by employing actuaries other than those of the pension scheme).

26.4.1 Risks of material misstatement

Auditors and directors should also discuss the risk of material misstatement in the financial statements arising from FRS 17 requirements.

TABLE 1: Examples of risks of material misstatement in relation to FRS 17

The risks below may not necessarily exist in every case, nor is this table intended to be an exhaustive list of all possible risks.

General

- directors may not have allocated sufficient resources to the FRS 17 process compliance.

Completeness of retirement benefit arrangements

- directors may not be aware of all schemes (for example, information about overseas schemes may not be well documented).

Subsidiaries

- directors of subsidiary entities may not fully understand the FRS 17 requirements.

Scheme changes

- scheme actuaries may not have been advised of important changes to schemes (for example, changes in benefit structures).

Consistency

- the treatment of scheme assets and liabilities related to bulk transfers may be inconsistent (leading to cut-off errors).

Actuarial assumptions

- key assumptions may be inconsistent (for example, the discount rate and the expected return on assets) or may be inappropriate (for example, benefit improvements).

Timetable

- the timetable for valuing scheme assets and liabilities may not be compatible with the entity's reporting timetable.

Surpluses

- directors may not have considered the recoverability of a surplus or may argue that it will be used for future benefit improvements (and therefore should not be accounted for in full).

Deficits

- the entity may be in breach of loan covenants when the deficit is taken into account and this may bring the entity's going concern into question.

Distributable profits

- the impact of any deficits in the group on distributable profits may not have been considered.

Actuarial updates

- changes since the most recent full actuarial valuation may give rise to imprecise liability calculations.

Source data

- actuaries may use incomplete or inaccurate source data (for example, in respect of membership records).

Asset values

- a timely, appropriate report on scheme assets may not be provided by trustees (for example, investments may be incomplete).

Multi-employer schemes

- it may be possible to allocate assets and liabilities to an individual reporting entity within the scheme and this may not have been identified.

Measurement and disclosure

- there may be a misallocation between the profit and loss account and the STRGL.

Deferred taxation

- directors may have failed to consider the allocation of deferred tax between the profit and loss account and the STRGL.

26.4.2   Communication

Effective communication between all the parties involved in FRS 17 compliance is essential to ensure a common understanding of what has to be done by each party and the timetable for its completion.

With the permission of directors, auditors communicate with actuaries at the audit planning stage to:

- inform actuaries of their intention to use their work as audit evidence;
- discuss the scope of their work, for example:
  - steps to produce the valuation within the reporting timescale,
  - procedures to establish the validity and completeness of the source data used in the valuation,
  - the possible variation in the liability and costs estimated by actuaries,
  - the impact of any significant events on the valuation,
  - the extent to which a fuller or more recent valuation may be required;
- ascertain the form and content of any reports to be issued in respect of FRS 17;
- confirm that actuaries:
  - will follow the FRS 17 requirements and their own professional guidance,
  - will include all the retirement benefits payable under schemes they have been engaged to advise upon,
  - understand the timetable for the preparation and audit of the financial statements,
  - will advise auditors of any matters occurring between the reporting entity's balance sheet date and the completion date of the valuation which would have a material effect on the valuation of scheme liabilities,
  - are content for directors to supply auditors with copies of the actuaries' draft or final FRS 17 reports.

Although actuaries are not professionally obliged to agree an engagement letter with directors, any terms of reference for their work may assist auditors in understanding the scope of their work.

For most FRS 17 purposes, actuaries can often update the most recent scheme valuation to reflect current conditions. Where significant changes have taken place, however, they may lead to material changes in the value of liabilities (for example, the impact of large bulk transfers or major new early retirement programmes). In such cases, auditors have to discuss the issues with directors and actuaries to determine whether actuaries need to carry out any additional work.

The entity auditors may also contact scheme auditors, fund managers or investment custodians who may be valuing the scheme assets.

Where the reporting entity prepares consolidated financial statements, there may be a large number of schemes. This may therefore involve a number of different trustees and actuaries with whom auditors may have to communicate. In practice, some responsibility passes to the subsidiary auditors, although it is important to establish that they are familiar with FRS 17 requirements (especially in the case of overseas subsidiaries). The reporting entity may appoint a lead actuary to communicate with the actuaries of the various schemes and collate FRS 17 information.

The Technical Release identifies a number of steps which auditors may take in respect of overseas schemes.

TABLE 2:   Steps in respect of overseas schemes

- consider how, if at all, the principles of FRS 17 apply to the overseas schemes (for example, pension schemes being state run);
- review the year end reporting timetable;
- determine whether overseas accounts staff are familiar with FRS 17 requirements;
- enquire if it is possible to communicate with overseas actuaries; and
- assess whether there are material schemes within overseas joint ventures or associates.

26.4.3 Materiality

ISA (UK and Ireland) 320 *Audit Materiality* accepts that there may be different materiality considerations depending on the aspect of the financial statements being considered. Auditors may judge, for example, that the expected degree of accuracy for note disclosures is lower than for the figures included in the primary financial statements. The level at which an omission or misstatement is material would therefore be higher.

This may be the case in the transitional period to full FRS 17 compliance. In the first two years, auditors' judgements of materiality relating to note disclosures may be based primarily on the relative significance of amounts in the context of the reporting entity's balance sheet. Auditors should recognise, however, that note disclosures in the first two years will be the basis for the comparative figures in the financial statements in the third year.

26.5   AUDIT EVIDENCE

26.5.1   *Understanding the schemes involved*

Given the potential material impact which FRS 17 could have on an entity's financial statements, it is important for auditors to understand which schemes are involved and the general nature of their provisions.

Auditors should therefore obtain from directors an understanding of the scheme rules which could have a significant influence on the entity's FRS 17 compliance (for example, the details of obligations to pay retirement benefits).

There could, however, be other benefits payable not covered in the scheme rules, for example:

- legal obligations to pay retirement benefits arising from informal agreements rather than formal contracts; and
- statutory requirements overriding the original scheme provisions.

Auditors should also take care to ensure that they receive the most up-to-date copy of the scheme rules.

Auditors may perform other procedures during their work which may help identify obligations to pay retirement benefits (for example, the review of board minutes or communications with employees).

26.5.2   *Scheme assets*

Scheme assets normally comprise one or more of the following:

- quoted securities;
- unquoted securities;
- unitised securities;
- insurance policies;
- loans and debt instruments; and
- freehold and leasehold properties.

Auditors may be able to obtain satisfactory evidence in respect of scheme assets without carrying out procedures on scheme asset records. Where there is a short period between the most recent scheme year end and the reporting entity's year end, and audited scheme financial statements are available, auditors may be able to obtain sufficient audit evidence by:

- asking directors to reconcile the scheme assets valuation at the scheme year end date with the assets valuation at the reporting entity's date being used for FRS 17 purposes;
- obtaining direct confirmation of the scheme assets from the investment custodian; and
- examining the key reconciling items (for example, contributions paid, benefits paid and estimated investment returns).

26.5.3   Using the work of the scheme auditors

Where the above reconciliation is not possible, it may be necessary to carry out procedures directly on the records of scheme assets. Although entity auditors could perform this work themselves (with the permission of directors and the scheme trustees), it may be more cost-effective to ask directors to arrange with the scheme trustees for the scheme auditors to carry it out, because of their familiarity with the scheme assets and accounting records. Entity auditors use the work of the scheme auditors in accordance with ISA (UK and Ireland) 600 *Using the Work of Another Auditor* (**see Chapter 38**).

Scheme auditors need to perform additional procedures to those carried out in the audit of the scheme financial statements if:

- the scheme and reporting entity have different accounting periods. This could involve additional procedures to update their work on the audit of the scheme to the reporting entity's balance sheet date. Where the period between the different period ends is short and the scheme period end precedes that of the entity, the entity auditors may be able to obtain sufficient appropriate audit evidence of the scheme assets at the entity period end by reviewing major movements in scheme assets since the scheme period end; and
- the scheme and reporting entity have the same accounting period but the scheme financial statements will be audited at a date later than that of the reporting entity. Arrangements may be necessary to supply the entity auditors with the evidence they require on a timely basis.

The entity auditors, with the permission of directors and scheme trustees, also need to communicate with the scheme auditors at the planning stage of the audit to:

- confirm in writing the nature and extent of the scheme auditors' work;
- agree the materiality to be applied;

- agree a timetable for scheme auditors to report to the entity auditors and the manner in which they are to report (entity auditors, where practicable, require scheme auditors to provide a report of factual findings resulting from the specified procedures).

26.5.4 Multi-employer schemes

A multi-employer scheme is one where a number of employers participate in a single defined benefit scheme. Sometimes there is no clear allocation of scheme assets to specific employers and it may be difficult to attribute a reasonable share of the assets and liabilities to each employer. In this situation, FRS 17 requires that these are treated defined contribution schemes provided certain disclosures are made.

Auditors should ask directors and others (for example actuaries) about how they concluded that the scheme was a multi-employer arrangement. An allocation of assets and liabilities may be possible where different employers within the scheme contribute at different rates.

Auditors should also understand the principal provisions of these schemes and those circumstances (for example, wind up of the scheme) which could cause a scheme deficit and:

- a liability or contingent liability for the reporting entity; or
- possible going concern problems for the entity.

26.5.5 Scheme liabilities

The Practice Note covers the actuaries' role in determining scheme liabilities either by a full actuarial valuation (see **Chapter 44**) or an annual update. Auditors will need to use the work of actuaries as audit evidence for FRS 17 purposes. The principles of ISA (UK and Ireland) 620 *Using the Work of an Expert* are followed closely by the Practice Note in setting out auditors' work (see **Chapter 38**).

26.5.6 Competence and objectivity of the actuary

Auditors should consider whether actuaries are members of the Institute of Actuaries, Faculty of Actuaries or Society of Actuaries. Where a foreign actuary is involved in FRS 17 work, these three bodies can advise on the acceptability of the standards of overseas actuarial professional bodies.

Actuaries' objectivity should also be evaluated, particularly where they are employees of, or related to, the reporting entity.

26.5.7   The actuary's work as audit evidence

Under ISA (UK and Ireland) 620, auditors need to consider a number of matters to evaluate the appropriateness of actuaries' work for FRS 17 purposes, including:

- the source data used;
- the assumptions and methods used; and
- the results of actuaries' work in the light of auditors' knowledge of the business and results of other audit procedures.

Actuarial source data is likely to include:

- scheme member data (for example, classes of member and contribution details); and
- scheme asset information (for example, values and income and expenditure items).

Directors are responsible for the source data used by actuaries. Auditors should discuss with directors and actuaries what has been done to establish that the data is relevant, reliable and sufficient. Where auditors have concerns over the scope of such procedures, they may wish to perform their own procedures.

The nature, timing and extent of any additional procedures depends on:

- the nature of the data and its sensitivity to the actuarial valuation;
- the source of the data and the extent to which it has already been subjected to audit procedures (for example, by entity auditors or the internal auditors); and
- actuaries' approach to verify the completeness and validity of the data.

26.5.8   Actuarial assumptions

Actuarial assumptions are estimates of future events that will affect the valuation of the scheme liabilities and the reporting entity's costs of retirement benefits (for example, mortality rates, termination rates, retirement age and changes in salary and benefit levels). FRS 17 states that the assumptions are the ultimate responsibility of directors but should be set upon advice given by actuaries.

Auditors will not have the same expertise as actuaries and are unlikely to be able to challenge the appropriateness and reasonableness of the assumptions. Auditors can, however, through discussion with directors and actuaries:

- obtain a general understanding of the assumptions and review the process used to develop them;

- compare the assumptions with those which directors have used in prior years; and
- consider whether, based on their knowledge of the reporting entity and the scheme, and on the results of other audit procedures, the assumptions appear to be reasonable and compatible with those used elsewhere in the preparation of the entity's financial statements.

26.5.9   *Assessing the results of the actuary's work*

There is no prescribed form for actuaries' reports on the results of their work. The pensions scheme figures required for FRS 17 are normally provided in a letter or written report. Actuaries may also provide a commentary on other matters, such as:

- the movements since the previous valuation in the figures required for inclusion in the balance sheet and the profit and loss account;
- the possible variation in the valuation of the scheme liabilities and the implications for the financial statements and the audit; and
- the sensitivity of the results, funding level, scheme maturity and investments to variations in the source data and assumptions.

Auditors should obtain copies of all written communications from actuaries to directors concerning the findings of their work.

Auditors should also discuss with directors whether actuaries have indicated that:

- any matters have occurred in the period from the reporting entity's balance sheet date up to the date on which the valuation was completed that would have a material effect on the valuation; or
- there was a departure from relevant professional requirements or guidance issued by their professional body.

Auditors may request actuaries to:

- provide specific confirmation on the above points;
- comment on the degree of precision attaching to the valuation and factors giving rise to potential material misstatement;
- indicate whether the FRS 17 amounts and disclosures in the financial statements adequately reflect the results of their work.

Where the results of actuaries' work is inconsistent with other audit evidence, auditors should discuss the inconsistency with the directors and actuaries. Additional procedures, such as requesting directors to obtain evidence from another actuary, may assist in resolving the inconsistency.

26.5.10 *Valuation of scheme liabilities and materiality*

The defined benefit asset (or liability) is based on the surplus (or deficit) of the value of the scheme assets over the value of scheme liabilities.

Generally accepted actuarial techniques may give a range of acceptable values. Auditors may be faced with a large range arising from an unusual event (for example, the outcome of a recent court case, which could potentially have a significant effect on the scheme, cannot be established with certainty before the approval of the financial statements).

Both the Practice Note and the Technical Release stress the need for auditors to check that financial statements contain sufficient disclosures about the actuarial assumptions. Auditors may, in exceptional circumstances, consider a fundamental uncertainty, explanatory paragraph in their report where the uncertainty caused by the range is unusually large.

26.5.11 *Disclosures*

The Practice Note makes clear that, where auditors have concerns regarding the disclosures in the financial statements or in the OFR, they should discuss their views with directors. If this does not lead to the matter being resolved, auditors may decide to communicate their concerns to those charged with governance (in accordance with ISA (UK and Ireland) 260 *Communication of Audit Matters to those Charged with Governance*) and consider the effect on their audit opinion (see **Chapter 9)**.

26.5.12 *Going concern*

When evaluating going concern, directors consider all relevant information of which they are aware at the time they approve the financial statements, including events known or expected to occur more than a year beyond the date on which they approve the financial statements (for example, a scheme is inadequately funded to a significant extent and the defined benefit liability to be recognised in the balance sheet may be material). In these circumstances, auditors would:

- enquire into the expected timing of the cash flows likely to arise as result of this liability and how directors would fund these payments; and
- consider whether the recognition of the defined benefit liability may cause the reporting entity to breach any existing loan covenant.

Under ISA (UK and Ireland) 570 *Going Concern* auditors should assess how directors have satisfied themselves that the going concern basis and any related disclosures are appropriate.

26.5.13 Recognition in the profit and loss account and the STRGL

The change in the defined benefit asset or liability is required to be analysed into a number of specified components. The nature, timing and extent of auditors' procedures in relation to these components depend on the materiality of the amounts involved and the risk of material misstatement of the financial statements.

TABLE 3: Profit and Loss Account and STRGL disclosures

Auditors should consider the following procedures in respect of Profit and Loss Account and STRGL disclosures:

Items charged to operating profit (current service cost, past service cost, gains and losses on settlements and curtailments)

- discuss with directors and actuaries the factors affecting current service cost (for example, a scheme closed to new entrants may see an increase year on year as a percentage of pay with the average age of the workforce increasing).

Items charged/credited to finance costs/income (expected return on scheme assets, interest on scheme liabilities)

- consider whether the interest costs reflect an average of the liabilities at the beginning of the year and movements during the year;
- ensure that the discount rate reflects the appropriate high quality corporate bond rate at the start of the year and is the same as the rate at which the scheme liabilities were measured at the end of the previous year;
- compare the expected return with market indices when dealing with quoted fixed interest and index-linked securities;
- consider discussing with directors and actuaries whether the equity risk premium (in a scheme with a majority of equities) is being over-estimated in the current year (where the actual return shows a consistent pattern, for example, always less than the expected return).

Items recognised in the STRGL (actuarial gains and losses, comprising: actual return less expected return on scheme assets, experience gains and losses arising on scheme liabilities, effects of changes in assumptions underlying scheme liabilities)

- discuss with directors and actuaries the underlying reasons for actuarial gains and losses (for example, employee turnover rates or unexpected changes in salaries/medical costs).

26.5.14   Expected return on scheme assets and discount rate

Auditors should pay particular attention to the amounts to be disclosed as the expected return on scheme assets and the rate used to discount the scheme liabilities.

TABLE 4:   Expected return on scheme assets and discount rate

Auditors should consider the following procedures in relation to expected return on scheme assets and discount rate:

- consider directors' judgement of the expected long term rate of return for each category of scheme assets and the current rate of return on a high quality corporate bond of equivalent currency and term to the scheme liabilities;
- review directors' discussions with actuaries to select a discount rate;
- review the 5-year historical table of the amounts recognised in the STRGL to help identify any systematic bias in the assumptions about the expected rate of return;
- obtain explanations from directors and actuaries to support the expected rate of return for all significant asset categories and consider whether any changes are consistent with, for example, changes in investment strategy; and
- discuss the choice of discount rate and get explanations for any change in the rate.

26.5.15   Disclosures

Auditors should consider the disclosures in the entity's financial statements where the reporting entity has more than one defined benefit scheme and whether disaggregation is required for the financial statements to give a true and fair view.

TABLE 5:   FRS 17 disclosures for an entity with more than one defined benefit scheme

Auditors should consider the following procedures for an entity with more than one defined benefit scheme:

- consider if disclosure has been made for each scheme or in groupings (helpful groupings may be based on the geographical location of the schemes and whether the schemes are subject to significantly different risks; and
- assess whether aggregated disclosure causes surpluses and deficits of different schemes being 'netted-off' or important information about arrangements whose costs are significantly different or more volatile compared with others being 'lost' by the presentation of averaged rates or aggregated values.

26.5.16   Distributable profits

Auditors should be aware of the potential problem arising where the individual financial statements of the reporting entity show a defined benefit liability so large that it reduces realised profits below that needed to cover any intended distribution.

ISA (UK and Ireland) 250 Part A *Consideration of laws and regulations in an audit of financial statements* requires auditors to obtain sufficient appropriate audit evidence about compliance with those laws and regulations relating directly to the preparation of, or the inclusion or disclosure of specific items in, the financial statements. This will include, for example, section 263 of the Companies Act 1985 (for a limited company), which specifies that a distribution cannot be made except out of profits available for the purpose.

If auditors become aware that there may be insufficient realised profits to make a proposed distribution, they normally discuss their concerns with directors and advise them of the potential consequences of making a potentially unlawful distribution. Directors and auditors may wish to consult their respective legal advisers. If directors are unable to dispel auditors' concerns and do not modify the proposed distribution, auditors should consider the implications of this disagreement for their report. This may result in auditors issuing a qualified or adverse opinion.

However, where companies have taken advantage of the transitional arrangements in FRS 17 only to make disclosures, ICAEW Technical Release 01/02 explains that the first time a company will need to take into account the effect of an FRS 17 deficit is in the declaration of interim dividends during the period in which FRS 17 is to be adopted in full (i.e., periods beginning on or after 1 January 2005). Furthermore, at the time of writing, there is no formal guidance on the extent to which a pension asset or liability recognised in accordance with FRS 17 affects distributable reserves. Where there is doubt as to the legality of any proposed dividend, companies should seek appropriate legal advice.

26.5.17   Management representations

ISA (UK and Ireland) 580 *Management Representations* requires auditors to obtain written confirmation of management representations on matters material to the financial statements when those representations are critical to obtaining sufficient appropriate audit evidence. Management representations cannot, however, be a substitute for other audit evidence.

Examples of typical representations which may be obtained by entity auditors are shown in Table 6.

TABLE 6: Typical management representations

- actuarial assumptions underlying the valuation of scheme liabilities are consistent with the entity directors' knowledge of the business;
- all significant retirement benefits, including any arrangements that:
  - are statutory, contractual or implicit in the employer's actions,
  - arise in the UK and the Republic of Ireland or overseas,
  - are funded or unfunded,
  - are approved or unapproved,
  - have been identified and properly accounted for; and
- all settlements and curtailments have been identified and properly accounted for.

26.6 SMALLER ENTITIES WITH INSURED SCHEMES

The Practice Note is intended to apply to auditors of all reporting entities and all types and sizes of defined benefit scheme (although some of the guidance may be more relevant to auditors of entities with significant and complex retirement benefit arrangements). These entities usually have well-resourced actuaries available but are often also subject to tight reporting deadlines (for example, listed companies).

The situation for smaller reporting entities is often quite different. Their retirement benefit arrangements may often be less complex and they generally enjoy a more relaxed reporting timetable. This may allow more time for directors and actuaries to comply with FRS 17 and allows auditors more time to obtain the necessary audit evidence.

A smaller reporting entity's occupational pension scheme is, however, sometimes administered by an insurance company with the only scheme asset an insurance policy (a 'fully insured scheme'). Scheme actuaries will usually be an employee of the insurance company and directors will probably ask the insurance company and its in-house actuary to provide the information for FRS 17 compliance.

In such circumstances, auditors should consider whether:

- the insurance company will be able to supply directors with values of the scheme assets and liabilities as at the entity balance sheet date, where it differs from the scheme year-end date;
- it will be appropriate for them to communicate with the insurance company's actuary;
- the basis to be used by the insurance company to value the insurance policies will represent 'the best approximation to fair value' under FRS 17: a surrender value will not be appropriate unless the trustees have

decided to surrender the policy or wind up the scheme;
- 'earmarked' insurance policies (for example, deferred annuity policies), excluded from the accounts of the scheme in accordance with statutory exemptions, will have been valued and included in the fair value of scheme assets to comply with FRS 17; and
- evidence will be available to support the basis for valuing the insurance policy as at the entity year balance sheet date.

Where the insurance company is unable to provide a valuation of an insurance policy as at the reporting entity balance sheet date, directors might decide to adjust the most recently obtained valuation for contributions received and benefits paid, also allowing for investment returns. The basis of this approach would need to be clearly disclosed in the notes to the financial statements.

The fact that auditors are not able to discuss matters with actuaries does not of itself give rise to a need to qualify the auditors' opinion on the financial statements as the auditors may be able to obtain sufficient appropriate evidence by:

- discussing the matters with directors; and
- reviewing any correspondence between directors and actuaries.

27 AUDIT OF ACCOUNTING ESTIMATES

27.1 AUDITING STANDARDS

ISA (UK and Ireland) 540 *Audit of Accounting Estimates* was issued in December 2004 and provides standards covering:

- auditors' duty with regard to accounting estimates;
- suitable audit approaches and procedures; and
- evaluation of results of audit procedures.

As with all ISAs (UK and Ireland), the text of the ISA has been supplemented with additional guidance from a UK and Ireland perspective. ISA (UK and Ireland) 540 supersedes SAS 420 *Audit of Accounting Estimates* has not yet been officially withdrawn.

ISA (UK and Ireland) 540 is effective for audits of financial statements for periods commencing on or after 15 December 2004.

In December 2004, the IAASB issued an Exposure Draft of a revision to ISA 540. The draft, entitled *Auditing Accounting Estimates and Related Disclosures (Other than Those Involving Fair Value Measurements and Disclosures)*, was developed in connection with the UK APB, and conforms the original ISA to the revised risk and fraud standards released by the IAASB. It was approved in September 2006 and subsequently it was decided to incorporate the requirements of ISA 545, *Auditing Fair Value Measurements and Disclosures* within it. The revised, renamed and redrafted ISA 540 was reissued for comment in December 2006. These changes are discussed further in section **27.5** below.

27.2 ACCOUNTING ESTIMATES

ISA (UK) 540 requires that auditors should obtain sufficient appropriate audit evidence regarding the accounting estimates material to the financial statements on which to base their audit opinion.

Accounting estimates are approximations which are deemed necessary because there is no precise means of measurement for a particular item in the financial statements. Examples include:

- stock provisions;
- bad debt provisions;
- depreciation;
- accrued revenue;
- deferred taxation provisions;
- provision for a loss from a lawsuit;
- profits or losses on construction contracts in progress; and
- warranty claim provisions.

The estimates in the financial statements are the responsibility of management and result from uncertainties regarding the outcome of events that have occurred, or are likely to occur. They involve the use of judgement and consequently the audit evidence available is less conclusive than with other items. When faced with estimates auditors must use their judgement in assessing the sufficiency and appropriateness of the evidence.

The processes involved in determining the estimate will depend on the nature of the item. For example, establishing an accrual for rent will involve taking the quarterly rental and apportioning it over the period concerned. On the other hand, establishing a provision for a slow moving stock item involves examining sales of the item over the period and since the year end, the costs associated with selling the item and the estimated selling price. In some cases specialist knowledge may be required to make an estimate, such as the amount of damages payable in a legal case.

Some estimates may be routinely made by management, and where this happens they should review regularly the formulae used to ensure they are still appropriate. For example, management should periodically reassess the estimated useful lives of fixed assets as part of its review of the appropriateness of the depreciation calculation.

Where the uncertainty associated with the item makes it impossible to estimate reasonably, the auditors need to consider the implications for their report.

27.3 AUDIT PROCEDURES

The ISA requires that auditors should obtain sufficient audit evidence as to whether an accounting estimate is reasonable in the circumstances and when required, is appropriately disclosed. To this end, auditors should adopt one, or a combination, of the following approaches in the audit of an accounting estimate:

(a)   review and test the process used by management to develop the estimate;

(b)   use an independent estimate for comparison with that prepared by management; or

(c)   review subsequent events which confirm the estimate made.

The guidance sets out the stages involved in reviewing and testing management's estimates. These are:

- evaluation of the data;
- consideration of the assumptions used by management;
- testing the calculations, normally by recalculation;
- comparison of prior year estimates with the actual result; and
- consideration of management's approval procedures.

Auditors should ensure that the data used by management to generate their estimates is consistent with that generated by the client's information systems and used in the financial statements. The accuracy of the data used should also be considered. Auditors may check the analysis of the data, for example the ageing of debtors, and may also use third party data to ensure accuracy. When examining an estimate of anticipated legal claims for example, auditors would normally communicate directly with the entity's lawyers.

When considering the assumptions used by management, auditors would normally consider whether the assumptions are:

- reasonable in light of actual results in the prior periods;
- consistent with those used for other accounting estimates; and
- consistent with management's plans.

Particular care should be taken when assumptions are particularly sensitive to change.

Auditors may be able to compare similar estimates in prior year financial statements with actual results for those periods. This should give comfort about the general reliability of the entity's estimates. In translating the comfort gained to the current year's estimates, auditors should consider whether the estimating formulae have been amended for the current period or whether an adjustment should be made given the auditors' knowledge of the client and the industry.

Auditors should consider whether the accounting estimates generated by the client are reviewed and approved by an appropriate level of management and evidenced as such.

The review of subsequent events may remove the need for the auditors to obtain other evidence to support an accounting estimate. For example, if an estimate is made concerning an insurance claim for loss of profits after a fire and is provisionally settled during the audit, this will provide evidence on the estimate and means that the auditors may reduce the attention they give to the process by which management derive the estimate. An estimate may become an accrual where it is fully supported by the subsequent evidence, for example, an estimate in respect of legal fees incurred before the year end becomes an accrual when those fees are rendered.

27.4   EVALUATION OF RESULTS

The ISA (UK and Ireland) requires that the auditors should make a final assessment of the reasonableness of the accounting estimate based on the auditors' knowledge of the entity and its industry and whether it is consistent with other evidence obtained during the audit and subsequent events.

If the auditors believe management's estimate to be unreasonable and management refuses to revise its estimate, the difference between management's estimate and the auditors' estimate must be considered with all other misstatements in assessing whether the effect on the financial statements is material.

27.5   ISA ED, AUDITING ACCOUNTING ESTIMATES, INCLUDING FAIR VALUE ACCOUNTING ESTIMATES, AND RELATED DISCLOSURES

In December 2004, the above Exposure Draft was issued by the IAASB. The Exposure Draft was written in conjunction with the UK APB and conforms ISA 540 to the revised audit risk and fraud standards. At that stage it was entitled *Auditing Accounting Estimates and Related Disclosures (Other than Those Involving Fair Value Measurements and Disclosures)*.

In addition, the draft revised ISA introduces requirements for greater rigour and scepticism when auditing accounting estimates. The ED gave guidance on how auditors should identify and document misstatements and gives indicators of possible management bias relating to accounting estimates. It introduced risk assessment procedures which are more comprehensive than those in the extant ISA, including understanding the process and relevant internal controls used by management to make accounting estimates, and reviewing the outcome of accounting estimates made in the prior period financial statements.

The draft ISA also introduced the concept of estimation uncertainty. This is defined as the susceptibility of a financial statements item to a lack of precision in its measurement because the outcome of future events is not known. The revised ISA focused auditors' work not only on accounting estimates that have a risk of material misstatement, but also on those that have a high estimation uncertainty.

The IAASB approved ISA 540 as a basis for applying the clarity drafting conventions in September 2006. However, as part of the redrafting process it had become clear that there was an element of repetition between ISA 540 and ISA 545, *Auditing Fair Value Measurements and Disclosures*. Therefore, ISA 540 was revised and redrafted to combine it with ISA 545 and was released as an Exposure Draft under its new title, *Auditing Accounting Estimates, Including Fair Value Accounting Estimates, and Related Disclosures* in December 2006.

In the UK the APB have requested that interested parties submit their comments to them for inclusion in the APB response to the IAASB.

28 AUDITING FAIR VALUE

28.1 INTRODUCTION

Assets, liabilities or components of equity may be presented or disclosed at fair value in the financial statements. The fair value used may arise from the initial recording of that asset, liability or equity or from a subsequent change in value. In the UK the use of fair value accounting is governed by Schedule 4 of the Companies Act 1985 as amended by the Companies Act 1985 (International Accounting Standards and Other Accounting Amendments) Regulations 2004 and for the consolidated financial statements of fully listed companies from 1 January 2005, by International Financial Reporting Standards.

The measurement of fair value can be simple, for example if assets are bought and sold in an active and open market, or more complex. Examples of fair values that can be difficult to determine include investment properties or complex financial derivatives. In these cases an estimation of fair value may be achieved by using the work of an expert valuer or a valuation model.

28.2 GUIDANCE

ISA (UK and Ireland) 545 *Auditing Fair Value Measurements and Disclosures* was issued in December 2004 and provides standards on the audit of fair value covering:

- understanding the entity's process;
- evaluating the entity's approach;
- using the work of an expert;
- audit procedures;
- disclosures; and
- communication with those charged with governance.

The text of the ISA (UK and Ireland) assumes that International Accounting Standards are used, but states that where other standards are used (such as UK Financial Reporting Standards) the auditing principles remain the same.

As with all ISAs (UK and Ireland), the text of the international ISA has been supplemented with additional guidance from a UK and Ireland perspective. There was no UK SAS equivalent prior to the publication of the ISA (UK and Ireland).

ISA (UK and Ireland) 545 is effective for audits of financial statements for periods commencing on or after 15 December 2004.

In December 2006, the IAASB issued an Exposure Draft of ISA 540, *Auditing Accounting Estimates, Including Fair Value Accounting Estimates, and Related Disclosures* as part of their Clarity Project. As part of their work on ISA 540 it had become clear that there were a number of similarities between that ISA and ISA 545, and so a decision was made to merge the two. Comments were requested by 30 April 2007. In line with their policy on updating ISAs (UK and Ireland) where the equivalent international version of the ISA is included in the IAASB's Clarity Project, the APB are not expected to amend the ISA (UK and Ireland) until the conclusion of the IAASB's project and the adoption of the revised ISAs for use in the European Union.

28.3   UNDERSTANDING THE ENTITY'S PROCESS

It is the responsibility of those charged with governance to establish procedures to allow the determination of fair values as necessary. This determination of procedures is often delegated to the entity's management, although responsibility remains with those charged with governance. This process may be simple, such as consulting published price quotations, or more complex involving assumptions and uncertainty.

In accordance with ISA (UK and Ireland) 315 *Understanding the Entity and its Environment and Assessing the Risk of Material Misstatement* auditors are required to gain an understanding of the process adopted by management and the related control activities in order to assess the risk of material misstatement (see **Chapter 22**). The risk of material misstatement should be assessed at the assertion level to allow the auditor to determine the nature, extent and timing of their audit tests.

When obtaining an understanding of the entity's fair value process auditors may consider the areas set out in **Table 1**.

TABLE 1: Areas to consider when gaining an understanding of an entity's fair value process

- the relevant control activities over the process used to determine fair value measurements, including, for example, controls over data and the segregation of duties between those committing the entity to the underlying transactions and those responsible for the valuation;
- the expertise and experience of those persons determining the fair value measurements;
- the role that information technology has in the process;
- the types of accounts or transactions requiring fair value measurements or disclosures (e.g., whether the accounts arise from the recording of routine and recurring transactions or whether they arise from non-routine or unusual transactions)
- the extent to which the entity's process relies on a service organisation to provide fair value measurements or the data that supports the measurement. When an entity uses a service organisation, auditors should refer to ISA (UK and Ireland) 402 *Audit Considerations Relating to Entities Using Service Organizations,* see **Chapter 37**;
- the extent to which the entity uses the work of experts in determining fair value measurements and disclosures;
- the significant management assumptions used in determining fair value;
- the documentation supporting management's assumptions;
- the methods used to develop and apply management assumptions and to monitor changes in those assumptions;
- the integrity of change controls and security procedures for valuation models and relevant information systems, including approval processes; and
- the controls over the consistency, timeliness and reliability of the data used in valuation models.

If auditors consider that the risk of material misstatement identified is a significant risk that requires special audit considerations, they should refer to ISA (UK and Ireland) 315.

There may only be limited control activities that can be effective in relation to fair value as fair value determinations often involve subjective judgements by management. As fair value measurements become more complex the likelihood of effective controls decreases whilst the risk of material misstatement increases.

28.4   EVALUATING THE ENTITY'S APPROACH

The auditor uses their knowledge of the business and financial reporting requirement to assess whether the fair value approach used by the entity is appropriate and consistently applied. For example knowledge of a client's business and future plans will assist with assessing the valuation applied to research and development work.

Auditors should pay particular attention to management's intentions, for example whether the intentions relied upon as part of the fair value process are realistic and relevant. Auditors may:

- consider management's past history of carrying out its stated intentions with respect to assets or liabilities;
- review written plans and other documentation, including budgets and minutes as appropriate;
- consider management's stated reasons for choosing a particular course of action;
- consider management's ability to carry out a particular course of action given the entity's economic circumstances, including the implications of any contractual commitments; and
- consider whether the course of action is allowed by UK or International Accounting Standards as relevant.

When a valuation method is not determined by statute or accounting standards, auditors should consider whether management's reasons for selecting a particular valuation method is appropriate. They should consider whether:

- management has sufficiently evaluated and appropriately applied any criteria that have been provided in accounting standards to support the selected method;
- the valuation method is appropriate to the item being valued; and
- the valuation method is appropriate for the business, industry and environment in which the entity operates.

The selected valuation method should be applied consistently, both for like assets and year on year. Where the valuation method has been changed in the period, auditors consider whether the change is justified either as a result of a change to the financial reporting rules or a change in the entity's circumstances, and whether the new method of valuation is more appropriate.

28.5   USING THE WORK OF AN EXPERT

Where valuation methods are complex or specialised, auditors may require the assistance of an expert when assessing the entity's methods and procedures. Where an expert is used, the auditor should refer to ISA (UK and Ireland) 620, *Using the Work of an Expert*, see **Chapter 39.**

In accordance with ISA (UK and Ireland) 620, the auditor should assess the expert's work. This will involve obtaining an understating of the significant assumptions and methods used, and considering whether they are appropriate, complete and reasonable given the auditors' knowledge of the business and the results of other audit procedures.

28.6 AUDIT PROCEDURES

Once the risk of material misstatement has been assessed, auditors should plan and perform their audit procedures. Procedures are likely to vary widely as a result of the many different types of fair value measurements that may occur. The three main types of procedure are:

- testing the entity's assumptions, the valuation model and the underlying data;
- developing independent fair value estimates to corroborate the entity's valuation; and
- considering the effect of subsequent events.

For some valuations it may merely be a case of consulting the same third party pricing data that the entity has used: for other areas the work performed will be more complex.

Whatever procedure is used, auditors should consider the results of their testing in relation to the rest of the evidence gained during the audit, for example is the discount rate used reasonable given the interest rates on borrowings by the entity.

28.6.1   *Testing the entity's assumptions, model and data*

When assessing an entity's fair value measurements, auditors may evaluate whether:

- the assumptions used by management are reasonable;
- the fair value measurement was determined using an appropriate model; and
- management used relevant information that was reasonably available at the time.

Assumptions
Auditors assess whether the assumptions used by the entity provide a reasonable basis for the fair value measurements and disclosures in the financial statements. To provide a reasonable basis the assumptions must be relevant, reliable, neutral, understandable and complete.

The assumptions will vary depending on the asset or liability being valued and the valuation method used, for example where discounted cash flows are

467

used assumptions will be required about the level of cash flows, the period over which they are measured and the discount rate applied.

Auditors should concentrate on significant assumptions, i.e., those that cover matters that materially affect the fair value measurement, and this will typically include those which are:

- sensitive to variation or uncertainty, such as long-term interest rates; and
- susceptible to misapplication or bias.

The auditor should encourage the entity to perform a sensitivity analysis on their fair value measurements, and should consider performing the analysis themselves if it is not completed by the entity.

Assumptions are often interdependent and should be assessed both individually and in conjunction with each other. Sometimes assumptions which appear reasonable on their own may not be consistent with others used in the same valuation. Assumptions should be consistent with:

- the general economic environment and the entity's economic circumstances;
- the plans of the entity;
- assumptions made in prior periods, if appropriate;
- past experience of the entity, although past experience may not be indicative of future conditions or events;
- other matters relating to the financial statements, for example assumptions used by management in other accounting estimates, whether fair value or not; and
- if applicable, the risk associated with the cash flows.

Auditors should obtain written confirmation of representations made by management or those charged with governance regarding the reasonableness of significant assumptions.

Model
Where a valuation model is used, auditors review the model and evaluate whether it is appropriate and the assumptions used are reasonable.

Data
The auditor should plan and perform audit procedures to determine whether the data used in deriving the fair value measurement is accurate, complete and relevant. They should also consider whether the fair value measurement has been properly calculated using that data and the entity's assumptions.

Typical audit procedures will include:

- verifying the source of the data;
- mathematical recalculation of the valuation; and
- reviewing the information for internal consistency.

28.6.2 Independent fair value estimates

Instead of testing the assumptions, model and data as stated above, auditors may choose to attempt to corroborate the entity's fair value measurement by using their own model to generate a valuation. Typically they would use the entity's assumptions and data in this model, and would, therefore, be required to plan and perform procedures to verify these as discussed in **28.6.1** above.

Alternatively, auditors could use their own model and assumptions, but they would still be required to understand the assumptions applied by the entity in order to consider how their valuation differs from that prepared by the entity.

28.6.3 Subsequent events

Transactions and events that appear after the period end, but before the completion of the audit, may provide evidence about fair value measurements. An example would be the sale of an investment property after the period end. Care should be taken, however, that the post balance sheet events may no longer reflect events at the balance sheet date, e.g., a property value may vary considerably month on month in a time of volatile markets.

28.7 DISCLOSURES

Auditors are required to consider whether the disclosures made about fair values are in accordance with the requirements of statute and financial reporting standards. This will include considering whether any additional information given voluntarily is appropriate and not misleading.

Auditors must also ensure that, where a change in valuation methods has occurred in the period, the details and reasons for this change have been properly disclosed.

28.8 COMMUNICATION WITH THOSE CHARGED WITH GOVERNANCE

As the assumptions used in fair value measurement can often have significant effects on the financial statements, auditors may choose to include details of the assumptions, the degree of subjectivity involved in their formulation and the relative materiality of items measured at fair value in their communications with those charged with governance.

29   AUDIT SAMPLING

29.1   AUDITING STANDARDS

ISA (UK and Ireland) 530 *Audit Sampling and Other Selective Testing Procedures* was issued in December 2004 and provides guidance on sampling covering:

- use of sampling;
- risk assessment;
- design of the sample;
- sample size;
- selecting the sample;
- performing audit procedures;
- errors; and
- evaluating results.

As with all ISAs (UK and Ireland), the text of the ISA has been supplemented with additional guidance from a UK and Ireland perspective. SAS 430 *Audit Sampling* has not yet been officially withdrawn.

ISA (UK and Ireland) 530 is effective for audits of financial statements for periods commencing on or after 15 December 2004.

29.2   USE OF SAMPLING

'When designing audit procedures, the auditor should determine appropriate means for selecting items for testing so as to gather sufficient appropriate audit evidence to meet the objectives of the audit procedures.' ISA (UK and Ireland) 530 paragraph 2.

The ISA (UK and Ireland) recognises that auditors do not normally examine all of the information available but reach conclusions on, for example, account balances using audit sampling.

In the ISA (UK and Ireland), audit sampling is defined as 'the application of audit procedures to less than 100 per cent of items ... [to] enable the auditor to obtain and evaluate evidence about some characteristic of the items selected in order to form ... a conclusion concerning the population from which the sample is drawn'. It does not include procedures where individual items which have a particular significance are examined, e.g., all items over £10,000, as here auditors are testing part of the population in its entirety and cannot use the results to draw conclusions about the rest of the population. Similarly, procedures such as walk-through tests are not sampling.

Auditors may use either tests of control or substantive procedures in their work. When performing tests of control, auditors identify a characteristic or attribute which indicates that a control has been implemented. This may be the signing of a purchase order or the completion of a credit check for new customers. The presence or absence of these attributes is then tested by auditors. Audit sampling for tests of control is generally appropriate when application of the control leaves audit evidence of performance, such as an approval stamp or the initials of an authorised person.

Substantive procedures can be broken down into substantive analytical procedures and tests of detail. Audit sampling will only relate to tests of detail.

29.3   RISK ASSESSMENT

ISA (UK and Ireland) 530 states that 'the auditor should use professional judgement to assess the risk of material misstatement ... and design further audit procedures to ensure that this risk is reduced to an acceptably low level'.

A population will have an inherent risk level as assessed by the auditor at the planning stage. The level of inherent risk will have a direct bearing on the sample size used. Where there is a high inherent risk the number of items tested from the population will be greater than in situations where inherent risk has been assessed as low. A higher sample size will result in lower sampling risk, increasing auditors' confidence levels that the population does not contain a material error. Other factors will also affect sample sizes, see **29.5** below

29.3.1   *Sampling risk*

Where sampling is used, auditors must accept a risk that the sample is not representative of the population from which it is drawn and that they may draw the wrong conclusion from the test.

Sampling risk may result in:

- a population such as a file of reconciliations, which is acceptable, being rejected because the sample happens to pick a large proportion of the items in error. This normally results in additional, unnecessary audit work but should not affect the validity of the final audit conclusion; or

- a population, which contains a material error, being accepted as satisfactory because the sample happens not to select any of the items that contain errors. This risk is more serious because there is the possibility that an unqualified audit report is issued when the financial statements contain material misstatement (although auditors should organise their other audit procedures so that it is, in fact, unlikely that such an error escapes detection).

Sampling risk does not only affect substantive procedures; tests of control may result in:

- too high an assessment of control risk, because the error in the sample is greater than that in the population; or
- too low an assessment of control risk, because the error in the sample is less than the error in the population as a whole.

Sampling risk may be reduced by using a rational (possibly a statistical) basis for planning, selecting and testing the sample and for evaluating the results. This will ensure that auditors have adequate assurance that the sample is representative of the population from which it is drawn.

29.3.2 Non-sampling risk

Non-sampling risk arises from factors that cause the auditor to reach an incorrect conclusion and is not related to the size of the sample. For example auditors may plan unsuitable audit procedures or misinterpret audit evidence and fail to recognise an error.

29.4 DESIGN OF THE SAMPLE

29.4.1 Deciding whether to sample

When designing audit procedures, the auditor must decide whether to:

- select all items in a population (100 per cent examination);
- select specific items; or
- use audit sampling.

Selecting all items

This is most appropriate for tests of detail, for example where the population constitutes a small number of large value items or where CAATs are used to test or reperform all the transactions in the period.

Selecting specific items

The decision to select specific items from population will be based on the auditor's knowledge of the client, the assessed risk of material misstatement and the characteristics of the population itself. Items selected may include:

- high value or key items (i.e., those which are themselves material, or have some other characteristic);
- all items over a certain amount;
- items to obtain information; and
- items to test control activities.

Audit sampling

Audit sampling may be applied to a class of transactions or account balances. Either non-statistical or statistic approaches may be used, see **29.9**.

29.4.2   Designing the sample

'When designing an audit sample, the auditor should consider the objectives of the audit procedure and the attributes of the population from which the sample will be drawn.

When designing an audit sample the auditor should also consider the sampling and selection methods' (ISA (UK and Ireland) 530 paragraphs 31 and 31-1)

Objectives

Auditors choose the audit procedures that are most likely to achieve the stated audit objectives. Once the procedures have been decided they design the most appropriate form of sampling. This involves identifying conditions that are to be regarded as errors. For example, in a test of controls operating over purchases, non-compliance with the approval procedures may be assessed as an error. By contrast the types of errors on a substantive test on sales invoices might be arithmetical inaccuracy and/or a failure to reflect them properly in the books of account.

Population

Auditors need to ensure that they are extracting the sample from the appropriate population to test the specific audit objectives. This is more difficult when the audit objective is testing for understatement, such as the understatement of creditors, as the sample is chosen from a related population. The relevant population for such a test of understatement might be suppliers' statements, post-period payments or a list of all suppliers during the period, rather than unpaid invoices. In these cases auditors need to take steps to ensure that the chosen population is complete, such as choosing suppliers' statements from a list taken from the purchase ledger.

The sampling unit is any of the individual items that make up the population and will vary according to the nature of the audit test. The auditors define the sampling unit in order to obtain an efficient and effective sample to achieve their audit objective. For example, when testing the validity of debtors the sampling unit is the individual customer balances or invoices.

Stratification

By dividing a population into discrete sub-populations, sample sizes can be reduced without increasing sampling risk. Populations are often subdivided by monetary value, meaning greater audit effort can be directed to larger value items. However, the results of audit procedures performed on a stratified population can only be projected to items in the same stratum; other items will have to be tested separately.

29.5 SAMPLE SIZE

'In determining the sample size, the auditor should consider whether sampling risk is reduced to an acceptably low level' (ISA (UK and Ireland) 530, paragraph 39

Sample size is affected by the level of sampling risk that auditors are willing to accept. The lower the acceptable risk, the greater the sample size will need to be.

Examples of some factors affecting sample sizes, taken from the ISA (UK and Ireland), are shown in **Table 1** and **Table 2**.

TABLE 1: Some factors influencing sample size for substantive tests	
Factor	*Impact on sample size*
Inherent risk [1]	• The higher the assessment of inherent risk, the more audit evidence is required to support the auditors' conclusion.
Control risk [2]	• The higher the assessment of control risk, the greater the reliance on audit evidence obtained from substantive procedures. • A high control risk assessment may result in the decision not to perform tests of control and reliance entirely on substantive procedures.
Detection risk [3]	• Sampling risk for substantive tests is one form of detection risk. The lower the sampling risk the auditors are willing to accept, the larger the sample size. • Other substantive procedures may provide audit evidence regarding the same financial statement assertions and reduce detection risk. This may reduce the extent of the auditors' reliance on the results of the substantive procedure using audit sampling.

	• The lower the reliance on the results of a substantive procedure using audit sampling, the higher the sampling risk auditors are willing to accept, and, consequently, the smaller the sample size.
Tolerable error rate	The higher monetary value of the tolerable error rate, the smaller the sample size and vice versa.
Expected error rate	If errors are expected, a larger sample usually needs to be examined to confirm that the actual error rate is less than the tolerable error rate.
Population value	The less material the monetary value of the population to the financial statements, the smaller the sample size that may be required.
Numbers of items in population	Virtually no effect on sample size unless population is small.
Stratification	If it is appropriate to stratify the population this may lead to a smaller sample size.

Notes

[1] Inherent risk is the susceptibility of an account balance or class of transactions to material misstatement, either individually or when aggregated with misstatements in other balances or classes, irrespective of related internal controls (see **Chapter 22**).

[2] Control risk is the risk that a misstatement that could occur in an account balance or class of transactions. The misstatement could be material, either individually or when aggregated with misstatements in other balances or classes, and would not be prevented, or detected and corrected on a timely basis, by the accounting and internal control systems (see **Chapter 22**).

[3] Detection risk is the risk that auditors' substantive procedures do not detect a misstatement that exists in an account balance or class of transactions, which could be material, either individually or when aggregated with misstatements in other balances or classes (see **Chapter 22**).

TABLE 2: Some factors influencing sample size for tests of controls	
Factor	*Impact on sample size*
Sampling risk	• The greater the reliance on the results of a test of control using audit sampling, the lower the sampling risk the auditors are willing to accept and, consequently, the larger the sample size. • The lower the assessment of control risk, the more likely the auditors are to place reliance on audit evidence from tests of control.
	A high control risk assessment may result in a decision not to perform tests of control.
Tolerable error rate	The higher the tolerable rate the lower the sample size and vice versa.
Expected error rate	• If errors are expected, a larger sample usually needs to be examined to confirm that the actual error rate is less than the tolerable error rate. • High expected error rates may result in a decision not to perform tests of control.
Number of items in population	Virtually no effect on sample size unless population is small.

29.6 SELECTING THE SAMPLE

ISA (UK and Ireland) 530 requires auditors 'to select items for the sample with the expectation that all sampling units in the population have a chance of selection'. In other words, all items in the population must have an opportunity of being selected although this need not be equal. For example, auditors will often choose samples so as to give higher value items a greater chance of selection.

The three most common methods of selecting a sample are:

• random selection, where each item has an equal chance of selection, using random number tables or CAATs;
• systematic selection, using a constant interval between selections and a randomly selected starting point. Where this method is being used it is important that the population is not structured in such a way that the sampling interval used corresponds to a particular pattern in the population; and
• haphazard selection, so long as there is no bias in the selection.

29.7 PERFORMING AUDIT PROCEDURES

Auditors perform the planned procedures on each item in the sample. If any item selected is not appropriate a replacement item should be chosen. However, auditors should consider whether the unsatisfactory item indicates an error. If procedures cannot be completed on a sample item, for example the supporting documentation has been lost, alternative audit procedures should be considered for that item. If no alternative procedures are possible, the item should be considered to be an error.

29.8 ERRORS

ISA (UK and Ireland) 530 states that auditors should 'consider the sample results, the nature and cause of any errors identified, and their possible effect on the particular audit objective and other areas of the audit.'

Before evaluating the results of a sample, auditors need to establish whether a matter detected is an error. There may be instances where such a matter does not meet the criteria for an error that were set in the planning of the test. For example, a substantive test of the validity of debtors may indicate that there has been a misposting between customer accounts. This does not lead to a misstatement of the total trade debtor balance; therefore in evaluating the sample it may be inappropriate to consider that this is an error. However, there may be implications for other areas of the audit, such as the recoverability of debtors.

The qualitative aspects of the error also need to be considered, particularly the nature and cause of the error, as they may have implications for other audit areas. It may be that all the errors fall within a particular time period or are at one location, in which case it may be possible to identify the extent of the error in the rest of the population. For example, if the member of staff who inputs the sales invoices on to the system was away from work for a month and the replacement was entering the net amount of the invoice instead of the gross amount, an exercise could be undertaken to quantify the extent of the error by comparing the total of that month's gross and net sales.

29.8.1 Tolerable error

This is the maximum error that is acceptable to the auditors, if they are to conclude that their audit objectives have been achieved. This is not necessarily the same as materiality, which relates to the financial statements as a whole rather than a particular balance or class of transactions, although it is related to materiality in the case of substantive testing. Where tests of control are being performed, the tolerable level of error will be the maximum rate of failure of an internal control that the auditors are prepared to accept.

29.8.2 Expected error

Before a test is performed an error may already be expected. Here, a larger number of items may need to be tested to conclude that the actual error in the population is not greater than the planned tolerable error. This may be the case where previous years' audit tests have produced errors or the review of the internal controls indicates this.

29.8.3 Projecting errors

> 'For tests of details, the auditor should project monetary errors found in the sample to the population, and should consider the effect of the projected error on the particular audit objective and on other areas of the audit' ISA (UK and Ireland) 530 paragraph 51

When projecting errors found in the sample for tests of detail to the population from which it was drawn, the method used must be consistent with that used to select the sample. Projection commonly involves extrapolating the errors in the sample and estimating any further error not detected due to the imprecision of the methods used.

To assess whether errors in the population might exceed the tolerable error, the projected population error (net of adjustments made by the entity) should be compared with the tolerable error, taking into account the results of other audit procedures relevant to that financial statement assertion.

Where the projected errors exceed the tolerable error, they reassess sampling risk and if they conclude that it is unacceptable (for example, they have insufficient confidence in the results of the sample) they should consider:

- extending their own audit procedures; or
- performing alternative procedures (which may involve reviewing a client's exercise to investigate errors).

This will enable them to conclude on the test and may result in identifying the need for an adjustment to the financial statements.

Anomalous errors, i.e., errors which arise from an isolated event that has not recurred other than on a specifically identifiable occasion, may be excluded when projecting errors to the population. This is because anomalous errors will not be representative of the population as a whole. However, their effect still needs to be considered in addition to the projection of non-anomalous errors.

Projection of errors is not appropriate for tests of control. On discovering errors in a test of control, auditors should consider whether the error is indicative of a general weakness in the control system.

29.9 EVALUATING RESULTS

Auditors should assess the results of the sample tested to determine if the objectives of the test have been met.

For tests of control, a high incidence of errors may lead auditors to increase their assessment of the risk of material misstatement. For tests of detail, high error rates may indicate that a class of transactions or an account balance is materially misstated.

Auditors should use judgement where the projected error in a sample, plus any anomalous error which was not subject to projection, is close to their assessment of tolerable error. Auditors should be aware that sampling risk may mean that selection of a different sample may have provided an error which was greater than tolerable error. Auditors should consider the results of other audit procedures when assessing whether an adjustment to the financial statements is required.

If auditors determine that test objectives have not been met, they may:

- request those charged with governance to investigate identified errors and the potential for further errors and to make any necessary adjustments; and/or
- modify the nature, timing and extent of further audit procedures. For example in the case of tests of controls, the auditor might extend the sample size, test an alternative control or modify related substantive procedures; and/or
- consider the effect on the audit report.

29.10 STATISTICAL AND NON-STATISTICAL SAMPLING

There are several similarities between statistical and non-statistical sampling. Both:

- examine less than the total population to reach a conclusion about the population;
- involve sampling risk;
- provide approximate, not exact, knowledge about the population;
- perform the same audit steps; and
- require audit judgement.

One major difference between statistical and non-statistical methods is that a statistical sample must be selected using an appropriate statistical basis from the population while, although desirable, this is not essential for non-statistical methods.

Not every audit sample is worth performing on a rigorous statistical basis. Non-statistical sampling may be used whenever auditors conclude that the additional costs of statistical sampling, such as set-up time, are in excess of the benefits to be obtained, for example, objectivity of sample selection and evaluation. Non-statistical sampling may be preferable in situations where the statistical selection is difficult to make because the records are not readily accessible or are in a form that makes it difficult to make a valid statistical selection. For example, at the physical stocktaking, when selecting items for test counting from floor to stock sheet there is no list of the population from which a statistical sample can be taken. In these cases, statistical sample sizes can still be used to get an idea of an appropriate sample size.

When using non-statistical methods, auditors also need to be satisfied that the selection is appropriate to obtain a reasonable conclusion and that they have not used these methods to exclude difficult items. Non-statistical sampling does not automatically solve problems or turn documents with errors into correct documents. Every item selected should be audited (and not replaced if not found). For example, a missing invoice should be investigated rather than inspecting the next available invoice. A conclusion about the population should be drawn from the sample evidence.

Approximate sample sizes should be generated for a population whether statistical or non-statistical methods are used. The sample size will depend on a number of factors such as population size, materiality and identified risk, and these will remain identical whichever sampling approach is used.

Statistical sampling is more likely to be used whenever auditors conclude that the benefits are greater than the costs. Examples of this include situations where:

- the set-up time and selection time are reasonable in relation to the time required to test the selected items and follow up on discrepancies (more likely to be true for larger tests than for smaller ones);
- the most extensive part of the test is a representative selection, not the selection of material or unusual items;
- records of the entire population are reasonably accessible for the purpose of making the selection (although even if they are not readily accessible, statistical sampling could be desirable if it is likely that a non-statistical selection would yield an inappropriate conclusion because of a failure to include inconvenient records in the selection); and

- the selection of the statistical sample can be effected easily, perhaps with the aid of computer-assisted techniques.

Even where the approach adopted does not meet the criteria for statistical sampling, elements of the statistical approach may still be used, for example the use of random selection of items to be tested using computer-generated random numbers.

30 MANAGEMENT REPRESENTATIONS

30.1 AUDITING STANDARDS

ISA (UK and Ireland) 580 *Management Representations* was issued in December 2004 and provides guidance on the need to gain written confirmation of management representations. The ISA contains guidance covering:

- management responsibilities;
- representations by management as audit evidence;
- documentation of representations; and
- refusal to provide written representations.

As with all ISAs (UK and Ireland), the text of the ISA has been supplemented with additional guidance from a UK and Ireland perspective. SAS 440 *Management Representations* has not yet been officially withdrawn.

ISA (UK and Ireland) 580 is effective for audits of financial statements for periods commencing on or after 15 December 2004.

In December 2006, the IAASB issued an Exposure Draft of a revision to ISA 580. The revision includes the required changes to bring the ISA in line with the drafting conventions set out in its Clarity Project as well as addressing concerns that auditors may be overly relying on written representations. Further details are provided in **30.8** below.

In November 2002, the Audit and Assurance Faculty of the ICAEW issued an Explanatory Note on Management Representation Letters (Audit 04/02). The aim of the Note is to help auditors increase the usefulness of management representation letters as audit evidence by suggesting methods to ensure that representations are reliable. The Explanatory Note is detailed in **30.9** below.

30.2 REQUIREMENT TO OBTAIN WRITTEN CONFIRMATION

During the course of their audit, auditors receive oral representations from management in response to particular enquiries. ISA (UK and Ireland) 580 requires that auditors obtain written confirmation of appropriate representations from management before they issue their report. In this context, management includes senior management, the directors and members of the audit committee.

Written confirmations may be in the form of:

- a representation letter from management;
- a letter from the auditors outlining their understanding of management's representations, duly acknowledged and confirmed by management; or
- minutes of meetings of the board of directors at which such representations are approved.

30.3 ACKNOWLEDGEMENT OF DIRECTORS' RESPONSIBILITY

ISA (UK and Ireland) 580 requires auditors to obtain evidence that those charged with governance acknowledge their collective responsibility for the fair presentation of the financial statements in accordance with the applicable financial reporting framework, and has approved the financial statements. This applies to all financial statements, not only those prepared by the auditors on behalf of the directors.

This acknowledgement can be achieved by the auditors receiving:

- relevant minutes from the directors' meeting;
- a written representation from the directors; or
- a signed copy of the financial statements which incorporates a statement of directors' responsibilities.

The last of these is generally included either in the directors' report or in a separate statement.

In group situations, acknowledgement of the directors' responsibilities applies to the group financial statements as well as those of the parent undertaking.

30.4   REPRESENTATIONS BY MANAGEMENT AS AUDIT EVIDENCE

In addition to the written confirmations of representations concerning the responsibility for the financial statements, ISA (UK and Ireland) 580 requires auditors to obtain them for 'matters material to the financial statements when other appropriate audit evidence cannot reasonably be expected to exist'.

It is suggested that auditors discuss these matters with those responsible for providing the written confirmation before they sign it to reduce the possibility of misunderstanding.

The auditors should assess the reasonableness of the representations on material matters. This may be achieved by:

- obtaining corroborative evidence from inside or outside the entity;
- assessing the representations for any inconsistency with other audit evidence obtained; and
- considering whether the individuals who made the representations can be expected to be well-informed on the matter.

The guidance accompanying the ISA (UK and Ireland) stresses that representations are not a substitute for other audit evidence that the auditors may reasonably expect to obtain and, were this to be the case, it could lead to a qualification to the auditors' report because of a limitation of scope.

This also applies to cases where there is a genuine limitation of scope and the auditors do not expect any other evidence to be available. For example, where auditors are appointed after the end of the reporting period and are unable to find any means of verifying material quantities of stock, management representations could never be sufficient evidence on their own to support quantities.

There will, however, be instances when no supporting evidence is available and cannot reasonably be expected to be available, and where written confirmation of the representation will constitute acceptable evidence. For example, when auditing a deferred tax provision auditors may need to accept representations about management's intentions in regard to future capital spending. Similarly, where the carrying value of one particular line of stock can only be supported by a proposed future marketing programme, representations concerning this are likely to be an essential part of the audit evidence. In such cases the auditors should ensure that nothing conflicts with the representations and that, when combined with other evidence, it supports an unqualified opinion.

In exceptional cases a matter may be so significant that the auditor makes reference to the representation in the audit report.

ISA (UK and Ireland) 580 also requires auditors to obtain written confirmation that management:

- acknowledges its responsibility for the design and implementation of internal control to prevent and detect error; and
- believes the uncorrected misstatements are not material to the financial statements both individually and in aggregate. This will typically involve a schedule of unadjusted misstatements being included in, or attached to, the representation letter.

As discussed in ISA (UK and Ireland) 570 requires auditors to consider the need for written confirmation of management representations regarding the going concern assumption, and these may be essential where there is no other evidence of the directors' assessment.

Where auditors prepare the financial statements in addition to auditing them, they may wish to obtain representations from management acknowledging the directors' responsibility for this in writing.

An example of a management representation letter from management to the auditors is shown in **Table 1** at **30.7**. It should be tailored for the circumstances of each client.

When consolidated financial statements are being produced there will be representations which are relevant to the group, in addition to those for the parent undertaking. Such representations may be obtained from either the directors of the parent undertaking or directly from those of the subsidiary. The method chosen will depend on the decision-making structure of the group. For example, where the parent company directors, or a proportion of them, are involved in the operational management of the subsidiary, the representations may be obtained directly from them by virtue of their day-to-day involvement.

30.5   CONTRADICTORY AUDIT EVIDENCE

Where there is a contradiction between the representation and other audit evidence, the ISA (UK and Ireland) suggests that the auditor 'should investigate the circumstances, and where necessary, reconsider the reliability of other representations'. This will usually be in the form of further enquiries of management about the reasons for the conflict. Management's response should be corroborated and if there is still a discrepancy further audit work may be necessary.

30.6 BASIC ELEMENTS OF A MANAGEMENT REPRESENTATION LETTER

The auditors need to ensure that when they request a management representation letter that it:

- is addressed to them;
- contains specified information, i.e., additional paragraphs may be needed;
- is appropriately dated; and
- is signed by someone with the appropriate level of authority.

In most cases, it will be appropriate for the chairman and the secretary to sign the letter on behalf of the Board based on the best of their knowledge and belief and having made appropriate enquiries of other members of management. Often the letter is discussed by the Board of directors before they approve the financial statements to ensure that all members are aware of the representations on which the auditors intend to rely in expressing their opinion on those financial statements.

The letter will normally be dated on the date of the audit report.

Where there is a delay in completing the audit after the date of receipt of the representation letter, auditors should consider whether there is a need to obtain further representations in respect of the intervening period and also whether they should extend their post balance sheet event review.

30.7 REFUSAL TO PROVIDE WRITTEN CONFIRMATION

ISA (UK and Ireland) 580 requires that where management refuses to provide the auditors with written confirmation of the representations, the auditors should consider whether this leads to a limitation of scope requiring either a qualified opinion or a disclaimer of opinion.

This will mean that the auditors need to reconsider any representations that they have relied on during the course of their audit.

TABLE 1:   Example letter of representation

ABC & Co 1 High Street London

Dear Sirs

Financial Statements at 31 March 20..

We confirm to the best of our knowledge and belief, and having made appropriate enquiries of other directors and officials of the company, the following representations given to you in connection with your audit of the company's financial statements for the year ended 31 March 20...

We acknowledge as directors our responsibility under the Companies Act 1985 for preparing the financial statements which give a true and fair view and for making accurate representations to you. All the accounting records have been made available to you for the purpose of your audit and all the transactions undertaken by the company have been properly reflected and recorded in the accounting records. All other records and related information, including minutes of all management and shareholder's meetings have been made available to you.

We acknowledge our responsibility for the design and implementation of internal control systems to prevent and detect error.

We confirm that we believe that the effects of the uncorrected financial statements misstatements listed in the attached schedule are not material to the financial statements, either individually or in aggregate.

The legal claim by XYZ Limited has been settled out of court by a payment of £.... No further amounts are expected to be paid and no similar claims have been received or are expected to be received.

In connection with deferred tax not provided, the following assumptions reflect the intentions and expectations of the company:

capital investment of £... is planned over the next three years;

there are no plans to sell revalued properties; and

we are not aware of any indications that the situation is likely to change so as to necessitate the inclusion of a provision for tax payable in the financial statements.

The company has not had, or entered into, at any time during the period any arrangement, transaction or agreement to provide credit facilities (including loans, quasi-loans or credit transactions) for directors or to guarantee or provide security for such matters.

There have been no events since the balance sheet date which necessitate

---

revision of the figures included in the financial statements or inclusion of a note thereto.

We confirm that the above representations are made on the basis of enquiries of management and staff with relevant knowledge and experience (and where appropriate, of inspection of supporting documentation) sufficient to satisfy ourselves that we can properly make each of the above representations to you.

As minuted by the board of directors at its meeting on ......

Chairman _____

Secretary _____

30.8 IAASB ED ISA 580 (REVISED AND REDRAFTED)

In December 2006, the IAASB issued a revised and redrafted Exposure Draft of the international version of ISA 580 for comment. As well as bringing ISA 580 in line with the redrafting conventions set out in their Clarity Project, the IAASB's aim was to 'enhance auditor performance on an audit of financial statements through more stringent requirements and expanded guidance' following concerns that auditors were becoming over-reliant on management representations.

The significant proposals in the Exposure Draft are:

- requirements for auditors to identify the relevant parties who are best placed to provide either general or specific written representations, which may be other than those charged with governance, where such people have relevant specialist knowledge;
- that ISA 200, *Objectives and General Principles Governing an Audit of Financial Statements* and ISA 210, *Terms of Audit Engagements* be amended to clarify the responsibilities of management, and that general written representations are obtained to require management to acknowledge these responsibilities;
- clarification that written representations on specific matters should only be sought 'when other sufficient appropriate audit evidence cannot reasonably be expected to exist', 'when the auditor considers it necessary to corroborate other audit evidence' or when required by another ISA; and
- guidance for auditors who wish to set a threshold amount whereby representations were only sought for matters with a higher monetary value than the threshold. Auditors are reminded to be mindful of situations where the aggregate of immaterial matters may become material.

The APB have requested comments from interested parties in the UK for inclusion in their response to the IAASB.

30.9 AUDIT 4/02: MANAGEMENT REPRESENTATION LETTERS, EXPLANATORY NOTE

In November 2002, the Audit and Assurance Faculty of the ICAEW issued an Explanatory Note on *Management Representation Letters* (Audit 04/02). The guidance was issued following a recent High Court decision concerning the audit of Barings Futures (Singapore) Pte Ltd (BFS) by Deloitte & Touche (D&T).

The guidance in the Note supplemented SAS 440 *Management Representations* and is still relevant under ISA (UK and Ireland) 580. It does not, however, constitute an Auditing Standard in its own right.

30.9.1 The case

Deloitte & Touche faced a claim in damages following their audit of BFS, and attempted to defend themselves by stating that management representations provided to them were recklessly fraudulent, as they were made by a director of BFS who had little knowledge of Nick Leeson's activities, despite being nominally his reporting superior.

However, their claim failed because they could not prove that the director signed the representation letter whilst:

- knowing that the statements were untrue; and
- knowing that he had no reasonable grounds for making the statements.

Despite Deloitte & Touche not winning their argument, the Judge did state that if they had been successful he would have held BFS vicariously liable for the director's actions.

30.9.2 Increasing the usefulness of representation letters as audit evidence

The Explanatory Note re-emphasises the requirement that auditors should discuss the contents of the representation letter with management, so that they understand what they are being asked to sign. Auditors should also consider whether the person signing the letter is in a position to enable them to sign the letter in full knowledge of the matters contained therein.

The Note suggests adding the following statement to all management representation letters to focus the attention of those signing the letter on whether proper enquiries have been made:

'We confirm that the above representations are made on the basis of enquiries of management and staff with relevant knowledge and experience (and, where appropriate, of inspection of supporting documentation) sufficient to satisfy yourselves that we can properly make each of the above representations to you.'

Auditors may also ask signatories what enquiries have been made of management and staff and how they went about this process. Where signatories have themselves obtained written representations from others, for example in relation to complex or specialist areas such as financial instruments, these may be attached to the management representation letter itself and referred to in the letter. Auditors may also wish to impress upon their clients that it is an offence under s389A of the 1985 Companies Act to knowingly or recklessly make a misleading or false statement to the company's auditors.

31 OPENING BALANCES AND COMPARATIVES

31.1 AUDITING STANDARDS

ISA (UK and Ireland) 510 *Initial Engagements – Opening Balances and Continuing Engagements – Opening Balances* was issued in December 2004 and provides guidance on the treatment of opening balances. At the same time ISA (UK and Ireland) 710 *Comparatives* was issued.

As with all ISAs (UK and Ireland), the text of the international ISAs have been supplemented with additional guidance from a UK and Ireland perspective. SAS 450 *Opening Balances and Comparatives* has not yet been officially withdrawn.

ISAs (UK and Ireland) 510 and 710 are effective for audits of financial statements for periods commencing on or after 15 December 2004.

31.2 AUDITORS' RESPONSIBILITIES

ISAs (UK and Ireland) 510 and 710 requires auditors to obtain sufficient evidence to ensure that accounts derived from the previous financial statements are:

- free from material misstatement; and
- incorporated appropriately in the current financial statements.

In the UK, auditors have no statutory responsibility to report specifically on corresponding or comparative amounts.

They do, however, have to report that the financial statements have been properly prepared under the Companies Act and as corresponding amounts are required by the Companies Act, this requirement imposes a responsibility to ensure that these amounts have been correctly extracted and, where appropriate, properly restated to achieve consistency and comparability.

31.3 OPENING BALANCES

As part of their audit evidence, auditors should confirm under ISA (UK and Ireland) 510 that:

- opening balances have been appropriately brought forward;
- opening balances are free from material error or misstatement; and
- appropriate accounting policies are consistently applied, or where there are changes these are adequately accounted for and disclosed.

Where such evidence cannot be obtained, auditors should consider the implications for their report. An example of the report is shown in **Table 1**.

TABLE 1:   Unable to obtain evidence regarding opening balances

Extract from independent auditors' report to the shareholders of XYZ Ltd

Basis of audit opinion
We planned our audit so as to obtain all the information and explanations which we considered necessary in order to provide us with sufficient evidence to give reasonable assurance that the financial statements are free from material misstatement, whether caused by fraud or other irregularity or error. However, the evidence available to us was limited because we were not appointed auditors of the company until (*date*) and in consequence it was not possible for us to perform the auditing procedures necessary to obtain sufficient appropriate audit evidence as regards (*specify and evaluate the balances involved*) included in the preceding years' financial statements at £..... Any adjustment to (*these figures*) would have a consequential effect on the profit for the year ended 31 December 20...

Qualified opinion arising from limitation in audit scope
In our opinion the financial statements:

- give a true and fair view in accordance with United Kingdom Generally Accepted Accounting Practice, of the state of the company's affairs as at 31 December 20.. and, except for any adjustments that might have been found to be necessary had we been able to obtain sufficient evidence concerning (*specify the balances involved*) as at 1 January 20.., of its profit for the year then ended; and
- have been properly prepared in accordance with the Companies Act 1985.

In respect alone of the limitation on our work relating to (*specify the opening balances involved*):

- we have not obtained all the information and explanations that we considered necessary for the purpose of our audit; and
- we were unable to determine whether proper accounting records had been maintained.

> In our opinion the information given in the Directors' Report is consistent with the financial statements.

31.3.1 Continuing auditors

Where their previous report was unqualified and their current audit has not cast any doubt on the opening balances, auditors may limit their procedures to ensuring that:

- the opening balances have been brought forward correctly; and
- the accounting policies have been consistently applied, or if there has been a change in policy that this is accounted for and disclosed properly.

In cases where the previous report was qualified, auditors should, in addition to those procedures noted above, consider whether the matter giving rise to the qualification has been resolved and properly dealt with in the current financial statements. Even if it is resolved it may still give rise to a qualification (see **31.4.1** below).

31.3.2 Incoming auditors

The guidance to the ISA (UK and Ireland) suggests that the sufficiency and appropriateness of the evidence incoming auditors require depends on:

- the entity's accounting policies;
- whether the previous financial statements were audited, and if so, whether the report was qualified;
- the nature of the opening balances and the risk of misstatement in the current financial statements; and
- the materiality of the opening balances relative to the current financial statements.

This means that in general more evidence is expected to support balances from previous years which affect the current year's results, for example, stock or debtors, where these are material. Where the level of activity has increased significantly and the relative importance of these figures is diminished, less evidence would be necessary.

Incoming auditors must carry out more extensive procedures than continuing auditors and these will include:

- consultations with management and review of the previous period's accounting records and control procedures; and
- substantive procedures on the opening balances, if other procedures on the current period to confirm the opening position do not provide sufficient evidence.

The situation where the previous financial statements were not audited, because of entitlement to audit exemption (see **Chapter 7**), is considered by guidance to the ISA (UK and Ireland). In such cases, where auditors are unable to obtain sufficient appropriate evidence from alternative procedures, they should consider the implications for their report. This will usually lead to a qualification, or in rare cases a disclaimer, on the basis of a limitation of scope depending on the effect of the unaudited figures on the financial statements. An example of such a qualified report where the company took advantage of audit exemption in the previous year is shown in **Table 2**.

TABLE 2:   Extract from example report where previous year's figures are unaudited (subject to audit exemption report)

To the shareholders of XYZ Limited

...

Basis of audit opinion
We conducted our audit in accordance with International Standards on Auditing (United Kingdom and Ireland) issued by the Auditing Practices Board, except that the scope of our work was limited as explained below.

An audit includes examination, on a test basis, of evidence relevant to the amounts and disclosures in the financial statements. It also includes an assessment of the significant estimates and judgments made by the directors in the preparation of the financial statements, and of whether the accounting policies are appropriate to the company's circumstances, consistently applied and adequately disclosed.

We planned and performed our audit so as to obtain all the information and explanations which we considered necessary in order to provide us with sufficient evidence to give reasonable assurance that the financial statements are free from material misstatement, whether caused by fraud or other irregularity or error. However, the evidence available to us was limited because we were appointed auditors during the year and we have been unable to carry out auditing procedures necessary to obtain adequate assurance regarding the opening balances and comparative figures because the financial statements for the year ended 31 December 20.. were unaudited. Any adjustments to the opening balances would have a consequential effect on the profit for the year. In addition, the amounts shown as corresponding amounts for the year ended 31 December 20.. may not be comparable with the figures for the current period.

In forming our opinion we also evaluated the overall adequacy of the presentation of information in the financial statements.

Qualified opinion arising from limitation in audit scope
Except for the financial effects of such adjustments, if any, that might have been

---

found to be necessary had we been able to obtain sufficient evidence concerning the opening balances as at 1 January 20.. and corresponding amounts, in our opinion the financial statements:

- give a true and fair view, in accordance with United Kingdom Generally Accepted Accounting Practice, of the state of the company's affairs as at 31 December 20.. and, of its profit/loss for the year then ended; and
- have been properly prepared in accordance with the Companies Act 1985.

In respect alone of the limitation on our work relating to opening balances:

- we have not obtained all the information and explanations that we considered necessary for the purpose of our audit; and
- we were unable to determine whether proper accounting records had been maintained.

In our opinion the information given in the Directors' Report is consistent with the financial statements.

Registered Auditors
Address
Date

In some cases it will be possible to hold discussions with the previous auditors to obtain information concerning their examination of particular areas and clarification of significant accounting matters, particularly if the previous report was qualified. However, there is no ethical obligation on the part of previous auditors to participate in such discussions. An alternative approach may be to use a questionnaire, similar in nature to that sent to other auditors in group audit situations (see **38.3.5**).

31.4 COMPARATIVES

As with opening balances, auditors should obtain evidence that comparatives are not materially misstated. ISA (UK and Ireland) 710 requires that evidence is obtained to confirm that:

- accounting policies are consistent, or if there has been a change that this is properly accounted for and disclosed;
- the comparative figures agree with those in the previous financial statements and are free from material error in the context of the current financial statements; and
- where comparatives have been adjusted because of material errors and misstatements that this is properly disclosed.

Where auditors are unable to obtain such evidence, they should consider the implications for their report.

For continuing auditors, as long as they have no concerns about prior year items, procedures are normally restricted to ensuring that the comparatives have been correctly brought forward and disclosed.

31.4.1 Qualified reports

The effect that a qualified report has on the report in the subsequent period will depend on:

- the nature of the qualification; and
- whether the matter has been resolved and correctly reflected in the financial statements.

The reasons for the qualification in one period may have knock-on effects into the next. The effect of a qualification on a subsequent period depends on whether or not the matter has been resolved. The guidance to ISA (UK and Ireland) 710 envisages three situations:

(a) when the matter is unresolved, and is material in the context of the current period's opening balances as well as comparatives, auditors should qualify the current period audit report in respect of opening balances and comparatives;

(b) where the matter is unresolved and does not effect the opening balances, but is material to the comparatives shown in the current financial statements, auditors should qualify their report in respect of the comparatives; and

(c) where the matter has been resolved, but is material to the current period, the auditors should include an emphasis of matter paragraph in their report on the current period explaining how it has been dealt with.

In (a) the qualified opinion would describe the matter and its effect on the current and preceding years' figures. An example of this would be where in a previous year the company had made a provision for the permanent diminution in value of a fixed asset which the auditors did not believe was necessary. In subsequent years they would qualify their report in respect of the consequential understatement of the depreciation charge and corresponding understatement of the asset and give an 'except for' opinion.

A further example would be a disagreement over the necessity for a provision against a debtor. **Table 3** shows the opinion paragraph that would be appropriate.

Where an auditors' report on the previous year contained a limitation of scope disclaimer covering all aspects of the report, it would be unlikely that they could satisfy themselves on the profit and loss account or the cash flow statement in the next year, even if they obtained sufficient evidence that the balance sheet for that year showed a true and fair view.

TABLE 3: Preceding period was qualified and the matter has not been resolved

Extract from independent auditors' report to the shareholders of XYZ Ltd

Qualified opinion arising from disagreement about accounting treatment
Included in the debtors shown on the balance sheet of 31 December 20.. and 31 December 20.. is an amount of £Y which is the subject of litigation and against which no provision has been made. In our opinion, full provision of £Y should have been made in the year ended 31 December 20.., reducing profit before tax for the year ended 31 December 20.. and net assets at 31 December 20.. and 31 December 20.. by that amount.

In our opinion the financial statements give a true and fair view, in accordance with United Kingdom Generally Accepted Accounting Practice of the company's profit [loss] for the year ended 31 December 20...

Except for the financial effect of not making the provision referred to in the preceding paragraph, in our opinion the financial statements:

- give a true and fair view, in accordance with United Kingdom Generally Accepted Accounting Practice, of the state of the company's affairs as at 31 December 20.. ; and
- have been properly prepared in accordance with the Companies Act 1985.

In our opinion the information given in the Directors' Report is consistent with the financial statements.

Where this occurs it normally affects areas such as stock and work in progress or debtors and creditors at the beginning of the period, uncertainty about which directly affects the profit and loss account and the cash flow statements. Where the effect is material either a qualification or disclaimer on the grounds of limitation of scope is needed depending on the effect of the limitation on the audit procedures and the significance of the amounts involved to the financial statements. An example of such a disclaimer is shown in **Table 4** of **Chapter 4**.

An example of (b) might be a limitation of scope in respect of the accounting records kept in the first six months of the year which had been destroyed by a fire but which had not led to a qualification in respect of the balance sheet. In the subsequent year there would be an 'except for' opinion in respect of the corresponding profit and loss figures as the auditors would still not have sufficient evidence on them.

Similarly, if there was a change in auditors in the previous period and that previous report contained the limitation of scope shown in **Table 6** of **Chapter 4**, the subsequent report will refer to this, as shown in **Table 4** below.

Situation (c) would result from a fundamental uncertainty which was not properly disclosed in the previous financial statements resulting in a disagreement which has now been resolved.

TABLE 4:   Previous qualification not affecting opening balances

Extract from independent auditors' report to the shareholders of XYZ Ltd

Basis of audit opinion
We conducted our audit in accordance with International Standards on Auditing (United Kingdom and Ireland) issued by the Auditing Practices Board, except that the scope of our work was limited as explained below . . . .

We planned and performed our audit so as to obtain all the information and explanations which we considered necessary in order to provide us with sufficient evidence to give reasonable assurance that the financial statements are free from material misstatement, whether caused by fraud or other irregularity or error. In forming our opinion we also evaluated the overall adequacy of the presentation of information in the financial statements. However, the evidence available to us was limited in relation to the comparatives in the current year's financial statements which are derived from the financial statements for the year ended 31 December 20... In our report on those financial statements we stated that, because we were appointed auditors on 30 June 20.., it was not possible for us to perform the auditing procedures necessary to obtain sufficient appropriate audit evidence concerning the quantities and condition of certain stock and work in progress included in the balance sheet at 31 December 20.. at £..... Any adjustment to this figure would have a consequential effect on the profit for the year ended 31 December 20.. and, consequently, our opinion on the financial statements for the year ended 31 December 20.. was qualified because of this limitation in audit scope. Accordingly the amounts shown as cost of sales and profit for the year ended 31 December 20.. may not be comparable with the figures for the current period.

Qualified opinion arising from limitation in audit evidence about comparatives
Except for the financial effects of any such adjustment, if any, as might have been determined to be necessary had we been able to satisfy ourselves as to the quantities and condition of stock and work in progress as at 31 December 20.., in our opinion the financial statements:

- give a true and fair view, in accordance with United Kingdom Generally Accepted Accounting Practice, of the state of the company's affairs as at 31 December 20.. and of its profit for the year then ended and
- have been properly prepared in accordance with the Companies Act 1985.

In our opinion the information given in the Directors' Report is consistent with the financial statements.

In contrast, where auditors issue a qualified report because of disagreement over an accounting policy, but this no longer exists following a change in accounting policy, which has been properly disclosed and adjustments made to the prior year, no qualification is necessary as the matter has been resolved and dealt with correctly.

Where an issue over which there was a disagreement has been resolved but not satisfactorily, for example, where the disagreement over the accounting policy was resolved by adjusting the current year's figures when the auditors considered a prior year adjustment was required, then both current period and comparatives would be qualified on the basis of disagreement.

For audits under the Companies Act 1985 there is no direct requirement to report on comparatives, apart from the fact that they are a 'disclosure requirement' under Sch 4. Any qualification should therefore be in terms of this requirement. If corresponding amounts are presented solely as good practice, the audit report reference should be made as an explanatory paragraph.

The guidance to the ISA (UK and Ireland) considers what auditors should do when they become aware of a material misstatement which affects the previous financial statements, which had an unqualified audit opinion. If the previous financial statements have been revised (see **Chapter 5**) the auditors need to ensure that the comparatives agree with the revised financial statements. Where the previous year's financial statements have not been reissued but the comparatives adjusted, no qualification is necessary as long as the matter is properly disclosed. Where no adjustment or disclosure has been made the auditors need to consider whether the misstatements in the opening balances will give rise to misstatements in this period's financial statements or whether the comparatives are materially misstated. Both of which, in the absence of adjustments, will lead to qualifications as discussed above.

31.5   INCOMING AUDITORS – COMPARATIVES

Where the comparative figures have been audited by other auditors, the new auditors assume responsibility for them as part of the financial statements as a whole. They should assess them in the light of their knowledge of the client and the previous financial statements.

If the comparative figures have not been audited, for example, advantage had been taken of the audit exemption regulations, auditors should ensure that the financial statements clearly disclose the fact that the comparatives are unaudited, but also need to ensure that they are not aware of any possible material misstatement in those figures. For accounts under the Companies Act, where additional procedures are not feasible, inability to do this will inevitably lead to a qualification of the comparatives on the basis of scope limitations as discussed above.

32 RELATED PARTIES

32.1 INTRODUCTION

In October 1995, the Accounting Standards Board issued FRS on related parties. This introduced a substantial increase in the scope and amount of disclosure of transactions with related parties from those already required by the Companies Act 1985. At the time of its exposure commentators noted that an accounting standard of this nature would make the auditors' task more difficult and called for guidance which was then issued in the form of SAS 460 *Related Parties*. In December 2004, the APB issued ISA (UK and Ireland) 550 *Related Parties*, effectively superseding SAS 460 for the audit of accounting periods beginning on or after 15 December 2005, although SAS 460 has not yet been officially withdrawn.

As part of its 'clarity project' (see **1.5.1**), and because of the involvement of related parties in a number of corporate scandals, the IAASB issued an exposure draft of a revision to ISA 550. The APB has now made its comments to the IAASB. Further details of the proposed revision and the APB's comments are given in **32.10** below.

FRS 8 requires certain disclosures of related party transactions, and the auditors' task is to obtain reasonable assurance that the disclosures made are complete and accurate. The nature of related party transactions makes them difficult to identify, and auditors may thus be faced with a high level of risk that they will not detect related party transactions which should be, but are not disclosed in the financial statements.

In addition, the definitions of related parties in the FRS are not easy to apply in practice. In deciding whether parties are related, it is necessary to consider the substance of the relationships either between individuals and the reporting entity or between different individuals. For example, members of a director's immediate family may be related parties if they are influenced or subject to influence by that director. In preparing financial statements directors must address the question of whether related party relationships exist in such circumstances and auditors must judge the reasonableness of this assessment. This may involve auditors in areas that are outside their normal areas of expertise.

For accounting periods beginning on or after 1 January 2005, the consolidated financial statements of listed companies must be prepared under IFRS. Under IFRS, the disclosure of related parties is made in accordance with the requirements of IAS 24. ISA (UK and Ireland) 550 is effectively split into two parts, one dealing with related parties under IAS 24 and one under FRS 8.

In November 2003, and following the very public failures of a number of companies who made use of so called 'business empires' and off-balance sheet arrangements, such as Special Purpose Entities, the APB published a study exploring some of the pitfalls of auditing these arrangements. The issues contained in the study are discussed in **32.11**.

32.2   AUDITING STANDARDS

ISA (UK and Ireland) 550 provides guidance covering:

* the existence and disclosure of related parties;
* evidence relating to transactions with related parties;
* disclosures relating to control of the entity; and
* management representations.

32.3   GENERAL REQUIREMENT

'The auditors should perform the audit designed to obtain sufficient appropriate audit evidence regarding the identification and disclosure ... of related parties and the effect of related party transactions that are material to the financial statements'.

In order to do this auditors need firstly to understand, as part of their knowledge of the business, the relevant disclosure requirements in legislation and accounting standards.

Generally, related party transactions may be difficult to detect. This may be due to:

* reticence on the part of the directors to disclose sensitive transactions;
* accounting systems not being designed to identify these transactions;
* a lack of controls over such transactions; and
* the complexity of the definition of a related party in FRS 8.

In certain instances, related party transactions may be concealed in whole, or in part, from auditors for fraudulent purposes. ISA (UK and Ireland) 240

The Auditor's Responsibility to Consider Fraud in an Audit of Financial Statements (see **Chapter 9**) provides guidance on the auditors' responsibility to consider fraud and error in financial statements and this includes fraudulent related party transactions.

The auditors' risk of not detecting related party transactions is compounded when transactions are:

- without charge;
- not self-evident to the auditors;
- with a party that auditors could not reasonably know was a related party; or
- actively concealed by the directors.

The ISA (UK and Ireland) stresses that directors are responsible for the identification and disclosure of related party transactions. However, in addition to their responsibility to ensure that the disclosures are complete and accurate, auditors should consider the effect they may have on other items within the financial statements, such as the tax liability. They must also be aware that the reliability of evidence may be reduced if it is obtained from related parties and also that transactions with them may be motivated by considerations other than ordinary business, such as window dressing.

32.4 MATERIALITY

FRS 8 requires the materiality of the transaction to the related party, where that party is a director or an entity controlled by an individual, to be considered in addition to that of the reporting entity. This may prove difficult for auditors to assess where they are not in full possession of the facts concerning the director's affairs. This additional assessment is not required by IAS 24.

This difficulty does not arise where companies are complying with the FRSSE (see **3.12.3**) as, when applying this, materiality only needs to be considered from the point of view of the entity itself.

32.5 EXISTENCE AND DISCLOSURE OF RELATED PARTIES

ISA (UK and Ireland) 550 requires auditors to assess the risk of undisclosed material related party transactions when planning their audit.

As transactions between related parties may not be at arm's length, there may be an actual or perceived conflict of interest. For this reason many entities will require that such transactions are authorised by those charged with governance. This means that such transactions are often recorded in the minutes of meetings of for example, meetings of directors. This is less likely for owner-managed entities where procedures are often less formalised.

The ISA (UK and Ireland) sets out a number of procedures that auditors should perform when reviewing information about related parties provided by the entity. These are set out in **Table 1**. Where there is an indication of an increased risk of material misstatement in relation to related parties, the auditors should perform additional tests to those listed as appropriate. Where there is a lower risk, the procedures may also be modified as necessary. Many of these procedures, such as review of prior year working papers, will often need to be carried out in any case as part of the auditors' planning to gain sufficient knowledge of the business.

TABLE 1:   Audit procedures in respect of completeness of related parties

- review prior year working papers for names of known related parties;
- review the entity's procedures for identification of related parties;
- enquire as to the affiliation of those charged with governance and officers with other entities;
- review shareholder records to determine the names of principal share-holders or, if appropriate, obtain a listing of principal shareholders from the share registers;
- review minutes of the meetings of shareholders and those charged with governance and other relevant statutory records such as the register of directors' interests;
- enquire of other auditors currently involved in the audit, or predecessor auditors, as to their knowledge of additional related party transactions;
- review the entity's income tax returns and other information supplied to regulatory agencies;
- review invoices and correspondence from lawyers for indications of the existence of related parties or related party transactions; and
- discover the names of all pension and other trusts established for the benefit of employees and the names of their management.

The extent of substantive testing required to obtain sufficient audit evidence following the procedures in **Table 1** will vary depending on the auditor's assessment of the entity's internal control over related party transactions. When assessing the control activities auditors should concentrate on controls over the authorisation and recording of related party transactions.

Auditors should also be aware of related party transactions which may not be included in the information provided by the entity. **Table 2** sets out a number of circumstances where auditors may wish to investigate further if they become aware of them during other audit testing.

TABLE 2: Examples of unusual circumstances

- transactions which have unusual terms such as very low interest rates;
- transactions which appear to lack a logical business rationale, such as the sale of an asset for what appears to be less than market value;
- transactions in which substance differs from form;
- transactions processed or approved in a non-routine manner or by personnel who do not ordinarily deal with such transactions, for example, a sale authorised by the chief executive rather than the sales manager;
- high volume or significant transactions with certain customers or suppliers compared to others;
- unrecorded transactions such as the receipt or provision of management services at no charge; and
- unusual transactions which are entered into shortly before or after the end of the reporting period, such as a large sale just before the year end which is later cancelled.

Where they discover previously undisclosed transactions auditors need to consider the effect of this on the reliance of other representations made by management.

32.6 EVIDENCE

ISA (UK and Ireland) 550 requires auditors to 'obtain sufficient appropriate audit evidence as to whether these transactions are properly recorded and disclosed.

The reliability of the evidence may be of concern when it is either:

- limited, such as an instruction from one group company to another to pay a management charge; or
- created by the related party, such as the confirmation of a loan.

In order to assess reliability where evidence is limited, the guidance suggests that auditors should consider:

- discussing the matter with management;
- confirming the terms and amount of the transaction with the related party; and
- corroborating the explanation with the related party.

Where the evidence is created by the related party, auditors should consider:

- inspecting any additional evidence held by the related party; or
- confirming explanations with persons associated with the transaction such as lawyers and bankers.

32.7   CONTROL DISCLOSURES

In addition to the disclosure of related party transactions, FRS 8 and IAS 24 require disclosure relating to the control of the entity. ISA (UK and Ireland) 550 expects auditors to obtain appropriate evidence in this respect usually via enquiry of management and it is suggested that this representation may be confirmed with the ultimate controlling party if considered appropriate.

32.8   DIRECTORS' REPRESENTATIONS

ISA (UK and Ireland) 550 requires auditors to obtain written confirmation from directors that information concerning related parties and control provided to them is complete and that the disclosures in the financial statements regarding related party transactions are adequate. A paragraph on directors' interests is already included in the example representation letter shown in **Chapter 30** and this needs to be extended to cover other related parties and control.

Where an entity requires its directors to confirm their interests in writing, the auditors should inspect these documents. In such cases the guidance suggests that the confirmations may be jointly addressed to the company and the auditors.

32.9   REPORTING

If auditors are unable to obtain sufficient appropriate evidence on related party matters or the disclosures are not adequate, ISA (UK and Ireland) 550 says that they should consider the implications for their report.

Where the auditors believe that there is more information which could have been obtained but they have been unable to do so, this is a limitation of scope which could lead to a qualified or disclaimed opinion as set out in **4.2.2**. For example, such a report would be appropriate where they suspect a related party transaction but have not been able to obtain all the evidence to which they are reasonably entitled to determine the matter.

In instances where auditors have sufficient evidence to know that the disclosure is incorrect or they consider the disclosures inadequate because the directors are unwilling to disclose information, they should consider giving a qualified or adverse opinion on the basis of disagreement (see **4.2.4**). Where the disclosures are required by the Companies Act, auditors are obliged to include the missing information in their report. The requirement of ISA (UK and Ireland) 700 to give details of all substantive factors that give rise to the disagreement and their implications for the financial statements imposes a similar requirement in respect of disclosures required by FRS 8 and this is supported by the guidance to the ISA (UK and Ireland) which notes that auditors should include the information that would be required where this is practicable. However, there is no help in interpreting 'practicable'.

32.10   ED ISA 550 REVISED

In January 2006, the IAASB issued an Exposure Draft of a revision to ISA 550. The amendments were thought necessary following the involvement of related parties in a number of corporate scandals, and place a greater emphasis on a risk-based approach to the consideration of related parties. The Exposure Draft requires auditors to obtain an understanding of the nature and business rationale behind relationships with third parties and the transactions entered into. This should provide sufficient information to identify, assess and respond to the risk of material misstatement resulting from these transactions.

The Exposure Draft also introduces requirements aimed at improving auditors' abilities to identify related parties and transactions not disclosed to them by management. These include seeking to identify transactions within the year that are significant and non-routine, and, if they do exist, considering whether they indicate the existence of previously undisclosed related parties.

For known related parties, auditors are required to obtain an understanding of the business rationale of the related party relationships themselves and the transactions entered into.

Further new requirements have been introduced in respect of:

- actions to be taken should auditors discover a related party that had not previously been disclosed to them;
- communication with those charged with governance;
- documentation; and
- assertions that related party transactions have been undertaken at 'arm's length'.

The APB sought comments from UK auditors before making their response on the Exposure Draft to the IAASB. The main comments made were:

- further clarification is required in relation to the need to perform a risk assessment on related party relationships and transactions, under ISA 315. This should include consideration of management's processes, the nature of the business and its ownership and the disclosures given in the financial statements;
- the requirement for auditors to obtain appropriate audit evidence about

disclosure of related party transactions where that disclosure "indicates or implies" that the transaction is at arm's length is likely to be onerous and costly. European Company Law changes will require that only those transactions not undertaken under normal commercial considerations are disclosed, meaning that there will be the implication that all other related party transactions will be at arm's length and therefore fall under the requirement set out in the proposed revision; and

• there is a lack of practical guidance to assist auditors when evaluating whether financial statements are misleading as a result of related party relationships and transactions.

Following receipt of comments from interested parties, the IAASB issued a redrafted version of ISA 550 in March 2007 and asked for further feedback to be submitted by 30 June 2007.

32.11   IMPROVING THE AUDITING OF ENTITIES UNDER COMMON CONTROL

32.11.1   Introduction

This study, published in November 2003, explores some of the pitfalls involved when auditing horizontal groups (or 'business empires') and off-balance sheet arrangements, which have featured prominently in a number of recent business collapses.

While such horizontal groups are legitimate they are not required to present consolidated financial statements. Consequently, financial statements of components of the empire may be misleading if there is inadequate disclosure of the effect of transactions with other parts of the empire.

Under UK Accounting Standards, 'Common control is deemed to exist when both parties are subject to control from boards having a controlling nucleus of directors in common'. Therefore, issues of common control are not limited to large listed companies, and they often feature in smaller family businesses.

Obtaining sufficient audit evidence concerning the proper disclosure of related party transactions can be difficult for auditors, and this is compounded when directors seek to avoid making the disclosures required by Accounting Standards. Indeed company law does not require those who control related entities to provide information to those who audit the companies that they control. Even when one firm is appointed to all the entities subject to common control, their duty of confidentiality may restrict them auditing the entities as if they were a single group.

33 OVERALL REVIEW OF FINANCIAL STATEMENTS

33.1 INTRODUCTION

The overall review is an audit step that has no equivalent under International Standards on Auditing (ISAs). Therefore SAS 470 has not been included in the process to replace the old auditing standards with their ISA (UK and Ireland) equivalents. At the time of writing it is not clear whether SAS 470 will be withdrawn, updated or remain extant in its present form. Historically, this has been seen by the APB as an important stage of the audit giving the auditors the opportunity to step back from the detail and assess the financial statements in the light of all their knowledge of the company gained both from the audit work carried out and from other sources.

33.2 AUDITING STANDARDS

SAS 470 *Overall Review of Financial Statements* contains three standards covering:

- SAS 470.1 – *The Purpose of Overall Review.*
- SAS 470.2 – *Compliance with Accounting Regulations.*
- SAS 470.3 – *Review for Consistency and Reasonableness.*

33.3 THE PURPOSE OF OVERALL REVIEW

SAS 470.1 requires that the auditors should 'carry out such a review of the financial statements as is sufficient, in conjunction with the conclusions drawn from other audit evidence obtained, to give them a reasonable basis for their opinion on the financial statements'.

This overall review is carried out in the final phase of the audit, once other evidence has been obtained. Such a review requires a person with 'appropriate levels of experience and skills'. As with other parts of the audit, auditors consider materiality when performing this review. The review complements their other evidence and is not intended to be the only procedure that the auditors carry out in order to give their opinion.

33.4   COMPLIANCE WITH ACCOUNTING REGULATIONS

SAS 470.2 requires that, as part of the review, 'auditors should consider whether the information in the financial statements is in accordance with statutory requirements and that the accounting policies employed are in accordance with accounting standards, properly disclosed, consistently applied and appropriate to the entity'.

In order to assess whether the accounting policies are appropriate, auditors need to assess them in the light of:

* common accounting policies in the particular industry;
* generally accepted accounting policies;
* whether any departures from applicable accounting standards are necessary for the financial statements to give a true and fair view; and
* whether the financial statements reflect the substance of the transactions, not merely their form.

To assist in ensuring that the financial statements comply with statutory requirements, accounting standards and other regulations, auditors may find that it is helpful to use a checklist. Use of such a checklist also provides evidence of this process being carried out.

33.5   REVIEW FOR CONSISTENCY AND REASONABLENESS

SAS 470.3 requires that 'the auditors should consider whether the financial statements as a whole and the assertions contained therein are consistent with their knowledge of the entity's business and with the results of other audit procedures performed, and the manner of disclosure is fair'.

In performing such a review the auditors may need to consider whether:

* the financial statements reflect the results of the audit;
* the review provides new information which affects the presentation of or disclosures in the financial statements;
* when compared with other available data, the information in the financial statements is as expected;
* the presentation of information in the financial statements is fair; and
* the aggregate of unadjusted misstatements, found during the current and previous years' audits, have any effect on the financial statements.

34 SUBSEQUENT EVENTS

34.1 INTRODUCTION

ISA (UK and Ireland) 560 *Subsequent Events* was issued in December 2004 and provides standards on the audit of post balance sheet events covering:

- events between the period end and the date of the audit report;
- events between the date of the audit report but before the financial statements are issued; and
- events discovered after the financial statements have been issued but before they are laid before members.

As with all ISAs (UK and Ireland), the text of the international ISA has been supplemented with additional guidance from a UK and Ireland perspective. SAS 150 *Subsequent Events* has not yet been officially withdrawn.

ISA (UK and Ireland) 560 is effective for audits of financial statements for periods commencing on or after 15 December 2004.

34.2 AUDITING STANDARDS

ISA (UK and Ireland) 560 states that 'the auditor should consider the effect of subsequent events on the financial statements and on the auditor's report'.

Subsequent events are those events (favourable or unfavourable) which occur between the balance sheet date and the date when the financial statements are authorised for issue.

Relevant events are those which:

- provide additional evidence on conditions existing at the balance sheet date, for which an adjustment should be made to the financial statements; or

- concern conditions which did not exist at the balance sheet date, but require disclosure because of their materiality. However the financial statements would not be adjusted for these events.

The ISA (UK and Ireland) also briefly considers the situation where facts are discovered after financial statements are laid before members, and this is covered in **34.6** below.

In December 2006 the IAASB issued an Exposure Draft of revision to the international version of ISA 560 as part of its clarity project. Details are given in **34.7** below.

34.3   BEFORE THE DATE OF THE AUDIT REPORT

'The auditor should perform audit procedures designed to obtain sufficient appropriate audit evidence that all events up to the date of the auditor's report that may require adjustment of, or disclosure in, the financial statements have been identified'.

It is important that auditors review matters of which they may have become aware during the course of their work and which may be susceptible to change after the period end. This review may be carried out in addition to those specific procedures which are necessary to confirm certain account balances, such as inventory cut-off or payments to creditors, although these procedures may be extended as part of this review.

The guidance provides some examples of procedures that may be performed as near as practicable to the date of the audit report. These are:

- enquiring into procedures that management has established to identify subsequent events;
- reviewing minutes of meetings of members, directors, and audit and executive committees held since the period end and enquiring about any matters discussed at meetings for which minutes are not available;
- reading the latest available information concerning the entity, including the accounting records and any management accounts;
- making enquiries of the entity's legal counsel concerning litigation and claims; and
- making enquiries of management as to whether any subsequent events have occurred which might affect the financial statements.

The extent of these procedures will depend on the length of the period between the balance sheet date and the date of the audit report.

Some examples of specific enquiries that auditors might make of the management are provided and include:

- the current status of items involving subjective judgement or which were accounted for on the basis of preliminary data – for example, litigation in progress;
- whether sales of fixed assets are planned or have occurred;
- whether new commitments, borrowings or guarantees have been entered into;
- whether the issue of new shares or debentures or an agreement to merge or liquidate has been made or is planned;
- whether any assets have been appropriated by government or destroyed, for example, by fire or flood;
- whether there have been developments regarding risk areas and contingencies;
- whether any unusual accounting adjustments have been made or are contemplated; and
- whether any events have occurred or are likely to occur which might bring into question the appropriateness of accounting policies used in the financial statements – for example, any that would bring the validity of the going concern assumption into question.

One area which is the frequent subject of specific enquiries by auditors is the appropriateness of the going concern assumption and this is considered in **Chapter 13**, 'Going concern'.

Where a part of the entity is audited by other auditors, the principal auditors should consider the other auditors' procedures for reviewing subsequent events up to the date planned for the principal auditors' report.

When the auditor becomes aware of an event which materially affects the financial statements, they should consider whether the events are properly accounted for and adequately disclosed in the financial statements.

34.4 BEFORE THE FINANCIAL STATEMENTS ARE ISSUED

There is occasionally a period of some time between the date of signature of the auditors' report and the issue of the financial statements. This will normally be caused by the time taken to print and process the financial statements. More rarely it may be because the statements are held back for issue with another document.

Once their report has been dated the auditors have no responsibility to perform procedures to review subsequent events. However, until the financial statements have been issued they can reasonably expect management to inform them of any events discovered which may affect the financial statements.

If the auditors become aware of subsequent events before the issue of the financial statements, they should establish whether the financial statements need amendment, discuss the matter with the directors and consider the implications for their report.

If the financial statements are amended the auditors should:

- perform additional procedures as appropriate;
- provide management with a new audit report on the amended financial statements, dated no earlier than the date the amended financial statements were approved; and
- extend their specific enquiries to the date of the new audit report.

If the financial statements are not amended, the auditors should consider the implications for their report and issue a qualified report if the original report has not been issued to the entity. When the original report has been issued, the auditors should request management not to issue the financial statements; but if these are issued, the auditors need to take action to prevent reliance on the audit report and may need to take legal advice.

34.5   PRIOR TO LAYING BEFORE THE MEMBERS

Once the financial statements have been issued auditors have no obligation to make any enquiry regarding the financial statements. However, auditors have a statutory right to attend the AGM and be heard on any part of the business of the meeting that concerns them as auditor. This will include making a statement about events after the date of the audit report and so the auditor needs to consider what to do in relation to such events.

34.6   REVISING OR WITHDRAWING FINANCIAL STATEMENTS

In situations where auditors become aware of events after the financial statements have been issued, if the facts would have led them to issue a different report they should consider whether the financial statements need amendment and consider the implications for their report. The guidance distinguishes between:

- events which occurred before the date of the audit report and of which the auditors should have been aware; and
- events which occurred after the date of the audit report.

In the first case, consideration should be given to revising the accounts (see **Chapter 5**). In the latter, there is no statutory procedure, but this normally involves attempting to have management withdraw the statements and, failing this, taking legal advice. This is a difficult area in which to give specific guidance, as much will depend on the circumstances.

When the financial statements need to be revised by management, the auditors should:

- carry out the necessary audit procedures;
- consider whether the Financial Services Authority's Listing Rules or the AIM rules require the information to be publicised, if appropriate;
- consider whether there are any requirements for reports to regulators;
- review management's procedures for informing those persons in receipt of the original financial statements of the situation; and
- issue a new report on the amended financial statements.

In the new audit report, having regard to the provisions for revising accounts, the auditors should:

- refer to the note which explains the subsequent event and the reasons for the amendment, or set out the reason in their report;
- refer to the earlier report issued by them on the financial statements; and
- date their report not earlier than the date of the amended financial statements.

In such circumstances auditors may wish to make use of their power under the Companies Act to address the general meeting at which the members consider the financial statements. The possibility of withdrawing their audit report is also one that is sometimes raised. However, it appears that this may not legally be effective.

34.7 IAASB CLARITY PROJECT REVISION TO ISA 560

As part of their Clarity Project (see **Chapter 1**), the IAASB issued an Exposure Draft of a revision to ISA 560 in December 2006. In addition to the changes required to apply the clarity drafting conventions, the IAASB is also seeking comments on:

- amendments to the application of ISA 560 to Securities Offering Documents;
- clarification of the restriction on subsequent events procedures and dual dating of the auditor's reports for amended financial statements (something which is not a concern for UK auditors); and
- additional guidance for the audit of small and public sector entities.

In the UK, the APB have requested that interested parties submit their comments to them for inclusion in the APB's response to the IAASB.

35 THE AUDIT OF SMALL BUSINESS

35.1 INTRODUCTION

The area of small business audits has been one which has exercised many minds over the last 20 years. The need for audits for small business has been the subject of much of the debate, although this has abated since the introduction of audit exemption regulations (see **Chapter 7**). As a result of these – and following subsequent changes to the exemption limits – small companies with turnover of less than £1 million and meeting the small criteria in ss246 and 247 of the Companies Act 1985 do not require an annual audit. There are, however, many small businesses which still require an audit because they do not qualify for the exemptions and even some which fall within the exemptions but for which its shareholders or some third party, for example a lender, requests an audit. The focus of the issue has changed more recently to how to perform such audits.

35.2 EXISTING GUIDANCE

In June 1997, Practice Note 13 *The Audit of Small Business* was issued by the Auditing Practices Board. This followed recognition in *The Audit Agenda* that although SASs must apply so that every audit 'provides a uniform and reliable quality of assurance', some guidance is necessary on the characteristics of 'owner-managed companies, including small businesses and how the SASs can be applied to them'. The objective of the guidance is to give helpful, realistic and practical advice on the way in which the audit of small businesses can be cost-effectively combined with the accountancy work which is normally also undertaken by the auditors of small businesses. As with other practice notes, the guidance is presented on a standard-by-standard basis. Although the Practice Note was issued prior to the APB adopting the ISAs (UK and Ireland) for the audit of periods beginning on or after 15 December 2004, the guidance it contains remains relevant under the new regime. Where the guidance refers to the old SASs, this commentary also includes references to the relevant ISA (UK and Ireland).

In January 2007, the APB issued two consultation papers entitled:

- *The Need for Guidance to Aid the Implementation of Auditing Standards on Smaller Entity Audits*; and
- *Draft Guidance on Smaller Entity Audit Documentation.*

These represent a significant change in the format of guidance for the audit of smaller entities and are discussed in **35.10** below.

35.3   CHARACTERISTICS OF SMALL BUSINESSES

The definition of a 'small business' cannot be a solely quantitative one, i.e., by reference to some measure of the size such as turnover. It also depends more upon qualitative characteristics.

The Practice Note defines as small any business in which:

(a)   there is a concentration of ownership and management in a small number of individuals (or one individual); and
(b)   one or more of the following are also found:
  - few sources of income and uncomplicated activities;
  - simple record-keeping; or
  - limited internal controls and potential for management override.

A restriction on the number of managers that an entity has may mean that there is only limited management time to devote to such matters as formal internal control procedures. However, this lack of formality may not necessarily mean an increased risk of fraud or error. Indeed, supervisory controls exercised on a day-to-day basis by the owner-manager may also have a significant beneficial effect.

On the other hand, owner-managers may have the ability to override controls, and this may have an adverse effect on the control environment and lead to an increased risk of misstatement. Auditors must assess this based upon their knowledge of the attitude and motives of the owner-manager. The Practice Note states that in auditing small businesses, as with any other audit, auditors should not assume that management is dishonest, but likewise should not assume unquestioned honesty.

Where a business has few sources of income and simple record-keeping procedures this may make it easier to acquire, record and maintain knowledge of the business. Accounting populations may be very easily analysed and many analytical review tests may be simple to perform, with easily corroborated explanations for any variations found. Analytical review procedures may, as a result, significantly reduce the amounts of tests of detail to be performed.

By contrast small businesses may have very informal accounting systems and completeness of records may therefore be a specific audit risk.

35.4 THE RELATIONSHIP BETWEEN SMALL BUSINESSES AND THEIR AUDITORS

Because they do not employ many people, small businesses often engage auditors to provide additional services such as accounting, advising on accounting and computer systems, taxation and other matters such as the preparation of budgets and forecasts and assisting with obtaining finance.

This in-depth involvement with a small business will allow auditors to keep their knowledge of the business up to date and help them to plan and conduct the audit as efficiently as possible.

Where assistance with the keeping of accounting records and the preparation of financial statements is given, auditors are able to use the information gained as audit evidence, which may reduce the need for separate audit procedures.

The Practice Note points out that provision of other services must always be limited by the knowledge that the client value of an audit derives from its objectivity. Auditors must always strive therefore to ensure that their relationship with small business does not prejudice their ability to form an objective opinion. To maintain this independence they must ensure that they do not take over the role of management. This is a particular problem where management are not aware of the nature and extent of their own responsibilities in certain areas (for example, choice of accounting policies and preparation of financial statements), which they may otherwise regard as part of the audit.

35.5 RESPONSIBILITIES

35.5.1 *SAS 110 Fraud and Error/ISA (UK and Ireland) 240 The Auditor's Responsibility to Consider Fraud in an Audit of Financial Statements*

The Practice Note sees the tendency of small businesses to be controlled by a single individual as making them more susceptible to the risk of fraud and error described in SAS 110 and ISA (UK and Ireland) 240. Auditors' knowledge of the owner-manager's general attitude to control issues and the way they exercise supervisory control will have a significant influence on their approach.

Examples of conditions or events typical of, but not exclusive to, small businesses, which may increase the likelihood of fraud or error or be indicative that it is occurring include the following set out in **Table 1** below:

TABLE 1:   Conditions which may indicate fraud or error

- the owner-manager has a specific motive to distort the financial statements, and has the ability to do so;
- there is confusion between personal and business transactions;
- the owner-manager's lifestyle is inconsistent with their remuneration;
- the owner-manager has not taken any holiday for a long period;
- there have been frequent changes in professional advisers;
- the audit start date is repeatedly delayed;
- there are demands to complete the audit in any unreasonably short period of time;
- accounting records are unavailable or have been lost;
- significant level of cash transactions with inadequate documentation;
- numerous unexplained aspects of audit evidence (e.g., differences with third-party confirmations, etc.);
- inappropriate use of accounting estimates;
- unusual transactions around the year end with a material effect on profit;
- unusual related party transactions; and
- excessive fees for agents or consultants.

35.5.2   SAS 120 Consideration of Law and Regulations/ISA (UK and Ireland) 250 Part A Consideration of Laws and Regulations in an Audit of Financial Statements

The laws and regulations governing small companies tend to be largely identical to those of larger entities. The difference anticipated by Practice Note 13 is the fact that small businesses tend to have less complicated activities, and thus are subject to a less complex regulatory environment. However, auditors must assess each situation on its own merits.

35.5.3   SAS 130 The Going Concern Basis in Financial Statements/ISA (UK and Ireland) 570 Going Concern

As discussed in **Chapter 13**, SAS 130 and ISA (UK and Ireland) 570 *Going Concern* contain features which allow them to be applied more easily to smaller businesses (or at least those with uncomplicated circumstances) in that the directors' assessment of going concern:

- does not have a minimum period;
- may be informal in nature; and
- does not have to be in great detail.

The Practice Note points out that where auditors assist an owner-manager with the assessment of going concern and the production of projections and budgets they must ensure that the owner-manager is aware that he remains responsible for this information and the reasonableness of the assumptions on which the information is based.

35.5.4   SAS 140 Engagement Letters/ISA (UK and Ireland) 210 Terms of Audit Engagements

One way of ensuring that owner-managers are aware of their responsibilities in areas such as going concern, as mentioned above, and their responsibilities for financial statements, even when these have been prepared by the auditors, is to ensure that this is stated in the engagement letter.

35.5.5   SAS 150 Subsequent Events/ISA (UK and Ireland) 560 Subsequent Events

Because of the lack of reporting deadlines often associated with small companies the length of time to be considered in a subsequent events review will often be greater.

In addition, accounting records and minutes may not have been written up since the year end and the auditors may need to rely on representations from the owner-managers. Here a representation letter, dated when the financial statements are approved and which ensures that the entire period since the year end has been covered, becomes increasingly important.

When the meeting at which the financial statements are approved is immediately followed by the annual general meeting (as is often the case with small companies) SAS 150 and ISA (UK and Ireland) 560 state that the interval is so short as to not require separate consideration.

35.6   PLANNING, CONTROLLING AND RECORDING

35.6.1   SAS 200 Planning/ISA (UK and Ireland) 300 Planning an Audit of Financial Statements

The basic considerations relating to planning are identical to entities of all sizes; however, planning the audit of a small business need not be a complex or time consuming exercise.

Where accountancy work is being performed the planning process must be properly co-ordinated in order to gain the most benefit from effort and cost. Planning should also be reconsidered as the accountancy work progresses.

Planning the audits of smaller businesses may also be easier in that much of the information may be obtained from:

- discussion with the owner-manager; and
- the knowledge of the audit engagement partner who is often involved in the provision of other services and will have some first-hand knowledge.

35.6.2   *SAS 210 Knowledge of the Business/ISA (UK and Ireland) 315 Understanding the Entity and its Environment and Assessing the Risks of Material Misstatement*

Often the provision of other services to small businesses enables auditors to gain additional information about the client's accounting system, activities, management style, plans for the future, etc. However, this information may be obtained incidentally, and therefore it is important to document such findings so that they can be taken into account when planning and conducting the audit.

The Practice Note states that documentation must be of a level sufficient to:

- facilitate proper planning of the audit; and
- enable any change of responsibility within the audit firm (either partner or staff) to occur smoothly.

35.6.3   *SAS 220 Materiality and the Audit/ISA (UK and Ireland) 320 Audit Materiality*

The levels of materiality used for the preparation of financial statements by auditors and the audit work itself are likely to be different as management will want to ensure that their accounting records are as accurate as possible, which involves a greater degree of accuracy than would be necessary to give an unqualified audit opinion.

In the case of small businesses, draft financial statements may not be available on which to assess planning materiality. Therefore it is important for any initial judgements to be revisited once the final figures are available.

To focus auditors' attention on the more significant financial statement items, while determining the audit strategy, materiality is generally assessed by reference to some measure of the size of the business. One method is to use a percentage of a figure in the financial statements, such as:

- profit or loss before tax (adjusted, if appropriate, for the effect of any abnormal levels of items of expenditure such as directors' remuneration);
- turnover; or
- balance sheet total.

If an entity is at or near 'break-even' point, as may more often be the case with small businesses, assessing materiality as a percentage of pre-tax results alone may be inappropriate and lead to excessive audit work.

35.6.4 *SAS 230 Working Papers/ISA (UK and Ireland) 230 Documentation*

Both the SAS and the ISA (UK and Ireland) state that the form and content of working papers are affected by a number of matters, two of which are of particular importance in the audit of a small business:

- the nature and complexity of the entity's business; and
- the needs in the particular circumstances for direction, supervision and review of the work of members of the audit team.

As a result, extensive documentation is likely to be unnecessary owing to the fact that small businesses often have simple management structures, few employees, informal accounting records, and few, if any, internal controls.

In addition, as audit teams are smaller, the amount of documentation needed to direct and supervise team members is less.

The level of documentation involved in any audit is a matter of professional judgement, and everything on an audit file should add to the clarity of understanding of the issues in question and enhance the quality of conclusions. While the requirements of neither the SAS nor the ISA (UK and Ireland) cover documentation relating to other services such as accountancy work, where this work is being used as a source of audit evidence the working papers should be of the standard expected by the SAS or ISA (UK and Ireland) as relevant.

It follows from this that if schedules drawn up primarily for the purpose of the accountancy work are also prepared with the needs of the audit in mind, the creation of working papers purely for the sake of the audit may be kept to a minimum.

35.6.5 *SAS 240 Quality Control for Audit Work/ISA (UK and Ireland) 220 Quality Control for Audits of Historical Financial Information and ISQC 1 Quality Control for Firms that Perform Audits and Reviews of Historical Financial Information, and Other Assurance and Related Service Engagements*

While the general principles set out in the SAS, ISA (UK and Ireland) and ISQC apply, the Practice Note points out that the requirements relating to quality control on individual audits are mostly only relevant to engagements where some of the work is delegated to one or more assistants. When small business audits are carried out entirely by the audit engagement partner (or a sole practitioner), questions of direction and supervision of assistants and review of their work do not arise.

35.7   ACCOUNTING SYSTEMS AND INTERNAL CONTROL

35.7.1   *SAS 300 Accounting and Internal Control Systems and Audit Risk Assessments/ISA (UK and Ireland) 315 Understanding the Entity and its Environment and Assessing The Risks of Material Misstatement and ISA (UK and Ireland) 330 The Auditor's Procedures in Response to Assessed Risks*

In applying SAS 300 *Accounting and Internal Control Systems and Audit Risk Assessment*, control risk is invariably assessed as high and therefore it is extremely unlikely that the audit of a small business will involve 'tests of controls'. In many small businesses there will be no formal system of internal control. This does not make such businesses 'unauditable' as it only raises the possibility of a risk of error. Such a risk may be offset by a number of factors and the absence of error may be established by reference to evidence obtained externally to the company. In fact, as explained above, a strong control environment will more often than not offset the potential problems that could result from lack of formal internal controls. Even where controls exist, they will not generally be ones that are easy to test. Thus it is rarely cost-effective to plan to rely on them. SAS 300 para 26 acknowledges that in these circumstances audit evidence may have to be obtained entirely through substantive procedures.

As small businesses tend to have few internal controls, the assessment of audit risk will often depend entirely on the assessment of inherent risk, as the risks identified here cannot be mitigated by a strong control environment. Therefore it is important that the assessment of inherent risk is performed carefully and in possession of full knowledge of the client, its business and trading position.

In addition, the risks of small businesses are often mitigated by the auditors' providing of other services, such as accountancy, and this should also be taken into account.

Auditors may also be involved in advising the client about their accounting systems and this may supply them with sufficient knowledge for the planning of the audit. Even if this is not the case the accounting systems of small businesses will usually be simple, informal and easily documented in short narrative notes.

35.8 EVIDENCE

35.8.1 *SAS 400 Audit Evidence/ISA (UK and Ireland) 500 Audit Evidence, 501 Audit Evidence – Additional Considerations for Specific Items and 505 External Confirmations*

Although the SAS and ISAs (UK and Ireland) recognise that audit evidence may be obtained from a number of sources (such as tests of control and substantive procedures), where segregation of duties is limited and evidence of supervisory control is lacking, evidence may be obtained entirely from substantive procedures. This would often be the case for small businesses.

As mentioned above, gaining assurance from accountancy procedures may lead to a reduction in the level of other audit procedures. This assurance may be gained through:

- examining prime documentation which supports a transaction or balance;
- calculating a balance for inclusion in the financial statements; or
- posting entries in the accounting records.

While the work may not be performed by those directly involved with the audit, it is important to ensure that the accountancy work is planned with the needs of the audit in mind.

While accountancy work may provide much of the assurance required, there will always be a need for some additional audit procedures in areas where it is unable to give assurance, for example, on the recovery of debtors, the valuation and ownership of stock, the carrying value of fixed assets and investments and the completeness of creditors. For convenience this work may be carried out at the same time as the accountancy work.

In the case of small businesses the completeness assertion may cause auditors particular problems. The two main reasons for this are:

- the owner-manager occupies a dominant position and may be able to ensure that some transactions are not recorded; and
- the business may not have internal control procedures that provide documentary evidence that all transactions are recorded.

Practice Note 13 states that auditors should plan and conduct the audit with an 'attitude of professional scepticism', and should not accept representations from management as a substitute for other audit evidence that would be expected to be available. However, unless the audit reveals evidence to the contrary, auditors are entitled to accept representations as truthful and records as genuine.

35.8.2   *SAS 410 Analytical Procedures/ISA (UK and Ireland) 520 Analytical Procedures*

The use of analytical review procedures when planning the audit of a small business may be limited due to lack of reliable information such as interim or monthly financial reports. Therefore analytical procedures at the planning stage may be more worthwhile once some of the accountancy work is completed. In some cases, a brief review of the general ledger or discussions with the owner-manager may prove sufficient.

When the activities of a business are uncomplicated and the number of variables to be considered is limited, analytical procedures may often be a very cost-effective way of obtaining audit assurance.

Such analytical review may also provide effective evidence regarding completeness, where expected results can be predicted with a reasonable degree of precision and confidence.

Practice Note 13 states that all auditors are required to perform a final analytical review to assess whether the financial statements are consistent with their knowledge of the business. However, due to the relative simplicity of small businesses many of the procedures performed are very similar to those used as substantive procedures. These may include:

- comparison to prior year;
- comparison to budget or forecast;
- review of trends in ratios;
- consideration of whether any changes in business are adequately reflected; and
- enquiry into unusual and unexplained features of the financial statements.

35.8.3   *SAS 430 Audit Sampling/ISA (UK and Ireland) 530 Audit Sampling and other Means of Testing*

The smaller populations normally encountered in small businesses may occasionally make it feasible to test:

- the whole population; or
- some part of the population – for example, all items above a given amount – applying analytical procedures to the balance of the population, if it is material.

Where auditors decide to sample a population, the same underlying principles apply to a small business as to a larger one.

35.8.4 SAS 440 Management Representations/ISA (UK and Ireland) 580 Management Representations

An important issue in respect of audit evidence in relation to completeness is that of acceptance of management representations. In many smaller businesses, the accounting system is often controlled by one or two individuals and the auditors may have difficulty in obtaining sufficient reliable evidence to assure themselves of the completeness of populations. This is particularly the case with cash businesses but may also apply to service industries or in businesses where stock is not purchased for specific customers. Auditors may also need to rely on representations when establishing that all expenditure is a valid charge on the business, given the confusion between the company and the owner in many small companies.

On their own, representations as to the completeness and accuracy of the accounting records cannot be sufficient. They may only be used if they are supported by or support the results of substantive tests of transactions and analytical review of costs and margins (or possibly one of them).

35.8.5 SAS 450 Opening Balances and Comparatives/ISA (UK and Ireland) 510 Initial Engagements – Opening Balances and Continuing Engagements – Opening Balances and ISA (UK and Ireland) 710 Comparatives

A small business which is a limited company may find itself in the position where its comparatives are taken from preceding period financial statements which were covered by the exemption from audit conferred on small companies.

Auditors will still need to obtain sufficient assurance about the opening balances and comparatives. Some information may be easily available (such as cash and debtors), but where they are unable to obtain the required evidence, they must consider qualifying their audit report. This issue is discussed in more detail above where a suitable report for use for these purposes is set out (see **Chapter 31**).

35.8.6 SAS 460 Related Parties/ISA (UK and Ireland) 550 Related Parties

Small businesses are as likely as larger businesses to enter into related party transactions, and the disclosures are identical. However, auditors of small businesses are more likely to be closely involved in the preparation of the financial statements, and will probably have a relatively detailed knowledge of the businesses' transactions, enabling them to identify those that are disclosable.

Where a small business is preparing accounts under the FRSSE, then the auditors' assessment of whether a related party transaction involving an individual related party is material is from the company's point of view only (see **3.12.3**).

35.9   REPORTING

35.9.1   *SAS 600 Auditors' Reports on Financial Statements/ISA (UK and Ireland) 700 The Auditor's Report on Financial Statements*

The modifications needed for auditors' reports either under the FRSSE or Sch 8 of the Companies Act 1985 are discussed in more detail above (see **3.12.3**).

35.9.2   *SAS 610 Reports to Directors or Management/ISA (UK and Ireland) 260 Communication of Audit Matters with those Charged with Governance*

Small businesses will often have simple, informal accounting systems and the scope for detailed internal control procedures based on segregation of duties will be limited. This is not necessarily a weakness, as the accounting system in place may be suitable for the size and complexity of the business and the degree of owner-manager involvement. Auditors must, therefore, ensure that recommendations to management are relevant and realistic to their business.

In addition, if management has not acted upon points made in previous management letters as the suggestions are not practical or cost-effective, auditors are likely to gain little from repeating the same recommendations again. However, they should continue to check that the recommendations remain valid.

35.10   CONSULTATION PAPERS ON SMALLER ENTITY AUDITS

In January 2007, the APB issued two consultation papers on proposals to revise guidance for the auditors of smaller entities. The two papers:

- *The Need for Guidance to Aid the Implementation of Auditing Standards on Smaller Entity Audits*; and
- *Draft Guidance on Smaller Entity Audit Documentation*

are discussed below. The comment period ended on 30 April 2007.

35.10.1 The Need for Guidance to Aid the Implementation of Auditing Standards on Smaller Entities

Practice Note 13 was issued prior to the development of ISAs (UK and Ireland) and hence requires either updating or withdrawing. It is the APB's view there have been a number of developments affecting the possible update of the Practice Note, namely:

- the proposed EU adoption of the ISAs coming out of the IAASB's Clarity Project (see **Chapter 1**), which include particular guidance on the application of each standard to smaller entities;
- IFAC's intention to develop explanatory guidance on the use of ISAs on SME audits; and
- the Professional Oversight Board's research which shows a drop in the number of small company audits following increases to the audit exemption threshold.

These developments have led the APB to suggest that Practice Note 13 be withdrawn rather than updated.

35.10.2 Draft Guidance on Smaller Entity Audit Documentation

Initial feedback on the implementation of ISAs (UK and Ireland) suggested significant increased costs to the auditors of SMEs in relation to the documentation requirements in ISA (UK and Ireland) 315 *Understanding the Entity and its Environment and Assessing the Risks of Material Misstatement* (see **Chapter 22**). For this reason the APB have decided to consult on example documentation which may be of use to the auditors of SMEs. The APB believes that providing example documentation is the best way to promulgate advice and guidance in this area. It states however, that the specific examples given are not meant to be mandatory.

The consultation paper sets out where the ISAs (UK and Ireland) give requirements for documentation and the key matters to be documented and provides example documentation for smaller entities in the following areas:

- understanding the entity (free form notes and based on a checklist);
- audit team planning meeting (excerpt from a meeting using a pre-set agenda);
- controls documentation (free form notes and based on a checklist and systems diagrams); and
- risk assessment (based on risks and based on assertions).

36   BANK CONFIRMATIONS

36.1   INTRODUCTION

This chapter reviews the confirmations that auditors may obtain from banks. These are generally of two types:

- bank letters for audit purposes, confirming balances, interest and other account information; and
- confirmations of ongoing facilities.

36.2   BANK LETTERS FOR AUDIT PURPOSES

36.2.1   Guidance

Practice Note 16 *Bank Reports for Audit Purposes* contains guidance on the form of the request letters and has been agreed with the British Bankers Association (BBA). In October 2005 a Consultation Draft of a revision to Practice Note 16 was issued by the APB suggesting a number of minor amendments. The comments made on this Consultation Draft called for extensive changes in some areas and the APB and the BBA are in ongoing discussions about how to resolve the issues arising. In October 2006, the APB reissued the Consultation Draft as interim guidance to clarify the status of Practice Note 16 and the changes are now incorporated within the relevant sections of this chapter.

In September 2002, the ICAEW's Audit and Assurance Faculty published Technical Release 3/02, *Bank Reports for Audit Purposes: Explanatory Note*, to assist auditors and banks in the prompt processing of requests for bank reports. The explanatory note was prepared by the British Bankers' Association and the CCAB and does not form an update or amendment to Practice Note 16, *Bank Reports for Audit Purposes*, but rather provides additional, non-mandatory guidance. Further details are given in **36.4** below. However, the proposals in the Consultation Draft of the revision to the Practice Note, and hence the interim guidance issued in October 2006, incorporate the guidance included in the Technical Release.

36.2.2   Authority

Customers have to give explicit authority to their banks before any information can be released to their auditors and the BBA has asked that, where possible, this takes the form of an ongoing standing authority rather than as a separate authority each time information is requested.

A single authority can cover several entities, for example in group situations, provided that each entity is specified, together with the relevant authorised signatures. An example of such a letter is shown in **Table 1** below.

TABLE 1:   Example of authority to disclose letter

XYZ Bank plc

(Parent Company Ltd, Subsidiary 1 Ltd, Subsidiary 2 Ltd)

I/we authorise XYZ Bank plc, including all branches and subsidiaries to provide our auditors ABC & Co any information that they may request from you regarding all and any of our accounts and dealings with you.

Authorised signatory

36.2.3   Authorities

The interim guidance to the Practice Note issued in 2006 clarifies that banks do not need a new authority to disclose information to auditors each time they are asked for confirmation of bank details. However, auditors are responsible for ensuring that standing authorities remain up to date, e.g., they cover all relevant entities or are amended if the auditor changes its name or status.

36.2.4   Disclaimers

The request letter indicates that the process of obtaining a confirmation does not create any contractual or other duty between the bank and the auditors. In addition, the bank may include a disclaimer stating that their response is given solely for the purposes of the audit and creates no responsibility to the auditors.

The APB is of the view that neither the statement in the request letter nor the disclaimer in the bank's reply significantly impairs the value of the confirmation. This is because the information supplied by a bank ought not to be regarded as inaccurate simply because legal action cannot be taken against the bank supplying it. Therefore, auditors can rely on this evidence as long as it is not:

- clearly wrong;
- suspicious; or
- inconsistent in itself or in conflict with other evidence gathered in the course of the audit.

36.2.5 Bank confirmation process

The Practice Note suggests that as part of their planning process, auditors consider the inherent and control risks in relation to relevant financial statement assertions when deciding whether to obtain a bank confirmation.

It notes that ordinarily auditors will wish to obtain confirmation of balances, facilities and security arrangements (referred to as 'standard information'), but recognises that there are clients with more complex relationships with their bankers and that in such cases auditors may require supplementary information. The decision on whether supplementary information is necessary will be based on the auditors' knowledge of the business and discussions with directors and management.

Instead of the request letter detailing all the possible areas in which responses are sought, the BBA has circulated the detailed listing of information which may be required. Where the request letter specifies the type of information, the recipient bank must always disclose the relevant details, in a specified order and where there is no information available this must be stated in the bank's response. **Table 2** and **Table 3** set out the instructions from the BBA in respect of 'standard' and 'supplementary' information.

TABLE 2: 'Standard' information as specified by BBA

1 Account and balance details
Give full titles of all bank accounts including loans (whether in sterling or another currency), together with their account numbers and balances. For accounts closed during the 12 months up to the audit confirmation date give the account details and date of closure.

Note: Also give details where your customer's name is joined with that of other parties and where the account is in a trade name.

State if any account or balances are subject to any restriction(s) whatsoever. Indicate the nature and extent of the restriction, e.g., garnishee order.

2 Facilities
Give the following details of all loans, overdrafts, and associated guarantees and indemnities:

- term;
- repayment frequency and/or review date;

- details of period of availability of agreed finance, i.e., finance remaining undrawn;
- detail the facility limit.

3 Securities

With reference to the facilities detailed in (2) above give the following details:

- any security formally charged (date, ownership and type of charge). State whether the security supports facilities granted by the bank to the customer or to another party.

Note: Give details if a security is limited in amount or to a specific borrowing or if to your knowledge there is a prior, equal or subordinate charge.

- where there are any arrangements for set-off of balances or compensating balances, e.g., back-to-back loans, give particulars (i.e., date, type of document and accounts covered) of any acknowledgement of set-off, whether given by specific letter of set-off or incorporated in some other document.

4 Additional banking relationships

State if you are aware of the customer(s) having any additional relationships with branches or subsidiaries of the bank not covered by the response. Supply a list of branches etc.

TABLE 3: 'Supplementary' information as specified by the BBA

Request for trade finance information

1 Trade finance

Give the currencies and amounts of the following:

(a) letters of credit;
(b) acceptances;
(c) bills discounted with recourse to the customer or any subsidiary or related party of the customer;
(d) bonds, guarantees, indemnities or other undertakings given to the bank by the customer in favour of third parties (including separately any such items in favour of any subsidiary or related party of the customer). Give details of the parties in favour of whom guarantees or undertakings have been given, whether such guarantees or undertakings are written or oral and their nature;
(e) bonds, guarantees, indemnities or other undertakings given by you, on your customer's behalf, stating whether there is recourse to your customer and/or to its parent or any other company within the group;
(f) other contingent liabilities not already detailed.

Note: For each item state the nature and extent of any facility limits and details of period of availability of agreed facility.

2 Securities

With reference to the facilities detailed in the above section give the following:

- details of any security formally charged (date, ownership and type of charge). State whether the security supports facilities granted by the bank to the customer or to another party.

Note: Give details if a security is limited in amount or to a specific borrowing or if to your knowledge there is prior, equal or subordinate charge.

- where there are any arrangements for set-off of balances or compensating balances e.g., back-to-back loans, give particulars (i.e., date, type of document and accounts covered) of any acknowledgement of set-off, whether given by specific letter of set-off or incorporated in some other document.

Request for derivative and commodity trading information

1 Derivatives and commodity trading

Give the currencies, amounts and maturity dates on a contract by contract basis of all outstanding derivative contracts including the following:

(a) foreign exchange contracts;
(b) forward rate agreements;
(c) financial futures;
(d) interest rate swaps;
(e) option contracts;
(f) bullion contracts;
(g) commodity contracts;
(h) swap arrangements (near and far dates);
(i) others (indicate their nature).

Note: Indicate the nature and extent of any facility limits, detail period of availability of agreed facilities.

2 Securities

With reference to facilities detailed in the above section give the following:

- details of any security formally charged (date, ownership and type of charge). State whether the security supports facilities granted by the bank to the customer or to another party.

Note: Give details if a security is limited in amount or to a specific borrowing or if to your knowledge there is prior, equal or subordinate charge.

- where there are any arrangements for set-off balances of compensating balances, e.g., back-to-back loans, give particulars (i.e., date, type of document and accounts covered) of any acknowledgement of set-off, whether given by specific letter of set-off or incorporated in some other document.

Request for custodian arrangements information

1 Custodian arrangements
Give details of the nature and quantity of any assets held but not charged.

The key steps for obtaining bank confirmations as agreed with the BBA are:

- the request is issued to the bank branch with which the client has their main business arrangement. It must be on the auditors' own note paper. The branch will normally respond on behalf of the bank, or if unable to supply a comprehensive response, the branch will advise the auditors of the names of the other branches with which the client is known to deal;
- the bank confirmation request will specify:
  - the names of the entities covered by the request;
  - the main account number and sort code of the principal entity or the holding company (see **36.2.7** below);
  - whether the auditors are requesting 'standard information' and, where appropriate, the nature of the supplementary information required;
  - details of any 'additional information' required;
  - the date for which information is required (the 'audit confirmation date');
  - a statement that the bank's response will not create a contractual relationship between the bank and the auditors;
  - a statement requesting the bank to advise the auditors if the authority is insufficient to allow the bank to provide full disclosure of the information requested; and
  - a contact name and telephone number.

An example request is given in **Table 4**.

TABLE 4:   Example bank confirmation request letter

XYZ Bank plc

Dear Sirs

In accordance with the agreed practice for provision of information to auditors, please forward information on our mutual client(s) as detailed below on behalf of the bank, its branches and subsidiaries. This request and your response will not create any contractual or other duty with us.

COMPANIES OR OTHER BUSINESS ENTITIES
(attach a separate listing if necessary)
(Parent Company Ltd,
Subsidiary 1 Ltd,
Subsidiary 2 Ltd)

Confirmation of ongoing facilities

AUDIT CONFIRMATION DATE (.. December 20..)

Information required	Tick
Standard	
Trade finance	
Derivative and commodity trading	
Custodian arrangements	
Other information (see attached)	

The Authority to Disclose Information signed by your customer is attached/ already held by you [*delete as appropriate*]. Please advise us if this authority is insufficient for you to provide full disclosure of the information requested.

The contact name is .... Telephone ....

Yours faithfully

Registered auditors/accountants

36.2.6   Timing of requests for information

The interim guidance issued in October 2006 recommends that auditors submit their requests for information at least one month before the period end date, an increase from the 14-day timescale set out in the original Practice Note. Where this notice is provided, banks will endeavour to provide the information within one month of the confirmation date. However, where there is a request for non-standard information or information has to be gathered from more than one branch, the bank's response period may increase to two months. The interim guidance also recommends that additional time is allowed at busy times of the year, i.e., for December or March year ends.

Where auditors of listed clients require a faster response than that outlined above, the guidance suggests that they discuss the possibility of accelerating a response with the bank directly.

36.2.7   Provision of account details

The interim guidance asks auditors to provide the names of all the entities covered by the request, together with the main account and sort code of the principal entity or the holding company. The aim of this is to aid the identification of the customer by the bank as entity names are often similar and identification is sometimes problematic. Banks will still be responsible for identifying all other relevant accounts.

This contradicts earlier guidance which warned against providing such information. The APB are of the opinion that where account details are taken from bank statements, this does not diminish the value of the evidence.

36.2.8   Non-BBA Banks

Where banks are not members of the BBA, auditors will need to specify the detailed information, as shown in **Table 2** and **Table 3**, required within the request letter.

36.3   CONFIRMATION OF ONGOING FACILITIES

As part of their consideration of 'going concern' (see **Chapter 13**), auditors will carry out a review of the ability of ongoing bank facilities to meet the entity's future cash needs. Where they consider existing banking facilities to be critical to the continuing operation of the entity, they may need to obtain a letter from the bank as to their intentions.

36.3.1   Procedures

As part of the reply to the standard request for a bank report for audit purposes, the auditors will have received details of any overdrafts and loans repayable on demand, specifying agreed facilities and dates of review. Where such facilities are in the process of being reviewed or they are to be reviewed within the time frame of the 'foreseeable future', and where the auditors consider their renewal as critical to their opinion, they may have to enter into correspondence with bankers to obtain confirmation.

Such correspondence should always be within the framework set out above for supplementary requests. This should encourage the banks to use standard disclaimers, which do not significantly impair the value of a response as audit evidence.

Table 5 contains suggested wording for a letter from the auditors to the bank requesting comfort as to the continuation of facilities, while **Table 6** provides an example of a letter from the bank to the auditors indicating their intentions concerning the facilities. It is suggested that this wording constitutes the minimum level of comfort acceptable from the bank, and is based on the guidance in SAS 130 *The Going Concern Basis in Financial Statements*. It is equally relevant following the publication of ISA (UK and Ireland) 570 *Going Concern*.

In both cases, it is important to ensure that the client is made aware that such confirmation is being sought.

TABLE 5: Comfort letter request

The Manager XYZ Bank Plc

Dear Sir

X Limited

We refer to your above named customer's instructions given in the authority .... already held by you and to your reply to our Standard Request for Bank Report for Audit Purposes dated ....

For the purpose of our audit, as part of a request for supplementary information, we would ask you to confirm that, based on the information provided to you by the company (specific documents should be listed) and subject to unforeseen circumstances, you see no reason why the company's facilities will not be renewed on existing terms when they fall due nor are you aware of any reason why such facilities will not continue to be made available (specify timing, e.g., six months after that date).

Yours faithfully

TABLE 6: Bank's response to comfort letter request

ABC & Co

Dear Sirs

X Limited

We refer to your letter of .... requesting confirmation as to continuing facilities.

The company's facilities are due for renewal on ..... No decision has been reached as to whether the facilities will be renewed and we will continue to monitor the situation in the light of information which is supplied to us. Renewal of the facility will be considered on the agreed renewal date.

Yours faithfully

36.3.2   Level of reliance to be placed on reply

A satisfactory reply from the bank does not absolve the auditors from properly considering the going concern position of a client company by reference to primary audit evidence. Further reference should be made to the matters discussed in **Chapter 13**.

36.4   AUDIT 3/02: BANK REPORTS FOR AUDIT PURPOSES, EXPLANATORY NOTE

In September 2002, the ICAEW's Audit and Assurance Faculty published Technical Release 3/02, Bank Reports for Audit Purposes: Explanatory Note, to assist auditors and banks in the prompt processing of requests for bank reports. The note provides additional, non-mandatory guidance to that included in Practice Note 16.

The Explanatory Note provides the following guidance:

- Auditors and banks should make use of the 'Bank Acknowledgement of Auditor Request' form (the 'acknowledgement') for all bank letters. An example is shown in **Table 6**. This aims to provide both banks and auditors with a point of contact to whom queries can be addressed. It should be attached to the back of the bank letter sent by auditors and returned to the auditor by the bank as soon as possible.
- All bank letters should be sent in envelopes headed 'Bank report for audit purposes'. A rubber stamp would be a suitable means.
- Banks should consult all relevant departments in compiling their report, and should not request account numbers from the auditors.
- Minor omissions or amendments to a bank report may be communicated by telephone or e-mail, although auditors may request written confirmation of these changes.
- Banks should not net off debit and credit balances.
- The fact that a bank does not have authority to disclose details of guarantees or other third party securities is not a reasonable excuse to delay their reply. Instead they should state that such guarantees or securities exist and the auditor can then gain information about these directly from the client by reviewing the relevant facility letter or bank agreement.
- A bank has the right to decline to give information about accrued interest or charges as this is not within the scope of the guidance agreed between the British Bankers' Authority and the Auditing Practices Board.

TABLE 6:   Bank Acknowledgement of Auditor Request

Part A - This part to be completed by the Auditor
This acknowledgement should be returned to:

Name _____

Position _____

Firm _____

Address _____

_____

_____

Tel No _____

E-mail * _____ * If available

Part B - This part to be completed by the Bank

Thank you for your request for a bank report for audit purposes in respect of
_____ (customer's name)

The request was received on:
_____ (day/month/year)

Your request is being processed and the letter will be completed once we have
gathered the information sought. In the event of your needing to contact us,
please address enquiries to:

Name _____

Position _____

Bank _____

Address _____

_____

_____

Tel No _____

E-mail * _____ * If available

37 OTHER OPERATIONAL ISSUES

37.1 INTRODUCTION

This chapter covers various guidance issued by the ICAEW and APB covering:

- debtors' confirmations;
- pending legal matters;
- paid cheques;
- stocktaking;
- service organisations; and
- auditing derivative financial instruments.

37.2 DEBTORS' CONFIRMATIONS

Guidance in this area comes from ICAEW Statement 901 – *Verification of Debtor Balances: Confirmation by Direct Communication* and the statement is directed towards the verification of trade debtors and is not intended to relate to debts from group companies or other special debts.

Further guidance is given in ISA (UK and Ireland) 505, External Confirmations (see **Chapter 24**).

As part of their procedures the auditors may decide to carry out a circularisation of the company's trade debtors to enable them to form an opinion as to the adequacy of the system of internal control over sales and its operation in practice. It will be a confirmation that the cut-off procedures are operating and should provide evidence as to whether the balances are genuine, accurately stated and not in dispute.

The auditors cannot approach the debtors directly as only the client can authorise third parties to divulge information to the auditors but generally, if asked, the management will authorise the circularisation. Where the client refuses, the auditors need to consider whether they are able to obtain sufficient alternative evidence and the implications for their report.

Where a circularisation is performed on a sample basis it may not provide sufficient evidence on its own, but may influence the extent of any other tests carried out.

There are two methods that can be used when requesting information from the debtor. These are:

- *positive*: where the debtor is requested to confirm the accuracy of the balance shown or state in what respect he disagrees; or
- *negative*: where the debtor only replies if the amount stated is disputed.

In either case the reply should be sent directly to the auditors. The choice of method will be a matter for the auditors' judgement, but there are certain factors which may influence this decision, including:

- the strength of the system of internal controls;
- whether there are any suspicions of irregularities;
- the number and size of accounts;
- whether there are amounts which are likely to be in dispute; and
- the number of bookkeeping errors.

Where there are doubts about the accuracy of the sales ledger or where there is a small number of large balances, more confidence will be gained from a positive circularisation. However, if errors are not expected or there is a large number of small balances then a negative one may be more appropriate.

In most cases, a sample of debtors' balances based on the complete population will be tested. However, the following should be considered when selecting the sample:

- old, unpaid accounts;
- accounts written off during the period;
- accounts with credit balances;
- accounts with nil balances; and
- accounts which have been paid by the date of the examination.

The request is usually accompanied by a statement of the account, either the normal monthly statement if the circularisation is carried out at the same time as these are sent out, or a specially printed one if the circularisation is at any other time. Where a positive response is required a pre-paid reply envelope is normally included.

The request may be as a specially prepared letter or as an attachment to the statement. The ICAEW Statement does not provide an example of such a letter, but one for a positive circularisation is shown in **Table 1.**

Where requests are returned as undelivered they should be sent to the auditors, who will need to consider what action to take.

When the positive method is used and replies are not received auditors should make every effort to ensure that some response is obtained. It may be that a member of the client's staff can be used to do this, but auditors will need to ensure that the clearance procedure is properly performed. It may be necessary to use other audit tests to provide evidence of the validity of the debtor where no reply is received in a positive circularisation, as every item selected must be concluded upon.

The responses may indicate inaccuracies in the part of the population that is not tested and further work may be necessary.

37.3 PENDING LEGAL MATTERS

ICAEW Statement 903 – *The Ascertainment and Confirmation of Contingent Liabilities Arising from Pending Legal Matters* covers the auditors' problems concerning contingencies arising from pending litigation against the company upon which they are reporting.

Further guidance is also given in ISA (UK and Ireland) 501 Audit Evidence – Additional Consideration for Specific Items (see **Chapter 24**).

TABLE 1: Example of positive debtors' circularisation letter

XYZ Plc Industrial House
Anytown
Name & Address

Dear Sir

As part of their normal audit procedures, we have been requested by our auditors, ABC & Co, to ask you to confirm direct to them the balance on your account at 31 December 20.. . This request is made for audit purposes only and remittances should be sent to us in the normal way.

According to our records the balance at that date in our favour was as shown by the enclosed statement of your account. If the balance is in agreement with that shown by your records, please sign the confirmation below and return it in the enclosed reply-paid envelope to ABC & Co. Please do this even if the account has been settled.

If the balance is not in agreement with that shown by your records will you please send the confirmation to our auditors showing, if possible, details of the items making up the difference.

Your co-operation in this matter is greatly appreciated.

Yours faithfully

XYZ Plc
ABC & Co
1 High Street
London
....

Dear Sirs

We confirm that according to our records a balance of £ .... was owing by us
to XYZ Plc at 31 December 20.. .

Name of company or _____ individual:

_____
Signed: _____
Position held: _____
Items making up difference if any: _____

It suggests procedures the auditors may use to verify the existence of claims, although they will not necessarily provide sufficient evidence of the likely amount that the company may be responsible for. These include:

- reviewing the system of recording claims and the procedure for bringing these to the attention of management;
- discussing with management arrangements for instructing solicitors;
- examining Board minutes and correspondence for potential claims;
- examining bills from solicitors or estimates of unbilled charges;
- obtaining a list of matters referred to solicitors with estimates of the possible ultimate liabilities; and
- obtaining written representations that there are no further matters of which the directors are aware.

Auditors may decide that they wish to obtain confirmation of these matters directly from the solicitors involved. This should be done with the client's authority and the Statement recommends that the letter should come from the client with a request that a copy of the reply be sent directly to the auditors.

The auditors may choose to make a non-specific enquiry, i.e., to enquire if there are any matters which are not listed of which the directors are aware, as this serves as a confirmation that the information received from the directors is complete. However, the Law Society has advised solicitors that it is unable to recommend them to comply with requests for information that are more widely drawn than the specific enquiry shown in **Table 2**.

The ICAEW considers that there may be circumstances in which non-specific enquiries are appropriate; however, it does not discuss how the opposing stands may be reconciled.

The correspondence and the other procedures adopted by the auditors may mean that undisclosed liabilities become apparent and it may be necessary to discuss these with management and their solicitors before considering the effect on their audit report.

TABLE 2: Extract from a letter to company solicitors requesting information on pending litigation

'In connection with the preparation and audit of our accounts for the year ended ... the directors have made estimates of the amounts of the ultimate liabilities (including costs) which might be incurred, and are regarded as material, in relation to the following matters on which you have been consulted. We should be obliged if you would confirm that in your opinion these estimates are reasonable.

Matter

Estimated liability including costs'

Where there are matters which are being dealt with by solicitors but the auditors are unable to take photocopies of documents because of legal privilege, they should prepare file notes of the evidence they have reviewed.

There are occasions when solicitors do not reply directly to requests on the grounds that letters written concerning the merits of litigation involving a client would be discoverable by the other party to the litigation.

The Audit Faculty of the ICAEW has issued Audit 2/95 an addendum to 3.903 dealing with this. They identify and make the following recommendations in two cases:

- *When solicitors refuse to write to auditors or clients* where it is advised that auditors should meet with the solicitors to discuss the matter and agree a file note that the auditor considers adequate to support the treatment of the matter in the financial statements.
- *When solicitors are prepared to write only to the clients* where the auditors should read and make notes of the relevant contents but will generally not photocopy the letter.

The file notes concerned in either of these cases must be non-specific and may only indicate that evidence has been obtained and the matter considered. Any fuller note may itself be discoverable.

37.4 PAID CHEQUES

Changes in legislation and audit practices have made it less important for auditors to review paid cheques returned to entities by their clearing bank.

37.4.1 Existing guidance

ICAEW Statement 3.909 (FRAG 27/93) *Paid cheques* aims to encourage auditors to:

- consider using alternative procedures;
- advise their clients to adopt more rigorous controls over cheque payments; and
- use cost-effective methods of examining paid cheques where they consider it to be necessary.

The statement does not provide detailed procedural guidance.

37.4.2 Audit evidence

Where adequate controls exist over purchasing and cheque payments it may not be necessary to examine returned cheques. In cases where controls are weak auditors may want evidence that:

- there has been no fraudulent endorsement of cheques;
- cheques are properly recorded and controlled; and
- the cash book accurately reflects details of them.

With regard to purchase ledger items, other forms of evidence may be sufficient such as the reconciliation of supplier statements. Evidence on other items may be obtained from analytical review or examination of supporting evidence.

Additionally the entity may use other forms of payment, such as electronic funds transfers, standing orders or direct debits.

37.4.3 Cheques Act 1992

Further controls against fraudulent endorsement comes from the Cheques Act 1992, which means that cheques crossed 'account payee' cannot be transferred by way of endorsement. Many banks now pre-print their cheques with this, which greatly reduces the risk and, in turn, the auditors' need to examine paid cheques.

37.4.4 Obtaining paid cheques

Where auditors decide that they need to review paid cheques they should aim to choose the most cost-effective method of obtaining this evidence. Discussions with the client and their bank will normally be necessary as to the most appropriate method. Options include:

- returning all paid cheques to the client;
- providing the auditors with an agreed number of paid cheques directly, the selection being left to the bank;
- providing photocopies of paid cheques;
- extracting cheques before they are stored and forwarding them to the auditors directly; and
- providing specific paid cheques at the auditors' request.

Where paid cheques are to be sent to the auditors directly by the bank, authority will have to be provided by the client.

37.5 STOCK

37.5.1 Introduction

The APB published Practice Note 25, *Attendance at Stocktaking* in January 2004 to supersede Auditing Guideline 405 which was some 20 years old. The Practice Note sought to give guidance on the application of SAS 300 *Accounting and Internal Control Systems and Audit Risk Assessment* and SAS 400 *Audit Evidence*, when determining the existence of stock but is equally as relevant to the ISA (UK and Ireland) equivalents.

The Practice Note covers:

- assessment of risks and internal controls;
- audit evidence;
- audit procedures before, during and after the stocktake;
- work in progress;
- the use of experts; and
- stock held by third parties.

Further guidance on the audit of stock is given in ISA (UK and Ireland) 501 Audit Evidence, Additional Considerations for Specific Items (see **Chapter 24**).

37.5.2 Assessment of risks and internal controls

ISA (UK and Ireland) 315 states that auditors should use professional judgement to ascertain levels of audit risk. Example factors to consider when assessing risks relating to existence of stock are set out in **Table 3**.

TABLE 3:   Example risk factors relating to existence of stock

- Reliability of accounting and stock recording systems including, in relation to work in progress, the systems that track location, quantities and stages of completion.
- Timing of stocktakes relative to the year end date, and the reliability of records used in any roll forward of balances.
- Location of stock, including stock on consignment and items held at third-party locations.
- Physical controls over stock, and its susceptibility to theft or deterioration.
- Objectivity, experience and reliability of the stock counters and of those monitoring their work.
- Degree of fluctuation in stock levels.
- Nature of stock, for example, whether specialist knowledge is needed to identify the quantity, quality and/or identity of stock items.
- Difficulty in carrying out the assessment of quantity, for example, whether a significant degree of estimation is involved.

The assessment of risk should also include consideration of frauds that influence stock levels. These may include the risk of false sales involving the movement of stock to another location, movement of stock to sites with different stocktaking dates, using inappropriate estimation techniques, or amendment or falsification of stock count sheets.

37.5.3   Audit evidence

Where stock is material or there is a risk of material misstatement, auditors will normally attend a stocktake. As well as giving evidence about the existence assertion, attending a stocktake may also provide evidence in respect of completeness and valuation of stock.

The main sources of evidence for the existence of stock are:

- evidence from audit procedures which confirm the reliability of the accounting records upon which the amount in the financial statements is based;
- evidence from tests of control over stock, including the reliability of stock counting procedures; and
- substantive evidence from the physical inspection tests undertaken by the auditors.

The amount and type of evidence required depends on the auditors' risk assessment.

Entities may or may not maintain detailed stock records. Where these are kept auditors should check that these records are up to date, that adequate stocktaking procedures are used, and that all material differences between physical and book stock are investigated and corrected.

Where no continuous stock records are maintained, the year-end stock figure will be derived from a full year-end stock count. In this situation it would be preferable for stocktaking to be completed at the year-end date but, where necessary, the count may be on a different date and updated for stock movements between that date and year-end.

In both situations attendance at the stocktake would be beneficial, either to confirm that accurate stock records are maintained or, where no stock records exist, to ensure that the count to determine year-end stock is accurate.

37.5.4 Audit procedures before, during and after the stocktake

Table 4 outlines example procedures that may be used before, during and after the stocktake. It does not provide an exhaustive list.

TABLE 4: Example audit procedures

Before the stocktake:

- performing analytical procedures and discussing findings with management;
- discussing client stocktaking arrangements and instructions with management;
- familiarisation with the nature and volume of the stock, the identification of high value items, the method of accounting for stock and the conditions giving rise to obsolescence;
- considering the location of the stock and assessing the implications of this for stock control and recording;
- considering the quantity and nature of work in progress, the quantity of stock held by third parties and whether expert valuers or stocktakers will be required;
- reviewing the system of internal control and accounting relating to stock;
- considering any involvement of internal audit; and
- considering the results of previous stocktakes and reviewing prior year work papers.

During the stocktake:

- ascertain whether client staff are following instructions;
- perform test counts to ensure that procedures and internal controls relating to the stocktake are operating effectively. Counting should be checked in both directions, i.e., from physical stock to stock sheet and vice versa;
- request recounts where results are not satisfactory;
- copy extracts of stocktaking records for subsequent testing;
- check the sequence of stock count records;

- consider whether the procedures for identifying damaged, obsolete and slow moving stock operate properly;
- ensure that stock held for third parties is separately identified and accounted for;
- consider the adequacy of cut-off procedures to ensure stock movements are included or excluded from the year end stock figure as necessary.

After the stocktake:

- follow up details of last serial numbers of goods inwards and outwards records to check cut-off;
- check copies of stock sheets are correctly reflected in final stock figures;
- review whether continuous stock records have been adjusted to the amounts physically counted and that differences have been investigated;
- follow up queries and notify senior management of serious problems encountered during the stocktake.

Some entities used computer-assisted techniques to perform stocktakes, for example, using hand held scanners. This may lead to there being no stock sheets, no physical count records and no paper records available at the time of the count. In such circumstances the auditors should consider the IT environment surrounding the stocktake and consider the need for specialist assistance to evaluate the techniques used and the controls in place.

37.5.5 Work in progress

Management may use accounting systems and internal controls to determine the completeness and accuracy of records of work in progress, and there may not be a stocktake. However, auditors may still find it beneficial to observe the work in progress as it may help with understanding the entity's control systems and processes and with determining the stage of completion of construction or engineering work in progress.

37.5.6 The use of experts

Auditors should determine whether expert help is required prior to attending the stocktake. Assistance may be required to substantiate quantities (e.g., a quantity surveyor) or to determine the nature and condition of specialist stock.

Where management involve a specialist third party stocktaker, common practice for farms, petrol stations and public houses, this does not eliminate the need for auditors to obtain audit evidence as to the existence of stock.

37.5.7 Stock held by third parties

If stock is located in public warehouses or with other third parties, the auditors normally obtain direct confirmation relating to quantities and ownership in writing from the custodian. If such stock is material auditors should consult ISA (UK and Ireland) 402 *Audit Considerations Relating to Entities Using Service Organisations* to ascertain how to obtain sufficient audit evidence (see **37.6**).

37.6 SERVICE ORGANISATIONS

ISA (UK and Ireland) 402 *Audit Considerations Relating to Entities Using Service Organisations* was issued in December 2004 and provides guidance on the procedures necessary to assess the impact of a reporting entity's use of a service organisation. As with all ISAs (UK and Ireland), the text of the ISA has been supplemented with additional guidance from a UK and Ireland perspective. SAS 480, *Service Organisations* is yet to be officially withdrawn. ISA (UK and Ireland) 402 is effective for audits of financial statements for periods commencing on or after 15 December 2004.

ISA (UK and Ireland) 402 *Audit considerations relating to entities using service organisations*, contains guidance covering:

- identification and assessment of service organisations;
- planning and risk assessment;
- accounting records;
- designing procedures and audit evidence; and
- reporting.

37.6.1 *Identification and assessment*

ISA (UK and Ireland) 402 requires auditors to identify whether the reporting entity uses service organisations and then to consider the impact of this on the client's internal control, their assessment of the risk of material misstatement and their procedures. The guidance notes that the outsourcing of an activity by an entity does not relieve its directors of their responsibilities nor does it alter those of the auditors. As not all outsourced activities have a significant effect on the reporting entity's financial statements auditors need to assess initially whether those activities are relevant to the audit and if so their effect on audit risk.

37.6.2 *Planning*

Identifying whether the use of service organisations is relevant to their audit should be part of the auditors' planning under ISA (UK) 402. Service organisations undertake a wide variety of activities including:

- information processing;
- maintenance of accounting records;
- facilities management;

- maintenance of safe custody of assets, such as investments; and
- initiation or execution of transactions on behalf of the entity.

Activities relevant to the audit are those that relate directly to:

- the preparation of the entity's financial statements, including the maintenance of material elements of its accounting records which form the basis for those financial statements; and
- the reporting of material assets, liabilities and transactions which are required to be included or disclosed in the financial statements (excluding the charge for provision of the service concerned); or
- are subject to law and regulations that are central to the entity's ability to conduct its business.

Auditors should obtain and document an understanding of the contract terms, whether agreed orally or in writing, and the way in which the reporting entity monitors the service organisation's activities so that it can meet its fiduciary and other legal responsibilities. This will assist the auditors in their consideration of the impact of the arrangement on the assessment of inherent risk (see **37.6.3**).

37.6.3   Assessing risk

Inherent risk will be affected by:

- the nature of the services provided;
- the degree to which authority is delegated to the service organisation;
- the arrangements for ensuring quality of the service provided;
- whether the activities involve assets which are susceptible to loss or misappropriation; and
- the reputation for integrity of those responsible for direction and management of the service organisation.

Auditors will consider these factors and assess inherent risk by financial statement assertion.

If, as a result of their assessment of inherent risk, the auditors decide that they expect to be able to rely on the operation of controls to reduce the extent of substantive procedures, they should then make an assessment of the control risk for material financial statement assertions.

The ISA (UK and Ireland) notes a number of factors relevant to the auditors' assessment of control risk, including:

- the extent and nature of controls operated by the user entity's personnel;
- undertakings by the service organisation for the operation of internal controls, and whether such controls are adequately specified, having

regard to the size and complexity of the activities undertaken by the service organisation;

- actual experience of adjustments to, or errors and omissions in, reports received from the service organisation;
- the way in which the user entity determines whether the service organisation complies with its contractual undertakings; and
- whether the service organisation provides information on the design and operation of systems of controls, possibly accompanied by reports from its external auditors.

Where the maintenance of accounting records has been outsourced, the ISA (UK and Ireland) notes that the following particular risk factors require consideration by the reporting entity's auditors:

- the knowledge and expertise of the service organisation's staff in matters relevant to the client's business;
- the practicality of control by the entity's management and the nature of controls actually implemented; and
- the use of quality assurance processes by the service organisation.

Examples of ways in which different activities undertaken by service organisations can affect the risk of misstatement are given in **Table 5**.

TABLE 5: Characteristics of service organisation activities which may increase risk		
Outsourced Accounting Functions		
Degree of risk	**Characteristics**	**Examples**
High	<ul><li>Complex transactions</li><li>Those undertaking accounting work need extensive business or specialist knowledge</li><li>Delegated authority to initiate and execute transactions</li><li>Effective controls only possible on 'real time' basis</li><li>Reversal of outsourcing costly/difficult</li><li>High cost of performance failure (eg misleading management reports leading to poor decision making</li><li>High proportion of finance functions outsourced</li></ul>	<ul><li>Maintenance of both accounting records and preparation of budgets and control reports</li><li>Accounting records of retail business</li></ul>

Medium	• Some business knowledge needed but parameters for necessary judgements can be identified and agreed in advance • Transactions can be initiated but execution requires approval from entity • Execution of transactions on instruction from entity • Analytical techniques insufficient for adequate degree of control • Discrete functions outsourced	• Outsourcing of accounting records by a supplier of raw materials • Credit control • Leasing arrangements
Low	• Little requirement for judgement in processing transactions • Non-complex transactions • Little business knowledge required • Analytical control techniques effective • Effects of failure can be contained • Easy to rearrange/find alternate service organisations • Low proportion of discrete functions outsourced	• Processing salary payments • Preparation of invoices • Data entry
Outsourced Investment Custody and Management		
High	• Transactions can be initiated on a discretionary basis • Entity does not maintain and cannot generate independent records of assets and interests, dividends or other income • Complex financial instruments • Custody and investment management undertaken by two separate entities but records are not independently generated, or one combined report is provided to the entity	• Discretionary trading, same custodian

Medium	• Combination of custody and execution of transactions/ collection of income but entity maintains or can generate (for example by reference to Extel) independent records of income • Custody and investment management undertaken by two unrelated entities which maintain independently generated records (ie derived from different source data) and report separately direct to the entity	• Custodian responsible for collection of dividends and reporting of income: entity reviews information • Independent custodian and investment manager
Low	• Entity initiates and maintains records of transactions • Separation of execution and custody functions • Low frequency of transactions and/or counterparties • Non-complex financial instruments • Analytical control techniques effective	• Custody of assets only • Execution of investment transactions pursuant to entity's instructions

37.6.4 Accounting records

The guidance states that auditors should assess whether the arrangements for maintaining all or part of the entity's accounting records by a service organisation has any effect on their reporting responsibilities in relation to accounting records.

The guidance notes that the wording of UK company law is such that it requires companies to keep records rather than cause them to be kept, and thus the wording of the contract with the service organisation will need to be reviewed to determine whether the entity retains ownership of those records. It is suggested that the auditors may wish to seek legal advice where there is any doubt on this matter.

37.6.5 Designing procedures and audit evidence

The ISA (UK) requires auditors to use their understanding of the arrangement to:

- assess whether they can obtain sufficient appropriate audit evidence on the relevant financial statement assertions from the records held at the reporting entity; and if not
- determine effective procedures to obtain audit evidence either by direct access to the records kept by the service organisation or through information obtained from the service organisation or its auditors.

Where auditors require evidence concerning balances representing assets held by or transactions undertaken by the service organisation, they may consider the efficiency and effectiveness of the following procedures:

- inspecting records and documents held by the reporting entity;
- establishing the effectiveness of controls;
- obtaining representations to confirm balances and transactions from the service organisation;
- performing analytical review procedures on the records maintained by the reporting entity or the returns from the service organisation;
- inspecting records and documents held by the service organisation;
- requesting the service organisation auditor or the reporting entity's internal audit function to perform specified procedures; and
- reviewing information from the service organisation and its auditors concerning the design and operation of its controls systems.

Where a report from the service organisation's auditors or from the reporting entity's internal auditors is being used by the auditors, they should consider the scope of the work performed and assess whether the report is sufficient and appropriate for its intended use.

The guidance considers whether the use of evidence from service organisations can be regarded as coming from an independent source. It notes that the nature of the activities undertaken by the service organisation may mean that the evidence may not be regarded as independent for audit purposes. It comments that, in such circumstances, auditors 'need to assess carefully the nature and source of information available to them in order to establish the most effective way to obtain evidence competent to support an independent opinion on its financial statements'. This may involve the auditors requesting access to the staff and records of the service organisation in order to do their own testing.

Auditors may wish to obtain a copy of the service organisation's statement on internal controls (see **42.8**) or the US's SAS 70 equivalent.

37.6.6 Reporting

If the auditors of the reporting entity decide that they need access to the service organisation's records in order to form an opinion on the financial statements and they are unable to obtain this evidence, the ISA (UK and Ireland) requires them to:

- include a description of the factors leading to the lack of evidence in the basis of opinion section of their report; and
- qualify their opinion or issue a disclaimer of opinion on the financial statements.

The guidance notes that auditors are unlikely to be able to obtain sufficient evidence if the following conditions exist:

- the reporting entity does not maintain adequate records of, or controls over, the activities undertaken by the service organisation; and
- no report from the service organisation's auditors concerning the operation of the system of controls has been made available; and
- the auditors are unable to carry out tests that they consider appropriate at the service organisation or it has not been possible for these tests to be carried out by the service organisation's auditors.

Examples of qualifications arising from limitations in scope are shown in **Table 4** and **Table 6** in **Chapter 4**.

37.7 AUDITING DERIVATIVE FINANCIAL INSTRUMENTS

37.7.1 *Introduction*

In April 2002 the APB issued Practice Note 23, based on the International Auditing Practice Statement (IAPS) on planning and performing the audit of derivative financial instruments, with amendments as necessary to reflect the Financial Reporting framework in the United Kingdom and the Republic of Ireland.

The Practice Note focuses on auditing derivatives held by end users. This may include banks and other financial sector entities where they are the end users. An end user is one that enters into a financial transaction for the purpose of hedging, asset/liability management or speculating.

FRS 13, *Derivatives and Other Financial Instruments*, defines a derivative financial instrument as a financial instrument that derives its value from the price or rate of some underlying item. Underlying items may be equities, bonds, commodities, interest rates, exchange rates or stock market and other indices. Derivative financial instruments include:

- futures;
- options;

- forward contracts;
- interest rate and currency swaps;
- interest rate caps, collars and floors;
- forward interest rate agreements;
- commitments to purchase shares or bonds;
- note issuance facilities; and
- letters of credit.

For many, the use of derivatives reduces exposure to change in exchange rates, interest rates and commodity prices. However, the characteristics of the derivatives may also result in increased business risk in some entities, which will, in turn, increase audit risk. These features include:

- little or no cash outflow/inflow is required until maturity of the transaction;
- no principle balance or other fixed amount is paid or received;
- potential risks and rewards can be substantially greater than the current outlays; and
- the value of the entity's asset or liability arising from the derivative may exceed the amount (if any) that the derivative is recognised at in the financial statements. This is because the UK and Republic of Ireland financial reporting framework does not allow derivatives to be shown at their fair value in the financial statements.

37.7.2   Responsibilities

As with any other item in the financial statements, the consultation draft states that it is management's responsibility to ensure that the preparation and presentation of the value of derivatives given in the financial statements is correct. In relation to derivatives, management are also responsible for:

- maintaining a system which will ensure that:
  - only authorised individuals can participate in the derivative market,
  - the use of derivatives is within the entity's agreed risk exposure levels;
  - risk and financial control is monitored; and
  - the entity is in compliance with applicable laws and regulations; and
- ensuring that the accounting system is able to report reliably on derivatives.

The purpose of an audit of financial statements is not to provide assurance on the adequacy of the entity's risk management related to derivatives or the controls over them. Rather the auditors' responsibility is to consider whether management's disclosures about derivatives in the financial statements are materially in accordance with all relevant legislation and accounting standards.

It is therefore important that clients are aware of this limitation on auditors' responsibilities. The engagement letter may set out these responsibilities in order to avoid any misunderstanding.

Auditors may need specialist skills or knowledge to ensure that they have the relevant professional competence to service a client holding derivative instruments. This knowledge will include:

- the operating characteristics and risk profile of the industry in which the entity operates;
- the derivative financial instruments used by the entity, and their characteristics;
- the entity's information system for derivatives, including services provided by a service organisation. This may require specialist knowledge about computer applications where significant information about these derivatives are transmitted, processed, maintained or accessed electronically;
- the methods of valuing the derivative; and
- the requirements of relevant legislation, regulations and applicable accounting standards for derivatives.

If this knowledge is not readily available within the audit team, auditors may seek the assistance of an expert from outside the team or outside the firm as necessary. This is more likely where the derivatives are particularly complex or valuations are based on complex pricing models. The consultation draft considers the knowledge of the business required in greater depth, looking in turn at general economic factors, the industry and the entity itself.

Auditors should understand how derivative activities are linked to the entity's day-to-day business activities. For example, because of the economic conditions that affect the price of the entity's raw materials, the entity may enter into a forward contract to hedge the cost of its stock.

37.7.3 Risks

The consultation draft considers the types of risk which auditors should consider when planning their audit procedures. The key financial risks are identified as:

- *Market Risk* relating to unfavourable changes in the value of the derivative on the market, together with related areas of *Price Risk* (including interest rate risk and foreign exchange risk) and *Liquidity Risk* that the instrument cannot be sold or disposed of;
- *Basis Risk* relating to changes in the Basis, or difference between the price of the hedged item and the related hedging instrument;
- *Credit Risk* that the customer or counterparty will not settle the obligation in full. This also includes *Settlement Risk*, that one party to the hedge will settle whilst the other fails;

- *Solvency Risk* that the entity will not have the funds available to honour outgoings as they fall due; and
- *Legal Risk*, relating to potential losses from legal or regulatory action.

These factors should be considered by auditors when assessing their client's inherent risk. Factors which might affect the auditors' assessment of inherent risk relating to the holding of derivatives include:

- the economics and business purpose of the entity's derivative activities. The auditors should understand the purpose of the activities. Different inherent risks will arise from derivatives held to reduce risk (hedging) or to increase profits (speculating);
- the complexity of the derivative's features. The more complex a derivative is, the more difficult it will be to determine its value, introducing increased valuation risk;
- whether the transaction giving risk to the derivative involved the exchange of cash. Derivatives not involving cash exchange at inception, or with irregular or end of term cash flows are often difficult to identify;
- an entity's experience with the derivative. Use of complex derivatives without sufficient expertise will increase inherent risk;
- whether the derivative is an embedded feature of an agreement. Management are less likely to identify embedded derivatives leading to a completeness issue;
- external factors affecting valuation, such as market fortunes or interest rate volatilities;
- whether the derivative is traded on national exchanges or across borders. Risk will be increased as a result of exchange rate changes or where cross border exchanges are subject to different laws and regulations.

Many derivatives have the associated risk that a loss may exceed the amount, if any, of the value of the derivative recognised on the balance sheet (off-balance sheet risk). In some cases the potential losses may be enough to cause significant doubt on the ability of the entity to continue as a going concern. Auditors should consider any sensitivity analyses or value-at-risk analyses performed by the entity as part of their evaluation of management's assessment of the entity's ability to continue as a going concern.

37.7.4 Types of audit procedures

When selecting audit procedures auditors should consider the following issues set out by the consultation draft:

- the assessed level of inherent risk;
- the accounting method used, i.e., if hedge accounting is used different procedures will be relevant to assess whether this is suitable;
- the sophistication of the accounting system used to record derivatives;
- the control environment in place;

- the role of internal audit;
- the use of service organisations; and
- the efficiency of using control procedures to reduce substantive testing.

The consultation draft continues to detail suggested substantive procedures which can be used to test derivative financial instruments.

37.7.5 Materiality

Particular care should be taken when assessing materiality for the testing of derivatives. As derivatives have little or no recorded balance sheet value, materiality should not be based on these values alone.

Despite their low financial recorded value errors in this area may give rise to high value misstatements. Auditors should be aware of this risk and assess materiality accordingly.

37.7.6 Other areas

Auditors usually obtain confirmation of oral representations from the board of directors. As a result of the often complex nature of derivative activities, auditors may prefer to obtain representations about derivatives from those responsible for the derivatives activity within the entity.

Auditors may consider the following areas for inclusion in a representation letter:

- management's objectives when entering into derivative activities, i.e. whether the derivatives are for hedging or speculation purposes;
- disclosures required by FRS 13;
- whether all transactions have been conducted at arm's length and at market value;
- the terms of derivative transactions;
- whether there are any side agreements associated with any derivative instruments; and
- whether the entity has entered into any written options.

When reporting to those charged with governance, the Practice Note sets out the following areas which the auditor may report:

- material weakness in the design or operation of the accounting or internal control systems;
- lack of management understanding of the nature or extent of the derivative activities or the related risks;
- a lack of formal policies covering the purchase, sale and holding of derivatives; and
- a lack of segregation of duties.

38 RELIANCE ON OTHERS

38.1 INTRODUCTION

This chapter examines situations where auditors rely on others for part of the audit evidence. It examines reliance on:

- internal audit;
- other auditors; and
- experts.

38.2 INTERNAL AUDIT

38.2.1 Auditing Standards

ISA (UK and Ireland) 610 *Considering the Work of Internal Audit* was issued in December 2004 and provides guidance covering:

- the effect of internal audit on external audit procedures;
- understanding of internal audit;
- assessment of internal audit;
- Evaluating specific internal audit work.

As with all ISAs (UK and Ireland), the text of the international ISA has been supplemented with additional guidance from a UK and Ireland perspective. SAS 500 *Considering the Work of Internal Audit* has not yet been officially withdrawn.

ISA (UK and Ireland) 610 is effective for audits of financial statements for periods commencing on or after 15 December 2004.

In December 2006, the IAASB issued a revision to the international version of ISA 610 as part of its Clarity Project. This is discussed in **38.2.5** below.

38.2.2   *Effect of internal audit on external audit procedures*

Internal audit is defined by the ISA (UK and Ireland) as 'an appraisal activity established within an entity as a service to the entity' and states that its functions include 'amongst other things, monitoring internal control'. It requires that external auditors consider the activities of this function and their effect, if any, on external audit procedures, although it does not relieve them of any of their responsibilities.

The activities of an internal audit function may include:

- review of the accounting and internal control systems;
- examination of financial and operating information;
- review of the economy, efficiency and effectiveness of operations;
- review of the compliance with laws, regulations and other external requirements and with management policies and directives; and
- special investigations.

Some of these activities will concern non-financial information and as such will not generally be of direct relevance to the external auditors. The level of precision that internal auditors work to may also be higher than that of the external auditors who are primarily concerned with material misstatement in the financial statements, but some of the methods used will be common.

Some entities will sub-contract the internal audit function to a third party but as this is still within the control of the entity, the external auditors may consider its impact on their own procedures.

38.2.3   *Understanding and assessment of internal audit*

'the external auditors should obtain a sufficient understanding of internal audit activities to identify and assess the risks of material misstatement of the financial statements and to design and perform further audit procedures.'.

Where an internal audit function is effective, external auditors may be able to reduce the extent of their own testing. However, they will not be able to rely solely on the work of internal audit to the extent of performing no additional testing themselves. Additionally, if internal audit is effective this may be a consideration in the external auditor's assessment of the entity's control environment and risk assessment.

Where internal audit is relevant to the risk assessment, the external auditor must obtain an understanding of the internal audit function and then carry out an assessment of the function. The ISA (UK and Ireland) sets out the criteria the auditors should use. External auditors should concentrate on the:

- organisational status of internal audit, including its ability to be objective and the level of management that it reports to;
- scope of the function, including the nature of assignments and whether management acts on its reports;
- technical competence of the persons performing the work; and
- application of due professional care, including whether the work is properly planned, supervised, reviewed and documented.

Coordination of the timing of the two auditors' work is best achieved by regular meetings throughout the year. This will normally ensure that the external auditors are made aware of any relevant matters as they come to light. The process also works in reverse, particularly at the end of the external audit when there may be matters in the report to management which are of concern to the internal audit.

38.2.4 Evaluating specific internal audit work

Where the external auditors use specific internal audit work 'they should evaluate and perform audit procedures on that work to confirm its adequacy for the external auditor's purposes'. This evaluation procedure may include consideration of whether:

- the work is carried out by adequately trained, proficient internal auditors;
- the work of assistants is properly supervised, reviewed and documented;
- sufficient appropriate evidence is obtained to give a reasonable basis for the conclusions reached;
- appropriate conclusions are reached;
- any reports are consistent with the results of the work performed;
- any exceptional or unusual matters found by internal audit are properly resolved; and
- any changes are required to the external auditors' procedures as a result of the work of the internal auditors.

Typical audit procedures employed by the external auditor may include:

- examination of items already examined by internal audit;
- examination of other similar items; or
- observation of internal audit procedures.

Table 1 gives examples of two scenarios and details the reliance that may be placed on the work of an internal audit department in each situation.

If the external auditors conclude that the internal auditors' work is not adequate for their purposes, they should consider what additional procedures of their own are necessary in order to have sufficient appropriate evidence to form an opinion.

TABLE 1:   Evaluating internal audit work

Case A

An internal audit function is staffed by a number of qualified accountants. Reports go to the audit committee. Their programme of work consists of among other things, systems checks and periodic audits of branch returns. External auditors receive reports as and when produced.

Case B

Internal audits are carried out on a part time basis by the controller of one subsidiary. Work is mainly of an ad hoc nature, looking at problem areas both in terms of control and efficiency and producing reports for the finance director.

Extent of reliance

Based upon the facts set out above, the possible extent of reliance in Case A would appear to be far greater than in Case B. The auditors may seek to rely on work performed on the internal controls systems by internal audit together with some of the checks carried out during the audits of branch returns.

In contrast, in Case B the opportunities for reliance on internal audit would be greatly reduced. Some reliance may be possible in areas reported on which have relevance to the external audit. However, because of the status of the internal audit and its method of operation there would probably be less reliance and a greater level of procedures in the relevant area.

38.2.5   IAASB Clarity Project Amendments to ISA 610

In December 2006, the IAASB issued an Exposure Draft of ISA 610 (Redrafted), *The Auditor's Consideration of the Internal Audit Function* for comment as part of its Clarity Project. There are no major changes to the substance of the ISA, rather it has been redrafted solely to apply the clarity drafting conventions set out by the IAASB.

In the UK, the APB have requested interested parties to submit their comments to them for inclusion in the APB response to the IAASB.

38.3   OTHER AUDITORS

38.3.1   Auditing Standards

ISA (UK and Ireland) 600 *Using the Work of Another Auditor* was issued in December 2004 and provides guidance covering:

- acceptance as principal auditors;
- professional experience of other auditors;

- procedures of principal auditors;
- significant findings of other auditors;
- co-operation between auditors.

As with all ISAs (UK and Ireland), the text of the international ISA has been supplemented with additional guidance from a UK and Ireland perspective. SAS 510 *The Relationship Between Principal Auditors and Other Auditors* has not yet been officially withdrawn.

ISA (UK and Ireland) 600 is effective for audits of financial statements for periods commencing on or after 15 December 2004.

In April 2005 the APB issued a proposed revision to ISA (UK and Ireland) 600 for comment. The Exposure Draft adopts the text of a proposed revision to ISA 600 issued by the IAASB, the issue of which has subsequently been delayed by its inclusion in the IAASB's Clarity Project. As a result no final version of the ISA (UK and Ireland) has been published to date. Details of the UK Exposure Draft are covered in **38.3.7** below.

Following research on the views of practitioners on how group audits are carried out in practice, the Audit and Assurance Faculty issued an eight point plan setting out practical guidance for increasing the quality of group audits in November 2005. This is detailed in **38.3.9** below.

38.3.2 Definitions

The ISA (UK and Ireland) uses the term 'principal auditors' to refer to the auditors who are reporting on a set of financial statements which include components on which they have not reported as auditors. This relates to where auditors of a parent company are not the auditors of one or more of its subsidiaries.

The ISA (UK and Ireland) does not deal with joint auditors or reliance by newly appointed auditors on the work of predecessors.

In the context of the UK Companies Act, the term 'components' encompasses companies, joint ventures and branches which form part of a group.

38.3.3 Acceptance as principal auditors

ISA (UK and Ireland) 600 requires that, before deciding to act for a particular organisation, 'the auditor should consider whether the auditor's own participation is sufficient to be able to act as principal auditors'. In order to do this, they should consider:

- the materiality of the portion of the financial statements which they audit;

- the degree of their knowledge regarding the business of the components;
- the nature of their relationship with the other auditors, particularly if they are an affiliated firm;
- their ability to perform additional procedures; and
- the risk of material misstatement of the components not audited by the principal auditors.

This is intended to ensure that the principal auditors are sufficiently involved with the rest of the group, albeit not directly with the components' audit. If they feel that they are not sufficiently involved they should either not accept appointment or take appropriate action to ensure that they have sufficient involvement.

38.3.4   The principal auditors' procedures

Principal auditors are required to consider the professional competence of the other auditor in the context of the assignment. There are various factors that affect the principal auditors' assessment of the other auditors, including:

- previous experience of their work;
- any affiliation of the other firm;
- membership of relevant professional bodies; and
- discussions with the other auditors.

The ISA (UK and Ireland) requires that the principal auditors obtain sufficient appropriate audit evidence that the work of the other auditors is adequate for the principal auditors' purposes. This involves, as part of the initial planning by the principal auditors, discussing with the other auditors what use is to be made of the other auditors' work and informing them of any specific areas which the principal auditors want addressed. Additionally, the principal auditors advise and obtain representations from the other auditors concerning compliance with:

- the independence requirements of both the entity (parent) and the component (subsidiary); and
- the relevant accounting, auditing and reporting requirements.

The principal auditors may use a consolidation questionnaire or checklist, to be completed by the other auditors, to provide audit evidence or may review the other auditors' working papers. The choice of method will depend on the circumstances of the particular case and may also depend on the assessment of the competence of the other auditors.

There may be situations where it is decided not to use any of the methods outlined above because of evidence previously obtained that acceptable quality control policies and procedures are complied with in the conduct of the other auditors' practice. This will most commonly be the case where the other auditors are affiliated to the principal auditors. The principal auditors will be able to rely more readily on an associated firm as the other auditors than where the other auditors are an independent firm. The quality control procedures of a national or international association should ensure that the work performed by the associate will be of a similar standard to that of the principal auditors (see **Table 2**).

The principal auditors should consider the significant findings of the other auditors. To do this they may use the methods noted above. They may also decide that discussions are needed between the two auditors and the management of the component. The principal auditors should also request copies of any reports to the management of the component by the other auditors. As a result the principal auditors may decide that additional procedures are necessary, performed by either the principal or the other auditors.

38.3.5   Co-operation between auditors

The ISA (UK and Ireland) requires that 'the other auditor, knowing the context in which the principal auditor will use the other auditor's work, should co-operate with the principal auditors'.

TABLE 2:   Reliance on other auditors

A & Co audit the parent company of a group, XYZ Plc, which has two subsidiaries, U Limited and W Limited.

U Limited is audited by the local office of A & Co. W Limited is audited by a smaller practice. U Limited and W Limited are both significant to the group accounts.

The degree of reliance that A & Co would be able to place on work of the subsidiary auditors would differ.

For the audit of U Limited, assuming this was carried out in accordance with common procedures and that their local office was subject to national quality control procedures, there would be no need for a comprehensive review of U Limited's audit.

In contrast for W Limited, they would not be able to rely on this and may need to carry out a full-scale review.

For UK subsidiaries (of a UK group), the other auditors have a statutory duty to communicate such information and explanations as may be reasonably required by the principal auditors. Where there is no such obligation, the other auditors should obtain the permission of the component's management before giving such assistance.

Where the other auditors have been unable to conclude on a matter, or feel that there is something that should be brought to the attention of the principal auditors, they should do so bearing in mind their statutory obligation as noted above.

There is no complementary obligation, but principal auditors may inform other auditors of such matters if they consider it appropriate after due consultation with those charged with governance at the parent entity.

38.3.6   Reporting considerations

Reliance on the work of other auditors does not relieve the principal auditors of any of their own responsibilities in reporting on the consolidated financial statements. They have sole responsibility for their report and should not refer to the other auditors in it.

There are two instances when the principal auditors should consider the implications of the other auditors' work on their own report. These are when:

- adequate evidence about the work of the other auditors cannot be obtained and the principal auditors have not been able to perform additional procedures in respect of these financial statements; or
- the other auditors intend to issue a qualified report or one containing additional explanatory material.

38.3.7   Exposure Draft ISA (UK and Ireland) 600 (Revised), The audit of group financial statements

Background

In April 2005 the APB issued a proposed revision to ISA (UK and Ireland) 600 entitled *The Audit of Group Financial Statements*, based on the text of a proposed revision to ISA 600 issued by the IAASB. This follows previous proposed revisions to ISA 600 by the IAASB which were issued in December 2003 and met with significant comment. The revised IAASB proposals addressed the concerns raised by the original respondents, however, the process of updating the international version of the ISA has now been subsumed within the IAASB's Clarity Project. As a result the issue of a revision to the ISA (UK and Ireland) has also been postponed.

The APB has commented on the version of ISA 600 arising from the IAASB's Clarity Project. In line with other comment letters issued to the IAASB, the APB requested comments from the auditing community in the UK before making its submission. The main comments are set out in **38.3.8** below.

Related auditors

The Exposure Draft introduces separate definitions for 'related auditor', 'unrelated auditor' and 'other auditor' as follows:

- a 'related auditor' is an auditor from the group auditors' firm or from a network firm who performs work on one or more components for purposes of the audit of the group financial statements and which operates under, and complies with, common monitoring policies and procedures;
- an 'unrelated auditor' is an auditor other than the group auditors or a related auditor who performs work on one or more components for the purpose of the audit of the group financial statements; and
- an 'other auditor' includes a related auditor and an unrelated auditor.

The distinction between related and unrelated auditors continues to affect the approach to be taken by the group auditor in relation to their work. The proposals are more stringent in relation to the:

- type of work to be performed on the components' financial information;
- group auditor's involvement in the work of the other auditors;
- group auditor's evaluation of the adequacy of the other auditors' work; and
- group auditors' communications with the other auditors.

Type of work to be performed

The type and extent of work to be performed on the financial information of a component will depend on the significance of the component and the group auditors' evaluation of the design and implementation of group-wide controls. The various levels are set out in **Table 3**.

TABLE 3: Work to be performed on the financial information of components

Significance

Work to be performed

Component likely to include significant risks of material misstatement of the group financial statements

Group auditors will request other auditors to perform either:

- an audit in accordance with ISAs using either a materiality level determined by the group auditor or a lower materiality level determined by the other auditor;
- an audit of specified account balances related to the identified specific risks; or
- specified audit procedures relating to the identified significant risks.

Component which is of individual financial significance to the group due to its size (see below)

Group auditors will request other auditors to perform an audit in accordance with ISAs using either a materiality level determined by the group auditor or a lower materiality level determined by the other auditor

Components which in aggregate represent less than five per cent of group assets, liabilities, cash flows, profit or turnover

Group level analytical procedures are likely to be sufficient for such components

Other components which are significant in aggregate

Group auditors may request other auditors to perform:

- an audit in accordance with ISAs using either a materiality level determined by the group auditor or a lower materiality level determined by the other auditor;
- an audit of specified account balances related to the identified specific risks;
- specified audit procedures relating to the identified significant risks; or
- a review of the financial information of the component.

The type of work performed will depend on:

- whether the component has been newly formed or acquired;
- whether significant changes have taken place in the component;
- whether internal audit has performed work at the component;
- the effectiveness of group-wide controls; and
- the risks posed by, or the individual financial significance of, the component in comparison with other components within this category.

A component of the group may be of individual financial significance to the group and thus the likelihood of the risk of material misstatement of the group financial statements arising from that component will increase. Group auditors may calculate a percentage of group assets, liabilities, cash flows, profit or turnover for each component to determine whether any are of financial significance. The Exposure Draft suggests that the choice of benchmark will depend on the nature and circumstances of the group, but states that a component representing 20 per cent or more of the relevant benchmark should be regarded as financially significant. Auditors may choose, however, to lower this percentage.

Involvement in the work of other auditors
The extent of the group auditors' involvement in the work performed by another auditor will depend on:

- the significance of the component,

- the professional qualifications and professional competence of the other auditor; and
- the quality control system of the other auditor's firm.

The Exposure Draft states that the group auditors' procedures will ordinarily include:

- meeting with component management to obtain an understanding of the component and its environment;
- performing risk assessment procedures and participating in the assessment of risks of material misstatement. These may be performed with the other auditors, or by the group auditors;
- determining and performing further audit procedures. These may be performed with the other auditors, or by the group auditors;
- participating in the closing or other key meetings between the other auditors and component management; and
- reviewing relevant parts of the other auditors' audit documentation.

Assessment of the adequacy of the work of other auditors

The Exposure Draft requires group auditors to evaluate the adequacy of the work of other auditors for the group auditors' purposes. The nature, timing and extent of the group auditors' evaluation will be affected by:

- whether a component is significant;
- whether the other auditors are related auditors and whether the group auditor and the related auditor applies the same audit methodology;
- the group auditors' evaluation of the professional qualifications, independence and professional competence of the other auditors and the quality control system of that firm; and
- the extent of the group auditors' involvement in the work of the other auditor.

The group auditor should review the work of other auditors in relation to significant components. Where the other auditor is an unrelated auditor, this task may be performed by a related auditor on the group auditors' behalf.

Communication with other auditors

The ISA (UK and Ireland) Exposure Draft contains more detailed requirements about the content of communications between group and other auditors and an appendix sets out examples of matters which may be included in the group auditors' letter of instruction.

Group auditors should communicate the type of work to be performed, the materiality level and the threshold above which the misstatements cannot be regarded as clearly trivial to the group financial statements and significant risks identified at the group level that are relevant to the work of the other auditors. They should also provide a list of related parties known to them and request the other auditor to be alert for unusual transactions.

Group auditors will request other auditors to confirm:

- that they have received the letter of instruction;
- that the other auditor will undertake the requested work;
- that the other auditor understands that the group auditor will consider, and may use, the other auditors' work for the purpose of the audit of the group financial statements; and
- in the case of an unrelated auditor, that the firm's quality control system complies with ISQC (UK and Ireland) 1, see **Chapter 20**, and whether there are any issues noted in recent monitoring reports that are likely to affect the work that the unrelated auditor will perform.

In addition, other auditors should confirm whether they understand the:

- relevant ethical requirements, and that they will comply with them;
- applicable financial reporting framework; and
- auditing and other standards applicable to the audit of the group financial statements.

At the conclusion of their work, the other auditors should send the group auditors a memorandum or report of the work they have performed setting out the items listed in **Table 4**.

TABLE 4:   Contents of the report by other auditors to group auditors

- whether they have complied with the quality control policies and procedures of their firm;
- whether they have complied with the relevant ethical requirements, including independence;
- whether they have complied with auditing or other standards applicable to the audit of the group financial statements;
- whether they have complied with the group auditors' other instructions;
- identification of the financial information of the component on which they are reporting;
- details of the work they have performed;
- uncorrected misstatements in the financial information of the component (not including misstatements below the threshold for clearly trivial misstatements);
- details of material weaknesses in internal control over financial reporting;
- other significant matters that they communicated or expect to communicate to those charged with governance;
- any other matters they wish to draw to the attention of the group auditors; and
- their findings, conclusions and opinions.

Acceptance and continuance as group auditor

In deciding whether to accept the position of group auditor, a firm should determine whether they will be able to obtain sufficient appropriate audit evidence on which to base their audit opinion. Where components in the group are audited by someone other than the group auditors the risk of not detecting a material misstatement will increase. This increase may be limited if the other auditors are related auditors.

To obtain sufficient audit evidence, the Exposure Draft requires group auditors to either perform the work on all components themselves or be involved in the work that other auditors perform.

Access to information

The Exposure Draft states that a firm should not accept an engagement to audit group financial statements if:

- their access to component information, those charged with governance of components, component management or other auditors (including relevant parts of their audit documentation) will be restricted; and
- the possible effect of their inability to obtain sufficient appropriate audit evidence is material and pervasive to the group financial statements, such that they are likely to disclaim an opinion on the group financial statements.

38.3.8 IAASB Clarity Project Amendments to ISA 600

As stated above, the publication of a revision to ISA (UK and Ireland) 600 has been postponed awaiting the outcome of proposed changes to the international version of the ISA as part of the IAASB's Clarity Project.

Following consultation with audit firms and other interested parties, the APB submitted their comments on the proposed changes to the IAASB in July 2006. The main points were:

- the removal of the distinction between related and unrelated auditors was supported, though some concern was voiced about the amount of evidence required to be obtained for those auditors which would previously have been classified as 'related'. Detailed evidence concerning ethical requirements and quality control systems of auditors in the same network may be unnecessary where control procedures and monitoring are common across the network;
- concern that the revised ISA was too prescriptive in the steps to be taken in some areas of a group audit. Although the level of specificity in the Exposure Draft was generally welcomed, there were concerns that a 'tick box' mentality may arise in some areas, specifically:
  - involvement in the work performed by other auditors;
  - communication with other auditors with regard to specific risks identified in components; and

- restrictions on access to information relating to acceptance and continuance requirements.
- further clarification is required on how to determine materiality levels for components; and
- additional consideration should be given to the implications for audit costs of the proposed changes.

38.3.9   *Promoting Best Practice in Group Audits*

In November 2005, the Audit and Assurance Faculty of the ICAEW published *Promoting Best Practice in Group Audits*, to provide practical guidance on increasing the quality of group audits. The guidance was based on the findings of research commissioned by the Faculty which sought the views of practitioners on how group audits are carried out in practice and looked for examples of good practice in firms.

The publication focuses on an eight point plan which deals with the challenges of project management, communication between auditors and dealing with the technical issues that specifically arise in relation to group audits. The eight point plan is set out below.

The Eight Point Plan
The Audit and Assurance Faculty's research concentrated on:

- establishing how group audits are currently handled;
- identifying best practice;
- providing practical guidance on the pitfalls to avoid; and
- providing a gap analysis of current practice and the main requirements of the proposed ISA (UK and Ireland) 600.

The eight point plan covers a range of issues which the Faculty believes are important to get right in order to make group audits as effective as possible. The key area is good project management with open lines of communication being established with other auditors. The plan is set out in **Table 5**.

TABLE 5: The Eight Point Plan

1. Get organised

- start early and establish clear milestones
- provide very clear instructions and requirements for deliverables to other auditors; an example of possible documentation to send to other auditors is set out in **Table 6**
- get audit committee and management buy-in to the audit process and ensure they understand their responsibilities
- consider asking for information on planning and risk assessment, including fraud risk, prior to the year end

---

- keep in regular contact with the key group parties
- use more telephone and conference calls rather than relying solely on letters and e-mail
- where appropriate, visit other auditors and subsidiary management

2. Analyse the group structure

- focus attention on the more unusual corporate structures
- if there are doubts about the group structure, verify it against publicly available information
- consider whether to accept an engagement where the group auditor is only directly responsible for a minority of the total group
- understand the accounting framework applicable to each component and any local statutory reporting requirements

3. Focus on the quality of other auditors

- consider the qualifications, independence and competence of other auditors up front, along with their quality control procedures
- for related auditors (those who have common quality control policies and procedures), group auditors may be able to rely on those common policies and procedures, particularly where they also adopt the same audit methodology
- for unrelated auditors, or related auditors where the group auditor is unable to rely on common policies and procedures, consider:
  - visiting the other auditor
  - requesting that the other auditor completes a questionnaire or representation
  - obtaining confirmation from a relevant regulatory body and/or
  - discussing the other auditor with colleagues from their own firm
- for an other auditor based overseas, consider whether they have enough knowledge and experience of ISAs (UK and Ireland)

4. Focus the group audit on high risk areas

- group auditors need to ask for enough information from other auditors to form their own conclusions on significant risks arising in components that affect the group financial statements. Focus attention on the five warning signs identified by respondents to the research:
  - recently acquired components
  - jurisdictions with under-developed financial reporting regimes
  - components which are 'just below the radar'
  - components that have a history of reporting late and
  - components that have had big swings in their profits
- consider the risks arising from the consolidation process itself, including the use of journals and incomplete information relating to adjustments between accounting frameworks or to align accounting policies
- discuss fraud risks with other auditors as appropriate

5. Understand internal controls across the group

- request details of material weaknesses in internal control identified by other auditors
- communicate material weaknesses in group-wide controls and significant weaknesses in internal controls of components to group management and those charged with governance of the group

6. Ensure staff understand the technical complexities of group audits and know when to bring in specialist help

- consider areas of particular concern, where it is important that practitioners are aware of the main issues and bring in expertise where it is needed:
  - differing accounting frameworks and policies
  - intra group transactions and balances
  - fair values in acquisitions
  - capturing post-balance sheet events
  - intangibles
  - the basis and calculation of share options and bonuses
  - deferred tax
- plan early any specialist involvement, for example the use of a tax expert to deal with international tax issues or a valuation expert for share options

7. Review other auditors' working papers

- group and other auditors should cooperate as regards sharing of information unless prohibited by law. Appropriate use of hold harmless letters may be used to manage risk
- get group management to obtain the consent of subsidiary management to communicate with the group auditor to deal with concerns about client confidentiality and sensitivity
- consider whether holding discussions with or visiting other auditors could deal with secrecy and data-protection issues

8. Review and update procedures, training and tools

- provide formal training on group audits to supplement on-the-job experience
- review standard questionnaires, if any, for effectiveness
- make sure that training materials and manuals are updated to reflect the new ISA (UK and Ireland) 600 in good time

TABLE 6: Possible documentation to send to other auditors

This is not a definitive list and should be tailored to the circumstances of the individual group.

Referral instructions

Including:

- timetable for the work;
- details of each of the components within the group together with required scope of work, arrangements for coordination of work at the planning stage and during the audit, including the group auditor's involvement in their work;
- any other known related parties;
- level of materiality and threshold for 'clearly trivial' misstatements;
- details of scope of work required for each component;
- details of specific risks and areas of focus for the group audit, including fraud risks and specific procedures required including work to be done on intra-group transactions and balances and the work to be done on subsequent events;
- description of any group-wide controls including any testing by the group auditor relevant to the work of other auditors, work by internal audit; and
- details of the applicable financial reporting framework, auditing standards and any other statutory reporting responsibilities, including group accounting policies and applicable laws and regulations.

Letter from other auditor acknowledging instructions

Including:

- the use that will be made of their work and that they will perform the work required;
- confirmation of independence and, for unrelated firms, of whether the quality control system complies with ISQC (UK and Ireland) 1 and any relevant issues noted in recent monitoring reports;
- confirmation of understanding of the applicable financial reporting framework and auditing standards.

Specimen reports to group auditor

Including:

- template for planning memorandum to describe proposed audit approach;
- template for clearance memos, summary memoranda and/or questionnaires to report findings including significant accounting, financial reporting and auditing matters including accounting estimates and related judgements, going concern matters;
- template for specimen management letter/report to those charged with governance of components including details of any material weaknesses in internal control and/or for reporting such issues to the group auditor;

- template for reporting uncorrected misstatements;
- template for reporting any actual fraud or information obtained that indicates a fraud may exist, including any suspected or alleged fraud affecting the component and any instances of non-compliance with laws and regulations that may have a material effect on the group financial statements;
- subsequent events review sign-off; and
- confirmation of independence including details of fees for non-audit services.

38.4 EXPERTS

38.4.1 Auditing Standards

ISA (UK and Ireland) 620 *Using the Work of an Expert* was issued in December 2004 and provides guidance covering:

- using the work of an expert;
- competence and objectivity of the expert;
- the expert's scope of work;
- assessing the work of the expert.

As with all ISAs (UK and Ireland), the text of the international ISA has been supplemented with additional guidance from a UK and Ireland perspective. SAS 520 *Using the Work of an Expert* has not yet been officially withdrawn.

ISA (UK and Ireland) 620 is effective for audits of financial statements for periods commencing on or after 15 December 2004.

38.4.2 Using experts

ISA (UK and Ireland) 620 requires that, 'when using the work performed by an expert, the auditor should obtain sufficient appropriate audit evidence that such work is adequate for the purposes of the audit'.

The term 'expert' refers to a person or a firm possessing specialist skills or knowledge in a field other than auditing and accounting. They are usually members of another profession such as surveyors, actuaries or engineers.

Where the firm of auditors employs the experts full-time they will still need to assess aspects of their work as if the experts were third parties with regard to the work and its results, although they may not need to consider the experts' skills and competence for each assignment. Auditors, however, need to have regard to the related ethical guidance when deciding if they can use employees of their firm as experts on an audit assignment. They must ensure that their objectivity and independence is not impaired, which would be the case where 'in house' experts are required to value an asset or a liability of the client company for inclusion in its balance sheet.

The types of evidence that auditors may obtain from experts will usually be a report, opinion or valuation, such as:

- valuation of an asset, for example property;
- determination of the quantity of an asset, for example minerals;
- determination of amounts using specialised techniques, for example actuarial valuation;
- measurement of work completed on contracts in progress; and
- legal opinions on interpretations of agreements.

The decision whether to use experts will depend on:

- the materiality of the financial statement assertion being tested;
- the risk of misstatement of the matter, bearing in mind its nature and complexity; and
- the quantity and quality of other audit evidence available on the matter.

Although the work of an expert may be used, the auditor retains sole responsibility for the audit opinion.

When it is the auditors who decide that the opinion of experts is required, they should discuss this with the management and if they refuse to agree to the appointment of experts then the auditors need to consider both obtaining other audit evidence and the implications for their audit report.

38.4.3   Competence and objectivity of experts

When planning to use the work of experts, auditors should assess the objectivity and professional qualifications, experience and resources of the experts.

The objectivity of the experts may be impaired if they are either employed by the entity or related to it in some way (for example, they are a shareholder).

Where the auditors are concerned about either the objectivity or competence of the expert they should discuss their reservations with those charged with governance. They may need to obtain alternative evidence or, if this is not possible, they should consider the implications for their report.

38.4.4   The experts' scope of work

Auditors should assess the appropriateness of the experts' work as audit evidence. The best way to achieve this is by reviewing the terms of reference of the experts, or their letter of instruction.

The letter of instruction should contain details of:

- the objectives and scope of the experts' work;
- the specific matters that the report is to cover;
- the intended use of the experts' work;
- the extent of the experts' access to the appropriate records; and
- information regarding the assumptions and methods intended to be used by the experts.

Where such details are not clear, the auditors may need to contact the experts directly to obtain sufficient evidence on the scope of the work to be carried out.

38.4.5   Assessing the work of experts

The auditors should assess the appropriateness of the experts' notes as audit evidence regarding the financial statement assertions being considered. This will involve assessment of:

- the source data used;
- the assumptions and methods used;
- the reasons for any changes in these from those used in the prior period;
- when the expert carried out the work; and
- the results of the work in the light of the auditors' knowledge of the business.

The auditors should ensure that the data used by the expert is sufficient, relevant and reliable and may consider reviewing or testing this data.

The experts' assumptions will not usually be challenged by the auditors as they do not have sufficient expertise, but they do need to understand the assumptions and consider whether they are reasonable given the auditors' knowledge of the business and the results of the other audit procedures.

Where the results of the experts' work are inconsistent with evidence obtained by the auditors, they should try to resolve this by discussion with the management. If they are unable to resolve the inconsistencies they will need to consider the implications for their audit report.

When the auditors are satisfied with the work of the experts there is no need for them to refer to this in their report.

38.4.6   Applying the guidance in practice

The different considerations in assessing the competence, objectivity and results of experts' reports may be seen by comparing the respective audit approaches to property carried in the accounts at valuation, which are supported by various levels of expert report. In summary, these are:

- full external valuation;
- valuation supported by limited review or a 'desk top' update by external valuers of a previous valuation;
- internal valuation by qualified directors supported by a full valuation report; or
- internal valuation by qualified directors not supported by a report.

External valuations
Where a valuation has been carried out by external experts, the auditors must:

- assess the competence and objectivity of the experts;
- agree on the scope of the work of the experts; and
- evaluate the findings of the experts.

Where the valuation is material to the accounts it will inevitably be the case that the auditors will need to discuss the valuation with the valuers.

Valuation supported by limited external evidence
In this case, there will be either a report or descriptive correspondence from external valuers, which must be assessed using the principles set out above. In particular, any limitations or qualifications should be examined to assess whether they undermine evidence already obtained. For example, a 'desk top' update is always qualified on the grounds that no site inspections have been carried out. If it is known that a site has been closed and severe dilapidation has taken place the auditors would question that valuation. If such an update assumes the same 'portfolio' but some sites have been sold, this must also cause the value to be questioned.

Internal valuation supported by full report
Where the directors are qualified valuers and support their valuation by a report setting out the assumptions that they have made in arriving at the figures (particularly in terms of rentals and yields), the auditors must initially assess this report using the same principles as they would for an external valuation. In assessing the other assumptions they may need to seek additional external evidence to support some of the assumptions (which the directors may in fact be able to provide). Where the effect is material, it will be necessary either to seek advice from other professionals or to use internal expertise to assess, for example, the reasonableness of assumptions concerning yields.

Auditors should avoid carrying out 'quasi-valuations' of their own. This course contains pitfalls, for example, using 'general' tables of yields as the only supporting evidence, as they cannot be easily attributed to a specific property. They should also be aware that special inducements can mean that quoted rentals are often in excess of the 'true rental'.

Unsupported internal valuations by qualified directors
In such cases the directors must be made to state their valuation and the underlying bases in writing. Where this is carried out the auditors will then assess it in the same way as at **38.4.6** above. If the directors are unable or unwilling to support their valuation the auditors must consider its materiality to their opinion.

38.4.7   Using the work of an actuary with regard to insurance provisions

Bulletin 1998/2 *Using the Work of an Actuary with Regard to Insurance Technical Provisions* was issued to provide guidance in the interpretation of SAS 520 in this particular situation. Although SAS 520 has been updated by ISA (UK and Ireland) 620, the guidance in the Bulletin remains relevant.

The Bulletin notes that auditors should consider the independence of the actuaries, their knowledge of the portfolio of business for which provision is being made and their experience of the market in which the insurer operates. When planning their audit, auditors should obtain information about the actuaries' approach to calculating the provisions in order to be able to assess their work.

Using their knowledge of the business and other evidence obtained in the course of their audit, auditors should consider whether the assumptions and methods of the actuaries are reasonable. If they are not satisfied that the actuaries' work provides sufficient appropriate evidence they should consider the implications for their report.

39 PREPARING FOR INTERNATIONAL FINANCIAL REPORTING STANDARDS

39.1 INTRODUCTION

Listed companies in the United Kingdom have been required to prepare their consolidated financial statements under International Financial Reporting Standards (IFRS) for year ends since 31 December 2005. From 31 December 2007 AIM-listed companies will also be required to produce their consolidated financial statements under IFRS. Other companies may adopt IFRS voluntarily at any time.

39.2 GUIDANCE

In 2004 the Audit and Assurance Faculty of the ICAEW published AUDIT 03/2004, *Auditing Implications of IFRS Transition* to give guidance on what auditors should expect management and audit committees to be doing as they manage transition to IFRS. It also sets out a number of issues that auditors should be aware of in the period up to the first audit under IFRS.

Following publication of AUDIT 03/2004, the Auditing Practices Board issued Bulletin 2005/3, *Guidance for Auditors on First-Time Application of IFRSs in the United Kingdom and Republic of Ireland*, providing further guidance in this area (see **39.6** below). The International Auditing and Assurance Standards Board (IAASB) has also issued a Questions and Answers paper to assist from an international perspective.

39.3 TIMETABLE

Where companies comply with IFRS for the first time they are required to include one full year of comparative figures, also under IFRS, using the standards extant at the reporting date. For example, management wishing to prepare IFRS financial statements for the year ended 31 December 2007, must show comparatives for the 31 December 2006 year end under IFRS, which in turn requires opening balances as at 1 January 2006 on an IFRS basis.

AUDIT 03/2004 contains guidance to assist auditors in assessing and commenting on their clients' transition process and their readiness for IFRS.

39.4   MANAGEMENT

Directors are responsible for ensuring that the company implements IFRS without any material impact on the business. They will need to review the impact on the business and ensure plans are in place to train staff, update systems and implement changes in reporting processes.

Management must identify gaps between current accounting policies and IFRS and then use this information to pinpoint changes required in financial data and additional information to meet the revised disclosure requirements. Once this has been completed they can formulate a detailed transition process.

Table 1 sets out a number of questions that auditors can ask clients to ascertain their readiness for IFRS conversion. The answers given may indicate risks which are likely to lead to a qualified audit report, and therefore should be considered as part of audit planning.

TABLE 1:   Questions to ascertain a client's readiness for IFRS conversion

- Has an estimate been made of the degree of resource with the necessary skill and knowledge required to manage the transition process?
- Is there sufficient access to the specialist expertise that will be required, for example for valuations?
- Has an estimate been made of the magnitude of change inherent in the transition process?
- Is management fully aware of the timetables and deliverables?
- Has the transition process been started?
- Is the impact analysis being carried out systematically and documented to a suitably high standard?
- Is there effective project management with senior management commitment and sponsorship?
- Is a thorough diagnostic exercise being undertaken to understand the accounting policy changes necessary before moving into the detail of restatement processes?
- Are changes on relevant accounting systems being tested as work is ongoing? Are these test results available?
- Is the entire group of companies (not just the head office) sufficiently involved in the process?
- Where IFRS are being adopted by individual companies, is there an understanding that there are other implications of IFRS transition

---

including reviewing deal structure, analysing the impact on reserves and dividends and reassessing impact on taxation?

- Is the building of data collection architecture and processes for the future being planned or implemented? Spreadsheets should not be seen as a long-term option.
- Are third party stakeholders being informed as soon as there is an understanding of the impact of the IFRS transition?
- Is a realistic view being taken on the reporting timetable, given the challenge of the IFRS transition to the company?
- Are there robust mechanisms in place to prevent and detect anyone taking advantage of the IFRS transition to deliberately misstate financial reports?

39.5 AUDIT COMMITTEES

Although many fully listed companies have already undergone transition to full IFRS reporting, the audit committees of AIM-listed companies will be expected to play a significant role in the transition process. However, overall responsibility for transition to IFRS rests with the directors. Auditors should discuss the quality and progress of the transition process with the audit committee at an early stage.

The audit committee should be suitably trained for the task, with relevant knowledge of IFRS. They should be able to determine the overall effectiveness of the transition plan as well as considering whether the committee's normal responsibilities in relation to financial statements has been satisfied.

Table 2 sets out questions that auditors can ask audit committees to assess how effective their role in relation to IFRS conversion is. The answers given may indicate risks which are likely to lead to a qualified audit report, and therefore should be considered as part of audit planning.

TABLE 2: Questions for the audit committee to assess the effectiveness of their role in relation to IFRS conversion

- Is the audit committee clear on its role and the degree of its involvement in the transition to IFRS?
- Has the audit committee considered whether there is sufficient training for the company's staff and its own members to develop their knowledge and skills?
- Has the audit committee reviewed the underlying accounting policy changes?
- Is the audit committee able to challenge management's choice of accounting policies and the robustness of the transition process?
- Is the audit committee aware of the requirements of IFRS and the Committee of European Securities Regulators' recommendations for disclosures during the transition to IFRS?

- Is the audit committee receiving regular reports on progress from the project implementation team?
- Has the audit committee considered the overall effectiveness of the company's implementation plan?
- Has the audit committee reviewed other matters that may affect the financial statements?
- When the audit committee reviews draft IFRS financial statements, will it consider whether the disclosures are appropriate in the light of the accounting policies chosen?
- Is the audit committee alert to the risk of the transition to IFRS being taken as an opportunity to deliberately misstate financial reports?
- Is the audit committee satisfied that the effect of the changes on transition to IFRS is being effectively communicated to external stakeholders?

39.6   AUDITORS

Auditors need to liaise regularly with their clients throughout the IFRS transition period to monitor progress being made against the timetable and to assess the quality of their clients' process and the judgements being made by management and audit committees. Where they believe the process is not adequate, or that there are failings in the judgements made, they should ensure that these are brought to the attention of management as soon as possible to limit the potential effects on the reporting timetable or audit report.

Bulletin 2005/3 provides guidance for auditors where IFRSs are being applied for the first time. The main areas are detailed below.

39.6.1   Quality control

ISQC 1 requires firms to have sufficient personnel with the capabilities, competence and commitment to ethical principles to enable them to issue appropriate reports. Therefore audit staff must have good knowledge and understanding of IFRSs and in the year of transition sufficient information to audit the reconciliations between UK GAAP and IFRSs.

ISA (UK and Ireland) 220 requires auditors to consult with specialists in relation to difficult or complex matters. The need for such consultations may be increased as transition to IFRSs take place and differences of opinion may be more common.

39.6.2   Ethical standards

Where auditors are asked to assist directors with their preparations for the introduction of IFRSs, care should be taken to ensure that auditors' independence and objectivity are not impaired. *Ethical Standard 5* prohibits accounting services being provided to listed audit clients except in exceptional circumstances. Valuation services are also prohibited where the valuation involves a significant amount of subjective judgement and is material to the financial statements.

39.6.3 *Planning*

Auditors should consider the implications of transition to IFRS when planning the audit. In particular they should:

- discuss with management the nature and timing of their involvement with the transition process, including any assistance or reporting required;
- determine what information and evidence will be needed to allow them to report on the financial statements prepared under IFRS and inform management of these requirements;
- ascertain the impact of the introduction of IFRS will have on the key systems which generate accounting information;
- consider whether the transition to IFRSs has impacted the benchmark upon which materiality has been assessed. This will give rise to a potential need to adjust the recording of uncorrected misstatements of prior periods;
- consider the audit of comparatives; and
- consider whether unadjusted audit differences under UK GAAP will affect opening balances and comparatives for the first period under IFRS.

Auditors should also be aware when planning their audits, that the wholesale change of accounting policies is likely to lead to increased risk, due in part to errors of understanding and limited practical experience but also because such changes may allow management to distort reported results by concealing losses behind new accounting policies or within new accounting systems and controls. Auditors should discuss these with management and determine management's views on any increased risk of error, using the entity's impact analysis and detailed plans for the implementation of IFRSs to aid identification of risks of misstatement in the financial statements.

In a group situation they should also ensure that accounting and disclosure choices offered by IFRS are being consistently applied in respect of each subsidiary.

39.6.4 *Engagement letters*

Auditors should clarify that the directors are responsible for considering and implementing the changes required for the introduction of IFRS, and the responsibility section of the engagement letter should make this clear. An example is given in **Table 3**.

TABLE 3: Example engagement letter paragraph

Responsibility for the implementation of International Financial Reporting Standards (IFRSs)
We are not responsible for ensuring that the company is prepared for the introduction of IFRSs, and this will only be considered in so far as it affects our audit responsibilities under statute and Auditing Standards.

As directors you are responsible for:

- analysing the impact of the introduction of IFRSs on the business;
- developing plans to mitigate the effects identified by this analysis;
- assessing any impact of the introduction of IFRSs on the appropriateness of adopting the going concern basis in preparing the financial statements (and preparation of relevant disclosures); and
- the preparation of financial statements as required under IFRSs, including comparative figures, and the full disclosures needed to give a true and fair view which will include reconciliations between the UK GAAP and IFRS figures.

39.6.5   Fraud and aggressive earnings management

Although fraud remains a possibility, transition to IFRS will afford increased opportunities for the manipulation of financial statements. Auditors should be particularly vigilant in relation to:

- restatement of the opening balances;
- increased pressure on management to deliver results;
- some aspects of IFRS which introduce more choices; and
- increased use of fair values.

In the year of transition to IFRSs the audit team discussion about fraud required by ISA (UK and Ireland) 240 should encompass the increased risk of fraud arising from transition.

39.6.6   Law and regulation

For each client, auditors must first ensure that the client has correctly assessed whether or not they are required to prepare their financial statements under IFRSs. At a time of such significant change the risk of non-compliance with laws and regulation is increased, and audit procedures should be planned to take account of this increased risk.

For entities in the financial sector, the transition to IFRSs may impact the requirement to maintain a certain level of regulatory capital. Auditors should consider whether this in turn affects going concern and whether a requirement to report to a regulator arises.

39.6.7 *Materiality*

The application of IFRSs may impact the basis on which materiality has been assessed, e.g. profit before tax and auditors should consider whether continuing use of the same basis is suitable. Where materiality was previously based on a value calculated under UK GAAP and the value has changed, i.e. for comparatives reworked under IFRS.

39.6.8 *Audit evidence*

Auditors will need to determine whether their audit work programmes require amendment for the IFRS environment. The transition to IFRS may require auditors to place more reliance on the work of experts in areas such as valuation of employee share options and non-traded financial instruments. Involvement of experts should be planned sufficiently in advance, and auditors should follow the requirements of ISA (UK and Ireland) 620, *Using the work of an expert*, in assessing and documenting the adequacy of the work of the expert (see **Chapter 38**).

In addition co-operation between principal and other auditors will be important in the year of transition to IFRSs, particularly where some group companies have not changed to IFRS. Principal auditors will need to clearly instruct the other auditors about the need to perform additional procedures as necessary.

39.6.9 *Analytical procedures*

Changes to IFRSs will mean that comparative data used for analytical review may be limited. Both historical data for that company or industry data available from third parties will be limited and there may be some requirement to reconstruct historical data as if IFRSs had been used at that time. This may not be possible or cost-effective, and auditors should be aware that analytical procedures may be less effective than in prior periods. Care should be taken to ensure that input data is relevant and internally consistent.

39.6.10 *Accounting estimates*

Where IFRSs require estimates to made that were not required under UK GAAP, the lack of track record and management experience in making such estimates will lead to greater risk of misstatements. Additional procedures may be required to audit these estimates. Particular care should be taken that management do not use hindsight when calculating estimates for comparative information as this will effectively be restating those estimates.

39.6.11   Fair values

IFRSs require certain assets and liabilities to be recognised at fair value rather than historical cost and this may be problematic as techniques will have to be determined and implemented for the first time. In addition, where entities elect to use fair value at transition as deemed cost, these amounts will not have been previously audited.

39.6.12   Opening balances

The Bulletin states that it is unlikely to be possible to audit the first financial statements under IFRSs without performing procedures on the opening IFRS balance sheet and then rolling these forward to the comparative figures and ultimately the first period IFRS reporting figures themselves. IFRS 1 requires first time adopters to prepare an opening balance sheet under IFRS at the date of transition, which is the beginning of the earliest period for which an entity presents full comparative information under IFRSs. Therefore for a 31 December year end applying IFRSs for the first time at the end of 2007, this will be as at 1 January 2006, the opening day of the comparative period.

The opening balance sheets for 2006 and 2007 should be prepared using IFRSs which are in force at the reporting date, subject to a number of exceptions set out in IFRS 1. These exceptions should be disclosed in the financial statements and auditors should ensure that the exceptions disclosed and those applied are the same. Although these figures must be disclosed they do not fall within the scope of the auditors' report, nor does the auditors' report make direct reference to the comparative figures. Auditors do have specific responsibilities relating to opening balances to the extent that they affect and determine current period figures in the financial statements only.

Auditors must also ensure that the reconciling items between UK GAAP and IFRSs balance sheets do not include errors and revisions of estimates in past results which should be accounted for as prior year adjustments.

39.6.13   Management representations

In the year of transition to IFRS representations are likely to confirm that the directors have obtained all necessary information from subsidiaries that are not IFRS companies to enable adjustments to be made to the financial statements for the purposes of consolidation into the group accounts.

39.6.14   Related party transactions

Auditors must be aware of the differences in required disclosure between the UK and IFRS standards in this area and complete their assessment of those disclosures accordingly.

39.6.15   Overall review of financial statements

Auditors are required by SAS 470 (of which there is no ISA (UK and Ireland) equivalent) to consider the effect of the aggregate uncorrected errors in both the current audit and that of the preceding period on the financial statements. The decision to leave errors uncorrected in the prior period will have been based on an assessment of materiality in the context of UK GAAP. Following transition, this assessment must be based on IFRS figures, and prior period unadjusted differences may now require restatement.

39.6.16   Going concern

Debt is sometimes subject to covenants based on values in the financial statements, such as the amount of reserves or another net asset value, and the introduction of IFRS may mean that these values change significantly. Auditors should be aware of the possibility of covenants being breached, and warn their clients that they may need to renegotiate covenants or obtain an approval for an increase in the company's borrowing powers from the shareholders prior to the introduction of IFRSs. Capital requirements for regulated entities may be similarly affected. Any impact on going concern should also be considered.

Auditors should be mindful of the fact that the requirements of IAS 1 relating to going concern are similar, but not identical for those in FRS 18 in respect of the period to be considered by directors and the disclosure requirements.

39.6.17   Audit reports

IAS 1 requires management to prepare financial statements that 'present fairly' the financial position, performance and cash flows of the company. Under the Companies Act, the term 'true and fair' remains. An amendment to the Companies Act clarifies that these terms should be read as having the same meaning.

Where, in the period leading up to transition, companies disclose details of the extent of their financial statements' compliance with IFRSs in the notes to the accounts, these will be subject to audit. Auditors will consider whether the disclosures are misleading and the effect on their audit report.

Following transition, group accounts for listed companies will be prepared under IFRS, but the parent company financial statements may still be prepared under UK GAAP. In such circumstances, because the financial statements are not comparable, both the financial statements and their respective audit reports will be included in the annual report.

39.6.18   Communication with management

Auditors should communicate with management throughout the transition process in accordance with ISA (UK and Ireland) 260, *Communication of audit matters to those charged with governance*. Auditors' appraisal of the company's IFRS readiness should include emphasis of those issues which are likely to affect the audit of the first financial statements under IFRS.

39.6.19   Interim financial information

As set out in **Chapter 15**, an entity should prepare its interim figures based on the accounting policies used in the last published annual accounts, except where they are to be changed in the subsequent annual financial statements. In such a situation the new accounting policies should be used. Therefore where listed companies are adopting IFRSs, their interim financial information must also be prepared using these standards. In addition the interim financial information must contain enough detail to enable a comparison to be made with the corresponding period for the preceding financial year, meaning comparatives must be restated.

Under UK GAAP, the ASB's Statement *Interim Reports* is persuasive rather than mandatory. Under IFRSs there are specific requirements governing the content and presentation of interim reports. This may lead to significant changes for some companies.

Much of the guidance above relating to the audit of annual financial statements is relevant to the review of interim financial information.

39.7   CLIENT SERVICE AND OTHER WORK FOR CLIENTS

There are many areas where auditors may assist their clients through the transition to IFRS and auditors may be asked by management to give assistance with the transition process as a separate engagement to the audit. Such assistance may include:

- IFRS training for client staff;
- commenting on areas where changes in accounting policy or disclosure are likely;
- assisting with preliminary diagnosis of the impact on financial reporting and accounting systems;
- reviewing accounting issue papers prepared by the client;
- providing technical guidance on IFRS standards and advising on the interpretation of IFRS;
- reviewing and discussing transition project scope and governance, including roles and responsibilities; and
- reviewing early draft IFRS financial statements.

Auditors must take care not to compromise their independence and objectivity when performing such work. They must ensure that the work they perform will not form part of the evidence on which their audit report will rely, and that the final decision on the appropriateness of accounting policies is made by the directors.

Auditors may also be asked to give early assurance on the company's state of readiness or on IFRS material that is being produced before the first set of IFRS financial statements. This may include requests for public reports to be made by the auditor. These areas may include:

- confirmation of appropriateness of accounting policies and interpretation of IFRS;
- confirmation of appropriateness of additional disclosure in the comparative financial statements relating to IFRS transition; and
- audit or review of the transition balance sheet, full year or interim comparative IFRS information.

In all these cases auditors should consider whether the request can be fulfilled through the terms of the current statutory audit engagement, or whether the work will require a separate review, assurance or agreed upon procedures engagement. Where such requests are received the list of issues in **Table 4** should be considered.

TABLE 4: Considerations for auditors requested to provide early assurance on IFRS financial statements

- Have you and your audit staff received sufficient IFRS training and do you have an adequate knowledge base to perform IFRS assignments?
- Have you satisfied yourself that your independence and integrity will not be compromised by performing this work?
- Have you agreed the timing of your involvement with your client's IFRS project with management?
- Have you considered the type of engagement that is appropriate depending on the involvement that the client has requested?
- Have you agreed the terms of the engagement and the form of any early reporting with management?
- Have you communicated your information needs to the company?
- Have you considered the implication of the IFRS transition for the preparation of the OFR?
- Have you considered how best to perform the required work when interpretations of IFRS continue to be issued prior to the company's first IFRS reporting date?
- Have you considered whether the company has mechanisms in place to prevent or detect fraud particularly in the following areas: restatement of comparative data, the choices made on accounting treatments and the use of fair value?

- Have you considered whether the base data from which the IFRS data has been prepared can be relied upon, or needs to be audited?
- Have you considered that the absence of comparative data will limit the effectiveness of analytical review?
- Do your working papers record properly and accurately your judgements and conclusions?
- Have you considered whether you need additional management representations on the IFRS financial statements, especially where management assumptions are key to valuations of assets and liabilities?
- Have you considered any concerns you may have on the timeliness and quality of the transition process and the potential consequences to the company? In particular, are you satisfied that your client's conversion project is capable of complete and accurate quantification of GAAP differences?
- Do you have a communication plan to enable you to discuss issues with the board, audit committee and management?

39.8   INTERNATIONAL GUIDANCE

The International Audit and Assurance Standards Board (IAASB) also published guidance for auditors on the first-time adoption of IFRS. This guidance is in the format of a number of questions and answers based on a single general scenario, and which should be referred to for a useful summary of some of the major issues affecting auditors.

40 REPORTING IN ACCORDANCE WITH GLOBAL INVESTMENT PERFORMANCE STANDARDS (GIPS)

40.1 GLOBAL INVESTMENT PERFORMANCE STANDARDS (GIPS)

Global Investment Performance Standards (GIPS) are voluntary ethical standards, which aim to ensure fair representation and full disclosure of an investment firm's performance history. GIPS were drafted by a committee of investment professionals representing countries throughout the world. Although this is a voluntary code, the acceptance of the GIPS as the global standard is expected to be widespread, and it has become increasingly common for investment managers to receive requests to provide information on historic performance results to prospective clients based on the standards set down in the GIPS, or an equivalent local standard.

40.2 REPORTING IN ACCORDANCE WITH GIPS

The Standards recommend that a firm's claim to be calculating and presenting performance history in compliance with GIPS is 'verified'. The Audit Faculty of the ICAEW have issued Technical Release Audit 1/00 *Guidance for Reporting in Accordance with Global Investment Performance Standards* to assist reporting accountants who are requested to report in accordance with the GIPS framework.

The Technical Release does not make reference to the term 'verification' since it is the Institute's view that the term implies a degree of checking and accuracy which is not consistent with the work to be performed as set out in the GIPS. The primary purpose of the work is to ensure that a firm has adhered to the standards set out in the GIPS. The suggested procedures attempt to strike a balance between ensuring the quality, accuracy and relevance of any performance statement and the cost to the investment firm of commissioning the independent review.

Section III of the GIPS set out the scope and purpose of the review and the procedures required (see **40.4**).

A report will be issued for the whole firm, as a GIPS review cannot be completed for a single composite. A composite is an aggregation of a number of portfolios into a single group that represents a particular investment objective or strategy.

The Technical Release is not mandatory when an accountant is asked to perform a review of a report of compliance, but if alternative procedures and reports are used, no reference should be made to the Technical Release in any report.

40.3   ENGAGEMENT LETTERS

To ensure that there is clear understanding of the scope and purpose of the engagement, the terms of the accountants' engagement should be agreed in writing. The engagement letter should include:

- the respective responsibilities of the investment management firm and the reporting accountants;
- the scope of the work which will be performed;
- the nature of the report;
- the agreed use of the report and the extent the report may be made available to the investment firm's existing and prospective clients;
- a reference to the likely need for client representations;
- an explanation of the limitations of the work to be performed; and
- limitations to the reporting accountants' liability.

The reporting accountant should exclude liability in respect of any loss or damage caused by the acts of the employees or directors of the investment firm. Liability to third parties or regulators should also be excluded, and reporting accountants would normally obtain a limitation in aggregate of any liability.

An example engagement letter is set out in **Table 1**.

TABLE 1: Engagement letter

The Directors
XYZ Asset Management

Dear Sirs

Following our recent meeting when you invited us to report on your policies over performance presentation and calculation of XYZ Asset Management ('the firm') for the period [date] to [date], we are writing to set out our proposed responsibilities, our understanding of the work to be performed, and the terms and conditions upon which we offer to perform such work.

Respective responsibilities of principals and reporting accountants
As the principals of XYZ Asset Management you are responsible for the design, implementation and maintenance of procedures that ensure that performance is reported in accordance with Global Investment Performance Standards (GIPS). You will describe the policies adopted in your business to ensure GIPS compliance in a report. It is our responsibility to form an independent opinion on whether these policies, insofar as they affect our opinion, were complied with in compiling composite reports for the period [date] to [date] and to report our opinion to you. This will include considering whether your statement appropriately reflects the extent to which processes and procedures designed to calculate and report in compliance with GIPS were followed during the period. Because reporting qualified compliance with GIPS is not envisaged, if there are material deficiencies in compliance or significant exceptions we will not issue an opinion. Instead we will draw these matters to your attention.

Scope of work
The work we shall perform will be conducted in accordance with the framework set out in the guidance issued by the Audit Faculty of the Institute of Chartered Accountants in England and Wales (Technical Release AUDIT 1/ 00) and included in Section III of GIPS. Our work will include obtaining an understanding of the policies and procedures in operation, enquiry of management, review of documents supplied to us and tests of certain specific procedures designed to ensure compliance with GIPS. Our work will be planned in advance. [In developing our plan we shall liaise with your Internal Audit Department to ensure that our work is properly coordinated with theirs.]

We shall not be responsible for a review of the compliance with policies beyond the period reported upon or for the identification of changes not disclosed by management.

Use of report
Our report will be addressed to you as principals of the company although we understand that you may wish to make the report available to existing or prospective clients using the reporting company's services, and we consent to the report being provided to them at their request for their information only. However, we will not accept any liability/responsibility to those parties or to any other party to whom this report is shown or into whose hands it may come.

You may not provide our report or copies thereof to any other third party. You agree to indemnify us against any liabilities, losses, expenses or other costs that we reasonably incur in connection with any claims against us by any such existing or prospective clients or any other third party. You agree not to use our report or references to it in material disseminated to the general public without our express written permission. In any cases where marketing literature is prepared which will refer either to us or to our report, you will seek our consent to those references in advance and we reserve the right to refuse.

Management representations
We may seek written representations from management in relation to matters for which independent corroboration is not available. We will also seek confirmation from you that any significant matters of which we should be aware have been brought to our attention.

Complaints procedure
[*Include relevant complaints procedures*]

Limitations of work
Procedures designed to address specified assertions are subject to inherent limitations and, accordingly, errors or irregularities may occur and not be detected. Such procedures cannot guarantee protection against fraudulent collusion especially on the part of those holding positions of authority or trust. Furthermore, our opinion will be based on historical information and the projection of any information or conclusions, contained in our opinion, to any future periods is subject to the risk that changes in procedures or circumstances may alter their validity.

Our work on the underlying accounting systems used to produce valuation information for performance calculation purposes will be restricted to a review of the design of processes and procedures to meet the input data requirements of GIPS and no detailed testing of those processes and procedures will be undertaken. Consequently, our work will not include tests of transactions in respect of any particular customer or composite. We will not carry out any independent examination work nor express an opinion on either the net asset value or the change in net asset value of any individual portfolio or composite.

Fees
Our fees will be based on the degree of skill involved, the experience of staff engaged and the time necessarily occupied on the work.

Limitation of liability
We accept no duty of care and deny any liability to anyone other than the firm. We will not be liable for any loss or damage caused by or arising from any fraudulent acts, fraudulent omissions, misrepresentations or wilful default on the part of the firm, its principals, employees or agents.

Any liability of our firm, its partners and staff from actions found against us to pay damages for losses arising as a direct result of breach of contract or negligence on our part in respect of services provided in connection with or arising out of the engagement set out in this letter (or any variation or addition thereto), whether in contract, negligence or otherwise shall in no circumstances exceed £x in aggregate: such amount including all legal and other costs which we may incur in defending any actions against us.

Applicable law
This engagement letter shall be governed by, and construed in accordance with, English law. The Courts of England shall have exclusive jurisdiction in relation to any claim, dispute or difference concerning the engagement letter and any matter arising from it. Each party irrevocably waives any right it may have to object to an action being brought in the Courts, to claim that the action has been brought in an inconvenient forum, or to claim that those Courts do not have jurisdiction.

Acknowledgement and acceptance
We shall be obliged if you will acknowledge receipt and your acceptance of this letter by [date].

Yours faithfully
Reporting Accountant

40.4   THE REPORTING ACCOUNTANTS' REVIEW

Guidance on the work to be undertaken by reporting accountants is included in GIPS section III, which is reproduced in **Table 2**. Professional judgement will be required to determine the nature, timing and extent of tests to be carried out. The reporting accountant may wish to place reliance on the work of the investment firm's own internal audit department or on the work of a local or previous reviewer, and the reporting accountant should consider the level of reliance that can be placed on evidence provided by such sources.

The level of work to be performed on the underlying accounting systems of the investment manager is restricted by GIPS to obtaining an understanding of the methods and policies used to record portfolio valuation information for performance calculation purposes. Because the underlying accounting records are not expected to be tested, let alone audited, the reporting accountant's opinion must explain the limitations of the review in this regard.

Therefore, it is likely that in the first year that GIPS are implemented the investment manager will rework their historical data to ensure that it conforms with the GIPS requirements. The principals' statement must make reference to this fact, and the accountants' report should state that it is corrected information, not information available for the first time, with reporting accountants ensuring that the status of the information is fully disclosed by the principals.

The reporting accountants will normally obtain written representations from the principals of the investment manager. Matters likely to be covered by the representation letter include:

- that any fraudulent or illegal acts, irregularities or uncorrected errors attributable to the client or its employees have been disclosed to the reporting accountants; and
- that the reporting accountants have been informed of all known instances of non-compliance with the policies in place.

TABLE 2: 'Verification' procedures outlined by GIPS

Pre-verification procedures
Knowledge of the firm: obtain samples of the firm's investment performance reports, and other available information regarding the firm, to ensure appropriate knowledge of the firm.

Knowledge of GIPS: understand the requirements and recommendations of GIPS, including any updates, reports or clarification of GIPS published by the Investment Performance Council, the body responsible for oversight of GIPS.

Knowledge of the performance standards: be knowledgeable of country-specific performance standards, laws and regulations applicable to the firm, and determine any differences between GIPS and the country-specific standards, laws and regulations.

Knowledge of firm policies: determine the firm's assumptions and policies for establishing and maintaining compliance with all applicable requirements of GIPS. As a minimum, reviewers must determine the following policies and procedures of the firm:

- investment discretion. The reviewer must receive in writing the firm's definition of investment discretion and the firm's guidelines for determining whether accounts are fully discretionary;
- definition of composites according to investment strategy. The reviewer must obtain the firm's list of composite definitions with written criteria for including accounts in each composite;
- timing of inclusion of new accounts in the composites;
- timing of exclusion of closed accounts in the composites;
- accrual of interest and dividend income;
- market valuation of investment securities;
- method for computing time-weighted portfolio return;
- assumptions on the timing of capital inflows/outflows;
- method for computing composite returns;
- presentation of composite returns;
- timing of implied taxes due on income and realised capital gains for reporting performance on an after tax basis;
- use of securities/countries not included in a composite's benchmark;
- use of leverage and other derivatives; and

- any other policies and procedures relevant to performance presentation.

Knowledge of valuation basis for performance calculations: understand the methods and policies used to record valuation information for performance calculation purposes. In particular, reviewers must determine that:

- the firm's policy on classifying fund flows (e.g., injections, disbursements, dividends, interest, fees, taxes, etc.) is consistent with the desired results and will give rise to accurate returns;
- the firm's accounting treatment of income, interest and dividend receipts is consistent with cash account and cash accruals definitions;
- the firm's treatment of taxes, tax reclaims and tax accruals is correct and the manner used is consistent with the desired method (i.e., gross- or net-of-tax return);
- the firm's policies on recognising purchases, sales and the opening and closing of other positions are internally consistent and will produce accurate results; and
- the firm's accounting for investment and derivatives is consistent with GIPS.

Verification procedures
Definition of the firm: determine that the firm is, and has been, appropriately defined.

Composite construction: ensure that

- the firm has defined and maintained composites according to reasonable guidelines in compliance with GIPS;
- all of the firm's actual discretionary fee-paying portfolios are included in a composite;
- the manager's definition of discretion has been consistently applied over time;
- at all times, all accounts are included in their respective composites and no accounts that belong in a particular composite have been excluded;
- composite benchmarks are consistent with composite definitions and have been consistently applied over time;
- the firm's guidelines for creating and maintaining composites have been consistently applied; and
- the firm's list of composites is complete.

Non-discretionary accounts: obtain a listing of all firm portfolios and determine on a sampling basis whether the manager's classification of the account as discretionary or non-discretionary is appropriate, by referring to the account agreement and the manager's written guidelines for determining investment discretion.

Sample account selection: obtain a listing of open and closed accounts for all composites for the years under examination. Reviewers may check compliance with GIPS using a sample of a firm's accounts. Reviewers should consider the following criteria when selecting the sample accounts for examination:

- number of composites at the firm;

- number of portfolios in each composite;
- nature of the composite;
- total assets under management;
- internal control structure at the firm (systems of checks and balances in place);
- number of years under examination; and
- computer applications, software used in the construction and maintenance of the composites, the use of external performance measurers and the calculation of performance results.

Account review: for selected accounts, determine

- whether the timing of the initial inclusion in the composite is in accordance with the policies of the firm;
- whether the timing of exclusion from the composite is in accordance with the policies of the firm for closed accounts;
- whether the objectives set forth in the account agreement are consistent with the manager's composite definition as indicated by the account agreement, portfolio summary and composite definition;
- the existence of the accounts by tracing selected accounts from account agreements to the composites;
- that all portfolios sharing the same guidelines are included in the same composite; and
- that shifts from one composite to another are consistent with the guidelines set forth by the specific account agreement or with documented guidelines of the firm's clients.

Performance measurement calculation: determine whether the firm has computed performance in accordance with the policies and assumptions adopted by the firm and disclosed in its presentations. In doing so, reviewers should

- recalculate rates of return for a sample of accounts in the firm using an acceptable return formula as prescribed by GIPS (i.e., time-weighted rate of return); and
- take a reasonable sample of composite calculations to assure themselves of the accuracy of the asset weighting of returns, the geometric linking of returns to produce annual rates of return and the calculation of the dispersion of individual returns around the aggregate composite return.

Disclosures: review a sample of composite presentations to ensure that the presentations include the information and disclosures required by GIPS.

Maintenance of records: maintain sufficient information to support the review report. The reviewer must obtain a representation letter from the client firm confirming major policies and any other specific representations made to the verifier during the examination.

40.5 THE REPORTING PACKAGE

The reporting package should comprise a report by the investment management firm concerning the policies they are claiming to comply with, and a report by the reporting accountants setting out the scope of their work and their opinion.

40.5.1 Report by the investment management firm

The report by the principals of the investment management firm should include:

- a statement of responsibility;
- representation that the whole firm has complied with GIPS for the whole period;
- the firm's policies as required by GIPS;
- details of significant changes to the policies during the period; and
- a statement that the procedures supporting the policies have been reviewed, and the extent to which the policies and procedures have been followed during the period.

A pro forma for the principals' report is given in **Table 3**.

TABLE 3: Principals' report

Report by the principals of XYZ Asset Management

Responsibilities of the principals

As the principals of XYZ Asset Management we are responsible for:

- the identification of policies relating to the presentation and calculation of investment performance in order to comply with the Global Investment Performance Standards (GIPS);
- the design, implementation and maintenance of procedures to provide reasonable assurance on an ongoing basis that the policies are followed.

We have reviewed the procedures [in operation during the period/applied retrospectively] to support the following policies and disclosures.

XYZ Asset Management Firm-wide GIPS assertions
XYZ Asset Management ('the firm') has complied [retrospectively] with the requirements of the Global Investment Performance Standards (GIPS) on a firm-wide basis in its application of processes and procedures to calculate and present composite reports and in compiling the performance results of each to the firm's composites for the periods from [date] to [date]. For the purpose of complying with GIPS, the firm has been defined as XYZ Asset Management. In particular, the following policies required by GIPS have been complied with in compiling composite reports for the period [date] to [date].

All of the firm's actual, discretionary, fee-paying portfolios are included in appropriate composites defined according to the investment strategy or investment objective. The firm's list and description of composites is available on request. The list of composites represents all of the composites of the firm for the period from [date] to [date].

The firm's policies for defining, creating and maintaining composites have been consistently applied.

Composites include new portfolios at the start of the next performance measurement period after the portfolio comes under management [or define alternative basis].

Composites exclude terminated portfolios after the last full performance period the portfolios were under management, but composites continue to include terminated portfolios for all periods prior to termination.

Accounting systems are designed to ensure input data requirements of GIPS have been complied with when computing portfolio returns.

Portfolio returns are calculated according to time-weighted total return methodology, with a minimum of [quarterly] valuation and accrual of income [for fixed income securities].

Portfolio returns within the composites are weighted using [beginning of period market values].

Composite returns for the required period are presented with all required disclosures.

.... (Principal's Signature)

40.5.2   Report by the reporting accountants

The reporting accountants' report should be addressed to the principals of the investment management firm, not the existing or prospective clients of that firm.

The reporting accountants' report should contain statements that:

- the report is intended for the use of the principals (the reporting accountant may wish to state that the report may be made available to third parties but without giving rise to any liability or duty to them);
- detail the scope of the report and the respective responsibilities of the principals and reporting accountants;
- the work performed is substantially less in scope than that of an audit and therefore no independent examination has taken place or any opinion expressed on the net asset values or change in net asset values of any individual portfolios or composites;

- no detailed testing of the processes and procedures relating to input data requirements has been performed, and work may have been limited to a review of the design of those processes and procedures;
- individual composite reports have not been subject to a detailed examination, and accordingly no opinion is expressed on them; and
- the report refers to a certain period, and the validity of the conclusions included may not be appropriate to future periods.

An example report is given in **Table 4**.

TABLE 4: Reporting accountants' report

Report by the independent reporting accountants to the principals of XYZ Asset Management

Use of this report
This report is intended solely for the use of the principals of XYZ Asset Management ('the firm') and for the information of its existing and prospective clients, without giving rise to any liability or duty on our part to such clients. The attention of existing and prospective clients of the firm is drawn to the engagement letter dated [date], which includes provisions relating to the scope of our responsibilities and the limitation of our liability, a copy of which is attached.

[*include more detail here on engagement terms if the engagement letter is not attached.*]

Scope
This report covers solely the application of the Global Investment Performance Standards (GIPS) by the firm, defined in your report, attached as [Appendix X] to this report. GIPS applies to the investment performance presentation and calculations operations carried out by the firm and does not extend to any other business or operation of XYZ Asset Management.

Our work was based upon obtaining an understanding of the policies and procedures applied by management in compiling performance reports for the period [date] to [date], assessment of whether such policies and procedures were appropriate to achieve compliance with GIPS, enquiry of management, review of documents supplied to us, and testing of such policies and procedures to confirm their operation. [Certain processes and procedures, as explained in the principals' report, were not in operation throughout the composite return period, but were applied retrospectively in order to bring the firm into compliance with GIPS in reporting performance for that return period.]

Individual composite presentations and returns calculations have not been subject to a detailed examination and accordingly we do not express an opinion on individual composite reports, including any such reports which may become attached to this report.

Our work on the underlying accounting system used to produce valuation

---

information for performance calculation purposes was restricted to a review of the design of processes and procedures to meet the input data requirements of GIPS and no detailed testing of those processes and procedures was undertaken. Our work did not include tests of transactions in respect of any particular customer or composite and we have not carried out any independent examination of, and do not express an opinion on the net asset value or the change in net asset value of, any individual portfolio or composite.

Respective responsibilities of principals and the reporting accountant
Your responsibilities as principals are set out in the attached engagement letter and in your report attached hereto. The policies described in your report are designed to achieve compliance with GIPS and are your responsibility as principals of XYZ Asset Management. It is our responsibility to form an independent opinion, based on work we have carried out, on whether these policies are designed to calculate and present performance reports in compliance with GIPS, and to ensure the composite construction requirements of GIPS have been complied with in compiling composite reports for the reporting period [date] to [date], and to report our opinion to you.
[*include principals' responsibilities here if not in principals' report.*]

Basis of opinion
Our review was conducted in accordance with the framework for reporting set out in the guidance issued by the Audit Faculty of the Institute of Chartered Accountants in England and Wales, Technical Release AUDIT 1/00, and procedures set out in Section III of GIPS, dated April 1999.

Procedures designed to address specific policies are subject to inherent limitations and, accordingly, errors or irregularities may occur and not be detected. Such procedures cannot guarantee protection against fraudulent collusion or misrepresentation especially on the part of those holding positions of authority or trust. Furthermore, this opinion is based on historical information and the projection of any information or conclusions to any future periods would be inappropriate.

Opinion
Based on the above, in our opinion:

- in compiling composite reports for the period from [date] to [date] the firm has complied, in all material respects, with all composite construction requirements of GIPS on a firm-wide basis;
- in compiling composite reports for the period [date] to [date] the firm's processes and procedures were designed to calculate and present composite reports in compliance with GIPS in conformity with policies set out by the principals in their report attached hereto.

Chartered Accountants   Address
Date

40.5.3 Material weaknesses

An investment management firm either complies with or does not comply with GIPS, and thus 'except for' opinions will be meaningless. If any material deficiencies are found, a reporting accountant will refuse to give any report.

However, an investment manager may have non-material deficiencies which, in the opinion of the reporting accountant, are not significant enough to render compliance invalid and where the issuing of an unmodified report will be appropriate.

41 AUDITING IN AN E-COMMERCE ENVIRONMENT

41.1 INTRODUCTION

E-commerce (electronic commerce) has seen unprecedented growth in the past couple of years, and few businesses have been left untouched by the advent of the Internet and the opportunities and risks resulting from the advance of the World Wide Web. E-commerce is the buying and selling of goods and services and the transfer of funds through digital communications. It also includes inter-company and intra-company functions, such as marketing, finance, manufacturing, selling and negotiating that enable commerce and use electronic mail, Electronic Data Interchange (EDI), file transfer, fax, video conferencing or interaction with a remote computer.

Whether clients have set up exclusively to take advantage of e-commerce opportunities (the so-called 'dot.com' businesses), or have expanded into e-commerce from a more traditional market place base, the different operating environment associated with e-commerce will require auditors to consider different audit risks and approaches.

Guidance in this area comes from a limited number of sources. In September 2000, the Audit and Assurance Faculty of the ICAEW issued, jointly with the Faculty of Information Technology, a guidance paper entitled *Implications of e-commerce for Auditors and Business Advisors*. This guidance paper sets out the main issues that an auditor or external adviser faces, and highlights the risks to which a business involved in e-commerce is exposed and the issues auditors may face, together with practical guidance on dealing with them.

In 2001 the APB issued Bulletin 2001/3, *E-business: Identifying financial statement risks* to provide additional guidance for auditors.

41.2 INVOLVEMENT IN E-COMMERCE

Businesses may be split between those who use e-commerce as an extension to their existing business, such as a hotel which takes reservations on-line, and those which are dependent entirely on e-commerce for their survival, such as a software vendor that sells only by clients downloading from its website. Auditors must be aware of this distinction, as entities of each type will have both different business models and audit risks resulting from e-commerce.

41.3 KNOWLEDGE OF THE BUSINESS

As with all entity types, auditors of businesses involved in or using e-commerce need to have sufficient knowledge of both the entity and its industry to enable them to understand the interaction of the events, transactions and practices with the financial statements and their effects on the audit. The auditors' knowledge of the industry in which their client is involved (e.g., selling books, travel and tourism or computer software) will help them to assess the impact of e-commerce on the business and also on their audit risk.

The growth of e-commerce may, however, have a significant impact on an entity's traditional business environment. To assess the impact of these changes auditors require appropriate IT skills and knowledge of the Internet. Understanding the business now involves not only understanding the business and the entity's business strategy, but also:

- understanding the e-commerce strategy and business model;
- understanding the technology; and
- assessing the IT skills and IT knowledge of its personnel.

The impact of e-commerce on an entity's business depends on the extent of its use. At the most basic level an entity may use its website as a static marketing tool with no connection to its internal systems. A more sophisticated e-commerce business may use its site to allow customers access to product information, place orders and make payments electronically. The most sophisticated user may provide an extranet to allow external parties to have direct selective and controlled access to its own systems through secure Internet pathways.

The types of enquiries an auditor may make of an entity which uses e-commerce together with the associated potential risks are set out in **Table 1**.

TABLE 1: Enquiries to be made of an e-commerce client to discover risk

Question	Potential risk
Is there a sufficient level of technical skill available, either within the entity or engaged by management (i.e., subcontractors)?	Lack of technical skill may mean that the website and any links into the entity's system are not developed or maintained to be sufficiently robust to handle a high volume of transactions. This may lead to excessive system 'down time' and loss of sales.
Is e-commerce a new business for the entity, or does it impact on traditional business channels?	E-business may provide additional growth opportunities for the entity. For some entities, entry into e-commerce may be the only way to ensure the continuation of the business.
Have the cost implications of electronic trading been fully evaluated by management and is the use of e-commerce supported by a justifiable business case?	Management may not have fully evaluated the costs and benefits of e-commerce. High set up costs may be poorly invested and cash receipts may be delayed, with an impact on profitability and cash flow.
What is the nature of the e-commerce business model (given that there is no standard for e-commerce businesses and the Internet based model is likely to vary significantly from that of the related 'traditional' business)?	A poorly constructed or ill thought-out business model may lead to failure to properly identify likely costs and business risks. If risks are unidentified they cannot be effectively controlled by management.
Have security issues been addressed by management?	Failure to address security issues could lead to corruption of a website or linked systems. This is particularly relevant where transactions initiated by customers impact directly on the financial statements. This may also lead to loss of confidence and loss of sales.
Has the entity's integration of Web applications with accounting systems been addressed business-wide to avoid unnecessary complexity?	Overly complex or poorly integrated systems and controls are likely to be less effective in controlling security risks and may lead to accounting systems breakdowns.

Has management considered e-commerce implementation difficulties and their resolution, and have past problems been properly dealt with?	Poorly developed implementation plans may lead to unforeseen additional cost, delay and loss of orders. Management attitude to resolving problems in the past may indicate a control weakness.
Is there an appropriate structure to measure the performance of e-commerce activities?	Failure to incorporate different performance measures into management reporting may lead to an inability to track business, trading and cost trends and take steps to mitigate associated risks promptly.
Have any concerns been expressed by management over the number of customers connecting to the business via the Internet, for example insufficient numbers to achieve the anticipated efficiencies or the ability of the entity's technology to deal with unexpectedly high levels of demand?	Where insufficient business is being generated there may be a going concern risk. Where systems are unable to cope with high demand there may be a loss of sales and customer goodwill. If systems are unable to cope with high demand, controls may also be breached.
How does management ensure control is maintained over transaction processing carried out by a service organisation?	Depending on the nature of the e-commerce operations that are outsourced, risks may include those related to maintenance of accounting records, completeness of income, credit risk and understatement of liabilities.
How are the authenticity and integrity of trading partners verified?	Retail customers may not be who they claim to be and use stolen credit card details to order goods and services. This may create a credit risk as banks may force retailers that do not make adequate checks to pay the full cost of fraudulent transactions. There is also risk of repudiation of contract.
Are there appropriate systems in place to ensure that the level of goods returned are monitored and recorded?	There is typically a higher level of returns of items purchased remotely than in a traditional retail environment. There is a risk that revenue is incorrectly recognised where returns are not recorded correctly.
How have management ensured that electronic contracts are legally binding?	Failure to ensure that electronic contracts are legally binding introduces the risk of repudiation, which affects credit risk and the risk of goods being returned.

Another area to consider is the extent to which the entity's industry is currently affected by e-commerce. In assessing this, auditors must be aware that some industries' involvement in e-commerce will be relatively mature, such as computer software and hardware suppliers, but in other cases there may be little experience to date. In addition, an entity may be adversely affected by the use of e-commerce in its, or a related, industry. Part of assessing knowledge of the business involves discovering the effects of external factors on the industry on which it operates. E-commerce may have wide-ranging effects. For example, the client may act as an intermediary between producer and consumer, and may be made redundant by the use made of the Internet by the producer to sell its product.

41.4   E-FRAUD

E-fraud is not new, nor is it fundamentally different from other types of fraud. What distinguishes it is the speed in which the e-commerce environment changes, meaning that both the opportunities for fraud and the procedures required to intercept it must change as quickly.

Parties intent on fraud will seek out and exploit weak controls. Many e-businesses, faced with fast growth, may be exposed by control systems which have not expanded at a rate to match the growth of the business.

Other reasons why auditors should pay particular attention to the possibility of fraud during the planning and execution of their audit include:

- the geographical remoteness of their customers and/or suppliers, of whom they are less likely to have built up a full knowledge;
- the ease with which anyone dealing with the business can assume a false identity;
- the increase in dealing with contractors and third parties over whom the entity has little or no control; and
- the increase in electronic documentation making the usual identification techniques, such as manual signatures, redundant.

41.5 LAW AND REGULATIONS

41.5.1 Relevant regulations

Businesses involved in e-commerce need to be aware of a number of relevant laws and regulations. Some of the main legislation relevant to e-business is set out in **Table 2**. In some cases, a business must take positive action to ensure that it complies with the regulations to avoid prosecution.

As this is an area in which legislation and regulations change rapidly, auditors must be aware of amendments and additions in order to fulfil the requirements of ISA (UK and Ireland) 250 Section A *Consideration of law and regulations in an audit of financial statements*. Areas where changes are likely include:

- taxation;
- privacy;
- intellectual property;
- cryptography;
- digital signatures; and
- acceptable business practices.

In addition, the laws and regulations governing an e-commerce entity are further complicated by the easy ability of such businesses to trade in many jurisdictions without having a presence and to move locations to avoid legal requirements.

TABLE 2: Laws and regulations of importance to businesses involved in e-commerce

The Data Protection Act 1998
This Act makes it necessary for most businesses to notify the Data Protection Commissioner if personal data is being processed electronically, or in a structured manual system. A business is also expected to have strong controls in place. A number of specific guidelines relate to websites, in particular to the collection of personal data and the use of 'cookies' (bookmarks which remember details about a site visited).

Computer Misuse Act 1990
Makes unauthorised access to a computer (including hacking) a criminal offence.

Copyright Design and Patents Acts
In many circumstances this makes copying software outside the terms of the licence a criminal offence. Criminal action may also result in a civil claim for damages.

Electronic Communications Act 2000
Allows for the eventual removal of obstacles in other legislation to electronic publication, such as the need for manual records or documentation. For example, the Act has a provision for the legal recognition of electronic signatures.

Regulation of Investigatory Powers Act 2000 (RIP Act)
Gives security services such as the police and MI5 the right to examine Internet traffic from any source which poses a security threat. This is likely to have most impact on Internet Service Providers (ISPs).

Health and Safety (Display Screen Equipment) Regulations 1992
Employers have a number of responsibilities for the safety of users who 'habitually use VDU screens as a significant part of their normal work'. Penalties for non-compliance include improvement notices, prohibition, fines and imprisonment.

41.5.2 Commercial law

Auditors will need to be aware of the legal framework in which transactions are taking place. Where transactions occur, for example over the Web, between buyers and sellers in different countries, the law in one of the countries must govern the transaction. However, there may be a number of complicating factors in identifying the appropriate framework. These include whether the supplier is based in the country from which the goods are issued, or whether the entity's website is hosted in a different country to that in which the entity itself is registered. In addition, some countries are passing legislation that allows an aggrieved customer to apply the law of the land in which they themselves are domiciled.

What constitutes a valid contract will also vary from country to country. In some countries both parties must sign a written agreement before a valid contract is said to exist. In the United Kingdom some agreements are required to be signed on paper, such as consumer credit agreements, but most do not. In addition, the Electronic Communications Act 2000 recognises digital signatures in other circumstances. These are all factors of which auditors must be aware when planning and executing their audit procedures.

41.5.3 Taxation

The main area of concern is the identity of the jurisdictions where taxation is levied. The customer, the ISP, the website and the supplier may all be located in different countries. Different taxes may need to be applied to the goods being ordered. Auditors need an awareness of these taxes and their impact on the financial statements.

41.6   AUDIT RISK

41.6.1   Issues relating to e-commerce

As stated in **41.3** above, an entity's involvement in e-commerce and use of the Internet may be at various levels of sophistication. The degree of sophistication will have a corresponding impact on the assessment of audit risk. Common business risks arise in the following areas:

- the identity and nature of relationships with e-commerce trading partners;
- the integrity of transactions;
- electronic processing of transactions and electronic record keeping;
- system reliability;
- privacy issues;
- returns of goods and product warranties; and
- taxation and regulatory issues.

Auditors must determine how the entity has applied its control framework to cover these risks.

In addition, e-commerce businesses may not have the controls to mitigate some of these risks because they may have experienced rapid growth and do not have either the human or physical resources to develop proper controls. This is because there is a temptation for businesses to ignore these constraints and attempt to grow, without due attention to the systematic risks in an e-commerce environment. Management's view of acceptable risk levels is significant to the security, completeness and reliability of the financial information produced.

Section **41.2** sets out the difference between entities which make use of e-commerce and those where e-commerce is central to their business, the 'dot.com' entities. For these businesses, auditors should also consider risks arising from:

- the lack of a traditional asset base;
- the accounting treatment of costs incurred to establish an infrastructure and the ongoing investment in web technology;
- cash flow information and business plans based on subjective judgements without a proven basis; and
- market pressure to achieve expectations leading to inappropriate judgements, for example.

41.6.2   Assessing risk

The advent of e-commerce has required a shift in the assessment of audit risk and the way auditors plan their audit procedures to reduce that risk to an acceptable level. In particular, the assessment of controls may assume a far greater importance as it may not be possible to obtain sufficient assurance without placing reliance on them.

It is management's responsibility, as in other areas, to identify e-commerce business risks and address them through the implementation of appropriate security and internal control measures. If the risks are not ultimately mitigated by adequate control procedures, the auditors must assess the affect on their audit and ultimately whether the entity is auditable.

When assessing the adequacy of the control environment for a business using e-commerce, auditors must use their knowledge of the business. In general, the greater the level of reliance the entity places on e-commerce and the Internet, the stronger and more complex the control environment will need to be. For example, where an entity's website is only used to provide information about the entity, without third-party interactive access, security controls need to be less extensive than those where the website is used to collect transaction information and process transactions with customers.

A further area of risk arises where a client moves away from direct physical control over the corporate data, for example:

- a third party may perform some or all of the recording and processing of accounting data. This may be the ISP, an Application Service Provider (ASP) who provides on-line access to standard packages for which a metered charge is made, or a Value Added Network (VAN) which provides the platform for electronic data interchange (EDI) for entities with incompatible hardware or software;
- data may originate from different parts of the world, and may be subject to different levels of controls depending on its origin;
- receipts and payments may be automated via BACS and other electronic funds transfer (EFT) methods;
- documents such as orders and invoices may be automated, making controls, such as authentication controls, more difficult to implement.

Management must ensure that third parties have sufficient controls to ensure the integrity and validity of their processing and the information they supply. Auditors will consider management's assessment of third-party controls when deciding what audit work is necessary.

Auditors may need to seek extra assurances from third parties or from third-party reviewers or auditors. They need to take particular care when assessing authorisation controls over payments and authentication controls over orders received which ensure that only valid transactions are actioned.

41.6.3   Accounting risks

The new business practices of dot.com entities also give rise to new accounting issues. These may have an impact on the assessment of audit risk. Typical accounting issues to consider include:

- the treatment of costs incurred to set up and improve web pages;
- ongoing maintenance costs;
- timing and recognition of sales revenue; and
- recognition and treatment of unusual transactions such as those involving barter arrangements.

41.6.4   Assessing the control environment

As explained above, it is likely that auditors will seek to place an increasing level of reliance on the controls over systems including those exercised by third parties. Auditors' assessments of the control environment extend to both the electronic and physical environment.

In establishing which controls may be relied upon, auditors consider a number of areas, the main ones being:

- the entity's security measures; and
- system reliability and authentication of financial records.

Security measures
Sophisticated measures such the encryption of data will not be successful if they operate within a generally insecure IT environment. Auditors must therefore address whether the environment meets basic security requirements before evaluating more detailed security measures. Typically, in fast growing areas such as e-commerce, management is focused on developing ways of carrying out transactions rather than building in safeguards and controls.

There are three acknowledged components to security. These are:

Confidentiality – a commercial organisation has a legal duty to ensure that its information is secure. E-commerce has effectively opened up corporate data to the whole world, requiring a business to protect against breaches of confidentiality and ensure that confidential information is not published on the Internet.
Integrity – this means ensuring that data is accurate, authorised, kept secure and not duplicated. This is likely to have a direct impact on financial data, as electronic and automatic handling of data may mean an increased risk of duplicate entries or incorrect order amounts not being noticed and corrected.
Dependence – the need for technical support is now 24 hours a day, meaning

that a business's back up and recovery procedures need to be fully tried and tested to ensure that there is no break in continuity of service and processing. This may include service level agreements with ISPs to guard against financial loss during excessive 'down–time'.

Encryption-based security

The use of encryption techniques results in a number of further risks. If encryption keys are lost information may not be accessible at a later date. This can pose both a business and an audit risk. Therefore, auditors should consider how encryption keys are safeguarded and their ability to access data and documents for testing as necessary. Where auditors are given copies of encryption keys they should have suitable internal procedures in place to make sure these are stored securely.

Ultimately, the use of encryption-based security does not absolve management from its responsibilities under company law to allow auditors access to data or to maintain adequate accounting records.

As part of their engagement letter, auditors should make clear that the establishment of appropriate security and controls, the addressing of encryption risk and the maintenance of audit access to documents and records is the responsibility of management.

System reliability and authentication of financial records

Audit procedures for traditional business activities tend to focus on controls over recording and storage. For entities involved in e-commerce the focus should be on the validity of the transaction – that is, those controls that apply to the actual initiation of transactions, such as the placing of an order by a customer, which generally prompt all other steps in processing the transaction. System controls, which ensure the integrity of the transaction at the time of its execution, are those controls that ensure that a transaction is accurate, valid and complete. The controls that auditors will be aiming to establish as present and working are likely to be those that:

- determine duplicate or fictitious identities;
- distinguish between browsing and order placement;
- validate all external inputs;
- prevent duplications or omissions;
- ensure that the payment is processed before the goods are despatched;
- address the causes of transaction failure, such as computer crashes or authentication problems which may lead to loss of information or interruption of service to customers;
- prevent incomplete processing;
- ensure details distributed to different systems are processed correctly and that multiple activities do not cause system breakdown; and
- ensure that records are properly entered and retained and that accounts balance both before and after transactions.

Auditors must also assess how the entity maintains the accessibility, integrity and retention of e-commerce records through real-time record keeping. Auditors will look for evidence of controls which act as a 'buffer' between the external 'shop front' interface and the accounting records of the entity to give comfort that financial data cannot be easily corrupted by those outside the organisation using the website.

As electronic records are more easily destroyed or altered, either unintentionally or maliciously, than their manual counterparts, auditors should consider the controls and policies in place to ensure ongoing security of information. They should also be aware of how system-based security measures such as digital signatures, electronic date stamps and record integrity checks are utilised to ensure data integrity.

Other control areas
Other controls auditors may consider include those designed to:

- ensure that all orders received will result in a valid sale not capable of repudiation;
- ensure that returned goods are correctly recorded; and
- establish privacy in accordance with legislative requirements.

41.7 AUDIT EVIDENCE

41.7.1 Difficulties in obtaining evidence

For entities with significant involvement in e-commerce, auditors may not be able to audit 'round the computer' – that is, verify inputs and outputs, and effectively bypass the processing that occurs in between. In a number of cases there is no alternative but to audit 'through the computer'. For example, although physical goods may be dispatched there is often very little conventional external audit evidence as the ordering and all the intervening steps are carried out 'on-line'. In addition, electronic records may not be as robust as physical records, which may present particular problems.

The audit trail available in e-commerce entities is therefore likely to vary significantly from that in the more traditionally organised industries. The two most common types of audit trail are access and transaction logs.

Although these logs are likely to be of significant use to auditors of an e-business, where a VAN or extranet is used there is a strong chance that the entity will not have access to some or all of them. Also in these cases, even where management has access, the level of detail included in them is likely to be such that it dissuades management from using them to control the business.

When using external processing auditors must be satisfied that a complete history exists of all events during the period and that the logs are a full list of all transactions processed. Therefore, they should suggest that service level agreements with external parties include the ability to retrieve and review audit trails or logs on demand, either for a particular date or range of dates. This should include an 'unusual activity log', which includes details of items such as apparently duplicated or very large orders.

41.7.2   Use of specialists

Auditors invariably require special skills to audit these systems. For each client auditors need to assess whether they possess the relevant skills within the practice to understand the business, assess risk and perform appropriate testing or, alternatively, how they may acquire such skills. This may involve using IS auditing specialists to perform evaluations of systems and carrying out computer-based tests of controls and computer-aided substantive audit procedures.

Where an external specialist is used, the guidance in ISA (UK and Ireland) 620 should be followed (see section **37.4**).

Although an e-commerce business may have complex computer systems they may not interface with accounting systems, which may be very simple and therefore require limited specialist skills to audit. An example is a vendor of computer software with complex search and download facilities on their site, but where payment for the download is made by credit card, the details of which are re-keyed and the cash collected by normal bank credit.

41.7.3   Types of evidence

Tests of control
Where, as is likely, auditors of e-commerce entities place significant reliance on the proven effective operation of controls, an IS audit specialist or an auditor with the requisite IT systems and e-commerce knowledge should be involved in the design and implementation of these tests.

The main objectives in assessing any internal controls remain the assessment of:

- the design of controls – that the accounting and internal control systems are capable of preventing or detecting material misstatements; and
- the operation of controls – that the systems exist and have operated effectively throughout the relevant period.

For e-commerce systems, auditors typically concentrate their efforts on the controls in place to ensure the security and authenticity of the originating transaction, such as the sales order received. Then they assess the reliability of the process within the computer system to prompt all the other steps in processing the whole transaction automatically. Typical controls over security and authenticity of inputs are detailed in section **41.6.4** above.

Because of the power and complexity of systems, there may be many effects of processing to which auditors must be alive. For example, where automatic processing of sales orders is linked directly to the accounting system it may affect auditors' consideration of matters such as:

- the completeness and accuracy of transaction recording;
- the timing of recognition of sales revenues; and
- recognition and recording of disputed transactions.

If there are doubts in these areas auditors may need to consider the reviews the client undertakes to ensure, for example, that items are reflected in the correct accounting period rather than the period in which the order is placed or that all resulting transactions are recorded by the automated system.

As the system's controls are likely to be so central to the process of collecting evidence and gaining assurance, auditors need to be sure that there is no possibility that these controls can be overridden. Where overrides occur auditors should review the appropriate reports to determine why they occurred and whether they received the required authorisation.

Where tests of controls are unable to provide sufficient evidence to reduce the amount of substantive tests, auditors may be able to obtain adequate audit evidence from increasing the number of substantive procedures planned. However, given the importance of effective controls for this type of entity, the successful operation of controls may be so central to the ability of the financial statements to show a true and fair view, that auditors have no alternative but to issue a qualified audit opinion.

Substantive procedures
ISA (UK and Ireland) 500 *Audit Evidence* requires auditors to consider the level of assurance required from substantive procedures following the assessment of relevant tests of controls. Whilst the level of assurance from substantive procedures may be reduced by planning and performing extensive work on the reliability of controls, the use of substantive procedures can never be eliminated.

Analytical review
Substantive procedures may comprise tests of detail, analytical procedures, or a combination of both. Particular issues exist when planning to use analytical procedures in the audit of e-commerce clients.

For these clients (especially for 'dot.com' companies) the traditional relationships between the financial statements' account balances may no longer be appropriate. The relationship between costs and revenues may be completely different and certain balances may disappear completely. For example, eliminating parts of the distribution network such as wholesalers will have a major effect on the commonly examined relationships. The impact may be on some, or all, of the following:

- stocks held;
- trade creditors;
- trade debtors;
- ratio analysis;
- forecasts and budgets;
- going concern considerations.

The problems are likely to be acute in early years of an e-commerce operation where the effect of constant change and, sometimes, fast growth, may mean that a different approach is needed each year. Auditors need to be aware of these changes and to adjust their analytical review procedures accordingly.

Where traditional analytical methods are no longer relevant, different non-financial measures may have to be used. These may include:

- website hits/impressions per week/month;
- percentage increase in subscriber base;
- incidence of returned goods compared to sales;
- direct costs per unit of each sale;
- advertising/marketing cost as a percentage of revenue; or
- burn rate – cash resources compared to monthly expenditure.

ISA (UK and Ireland) 520 *Analytical Procedures* requires analytical review at both the planning and overall review stage of the audit. For analytical review at the planning stage, given the speed of change it may be preferable to investigate trends and result with reference to management budgets and forecasts for the period, rather than making comparisons with prior year figures.

41.7.4 Materiality

Materiality benchmarks are often established in relation to turnover levels for traditional entities. However, for e-businesses it is increasingly unlikely that there is a performance history that can be reliably used to establish materiality. Therefore, auditors may have to extend their assessment beyond quantitative measures.

41.7.5   Other performance indicators

For e-commerce entities, financing from third parties is often obtained on the basis of non-financial measures and projections such as the number of registered users or the number of 'hits' on a website. Entities may also publish this data with their financial statements. These non-financial indicators should be clearly presented to ensure that they do not mislead readers, who may not be aware of uncertainties as to the accuracy or meaning of the figures.

This data will be part of the 'other information' read by auditors in line with ISA (UK and Ireland) 720 *Other information in documents containing audited financial statements*, see **Chapter 14**.

41.7.6   Work papers

As clients move increasingly to a paperless office, auditors are increasingly keen to follow the same route for their audit work papers. There are a number of unresolved issued in this area. These include the need to ensure safe and secure storage and prevent unauthorised changes to data. In addition, the use of electronic sign offs is an area of concern upon which no official guidance has yet been issued.

41.8   GOING CONCERN

Many e-commerce start-ups have reported significant losses in early phases. Therefore, auditors should be alert to the risk of business failure and should use their professional judgement to assess the appropriateness of the going concern assumption. They should have regard to non-recurring events, break-even forecasts and the entity's business plans. In particular, they should consider the business's arrangements to ensure the viability of continued activity.

Auditors should also consider the impact of e-commerce on the ability of an entity to continue as a going concern even when that entity is not itself involved in e-business. Risks may arise as a result of the entity falling behind developments in the industry or by the industry itself being rendered obsolete by e-commerce.

41.9   CERTIFICATION

As discussed above, the rapid growth of the Internet has prompted many reliability, security and privacy issues. The publicity given to these risks has created an environment of scepticism around trading on the Internet, both in the business-to-business (B2B) and the business-to-consumer (B2C) markets.

E-commerce entities are therefore keen to promote their businesses as having adequate systems to meet the security needs of their customers and suppliers. One way to do this is to gain a certification of security for their systems and display this on their website.

There are a number of certification schemes operated by trade associations and consumer groups. Some are self-certifying, but some, such as the WebTrust seal marketed by the ICAEW, require independent verification of the procedures put in place by the e-business to minimise the effect and occurrence of security breaches. With some schemes regular verification is required to maintain the seal. There is no common standard applied by all certification bodies, but the DTI is encouraging an environment in which seal providers subscribe to a minimum set of standards.

It is therefore important for the auditor and customer to understand the assurance that the seal provides and, more importantly, what it does not. Often clicking on the seal itself will provide much of this information. If the external auditor has been involved in awarding a WebTrust seal to the client, the work performed for this task will have provided a detailed knowledge of the security issues and the controls in place to mitigate them. This will be of relevance to their assessment of audit risk.

42 REPORTS FOR SPECIAL PURPOSES AND TO THIRD PARTIES

42.1 INTRODUCTION

Managing auditors' own risk has become increasingly important in recent years and one major area of concern is reliance by parties other than those with whom the auditor has contractual relations. For example where loans and other facilities are made available to businesses, the extent to which the auditor is responsible to the lender is often ambiguous. This becomes more difficult and potentially more dangerous where auditors have an obligation to report to other third parties, for example Regulatory Authorities. Managing the terms under which third parties can, or more importantly cannot, place reliance on reports is an area in which increasing guidance has been produced. This chapter provides an overview of this guidance and covers a number of areas where it is likely to happen.

42.2 DEVELOPMENT OF GUIDANCE

In November 2000, the Consultative Committee of Accountancy Bodies (CCAB) issued a Statement which contains guidance aimed at helping all parties involved in financing arrangements. This addresses issues such as the appropriate form of report, firms' duties of care and reporting in connection with covenants in loan agreements and other facilities.

The Statement was reissued by the Audit and Assurance Faculty of the ICAEW as Technical Release 4/00 *Firms' reports and duties to lenders in connection with loans and other facilities to clients and related covenants.* Audit 4/00 replaced Practice Note 4 issued by the Auditing Practices Board, *Reliance by Banks on Audited Financial Statements.* The guidance deals with non-statutory audits and reviews and is, therefore, of greater relevance to those companies taking advantage of the increase in the statutory audit exemption threshold (see **7.1**).

The guidance also deals with reports on client's compliance with loan covenants, including the scope of work to be performed and the format of the report to be given.

The Statement is based on current law governing duties of care, and notes that the ongoing review of company law may necessitate revision of this statement in due course.

Since 2001 a number of further publications have been issued addressing various aspects of liability to third parties. The main additional guidance is contained in:

- ICAEW Technical Release Audit 1/01: *Reporting to Third Parties* (see **42.9** below);
- ICAEW Technical Release Audit 2/01: *Requests for References on Clients' Financial Status and their Ability to Service Loans* (see **42.9** below);
- ICAEW Technical Release AAF 01/06: *Assurance Reports on Internal Controls of Service Organisations Made Available to Third Parties* (see **42.8** below);
- ICAEW Technical Release AAF 03/06: *The ICAEW Assurance Service on Unaudited Financial Statements* (see **42.7** below); and
- ICAEW Technical Release AAF 04/06: *Assurance Engagements: Management of Risk and Liability* (see **42.3** below).

In 2005, the Audit and Assurance Faculty completed a study of the legal cases involving claims by third parties against auditors. The review, *Audit liability: Claims by third parties*, was conducted in conjunction with the law firm Simmons & Simmons and summarises the key matters arising from the relevant cases. It is considered in **42.10** below.

The joint ICAEW/Association of British Travel Agents (ABTA) working group has developed a package of reporting arrangements, designed to help ABTA regulate its members and be consistent with the new AUDIT1/01 framework. These form Technical Release AUDIT 2/02, new arrangements for reporting to the ABTA.

In 2003 further guidance was issued by the ICAEW to develop the guidance in Audit 1/01 for specific circumstances:

- Audit 2/03: New Arrangements for Reporting to the Civil Aviation Authority (CAA) in connection with the Civil Aviation (Air Travel Organisers' Licensing) Regulations 1995;
- Audit 3/03: Public Sector Special Reporting Engagements – Grant Claims (see **Chapter 47**);
- Audit 4/03: Access to Working Papers by Investigating Accountants (see **Chapter 19**); and
- Audit 5/03: Reporting to Regulators of Regulated Entities (see **Chapter 48**).

On the international stage, the IAASB has reissued ISA 920 as International Standard on Related Services (ISRS) 4400, *Engagements to Perform Agreed-Upon Procedures Regarding Financial Information*. This is discussed in **42.11** below.

Following the publication of the other Technical Releases listed above, the ICAEW published AAF 04/06, *Assurance Engagements: Management of Risk and Liability* in November 2006. The general principles in this guidance are based on the IAASB's *International Framework for Assurance Engagements* and ISAE 3000, *Assurance Engagements other than Audits or Reviews of Historical Financial Information*. This is considered in the next section as it provides general guidance which can be applied to all cases.

42.3   GENERAL GUIDANCE

AAF 04/06 provides principles for reporting accountants to consider in relation to managing their risk and liability when agreeing to undertaken assurance engagements and providing assurance reports to third parties. It does not seek to provide detailed advice on the planning and conduct of the work involved in such engagements or how to manage risk and liability in particular circumstances. Such detail will be provided in other technical releases which will cross-refer to this over arching guidance.

42.3.1   Accepting an engagement

Reporting accountants should have appropriate engagement acceptance procedures to assess the risks associated with taking on a particular engagement. Reporting accountants should consider the:

- purpose for which the work is being sought;
- party or parties seeking to benefit from the work, whether they are directly party to the engagement or not yet identified;
- use that will be made of the work; and
- professional competence of the engagement team.

42.3.2   Managing professional liability

AAF 04/06 outlines the following arrangements into which reporting accountants may enter:

- a tri-partite or multi-partite engagement contract with the client and the third parties, accepting that they owe a duty of care not only to the client but also to those third parties. Provisions to limit liability may be appropriate;
- an engagement with the client, with the option for third parties to join the duty of care if they accept the relevant terms of the engagement letter.

Again liability may be limited;

- an engagement with the client alone, but allowing access to the audit report for third parties as long as they:
  - acknowledge in writing that the reporting accountant owes them no duty of care; and
  - agree in writing that no claims will be brought against the reporting accountant in relation to the assurance report; and
- an engagement with the client alone, disclaiming any liability or duty to others by notice in the assurance report. This may be in conjunction with the client indemnifying the reporting accountant if a third party makes a claim against the reporting accountant, although such indemnities may not be commercially attractive or reliable if the client is not financially stable.

Alternatively if the risks are too high or reporting accountants are unable to reach acceptable terms with the client or third parties, reporting accountants may decline to accept the engagement.

42.3.3   Agreeing the terms of the engagement

Reporting accountants must manage their relationship with the client and any third party, and clarify that any assurance engagements are separate from statutory audit engagements. Depending on the type of contractual arrangement agreed upon (see **42.3.2**), reporting accountants will need to agree specific terms with all parties to the engagement and record them in writing in the engagement letter. The engagement letter should include details of the purpose of the report to be issued, its agreed use and any accompanying disclosure restrictions setting out the extent to which, the context in which, and the basis on which the report may be made available by the client to the third parties.

It is often useful to include a draft pro forma report as an appendix to the engagement letter.

42.4   DUTIES TO LENDERS

As set out above, the position of the auditor in relation to the provider of loans and other facilities can be ambiguous. Technical Release 4/00 *Firms' reports and duties to lenders in connection with loans and other facilities to clients and related covenants* provides guidance in relation to various aspects of the relationship of auditors with providers of finance to their clients.

42.4.1   Case law

The guidance issued in Technical Release 4/00 is based on case law. In his judgement in the case of *Caparo Industries plc* v *Dickman* (1990) 2 WLR 353,

Lord Bridge stated that a duty of care to a third party will exist if the person who owes the duty of care is aware:

- of the transaction to be undertaken by the third party;
- that the advice given will be passed to the third party, either directly or indirectly; and
- that it is likely that the third party will rely on that information in deciding whether to enter into the transaction.

Since this judgement, banks and other lenders have sought to document a direct and sufficient relationship between themselves and their customer's auditors so as to be able to rely on statutory audit reports.

42.4.2 Duties of care for the statutory audit report

An auditor's duty of care in respect of their audit report would not normally be expected to extend beyond that owed to their client. However, the general trend of authorities since *Caparo* makes it clear that, unless there is an effective disclaimer, an auditor may owe a duty of care to a lender or other third party. The test is whether the auditor, in making the statements in their audit report, assumed a responsibility to a lender who may subsequently be given a copy of those statements. The important issue is not whether the auditor in question intended to assume the responsibility towards the third party, but rather whether a reasonable auditor would have assumed the responsibility in those circumstances.

Therefore, auditors must be aware that they may inadvertently accept responsibility unless steps are taken to limit their exposure. Auditors may assume responsibility without their knowledge by the client having discussions with the lender, or the lender being passed a set of the most recent audited financial statements, if it is deemed that a reasonable auditor would assume such responsibility.

Lenders will seek to establish a relationship with the auditors. In this regard, certain banks have included a clause in the conditions attached to a loan, which requires the auditor of the borrower to provide written acknowledgement to the bank that the bank may rely on the audited financial statements of the borrower in connection with the facilities offered. Where auditors are aware, or are in receipt, of a request to provide acknowledgement, they should not let it go unanswered.

In addition, banks may write directly to auditors stating that they do intend to rely on audited financial statements in connection with a proposed transaction. In this situation, a duty of care will be created unless the auditor vigorously denies it. A firm should normally disclaim all responsibility in this situation in writing. An example response is shown in **Table 1**.

TABLE 1:   Example disclaimer of responsibility to lenders for audit or review reports

[Lender plc]

Dear Sirs

XYZ plc – [Loan/transaction reference]

We acknowledge receipt of your letter of 31 March 20.., in which you state your intention to rely on the financial statements of XYZ plc for the year ended 31 December 20.. and our audit [review] report thereon, in connection with the above-mentioned loan agreement.

Our audit [review] of the financial statements was neither planned nor conducted for the purpose of (or in contemplation of) the loan agreement (and transaction) referred to above. In particular, the scope of our work was set, and judgements made, by reference to our assessment of materiality in the context of the financial statements taken as a whole, rather then in the context of your needs. For this reason, our work would not necessarily have addressed or reflected matters in which you may be primarily interested as lenders. Therefore, we cannot accept any responsibility to you in relation to our report and disclaim all liability to you in connection therewith (and your lending decision in relation to the proposed transaction and any other actions you may take).

Should you require any specific assurances from us regarding any matters in which you may be primarily interested as a lender, we should be happy to discuss them with you in the context of an engagement between ourselves, Lender plc and XYZ plc which would be entirely separate from our audit [review] of XYZ plc's financial statements.

Yours faithfully

cc. XYZ plc

42.4.3   Draft accounts

The courts have held that reliance on draft audited accounts was not actionable, since a reasonable auditor would not intend such reliance to occur. However, there may be circumstances in which a duty of care may arise and care must be taken, therefore, when circulating draft audited accounts. The status of the accounts must be clearly stated and the giving of assurances or representations about the reliability of the accounts (or whether the final position is likely to differ greatly from that shown in the draft) should be avoided.

42.4.4 Disclaimer of responsibility

Disclaimers of responsibility can only be relied upon if they pass the reasonableness test set out in s2 of the Unfair Contract Terms Act 1977. If the disclaimer is not reasonable it will be void.

Disclaimers can be worded to pass the reasonableness test and are therefore an effective way of limiting an auditor's liability to lenders and other third parties who seek to claim reliance on a report. They may also be useful in avoiding any doubt that a firm does not have a duty of care to a lender or third party to whom a report is shown or a reference to a report is made.

However, it is important to note that a disclaimer of responsibility does not exempt an auditor or an accountant issuing a review report from carrying out their work in accordance with Auditing Standards or other applicable standards.

42.4.5 The Contracts (Rights of Third Parties) Act 1999

The Contracts (Rights of Third Parties) Act 1999 came into force on 11 November 1999 and applies to all contracts entered into after 10 May 2000. Under the Act, a third party to a contract has the right to enforce a term of that contract if it confers a benefit or right to the third party. This equates to a partial abolition of the concept of 'privity of contract', which has been a central feature of the English law of contract for more than 100 years.

Therefore, if a reference is made to the provision of a set of financial statements to a lender, or to a lender requiring the financial statements for a specific purpose, within a contract between an auditor and their client, a benefit may have been conferred upon the lender.

Audit engagement letters should state clearly that they do not confer any rights on any third party and that, for the avoidance of doubt, any rights conferred on third parties pursuant to the Contracts (Rights of Third Parties) Act 1999 shall be excluded.

The Act does not apply to Scotland, which has long recognised the concept of *ius quaesitum tertio*, a right vested in and secured to a third party in and by a contract between two parties. Accordingly, a third party has the right to enforce a contract between two parties if the intention to confer a benefit on that third party can be gathered from the terms of the document.

42.4.6 Separate engagements to provide specific assurances to lenders

If a firm decides that it is able to provide specific assurances to a lender, it should be the subject of a separate engagement between the firm, the client and the lender. There should be a separate engagement letter in place for this work, normally the subject of separate financial arrangements.

A firm should also consider whether entering into such an agreement with both client and lender could present it with a conflict of interest. Reference should be made to the ethical guidance of the Institute which governs the firm.

42.5 COVENANTS IN AGREEMENT FOR LOANS AND OTHER FACILITIES

Agreements for certain financing arrangements often contain a number of covenants with which the borrower is expected to comply. Typically, the directors of the borrower are required to prepare a periodic statement or report, a 'Statement of Covenant Compliance', to confirm continuing compliance with the covenant terms agreed when arranging the finance.

Imposed covenants will be either financial or non-financial. Non-financial covenants tend to be more common and take the form of commitments by the borrower as to its future actions. Financial covenants may also need to be maintained by the borrower. These will often be financial statement ratios, the intention of which is to provide the lender with some assurance as to the continuing financial condition of the business.

A list of common financial and non-financial covenants is given in **Table 2**. In specialised industries, lenders may require the maintenance of industry key performance indicators (KPIs), which are derived from management information outside the financial statements, such as room occupancy rates for hotels or pollution levels for heavy industry.

TABLE 2:   Common covenants for borrowings

Financial

- cash flow to total debt service;
- dividend cover;
- minimum share capital and reserves;
- PBIT-based interest cover;
- gearing;
- cash flow-based interest cover;
- net current assets/borrowings;
- proportion of debtors below certain days outstanding;
- current ratio;
- quick asset ratio;
- EBITDA;
- gross profit margin;
- rent roll ratios.

Non-financial

- first charge over specified assets;
- audited annual accounts within a specified period;
- cross default clauses;
- monthly management accounts within a specified period;
- restrictions on changes to ownership;
- restrictions on additional borrowings (from other sources);
- maintenance of adequate fire, theft and other insurances;
- restrictions in mergers/acquisitions;
- restrictions on asset disposals;
- no capital expenditure beyond certain limits without approval;
- compliance with environmental laws and regulations;
- compliance with other laws and regulations;
- no redemption of preference shares while loans outstanding;
- charges over key-man insurance;
- key-man critical illness policy;
- limits on directors' remuneration.

42.5.1 The lender's requirement for evidence of covenant compliance

The lender will require from the directors of the borrower, a written confirmation that they have complied with all covenants for the period under review. This confirmation should set out the computation of the relevant financial covenants for the applicable accounting date. Simple calculations of gearing and interest cover are often self-evident and can easily be re-performed by the lender to ensure compliance. However, where information for covenants is not readily available to the lender, or it is not contained in the borrower's financial statements, the lender may require a report from the borrower's auditors.

Auditors are not compelled to accept such an engagement, as they cannot be bound to comply with the terms of an agreement to which they are not party. Therefore, if auditors become aware that a client is negotiating a loan or other facility, it is good practice to enquire whether the draft loan agreement seeks to place any reporting obligations on them.

Where a requirement to report is found, auditors should write to the lender to clarify the basis of preparation. This is particularly important if the lender approaches the auditor directly, rather than through the borrower. An example letter for this purpose is set out in **Table 3**.

TABLE 3: Example letter to lender setting out basis on which reports under a loan agreement will be provided

[Lender plc]

Dear Sirs

XYZ plc – [Loan Agreement Reference]

XYZ plc has provided us with a copy of [and you have written to us in connection with], the Loan Agreement referred to above, Clause X of which contemplates that reports will periodically be provided to you by the auditors of XYZ plc in connections with XYZ plc's compliance with certain covenants. As auditors of XYZ plc, we confirm that, provided that XYZ plc authorises us to do so and you sign an engagement letter with us substantially in the attached form, we will report to you on the following matters:

- whether the financial information contained in the Statement of Covenant Compliance prepared by the directors of XYZ plc has been accurately extracted from the sources identified therein and, where applicable, agrees with the underlying accounting records;
- whether the calculations shown in the Statement, made in accordance with Clause X of the loan agreement, are arithmetically accurate; and
- where the elements and composition of the financial information contained in the Statement are the subject of objective accounting definition in the Loan Agreement, or have subsequently been agreed by Lender plc and XYZ plc, whether the financial information is presented in compliance with the relevant definitions and agreement.

As regards our audit work on XYZ plc's financial statements for future periods, our work will be carried out in accordance with our statutory and professional obligations and will not be planned or conducted in contemplation of your requirements or any matters which might be set out in the Loan Agreement. In particular, the scope of our audit work will be set and judgements made by reference to our assessment of materiality in the context of the audited accounts taken as a whole, rather than in the context of your needs. For this reason, our work will not necessarily address or reflect matters in which you may be primarily interested as lenders. Therefore, we cannot accept any responsibility to you in relation to our audit opinions and disclaim all liability to you in connection therewith.

Yours faithfully

cc. XYZ plc
Enc. Form of engagement letter [see Table 4]

42.5.2 The firm's duty of care when reporting on the directors' statement of covenant compliance

Auditors accepting an engagement to report on compliance with covenants acknowledge a duty of care to the lender. Firms will use their established risk management techniques to control this duty. One key method of achieving this is to issue an engagement letter which limits the use of the report to the intended addressee of the report, includes a disclaimer of responsibility to all other parties and specifies liability limits.

In addition, an engagement letter normally includes an exclusion of liability to the lender in respect of their normal audit or review report. This ensures that no responsibility to lenders is assumed for these reports.

Firms must consider whether the engagement is between themselves and the lender, or if it is a separate engagement between themselves and their client. In either case, a separate engagement letter is sent. An example wording is set out in **Table 4**.

The example wording also includes clauses excluding liability in respect of any loss or damage caused by, or arising from, fraudulent acts, misrepresentation or concealment on the part of the client entity, its directors, employees or agent, and excluding all liability to third parties.

TABLE 4:   Example engagement letter

[Lender plc]

[Other addressees as provided for in the second paragraph of the letter]

Dear Sirs

XYZ plc – [Loan Agreement reference]

Under the terms of Clause [X] of the agreement dated [date] between XYZ plc and Lender plc ('the Loan Agreement'), the Directors of XYZ plc are required to procure that their auditors report to you in connection with the Directors' Statement of Covenant Compliance ('the Statement'), prepared in accordance with Clause [X] of the Loan Agreement. At the request of the Directors of XYZ plc, we are writing to set out our understanding of the work you wish us to perform and the terms and conditions upon which we are prepared to provide such a report for your use. A copy of this letter is being sent to the Directors of XYZ plc to confirm their authorisation and understanding of the basis on which we will report to you.

[This engagement letter is addressed to Lender plc, as lead manager/arranger of the facility/syndication agreement, and to each of the other lenders participating in the facility/syndication agreement whose names, as set out in Attachment 1, have been notified to us by Lender plc as having validly authorised it to

---

accept this engagement letter on their behalf. By signing and accepting the terms of this engagement letter, Lender plc confirms that it will ensure that it receives prima facie authority from each other lender identified in Attachment 1, as participating in the facility/syndication agreement authorising it to enter into this engagement letter on the relevant lender's behalf.]

Respective responsibilities of directors and auditors
The Directors of XYZ plc are responsible for ensuring that XYZ plc complies with all of the terms and conditions of the Loan Agreement including each of the Covenants set out in Clauses [X] to [X] thereof. Under Clause [X] thereof, the Directors are responsible for preparing their Statement of Covenant Compliance. Our responsibility is to prepare a report to you on the computation of those financial covenants which pertain to accounting matters as identified below.

We are auditors of XYZ plc and have audited the annual accounts of XYZ plc ('the audited accounts') and reported to its members in accordance with our responsibilities under the Companies Act on [date]. Our audit of the accounts of XYZ plc was not intended to address compliance with financial covenants or other matters in which the addressees of this letter may be primarily interested. In particular, the scope of our audit work was set and our judgements made by reference to our assessment of materiality in the context of the audited accounts taken as a whole, rather than in the context of the report contemplated in this letter. Accordingly, we do not acknowledge any responsibility, and deny any liability, to the addressees of this letter in relation to the audited accounts.

Basis of report
Our work will be conducted in accordance with the framework for reporting in connection with loan covenants set out in guidance issued by the Consultative Committee of Accountancy Bodies and published as Audit Technical Release 4/00 by the Institute of Chartered Accountants in England and Wales [*or alternative CCAB member*]. We will read the Statement prepared by the Directors. Our work will be based on obtaining an understanding of the compilation of the Statement and by enquiry of management, reference to the Loan Agreement, comparison of the financial information in the Statement to the sources from which it was obtained and re-computation of the calculations in the Statement. [The specific procedures that we have agreed to conduct are set out in the Appendix to this letter.] Other than as set out herein, we will not carry out any work by way of audit, review or verification of the financial information nor of the management accounts, accounting records or other sources from which that information is to be extracted for the purpose of providing you with our report.

Use of report
Our report will be provided solely for your use in connection with the Loan Agreement and should not be made available to any other party without our written consent. The report is confidential to you and will be provided only for the purpose of your assessment of XYZ plc's compliance with the terms of Clause [X] of the Loan Agreement. We accept no liability to any other party who is shown or gains access to our report.

Obligations and liabilities

We undertake that we will exercise reasonable professional skill and care in the performance of our work as set out in this letter in accordance with applicable professional standards. This engagement is undertaken subject to certain terms excluding liability where information is or has been misrepresented to us, or withheld or concealed from us, and providing for our aggregate liability to the addressees of this letter and XYZ plc to be limited to a maximum aggregate amount of £[X] and subject to that cap, to the part of any loss suffered which is proportional to our responsibility.

It is agreed that the allocation between addressees of the limit of liability specified above will be entirely a matter for the addressees, who shall be under no obligation to inform us of it, provided always that if (for whatever reason) no such allocation is agreed, no addressee shall dispute the validity, enforceability or operation of the limit of liability on the ground that no such allocation was agreed.

Our detailed Terms of Business are set out in the attachment to this letter which shall apply as if set out in full herein.

Acknowledgement and acceptance

We will be grateful if, having considered the provisions of this letter together with the attachments and having concluded that they are reasonable in the context of all the factors relating to our proposed engagement, you will indicate your agreement to these arrangements by signing and returning to us the enclosed copy of this letter.

Yours faithfully

The terms and conditions contained in this letter and the attached Terms of Business are agreed and accepted on behalf of Lender plc by:

.... (authorised person)
Authorised and accepted on behalf of XYZ plc by:
.... (authorised person)

42.5.3 The firm's consideration of acceptance of the engagement

Before accepting the engagement the auditor must ensure that the respective responsibilities of the borrower and the auditor are clearly defined. It is the responsibility of the directors of the borrower to prepare the financial information and the Statement of Covenant Compliance, and the auditors' responsibility is to report on that information to the extent that it relates to financial and accounting matters.

The Statement of Covenant Compliance will normally set out the calculations of financial ratios, etc., as provided for under the loan agreement. The loan agreement will usually require the borrower to comply with the covenants at all times during the period being reported upon, but the auditors' report will only refer to compliance at specific dates. A firm would not normally accept an engagement which requires confirmation of compliance with covenants over an extended period of time, or for which confirmation that the borrower will comply with covenants in the future based on prospective information is required.

Firms should also consider carefully the implications of accepting an engagement to report on a Statement of Covenant Compliance based on financial covenants whose terms are imprecise.

42.6   ENGAGEMENTS TO REPORT ON COVENANT COMPLIANCE

42.6.1   Scope of work performed

The scope of work will vary from engagement to engagement and should be agreed with both the client and the lender. Typical procedures will include:

- reading the relevant clauses of the loan agreement and gaining an understanding of the operation of the covenants;
- reading the directors' Statement of Covenant Compliance;
- agreeing the financial information in the Statement to the sources from which it has been extracted;
- re-computing the calculations and ratios set out in the Statement in order to ascertain their arithmetical accuracy; and
- obtaining a representation from the client as to the completeness of disclosure in the Statement.

Firms will not undertake procedures to confirm the reliability of the financial information in the Statement nor of the sources from which the data has been extracted. In addition, they will not report on non-financial information in the Statement, such as directors' judgements on future business trends.

An example representation letter is provided in **Table 5**.

TABLE 5:   Example representation letter

[Auditors' name and address]

Dear Sirs

[Loan Agreement Reference]

In connection with your proposed report in accordance with the arrangements set out in your letter of [date], we are writing to confirm to the best of our knowledge and belief the following representations we have made to you and on which you need to rely in providing your report on the Statement of Covenant Compliance ('the Statement') to Lender plc.

We are responsible for preparing the Statement, accurately reflecting the matters contained therein at the relevant dates.

The Statement is complete and accurate and reflects all matters of significance relating to Lender plc's assessment of XYZ plc's compliance with the Covenants set out therein as at the relevant dates and all significant matters relevant to that assessment have been brought to your attention.

Throughout the period since [date] the Company has at all times been in compliance with the terms of the Loan Agreement or, if not, all such instances of non-compliance have been notified to Lender plc in accordance with the terms of the Loan Agreement. Copies of such notifications have been made available to you.

[No events have occurred subsequent to [date of last audited financial statements] that would have required adjustment to, or disclosure in, the audited financial statements had their approval by the Board been deferred until the date of this letter.]

Yours faithfully

.... (signature of authorised person on behalf of XYZ plc)

42.6.2   The report

The report should be prepared in accordance with the engagement letter. The report will:

- identify the addressees who can rely on it;
- contain a statement concerning the scope of the report and the respective responsibilities of the directors and auditors;
- refer to the Statement of Covenant Compliance;
- set out the basis for the report;
- provide a description of the procedures undertaken (either in the body of the report or in an appendix);

- report on the arithmetical accuracy of the extraction and calculation of the financial information within the Statement; and
- where the elements and composition of the financial information in the Statement are the subject of objective accounting definition in the loan agreement, or have been subsequently agreed by the parties, report whether the financial information is presented in compliance with the relevant definitions and agreement.

An illustrative form of report is given in **Table 6**.

TABLE 6:   Example report

[Lender plc]

[Other addressees as provided for in the engagement letter]

Dear Sirs

XYZ plc – [Loan Agreement reference]

We refer to the above-mentioned agreement ('the Loan Agreement'). Under the terms of Clause [X] thereof, XYZ plc is required to comply with specified financial covenants and to supply the addressees of this letter with information in connection therewith reported upon by its auditors.

The directors of XYZ plc have prepared a Statement of Covenant Compliance ('the Statement'), a copy of which is appended to this letter.

This report letter is provided pursuant to, and must be read in conjunction with, our engagement letter dated [date] and is subject to the terms and limitations set out therein.

Basis of report
Our work was conducted in accordance with the framework for reporting in connection with loan covenants set out in guidance issued by the Consultative Committee of Accountancy Bodies [and published as Audit Technical Release 4/00 by the Institute of Chartered Accountants in England and Wales, *or alternative CCAB member*]. We have read the attached Statement prepared by the Directors. Our work was based on obtaining an understanding of the compilation of the Statement by enquiry of management, reference to the Loan Agreement, comparison of the financial information in the Statement to the sources from which it was obtained and re-computation of the calculations in the Statement. [The specific procedures we performed are set out in the Appendix to this letter.] For the purpose of providing you with this letter, other than as set out herein, we have not carried out any work by way of audit, review or verification of the financial information nor of the management accounts, accounting records or other sources from which that information has been extracted.

Report

Based solely on the procedures described above, we confirm that:

- the financial information contained in the accompanying Statement has been accurately extracted from the sources identified therein and, where applicable, agrees with the underlying accounting records;
- the calculations shown in the Statement made in accordance with Clause [X] of the Loan Agreement are arithmetically accurate; and
- the financial information in the Statement is presented in compliance with the relevant accounting definitions as to its elements and composition set out in Clause [X] of the Loan Agreement [and as agreed between Lender plc and XYZ plc and confirmed to us in a letter dated [date]].

Our report as set out herein is confidential to the addressees of this letter and should not be made available to any other party without our written consent. It is provided solely for the purpose of your assessment of XYZ plc's compliance with the terms of [Clause [X] of] the Loan Agreement. We accept no liability to any other party who is shown or gains access to this letter.

Yours faithfully

cc. XYZ plc

42.7 DUTIES OF CARE FOR NON-STATUTORY AUDITS OR REVIEWS

42.7.1 Background

Small companies which take advantage of the statutory audit exemption may still decide to have their financial statements reviewed for other purposes. The review report will not be on the public record and the firm performing the review will include a restriction on the use of its report, requiring written consent to be obtained before the report can be given to any third party. In August 2006, the Audit and Assurance Faculty of the ICAEW issued guidance in this area in AAF 03/06 *The ICAEW Assurance Service on Unaudited Financial Statements*. AAF 03/06 uses the IAASB's *International Framework for Assurance Engagements* as its reference as well as other guidance and standards on similar types of assurance engagements.

In an assurance engagement accountants express a conclusion on the financial statements, in those covered by AAF 03/06 the accountants give a negative form of conclusion on the unaudited financial statements. This is known as a limited assurance engagement, as opposed to reasonable assurance engagements where positive assurance is given, usually in terms of a true and fair view. The giving of a conclusion separates assurance engagements from compilation reports where no conclusion is given on the information compiled, or agreed upon procedure reports, where the report is purely factual. This is illustrated in **Table 7**.

TABLE 7:   Types of engagement

Type of engagement	Assurance Engagement		Compilation Engagement	Agreed Upon Procedures Engagement
	Reasonable Assurance	**Limited Assurance**		
Level of assurance/ type of conclusion	Positive opinion, usually 'true and fair'	Negative opinion, guidance given in AAF 03/06	Confirm facts of compilation only, no conclusion given	Purely factual, no conclusion given

42.7.2   Accepting the engagement

The terms of the engagement should be agreed in writing. Example engagement letter wording is given in **Table 8**. The assurance report may be received by people not party to the engagement and accountants should assess the risks of litigation arising from third parties prior to accepting the engagement. The engagement letter should be suitably worded to ensure that no liability is assumed to any third party.

TABLE 8:   Example extracts from an engagement letter for limited assurance engagement

Scope of our work
You have asked us to report to you on a limited assurance basis on the unaudited financial statements of the company. We shall plan our work on the basis that the company is not required by statue or regulation to have an audit of its financial statements for the year ended [date], unless you inform us in writing to the contrary. In carrying out this engagement we will make enquiries, perform analytical procedures and assess the consistency of application of your accounting policies in accordance with Generally Accepted Accounting Practice in the United Kingdom ('UK GAAP'). We will perform limited examination of evidence relevant to certain balances and disclosures in the financial statements where, after performing the above work, we become aware of matters that might indicate material misstatements in the financial statements.

Our work will be undertaken and our report will be made in accordance with AAF 03/06 issued by the Institute of Chartered Accountants in England and Wales.

Our conclusion on the unaudited financial statements cannot be regarded as providing assurance on the adequacy of the company's systems or on the incidence of fraud, non-compliance with laws and regulations or weaknesses in internal controls. Engaging us to perform this assurance engagement on the unaudited financial statements does not relieve the directors of their responsibilities in these respects.

You have advised us that the company is exempt from an audit of the financial statements. We will not carry out any work to determine whether or not the company is entitled to audit exemption. However should our work indicate that the company is not entitled to the exemption, we will inform you of this.

Our work will not be an audit of the financial statements in accordance with International Standards on Auditing (UK and Ireland). Consequently, it does not include a comprehensive assessment of the risk of material misstatement, a consideration of fraud or of laws and regulations, to the gaining of an understanding of, or the testing of, internal control in accordance with International Standards on Auditing (UK and Ireland). It does not include the gathering of evidence in relation to all material areas of the financial statements and in respect of all relevant assertions.

Since we will not carry out an audit nor confirm the accuracy or reasonableness of the accounting records maintained by the company, we can only provide a limited assurance report as to whether the financial statements present a true and fair view.

Furthermore, as the Board of Directors, you have a duty to prepare financial statements that comply with the Companies Act 1985 and applicable accounting standards. Where we identify that the financial statements do not conform to UK GAAP or if the accounting policies adopted are not immediately apparent this will need to be disclosed in the financial statements.

We have a professional responsibility not to be associated with financial statements which may be false or misleading. Therefore, although we are not required to search for such matters, should we become aware, for any reason, that the financial statements may be misleading, we will discuss the matter with you with a view to agreeing appropriate adjustments and/or disclosures in the financial statements. In circumstances where adjustments and/or disclosures that we consider appropriate are not made or where we are not provided with appropriate information, and as result we consider that the financial statements are misleading, we will withdraw from the engagement.

Basis of the accountants' report
Our report is prepared on the following basis:

- our report is prepared solely for your confidential use. It may not be relied upon by anyone else; and
- except to the extent required by court order, law or regulation, or where required in any court proceedings in which you may be involved, our report must not be made available, copied, referred to or recited to any other person, or included in any other document, nor may you make reference to us or the services, without our prior written permission.

Liability provision
We (that is, [name of firm]), will perform the engagement with reasonable skill and care and we acknowledge that in respect of liability (if any) on our part to the Company for losses, damages, costs or expenses ('losses') caused by our breach of contract, negligence, fraud or other deliberate breach of duty, the following provisions will apply:

- we will not be liable if such losses are due to the provision of false, misleading or incomplete information or documentation or due to the acts or omissions of any person other than us, except where, on the basis of the work normally undertaken by us within the scope set out in these terms of engagement, it would have been reasonable for us to discover such defects;
- we will accept liability without limit for the consequences of our own fraud or other deliberate breach of duty and for any other liability which it is not permitted by law to limit or exclude; and
- subject to the previous provisions of this liability paragraph, our total aggregate liability whether in contract, tort (including negligence) or otherwise, to the Company, for losses arising from or in connection with the work which is the subject of these terms (including any addition or variation to the work), shall not exceed in aggregate the amount of [£agreed amount].

The Company and the directors of the Company will not bring any claims or proceedings against any of our individual partners, members, directors or employees. This clause is intended to benefit such partners, members, directors and employees who may enforce this clause pursuant to the contracts (Rights of Third Parties) Act 1999 ('the Act'). Notwithstanding any benefits or rights conferred by this agreement on such partners, members, directors or employees by virtue of the Act, we and the directors of the Company may together agree in writing to vary or rescind the agreement set out in this letter without the consent of any such partners, members, directors or employees. Other than as expressly provided in this paragraph, the provisions of the Act are excluded.

Any claims, whether in contract, negligence or otherwise, must be formally commenced within [years] after the party bringing the claim becomes aware (or ought reasonably to have become aware) of the facts which give rise to the action and in any event to later than [years] after any alleged breach of contract, negligence or other cause of action. This expressly overrides any statutory provision which would otherwise apply.

As part of their risk management process, accountants should consider whether there are third parties who may seek to rely on their report. Depending on circumstances, and similar to the general guidance for managing professional liability set out in **42.3.2** above, accountants may:

- accept that they owe a duty of care to the third parties and enter into a tri-partite or multi-partite engagement contract with the client and the third parties. Provisions to limit liability may be appropriate;
- proceed with an engagement with the client alone, but allowing access to the report for third parties as long as they:
  - acknowledge in writing that the reporting accountant owes them no duty of care; and
  - agree in writing that no claims will be brought against the reporting accountant in relation to the assurance report;
- engage with the client alone, disclaiming any liability or duty to others by notice in the assurance report. This may be in conjunction with the client

indemnifying the reporting accountant if a third party makes a claim against the reporting accountant; or

- decline to accept the engagement.

42.7.3 Reliance by third parties

During the performance of the engagement, or after the report has been issued, accountants may become aware of third parties, such as banks or lenders, who may request sight of the report. In such cases, accountants may decline the request, or access may be agreed if the third party acknowledges in writing that they owe the accountant no duty of care.

When accountants become aware that a third party has obtained a copy of their report they should consider writing to the third party informing them that they did not undertake the work for the use of third parties and that they do not accept any responsibility to them and that all liability is denied.

42.7.4 Reporting

Accountants' reports help addressees derive comfort from the involvement of an independent accountant. They also assist in clarifying the scope of the engagement and ensuring that readers are aware that a full audit has not taken place. **Table 9** includes an example report to directors. **Table 10** shows a report addressed to directors and third parties.

TABLE 9: Example accountants' report to directors

Accountants' independent assurance report on the unaudited financial statements of [entity name]

To the Board of Directors of [entity name] ('the Company')
We have performed certain procedures in respect of the Company's unaudited financial statements for the year ended [date] as set out on pages [x] to [x], made enquiries of the Company's directors and assessed accounting policies adopted by the directors, in order to gather sufficient evidence for our conclusion in this report.

This report is made solely to the Company's directors, as a body, in accordance with the terms of our engagement letter dated [date]. It has been released to the directors on the basis that this report shall not be copied, referred to or disclosed, in whole (save for the directors' own internal purposes or as may be required by law or by a competent regulator) or in part, without our prior written consent. Our work has been undertaken so that we might state to the directors those matters that we have agreed to state to them in this report and for no other purpose. To the fullest extent permitted by law, we do not accept or assume responsibility to anyone other than the Company and the Company's directors as a body for our work, for this report or the conclusions we have formed.

Respective responsibilities
You have confirmed that you have met your duty as set out in the directors' statement on page [x]. You consider that the Company is exempt from the statutory requirement for an audit for the year. Our responsibility is to form and express an independent conclusion, based on the work carried out, to you on the financial statements.

Scope
We conducted our engagement in accordance with the Institute of Chartered Accountants in England & Wales Interim Technical Release AAF 03/06. Our work was based primarily upon enquiry, analytical procedures and assessing accounting policies in accordance with Generally Accepted Accounting Practice in the UK[/the Financial Reporting Standard for Smaller Entities]. If we considered it to be necessary, we also performed limited examination of evidence relevant to certain balances and disclosures in the financial statements where we became aware of matters that might indicate a risk of material misstatement in the financial statements.

The terms of our engagement exclude any requirement to carry out a comprehensive assessment of the risks of material misstatement, a consideration of fraud, laws, regulations and internal controls, and we have not done so. We are not required to, and we do not, express an audit opinion on these financial statements.

Conclusion
Based on our work, nothing has come to our attention to refute the directors' confirmation that in accordance with the Companies Act 1985 the financial statements give a true and fair view of the state of the Company's affairs as at [date] and of its profit [/loss] for the year then ended and have been properly prepared in accordance with Generally Accepted Accounting Practice in the UK [/the Financial Reporting Standard for Smaller Entities].

Name of firm
Chartered Accountants
Location
Date

TABLE 10: Example accountants' report to directors and other parties

Accountants' independent assurance report on the unaudited financial statements of [entity name]

To the Board of Directors of [entity name] ('the Company') and [Third party]
We have performed certain procedures in respect of the Company's unaudited financial statements for the year ended [date] as set out on pages [x] to [x], made enquiries of the Company's directors and assessed accounting policies adopted by the directors, in order to gather sufficient evidence for our conclusion in this report.

This report is made solely to the Company's directors, as a body, and to [third party], [as a body], in accordance with the terms of our engagement letter dated [date]. It has been released to the directors and [third party] on the basis that this report shall not be copied, referred to or disclosed, in whole (save for the directors' own internal purposes or amongst the directors and [third party] or as may be required by law or by a competent regulator) or in part, without our prior written consent. Our work has been undertaken so that we might state to the directors and [third party] those matters that we have agreed to state to them in this report and for no other purpose. To the fullest extent permitted by law, we do not accept or assume responsibility to anyone other than the Company and the Company's directors as a body and [third party] [as a body] for our work, for this report or the conclusions we have formed.

Respective responsibilities

The Company's directors have confirmed that you have met their duty as set out in the directors' statement on page [x]. They consider that the Company is exempt from the statutory requirement for an audit for the year. Our responsibility is to form and express an independent conclusion, based on the work carried out, to the Company's directors and [third party] on the financial statements.

Scope

We conducted our engagement in accordance with the Institute of Chartered Accountants in England & Wales Interim Technical Release AAF 03/06. Our work was based primarily upon enquiry, analytical procedures and assessing accounting policies in accordance with Generally Accepted Accounting Practice in the UK[/the Financial Reporting Standard for Smaller Entities]. If we considered it to be necessary, we also performed limited examination of evidence relevant to certain balances and disclosures in the financial statements where we became aware of matters that might indicate a risk of material misstatement in the financial statements.

The terms of our engagement exclude any requirement to carry out a comprehensive assessment of the risks of material misstatement, a consideration of fraud, laws, regulations and internal controls, and we have not done so. We are not required to, and we do not, express an audit opinion on these financial statements.

Conclusion

Based on our work, nothing has come to our attention to refute the directors' confirmation that in accordance with the Companies Act 1985 the financial statements give a true and fair view of the state of the Company's affairs as at [date] and of its profit [/loss] for the year then ended and have been properly prepared in accordance with Generally Accepted Accounting Practice in the UK [/the Financial Reporting Standard for Smaller Entities].

Name of firm
Chartered Accountants
Location
Date

42.8   REPORTS ON INTERNAL CONTROLS OF SERVICE ORGANISATIONS

42.8.1   Background

Many entities use service organisations to perform various tasks for them. These services may vary from performing a certain task, such as preparing the payroll, to replacing entire business units. Many of the functions undertaken by service organisations affect an entity's financial statements and so auditors may seek information about the control procedures put in place by the service organisation.

Reporting accountants may be asked by service organisations to provide a report on their internal controls which they can supply to their customers and the customers' auditors.

In June 2006 the Audit and Assurance Faculty of the ICAEW issued AAF 01/06 *Assurance Reports on Internal Controls of Service Organisations Made Available to Third Parties* specifically in relation to financial service activities, including:

- custody;
- investment management;
- pension administration;
- property management;
- fund accounting; and
- transfer agency.

The guidance may be applied to other areas, such as payroll processing, but further considerations may be required.

AAF 01/06 replaces the original guidance in this area contained in AUDIT 4/97 *Reports on Internal Controls of Investment Custodians Made Available to Third Parties, FRAG 21/94 (Revised)* and is effective for periods ending on or after 31 March 2007.

42.8.2   Responsibilities of the service organisation

The directors of the service organisation are required to identify control objectives and the controls procedures which they consider appropriate to ensure that these control objectives are met. Their key responsibilities are:

- accepting responsibility for internal control;
- evaluating the effectiveness of the service organisation's controls procedures using suitable criteria;
- supporting their evaluation with sufficient evidence, including documentation; and

- providing a written report of the effectiveness of those control procedures for the relevant period.

The appendices to AAF 01/06 include a list of detailed control objectives for the financial services activities listed in **42.8.1** above. The list is not exhaustive and the directors of the service organisation are responsible for considering whether the objectives are sufficient for their organisation. The directors are required to make a statement in their report that they have referred to the examples in the appendices.

Service organisations are also responsible for:

- providing the reporting accountants with access to appropriate service organisation resources, such as service organisation personnel, systems documentation, contracts and minutes of management or audit committee meetings;
- disclosing to the reporting accountants any significant changes in control procedures that have occurred since the service organisation's last examination or within the last 12 months if the service organisation has not previously engaged reporting accountants to issue an assurance report;
- disclosing to the reporting accountants and the affected customers any illegal acts, fraud, or uncorrected errors attributable to the service organisation's management or employees that may affect its customers and the entity's whistle-blowing arrangements;
- disclosing to the reporting accountants any relevant design deficiencies in control procedures of which it is aware, including those for which the directors believe the cost of corrective action may exceed the benefits;
- disclosing to the reporting accountants all significant instances of which it is aware when control procures have not operated with sufficient effectiveness to achieve the specified control objectives; and
- providing the reporting accountants with a letter of representation.

42.8.3   Accepting the engagement

As with other reports where third parties may be seeking to place reliance on their report, reporting accountants may:

- accept that they owe a duty of care to the third parties and enter into a tri-partite or multi-partite engagement contract with the client and the third parties. Provisions to limit liability may be appropriate. A multi-partite engagement contract may be difficult where the service organisation has numerous customers;
- engage with the service organisation with the ability for its customers to be afforded the same duty of care agreed between the reporting accountant and the service organisation if they subsequently accept the relevant terms of the engagement letter, including any limitations on liability;

- proceed with an engagement with the client alone, but allowing access to the report for third parties as long as they:
  - acknowledge in writing that the reporting accountant owes them no duty of care; and
  - agree in writing that no claims will be brought against the reporting accountant in relation to the assurance report;
- engage with the client alone, disclaiming any liability or duty to others by notice in the assurance report. This may be in conjunction with the client indemnifying the reporting accountant if a third party makes a claim against the reporting accountant; or
- decline to accept the engagement.

Reporting accountants will always disclaim liability to the auditors of the service organisation's customers, as auditors will have responsibility for their own audit report.

Example extract terms of engagement are shown in **Table 11**.

TABLE 11:   Extracts of example engagement letter paragraphs for assurance reports on internal controls of service organisations

Responsibilities of directors
The Board of Directors ('the Directors') of [entity name] in relation to which the reporting accountant's assurance report is to be provided ('the Organisation') are and shall be responsible for the design, implementation and operation of control procedures that provide adequate level of control over customer's assets and related transactions. The Directors' responsibilities are and shall include:

- acceptance of responsibility for internal controls;
- evaluation of the effectiveness of the service organisation's control procedures using suitable criteria;
- supporting their evaluation with sufficient evidence including documentation; and
- providing a written report ('Directors' Report') of the effectiveness of the service organisation's internal controls for the relevant financial period.

In drafting this report the Directors have regard to, as a minimum, the criteria specified within the Technical Release AAF 01/06 issued by the Institute of Chartered Accountants in England & Wales ('the Institute') but they may add to these to the extent that this is considered appropriate in order to meet customers' expectations.

Responsibilities of reporting accountants
It is our responsibility to form an independent conclusion, based on the work carried out in relation to the control procedures of the Organisation's [ ] function carried out at the specified business units of the Organisation [located at [ ]] as described in the Directors' Report and report this to the Directors.

Scope of the reporting accountants' work

We conduct our work in accordance with the procedures set out in AAF 01/06, issued by the Institute. Our work will include enquiries of management, together with tests of certain specific control procedures which will be set out in an appendix to our report.

In reaching our conclusion, the criteria against which the control procedures are to be evaluated are the internal control objectives developed for service organisations as set out within the AAF 01/06 issued by the Institute.

Any work already performed in connection with this engagement before the date of this letter will also be governed by the terms and conditions of this letter.

We may seek written representations from the Directors in relation to matters on which independent corroboration is not available. We shall seek confirmation from the Directors that any significant matters of which we should be aware have been brought to our attention.

Inherent limitations

The Directors acknowledge that control procedures designed to address specified control objectives are subject to inherent limitations and, accordingly, errors or irregularities may occur and not be detected. Such procedures cannot guarantee protection against fraudulent collusion especially on the part of those holding positions of authority or trust. Furthermore, the opinion set out in our report will be based on historical information and the projection of any information or conclusion in our report to any future periods will be inappropriate.

Use of our report

Our report will, subject to the permitted disclosures set out in this letter, be made solely for the use of the Directors of the Organisation, and solely for the purpose of reporting on the internal controls of the Organisation, in accordance with these terms of our engagement.

Our work will be undertaken so that we might report to the Directors those matters that we have agreed to state to them in our report and for no other purpose.

Our report will be issued on the basis that it must not be recited or referred to or disclosed, in whole or in part, in any other document or to any other party, without the express prior written permission of the reporting accountants. We permit the disclosure of our report, in full only, to customers [of the Organisation using the Organisation's [financial services] ('customers') [(as defined in appendix [ ] to this letter,] and to the auditors of such customers, to enable customers and their auditors to verify that a report by reporting accountants has been commissioned by the Directors of the Organisation and issued in connection with the internal controls of the Organisation without assuming or accepting any responsibility or liability to them on our part.

To the fullest extent permitted by law, we do not and will not accept or assume responsibility to anyone other than the Directors as a body and the Organisation for our work, for our report or for the opinions we will have formed.

Liability provisions

We will perform the engagement with reasonable skill and care and acknowledge that we will be liable to the Directors as a body and Organisation for losses, damages, costs or expenses ('losses') suffered by the Directors as a body and the Organisation as a result of our breach of contract, negligence, fraud or other deliberate breach of duty. Our liability shall be subject to the following provisions:

- we will not be so liable if such losses are due to the provision of false, misleading or incomplete information or documentation or due to the acts or omissions of any person other than us, except where, on the basis of the enquiries normally undertaken by us within the scope set out in these terms of engagement, it would have been reasonable for us to discover such defects;
- we accept liability without limit for the consequences of our own fraud or other deliberate breach of duty and for any other liability which it is not permitted by law to limit or exclude;
- subject to the previous provisions of this Liability paragraph, our total aggregate liability, whether in contract, tort (including negligence) or otherwise, to the Directors as a body and the Organisation, arising from or in connection with the work which is the subject of these terms (including any addition or variation to the work), shall not exceed the amount of [to be discussed and negotiated].

To the fullest extent permitted by law, the Organisation agrees to indemnify and hold harmless [name of reporting accountants] and its partners and staff against all actions, proceedings and claims brought or threatened against [name of reporting accountants] or against any of its partners and staff by any persons other than the Directors as a body and the Organisation, and all loss, damage and expense (including legal expenses) relating thereto, where any such action, proceeding or claim in any way relates to or concerns or is connected with any of [name of reporting accountants]'s work under this engagement letter.

The Directors as a body and the Organisation agree that they will not bring any claims or proceedings against any of our individual partners, members, directors or employees. This clause is intended to benefit such partners, members, directors and employees who may enforce this clause pursuant to the Contracts (Right of Third Parties) Act 1999 ('the Act'). Notwithstanding any benefits or rights conferred by this agreement on such partners, members, directors or employees by virtue of the Act, we and the Directors as a body may together agree in writing to vary or rescind the agreement set out in this letter without the consent of any such partners, members, directors or employees. Other than as expressly provided in this paragraph, the provision of the Act are excluded.

Any claims, whether in contract, negligence or otherwise, must be formally commenced within [years] after the party bringing the claim become aware (or ought reasonably to have become aware) of the facts which give rise to the action and in any event no later than [years] after any alleged breach of contract, negligence or other cause of action. This expressly overrides any statutory provision which would otherwise apply.

This engagement is separate from, and unrelated to, our audit work on the financial statements of the Organisation for the purposes of the Companies Act 1985 (or its successor) or other legislation and nothing herein creates obligations or liabilities regarding our statutory audit work, which would not otherwise exist.

[*Appendix*
List of customers to whom the assurance report may be made available.]

Reporting accountants may become aware of third parties other than the service organisation's customers who may request sight of the report. In such cases, accountants may decline the request, or access may be agreed if the third party acknowledges in writing that they owe the accountant no duty of care.

42.8.4 *Reporting accountant's procedures*

Reporting accountants will read the directors' description of the controls procedures and undertake procedures to determine whether that description is a fair presentation. Procedures may include:

- discussing aspects of the control framework and relevant control procedures with management and other personnel;
- determining who the customers are and how the services provided by the service organisation are likely to affect the customers;
- reviewing standard terms of contracts with the customers to gain an understanding of the service organisation's contractual obligations;
- observing the procedures performed by the service organisation's personnel;
- reviewing the service organisation's policy and procedure manual and other systems documentation; and
- performing walkthrough tests on selected transactions and control procedures.

Reporting accountants should consider whether the control procedures are suitably designed. Their assessment may include:

- considering the linkage between the control procedure and the associated control objectives;
- considering the ability of the control procedures to prevent or detect errors; and
- performing further procedures such as enquiries of personnel, inspection

of documentation and observation of control procedures to determine whether they are adequately designed and operated as prescribed.

Where reporting accountants become aware that the control objectives are incomplete or inappropriate they discuss their findings with the directors and request that the directors amend their report accordingly. If the directors refuse to make suitable amendments, reporting accountants will highlight this fact in their report.

42.8.5 Reporting

The engagement performed by the reporting accountant is a reasonable assurance engagement, that is sufficient evidence is obtained to allow them to express a positive conclusion on the directors' report (see **Table 7**).

The report concludes on the fairness of the description and the design and operating effectiveness of controls procedures over a specified period. An example report is given in **Table 12**.

TABLE 12:   Example report on internal controls of service organisations

To the directors of [name of entity]

Use of report
This report is made solely for the use of the directors, as a body, of [name of entity], and solely for the purpose of reporting on the internal controls of [name of entity], in accordance with the terms of our engagement letter dated [date] [and attached as appendix [ ]].

Our work has been undertaken so that we might report to the directors those matters that we have agreed to state to them in this report and for no other purpose. Our report must not be recited or referred to in whole or in part in any other document nor made available, copied or recited to any other party, in any circumstances, without our express prior written permission.

We permit the disclosure of this report, in full only, by the directors at their discretion to customers [of [name of entity] using [name of entity]'s [financial services] ('customers'),] and to the auditors of such customers, to enable customers and their auditors to verify that a report by reporting accountants has been commissioned by the directors of [name of entity] and issued in connection with the internal controls of [name of entity], and without assuming or accepting any responsibility or liability to customers or their auditors on our part.

To the fullest extent permitted by law, we do not accept or assume responsibility to anyone other than the directors as a body and [name of entity] for our work, for this report or for the conclusions we have formed.

Subject matter

This report covers solely the internal controls of [name of entity] as described in your report as at [date]. Internal controls are processes designed to provide reasonable assurance regarding the level of control over customers' assets and related transactions achieved by [name of entity] in the provision of [outsourced activities] by [name of entity].

Respective responsibilities

The directors' responsibilities and assertions are set out on page [ ] of your report. Our responsibility is to form an independent conclusion, based on the work carried out in relation to the control procedures of [name of entity]'s [ ] function carried out at the specified business units of [name of entity] [located at [ ]] as described in your report and report this to you as the directors of [name of entity].

Criteria and scope

We conducted our engagement in accordance with International Standard on Assurance Engagement (ISAE) 3000 and the Institute of Chartered Accountants in England & Wales Technical Release AAF 01/06. The criteria against which the control procedures were evaluated are the internal control objectives developed for service organisations as set out within the Technical Release AAF 01/06 and identified by the directors as relevant control objective relating to the level of control over customers' assets and related transactions in the provision of [outsourced activities]. Our work was based upon obtaining an understanding of the control procedures as described on page [ ] to [ ] in the report by the directors, and evaluating the directors' assertions as described on page [ ] to [ ] in the same report to obtain reasonable assurance so as to form our conclusion. Our work also included tests of specific control procedures, to obtain evidence about their effectiveness in meeting the related control objectives. The nature, timing and extent of the tests we applied are detailed on pages [ ] to [ ].

Our tests are related to [name of entity] as a whole rather than performed to meet the needs of any or any particular customer.

Inherent limitations

Control procedures designed to address specific control objectives are subject to inherent limitations and, accordingly, errors or irregularities may occur and not be detected. Such control procedures cannot guarantee protection against (among other things) fraudulent collusion especially on the part of those holding positions of authority or trust. Furthermore, our conclusion is based on historical information and the projection of any information or conclusions in this report to any future periods would be inappropriate.

Conclusion

In our opinion, in all material respects:

- the accompanying report by the directors describes fairly the control procedures that relate to the control objectives referred to above which were in place as at [date];
- the control procedures described on pages [ ] to [ ] were suitably designed such that there is reasonable, but not absolute assurance that the specified

control objective would have been achieved if the described control
procedures were complied with satisfactorily [and customers applied the
control procedures contemplated]; and
- the control procedures that were tested, as set out in the attachment to this
  report, were operating with sufficient effectiveness for us to obtain
  reasonable, but not absolute, assurance that the related control objectives
  were achieved in the period [x] to [y].

Name of firm
Chartered Accountants
Location
Date

42.9   REPORTS TO OTHER THIRD PARTIES

42.9.1   Introduction

The Audit and Assurance Faculty increased the scope of the original
guidance on reporting to lenders to other third parties by publishing two
further Technical Releases: Audit 1/01, *Reporting to third parties* and 2/01
*Requests for references on clients' financial status and their ability to service
loans.*

The aim of Audit 1/01 is to establish the same type of approach as set out in
Audit 4/00 for all special reporting engagements. Firms should be on their
guard to avoid circumstances that may result in a duty of care for the
statutory audit report becoming established with a third party without
sufficient disclaimers being put in place.

The guidance in Audit 2/01 is only appropriate where there is no need to
perform any work, research or investigation to produce the reference. If
further work is required, then a formal engagement should be agreed under
Audit 1/01.

42.9.2   Audit 1/01: Reporting to third parties

Accountants have no obligation to sign reports requested by third parties
such as trade bodies or regulators, but may wish to do so in order to assist
their clients. Accountants should endeavour to become familiar with third
parties' demands for customised reports as early as possible in the
relationship with their client so that appropriate engagement terms can be
negotiated.

Technical Release Audit 1/01 aims to help accountants to manage their risk
in relation to providing such reports. However, it does not cover corporate
finance engagements, reports made under UK company legislation, which
will be covered by Practice Note 8, reports relating to public sector entities
or requests for references, which are covered by Audit 2/01.

The Technical Release sets out, under a number of headings, the process accountants should follow in response to requests from third parties. The process is illustrated by the flowchart in **Table 13**.

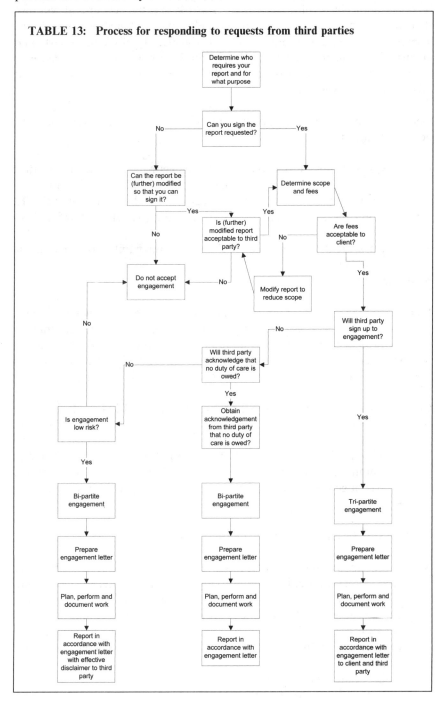

TABLE 13: Process for responding to requests from third parties

Determine who will rely on the accountants' work and for what purpose

When accountants become aware that a report has been requested, and will be relied upon, by a third party there is a risk that the accountant will owe that third party a duty of care unless an effective disclaimer is put in place. Therefore the accountant must determine the identity of the third party and details of the reliance they wish to place on the report, as well assessing the extent of loss the third party could suffer if they relied on the report and it proved to be misleading.

Once accountants have an understanding of the risks involved they can decide whether to:

- contract with the third party for the engagement and accept that they have a duty of care to the third party and limit liability if appropriate;
- contract with their client for the engagement and ensure that the third party confirms in writing that no duty of care exists before allowing them access to the report;
- contract with their client but disclaim or limit liability or duty to the third party in their report; or
- not accept the engagement.

If accountants regard a report as high risk they should only agree to provide the report if the third party either is a party to the engagement contract or has acknowledged that the accountants owe no duty of care to them in writing. Accountants should not allow their reports to be provided to third parties unless the extent of their liability to that party is clear.

Consider the form of the report requested by the third party

Accountants are not bound by any form of report agreed between the client and the third party without the accountants' consent. The form of report requested by the third party may not be appropriate for the accountant, and the accountant should not accept arguments that the form of the report cannot be changed (even where the report is of a 'standard' format in a pre-printed form).

Accountants should be wary of the following:

- wording giving an opinion on a matter as a statement of fact when that matter, by its nature, is inherently uncertain or a matter of judgement;
- the use of the term 'true and fair' when financial information is not prepared under the framework of Financial Reporting Standards;
- 'fair and reasonable' opinions, which are usually associated with investment banks making recommendations to shareholders in respect of transactions;
- wording that might suggest that the third party is able to rely on the statutory audit of the client;

- opinions that are open-ended or otherwise cannot be supported by the work carried out by the accountants;
- opinions which accountants do not have the necessary competence to provide, such as actuarial opinions or property valuations;
- opinions on matters beyond the accountants' knowledge and experience, particularly in relation to the detailed and specific operation circumstances of the client;
- wording that is open to interpretation;
- reports on internal controls where there are inadequate criteria for a sound control system;
- reports without addressees;
- reports on financial information which is not explicitly approved by the client;
- qualifications in covering letters only; and
- opinions which would impair the accountants' independence.

Accountants must only sign reports if they have performed sufficient work to support the statements they are asked to make. In some circumstances, such as reports on future solvency or performance of the client, statements cannot be supported by any amount of work, and accountants should refuse to sign such reports. Instead an agreed upon procedures form of report may be given, see below.

Agree the work to be performed and the form of the report to be given
In agreeing the work to be performed and form of report, accountants must make clear to clients and third parties that these engagements are separate from the statutory audit engagement and will be subject to separate terms and a separate fee. The terms for the report to third parties may include a limitation of liability.

The accountant must agree the form of report that is appropriate and the timescale in which it is to be delivered. The timescale must be realistic in relation to the amount of work the accountant will need to perform to provide the required opinion.

No UK auditing standards cover the forms of report which may be given, though some guidance is available in international standards. International standards break the types of report down into four types:

- *high level of assurance*, where a conclusion is expressed in positive terms;
- *moderate level of assurance*, requiring performance of limited procedures and possibly involving the provision of negative assurance in the style of 'nothing has come to our attention...';
- *agreed upon procedures*, which involves performing certain defined procedures on factual information and reporting findings without any form of opinion on the implications of the work done; and

- *compilation engagements*, which involve preparing financial information on behalf of clients.

Where reports are to be given to third parties an agreed upon procedures report is usually most suited to the requirements of the client and the third party. Accountants must consider the level of risk of giving the type of report requested by the third party (even after appropriate liability limits are set) and consider whether the engagement should be accepted.

Agree appropriate terms of agreement

The accountant should agree terms of engagement in writing with both the client and third party. If the third party refuses to sign an engagement letter, the accountant should either refuse to provide a report, or do so only subject to a disclaimer of liability to the third party. Disclaimers must be reasonable to be effective. An example disclaimer notice is given in **Table 14**:

TABLE 14:   Example disclaimer notices

Where the third party does not sign the engagement letter:

Our Report is prepared solely for the confidential use of [client name] and solely for the purpose of [details]. It may not be relied upon by [client name] for any other purpose whatsoever. Our Report must not be recited or referred to in whole or in part in any other document. Our report must not be made available, copied or recited to any other party [without our express permission]. [Accountant name] neither owes nor accepts any duty to any other party and shall not be liable for any loss, damage or expense of whatsoever nature which is caused by their reliance on our report.

Where the third party signs the engagement letter:
Our Report is prepared solely for the confidential use of [client name] and [name of third party], and solely for the purpose of [details]. It may not be relied upon by [client name] or [name of third party] for any other purpose whatsoever. Our Report must not be recited or referred to in whole or in part in any other document. Our Report must not be made available, copied or recited to any other party [without our express written permission]. [Accountant name] neither owes nor accepts any duty to any other party and shall not be liable for any loss, damage or expense of whatsoever nature which is caused by their reliance on our Report.

Example engagement letter extracts for an agreed upon procedures engagement are set out in **Table 15**.

TABLE 15: Example extracts from an engagement letter for an agreed upon procedures engagement

Services to be provided
We will complete the specified limited scope procedures set out below:

(describe the nature, timing and extent of the procedures to be performed, including specific reference, where applicable, to the identity of the documents and records to be read, individuals to be contacted and parties from whom confirmations will be obtained.)

The above procedures will be performed solely for your purposes. You are responsible for determining whether the scope of our work specified above is sufficient for your purposes.

Upon completion of the procedures we will provide you with a report of our findings in the form of that attached to this letter, solely for your information. Our report is not to be used for any other purpose or disclosed to any other third party without our consent. [We consent to the report being released to [third party name] provided that [third party name] acknowledges in writing that we owe no duty of care to [third party name] and we will not be liable to [third party name] for any reliance it chooses to place on the report.]

We have agreed that, under this engagement, we will not perform an audit or any verification procedures other than those which are specified in the scope section above. [If we were to perform additional procedures or if we were to perform an audit or any more limited review, other matters might come to our attention that would be reported to you.] Our report will not extend to any financial statements of the Company taken as a whole.

Audit work
Our audit work on the financial statements of the Company is carried out in accordance with our statutory obligations and is subject to a separate engagement letter. Our audit report is intended for the sole benefit of the Company's shareholders as a body, to whom it is addressed, to enable them to exercise their rights in general meeting. Our audits of the Company's financial statements are not planned or conducted to address or reflect matters in which anyone other than such shareholders as a body may be interested.

We do not, and will not, by virtue of this report or otherwise, assume any responsibility whether in contract, negligence or otherwise in relation to our audits of the Company's financial statements; we and our employees shall have no liability whether in contract, negligence or otherwise to [third party name if addressee to this letter, or to] any [other] third parties in relation to our audits of the Company's financial statements.

Scope of our work
The scope of our work and the procedures we shall carry out in preparing our report, together with the limitations inherent therein, are outlined above. If the scope and procedures do not meet your requirements, please tell us so that we

> can discuss a different scope or additional or alternative procedures. [You should understand that there is no guarantee that these procedures will result in the identification of all matters which may be of interest to you.]
>
> Our work will be based primarily on internal management information and will be carried out on the assumption that information provided to us by the management of the Company is reliable and, in all material respects, accurate and complete. We will not subject the information contained in our reports and letters to checking or verification procedures except to the extent expressly stated. This is normal practice when carrying out such limited scope procedures, but contrasts significantly with, for example, an audit. Even audit work provides no guarantee that fraud will be detected. You will therefore understand that the Services are not designed to and are not likely to reveal fraud or misrepresentation by the management of the Company. Accordingly we cannot accept responsibility for detecting fraud (whether by management or by external parties) or misrepresentation by the management of the Company.

Any engagement letter should include the following:

- an unambiguous description of the scope of work and form of report to be given;
- a description of the client's obligations and responsibilities;
- a statement that the engagement is separate from the statutory audit and that no duty of care will arise in relation to the statutory audit;
- if agreed, an appropriate liability cap;
- details of the addressee for the report, together with details of restrictions on who is entitled to see and rely on the report; and
- a copy of the report that will be provided.

Example wording for a liability cap is set out in **Table 16**.

TABLE 16:   Example liability cap

The aggregate liability, whether to [client name] or [third party name] or any other party, of whatever nature, whether in contract, tort or otherwise, of [Accountant's name] for any losses whatsoever and howsoever caused arising from or in any way connected with this engagement [and this transaction] shall not exceed [amount] (including interest).

Perform the work
The work for a third party report is separate to that for the statutory audit, and the audit team should put together a separate working paper file for this engagement.

Report
The report should reflect the terms set out in the engagement letter, and

should not include undefined terms such as 'review' without specifying what the terms mean.

Accountants should not modify the wording of their reports at the client's or third party's request unless the modification is appropriate and they have the opportunity to perform any additional work that is required to support the change in wording. If a different form of report is required to that set out in the engagement letter, the accountants should either reissue their terms of engagement or refuse to report, giving their reasons in writing.

Illustrative contents of a report of factual findings for an agreed upon procedures engagement are set out in **Table 17**.

TABLE 17: Illustrative contents of a report of factual findings for an agreed upon procedures engagement

These include:

- addressee;
- identification of the applicable engagement letter and specific information to which the agreed upon procedures have been applied;
- a statement that the procedures performed were those agreed with the client (and third party, if applicable);
- identification of the purpose for which the agreed upon procedures were performed;
- a listing of the specific procedures performed;
- a description of the accountants' factual findings, including sufficient details of errors and exceptions found;
- a statement that the procedures performed do not constitute either an audit or a review;
- a statement that had the accountants performed additional procedures, an audit or a review, other matters might have come to light that would have been reported;
- a statement that the report is restricted to those parties that have agreed to the procedures performed;
- a statement that the report relates only to the matters specified and that it does not extend to the entity's financial statements taken as a whole; and
- the date of the report.

42.9.3 Audit 2/01: Requests for references on clients' financial status and their ability to service loans

Accountants may be asked to provide references to banks, building societies and a range of other bodies about their clients' financial position, ability to pay debts as they fall due or service a loan. This is particularly relevant for individuals or small businesses that may not have audited accounts. Audit 2/01 provides guidance on how reporting accountants can manage their risks effectively when asked to perform such procedures.

The guidance is only appropriate where the accountant does not have to perform any additional work, research or investigation to give the reference. Where extra procedures have to be performed the guidance in Audit 1/01 should be followed.

The main issues

Third parties would like accountants to confirm that their client will have sufficient future income to service a loan or other commitment. However, no amount of enquiry can provide accountants with the assurance required to give such a confirmation.

Reporting on the present solvency of a client is only possible if the accountant is engaged to report on accounts, computations and projections as at a stated date. It is likely that the costs involved in producing such a report will be prohibitive to any third party.

References covered by Audit 2/01 require no extra work, and therefore incur no fee. This avoids the possibility of an implied contract. The fact that no extra work has been performed is stated in the reference.

Accountants may legitimately refuse to give a reference if they think the risks of doing so are too high, e.g. if the amounts involved are judged to be too large.

Unincorporated entities

Lenders who are entering into agreements with individuals and other unincorporated small borrowers, will not have audited reports to consider when making their lending decision. Accountants can, however, supply information that might be useful to a lender. This will include:

- the length of time the accountant has acted for the client;
- the net income or profits declared to the Inland Revenue; and
- a statement that the accountant has no reason to suppose that the client would have entered into a commitment which they would not expect to fulfil.

The third item above is a matter of judgement and will be based on the accountants' past experience of the client and the client's attitude to commercial obligations. Where accountants have insufficient knowledge of their client (for example, they have only just started to act) or there is any doubt about the judgement, they can decline to comment.

If the accountants' knowledge of the client is out of date, this will also be noted in the report.

Reporting

Accountants should report in a manner suitable for the particular circumstances. Third parties may provide a standard form of report, but accountants should amend the wording if necessary to reflect any limitations to the information requested.

Accountants should ensure that all technical terms are sufficiently defined, and should refer the third party to information provided directly by the client if this is more appropriate.

An example report is given in **Table 18**.

TABLE 18: Example of an accountants' reference in connection with a lending application made by an individual or other small borrower

Without responsibility

[Name of lender]

[Address]

Dear Sirs

REFERENCE IN CONNECTION WITH THE LENDING APPLICATION MADE BY [name of client and application reference, as appropriate]

Our above named client has approached us for a reference in connection with the proposed loan by you of [amount] [repayable by monthly instalments of amount over number years].

We have acted in connection with our client's [personal/business/corporate tax] affairs since [date]. However, it should be noted that our knowledge of our client's affairs may not be fully up to date. In addition, we have not carried out any specific work with regard to this statement.

Our client's net income [insert definition] declared by our client to the Inland Revenue as at [date] amounted to [amount]. (To be adapted for borrowers who are not individuals)

(Income/profits for previous years and identification of those agreed with the Inland Revenue may be added)

Whilst we have no reason to believe that our client would enter into a commitment such as that proposed which our client did not expect to be able to fulfil, we can make no assessment of our client's continuing income or future outgoings.

Whilst the information provided above is believed to be true, it is provided without acceptance by [Accountant's name] of any responsibility whatsoever, and any use you wish to make of the information is, therefore, entirely at your own risk.

```
Yours faithfully

Signed ....................
Dated  ....................
```

42.10   AUDIT LIABILITY: CLAIMS BY THIRD PARTIES

In June 2005, the Audit and Assurance Faculty of the ICAEW, in conjunction with the law firm Simmons & Simmons, published a review of the legal cases involving claims by third parties against auditors. It sets out the key matters arising from the cases of which auditors in practice should take note.

All the cases have in common an institution seeking assurance or reassurance from a company's auditors as to that company's financial strengths at a particular point in time, whether by reference to its audited accounts or by means of some other independent confirmation from the auditors that the company is financially sound.

As stated in **42.3** above, the case law surrounding auditors' duty of care was set out in the *Caparo v Dickman* judgement. That case set out that there would only be sufficient grounds to establish a duty of care to a third party where:

- the work produced was required for a purpose made known to the auditor; and
- the auditor knew, or should have known, that its work would be communicated to the non-client party for that purpose; and
- the auditor, knew or should have known, that its work would be likely to be relied upon by that third party for that purpose, without independent enquiry.

The main categories of cases where the application of these principles has been considered in the paper are:

- potential investors;
- creditors and lenders;
- regulators and trade bodies; and
- affiliates/associates of the audit client.

42.10.1   *Potential investors*

A duty of care to potential investors may occur other than in written form. In *ADT v Binder Hamlyn*, ADT, the potential investor, argued that a duty of care had been created when the audit partner made a comment in a meeting that the firm stood by its earlier unmodified audit opinion. ADT stated that they made further investment in Britannia Securities Group plc as a result of this affirmation and therefore sought damages from Binder Hamlyn when that investment lost money. By orally restating the true and fair opinion to the potential investor, the audit partner had assumed a duty of care to ADT which did not exist from the earlier audit report itself, as this had been prepared only with the shareholders of Britannia in mind.

An important element of the *Caparo* decision is whether the third party would have had another way of obtaining the assurance it sought from the auditor. In *Barker v Grant Thornton*, where potential investors are suing the auditor, no duty of care was found to exist as it was reasoned that it would have been practical for the investor to have instructed investigating accountants to obtain the necessary assurance for them rather than rely on the statutory audit report. In addition, Grant Thornton had already specifically disclaimed responsibility to the investor.

In *Yorkshire Enterprises Ltd v Robson Rhodes*, however, as the auditors were aware that they were completing the audit promptly because the financial statements were to be passed on to venture capitalists, it was not judged reasonable to require the investors to instruct their own investigating accountants. In addition, Robson Rhodes had not specifically disclaimed responsibility to Yorkshire Enterprises.

Two other cases set out in the study, *Electra Private Equity Partners v KPMG* and *Man Nutzfahrzeuge Aktiengesellschaft and Others v Ernst & Young and Others* demonstrate that auditors may have a duty of care to a third party not by what they said or did when auditing the financial statements, but merely on the basis of what they were told during the audit, for example that the audited financial statements were to be relied upon as the basis of a proposed sale. Such cases make the use of a disclaimer of the type recommended by Audit 1/03.

Another case where actuaries were sued by a potential investor in a client highlights the need for caution when auditors or other professional advisors are asked to provide copies of their reports to third parties. Although the courts eventually found for the actuaries, the absence of a statement clarifying that no responsibility was being assumed to the third party in providing a copy of the report caused a lengthy protraction of the case.

42.10.2 Creditors and lenders

The same principles apply to those that lend money rather than invest in a company. The case of *Royal Bank of Scotland v Bannerman Johnstone Maclay* it was sufficient that auditors should have been aware that a lender would rely on audited financial statements to create a duty of care. This case is discussed in **Chapter 3**.

42.10.3   Regulators and trade bodies

In a similar manner, in *Andrew & Others v Kounnis Freeman*, the auditors ought to have known that the audited financial statements which they forwarded to the Civil Aviation Authority (CAA) would be relied upon by the CAA in determining whether to renew a company's ATOL licence, and by sending the audited financial statements they assumed a duty of care.

In another case audited financial statements were forwarded by the client to ABTA and IATA. In addition they were sent to the provider of bond facilities to the travel agent. A travel agent is required to hold such bonds in order to be a member of ABTA and IATA. A duty of care was found to exist between the auditor and the bond provider, despite the auditor not knowing who would be providing the bond facilities. In this situation it was sufficient that the auditor, with experience of clients in the travel business, should be aware that a bond provider would be required and that this provider would need sight of the audited financial statements.

42.10.4   Affiliates or associates of the audit client

As well as separate third parties pursuing claims against auditors, there are situations where a claim is made by entities affiliated or associated with the audit client. In *Barings plc (in administration) and Others v Coopers & Lybrand and Others,* Barings sought damages from the auditors of one of its own indirect subsidiaries. It was judged that Coopers & Lybrand knew that their audit report on the subsidiary would be required to allow directors of the parent company to prepare group financial statements which showed a true and fair view. In addition, the auditors of the subsidiary had liaised directly with the auditors of the parent company, reporting to them any matters of significance so that they could inform the parent company management. Both these matters created a duty of care between the subsidiary auditors and the parent company, independent of the duty of care the subsidiary auditors had to their own client.

42.11   ISRS 4400

International guidance in the area of reports to third parties is provided by International Standard on Related Services (ISRS) 4400, *Engagements to Perform Agreed-Upon Procedures Regarding Financial Information.* ISRS 4400 was previously issued by the IAASB as ISA 920 and contains guidance on auditors' professional responsibilities when an engagement to perform agreed-upon procedures is undertaken.

In an agreed-upon procedures engagement, auditors will carry out procedures of an audit nature on which they and the entity, together with any relevant third parties, have agreed, and report on their findings. This report will be factual in nature and no assurance is expressed.

ISRS 4400 contains detailed guidance on:

- defining the terms of the engagement;
- planning,
- documentation;
- procedures and evidence; and
- reporting.

PART 5
SPECIALIST AUDITS

43 CHARITIES

43.1 LEGAL BACKGROUND

There are now a number of different regulators with responsibility for charities throughout the UK, and each is at a different stage in establishing its regulatory regime. The Charity Commission regulates charities in England and Wales, the Office of the Scottish Regulator governs charities registered in Scotland and also, to some extent, English or Welsh charities operating in Scotland. Northern Ireland is likely to have its own Charity Commission during 2007. This chapter mainly addresses the regime governing English and Welsh charities.

The Charities (Accounts and Reports) Regulations 2005 were issued in March 2005 and were applicable to all accounting periods beginning on or after 1 April 2005. The revised Charities SORP was also issued in 2005, and effective for accounting periods commencing 1 April 2005. In April 2002 the APB issued a revision to Practice Note 11, which was originally issued in October 1996, and Bulletin 2005/1, *Audit Risk and Fraud – Supplementary Guidance for Auditors of Charities*, dealing with ISAs as they affect charities was issued in 2005.

Charities that are subject to alternative legislative requirements to the Charities Act (such as the Companies Act for charities that are limited companies), or alternative SORPS to the Charities' SORP (for example, RSLs) should follow the accounting and auditing requirements in the alternative legislation or SORP. For charities which are limited companies, the DTI consider the SORP to be indicative of the accounting practices necessary for charities to produce financial statements which show a true and fair view. This chapter deals mainly with charities applying the Charities SORP or subject to the Charities Act 1993 accounting and auditing requirement.

In charitable companies the directors are also the charity trustees and the term 'trustees' has been used throughout to refer to both.

The Companies Act 2006 and the Charities Act 2006 will make significant changes to the audit and reporting regimes for charities which are not large companies. The changes in the Charities Act 2006 are effective from 27 February 2007, with requirements relating to financial years effective for financial years commencing on or after that date. Schedule 9, Pt. 1 of the Companies Act 2006 will remove the special provisions about accounts and audit of charitable companies. Charitable companies that qualify as a small company under company law will become subject to the scrutiny regime of the Charities Act 2006. This will mean that, in due course, company charities will be subject to the same independent examination and audit regime, depending upon their gross income and gross assets, as all other charities. Once these changes take effect only those charitable companies that do not qualify as small companies will remain subject to the audit regime of the Companies Acts.

Furthermore charities established in Scotland register separately as Scottish charities. The Charity Accounts (Scotland) Regulations 2006 apply to all charities with a financial year which begins on or after 1 April 2006. For accounting periods commencing before 1 April 2006 charities should continue to maintain accounting records and prepare accounts in accordance with the Charity Accounts (Scotland) Regulations 1992. The exemptions applicable to Scottish charitable corporations, local authority trusts, and registered housing associations as contained in statutory instruments 1993/1624, 1995/645 and 2000/49, and the exemption orders in 1993 and 2005 for designated religious bodies also continue to apply for accounting periods commencing before 1 April 2006. The OSCR Publication 'Scottish Charity Accounts – A Brief Guide' provides further guidance.

43.1.1 General

The Charities Act 2006 brings in a new regime for charities and is relevant for all accounting periods commencing on or after 27 February 2007.

For periods prior to this date, all charities, whether incorporated or not, with gross income in excess of £250,000 have to be audited (see **43.2** to **43.23**).

In England and Wales, registerable charities, which are not limited companies, with income or expenditure up to £250,000 in both their current year and the two preceding years, may elect to have their accounts independently examined instead of audited (see **43.1.2**).

Registerable charities which are not limited companies with income or expenditure up to £250,000 in both the current year and the preceding two years may elect to have their accounts independently examined instead of audited (see **43.1.2**).

Limited company charities with income between £90,000 and £250,000 are required to have an audit exemption report prepared (see **43.24**).

For financial years commencing on or after 27 February 2007, the audit threshold increases to:

- £500,000 gross annual income for all charities; or
- an aggregate value of assets over £2.8 million and gross annual income over £100,000 for non-company charities; or
- a balance sheet total over £2.8 million for charitable companies.

Registerable charities which are not limited companies with income or expenditure up to £500,000 in the relevant year may elect to have their accounts independently examined instead of audited (see **43.1.2**). This test used to have to apply to both the current year and the preceding two years.

Limited company charities with income between £90,000 and £500,000 and assets of £2.8 million or less will be required to have at least an audit exemption report prepared (see **43.24**). A charitable company with income of £90,000 or less will need neither an audit or an accountant's report unless its assets are over £2.8 million.

43.1.2 Independent examination

In England and Wales, for accounting periods commencing on or after 27 February 2007 unincorporated charities whose gross income is £500,000 or less in the relevant financial year and whose gross assets are £2.8 million or less at the end of the year may elect to have an independent examination.

Where gross assets exceed £2.8 million, provided gross income is less than £100,000, unincorporated charities may still elect to have an independent examination.

There is, however, no requirement for independent scrutiny where the gross income for the year in question is £10,000 or less.

The 2006 Act also introduces the requirement, where the gross income of the charity exceeds £250,000 and the charity is not subject to statutory audit (i.e. gross income does not exceed £500,000 and gross assets are £2.8 million or less), for the independent examiner to be a member of a specified accountancy body.

An independent examination does not have to be carried out by a professionally qualified individual but should be by a person suitable to the circumstances of the charity. The Regulations describe the examiner as 'an independent person who is reasonably believed by the trustees to have the requisite ability and practical experience to carry out a competent examination of the accounts'.

The independent examiner's report to the charity's trustees is intended to provide a moderate level of assurance (negative assurance) and should:

- specify that it is a report in respect of an examination carried out under the Charities Act and in accordance with any directions given by the Commissioners which are applicable;
- state whether or not any matter has come to the examiner's attention which gives him reasonable cause to believe that in any material respect:
  – accounting records have not been kept in accordance with the Act;
  – the accounts do not accord with the records;
  – state whether the accounts do not accord with the records; or
  – the accounts do not comply with the Regulations;
- state whether or not any matter has come to his attention which should be drawn to the attention of the trustees;
- disclose any material expenditure or action which appears not to be in accordance with the trusts of the charity; and
- disclose any information or explanation provided or any information in the accounts which is materially inconsistent with the trustees' report.

43.1.3   Whistle-blowing duties for auditors of unincorporated charities

The Regulations also give auditors and independent examiners of unincorporated charities similar rights and duties to those of regulated entities e.g., banks and financial services companies, to report directly to the regulator. Under this *whistle-blowing* requirement, they have to report in writing, under s8 (general power to institute inquiries) or s18 (power to act for protection of charities) of the 1993 Act, any matters which may be of material significance to the Charity Commission's function as a regulator, which came to light as a result of their work.

No similar requirement exists for auditors of incorporated charities which are limited companies, although the Practice Note makes it clear that the expectation that auditors of incorporated charities will report in the public interest effectively mirrors the requirement for unincorporated charities. The Charities Act 2006 will make the same duties and safeguards apply to auditors of limited companies.

The revised Practice Note has provided additional guidance in this area, and this is detailed in the section of this chapter that covers SAS 620/ISA (UK and Ireland) 250, Part B.

43.2 GUIDANCE

The major source of guidance for auditors is Practice Note 11 *The Audit of Charities*, which is designed to provide guidance on the application of the various SASs to charities. Table 1 sets out the SASs which the Practice Note covers.

TABLE 1: SASs considered by Practice Note 11

Responsibility

SAS 110 – *Fraud and Error.*
SAS 120 – *Consideration of Law and Regulations.*
SAS 130 – *The Going Concern Basis in Financial Statements.*
SAS 140 – *Engagement Letters.*
SAS 160 – *Other Information in Documents Containing Audited Financial Statements.*

Planning, controlling and recording

SAS 210 – *Knowledge of the Business.*
SAS 220 – *Materiality and the Audit.*

Accounting systems and internal control

SAS 300 – *Accounting and Internal Control Systems and Audit Risk Assessments.*

Audit evidence

SAS 400 – *Audit Evidence.*
SAS 410 – *Analytical Procedures.*
SAS 420 – *Audit of Accounting Estimates.*
SAS 440 – *Management Representations.*
SAS 450 – *Opening Balances and Comparatives.*
SAS 460 – *Related Parties.*
SAS 470 – *Overall Review of Financial Statements.*

Using the work of others

SAS 510 – *The Relationship between Principal Auditors and Other Auditors.*
Reporting
SAS 600 – *Auditors' Reports on Financial Statements.*
SAS 610 – *Reports to Directors or Management.*
SAS 620 – *The Auditors' Right and Duty to Report to Regulators in the Financial Sector.*

Although the Practice Note was issued prior to the APB adopting the ISAs (UK and Ireland) for the audit of periods beginning on or after 15 December

2004, the guidance it contains remains relevant under the new regime. Where the guidance, and this commentary, refers to the old SASs, this commentary also includes references to the relevant ISA (UK and Ireland).

Following the publication of the ISAs (UK and Ireland), the APB issued Bulletin 2005/1 *Audit Risk and Fraud – Supplementary Guidance for Auditors of Charities*, which considers the impact of the new risk and fraud ISAs (UK and Ireland). The Bulletin is considered alongside the sections covering the risk and fraud ISAs (UK and Ireland) below.

43.3   BACKGROUND

The Practice Note only covers audits of charities and considers independent examinations as a different type of engagement. It points to the problems presented by charities given:

- the diversity of accounting requirements which depend on size and corporate status;
- the regulatory framework which depends on where a charity is established and what it does, including the duty to report in certain circumstances to the Charities Commission;
- its governing document and the extent of its objects and powers;
- the fact that they may be responsible for public money;
- the wide public interest in them; and
- their special features, such as voluntary income, restricted funds and charitable status.

43.4   SAS 110 FRAUD AND ERROR/ISA (UK AND IRELAND) 240 THE AUDITOR'S RESPONSIBILITY TO CONSIDER FRAUD IN AN AUDIT OF FINANCIAL STATEMENTS

Bulletin 2005/1 sets out how ISA (UK and Ireland) 240 can be applied to the audit of charities.

In applying ISA (UK and Ireland) 240 (as well as SAS 110) to charities, auditors must be aware that the trustees are responsible for the prevention or detection of fraud in relation to the charity. However, the planning process of the audit must include an assessment of the possibility of fraud being committed by any of the people involved in the operation of the charity as well as by third parties. Certain features of charities may increase the risk of fraud, namely:

- widespread branches or operations, such as those established in response to emergency appeals in countries where there is no effective system of law and order;
- the use of volunteer and/or inexperienced staff;
- transactions often undertaken in cash;
- unpredictable patterns of giving by members of the public, both in terms of timing and point of donation; and
- the limited involvement of trustees in key decision making or monitoring.

Auditors are required by ISA (UK and Ireland) 240 to consider whether one or more fraud risk factors are present and to investigate whether unusual or unexpected relationships may indicate risks of material misstatement due to fraud. Analytical procedures may not be easily applied to the audit of charities, as the financial statements can be very difficult to predict.

The Practice Note points out that even where fraud has been reported to the trustees, the audit report must include details of any fundamental uncertainty or disagreement over disclosure of a suspected or actual instance of fraud or error.

The Practice Note lists the various authorities which regulate charities as being the proper authorities to which reports of frauds in the public interest should be made. For example, for charities established in England and Wales, except where exempt, the proper authority is the Charities Commission.

43.5 SAS 120 CONSIDERATION OF LAW AND REGULATIONS/ISA (UK AND IRELAND) 250 PART A CONSIDERATION OF LAWS AND REGULATIONS IN AN AUDIT OF FINANCIAL STATEMENTS

Because there are laws and regulations specifically made to cover charities and their activities, including laws which affect charities which undertake fundraising, auditors must have an understanding of applicable law and regulation. Auditors must be aware of the risk of money laundering given the relatively large sums of cash which many charities receive.

As in SAS 120 and ISA (UK and Ireland) 250 the Practice Note examines this area from the point of view:

- of laws relating directly to the preparation of financial statements; and
- those which provide a legal framework within which the entity conducts its business.

43.5.1   *Laws relating directly to the preparation of financial statements*

Auditors here must be aware of, in particular, the 1995 Accounting Regulations and the Charities SORP. In addition, charities may also be subject to Companies Act requirements and those which relate to housing associations.

Auditors should also check whether the charity's governing document contains any special disclosure or reporting requirements.

43.5.2   *Laws central to a charity's conduct of business*

Guidance is given on the interpretation of 'central' in the context of charities. Laws and regulations are seen to be central by the Practice Note if a breach would lead to:

- the appointment of a receiver or manager by the Charities Commission;
- the loss of necessary licences to continue a major part of its operations; or
- financial effects resulting in liabilities which exceed available resources.

These laws will to a large extent be dependent on the charity's activities. They may be subject to:

- Charities Act requirements relating to fundraising, property and borrowing transaction;
- laws on raising funds through lotteries;
- laws relating to house to house or street collections;
- Trustee Investments Act;
- Children's Act requirements;
- Registered Homes Act;
- Environmental Protection Act; and
- food safety and hygiene regulations.

Auditors must be aware of the objects of the charity and the fact that the Charities Commission has powers to suspend or remove trustees, officers, agents or employees and to freeze the property and appoint a receiver and manager if they consider that the charity's property requires protection.

Auditors must also be aware of tax as, although most activities of a charity do not attract taxation, trading other than directly or indirectly in furtherance of the charity's objects may well give rise to a tax liability. In addition, the VAT position is different to that relating to corporation tax as exemptions do not generally apply.

Similar considerations to those for other companies apply where breaches of law and regulations are found.

43.6 SAS 130 GOING CONCERN BASIS IN FINANCIAL STATEMENTS/ISA (UK AND IRELAND) 570 GOING CONCERN

This can be a difficult area in the audit of charities as many charities have an apparent financial weakness which is often compounded by the uncertainty of future income. Their ability to raise revenue will often be outside their direct control, and be dependent on such matters as the voting of grants and spending of the public.

It may also be difficult for a charity to cut back on a project or grant funding in the event of a liquidity problem, and although it may have an apparently large bank balance it may be unable to meet general liabilities because the balance in question belongs to a restricted fund.

The Practice Note provides examples of conditions which may indicate that the charity is not a going concern. These include:

- inability to finance its operations from its own resources;
- decision by the trustees to curtail or cease activities;
- loss of essential resources or key staff;
- loss of operating licence;
- significant changes in strategy of major funders; and
- significant decline in donations by the public.

Similar considerations apply to charities as to commercial entities. Auditors must assess whether there is sufficient disclosure of relevant circumstances to enable financial statements to give a true and fair view on this issue. The trustees' report may also contain disclosures giving indications of factors such as future expected income based on past donations or patterns of giving.

In considering going concern, the Practice Note suggests it may be helpful for the auditors to include the following points in discussions with trustees:

- the nature of management information systems covering future income and expenditure;
- the level of forecast future expenditure, analysed between committed and discretionary;
- the level of 'known' future income (deriving from sources such as endowments, investments, and Deeds of Covenant – after allowing for Deeds terminated due to unforeseen circumstances);
- shortfall of income on forecast expenditure needing to be made up by

voluntary donations of cash or other resources;
- past patterns of income and expenditure;
- where the charity relies on a major donor, whether it is practical to obtain comfort in relation to their future support;
- level of uncommitted reserves available;
- lists of projects supported or awards made in the year and planned for the following year;
- comparison of previous budgets to actual performance;
- the reasonableness of the assumptions underlying the current budgets;
- any reliance on support by the charity's bankers, major donors, or public authorities;
- any reliance on a particular client group; and
- any special operating licences or similar conditions.

The going concern concept does not apply to the preparation of financial statements on a receipts and payments basis (allowed for small unincorporated charities in England and Wales which are within the income thresholds defined by legislation). In these circumstances auditors should consider whether there are matters that affect the charities' ability to continue operational existence for the foreseeable future. Auditors should not issue their report unless they are satisfied with explanations received from trustees concerning future funding arrangements. If they are not satisfied they may find it appropriate to include an explanatory paragraph in their report. They will not qualify their report on the proper presentation of the receipts and payments account.

43.7   SAS 140 ENGAGEMENT LETTERS/ISA (UK AND IRELAND) 210 TERMS OF AUDIT ENGAGEMENTS

Engagement letters will normally be sent to the trustees although they may be sent to a different appointing authority. The engagement may cover reports on other funds or on the disposition of local authority grants. Auditors will need to check documentation relating to funds received by the charity for consideration requiring special reports. Where trustees are not involved in the day-to-day running of the charity, the Practice Note suggests that auditors may send an additional copy to the chief executive or person responsible for that day-to-day management.

43.8 SAS 160 OTHER INFORMATION/ISA (UK AND IRELAND) 720 OTHER INFORMATION IN DOCUMENTS CONTAINING AUDITED FINANCIAL STATEMENTS

The Practice Note lists the types of other information that may be in documents containing audited financial statements.

The Charities SORP requires trustees of charities with gross income exceeding £250,000 to state in their report that the major identified risks to which the charity is exposed have been reviewed and that systems have been put in place to mitigate such risks. Smaller charities are not required to give this information, but it is considered good practice to make a statement about risk assessment and mitigation. Whilst auditors are not expected to verify any risk management statement made by trustees, they should consider the disclosures made in relation to their knowledge of the charity's circumstances and systems.

The Practice Note suggests that where corporate governance statements are made the guidance in Bulletin 1995/1 is referred to (see Chapter **15**).

43.9 SAS 210 KNOWLEDGE OF THE BUSINESS/ ISA (UK AND IRELAND) 315 UNDERSTANDING THE ENTITY AND ITS ENVIRONMENT AND ASSESSING THE RISKS OF MATERIAL MISSTATEMENT

Auditors will need knowledge of the special features of charity audits, and in planning they will need to be aware of the following:

- the existence of special regulations governing the conduct of charities;
- sources of income which may include grants from public authorities or funds held on trust. Breaches of the conditions relating to the use of such income can have serious implications to the charity;
- tax relief dependent upon a charity complying with the governing document submitted to the Inland Revenue;
- activities of the charity which bring it within the scope of other regulations, as well as those relating to charities;
- the level of involvement in the administration of the charity which can be expected of trustees; and
- the way in which the charity is managed on a day-to-day basis.

In terms of the regulatory framework the factors considered under SAS 120/ ISA (UK and Ireland) 250 Part A above will apply.

Auditors must be aware of the way in which the charity conducts its operations, whether through:

- groups of distinct legal entities;
- associated undertakings;
- what are effectively branches; or
- by subcontracting to non-controlled organisations.

Depending on the structure, the accounting requirements will be different.

Overseas operations can also present difficulty as there is a wide range of structures which charities can adopt. Auditors must determine the legal status and decide whether their accounts need to be incorporated within the main accounts of the charity.

The source of much information about a charity will be its officers and trustees together with its governing document. For larger charities sources of information may include specialist publications and umbrella organisations which provide statistics and industry norms.ISA (UK and Ireland) 315 requires auditors to use their understanding of the entity and its environment to assess the risk of material misstatement in the financial statements. Bulletin 2005/1 gives details of the areas that auditors of charities should consider.

43.10   SAS 220 MATERIALITY/ISA (UK AND IRELAND) 320 AUDIT MATERIALITY

Materiality should be considered with regard to the applicable laws and regulations and any additional reports the auditors are required to make – for example, in respect to restricted funds. The general principles underlying the consideration of materiality apply to audits of charities in a similar way to other entities.

43.11   SAS 300 INTERNAL CONTROL/ISA (UK AND IRELAND) 315 UNDERSTANDING THE ENTITY AND ITS ENVIRONMENT AND ASSESSING THE RISKS OF MATERIAL MISSTATEMENT AND ISA (UK AND IRELAND) 330 THE AUDITOR'S PROCEDURES IN RESPONSE TO ASSESSED RISKS

ISA (UK and Ireland) 315
SAS 300 and ISA (UK and Ireland) 315 require auditors to obtain an understanding of the accounting and internal control systems sufficient to

plan the audit and develop an effective audit approach. There is a wide variation between different charities in terms of size, activity and organisation so that there can be no standard approach to internal control and risk. Even large national charities with sophisticated control systems may have local branches that are run by voluntary staff on an informal basis.

43.11.1 Inherent risk

The Practice Note lists the factors which may affect the auditors' assessment of inherent risk. These include:

- the significance of donations and cash receipts;
- fundraising by non-controlled bodies;
- the extent of donations by credit card or over the internet;
- the valuation of donations in kind;
- uncertainty over completeness of income;
- operational limitations imposed by governing documents;
- restricted funds;
- difficulties in identifying and quantifying liabilities arising from constructive obligations;
- sensitivity of key statistics, such as the proportion of resources used for administration purposes;
- trading activities; and
- complexities of tax rules relating to charities.

43.11.2 Control environment

Auditors must assess the adequacy of controls in relation to the circumstances of each charity. Here, the attitude rather than involvement of the trustees is likely to be fundamental.

The features of a sound control environment – for example, clearly defined authority, segregation of duties, competent staff, budgetary controls – are similar to those that apply in commercial organisations.

Auditors may also need to ensure that there is control over grants made to other bodies.

Bulletin 2005/1 provides details of factors that auditors should consider when assessing the control environment of a charity. These include the:

- amount of time committed by trustees to the charity's affairs;
- skills and qualifications of individual trustees;
- frequency and regularity of trustee meetings and the level of attendance at these meetings;
- form and content of trustee meetings;
- independence of trustees from each other;

- division of duties between trustees;
- supervision by the trustees of relatively informal working arrangements which are common when employing volunteers;
- degree of involvement in, or supervision of, the charity's transactions on the part of individual trustees;
- level of delegation by trustees to senior management and the formality of this delegation; and
- the committee structure of the organisation.

In addition, auditors should review any risk register maintained by the charity to ascertain what the trustees determine to be the business risks faced by the charity and what control systems they have established to mitigate those risks. The auditors' assessment of related business processes, in line with the requirements of ISA (UK and Ireland) 315, should include ensuring that systems accurately capture details of restrictions on income.

43.11.3   Control activities

Tables 2 to 6 show examples of control activities which the Practice Note considers may be applicable to charities and of which auditors should gain an understanding to enable them to assess the risk of material misstatement at the assertion level and design further audit procedures responsive to those assessed risks.

TABLE 2: Controls over cash donations	
Source	*Examples of Controls*
Collecting boxes and tins	<ul><li>numerical control over boxes and tins</li><li>satisfactory sealing of boxes and tins so that any opening prior to recording cash is apparent</li><li>regular collection and recording of proceeds from collecting boxes</li><li>dual control over counting and recording of proceeds</li></ul>
Other cash receipts	<ul><li>clear directions to staff on how to handle cash donations</li><li>advice to donors on where to make donations securely</li></ul>
Postal receipts	<ul><li>unopened mail kept securely</li><li>dual control over the opening of mail</li><li>immediate recording of donations on opening of mail or receipt</li><li>agreement of bank paying in slips to record of receipts by an independent person</li></ul>
Receipts over the internet	<ul><li>sending a confirmation receipt to the donor</li><li>controls over the writing up of daybooks</li></ul>

TABLE 3: Controls over other donations	
Source	*Examples of controls*
Gift aid/Deeds of Covenant	• regular checks and follow up procedures to ensure due amounts are received • regular checks to ensure all tax repayments have been obtained
Legacies	• comprehensive correspondence file maintained in respect of each legacy • numerically controlled searches of agency reports of legacies receivable • regular reports and follow up procedures undertaken in respect of outstanding legacies • security of chattels received as legacies and procedures to establish their value and proper realisation
Donations in kind	• in case of charity shops, separation of recording, storage and sale of stock • all types of activity: immediate recording of donated assets

TABLE 4: Controls over other income	
Source	*Examples of controls*
Fund-raising activities	• records maintained for each fund-raising event • other controls maintained over receipts appropriate to the type of activity and receipt (see Tables **2** and **3**) • controls maintained over expenses as for administrative expenses
Central and local government grants and loans	• regular checks that all sources of income or funds are fully utilised and appropriate claims made • ensuring income or funds are correctly applied in accordance with the terms of the grant or loan • comprehensive records of applications made and follow up procedures for those not discharged

TABLE 5: Controls over fixed assets	
Source	*Examples of controls*
Existence of assets	• a register of fixed assets maintained, including donated assets
Valuation	• donated assets recorded at approximate market value, where appropriate • depreciation calculated and recorded in accordance with proper assessment of future benefits derived from assets' use

TABLE 6: Controls over use of funds	
Source	*Examples of controls*
Restricted funds	• separate records maintained of relevant revenue, expenditure and assets • terms controlling application of funds • oversight of application of fund monies by independent personnel or trustees
Grants to beneficiaries	• records maintained covering requests for material grants received and their treatment • appropriate checks made on applications and applicants for grants, and that amounts paid are *intra vires* • records maintained of all grant decisions, checking that proper authority exists, that adequate documentation is presented to decision making meetings, and that any conflicts of interest are recorded • controls to ensure that grants made are properly spent by the recipient for the specified purpose, for example, requirements for returns with supporting documentation or auditors' reports concerning expenditure, or monitoring visits

Where charities have UK or overseas branches, control activities may include:

- regular reports to head office by any branch, office or individual, checks to ensure these are received and a mechanism for monitoring branch activities;
- prompt investigations of reports of misuse of the charity's name;
- internal controls of a standard equivalent to those in the main charity for any branch where trustees have direct control;

- accounts and procedures manuals for branches;
- acknowledgements of remittances to and from branches abroad;
- clear instructions on receipt and transfer of income to identify when it is branch funds or main charity funds;
- controls over recruitment of staff in branches;
- defined authorisation limits and responsibilities for local staff;
- periodic checks from head office or internal audit of material amounts;
- retention of documents for local inspection or for periodic transmission to head office; and
- treasury operations to ensure that overseas funds are held in a hard currency and foreign exchange exposure is minimised.

In accordance with ISA (UK and Ireland) 315 auditors are required to assess the risk of material misstatement at the financial statements level, for classes of transactions, account balances and transactions. There are many factors which may affect the risk of material misstatement in charities including the:

- complexity and extent of regulation;
- valuation of donations in kind;
- uncertainty of future income; and
- special consideration that must be made of restricted funds.

Further examples are provided in Bulletin 2005/1. Auditors must then consider whether any of these risks are significant risks for which special audit consideration must be given, including the evaluation of related controls and the planning and performance of related procedures.

ISA (UK and Ireland) 330

ISA (UK and Ireland) 330 requires auditors to plan and perform specific audit procedures where they have identified a significant risk of material misstatement. Common areas for the risk of material misstatement for charities are:

- ensuring completeness of incoming resources;
- overseas operations; and
- restricted funds.

Completeness of income

Typically income from charities comes from a number of different sources, such as grants and public donations, and its amount and timing is often difficult to predict. Trustees cannot be expected to have responsibility for funds until they are, or should be, within the control of the charity, but as soon as this happens, trustees should implement procedures to ensure appropriate recording and safeguarding of the funds.

The Bulletin suggests the following possible substantive procedures for completeness of incoming resources:

- where professional fundraisers have been used to generate funds, auditors can review terms of the agreement between the charity and the fundraiser and other relevant documentation to ensure that all funds have been accounted for;
- check the arrangements for the transferral of funds from branches, associates or subsidiaries to the main charity, to determine when funds are recognised;
- review correspondence with solicitors to determine when legacy income is reasonably certain, its value can be measured and it can therefore be recorded;
- where informal groups raise funds for a charity, without the charity's knowledge, charities have no obligation to record the income until it is received, and so auditors should ensure that funds are not recorded prior to this time;
- examination of grant applications and correspondence to determine completeness of grant income, including direct confirmation about the amounts receivable from the grant provider; and
- auditors should consider the procedures in place for recognising and valuing non-cash donations, such as goods and services. They should also review the disclosures in the financial statements regarding the basis of valuation of non-cash donations to ensure it is reasonable.

Substantive procedures may be limited by the uncertainty affecting donations, but they may be of use to corroborate other evidence.

Overseas operations

Where overseas operations exist, auditors will be required to obtain evidence of material expenditure overseas and gain an understanding of when overseas expenditure has occurred. Where the overseas operations are part of the charity, the expenditure will not be incurred when money is transferred to the overseas branch, but when the expenditure is actually made by that branch.

The Bulletin suggests the following procedures:

- consideration of internal control procedures put in place by the charity, and how adherence to procedures is monitored;
- obtaining evidence from field officers' reports as to work undertaken;
- comparison of accounting returns of expenditure with field reports and plans for consistency and reasonableness;
- analytical review of accounting returns received from overseas branches or local agents;
- consideration of any inspection or internal control visit reports undertaken by any internal audit function; and

- consideration of audit work undertaken by local auditors.

Where material assets are held or material funds are applied by overseas operations, the Bulletin suggests that auditors make site visits to obtain evidence.

Where a charity makes a grant to an autonomous overseas charity, auditors ensure:

- receipt of the funding; and
- that the charity has exercised reasonable diligence in ensuring that the funds are used for charitable purposes.

Restricted funds
Restricted funds which are subject to specific rules about their application may give rise to a significant risk of material misstatement. Auditors should consider:

- the terms or conditions attached to the restricted funds;
- any funds in deficit;
- any income funds held in illiquid assets, preventing application of the fund; and
- capital being expended without authority.

The Bulletin suggests the following audit procedures:

- consideration of internal control procedures put in place by the charity to identify restricted funds;
- consideration of the methods used in cost allocation;
- comparison of expenditure with the terms of the restricted funds;
- consideration of the recoverability of negative balances; and
- consideration of the ability of the fund to meets its obligations in view of its underlying assets.

43.12 SAS 400 EVIDENCE/ISAS (UK AND IRELAND) 500 AUDIT EVIDENCE, 501 AUDIT EVIDENCE – ADDITIONAL CONSIDERATIONS FOR SPECIFIC ITEMS AND 505 EXTERNAL CONFIRMATIONS

Charities also provide certain difficulties in collection of evidence in different areas:

The Practice Note sees completeness of income as being the major problem.

It suggests that the best way to obtain evidence is to ascertain a system of control, and test it.

The Practice Note warns about diversion of donations to bank or building society accounts not owned by a charity. The question of when income accrues to a main charity where it had affiliated leagues of friends and similar independent bodies will also arise. Here, auditors will need to check agreements made between charities under the 1992 Charities Act with particular emphasis on when the money is to be transmitted to the charity.

A combination of testing of reliance on internal controls, analytical review procedures and substantive testing of accounting records will normally provide auditors with sufficient appropriate evidence. Where this is not the case they will need to consider the implications for their report in relation to a limitation of scope.

Other areas where collection of evidence may give rise to problems are:

- verification of expenditure;
- recognition and measurement of donations made by way of goods, other assets or services;
- overseas branch and operation; and
- the accounting of retail operations run by volunteers.

43.13   SAS 410 ANALYTICAL PROCEDURES/ISA (UK AND IRELAND) 520 ANALYTICAL PROCEDURES

The Note sets out certain analytical procedures which auditors may find useful:

- comparison of actual income and expenditure to prior year figures and trends;
- comparison of actual to budgeted results;
- comparison of actual expenditure to the auditors own estimate of expenditure;
- comparison of results of an individual branch to those of similar branches of the main charity;
- checking charity shop sales revenue to notional revenue based on estimated sales value of stocks sold;
- comparison of sales per square foot of selling space to retail sale statistics for similar shops;
- analyses of efficiency ratios such as staff or administration costs as a percentage of benefits delivered or grants made; and
- comparison of actual donations received to the amount which would be expected on the basis of available charity statistics.

43.14 SAS 420 ACCOUNTING ESTIMATES/ISA (UK AND IRELAND) 540 AUDIT OF ACCOUNTING ESTIMATES

Accounting estimates in the financial statements of charities should be audited using similar principles to other entities, bearing in mind the accounting requirements of the SORP. Examples of instances where estimates may be used include:

- ascertaining the value of legacy income (though this should only be recognised where the amount is reasonably certain);
- allocation of costs in the Statement of Financial Activities;
- valuations of donations in kind; and
- valuation of fixed assets where no market price exists.

Auditors will ensure that techniques selected by the trustees enable the financial statements to give a true and fair view and that the financial statements disclose a description of the estimation techniques used, in order to comply with FRS 18, *Accounting Policies* and the Charities SORP.

43.15 SAS 440 MANAGEMENT REPRESENTATIONS/ISA (UK AND IRELAND) 580 MANAGEMENT REPRESENTATIONS

A representation letter in respect of the financial statements of the charity is normally signed by the trustees who are responsible for the contents and presentation of the financial statements.

Where day to day management of the charity is delegated to senior management by trustees and representations are taken from those staff, auditors should ensure that the staff involved have the necessary authority and all such representations are considered and approved by the trustees.

43.16 SAS 450 OPENING BALANCES AND COMPARATIVES/ISAS (UK AND IRELAND) 510 INITIAL ENGAGEMENTS – OPENING BALANCES AND CONTINUING ENGAGEMENTS – OPENING BALANCES AND 710 COMPARATIVES

Because of the possibility that charities will qualify by reason of size for an audit where previously they were exempt, cases will arise where charities will not have had opening balances audited and the receipts and payments basis of accounting may have been used. If either or both occurs, auditors will normally need to qualify their reports on the basis of limitation of audit scope. Such a qualification is shown in **Table 10**.

43.17   SAS 460 RELATED PARTIES/ISA (UK AND IRELAND) 550 RELATED PARTIES

It is a fundamental principle of trust law that a trustee should not benefit directly or indirectly from his or her trust. Neither charity trustees nor persons connected with them should transact business with the charity unless expressly permitted by the charities governing document or an appropriate authority. There are also disclosure requirements in the Charities SORP and in the regulations.

43.18   SAS 470 OVERALL REVIEW OF FINANCIAL STATEMENTS

Auditors should consider whether the accounting policies are appropriate to the charity, consistently applied and adequately disclosed, as well as whether the results for the year are fairly presented.

Particular consideration should be given to:

- disclosure of income from fundraising activities;
- capitalising expenditure on fixed assets;
- apportioning administrative expenditure;
- recognising income from donations and legacies;
- treatment of exceptional items;
- presentation of special or irregular income or expenditure; and
- disclosure of restricted funds.

There is no ISA (UK and Ireland) equivalent for this SAS.

43.19   SAS 480 SERVICE ORGANISATIONS/ISA (UK AND IRELAND) 402 AUDIT CONSIDERATIONS RELATING TO ENTITIES USING SERVICE ORGANIZATIONS

The requirements for auditors to review arrangements between charities and their service organisations does not vary from that which exists where a company is audited.

The use of service organisations by charities is not uncommon and includes services provided to the charity such as:

- maintenance of accounting records;
- payroll services;
- fundraising;
- custodianship of assets; and
- investment management services.

43.20 SAS 510 RELATIONSHIP BETWEEN PRINCIPAL AUDITORS AND OTHERS/ISA (UK AND IRELAND) 600 USING THE WORK OF ANOTHER AUDITOR

Where other auditors are used because they act for local branches, subsidiaries or other units, principal auditors must assess the degree of reliance they intend to place on the other auditors' work. Where the charity is a limited company, there is a statutory obligation on auditors of any subsidiary undertaking that is a company to communicate such information and explanations as may be reasonably required by the principal auditors. Where the charity is unincorporated, auditors have rights under section 44(1)(d) of the 1993 Act of access to books, documents and records which relate to the charity. This extends beyond those actually in the ownership of the charity. Generally, the principal auditors will take steps including:

- agreeing with the client a standard mandate to be issued to the secondary auditors covering the scope of work to be undertaken and reports to be issued;
- issuing a standard questionnaire to be completed by the subsidiary auditors; and
- obtaining a report of principal findings direct from subsidiary auditors.

Similar considerations apply where auditors rely on the work of others to undertake audit work relating to overseas branches or subsidiaries of a charity.

43.21 SAS 600 AUDITORS' REPORTS ON FINANCIAL STATEMENTS/ISA (UK AND IRELAND) 700 THE AUDITOR'S REPORT ON FINANCIAL STATEMENTS

The 1995 regulations determine that audit reports should be addressed to the trustees unless the auditor has been appointed by the Charity Commission. Companies and Friendly Societies statutes require audit reports to be addressed to the members.

The trustees' responsibilities may vary depending upon the constitution of the particular charity. The Companies Act and the Friendly and Industrial and Provident Societies Act establish duties under law. Where a charity is not subject to regulation, the Practice Note recommends the form of words shown in **Table 7.**

TABLE 7:   Example statement of trustees' responsibilities

'Law applicable to charities in England & Wales/Scotland/Northern Ireland requires the trustees to prepare financial statements for each financial year which give a true and fair view of the charity's financial activities during the year and of its financial position at the end of the year (unless the charity is entitled to prepare modified accounts on a receipts and payments basis). In preparing financial statements giving a true and fair view, the trustees should follow best practice and:

- select suitable accounting policies and then apply them consistently;
- make judgments and estimates that are reasonable and prudent;
- state whether applicable accounting standards have been followed, subject to any material departures disclosed and explained in the financial statements; [For large charitable companies.]
- state whether applicable accounting standards and statements of recommended practice have been followed, subject to any departures disclosed and explained in the financial statements; [For unincorporated charities required to produce financial statements on an accruals basis.]
- prepare the financial statements on the going concern basis unless it is inappropriate to presume that the charity will continue in operation.

The trustees are responsible for keeping proper accounting records which disclose with reasonable accuracy the financial position of the charity and which enable them to ensure that the financial statements comply with the [applicable law/regulations/trust deed]. They are also responsible for safeguarding the assets of the charity and hence for taking reasonable steps for the prevention and detection of fraud and other irregularities.'

Where charities are required to prepare statements which show a true and fair view then compliance with accounting standards is necessary.

The Practice Note puts forward the argument that since the Charities SORP has been developed and issued under the code of practice established by the Accounting Standards Board for the production and issue of SORPs it is authoritative guidance on the application of accounting standards to charities.

As the 1993 Act requires trustees to state whether financial statements have been prepared in accordance with SORP this provision, taken with the general status of the SORP, implies a strong presumption that the financial statements will need to follow the SORP in order to give a true and fair view.

In addition, FRS 2 and the SORP indicate that it is necessary for reporting entity to prepare consolidated financial statements in certain circumstances.

The Practice Note gives examples of certain opinions. The unqualified opinion and the one relating to limitation of scope are reproduced in **Tables 8** and **9**.

TABLE 8: Unqualified opinion: unincorporated charity in England and Wales preparing financial statements under s42(1) of the Charities Act 1993

Report of the independent auditors to the trustees of XYZ charity
We have audited the financial statements of XYZ charity for the year ended [date] on pages ... to .... These statements have been prepared under the historical cost convention as modified by the revaluation of certain fixed assets and the accounting policies set out therein.

Respective responsibilities of trustees and auditors
The trustees' responsibilities for preparing the Annual Report and the financial statements in accordance with applicable law and United Kingdom Accounting Standards are set out in the Statement of Trustees' Responsibilities.

We have been appointed as auditors under section 43 of the Charities Act 1993 and report in accordance with regulations made under section 44 of that Act. Our responsibility is to audit the financial statements in accordance with relevant legal and regulatory requirements and the United Kingdom Auditing Standards.

We report to you our opinion as to whether the financial statements give a true and fair view and are properly prepared in accordance with the Charities Act 1983. We also report to you if, in our opinion, the Trustees' Annual Report is not consistent with the financial statements, if the charity has not kept proper accounting records or if we have not received all the information and explanations we require for our audit.

We read other information contained in the Trustees' Annual Report and consider whether it is consistent with the audited financial statements.. We consider the implications for our report if we become aware of any apparent misstatements or material inconsistencies with the financial statements. Our responsibilities do not extend to any other information.

Basis of audit opinion
We have conducted our audit in accordance with United Kingdom Auditing Standards issued by the Auditing Practices Board. An audit includes examination, on a test basis, of evidence relevant to the amounts and disclosures in the financial statements. It also includes an assessment of the significant estimates and judgements made in the preparation of the financial

---

statements, and of whether the accounting policies are appropriate to the charity's circumstances, consistently applied and adequately disclosed.

We planned and performed our audit so as to obtain all the information and explanations which we considered necessary in order to provide us with sufficient evidence to give reasonable assurance that the financial statements are free from material misstatement, whether caused by fraud or other irregularity or error. In forming an opinion we also evaluated the overall adequacy of the presentation of information in the financial statements.

Opinion
In our opinion the financial statements give a true and fair view of the charity's state of affairs as at 31 December 20.. and of its incoming resources and application of resources in the year then ended and have been properly prepared in accordance with the Charities Act 1993.

Registered Auditors
Address
Date

TABLE 9:   Qualified opinion – limitation of scope of auditors' work: unincorporated charity in England and Wales preparing financial statements under s42(1) of the Charities Act 1993

Report of the independent auditors to the trustees for XYZ charity
We have audited the financial statements of XYZ charity for the year ended [date] on pages ... to .... These statements have been prepared under the historical cost convention as modified by the revaluation of certain fixed assets and the accounting policies set out therein.

Respective responsibilities of trustees and auditors
The trustees' responsibilities for preparing the Annual Report and the financial statements in accordance with applicable law and United Kingdom Accounting Standards are set out in the Statement of Trustees' Responsibilities.

We have been appointed as auditors under section 43 of the Charities Act 1993 and report in accordance with regulations made under section 44 of that Act. Our responsibility is to audit the financial statements in accordance with relevant legal and regulatory requirements and the United Kingdom Auditing Standards.

We report to you our opinion as to whether the financial statements give a true and fair view and are properly prepared in accordance with the Charities Act 1983. We also report to you if, in our opinion, the Trustees' Annual Report is not consistent with the financial statements, if the charity has not kept proper accounting records or if we have not received all the information and explanations we require for our audit.

We read other information contained in the Trustees' Annual Report and consider whether it is consistent with the audited financial statements. We consider the implications for our report if we become aware of any apparent misstatements or material inconsistencies with the financial statements. Our responsibilities do not extend to any other information.

Basis of audit opinion
We have conducted our audit in accordance with United Kingdom Auditing Standards issued by the Auditing Practices Board, except that the scope of our work was limited as explained below.

An audit includes examination, on a test basis, of evidence relevant to the amounts and disclosures in the financial statements. It also includes an assessment of the significant estimates and judgements made in the preparation of the financial statements, and of whether the accounting policies are appropriate to the charity's circumstances, consistently applied and adequately disclosed.

We planned and performed our audit so as to obtain all the information and explanations which we considered necessary in order to provide us with sufficient evidence to give reasonable assurance that the financial statements are free from material misstatement, whether caused by fraud or other irregularity or error. However, the evidence available to us was limited because, £x of the expenditure recorded in the financial statements concerns the charity's project to construct a community centre at [location], and records relating to this project were destroyed in the accident at the site reported in note x. There were no satisfactory audit procedures that we could adopt to confirm that expenditure in respect of the project was properly recorded.

In forming an opinion we also evaluated the overall adequacy of the presentation of information in the financial statements.

Qualified opinion arising from limitation in audit scope
Except for any adjustments that might have been found to be necessary had we been able to obtain sufficient evidence concerning expenditure on [project], in our opinion the financial statements give a true and fair view of the charity's state of affairs as at 31 December 20.. and of its incoming resources and application of resources in the year then ended and have been properly prepared in accordance with the Charities Act 1993.

In respect alone of the limitation on our work in relation to [project]:

- we have not obtained all the information and explanations that we considered necessary for the purpose of our audit; and
- we were unable to determine whether proper accounting records had been maintained.

Registered Auditors
Address
Date

TABLE 10:   Qualified opinion – limitations of scope and additional emphasis where unincorporated charity not previously subject to audit and changed basis of preparation (to replace last two paragraphs in Table 8)

We planned our audit so as to obtain all the information and explanations which we considered necessary in order to provide us with sufficient evidence to give reasonable assurance that the financial statements are free from material misstatement, whether caused by fraud or other irregularity or error. However, the evidence available to us was limited because the financial statements for the year ended 31 March 20.. were not subject to an audit.

We were appointed auditors on ..... As a result it was not possible for us to perform the auditing procedures necessary to obtain sufficient appropriate audit evidence in respect of the financial position of the charity as at 31 March 20.. . Any adjustment to the figures shown in the balance sheet at that date would have a consequential effect on the incoming resources and application of resources for the year ended 31 March 20.. . In addition there were no satisfactory audit procedures which we could adopt to confirm that the transactions recorded in the receipts and payments account for the year ended 31 March 20.. were fairly stated.

Change in basis of preparation of the financial statements
The financial statements for the year ended 31 March 20.. were prepared on a receipts and payments basis. In forming our opinion, we have considered the adequacy of the disclosures made in the financial statements concerning the change in the preparation to the accruals basis. Details of the financial effect of the change in basis of accounting, including reconciliation of the figures previously reported in the receipts and payments account and statement of assets and liabilities for the previous year to the re-stated statement of financial activities and balance sheet are set out in note x. In view of the information provided in the note, our opinion is not qualified in this respect.

In forming our opinion we also evaluated the overall adequacy of the presentation of the information in the financial statements.

Qualified opinion arising from limitation in audit scope
In our opinion, the financial statements give a true and fair view of the state of the charity's affairs at 31 March 20.. and, except for any adjustments that may have been found to be necessary had we been able to obtain sufficient evidenceconcerning the opening balances at 1 April 20.., of its incoming resources and application of resources in the year ended 31 March 20... Except for any adjustments to the comparatives which might have been found to be necessary had we been able to obtain sufficient evidence concerning the elements of the receipts and payments account for the year ended 31 March 20.., the financial statements have been properly prepared in accordance with the Charities Act 1993.

In respect alone of the limitation on our work in relation to the financial statements for the year ended 31 March 20..:

- we have not obtained all the information and explanations that we considered necessary for the purpose of our audit.

Registered Auditors
Address
Date

43.22 SAS 610 (REVISED) COMMUNICATION OF AUDIT MATTERS TO THOSE CHARGED WITH GOVERNANCE/ISA (UK AND IRELAND) 260 COMMUNICATION OF AUDIT MATTERS WITH THOSE CHARGED WITH GOVERNANCE

The Practice Note suggests that the auditors' work on the charity's system of internal control may identify information on these systems which would assist the trustees in seeking to establish and maintain effective and efficient systems. Even if management letters are addressed to the executives responsible for the day-to-day running of the charity, a copy of the report should be sent to the trustees.

43.23 SAS 620 AUDITORS' RIGHT AND DUTY TO REPORT TO REGULATORS IN THE FINANCIAL SECTOR/ISA (UK AND IRELAND) 250 PART B THE AUDITOR'S RIGHT AND DUTY TO REPORT TO REGULATORS IN THE FINANCIAL SECTOR

The Practice Note suggests that as auditors have a duty to report to regulators in relation to unincorporated charities then SAS 620 or ISA (UK and Ireland) 250 applies, although on a strict reading of SAS 620 or ISA (UK and Ireland) 250 they only apply to auditors who have a duty to report to Regulators in the financial sector. Nonetheless the Practice Note goes on to give guidance setting out that the auditors report is to assist the Charity Commission in its supervisory functions relating to:

- the proper direction and management of charities;
- charities compliance with legal and constitutional requirements; and
- the prevention of abuse or misappropriation of charities' funds.

Although auditors of charitable companies have no such duty, the DTI has indicated that it intends to introduce legislation to remedy this in due course.

Auditors do not need to perform additional work as a result of the statutory duty although they will need to make members of audit teams aware of reportable matters which are likely to be encountered.

Auditors must report matters which they have reasonable cause to believe are, or are likely to be, of material significance in relation to the Commissioners power to institute enquiries or to act for the protection of charities.

Additionally, where auditors cease to hold office, for any reason, they are required to make a statement as to whether there are any matters concerning their ceasing to hold office which should be brought to the attention of the trustees. A copy of this statement should be sent to the Charity Commission.

As in the financial services sector, 'material significance' does not have the same meaning as 'material' in the context of the audit of financial statements. For example, dishonesty by a trustee may not be significant in financial terms but would have a significant effect on the commissioner's consideration of whether the person concerned should be allowed to continue to act as a charity trustee.

The statutory duty on the auditors to report to the Charity Commission will primarily arise from the identification of a significant loss or misapplication of a charity's property or funds or from the identification of a significant risk to property or funds resulting from maladministration or misuse of assets. Matters that the Charity Commission consider materially significance are set out in an Appendix to the Practice Note.

The Practice Note points out auditors might, in the course of the audit, become aware of:

- a lack of prudence or significant inadequacy in the arrangements made by trustees for the direction and management of the charity's affairs (**Table 11**);
- a significant breach of legislative requirement or of the charity's trusts (**Tables 12** and **13**); and
- circumstances indicating a probable deliberate misuse of charity property (**Table 14**).

TABLE 11:   Examples of a lack of prudence or inadequate arrangements

- evidence of incompetence or lack of judgement;
- evidence of indifference or recklessness;
- failure of the trustee body to exercise proper control over the administration and management of the charity's affairs;
- the trustee body is accustomed to 'rubber stamp' decisions made by a dominant chief executive or senior member of staff;

- uncertainty exists as to who are the charity trustees;
- functions delegated to third parties are not monitored and controlled; and
- important issues of policy or strategy not properly decided by the trustee body.

TABLE 12: Examples of constitutional failures

- trustee body not properly constituted;
- important issues of policy or strategy not properly decided by the trustee body;
- decisions which require professional advice are taken without advice, or such advice is arbitrarily overridden;
- evidence of a material application of funds for purposes outside the charity's objects or contrary to any special trust; and
- speculative or reckless investment.

TABLE 13: Examples of trustees acting outside power

- any charity trustee receiving remuneration without proper powers or consents;
- the charity entering into any transaction with any person connected with the charity without proper authority which could give rise to a conflict of interest or be to the benefit of that connected person and/or to the detriment of the charity;
- a failure in obtaining proper consent in respect of property transactions with connected persons;
- a failure to obtain Inland Revenue agreement for any non-qualifying loan or investment;
- evidence that any charity trustee is a person disqualified from acting as a charity trustee under s72 of the Charities Act 1993;
- evidence of a material breach of The Charitable Institutions (Fund-Raising) Regulations 1994, SI 1994 No 3024;
- evidence of a material failure to account for any material liability to any direct or indirect tax;
- the auditors have been obstructed by the action or inaction of any charity trustee in obtaining all information or explanations necessary for the purposes of the statutory audit;
- the auditors have been prevented from continuing with or completing the audit as a result of insufficient records being available or insufficient explanations being given in answer to questions raised;
- there has been a breach of the duty to keep accounting records as required by s41 of the Charities Act 1993 which is so material or pervasive that the auditor is unable to express an opinion on the financial statements.

TABLE 14:   Examples of the abuse or misuse of funds

- evidence exists of false accounting;
- evidence exists of theft or misappropriation by any charity trustee, employee, volunteer, agent or third party and this matter has not been reported to the Police Authorities or the Commissioners;
- evidence exists that gives reasonable cause to doubt the honesty or integrity of a charity trustee or the trustee body.

Examples of items which fall into each of the categories described above are set out in Tables 11 to 14 above.

Once auditors have identified a matter that is of "material significance" the report should be made to the Charity Commission without undue delay. Matters found will normally be discussed with Trustees, but these discussions should not cause a delay in the auditors' report to the Commission. Where matters have already been rectified by the trustees, a report to the Commission will not normally be required, unless there has been significant pecuniary loss to the charity or the matter casts doubt on the honesty and integrity of the trustees.

In addition to those examples, auditors need to take into account any requirements for the trustees to notify certain matters or events to the Commissioners on an ad hoc basis. Examples of matters that fall to be notified to the Commissioners by the trustees, or upon which the trustees must obtain authority from the Commissioners before action, include:

- certain dispositions of charity land;
- failure to observe proper process in relation to commencing, ceasing or varying the activities of a charity;
- the establishment of common deposit funds or common investment schemes;
- action proposed or contemplated by the trustees which the latter consider to be expedient in the interests of the charity but which is not authorised by the governing document;
- the making of ex gratia and similar payments, or the waiving of entitlements to receive property, which are outside the powers of the trustees but which they consider they have a moral obligation to make or waive; and
- any changes to the particulars registered for the charity such as the governing document.

43.24 SUMMARISED FINANCIAL STATEMENTS

The Practice Note contains guidance on auditors' reports on summarised financial statements produced by charities.

Where the charity is unincorporated there is no statutory requirement for auditors to report on summarised financial statements, but the SORP states that where the summarised version has been derived from the full accounts there should be an accompanying statement of their consistency from the auditors or independent examiners. Where the charity is incorporated the requirements of s240 of the Companies Act regarding non-statutory financial statements also apply.

Inconsistency may be indicated by:

- inaccurate extraction from the full financial statements;
- summarising information in such a way that it becomes unduly selective; and
- omission of fundamental information.

Where the auditors' report on the full financial statements was qualified, the Practice Note suggests that auditors may wish to refer to the matter in their report on the summarised financial statements.

An example of an auditors' report on summarised financial statements is shown in **Table 15**.

TABLE 15:   Auditors' statement on summarised financial statements

Independent auditors' statement to the trustees of XYZ charity
We have examined the summarised financial statements of XYZ charity.

Respective responsibilities of trustees and auditors
The trustees are responsible for preparing the summarised financial statements in accordance with the recommendations of the Charities SORP.

Our responsibility is to report to you our opinion on the consistency of the summary financial statements with the full financial statements and Trustees' Annual Report. We also read the other information contained in the [*summarised Annual Report*] and consider the implications for our report if we become aware of any apparent misstatements or material inconsistencies with the summary financial statement.

Basis of opinion
We conducted our work in accordance with Bulletin 1999/6 *The auditors' statement on the summary financial statement* issued by the Auditing Practices Board for use in the United Kingdom.

> *Opinion*
> In our opinion the summarised financial statements are consistent [are not consistent] with the full financial statements and Trustees' Annual Report of XYZ charity for the year ended 31 December 20. [in the following respects ...].
>
> Registered Auditors
> Address
> Date

43.25   AUDIT EXEMPTION REPORTS

Incorporated charities with gross income between £90,000 and £250,000 are subject to an audit exemption report under s249A(2).

Standards and guidance on these reports are contained in the Statement of Standards for Reporting Accountants *Audit Exemption Reports* published by the APB.

The Statement introduces 17 'standards' in bold type, which we refer to under their paragraph number and which it refers to as basic principles and essential procedures covering:

- objective of the engagement;
- agreeing terms of engagement;
- ethical considerations;
- planning;
- documentation;
- work delegated to assistants;
- procedures;
- reporting;
- modification of the report; and
- circumstances which may lead to resignation.

The Statement stresses that where accountants have assisted in the preparation of the accounts from the accounting records, little further work may be required in order to give the report, so long as they are satisfied that their procedures comply with the standards.

43.25.1   Objective of the engagement

Reporting accountants are required to express an opinion on three matters:

- agreement of the accounts to the underlying accounting records;
- compliance of the accounts with the form and content rules of Schedule 4 of the Companies Act 1985; and
- eligibility for the exemption.

The only assurance given by the report is on these matters, and the reporting accountants' work should be carried out so as to provide a 'reasonable basis on which to express the opinions' (paragraph 1).

The limited nature of the audit exemption report means that reporting accountants do not consider the completeness, accuracy and validity of the accounting records and nor do they consider the truth and fairness of the accounts. It is not necessary to ensure compliance with accounting standards or to assess the appropriateness of the going concern basis.

43.25.2 Agreeing terms of engagement

The terms of the engagement must be agreed in writing by the trustees and the reporting accountants (paragraph 2). The engagement letter should include paragraphs on:

- the respective responsibilities of trustees and reporting accountants;
- the scope of the reporting accountants' work;
- the circumstances in which, and the form in which, the report can be issued; and
- the terms of any other non-statutory services being provided (such as assistance in the preparation of the accounts).

An example of the engagement letter is shown in **Table 16**.

TABLE 16: Engagement letter for audit exemption report

To the trustees of ...

The purpose of this letter is to set out the basis on which we are engaged:

(a) to act as reporting accountants to prepare a report for the purposes of s249A(2) Companies Act 1985 (the Act), in respect of the company's accounts for the year ended ..., in accordance with s249C of the Act; and

(b) to provide other professional services to the company;

and the respective responsibilities of the directors and trustees and of ourselves.

1 *Responsibilities of the directors and trustees*
1.1 As directors of the charitable company, you are responsible for ensuring that the company maintains proper accounting records and for preparing accounts which give a true and fair view and which have been prepared in accordance with the Act.

1.2 You are also responsible for determining whether, in respect of the year, the company meets the conditions for exemption from an audit of the accounts set out in s249A of the Act, and for determining whether, in respect of the year, the exemption is not available for any of the reasons set out in s249B.

1.3 If, in respect of the year, the availability of the exemption from an audit of the accounts is conditional upon your causing a report in respect of these accounts to be prepared for the purposes of s249A(2), you are responsible for deciding whether that report shall be made and for appointing us as reporting accountants to make that report to the shareholders of the company.

1.4 As trustees of a charitable company, you are under a duty to prepare an annual report for each financial year complying in its form and content with regulations made under the Charities Act 1993. In preparing the annual report you are also required to have regard to the Statement of Recommended Practice (SORP) *Accounting by Charities*, issued in October 1995 by the Charity Commissioners for England and Wales.

2 *Responsibilities of the reporting accountants*
2.1 We shall plan our work on the basis that a report for the purposes of s249A(2) is required for the year, unless you inform us in writing that either:

(a) the company requires an audit of the accounts; or
(b) the company requires neither an audit nor such a report.

2.2 Should you instruct us to carry out an audit, then a separate letter of engagement will be required.

Audit exemption reports
2.3 Should you inform us that the company requires neither an audit nor a report, then we shall have no responsibilities to the company, except those specifically agreed upon between us in respect of other professional services.

2.4 As reporting accountants, we have a statutory responsibility to report to the shareholders of the company whether in our opinion:

(a) the accounts are in agreement with the accounting records kept by the company under s221 of the Act; and
(b) having regard only to, and on the basis of, the information contained in those accounting records, the accounts have been drawn up in a manner consistent with the accounting requirements specified in s249C(6) of the Act, so far as they are applicable to the company.

2.5 We also have a statutory responsibility to state that, having regard only to, and on the basis of, the information contained in the accounting records kept by the company under s221, in our opinion the company satisfied the conditions for exemption from an audit of the accounts specified in s249A(4) of the Act and did not, at any time within the year, fall within any of the categories specified in s249B(1), of companies not entitled to the exemption.

2.6 We do not have any responsibility to report whether any shareholder of the company has notified the company that he or she requires an audit, consequently we have no responsibility to carry out any work in respect of this matter.

2.7 Should our work lead us to conclude that the company is not entitled to exemption from an audit of the accounts, or should we be unable to reach a conclusion on this matter, then we will not issue any report and will notify you in writing of the reasons. In these circumstances, if appropriate, we will discuss with you the need to appoint an auditor.

3 *Scope of the reporting accountants' work*

3.1 Our engagement will be conducted in accordance with the Statement of Standards for Reporting Accountants issued by the Auditing Practices Board. Our procedures will consist of comparing the accounts with the accounting records kept by the company, and making such limited enquiries of the officers of the company as we may consider necessary for the purposes of our report.

3.2 Our work as reporting accountants will not be an audit of the accounts in accordance with Auditing Standards. Accordingly, we will not seek any independent evidence to support the entries in the accounting records, the existence, ownership or value of assets, or the completeness of income, liabilities and disclosures in the accounts. Nor will we make any assessment of the estimates and judgements made by you in your preparation of the accounts. Consequently our work as reporting accountants will not provide any assurance that the accounting records or the accounts are free from material misstatement, whether caused by fraud, other irregularities or error.

3.3 We have a professional responsibility not to allow our name to be associated with accounts which we consider may be misleading. Therefore, although we are not required to search for such matters, should we become aware, for any reason, that the accounts may be misleading, and the matter cannot be adequately dealt with by means of modification of our report, we will not issue any report and will withdraw from the engagement, and will notify you in writing of the reasons.

3.4 As part of our normal procedures, we may request you to provide written confirmation of any information or explanations given by you orally during the course of our work.

3.5 We attach to this letter a specimen of the form of report, setting out, in the manner specified by the professional standards, the opinions required by the Act.

4 *Accounting and other services*

4.1 You have asked us to assist you in the maintenance of the accounting records and in the preparation of the accounts, as follows:

(*describe the work to be performed or refer to a separate letter of engagement*)

4.2 You have also asked us to provide other professional services, in respect of . . .

(*describe the other services*)

4.3 Our engagement with the company as reporting accountants for the purpose of preparing the report is a statutory responsibility and is distinct, and entirely separate, from any obligations or responsibilities arising out of the contractual arrangements agreed between us under which we are to provide the professional services described in 4.1 to 4.2 above.

5 *Limitation of liability*
(*The reporting accountants can agree with the directors a limit on any liability arising out of the work. In such circumstances, legal advice may be required regarding the form of words to be included in the engagement letter.*)

6 *Fees*
6.1 Our fees are computed on the basis of time spent on the company's affairs by the partners and our staff, and on the level of skills and responsibility involved. Our fees will be charged separately for each of the main classes of work described above, will be billed at appropriate intervals during the year and will be due on presentation.

Audit exemption reports
6.2 If, in the circumstances described in 2.7, we do not issue any report, or if, in the circumstances described in 3.3, or for any other reason, it becomes necessary for us to withdraw from the engagement, our fees for work performed will be payable to the company.

7 *Agreement of terms*
7.1 We shall be grateful if you could confirm in writing your agreement to the terms of this letter, or let us know if they are not in accordance with your understanding.

Yours faithfully
...

The guidance notes that as the preparation of an audit exemption report is not an audit engagement, the reporting accountants may limit their liability arising out of the work. It suggests legal advice is sought on this matter. This raises various issues including whether the extent and nature of any proposed limitation is effective in law and whether it is acceptable to the company for whom the report is being prepared.

43.25.3   *Ethical considerations*

The APB believes that users will expect the reporting accountants to have complied with their professional body's ethical guidance – for example, the integrity, objectivity and independence rules of the ICAEW. In addition, the Act requires reporting accountants to be independent of the company.

43.25.4   *Planning*

Paragraph 4 requires reporting accountants to 'plan their work so that an effective engagement is performed'. As part of this it will be necessary to obtain the trustees' confirmation that the company has not fallen and will not fall, if the period has not ended, into any of the categories where the exemption is not available and that they will require an audit exemption report to be prepared. When giving this confirmation, the trustees also need to have considered whether they have given any undertakings to have the accounts audited, for example a covenant attached to a bank loan.

As the procedures that the reporting accountant will adopt depend on the nature of the accounting records and the extent of any accounts' preparation assistance, obtaining an understanding of these is vital part of the planning.

43.25.5 Documentation

As with any assignment, the working papers should record the planning and procedures and be sufficient to support the opinion and demonstrate compliance with the applicable standards.

43.25.6 Work delegated to assistants

Where reporting accountants delegate work, paragraph 6 expects this to be directed, supervised and reviewed 'in a manner which provides confidence that such work is done competently and in accordance with these standards'. This is similar to SAS 240.4 and ISA (UK and Ireland) 220 on quality control for individual audit assignments. The reviewer should be of at least equal competence to ensure that the objectives of the engagement are met.

43.25.7 Procedures

The five standards under this heading cover each of the three aspects of the audit exemption report and any discussions with the trustees, including what to do if it is found that the exemption criteria have not been met. The standards on the various aspects of the report only require the performance of such procedures as are necessary to provide a reasonable basis on which to express an opinion on each requirement. The accompanying guidance goes into more detail.

In order to form an opinion on whether the accounts are in agreement with the accounting records, reporting accountants need to agree all balances in the accounts to the general ledger, via the trial balance. The guidance recommends that the posting of the books of prime entry to the general ledger should be agreed on a test basis, but provides no assistance in deciding the number of items to test – it merely says that regard will have to be had to the 'need to obtain a reasonable basis for the opinion expressed'.

In practice, the number chosen will depend, as with an audit engagement, on the amount of assurance that is required from the procedure. The more reliance that can be placed on, for example, analytical review and the presence of systems over which controls are exercised, the less need there is to test large numbers of items.

There is no requirement, either in the legislation or in the Statement, for reporting accountants to check the accuracy of the accounting records back to source documents, or even whether proper accounting records have been kept. Where the source documents are the only records they constitute the accounting records.

Where the reporting accountants have assisted in the preparation of the accounts the amount of work that is necessary depends on the precise nature of this preparation work. For example, if they have prepared accounts from the books of prime entry or the source documents, then so long as the work has been reviewed adequately, no further work is necessary to form an opinion that the accounts agree to the accounting records. However, if the company has carried out accountancy work to the extent of extracting a trial balance then the accountants must carry out procedures to test this extraction back to the ledgers and books of prime entry.

No work is required to obtain evidence to support:

- the entries in the accounting records;
- the existence, ownership or value of assets; or
- the completeness of income, liabilities or disclosures.

Accounts drawn up in a manner consistent with the specified accounting requirements

Reporting accountants are required to form an opinion on whether the accounts have been prepared in the form set out in Schedule 4 of the Act. This assessment should be based on whatever accounting records have been kept by the company. There is no need to assess and report on the adequacy of the company's accounting records.

To assess compliance with the form and content rules of Schedule 4, reporting accountants must ensure the presentation of each item in the accounting records is:

- in an appropriate caption, in one of the prescribed formats with an appropriate description; and
- on a basis permitted by Schedule 4.

Other requirements of the Schedule should also be complied with – for example, the need to provide depreciation. To assist in this, completion of a Companies Act disclosure checklist similar to that for an audit should be used. There is no need to obtain evidence to support any estimates or judgements made by the trustees in the accounts.

Entitlement to exemption from audit
Similarly, where reporting on the entitlement to the exemption, reporting accountants only need consider the information in the accounting records, no further verification being necessary. However, this consideration cannot be restricted to the position at the balance sheet date. The examination must be sufficient to ensure that the various criteria, for example that thecompany was not a parent or subsidiary undertaking, have been satisfied for the whole period.

The guidance suggests that, in most cases, reporting accountants will have sufficient knowledge of their clients to be able to make this assessment easily. However, it does stress that they should remain alert to any information which would affect the entitlement which comes to light during their work.

Discussions with the trustees
Paragraph 10 notes two occasions when reporting accountants should discuss their concerns with the trustees. These are when they:

* have doubts that their procedures have provided sufficient evidence to give affirmative opinions on the matters specified for their report; or
* have become aware of information that leads them to believe that the accounts may be misleading.

In the first situation the guidance suggests that by discussing the matter with the trustees appropriate evidence will be forthcoming or amendments made to the accounts. Where evidence or explanations are provided by the trustees, the reporting accountants are not required to obtain independent verification of this.

In the second case, the standards have been developed on the basis that although there is no need for reporting accountants to obtain evidence that the accounts are not misleading, they would wish to clarify any matter which might indicate this, as they would not wish their name to be associated with documents they believe to be misleading.

There are no provisions in the legislation for the report to be qualified in respect of the criteria for audit exemption. This means that where reporting accountants become aware that the company does not satisfy the criteria they should notify the trustees in writing, as soon as possible, that they are unable to give the report, giving reasons, and informing them that an audit is required.

43.25.8 *Reporting*

Once reporting accountants are satisfied that they have sufficient evidence to form an affirmative opinion on the matters set out in the legislation, paragraph 12 requires them to issue a report containing this opinion. An example of the report is set out in **Table 17**.

TABLE 17:   Audit exemption report

Accountants' report to the members on the unaudited accounts of XYZ Charity (a company limited by guarantee)
We report on the accounts for the year ended ... set out on pages ... to ....

Respective responsibilities of trustees and reporting accountant
As described on page ... the company's directors are responsible for the preparation of the accounts, and they consider that the company is exempt from an audit. It is our responsibility to carry out procedures designed to enable us to report our opinion.

Basis of opinion
Our work was conducted in accordance with the Statement of Standards for Reporting Accountants, and so our procedures consisted of comparing the accounts with the accounting records kept by the company, and making such limited enquiries of the officers of the company as we considered necessary for the purposes of this report. These procedures provide only the assurance expressed in our opinion.

Opinion
In our opinion:

- the accounts are in agreement with those accounting records kept by the charitable company under s221 of the Companies Act 1985;
- having regard only to, and on the basis of, the information contained in those accounting records:
  (a) the accounts have been drawn up in a manner consistent with the accounting requirements specified in s249C(6) of the Act; and
  (b) the charitable company satisfied the conditions for exemption from an audit of the accounts for the year specified in s249A(4) of the Act as modified by s249A(5) and did not, at any time within that year, fall within any of the categories of companies not entitled to the exemption specified in s249B(1).

Reporting Accountants
Address
Date

Paragraph 13 covers the format of the report and is similar to SAS 600.2. Unless the trustees have made a statement acknowledging their responsibilities, the company is not entitled to the audit exemption. The responsibility statement which should be referred to in the audit exemption report covers the trustees' responsibilities for:

- ensuring that the company keeps accounting records which comply with s221 of the Act; and
- preparing accounts which give a true and fair view and which otherwise comply with the Act.

As with audit reports accompanying financial statements filed at Companies House, the reporting accountants should sign in manuscript the audit exemption report filed with unaudited accounts.

43.25.9 Modification of the report

There are three ways in which the report may be modified. These are by:

- disagreement;
- limitation of scope; or
- use of an explanatory paragraph.

Disagreement
Reporting accountants should modify their report where they conclude that, in relation to a particular matter, the accounts either:

- are not in agreement with the company's accounting records; or
- are not drawn up in a matter consistent with Schedule 4.

This modification will be a negative opinion in respect of the relevant part of the opinion part of the audit exemption report. An example is shown in Table 18.

The reporting accountants will need to consider the implications of this negative opinion on other parts of their report, particularly whether it casts doubt on the entitlement to audit exemption. However, it should not mean that any additional work is required in respect of other parts of the accounts or the accounting records.

Limitation of scope
Limitations of scope affect audit exemption reports in a similar way to an audit report and may be imposed by the trustees or by circumstances. Where this 'prevents reporting accountants from obtaining a reasonable basis for an opinion' on either the consistency with Schedule 4 or the agreement with accounting records, paragraph 15 requires a qualified opinion on the relevant matter.

Where the limitation of scope is caused by the absence of part of the accounting records it may be possible, either by reconstruction from source documents or by comparison with other records, to form an opinion on whether the company is entitled to audit exemption. However, reporting accountants may not be able to give an unmodified opinion on agreement with the accounting records or compliance with Schedule 4.

TABLE 18:   Extract from audit exemption report containing a disagreement

Opinion – including disagreement
As stated in note … , the trustees have made no provision in the accounts for the depreciation of fixtures and fittings shown in the balance sheet at £… . Paragraph 18 of Schedule 4 to the Companies Act 1985 requires that any fixed asset which has a limited useful economic life be depreciated.

In our opinion:

- the accounts are in agreement with the accounting records kept by the company under s221 of the Companies Act 1985;
- having regard only to, and on the basis of, the information contained in those accounting records:
  - (a) because of the absence of the provision for depreciation referred to above, the accounts have not been drawn up in a manner consistent with the accounting requirements specified in s249C(6) of the Act; and
  - (b) the charitable company satisfied the conditions for exemption from an audit of the accounts for the year specified in s249A(4) of the Act and did not at any time within that year, fall within any of the categories of companies not entitled to the exemption specified in s249B(1).

Reporting Accountants
Address
Date

The qualification that will result from a limitation in scope is an 'except for' opinion on the matter concerned. An example of this is shown in Table 19.

43.25.10   Use of explanatory paragraph

As noted in **43.24.7** on discussions with trustees, the standards are developed on the basis that reporting accountants would not wish their name to be associated with something which they believed was misleading. Recognising that discussions with trustees may not lead to a resolution of the matter, paragraph 16 provides for the use of an explanatory paragraph in the report. This is not a qualification as it concerns matters outside the scope of the reporting accountants' work and opinion. Reporting accountants need to be sure that this matter is outside the scope of their examination and has no affect on the eligibility for the exemptions. The explanatory paragraph in the basis of opinion section of the report should highlight the issue and provide readers with a proper understanding of the basis of the opinion. Table 20 is an example of an explanatory paragraph.

TABLE 19:   Extract from audit exemption report including limitation of scope

...

Basis of opinion
Our work was conducted in accordance with the Statement of Standards for Reporting Accountants and so our procedures consisted of comparing the accounts with the accounting records kept by the company, and making such limited enquiries of the officers of the company as we considered necessary for the purposes of this report. These procedures provide only the assurance expressed in our opinion.

Owing to flood damage, certain accounting records relating to donations for the first month of the year have been destroyed, and so we have been unable to compare the donations shown in the accounts with those accounting records.

Opinion – including limitation on scope
In our opinion:

- except for the uncertainty relating to donations, which arises from the limitation on the scope of our work described above, the accounts are in agreement with those accounting records kept by the company under s221 of the Companies Act 1985;
- having regard only to, and on the basis of, the information contained in those accounting records:
  - (a) the accounts have been drawn up in a manner consistent with the accounting requirements specified in s249C(6) of the Act; and
  - (b) the company satisfied the conditions for exemption from an audit of the accounts for the year specified in s249A(4) of the Act and did not, at any time within that year, fall within any of the categories of companies not entitled to the exemption specified in s249B(1).

Reporting Accountants
Address
Date

The absence of an explanatory paragraph does not mean that there are no such matters, only that none have come to the attention of the reporting accountants.

The situation used in **Table 17** is reasonably clear-cut, but there may be instances where there is less certainty as to whether the reporting accountants' suspicions are significant enough for an explanatory paragraph to be used. For example, if the debt had been outstanding for nine months but the debtor was still trading, a judgement is necessary on whether an explanatory paragraph is necessary because the accounts may be misleading. Such a judgement should be based upon the degree of certainty that the accounts are misleading which is possessed by the reporting accountants.

TABLE 20:   Extract from an audit exemption report including explanatory paragraph

...

Basis of opinion

...

Trade debtors

In carrying out our procedures it has come to our attention that the balance sheet total of debtors includes a debt of £ ... which has been outstanding for in excess of one year. XYZ Limited has no security for this debt. The trustees have made no provision against the debt being irrecoverable and they have informed us that they are satisfied that it will be recovered in full. We are not required to and have not performed any procedures to corroborate the trustees' views, and we therefore express no opinion on this matter.

Opinion

...

---

44 PENSION SCHEMES

44.1 GUIDANCE FOR AUDITORS OF PENSION SCHEMES

Pension schemes operate in a complex legal environment and the APB has provided specific guidance to auditors of schemes in Practice Note 15 *The Audit of Occupational Pension Schemes in the United Kingdom (revised)* (PN15). In March 2007 the APB announced the publication of a revision of PN15. Richard Fleck, APB Chairman, commented on the revised version:

> 'Although there have been a number of changes in the regulatory arrangements for occupational pension schemes since the previous version of PN 15 was issued in 2004, the substance of the guidance in the Practice Note has not needed major revision'.

The principal revisions as set out in the preface to PN15 are:

- the guidance is now based on ISAs (UK and Ireland);
- reference is made to the Pensions Regulator. The role of the Regulator is explained later in this chapter;
- the introduction of materiality to the reporting on contributions as explained in this chapter;
- the inclusion of guidance for other reporting situations. The final section of this chapter gives an overview of this;
- a summary of the legal and regulatory framework includes reference to the Pensions Act 2004, the Finance Act 2004 and the Finance Act 2005; and
- a new appendix in respect of non-statutory audits.

The guidance in this chapter is based on the revised PN15 which explains the application of auditing standards issued by the APB to the audit of occupational pension schemes in the United Kingdom. It is, therefore, essential that auditors are familiar with the content of PN15 before accepting an appointment from the trustees of a pension scheme.

This chapter is intended to guide auditors of pension schemes to the key items addressed in PN15 and to provide details of where other relevant information can be obtained.

44.2   LEGAL BACKGROUND

ISA (UK and Ireland) 250 Consideration of Law and Regulations in an Audit of Financial Statements sets out the auditors' responsibilities to consider laws and regulations. The legislative framework for pension schemes is dominated by the Pension Schemes Act 1993, the Pensions Act 1995 ('PA 1995'), the Pensions Act 2004 ('PA 2004') and Regulations that accompany them.

The Pensions Schemes Act 1993 is consolidating legislation addressing the contracting out of the additional element of the state scheme (currently the State Second Pension) and the protection of members through the disclosure of information to them and by placing restrictions on employer-related investment.

PA 1995 and PA 2004 are both reforming legislation and primarily enabling Acts with detailed requirements set out in Regulations made under them. The principal Regulations that pension scheme auditors need to be aware of are:

- The Occupational Pension Schemes (Disclosure of Information) Regulations 1996 ('the Disclosure Regulations');
- The Occupational Pension Schemes (Scheme Administration) Regulations 1996 ('the Administration Regulations');
- The Occupational Pension Schemes (Requirement to obtain Audited Accounts and a Statement from the Auditor) Regulations 1996 ('the Audited Accounts Regulations'); and
- The Administration Regulations and the Audited Accounts Regulations have been subsequently amended by The Occupational Pension Schemes (Administration and Audited Accounts) (Amendment) Regulations 2005 ('the Amending Regulations').

PA 1995, PA 2004 and the Regulations set out the basis on which auditors are appointed, auditors' responsibilities and the form and content of pension scheme financial statements and annual reports. They also set out responsibilities for trustees such as obtaining the annual report and financial statements and the establishment and operation of internal controls.

PA 2004 also introduced the Pensions Regulator ('the Regulator'). The Regulator replaced the Occupational Pensions Regulatory Authority ('OPRA') from April 2005.

The Regulator, which is sometimes abbreviated to 'TPR' or 'tPR', has a range of powers, which include issuing:

- codes of practice, as explained further below;
- improvement notices: the ability to prevent those responsible for the scheme contravening pensions legislation;
- third party notices: the ability to take action against a third party who is preventing a person from complying with the law;
- contribution notices: to order contributions from parties attempting to avoid employer debt to a defined benefit scheme; and
- financial support directions: to secure financial support from a party associated with the principal employer if the employer is either a service organisation or insufficiently funded.

Codes of practice are primarily directed at trustees. They are not statements of law, but are an indication of what is considered to be best practice. Any departure from them should, therefore, be justifiable and not be in breach of any underlying legal requirements. All professionals involved with pension schemes should be aware of the issue of codes of practice and should refer regularly to the Pension Regulator's website (*www.thepensionsregulator. gov.uk*). There have been ten codes of practice issued to date. Those which are particularly relevant to the responsibilities and work of a pension scheme auditor are:

01 Reporting breaches of the law
03 Funding defined benefits
05 Reporting late payment of contributions to occupational money purchase schemes
07 Trustee knowledge and understanding
09 Internal controls

The codes of practice referred to above are explained in more detail in the relevant parts of this chapter.

PN15 provides comprehensive information on whistle-blowing and this should be referred to in addition to the information available from the Regulator.

Code of practice 01 explains the 'whistle-blowing' requirements and this, together with further guidance issued by the Regulator, should be understood by the scheme auditor. Section 70 of PA 2004 imposes on the auditor and virtually everyone associated with the running of a scheme a duty to whistle-blow to the Regulator from 6 April 2005.

In explaining the legal environment in which pension schemes operate, code of practice 01 refers to 'enactments or rule of law', which are broadly defined to include the Theft Act, trust law and common law. Auditors of pension schemes must, therefore, maintain an understanding of many legal requirements. In addition, there must also be familiarity with the scheme's own rules and regulations which are set out in the trust deed and rules.

The duty to report to the Regulator arises where the trustees and others associated with the scheme have failed to comply with their legal duties. The Regulator has, however, indicated that it expects most reporting to be by trustees and, if a report has already been made, auditors should only report if there is additional information to be provided. Auditors are not required to undertake any additional work other than to fulfil their responsibilities.

44.3   ACCOUNTING GUIDANCE

The accounting guidance for pension schemes is contained in the Statement of Recommended Practice *Financial Reports of Pension Schemes* ('the SORP'). The SORP is issued by the Pensions Research Accountants Group ('PRAG') who also issue other guidance for the accounting and governance of pension schemes. Auditors of pension schemes should refer to the PRAG website (*www.prag.org.uk*) for details of the latest guidance.

An exposure draft of a revision to the SORP to reflect changes in the legislative environment and UK Generally Accepted Accounting Practice was issued in December 2006 and is expected to apply to periods commencing on or after 6 April 2007 with early adoption recommended.

Auditors are required by Regulation 3 of the Audited Accounts Regulations to report whether the financial statements contain the information specified in the Schedule to those Regulations. The Schedule sets out the format in which the financial information should be presented and certain disclosures that need to be made. One disclosure is whether the financial statements have been prepared in accordance with the SORP and if not, an indication of material departures.

PN15 explains that it is normally necessary to follow the guidance in the SORP in order for pension scheme accounts to show a true and fair view. Auditors must, therefore, be familiar with the requirements of the SORP and be prepared to refer to any material non-compliance with it in the audit opinion.

44.4   SCHEMES EXEMPT FROM AUDIT

A number of categories of scheme are exempt under the Administration Regulations from the requirement to appoint an auditor. The principal exemptions relate to:

- occupational schemes with fewer than two members;
- certain public sector schemes;
- occupational money purchase small schemes (prior to the Finance Act 2004 and the Amending Regulations these were known as Small Self

Administered Schemes) meeting specified criteria in respect of unanimous decision making and membership of the trustee board;

- occupational schemes in which the only benefits provided are death benefits and under which no member has accrued rights; and
- unfunded occupational schemes.

Any of the above schemes may be audited on a 'voluntary basis', for example where the trustees request an audit to be performed or where the scheme rules require an audit.

In addition, schemes which invest only in one or more insurance policies which specifically allocate benefits to individual members (ear-marked schemes) only require an auditors' statement about contributions.

44.5 CONSIDERATION OF FRAUD

Although PN15 comments that the risk of fraudulent financial reporting is low given the nature of pension schemes it also states that the potential for fraud cannot be ignored. The most likely risk is the misappropriation of assets and PN15 explains that, even if activities are delegated, the trustees retain responsibility for the prevention and detection of fraud.

Examples of the type of fraud that may occur in a pension scheme are:

- misappropriation of assets;
- non-payment of employee and/or employer contributions to the scheme;
- use of assets of the scheme either directly or as collateral for borrowing by either the employer or an associate of the employer;
- misapplication of the assets of a scheme to meet the obligations and expenses of either another scheme or of the sponsoring employer;
- dealing in scheme assets by the investment manager without the required mandate or authorisation;
- lending of scheme assets by the custodian without authorisation;
- exchange of assets without sufficient valuable consideration (for example selling assets such as property at below market value);
- assets of the scheme used for the personal preferment of the trustees or used for the personal preferment of an individual scheme member;
- benefit claims by members or their beneficiaries to which they are not entitled (for example failure to notify a scheme of the death of a true beneficiary); and
- creation of fictitious scheme records by the administrator (for example dummy beneficiary records).

PN15 states that auditors usually rebut the presumption that revenue recognition gives rise to a risk of material misstatement due to fraud. This is due to the nature of the income, the not for profit nature of a pension scheme and the limited scope for revenue manipulation.

There are circumstances that increase the risk of fraud and auditors need to be aware of these when planning the audit. These include:

- trustees or scheme management displaying a significant disregard for the various regulatory authorities;
- trustees or scheme management having little or no involvement in the day-to-day administration of the scheme;
- trustees or scheme management having ready access to the scheme's assets and an ability to override any internal controls;
- trustees or scheme management failing to put in place arrangements to monitor activities undertaken by third parties, including the employer;
- trustees or scheme management displaying a lack of candour in dealings with members, the actuary or the auditors on significant matters affecting scheme assets;
- the sponsoring employer operating in an industry with increasing business failures, or itself having financial difficulties; and
- significant levels, or unusual types, of related party transactions (including employer-related investments) involving unaudited entities or entities audited by other firms.

To properly assess the above circumstances, scheme auditors should be interacting with the trustees and those responsible for the management of the scheme, conducting analytical procedures and holding a fraud brainstorming discussion. As with all other entities, an appropriate response to identified fraud risks should be determined and management representation sought on fraud.

44.6 COMMUNICATION WITH TRUSTEES

Scheme auditors must ensure that there is interaction with trustees at various stages of the audit. As well as being a requirement of ISA (UK and Ireland) 260 *Communication of audit matters with those charged with governance,* it is fundamental to the planning of the audit and compliance with ISA (UK and Ireland) 315 *Understanding the entity and its environment and assessing the risks of material misstatements.*

Auditors will communicate with the trustees on a range of matters including:

- independence;
- scope of the audit, the audit plan and any additional procedures;
- timetable;
- fees;

- access to third parties and information;
- fraud;
- procedures, controls and internal audit;
- establishing expectations for analytical procedures and discussing the results of such procedures;
- changes to the scheme;
- issues arising from a review of the minutes;
- unadjusted errors other than those that are clearly trivial; and
- communication with the Regulator.

At the end of the audit process auditors will also communicate with trustees. Trustees should be notified of all breaches of duties relevant to the administration of the scheme discovered in the course of the audit work. These duties include those imposed by any enactment or rule of law on the trustees or managers, the employer, any professional adviser or any prescribed person acting in connection with the scheme. The notification to the trustees should be made, regardless of whether the matter gave rise to a statutory duty to report to the Regulator. If there are no matters that need to be notified, the trustees should be advised in writing accordingly.

44.7 CONTROL ACTIVITIES

ISA (UK and Ireland) 315 *Understanding the entity and its environment and assessing the risks of material misstatement* requires auditors to understand the systems and controls of entities being audited. PN15 sets out the features of an effective control environment, examples of control activities and the factors that increase the risk of material misstatement. In considering the risk of material misstatement, auditors should refer to the appendices of PN15 which explain the risks which apply to different benefit structures.

Auditors should also consider the ability of the trustees and in doing so reference should be made to code of practice 07 'Trustee Knowledge and Understanding'. The Regulator intends that trustees should, amongst other areas, be familiar with their powers and the manner in which their scheme operates. The code of practice explains how trustees might approach the task of determining the elements of knowledge and understanding which are appropriate for them and how they might acquire the knowledge and understanding needed. This is, therefore, a part of the assessment of the environment. Many pension schemes delegate activities, most commonly administration and investment management, to third parties. Of particular relevance to pension scheme auditors is, therefore, ISA (UK and Ireland) 402 *Audit considerations relating to entities using service organisations*. The responsibility for the operation of the scheme does, however, remain with the trustees when they have outsourced activities and they are responsible for ensuring that scheme has appropriate procedures and controls. Any weaknesses or gaps in the controls operated by trustees may lead to additional audit risk. In such circumstances, auditors will need to design audit procedures to address that risk.

It must be emphasised that the systems and control activities that need to be understood are those operated by the trustees and which are under their direct control. Section 249A of PA 2004 and *The Occupational Pension Schemes (Internal Control) Regulations 2005* impose on trustees a statutory obligation to operate internal controls and in considering the internal controls auditors should refer to code of practice 09 Internal Controls and the PRAG Publication, 'Outsourcing for Trustees'.

It is necessary for scheme auditors to gain an understanding of how the scheme's use of a service organisation affects the scheme's internal control. The following should, therefore, be documented and understood:

- the services provided;
- selection procedures;
- contractual terms and the relationship;
- contingency plans;
- interaction of the control systems of the scheme and the service organisation;
- the scheme's controls relevant to the service organisation and how risks are identified and controlled;
- the capability of the service organisation; and
- information available to the trustees in respect of the service organisation's operations including general and IT controls.

The directors of the service organisation may provide information to the trustees by producing an 'internal control report' in accordance with *AAF 01/06 Assurance report on internal controls of service organisations made available to third parties* ('AAF 01/06') (see **Chapter 42**).

The essential content of an internal control report under AAF 01/06 is for the service organisation to explain how control procedures achieve control objectives. Control objectives are set by the management of the service organisation, but AAF 01/06 provides mandatory objectives for pension scheme administrators, custodians and investment managers. An internal control report produced under AAF 01/06 will also contain a report from a Reporting Accountant providing an opinion on the fairness of the description and the design and operating effectiveness of control procedures.

Trustees should seek to obtain such reports from service providers and incorporate the assessment of them into their control procedures.

Having gained an understanding of the service organisation's controls, it may be concluded that these controls do not impact on the overall assessment of the audit risk in respect of the scheme. This could, for example, be because either the activities are not significant to the audit of the scheme or because the trustees have appropriate controls in place over their use of the service organisation.

If, however, the activities of the service organisation do result in audit risk, appropriate audit procedures will need to be designed.

The nature of the procedures will be specific to each scheme and are dependant upon the service and the risks that have been assessed. Access to the service organisation will not always be necessary as the trustees may either hold sufficient documentation, or the service organisation provides periodic reports which contain adequate information. The internal control reports provided to trustees may also provide useful information to the scheme auditor.

44.8 CONTRIBUTIONS

Scheme auditors are required by the Audited Accounts Regulations to make a statement about contributions. This is separate to the opinion that is given on the financial statements. The statement for periods beginning on or after 22 September 2005 is whether contributions have, in all material respects, been paid at least in accordance with the payment schedule or the schedule of contributions.

Auditors need to understand the basis under which contributions are paid to the scheme by the employer. Money purchase schemes are required to have a payment schedule under section 87 of PA 1995 and a defined benefit scheme is required to have a schedule of contributions under section 58 of PA 1995 ('the schedule(s)').

Following the replacement of the Minimum Funding Requirement with Scheme Specific Funding the form and content of the schedule of contributions has changed and pension scheme auditors need to be familiar with the requirement relevant to the scheme:

Schedule of Contributions under the Minimum Funding Requirement
The schedule is prepared in accordance with the Occupational Pension Schemes (Minimum Funding Requirement and Actuarial Valuations) Regulations 1996.

Schedule of Contributions under the Scheme Specific Funding regime
The schedule is prepared in accordance with the Occupational Pension Schemes (Scheme Funding) Regulations 2005.
A schedule of contributions produced under the Scheme Specific Funding Regime is required to show separately any deficit funding and 'other' contributions due from the employer. It must also be signed by the trustees and the employer.

Auditors need to ascertain when a schedule becomes effective. PN15 provides guidance on the issues that need to be considered, but it is important to be aware that a schedule of contributions cannot be effective until it is certified by the actuary and that it cannot be backdated.

Code of practice 03 'Funding defined benefits' and code of practice 05 'Reporting late payment of contributions to occupational money purchase schemes' provide guidance for trustees on the monitoring of contributions and the reporting responsibilities in the event of late or incorrect payments being made.

In order to make their statement about contributions, auditors obtain the schedule and undertake procedures to obtain sufficient appropriate evidence to conclude whether or not contributions payable have, in all material respects, been paid at least for the amounts and within the timeframe set out in the schedule.

Auditors need to consider a range of issues, including:

- changes in rates of contributions payable and the extent to which these have been included in the schedule;
- changes in the definition of salary on which the contributions are based;
- whether the schedule is sufficiently clear;
- whether the schedule complies with legal requirements and guidance issued by the Regulator;
- whether there have been any member complaints about incorrect contributions;
- the scheme's systems for recording and monitoring contributions; and
- any reports to the Regulator of late or inaccurate contributions.

As the statement about contributions is separate to the audit opinion, PN15 indicates that it should be a separate report.

PN15 also recommends that a summary of contributions paid during the scheme year under the schedule is produced by the trustees and included with the annual report ('the summary').

The summary, an example of which is included in the appendices to PN15, shows details of contributions payable during the year together with a reconciliation to the contributions shown in the fund account. The significance of the summary is that it enables the reader of the annual report and financial statements to identify which contributions the auditors' statement refers to.

As the schedule refers to both the quantum and the timing of the payment of contributions materiality must be considered in terms of both value and time. It is normal to apply materiality to values and the pension scheme auditor should consider this in the same manner as for any other transaction stream. The application of materiality to timing is more complex.

The application of materiality is a matter of judgement for individual pension scheme auditors and the only guidance provided by PN15 is that there should be regard to the frequency of the breaches and the cumulative, as well as the individual, impact of the breaches.

In considering the application of materiality to timing there are, however, some salient factors which may be considered:

- the statement about contributions is on an aggregate basis and so materiality should not be applied based on the perception of a single member's contribution;
- late contributions are usually more significant in a defined contribution arrangement; and
- the manner of the monitoring of contributions, the identification of any late contributions and the timeliness of such identification.

In the event that the auditors' statement on contributions is qualified, trustees should have already considered the need to report to the Regulator because of their responsibility to monitor the receipt of contributions. In such circumstances the auditor will need to consider the following:

- if a report has been made by the trustees, did it contain all relevant information that the Regulator would expect?
- if the trustees were aware of the issue giving rise to the qualification, have they documented why a report was not made to the Regulator and is the conclusion reasonable?
- if the trustees were not aware of the issue, are their monitoring procedures insufficient and are there wider implications?

Depending upon the results of the above, it may be necessary for a report to be made to the Regulator by either the trustees or the auditor. A qualified statement about contributions does not automatically result in a report to the Regulator. A report by the trustees to the Regulator on the timing of contributions is, however, more likely to result in a qualified statement about contributions, but the pension scheme auditor should give the matter proper consideration.

44.9   SCHEMES IN THE PROCESS OF WINDING UP

Schemes in winding up are not exempt from the requirement to produce an annual report and audited financial statements until the wind up is complete. The Administration Regulations do not require the appointment of an auditor if the membership is less than two, so potentially the statutory requirement for an audit can cease before the wind up is finalised. However, trust law and best practice indicate that financial statements should still be prepared. In these circumstances, the audit becomes non-statutory and auditors need to consider whether the existing engagement terms remain appropriate.

A schedule of contributions is no longer required once the wind up of a defined benefit pension scheme commences and auditors should only express an opinion in their statement about contributions on compliance with the schedule of contributions up to the date the wind up commences. In relation to subsequent periods, the statement concerns compliance with the scheme rules and, where appropriate, the recommendations of the actuary.

For a money purchase scheme, the payment schedule is still required during the wind up period. Trustees should revise the payment schedule to reflect the basis on which contributions are payable from the start of winding up, which is normally nil. Auditors express an opinion on the payment schedule in force up to the commencement of winding up and thereafter on the revised schedule if one has been produced.

Once winding up is formally concluded the auditors' appointment automatically lapses without the need for formal resignation. Evidence of winding up should be obtained, but, if no such evidence is available, auditors should consider formal resignation. Where no audit work has been performed for several months, it may be appropriate for auditors to include in the statement on resignation that they are not able to know of any circumstances which might affect members' interests.

44.10   OTHER REPORTING SITUATIONS

There are situations when audited financial statements are required for periods other than the usual agreed accounting reference date. These will normally coincide with the requirement for an actuarial valuation such as:

- the determination of the Pension Protections Fund Levy;
- a claim against an employer under section 75 of PA 1995 due to an employer ceasing to participate in a multi-employer scheme;
- following a bulk transfer into or out of a scheme and/or a significant change in membership; and
- for the purpose of the Pension Protection Fund following the entry of the scheme into the assessment period.

The financial statements in all of these situations should be prepared in accordance with the Audited Accounts Regulations. A trustee report is not usually required and the notes to the financial statements should specify the purpose for which the financial statements have been prepared. Auditors will report on the financial statements in the usual manner, again specifying the purpose for which they have been prepared. There is not usually a requirement to give a separate statement about contributions. PN15 provides detailed guidance and examples of reports.

45 SOLICITORS' ACCOUNTS RULES

45.1 BACKGROUND

The Rules dealing with solicitors' accounts are contained in the Solicitors' Accounts Rules 1998 (SAR98).

SAR98 covers solicitors, registered European Lawyers and registered foreign lawyers (in partnership with solicitors or registered European Lawyers) who practice in England and Wales, who are employed by a practice or who are employed as in-house solicitors.

Solicitors who practice outside England and Wales continue to be bound by the Solicitors' Overseas Practice Rules 1990, Rules 12–16. These are similar in principle to SAR98, but are less detailed and less onerous in their requirements.

All practising solicitors who handle clients' money are required to deliver a report confirming their compliance with SAR98. This must be given by an authorised reporting accountant on an annual basis to the Law Society within six months of the solicitor's firm's year end.

45.1.1 Objective

The object of SAR98 is to ensure:

- compliance with the Law Society's Practice Rule 1 as to the solicitor's integrity, the duty to act in the client's best interests, and the good repute of the solicitor and the solicitor's profession;
- the fair treatment of clients' money and controlled trust money, including the distinction between clients' money, controlled trust money, and solicitor's own money; and
- that solicitors maintain adequate bookkeeping and recording systems.

The responsibility for maintaining the accounting systems lies with the partners and, as with companies where all directors are responsible, even if delegated to one particular person, all partners are responsible.

Breaches of the Rules must be rectified immediately upon discovery, including the replacement of money improperly withheld or withdrawn from a client account. The duty to remedy breaches rests not only on the person causing or discovering the breach but also on all the partners. This duty extends to replacing missing client money or controlled trust money from partners' own resources, even if the money has been misappropriated by an employee or fellow partner and whether or not a claim is made on the solicitors' indemnity or compensation funds.

SAR98 strongly recommends that accounting records are written up at least weekly, even in the smallest practice, and daily in the case of larger firms.

The basic principle is that any money received from a client by a solicitor must be paid into a client account unless it is received in respect of a bill rendered to the client for time costs or disbursements that have already been paid by the solicitor. Money may only be withdrawn from a client account in accordance with the client's instructions, or to settle a solicitor's fee after a fee invoice has been given to the client.

The books of account maintained by the solicitor must show the current balance on each client's ledger and balances must be reconciled with the cash books and the bank statements every five weeks. The records must be kept for a period of six years and any bank statements must be kept as issued and printed by the bank.

Solicitors are responsible for accounting to their clients for any interest earned on the clients' money while it is held by the solicitor unless the amount of interest is £20 or less. This applies even where the money is held in a general client account for specified periods of time. The accounting system should have the ability to highlight this.

The Council of the Law Society has the power to order an inspection of the books of account and records in order to ascertain that they are in accordance with SAR98.

45.2   EXISTING GUIDANCE

The accountant's report has to be prepared by a registered auditor and strict rules for its compilation are set out in SAR98. Although it is called an accountant's report, many of the procedures involved are of an auditing nature. As the opinion confirms whether the rules have been complied with, it is a less judgemental exercise than an audit of financial statements. It is restricted to an examination of both client and office ledgers and the related bank accounts, and it does not involve the audit of a profit and loss account and balance sheet of the practice. No accounts have to be filed with the Law Society.

In April 2001 the Law Society added a new rule, 42(1)(P), requiring accountants to check, as part of their SAR work, that the solicitor's practice holds PI insurance for the period from 1 September 2000 onwards for the purposes of the Solicitor's Indemnity Insurance Rules 2000.

45.3 ENGAGEMENT LETTER

There is a formal requirement for engagement letters to be issued to and agreed with solicitors and both parties must keep these for three years. The engagement letter should include a paragraph designed to release the reporting accountants from their duty of confidentiality in certain cases where it is necessary to report directly to the Law Society under the 'whistle-blowing' provision. An example of suitable paragraphs for inclusion in the engagement letter is shown in **Table 1** below.

TABLE 1: Paragraphs to include in an engagement letter concerning whistle-blowing

In accordance with rule 38 of the Solicitors' Accounts Rules 1998, we are instructed as follows:

(a) that we may, and are encouraged to, report directly to the Law Society without prior reference to you should we, during the course of carrying out work in preparation of the accountant's report, discover evidence of theft or fraud affecting client money, controlled trust money, or money in a client's own account operated by a solicitor, registered foreign lawyer, or recognised body as signatory; or information which is likely to be of material significance in determining whether any solicitor, registered foreign lawyer or recognised body is a fit and proper person to hold client money or controlled trust money, or to operate a client's own account as signatory;

(b) to report directly to the Law Society should our appointment be terminated following the issue of, or indication of intention to issue, a qualified accountant's report, or following the raising of concerns prior to the preparation of an accountant's report;

(c) to deliver to you with our report the completed checklist required by rule 46 of the Solicitors' Accounts Rules 1998; to retain for at least three years from the date of signature a copy of the completed checklist; and to produce the copy to the Law Society on request;

(d) to retain these terms of engagement for at least three years and to produce them to the Law Society on request; and

(e) following any direct report made to the Law Society under (a) or (b) above, to provide to the Law Society on request any further relevant information in our possession.

To the extent necessary to enable us to comply with (a) to (e) above, you waive your right of confidentiality. This waiver extends to any report made, document produced or information disclosed to the Law Society in good faith pursuant to these instructions, notwithstanding that it may subsequently transpire that we were mistaken in our belief that there was cause for concern.

45.3.1   'Whistle-blowing'

Under SAR98 reporting accountants may report directly to the Law Society, without reference to the solicitors, where they discover evidence of theft or fraud affecting client's money or trust money, or information which is likely to be of material significance in determining the fit and proper status of any solicitor.

Matters which may indicate a requirement on the reporting accountant to report to the Law Society include:

- false accounting, theft or misappropriation by any solicitor in the firm;
- evidence of theft or misappropriation by any employee, fee-earner, consultant or third party not reported to the police authorities;
- evidence leading to concerns about honesty or integrity of any solicitor;
- evidence of attempted tax evasion (either direct or indirect taxes);
- failure to properly control client money;
- failure to keep proper accounting records under the SAR98 which is so significant that the reporting accountant is unable to express an opinion in his report;
- failure to take professional advice without due consideration;
- evidence of indifference or recklessness in connection with client or controlled trust money or operation of a client's own account as signatory; or
- any other matters or indications of fraud or theft in connection with client or controlled trust money or operation of a client's own account as signatory.

45.3.2   Termination of appointment

Reporting accountants are also required to communicate with the Law Society on the termination of their appointment where this has arisen from the issue of, or an indication of the intention to issue, a qualified accountant's report.

45.3.3   Independence

Reporting accountants must note in their report any possible connections with the solicitors that may influence their independence.

As part of the SAR98 report, the reporting accountant must complete a questionnaire concerning whether the reporting accountant, his principals, directors or employees of the accountancy practice:

- are related to the solicitor;
- normally maintain the solicitor's client accounts;
- place substantial reliance on the solicitor for referral of clients;

- are clients or former clients of the solicitor; and
- whether there are any other circumstances which may affect the reporting accountant's independence.

The Law Society has indicated that the disclosure of this information is stated to relate only to that information which is within the personal knowledge of the person signing the report. They have also said that they do not expect detailed investigations to be undertaken for everyone in the firm, but they do expect reasonable enquiries to be made of those directly involved in the work. For example, if the engagement partner is aware that one of his fellow partners is related to a solicitor covered by the report, this should be noted. If he is not aware of the relationship then it need not be noted, as it could not influence the reporting accountant's independence.

45.3.4 Place of examination

SAR98 requires that the examination of the solicitor's accounting records, files and other relevant documents should be performed at the solicitor's office and not at those of the reporting accountants. They do permit an initial electronic transmission of data to the reporting accountants at their offices where this is to reduce the amount of time spent at the solicitor's premises.

45.4 PROCEDURES

SAR98 sets out the matters that should be checked. These cover:

- the adequacy of the accounting system;
- checking that any client money or controlled trust money is properly dealt with;
- ensuring that receipts and payments of client money and controlled trust money are properly recorded;
- the adequacy of the system of recording and transferring costs;
- examining financial transactions on client and controlled trust accounts, to ensure they comply with SAR98;
- checking the reconciliations required at two dates;
- ensuring that the reconciliations have been performed at the appropriate intervals throughout the period and have been retained;
- checking that any inter-client transfers have been dealt with in accordance with SAR98; and
- where acting for both purchaser and lender in a conveyancing transaction, that client funds are clearly identifiable.

Where the solicitors use a computerised accounting system, testing may be carried out on a sample basis so long as the reporting accountants are satisfied that the system is adequate and the fact is mentioned in their report.

The Law Society issues guidelines for procedures and systems for accounting for clients' money, and the reporting accountants are required to report on material departures from them, which are identified during their work on SAR98. However, they are not required to undertake a detailed check on compliance with these guidelines.

45.5   PROBLEM AREAS

Reporting accountants should ensure that they are aware of the following problem areas as part of their knowledge of the business, as they are the common areas in which solicitors breach the SARs.

45.5.1   Debit balances

No client account may go into debit in the solicitor's ledger. Each client should be treated in isolation and it is not permissible to net off debits and credits on the client ledger. This would indicate a shortage of funds that should be disclosed.

The Law Society does not allow debit balances to be offset against credit balances when stating the liabilities to clients and controlled trusts as shown by the ledgers on the accountant's report form.

45.5.2   Client confidentiality

Solicitors may refuse to allow the accountant access to certain documents on the grounds of client confidentiality and where this is the case the accountant should qualify the report, setting out the circumstances.

45.5.3   Trivial breaches

During the course of the examination, clerical and bookkeeping errors may come to light. Most of these will be classified as trivial breaches and will not lead to a qualification of the accountant's report as long as they have been rectified on discovery and that there was no loss to any client as a result. However, the term 'trivial breach' is not defined and will be a matter of judgement. The factors that should be considered include:

- the amount involved;
- the nature of the breach;
- whether the breach is deliberate or accidental;
- how often the same breach has occurred; and
- the time outstanding before correction.

The notes to SAR98 state that the Law Society receives a number of accountant's reports which make reference to trivial breaches but also show a significant difference between liabilities to clients as shown in the ledger an client money in bank accounts. Where this is the case, the notes to SAR98 require that an explanation for the difference must be given.

45.5.4 *'Without delay'*

'Without delay' is defined in SAR98 as meaning the day of receipt or the next working day. This means that solicitors must have procedures to ensure that cheque receipts are banked 'without delay'. Any cheques that are not banked within this time period will constitute a breach of SAR98.

45.5.5 *Other areas*

Other problem areas include ensuring that the specific rules are properly applied to:

* interest on clients' money;
* trust money;
* legal aid receipts; and
* designated deposit accounts.

45.6 REPORTING

The accountant's report confirms that the solicitor has complied with the SAR98. Its form is set out in SAR98 and requires details of:

* the solicitor(s) covered by the report;
* the period covered by the report;
* the results of the reconciliations at the chosen dates; and
* any qualification.

The report may be qualified in respect of matters:

* on which the accountant has been unable to satisfy himself or herself, giving the reasons for that inability; or
* where it appears to the accountant that there have been breaches of SAR98.

There is some space on the standard form for details of the qualification. The details given should be sufficient to enable the Law Society to understand the nature of the breach. If necessary, a separate letter may contain these details but this must be referred to in the report.

As noted in **45.3.3** any possible connections with the solicitors which might influence independence must be detailed on the report.

45.7 CHECKLIST

As well as reporting to the Law Society, reporting accountants are required to complete a checklist which is kept by the solicitor and which may be reviewed by the Law Society. The checklist covers the results of the test checks made by the reporting accountants on client money and controlled trust money in the following areas:

- each office's accounting system;
- postings to ledger accounts and casts;
- receipts and payments of client money and controlled trust money;
- the system of recording costs and making transfers;
- examination of client files for verification of transactions and entries in accounting records;
- extraction of client ledger balances for clients and controlled trusts;
- reconciliations;
- payments of client money and controlled trust money;
- office accounts – client money and controlled trust money;
- client's money and controlled trust money not held in client account;
- inter-client transfers;
- instances where the firm acts for both borrower and lender in a conveyancing transaction; and
- information and explanations requested.

Reporting accountants have to confirm whether the results of their tests are satisfactory in each of these areas and, if not, indicate that any breaches have been mentioned in the accountant's report. Where, as a result of these tests, the position has been found to be unsatisfactory, further details are to be reported at the end of the checklist.

46 INVESTMENT BUSINESSES

46.1 INTRODUCTION

This Chapter covers the audit considerations in respect of the financial statements, client assets and conduct of business rules for investment businesses. The guidance is taken from Practice Note 21 *The Audit of Investment Businesses in the United Kingdom* as supplemented by APB Bulletin 2001/7 *Guidance for Auditors of Investment Business*. This Practice Note also covers auditors' reports to the FSA, which is covered in **Chapter 8**, 'Reports to the FSA on investment businesses'.

The APB issued Practice Note 21 in June 2000, to supersede Practice Note 1 *Investment Businesses* and Practice Note 5 *The Auditors' Right and Duty to Report to SIB and Other Regulators of Investment Businesses*. Practice Note 21 was supplemented in December 2001 by APB Bulletin 2001/7 which takes into account the changes that came about at N2 (1 December 2001) when the FSA took over the regulation of firms previously regulated by the Securities and Futures Authority (SFA), the Investment Management Regulatory Organisation (IMRO) and the Personal Investment Authority (PIA).

In April 2005 the APB issued Bulletin 2005/2, *Audit Risk and Fraud – Supplementary Guidance for Auditors of Investment Businesses*, to supplement Practice Note 21 following the publication of the ISAs (UK and Ireland) relating to audit risk and fraud. The relevant sections of this chapter have been updated to reflect the guidance in the Bulletin. In March 2006 the APB issued an Exposure Draft of a full revision to Practice Note 21. The main changes to the earlier Practice Note are summarised in **46.5**.

Although the old Practice Note and Bulletin 2001/7 were issued prior to the APB adopting the ISAs (UK and Ireland) for the audit of periods beginning on or after 15 December 2004, the other guidance within them remains relevant under the new regime. Where the guidance refers to the old SASs, this commentary also includes references to the relevant ISA (UK and Ireland).

46.2   RULES AND REPORTING REQUIREMENTS

Investment businesses incorporated in Great Britain are subject to the same requirements of the Companies Act for a statutory audit of financial statements as any other company. The scope of the audit is no different, but regulated businesses are not able to take advantage of the exemptions available for small and medium-sized entities. Investment businesses trading as sole traders and partnerships are subject to additional requirements under the FSA Handbook of Rules and Guidance (the FSA Rules) that they would not be subject to were they not regulated.

In addition to the requirements for a statutory audit, investment businesses are governed by the FSA Rules, the primary objective of which is investor protection. The main categories of the FSA Rules are:

- High Level Standards to ensure that firms follow the FSA's Principles for Business and meet Threshold Conditions as well as ensuring that those within the firm performing Controlled Functions meet the requirement of the Approved Persons regime;
- Business Standards consisting of:
  - Interim Prudential Sourcebooks containing financial rules, designed to ensure that the business is financially sound, has appropriate controls and is able to meet its commitments;
  - Client Assets rules, requiring segregation of money and investments held for clients and also covering arrangements for custody;
  - Conduct of Business rules, to ensure that the business deals fairly, honestly and with due skill, care and honesty with its clients;
  - Market Conduct rules, containing the FSA code of market conduct, price stabilising rules, interprofessional conduct and endorsement of the takeover code;
  - Regulatory Process rules, containing details of the authorisation, supervision, enforcement and decision making processes; and
  - Redress rules, covering dispute resolution, compensation and complaints against the FSA.

Compliance with the FSA Rules is monitored in a number of ways, the principal ones being:

- internally, by the business itself;
- by submitting regular returns to the FSA;
- by monitoring and inspection by the FSA;
- reports to the FSA by the business's auditors.

Therefore, auditors constitute an important part of the system of supervision, and issue reports in the following areas:

- the usual true and fair opinion on the financial statements;

- an opinion on whether the entity fulfils the FSA's requirements for financial resources;
- whether the accounting records and control systems meet the FSA's requirements;
- whether the entity has complied with the rules concerning client assets; and
- interim profits for capital adequacy purposes.

The Practice Note splits these reports into three types:

- the audit of financial statements;
- review reports on interim profits; and
- reports to the FSA.

The audit of financial statements and the review of interim profits are discussed further in this chapter. **Chapter 8** contains details about reporting to the FSA, in addition to guidance on ad hoc reporting to the FSA as set out in Section B of ISA (UK and Ireland) 250.

In addition, the Practice Note contains detailed guidance on considerations in relation to client assets and this is covered in section **46.4** below.

The introduction of the CREST system of on-line share settlement in July 1996 has meant that auditors of investment businesses which are CREST users, such as stockbrokers, fund managers or custodians, need to understand the nature of the system. Guidance for auditors comes from Audit 2/96 *Guidance for auditors of CREST users*, issued by the Audit Faculty of the Institute of Chartered Accountants in England and Wales, which gives an overview of how the system operates, its regulatory structure and some of the key audit issues. It is discussed in **46.7** below.

46.3   THE AUDIT OF FINANCIAL STATEMENTS

The Practice Note sets out guidance for the audit of financial statements on a SAS-by-SAS basis. This chapter sets out some of the major areas of which to be aware when auditing an investment business.

46.3.1   *SAS 100 Objective and general principles governing an audit of financial statements/ISA (UK and Ireland) 200 Objective and general principles governing an audit of financial statements*

In addition to the ethical guidance issued by auditors' professional bodies, there are additional independence rules laid down by the FSA. Therefore, auditors should be aware of the increased threat to their independence and review these prior to accepting any regulated audit engagement.

46.3.2   SAS 110 Fraud and error/ISA (UK and Ireland) 240 The auditor's responsibility to consider fraud in an audit of financial statements

Key indicators of potential fraud and error particularly relevant to investment businesses will include:

- backlogs in key reconciliations;
- inadequate segregation of duties between back, middle and front office staff;
- inadequate management understanding of complex products;
- inadequate definition of responsibilities and supervision of staff;
- inadequate whistle-blowing arrangements;
- high management and staff turnover;
- ineffective oversight of offshore operations;
- lack of an effective audit committee;
- ineffective personnel practices and policies;
- inadequate communication of information to management; and
- elements of remuneration packages linked to revenue or profits.

46.3.3   SAS 120 Consideration of law and regulations/ISA (UK and Ireland) 250 Part A Consideration of laws and regulations in an audit of financial statements

SAS 120 requires auditors to perform procedures that identify possible or actual non-compliance with regulations which are central to the entity's ability to conduct its operations. The SAS defines laws and regulations which are central to the entity's ability to conduct its business as those where either compliance is required to obtain a licence to operate, or where non-compliance could be reasonably expected to result in the entity ceasing to operate.

The Practice Note suggests the following procedures to help identify such possible or actual breaches of non-compliance for an investment business:

- obtain a general understanding of the legal and regulatory framework applicable to the entity and industry, and of the procedures followed to ensure compliance with the framework;
- inspect correspondence with the relevant regulators;
- enquire of the directors whether they are on notice of any possible instances of non-compliance with law or regulations;
- include in the representation letter confirmation that the directors have disclosed to the auditors all those events of which they are aware which involve possible non-compliance, together with the actual or contingent consequences arising therefrom;
- hold discussions with the investment business's Compliance Officer and other personnel responsible for compliance; and

- review any work on compliance matters carried out by internal audit.

46.3.4 SAS 130 The going concern basis in financial statements/ISA (UK and Ireland) 570 Going concern

Paragraph 31 of SAS 130 sets out the areas for consideration in assessing whether an entity is a going concern. For investment businesses the attitude of the FSA towards an entity and continuing authorisation of the entity by the FSA are paramount to continuing as a going concern. Therefore, the following items should also be considered:

- FSA censures or fines;
- FSA capital shortages;
- non-routine visits from the FSA;
- reputation and other indicators; and
- general non-compliance with the FSA Rules.

Any doubts about an entity's ability to continue as a going concern may be reportable to the FSA under the guidance in SAS 620.

46.3.5 SAS 140 Engagement letters/ISA (UK and Ireland) 210 Terms of audit engagements

The FSA Rules have various requirements in relation to accepting engagements. There is no requirement for auditors to be approved by the FSA before they can be appointed. However, investment businesses must take reasonable steps to ensure that the auditors it is planning to appoint or has appointed, have suitable skills, experience and independence with the nature, scale and complexity of the firm's business and the requirements and standards under the regulatory system to which the business is subject.

To enable the business to assess the ability of an auditor, the FSA may seek information about the auditor's relevant experience and skills. The FSA will normally seek such information by letter from an auditor who has not previously audited any FSA regulated firm. The auditor should reply fully to the letter and the regulated firm should not appoint any auditor who does not reply to the FSA. The FSA may also seek further information on a continuing basis from auditors as it deems necessary.

46.3.6 SAS 200 Planning/ISA (UK and Ireland) 300 Planning an audit of financial statements

Auditors will usually complete their work on the annual accounts at the same time as the work required to report to the FSA, in an effort not to duplicate audit effort. Auditors must also ensure that their work is planned to meet the short timescales for reporting imposed by the FSA.

46.3.7   SAS 210 Knowledge of the business/ISA (UK and Ireland) 315 Understanding the entity and its environment and assessing the risks of material misstatement

Auditors must seek to understand the complex business and regulatory regime within which investment businesses operate. This will include:

- obtaining a general understanding of the applicable legal and regulatory framework and the procedures followed to ensure this framework is complied with;
- reviewing the firm's Scope and Permission Notice; and
- inspecting correspondence with regulators.

Auditors should not accept work that they are not competent to undertake and may consider using technical specialists for more involved areas – for example, when considering trades in complex products or for a business heavily involved in e-commerce. The use of specialists is particularly important in assessing valuations of particular derivative instruments for which there is no independent fair market valuation. Guidance on the use of specialists is given in section **38.4**.

46.3.8   SAS 300 Accounting and internal control systems and audit risk assessments/ISA (UK and Ireland) 315 Understanding the entity and its environment and assessing the risks of material misstatement and ISA (UK and Ireland) 330 The auditor's procedures in response to assessed risks

Investment businesses differ greatly in their size and the complexity of their operations, and therefore the reliance auditors place on internal control systems varies. Where client assets exist this is likely to be an area where detailed internal controls are relevant. Whilst client assets are not, in principle, part of the financial statements, any material deficiency could be indicative of poor control and may have an impact on the financial position of the business.

When the systems are designed, their dual purposes should be borne in mind. There are considerations both for the entity itself and for the protection of investors' interests. Detailed guidance on the requirements for the accounting records is included in each set of the FSA Rules.

As part of their consideration of the risk of material misstatement, auditors should understand the selection and application of the entity's accounting policies and consider whether they are appropriate. This is likely to be in conjunction with auditors' assessment of the entity's objectives, strategies and the related business risks. In addition, auditors should obtain an understanding of the measures used by management to review the business's performance. This will assist them in understanding the pressures faced by the firm and which may prompt management to misstate the financial statements.

The risk of material misstatement should be assessed at the financial statements level and at the assertion level for classes of transactions, account balances and disclosures. Auditors should determine which, if any of these risks are significant risks which require special audit consideration, and for each significant risk they should evaluate the design of the entity's related controls.

Auditors should obtain an understanding of the control environments. Factors to be considered when assessing the control environment of an investment business are shown in **Table 1**.

TABLE 1: Factors to consider when assessing the control environment

- the nature and status of the investment business's clients and any changes in their status which may affect the application of investor protection requirements;
- a change in the market environment (e.g., an increase in competition);
- the introduction of new clients, products or marketing methods;
- claims made in promotional literature (particularly in relation to performance);
- the risk profile of the business undertaken by the entity;
- the complexity of products;
- the consistency, across geographical location, of products sold and methods used;
- the legal and operational structure of the investment business;
- financial and managerial support provided to and by any other group companies;
- the number of branches and sales offices;
- the use of appointed representatives;
- management's attitude towards control, regulation and investor protection;
- the roles and responsibilities allocated to the finance and compliance functions;
- the recruitment, training, competence and supervision of personnel; and
- the integrity, competence and experience of management.

The auditors' understanding of an entity's control activities should allow them to assess the risks of material misstatement at the assertion level and to design further audit procedures in response to assessed risks.

Many investment businesses will have computer-based systems and in these situations management should understand the interaction between manual and computer controls. Normally, the greater the degree of computerisation, the greater the emphasis that will be required on the general and application controls of the computerised function, as part of the overall system of control.

Whatever the system of control, it should be fully documented so that it may be understood and operated effectively and consistently. Failure to maintain such documentation may be a reportable matter under the FSA Rules.

The effective operation of a control system may be assisted by an internal audit or a compliance department. The auditors will need to consider the terms of reference of these departments, their independence from operations, the quality of the staff and their reporting procedures (see **Chapter 38**).

Once the risk of material misstatement has been assessed, auditors are required to plan procedures specifically related to those identified risks. Bulletin 2005/2 sets out a number of potential substantive procedures in the following areas:

- fees and commissions receivable;
- commissions payable;
- trading of securities and other instruments and related gains and losses;
- valuation of investments; and
- liabilities for breaches.

46.3.9   SAS 440 Management representations/ISA (UK and Ireland) 580 Management representations

Possible additions to the standard management representation letter for investment businesses include:

- acknowledging management's responsibility for establishing and maintaining accounting records and systems of control in accordance with the FSA Rules;
- confirming that management has made available to the auditors all correspondence and notes of meetings with the FSA relevant to the auditors' examination;
- that all complaints have been drawn to the attention of the auditors; and
- where applicable, representation that no client money or client investments were held by the investment business.

46.3.10   SAS 480 Service organisations/ISA (UK and Ireland) 402 Audit considerations relating to entities using service organizations

It is common for investment businesses to outsource some of their functions, including:

- safe custody of investments by a custodian;
- settlement or clearing of trades;
- maintenance of accounting records;
- product administration (such as unit trusts, savings schemes, PEPs or ISAs); and
- investment management.

Auditors must consider where to obtain their audit evidence where activities are outsourced. Evidence may be obtained from the investment business itself, by contacting or visiting the third party, or by relying on the assurances of the third party's auditors. Investment business should take reasonable steps to ensure that, where applicable, each of its appointed representatives and material outsourcers give auditors the same right of access to their accounting and other records as the firm itself is required to give to their auditors. See further details on SAS 480 and ISA (UK and Ireland) 402 in **Chapter 37**.

The investment business is required to comply with the FSA Rules whether or not its activities are outsourced.

46.3.11 *SAS 600 Auditors' reports on financial statements/ISA (UK and Ireland) 700 The auditor's report on financial statements*

Details of auditors' reports to the FSA as the regulator of investment business are covered in **Chapter 8**.

46.3.12 *SAS 610 Reports to directors or management/ISA (UK and Ireland) 260 Communication of audit matters with those charged with governance*

The FSA Rules require auditors to submit to investment businesses on an annual basis a report or letter commenting on the business's internal controls or stating that they have no comments. Such a report or letter need only cover such matters that have come to the auditors attention while undertaking the work to produce their audit report to the FSA.

46.4   CLIENT ASSETS

The main purpose of the FSA Rules in this area is to ensure that the investment business safeguards client assets, both in its day-to-day business and in the event of its insolvency. Section 9 of the FSA's Conduct of Business contains the FSA's rules with which an investment business must comply and on which auditors are required to report under Section 9 of the FSA's Interim Prudential Sourcebook for Investment Businesses.

Appendix 4 of the Practice Note sets out the relevant planning considerations for each category of client assets:

- client investments; and
- client money.

It also considers where there are no client assets. As part of the auditors' report on the investment business, the auditors confirm that the entity has complied with the FSA Rules. It is the auditors' responsibility to plan and perform their audit of these areas to be able to fulfil their reporting obligations.

Further guidance on auditors' reports to the FSA on client assets is set out in **Chapter 8**.

46.4.1   Client investments

Client investments may be any of the following, held by an investment business on behalf of a client:

- shares and stocks in the capital of a company;
- debentures;
- government and public securities;
- warrants or other instruments entitling the holder to subscribe for investments;
- certificates representing securities; or
- units in a collective investment scheme.

In addition, arranging custody for a client as well as actually providing the custody is also covered by the legislation.

Accounting records
Auditors must consider whether the investment business has promptly recorded in its books and records all transactions undertaken by it in the period. This includes the purchase and sale of investments of behalf of its clients, as well as the movement of documents (including the business's own documents, due to the risk of mixing clients' documents with the investment business's own). Auditors should also consider whether records are in agreement with the statements sent out to clients, if reconciliations are carried out in accordance with the FSA Rules and whether other benefits accruing to clients, such as bonus or scrip issues, are correctly accounted for.

Evidence that the matters set out in **Table 2** are being properly carried out is likely to give auditors comfort in respect of these control objectives.

TABLE 2: Matters on which evidence is required in respect of accounting records

- that documents of title are recorded immediately on receipt;
- that documents of title are not released to clients, registrars, brokers, etc., without the records being amended;
- records are kept in respect of each document setting out date of receipt and despatch, the nature of the document, details of the investment to which it relates and the client to whom the investment belongs;
- that the statements are correct and regularly dispatched to clients;
- that client correspondence and queries are promptly and properly dealt with; and
- that bonus and scrip benefits are properly allocated to clients.

Accounting systems and controls

The Practice Note stresses the importance of the control environment to the effectiveness of the system of internal control that operates in the investment business. One element of this is to ensure that lapses in procedures are dealt with immediately, rather than ignored.

The auditors should consider the following areas in detail as part of their audit of client investments:

- safe custody and proper control of client investments including the sending of periodic statements;
- proper registration and segregation of client investments; and
- compliance with reconciliation requirements.

The appendix to the Practice Note gives details of the objectives to be tested and typical evidence to be gained by auditors in each of these areas.

46.4.2 Client money

Definition

Client money is defined by the FSA Rules as:

> 'money of any currency which, in the course of carrying on designated investment business, a firm holds in respect of any investment agreement entered into, or to be entered into, with or for a client, or which a firm treats as client money in accordance with the client money rules'.

The definition of client money specifically includes the cash component of an ISA.

It is important for auditors to understand what constitutes client money for the particular investment business on which they are reporting. They need to be aware of the possibility that the management of the entity has not correctly identified what is client money.

Auditors should be aware that different types of clients are identified in the FSA Rules and although, in general, all money received from private clients must be treated as client money, there are certain limited exemptions to what is deemed to be 'client money'. Auditors should consult the relevant the FSA Rules in individual cases.

In relation to banks, the application of client money rules is limited in certain respects. Where a bank holds the money of its investment business clients in accounts with itself, it is not considered to be holding client money. The client money rules will apply, however, if the bank passes the money outside the bank. Again, the auditor should refer to the FSA Rules.

Client bank accounts

All client money must be held in accounts at an approved bank, and the rule books require investment businesses to perform a risk assessment on the bank prior to opening the accounts and regularly throughout the period of holding the account. The auditor must ensure that the investment business has adhered to all relevant rules pertaining to the client bank account including:

- ensuring the account is named so as to make it clear that the money in the account does not belong to the business;
- checking that the bank has no right of set off over the accounts; and
- ensuring that any interest accrued is paid into that account.

Auditors will request written confirmation of adherence to these rules from the bank.

Detailed audit objectives and examples of audit evidence in respect of:

- adequate accounting records;
- adequate systems and controls as regards:
    - proper holding of client money;
    - payment into and withdrawal from client bank accounts;
    - proper accounting for interest; and
- compliance with the relevant regulations at specified dates

are set out in an appendix to the Practice Note.

46.4.3   *No client assets*

Auditors must be aware of situations where investment businesses do not hold client assets, either by their own choice or under the terms of their authorisation by the regulator. In these cases there should be controls to ensure that where client assets are received they are immediately returned to the investor.

Where no client assets are held, the FSA will require a report from the auditors that this is the case. Possible procedures for this purpose are detailed in **Table 3**.

TABLE 3: Procedures to verify that no client assets are held

- ensure that procedures are in place to train staff about the existence and importance of client assets;
- enquire how settlements are made on clients' behalf;
- review the investment business's cash book to ensure that no client money transactions pass through it;
- review client files for indications that client assets may exist;
- review client files for agreements on how custody is to be managed and review agreements with any custodians to ensure that money is not classed as, or treated as, client money;
- if an investment business has no client assets because it does not act for private clients, review client lists to confirm that no private clients are included;
- enquire how dividends, especially unclaimed dividends, and rights issues are dealt with (these should not be written off to the investment business's own profit and loss account even if not material);
- ensure reviews occur at regular intervals to confirm that client money is not held;
- enquire about the action taken if any client money is received; and
- obtain representations from management that no client money is held.

46.4.4 Other audit considerations

The auditors must test compliance with certain of the FSA Rules at particular dates during the period under review. For example, reconciliations should be performed at the relevant date as laid down in the FSA Rules and this should be checked by the auditors. Other requirements may be tested at any time during the accounting period – for example, the use of appropriately designated client bank accounts.

Guidance on trivial breaches is contained in **Chapter 8**.

46.5 ED PRACTICE NOTE 21 (REVISED)

Following the introduction of the ISAs (UK and Ireland), the APB issued Bulletin 2005/2, *Audit Risk and Fraud – Supplementary Guidance for Auditors of Investment Businesses* as a supplement to Practice Note 21. At the time of its publication, the APB stated that it would add a full scale revision of Practice Note 21 to its work programme.

In March 2006, the APB issued an Exposure Draft of the full revision to Practice Note 21, which when finalised will replace both the old Practice Note and Bulletin 2005/2. The major additions in the revised version are set out below.

46.5.1   ISA (UK and Ireland) 210 Terms of audit engagement

The draft revision suggests that audit engagement letters may additionally refer to:

- section 346 of FSMA 2000 which makes it a criminal offence for an authorised person or its officers, controllers or managers to provide false or misleading information to an auditor; and
- the need for the entity to make the auditors aware of any review, investigations or reports that may be relevant to the audit of the financial statements.

46.5.2   ISA (UK and Ireland) 250 Consideration of laws and regulations in an audit of financial statements – Section A

ISA (UK and Ireland) 250 Section A states that laws and regulations relevant to the audit can be regarded as falling into two main categories:

- those relating to the preparation of the financial statements; and
- those which provide a legal framework within which the entity conducts its business and which are central to its ability to continue to conduct its business.

Any laws and regulations which do not fall within these categories need not be taken into account when planning and performing the audit work.

The second category is crucial to investment businesses as non-compliance with those regulations central to the entity's business may cause the Regulator to revoke or restrict authorisation. In order to obtain an understanding of these regulations, auditors:

- obtain a general understanding of the legal and regulatory framework and the procedures followed to ensure compliance with it;
- inspect correspondence with the relevant regulators;
- ask the directors whether they are on notice of any possible instances of non-compliance; and
- obtain written confirmation from the directors that they have disclosed to the auditors all those events of which they are aware which involve

possible non-compliance, together with the actual or contingent consequences which may arise.

In addition, auditors should:

- hold discussions with the entity's Compliance Officer and other personnel responsible for compliance;
- review any work on compliance matters carried out by internal audit;
- review breaches, complaints and gifts registers;
- review results of compliance monitoring; and
- review any FSA risk mitigation programmes.

It is also important that auditors have an understanding of the Conduct of Business Rules. Although auditors have no direct reporting responsibility under the rules, breaches may give rise to material fines or the restriction of authorisation by the FSA. Breaches of the Conduct of Business Rules may also warrant reporting to the regulator under the statutory duty provisions (see **Chapter 8**).

46.5.3 *ISA (UK and Ireland) 250 Consideration of laws and regulations in an audit of financial statements – Section B*

Reports to the regulator are considered in **Chapter 8**.

46.5.4 *ISA (UK and Ireland) 260 Communication of audit matters to those charged with governance*

ISA (UK and Ireland) 260 covers issues which may arise if reports to directors or management are to be made available to third parties. For investment businesses, the FSA may request copies of such reports from the entity or direct from the auditor. Auditors must obtain the consent of their client before providing copies to the FSA.

It is therefore preferable that auditors include statements in their reports to management that:

- the report has been prepared for the sole use of the entity;
- it must not be disclosed to a third party, or quoted or referred to, without the written consent of the auditors; and
- no responsibility is assumed by the auditors to any other person.

The auditors' engagement letter may also make reference to the fact that reports to those charged with governance are required to be sent to the FSA.

46.5.5   ISA (UK and Ireland) 315 Obtaining an understanding of the entity and its environment and assessing the risks of material misstatement

ISA (UK and Ireland) 315 requires auditors to obtain 'a sufficient understanding of control activities to assess the risk of material misstatement at the assertion level'. The draft revision to the Practice Note states that different systems and controls may be deemed adequate for different investment businesses. However, all systems should ensure that the following general control objectives are met:

- the business is planned and conducted in an orderly, prudent and cost-effective manner in adherence to established and documented policies;
- transactions and commitments are entered into only in accordance with management's general or specific authority;
- client assets are safeguarded and are completely and accurately recorded;
- the assets of the business are safeguarded and the liabilities controlled;
- the risk of loss from fraud, other irregularities and error is minimised, and any such losses are promptly and readily identified;
- management is able to monitor on a regular and timely basis the investment business's position relative to its risk exposure;
- management is able to prepare complete and accurate returns for the regulator on a timely basis in accordance with the rules; and
- issues relating to compliance with the rules are resolved in a timely manner to the satisfaction of the FSA.

46.5.6   ISA (UK and Ireland) 402 Audit considerations relating to entities using service organisations

For each outsourced activity, the ISA (UK and Ireland) requires auditors to determine the significance of the outsourced activities to the entity and their relevance to the audit. Investment businesses commonly outsource a number of functions which are relevant activities in accordance with ISA (UK and Ireland) 402, such as safe custody of investments, settlement or clearance of trades or product administration.

46.5.7   ISA (UK and Ireland) 540 Audit of accounting estimates

Accounting estimates are used for valuation purposes in some investment businesses, for example with over-the-counter derivatives and illiquid trading positions which cannot be readily substantiated by a fair market valuation. ISA (UK and Ireland) 540 requires auditors to design and perform audit procedures to obtain sufficient appropriate audit evidence that the estimates are reasonable. This will include one or more of:

- reviewing and testing the process used by management to develop the estimate;

- using an independent estimate for comparison with that prepared by management; and
- reviewing subsequent events which provide audit evidence of the reasonableness of the estimate made.

46.5.8 ISA (UK and Ireland) 545 Auditing fair value measurements and disclosures

As with accounting estimates, fair value measurements are often important to investment businesses. As part of the understanding of the entity and its environment, auditors should obtain an understanding of the entity's process for determining fair value measurements and disclosures and the related control activities.

46.6 HIGH LEVEL STANDARDS AND CONDUCT OF BUSINESS RULES

The prime responsibility for ensuring compliance with, and reporting breaches of, the FSA's High Level Standards and Conduct of Business rules (other than audit requirements under Section 9 of the Conduct of Business Sourcebook described in **46.4** above) lies with the management of the investment business. The FSA performs periodic inspections of investment businesses to review compliance with the FSA Rules.

The FSA's High Level Standards Sourcebook covers such matters as:

- Principles for Businesses;
- Senior Management Arrangements, Systems and Controls;
- Threshold Conditions;
- Statements of Principle and Code of Practice for Approved Persons; and
- The Fit and Proper Test for Approved Persons.

The FSA's Conduct of Business Sourcebook covers such matters as:

- clear, fair and not misleading communication;
- inducements and soft commission;
- reliance on others;
- Chinese walls;
- financial promotion;
- the internet and other electronic media;
- accepting customers;
- client classification;
- terms of business and client agreements with customers;
- advising and selling;
- product disclosure and the customer's right to cancel or withdraw;
- dealing and managing investments;

- reporting to customers;
- client assets;
- operators of collective investment schemes;
- trustee and depository activities.

46.6.1   Impact on the audit

Auditors have no direct reporting responsibility in respect of the FSA's High Level Standards and Conduct of Business (other than Section 9) rules, although breaches of such rules may have implications for the financial statements of the investment business, other aspects of the annual reporting requirements, or ad hoc reports. Therefore some enquiry into possible breaches is called for. Examples of such situations are:

- FSA Rule breaches, which could give rise to fines or claims by investors; or
- a restriction or withdrawal of authorisation, which could threaten the business's viability as a going concern.

46.6.2   Audit approach

Staff involved in the audit should have a general understanding of the High Level Standards and Conduct of Business rules to enable them to spot possible breaches which come to their attention. They should assess the control environment that exists, considering such areas as:

- the adequacy of procedures and training to inform staff of the requirements of the FSA and to ensure that they meet those requirements;
- the adequacy of authorities and supervision;
- the review of compliance by senior management;
- procedures to ensure possible breaches are investigated by an appropriate person and are brought to the attention of senior management; and
- the authority of, and resources available to, the compliance officer.

Possible areas, outside client assets, where compliance problems commonly occur and may have an effect on the audit include:

- conducting business outside the scope of its authority: such action could result in fines, suspension or loss of authorisation;
- customer complaints: a significant level of complaints should put auditors on guard;
- poor controls over appointed representatives: the business is liable for the acts of its representatives;
- personal dealings of its employees: the business could be liable if clients believe they are dealing with the business when in fact they are dealing with its employees;

- misclassification of customers as 'business' or 'private' investors: incorrect classification could result in claims;
- unauthorised deposit taking; and
- lack of or incomplete customer agreements.

It would normally be inappropriate to perform any direct testing for compliance with the High Level Standards and Conduct of Business rules, as it is beyond the auditors' responsibility and they may not be technically competent enough to perform the work. Ensuring compliance with such rules is part of the monitoring function of the FSA. However the general steps that may be taken to assess the impact of any breaches on the auditors' report are:

- consideration of the investment business's compliance framework, including operational manuals and the documentation of its procedures and controls;
- review of the scope and results of the internal compliance monitoring and review;
- examination of the records maintained of any breaches and notifications to the FSA;
- examination of correspondence with the FSA and the results of the most recent inspection visit;
- review of the register of complaints from customers; and
- review of monitoring returns and questionnaires submitted to the FSA.

Where auditors become aware of a possible breach of the High Level Standards or Conduct of Business rules they should identify its cause and consider whether it imposes any reporting requirements on them.

Auditors should enquire of management and staff whether any breaches have occurred and obtain appropriate representations in writing from management.

46.7 REVIEW REPORTS ON INTERIM PROFITS

All bodies subject to the Investment Services Directive are required to maintain adequate capital resources, as defined by the EC Capital Adequacy Directive. The reserves of an investment business are permitted to include interim profits as long as the interim profits have been verified. External auditors may be requested to perform this verification and report on interim profits for capital adequacy purposes.

The engagement to 'verify' interim profits is essentially a review engagement and the opinion may be given in terms of negative assurance. The report is addressed to the directors of the entity.

Auditors must state in their report that they have followed the review procedures specified by the FSA or, if they have varied the procedures used, the alternative procedures should be listed in their report. Alternatively, reference may be made to the engagement letter, where the alternative procedures may have been listed.

The FSA states in the FSA Rules the procedures they wish auditors to perform. As a minimum, auditors should:

- satisfy themselves that the figures forming the basis of the interim profits have been properly extracted from the underlying accounting records;
- review the accounting policies used in arriving at the interim profits to obtain comfort that they are consistent with those used when drawing up the annual financial statements, and adhere to the rules of the regulator involved;
- perform analytical review on the results to date, including comparisons of actuals to date with budget and prior period;
- discuss the overall performance and financial position of the business with management;
- ensure the implications of current and prospective litigation and claims, changes in business activities and provisions for bad and doubtful debts are included in the interim profit figure; and
- follow up problem areas of which they are already aware.

Auditors must also make it clear that the report is for the use of the FSA and for the purpose of the calculation of capital adequacy only.

An example review report is given in **Table 4**. This should be adapted where the entity is unincorporated, or a sole-trader, or where procedures have not been specified by the engagement letter.

TABLE 4:   Example review report on interim profits for a FSA regulated investment business

Review report by the independent auditors to the board of directors of XYZ Limited ('the company')
In accordance with our engagement letter dated [date], a copy of which is attached, we have reviewed the company's statement of interim profits for the period from [date] to [date] set out on pages [x] to [x] of the attached reporting statement. That statement is the responsibility of, and has been approved by, the directors. Our review did not constitute an audit, and accordingly we do not express an audit opinion on the interim profits. It has been carried out having regard to the guidance in Appendix 58 of the FSA's Interim Prudential Sourcebook for Investment Businesses.
Based on review procedures performed, nothing has come to our attention that causes us to believe that:

> - the interim profits have not been calculated on the basis of the accounting policies adopted by the company in drawing up its annual financial statements for the year ended [date of last annual financial statements];
> - those accounting policies are not in accordance with the principles set out in rule 10-41 of the SFA Rule Book; and
> - the interim profits after tax amounting to £[x] are not reasonably stated.
>
> [Date]

46.8 CREST

Auditors of entities which use CREST need to obtain an understanding of the nature of the processing system and the controls necessary to ensure the investment assets are properly safeguarded. They also have to be reasonably satisfied as to the assets' existence and ownership and year end balances for their statutory reports and those to the FSA concerning the keeping of adequate books and records.

Audit 2/96 covers three areas where CREST may impact on the audit approach. These are:

- understanding the business;
- evaluating internal controls; and
- detailed audit procedures.

46.8.1 *Understanding the business*

The following matters may need to be considered in seeking to comply with SAS 210.1 or ISA (UK and Ireland) 315 where CREST is used (see **16.2**):

- the extent of the interaction between the entity and CREST, including:
  - whether securities are held as principal by the entity or whether the organisation conducts investment business on behalf of other clients as agents;
  - the volume and value of transactions settled;
  - the materiality of unsettled transactions and balances relative to the entity's financial position; and
  - its relationship with other parties within CREST;
- the manner in which the entity interacts with CREST, including:
  - the entity's status within CREST as a user, member or registrar;
  - the structure of the member's accounts that 'contain' the entity's investments;
  - details of the connection to CREST, such as gateway and network provider; and
  - the systems used to interact with CREST, whether standard interface, bespoke or off-the-shelf in-house systems.

Specialists, such as computer audit staff, may need to be involved to assess the systems in the first year that CREST is used by the entity, and the effort required is likely to be greater when in-house systems are used. Once the systems have been ascertained and documented, the guidance in ISA (UK and Ireland) 315 (see **Chapter 22**) should be followed to develop an appropriate audit approach.

46.8.2   Evaluating internal controls

The types of internal controls which need to be considered in relation to CREST include:

- access and authorisation controls with regard to the CREST computer systems;
- adequate audit trail controls which identify CREST transactions;
- other IT controls such as security, disaster planning and authorised upgrading of the system;
- organisational and segregational controls over CREST transactions; and
- management controls such as reconciliations and follow-up of exception reports.

Auditors will need to consider controls at CREST as well as the procedures within the entity being audited in accordance with ISA (UK and Ireland) 402 *Audit considerations relating to entities using service organizations*. More reliance will need to be placed on CREST systems where the entity's records or systems are unreliable. The guidance notes that CREST Co will be commissioning its own auditors to produce an annual report on controls which will be made available to CREST members and their auditors, where it is necessary to consider CREST's own controls.

46.8.3   Detailed audit procedures

The extent and nature of detailed audit procedures will depend on the auditors' assessment of risk and the strength of the entity's systems and controls. The Technical Release notes several matters which the auditors may wish to take into account when planning their work on a CREST user. At present, CREST does not produce hard-copy confirmations, although they have indicated that this may change if there is sufficient demand. Auditors will therefore need to find alternative evidence. The guidance suggests that this may be obtained by:

- the auditors being authorised to use the entity's systems to obtain confirmation;
- auditors installing their own CREST link and having the entity's permission to have read-only access to their records;
- independent confirmation with the counterparty; or
- work on the entity's own systems and reconciliations.

47 REGISTERED SOCIAL LANDLORDS

The Housing Act 1996 introduced the concept of the 'registered social landlord' (RSL) in England and Wales, which can include housing associations, local housing companies, registered housing charitable trusts and housing care and support agencies.

Social landlords wishing to have access to social housing grants and certain other grants must be registered with the relevant regulatory body (see **47.2.5**). As a result, they are subject to monitoring and regulation by the regulatory body and their objects and constitution need to meet various conditions. RSLs operate under a variety of legal frameworks, including industrial and provident societies, limited companies and charitable trusts.

Every RSL is required, under legislation, to have an annual independent audit, although the specific auditing requirements vary depending on the legal status of the RSL. For example, some registered social landlords may be eligible to apply exemptions applicable to small companies, charities and industrial and provident societies. In such cases they must supply an accountant's report. The thresholds have been amended by SI 2006/265 The Friendly and Industrial and Provident Societies Act 1968 (Audit Exemption) (Amendment) Order 2006 and the Charities Act 2006. Advantage of these exemptions is only possible if permitted under the Rules of the registered social landlord.

Auditors of RSLs must be registered auditors, i.e. eligible under the Companies Act 1989 and registered with a supervisory body recognised under that Act.

47.1 EXISTING GUIDANCE

47.1.1 Practice Note 14

Practice Note 14 *The Audit of Registered Social Landlords in the United Kingdom (Revised)* provides guidance on how Statements of Auditing

Standards should be applied to audits of the financial statements of RSLs. The Practice Note does not have an effective date and so should be applied to any audits of RSLs commencing after its date of issue of March 2006.

The March 2006 version of Practice Note 14 (Revised) replaced the November 2003 version which in turn had replaced the first Practice Note 14 issued in September 1997. The latest Practice Note is based on legislation (including the Housing Act 2004) and regulations in effect at 31 December 2005. The two revisions take account of regulatory developments affecting RSLs since Practice Note 14 was originally issued. However, the main changes arise from the replacement of Statements of Auditing Standards (SASs) by International Standards on Auditing (ISAs) (UK and Ireland), which apply to all audits undertaken in the United Kingdom and the Republic of Ireland in respect of periods commencing on or after 15 December 2004.

Although the Housing Act 1996 introduced the term RSL in respect of England and Wales, Practice Note 14 (Revised) also uses the term RSL for housing associations in Scotland and Northern Ireland.

The Practice Note follows the framework of the ISAs and provides a commentary on the application of each ISA to the audit of RSLs. The introduction to the Practice Note stresses that it is designed to ensure the consistent application of ISAs across the social housing sector rather than provide detailed explanatory material to assist auditors on all aspects of RSL audit work. Section **47.3** below summarises the applicability of ISAs to RSL audits as interpreted by the Practice Note and should be read in conjunction with the Practice Note in order to get a full understanding of the implications for the audit of RSLs.

47.1.2   Regulatory Circulars and Good Practice Notes

Regulatory circulars and good practice notes issued by the RSL regulatory bodies (e.g., the Housing Corporation in England) require RSLs to submit a copy of their auditor's management letters, together with the RSL's responses, to the relevant regulatory body. There are usually strict timescales for submitting management letters and responses, e.g within six months of the financial year end for RSLs regulated by the Housing Corporation.

Two documents which auditors of RSLs in England should be aware of are:

- Good Practice Note 7, *External audit of housing associations* – (GPN 7); and
- Circular R2-25/01, *Internal Controls Assurance*,

both of which are issued by the Housing Corporation and are available on *www.housingcorp.gov.uk*.

RSLs in Wales, Scotland and Northern Ireland will have similar guidance in respect of external audit and internal controls assurance.

GPN 7 was first issued in November 2003 and applies to RSLs registered in England. This Good Practice Note replaced the external audit sections of the 1995 Code of Audit Practice for Housing Associations (now replaced in its entirety). It provides guidance to housing associations in respect of complying with statutory and regulatory requirements. Whilst not aimed directly at the auditors of RSLs, they should become familiar with its contents as follows:

- requirement to have an external audit;
- eligibility to be external auditor;
- selecting an external auditor;
- engagement of an external auditor;
- respective responsibilities of the association and the external auditor;
- the auditor's report;
- the auditor's management letter;
- other communication from the external auditor;
- other services provided by the external auditor;
- reviewing the external auditor's performance and changing the auditor;
- tendering the audit service;
- audit committees; and
- groups.

GPN 7 is being revised in 2007 to reflect changes in legislation (e.g. Housing Act 2004, Companies (Audit Investigations and Community Enterprise) Act 2004, Companies Act 2006 and Charities Act 2006), International Standards on Auditing, Ethical Standards for Auditors and general good practice. A new section on small housing associations is expected in the revision.

There are also plans to revise the internal controls assurance circular during 2007.

47.2 BACKGROUND

47.2.1 *The nature of RSLs*

RSLs are not-for-profit organisations, managed under the oversight of a board or committee of management, independently from local and central government. They provide social housing accommodation (usually made available at less than market rents and allocated to applicants in greatest housing need) and other related services.

They provide an alternative to local authority and private sector rented housing, undertaking new building, refurbishing existing property or acquiring existing satisfactory properties, with the aim of providing rented accommodation. Under certain conditions such housing may be sold to tenants (e.g., right to buy and shared ownership).

RSLs may be constituted in various ways, for example, as:

- industrial and provident societies (either as exempt charities or non-charitable); or
- limited companies (either as registered charities or non-charitable).

It is important that auditors understand the statutory framework of their RSL clients as this will affect audit reporting requirements. This does differ slightly between England, Wales, Scotland and Northern Ireland. The majority of RSLs in the United Kingdom are registered with the Housing Corporation under the Housing Act 1996 and the term given to that body is the 'Regulator'. Under certain pieces of legislation, the Regulator has the power to determine the accounting requirements of RSLs which will be important for the auditors to understand. Practice Note 14 (Revised) contains useful guidance in its appendices covering legislation throughout the United Kingdom relevant to RSLs.

The constitution of all RSLs or the legal rules under which they are incorporated must prohibit them from distributing any surpluses or assets to the members or the board, even if they are non-charitable.

The majority of RSLs are industrial and provident societies and most reference is made to a consolidating piece of legislation, the Industrial and Provident Societies Act 1965. As industrial and provident societies, they fall under the administrative jurisdiction of the mutual societies division of the Financial Services Authority (FSA) which took over this role from the Registry of Friendly Societies. This means that their constitution comprises 'rules' which must be registered with the FSA. They will be governed by a voluntary board which is appointed by the members. The Industrial and Provident Societies Act 1965 contains some basic requirements for the accounts and audit. The Friendly and Industrial and Provident Societies Act 1968 sets out the main accounting and audit requirements. It requires proper financial records to be kept and that all financial statements agree with those records, that there is a satisfactory system of internal control over transactions and that the financial statements show a true and fair view of the RSL's financial position. Industrial and provident societies which are charitable are known as exempt charities which means they are subject to the Charities Act but are not regulated by the Charity Commission.

RSLs which are limited companies are incorporated under the Companies Act 1985 and are generally companies limited by guarantee without share capital. They will therefore need to comply with the Companies Act 1985 but also the accounting determinations issued by the relevant regulator, e.g., the Housing Corporation. RSL charitable companies are also regulated by the Charity Commission but as RSLs, the Statement of Recommended Practice in the RSL sector takes precedence over the Charity SORP.

47.2.2 Responsibilities of the Board or the Committee of Management

Although day-to-day management of the RSL may be delegated to subcommittees or staff, the board retains full responsibility for seeing that those functions are properly carried out.

The roles and responsibilities of the board noted in the Practice Note normally include:

- defining and monitoring compliance with the governing documents, values and objectives of the RSL;
- establishing plans to achieve those objectives;
- approving each year's budget and financial statements prior to publication;
- establishing and overseeing an appropriate framework of delegation and effective systems of control;
- taking key decisions on matters that will, or might, create significant risks for the RSL;
- monitoring the performance of the RSL in relation to these plans, budgets and decisions;
- appointing and, if necessary, dismissing the chief executive and being represented in the appointment of key second tier managers;
- appointing and agreeing the remuneration of the auditors;
- satisfying themselves that the affairs of the RSL are conducted lawfully and in accordance with performance standards set by the Regulators; and
- overseeing the RSL's relationship with its regulatory body.

GPN 7 (see **47.1.2** above) is being revised and is likely to make reference to amendments made to the Companies Act 1985 as a result of the Companies (Audit, Investigations and Community Enterprise) Act 2004. These amendments confer rights to auditors and define offences relating to the provision of information to auditors. Under this legislation, it is an offence for directors not to give adequate or accurate information to auditors and directors are required to disclose whether they have complied in their Board report. For registered social landlords, this legislation is only applicable to those registered under the Companies Act but the revision to GPN 7 is likely to refer to the Companies Act section 234ZA statement as being one of good governance for all housing associations.

47.2.3   Responsibilities of audit committees

In October 2004, the Housing Corporation published "Improving the Effectiveness of Audit Committees: a Good Practice Guide". This publication addresses how audit committees can operate effectively and contribute to good governance in housing associations. It is also useful guidance for external auditors covering areas such as:

- understanding what goes into external audit management letters;
- assessing auditor performance and effectiveness;
- the independence of auditors; and
- the audit committee's role with regard to accounting policies;

The guidance covers many other areas regarding good governance and internal audit arrangements.

47.2.4   Financial reporting requirements

The financial statements of RSLs are prepared in accordance with the requirements of applicable law and regulations contained in accounting orders or determinations issued under the relevant statutes. The precise nature of the requirements is determined by two factors:

- how the RSL is constituted (for example, as a registered charity, industrial and provident society, or non-profit making company); and
- whether the RSL is registered by the relevant regulatory body.

Generally, each RSL is required to prepare financial statements which give a true and fair view and hence should comply with applicable accounting standards. The Statement of Recommended Practice *Accounting by Registered Social Landlords* (the RSL SORP) supplements these general accounting principles and provides authoritative guidance on their application. Therefore, in order to give a true and fair view, financial statements of RSLs are normally prepared following the provisions of the RSL SORP.

Although there is no specific legal requirement that RSLs should comply with accounting standards or with the RSL SORP, the various regulations require the board of an RSL to state whether its financial statements have been prepared in accordance with applicable accounting standards and statements of recommended practice, which implies that the RSL SORP should be applied.

The latest version of the RSL SORP is *Accounting by Registered Social Landlords Update 2005* which was issued in May 2005. Since then changes in financial reporting standards and other accounting practice have continued as well as developments in the social housing sector. Therefore, a SORP

Working Party continues to work on updates to the RSL SORP. This is being completed in a number of phases.

The Update to the 2005 SORP began with a consultation process in 2006 with responses received in October 2006. However, this resulted in a wide range of differing opinion on areas such as accounting for shared ownership properties and mixed tenure developments. The SORP Working Party is working on a revised draft of the SORP which will be issued for a second consultation process during 2007. It is not yet certain when this will be finalised but an agreed version is likely to appear towards the end of the 2007 calendar year. The effective date is likely to be for accounting periods beginning on or after 1 January 2008 or possibly 1 April 2008, but earlier adoption will again be encouraged. The majority of RSLs will therefore need to implement the changes in their 31 March 2009 financial statements but some are likely to adopt the changes for 31 March 2008.

Another update to the SORP is then expected in 2009 which will take into consideration the ASB's revised approach to conversion in respect of International Financial Reporting Standards.

There is also the '*Statement of Principles for Financial Reporting: Proposed Interpretation for Public Benefit Entities*'. This was published as an Exposure Draft in August 2005 and could have a significant impact on RSL financial accounting, mainly in respect of the treatment of social housing grant, i.e., as a revenue grant instead of capital. After a final consultation period during 2007, it is possible that this will be issued in final form during 2007 and will be applicable to accounting periods beginning on or after 1 April 2008 with earlier adoption encouraged.

47.2.5 *Responsibilities of auditors*

Although RSLs may be subject to different legislation, the statutory duties of their auditors are similar. The auditors are required to:

- express an opinion as to whether the financial statements give a true and fair view and have been properly prepared in accordance with the appropriate statutory requirements; and
- state in the auditors' report:
  - where proper books of account have not been kept;
  - where a satisfactory system of control over transactions has not been maintained; and
  - if the financial statements are not in agreement with the books and records of the RSL.

There may also be a requirement imposed by the relevant regulatory body to report to them on certain returns of RSLs e.g. as requested by the Housing

Corporation. Similarly with regard to funders, loan covenants may include the need for the auditors to report on compliance with financial covenants.

47.2.6   Features of RSL audits

Internal controls

Internal controls are particularly relevant because:

- RSLs are in receipt of substantial amounts of public funding in the form of grants; and
- legislation requires auditors to state in their report on the financial statements if the RSL has failed to maintain a satisfactory system of internal control.

Other guidance

There are housing federations which represent the best interests of RSLs in the United Kingdom. Auditors should be aware of guidance issued by these federations, for example, codes of governance.

The long-term nature of the business

The main income source, rents, is fairly predictable, and thus analytical procedures are often a useful audit tool.

Substantial debt financing

It is common for RSLs to have significant amounts of borrowing. Therefore it is important for RSLs and their auditors to assess their medium-term financial forecasts to ensure that the going concern basis remains appropriate. Such debt financing brings with it loan covenant compliance requirements and the importance of accounting under Financial Reporting Standard 25 (FRS 25) if there are any breaches during the year.

Complex direct tax, indirect tax and employee tax rules

RSLs are heavily involved in property transactions and this brings with it complex corporation tax and VAT requirements. As many RSLs are charitable they need to be aware of their primary purpose when considering property development contracts involving mixed tenure (e.g., developments where a scheme may include an element of commercial units and units for outright sale). Other examples of complexities include:

- group structures and most often the inability to be considered a group for tax purposes, i.e., group relief;
- conflicts between RSL accounting requirements under accounting standards, and the RSL SORP and the tax treatment, e.g., first tranche shared ownership sales;
- transfer pricing, loan relationships and gift aid which can add complexity when linked to property transactions following 2006 Budget changes;
- partial exemption treatment for VAT purposes;

- the use of development company subsidiaries outside the VAT group to maximise the recovery of VAT on professional fees;
- potential difficulties for stock transfer associations in claiming input VAT on certain property refurbishment costs;
- the effect of employee tax for employees transferring from local authorities and tax deduction requirements on payments made to overseas landlords, e.g., under temporary leasing arrangements;
- construction industry scheme administration; and
- self employed tax rules when using consultants, especially in busy property development departments.

Supported housing

RSLs involved in supported housing and providing care services have access to various sources of funding, e.g., in England, 'Supporting People'. A large amount of this funding is available through contracts with local authorities. These contracts can be complex and the available funding may not always be sufficient to deliver the service.

Housing properties

A significant number of RSLs including many established by means of Large Scale Voluntary Transfers, carry their housing properties at an existing use valuation. A professional valuation is obtained and, as set out in ISA (UK and Ireland) 620 *Using the work of an expert*, auditors consider the proper inclusion of the valuation in the accounts, the information on which the valuer has relied and the reasons for any changes in the valuation from the previous period.

Judgement is needed on the depreciation policy to be adopted in respect of housing properties. This covers the useful economic lives of housing properties which for most RSLs can cover long periods depending on property type, location and construction method. Determining the amount of cost attributable to land (which is not depreciated) and to buildings can be difficult where the properties have been in ownership for many years and records may not provide the split.

Capitalisation of works to existing properties

The principles of FRS 15 are followed and further guidance is given in the RSL SORP. The RSL SORP recommends that works which result in an increase in the net rental income stream should be capitalised as improvements. This may arise from works carried out to existing properties, through a combination of increased rents, reduction in future maintenance costs or a significant extension to the life of the property. It is often difficult to demonstrate that any enhancement of the economic benefits of tangible fixed assets is in excess of the previously assessed standard of performance anticipated when the assets were first acquired, constructed, last replaced or revalued and should be capitalised. RSLs might therefore consider component accounting but this has implications for record keeping.

Impairment

FRS 11 is an important standard to consider in RSL audits. Impairments can result from a major reduction in the service potential of a property which may arise from a reduction in demand in the local area. Such impairments are recognised immediately in the income and expenditure account. Impairment reviews are also required where the estimated economic life of housing properties for depreciation purposes is 50 years or more, or no depreciation is charged because it is considered immaterial.

47.2.7   The auditors' relationship with the Regulators

The Housing Act 1996, Schedule 1, Part III, sets out the general requirements in respect of accounts and audit. The Housing Act 2004 inserted an additional Section 19A to the Housing Act 1996 regarding disclosure of information by auditors to the relevant authority. This states that a person who is, or has been, an auditor of a registered social landlord does not contravene any duty to which he is subject merely because he gives to the relevant authority:

(a)   information on a matter of which he became aware in his capacity as auditor of the registered social landlord; or

(b)   his opinion on such matter,

if he is acting in good faith and he reasonably believes that the information or opinion is relevant to any functions of the relevant authority.

The above applies whether or not the person is responding to a request from the relevant authority.

47.3   ISA (UK AND IRELAND) 210: TERMS OF AUDIT ENGAGEMENTS

Engagement letters should set out additional auditor responsibilities in relation to RSLs, which may arise:

- under statute – such as additional returns to be reviewed;
- from recommendations issued to RSLs within the various codes and other recommendations from the relevant regulatory body or relevant housing federation; or
- by agreement with the RSL.

Statutory requirements may also result in additional returns which an RSL may require its auditors to review or sign, such as a service charge summaries under the Landlord and Tenant Act 1985. The recommendations made to RSLs by their regulatory bodies are not themselves binding on auditors, but RSLs and their auditors will generally agree to increase the scope of the auditors' work to ensure that the RSL complies with best practice.

An example of an audit engagement letter is shown in **Table 1**.

TABLE 1: Example engagement letter for RSL – drafted for an Industrial and Provident Society and should be amended for other types of constitution

To the Board of [name of RSL]

The purpose of this letter is to set out the basis on which we are to act as auditors of the RSL and the respective areas of responsibility of the Board, comprising of those charged with governance of the RSL, and of ourselves.

1 Responsibilities of the Board and auditors
1.1 The Board is responsible for preparing Financial Statements in accordance with applicable law and United Kingdom Generally Accepted Accounting Practice for each financial year which give a true and fair view of the state of affairs of the Association and of the surplus or deficit for that period. In preparing those Financial Statements, the Board is required to:

- select suitable accounting policies and then apply them consistently;
- make judgements and estimates that are reasonable and prudent;
- state whether applicable accounting standards have been followed, subject to any material departures disclosed and explained in the financial statements; and
- prepare the financial statements on the going concern basis unless it is inappropriate to presume that the RSL will continue in business.

The Board is responsible for keeping proper accounting records which disclose with reasonable accuracy at any time the financial position of the RSL and to enable it to ensure that the financial statements comply with the Industrial and Provident Societies Acts 1965 to 2002, Schedule 1 to the Housing Act 1996 and the Accounting Requirements for Registered Social Landlords General Determination 2006. It has general responsibility for taking reasonable steps to safeguard the assets of the RSL and to prevent and detect fraud and other irregularities.

1.2 As Board members, you are under a duty to prepare an annual report for each financial year complying in its form and content with regulations as made under the Accounting Requirements for Registered Social Landlords General Determination 2006. You are also required to have regard to the Statement of Recommended Practice, Accounting by Registered Social Landlords, (the SORP) as updated from time to time, issued jointly by the National Housing Federation in England, the Scottish Federation of Housing Associations and the Welsh Federation of Housing Associations. RSL financial statements and accounting practices are expected to comply fully, where appropriate, with the SORP.

1.3   We have a statutory responsibility to report to the members whether in our opinion the financial statements give a true and fair view of the state of the

---

RSL's affairs and of the surplus or deficit for the year, and whether they have been properly prepared in accordance with the Industrial and Provident Societies Acts 1965 to 2002, Schedule 1 to the Housing Act 1996 and the Accounting Requirements for Registered Social Landlords General Determination 2006, as amended, (or other relevant legislation). In arriving at our opinion, we are required to consider the following matters, and to report on any in respect of which we are not satisfied:

- whether proper accounting records have been kept by the RSL;
- whether the RSL's balance sheet and income and expenditure account are in agreement with the accounting records;
- whether the RSL has maintained a satisfactory system of control over its transactions;
- whether we have obtained all the information and explanations which we consider necessary for the purposes of our audit; and
- whether the information in the Board's report is consistent with that in the audited financial statements.

1.4 We have a professional responsibility to report if the financial statements do not comply in any material respect with applicable accounting standards, unless in our opinion the non-compliance is justified in the circumstances. In determining whether or not the departure is justified we consider:

- whether the departure is required in order for the financial statements to give a true and fair view; and
- whether adequate disclosure has been made concerning the departure.

1.5 Our professional responsibilities include:

- providing in our report a description of the Board's responsibilities for the financial statements where the financial statements or accompanying information do not include such a description; and
- considering whether other information in documents containing audited financial statements is consistent with the financial statements.

2 Scope of audit

2.1 Our audit will be conducted in accordance with International Standards on Auditing (UK and Ireland) issued by the Auditing Practices Board (APB) and will have particular regard to the APB's Practice Note, '*The audit of registered social landlords in the United Kingdom*' and the Housing Corporation's Good Practice Note '*External audit of housing associations*'. It will include such tests of transactions and of the existence, ownership and valuation of assets and liabilities as we consider necessary.

2.2 We shall obtain an understanding of the accounting and internal financial control systems in order to assess their adequacy as a basis for the preparation of the financial statements and to establish whether proper accounting records have been maintained by the RSL.

2.3 We shall expect to obtain such appropriate evidence as we consider sufficient to enable us to draw reasonable conclusions therefrom. The nature and extent of our tests will vary according to our assessment of the RSL's accounting system and where we wish to place reliance on it, the system of internal control, and may cover any aspect of the business operations.

2.4 Our work will be planned in advance and incorporated into an audit plan. This may be varied on the basis of our findings during the course of an audit and from year to year. Accordingly, we may modify our audit scope, rotate our audit emphasis and propose matters of special audit emphasis, as the circumstances dictate.

2.5 Our audit includes assessing the significant estimates and judgements made by the Board in the preparation of the financial statements and whether the accounting policies are appropriate to the RSL's circumstances, consistently applied and adequately disclosed.

2.6 The concept of materiality affects our audit planning and our consideration of matters arising from our audit. We take into account both qualitative and quantitative factors when assessing materiality.

2.7 In forming our opinion we will also evaluate the overall presentation of information in the financial statements.

3. Internal audit
3.1 In developing our audit plan, we will liaise with your internal auditors to ensure that our work is properly co-ordinated with theirs. It is our policy to rely upon internal audit work whenever possible, while ensuring that adequate audit coverage is achieved of all significant areas.

4. Management representations
4.1 The information used by the Board in preparing the financial statements will invariably include facts or judgements which are not themselves recorded in the accounting records. As part of our normal audit procedures, we shall request appropriate Board members, or senior officials/management to provide written confirmation each year of such facts or judgements and any other oral representations which we have received during the course of the audit on matters having a material effect on the financial statements. We will also ask you to confirm in that letter that all important and relevant information has been brought to our attention. In addition, we shall present to the Board a schedule of any unadjusted misstatements that have come to our attention in the course of our audit work, and if you decide not to adjust the financial statements for these misstatements we shall request you to explain in writing your reasons for not making the adjustments.

5. Detection of fraud, error and non-compliance with laws and regulations
5.1 The responsibility for safeguarding the assets of the RSL and for the prevention and detection of fraud, error and non-compliance with law or regulations rests with yourselves. However, we shall endeavour to plan our audit so that we have a reasonable expectation of detecting material misstatements in the financial statements or accounting records (including any material misstatements resulting from fraud, error or non-compliance with law or regulations), but our examination should not be relied upon to disclose

all such material misstatements or frauds, errors or instances of non-compliance as may exist.

6. Reports to management
6.1 At the conclusion of the audit, or sooner if appropriate, we shall prepare a report to The Board that will include comments on:

- any expected modification of the auditors' report,
- unadjusted misstatements,
- material weaknesses to the accounting and internal control systems identified during the audit,
- the qualitative aspects of the RSL's accounting practices and financial reporting,
- matters specifically required by other Auditing Standards, and
- any other relevant matters relating to the audit.

6.2 Our audit is not designed to identify all significant weaknesses in the RSL's system of internal controls. Our review of internal control systems is only performed to the extent required to express an opinion on the RSL's financial statements and therefore our comments on these systems will not necessarily address all possible improvements which might be suggested as a result of a more extensive special examination.

7. Other requirements
7.1 In order to assist us with the examination of your financial statements, we shall request early sight of all documents or statements (including the Chairman's statement, operating and financial review and the Board report) which are due to be issued with the financial statements. We are also entitled to attend all general meetings of the RSL and to receive notice of all such meetings.

7.2 Once we have issued our report we have no further direct responsibility in relation to the financial statements for that financial year. However, we expect that you will inform us of any material event occurring between the date of our report and that of the Annual General Meeting which may affect the financial statements.

8. Summary Financial Statements
8.1 As Board members of the RSL, you are responsible for any summary financial statements. Our responsibility is to report to the members whether in our opinion the summary financial statement is consistent with the full financial statements and report of the RSL for the year. Our work will be conducted in accordance with Bulletin 1999/6 'The auditors' statement on the summary financial statement' issued by the Auditing Practices Board.

9. Adoption of Housing Corporation Circular R2-25/01
9.1 We are not required to report on your compliance with the requirements of Circular R2-25/01. Our responsibilities in respect of this statement on internal control are governed by ISA (UK and Ireland) 720 'Other information in documents containing audited financial statements' which requires that;

- We should read the other information. If as a result we become aware of any apparent misstatements therein, or identify any material inconsistencies with the audited financial statements, we should seek to resolve these with you;
- If we identify an inconsistency between the financial statements and the other information, or a misstatement within the other information, we should consider whether an amendment is required to the financial statements or to the other information and should seek to resolve the matter through discussion with the directors;
- If, after discussion with the directors, we conclude that;
- The financial statements require amendment and no such amendment is made, we should consider the implications for our reports;
- That the other information requires amendment and no such amendments is made, we should consider appropriate action including the implications for our report.

10. Electronic communications

10.1 We acknowledge that as the Board of the RSL you may wish to publish the RSL's financial statements and the auditors' report on the RSL's website or distribute them to shareholders by means such as e-mail. Your responsibilities concerning the preparation, dissemination and signing of the financial statements do not change simply because the financial statements are reproduced or distributed electronically; it is your responsibility to ensure that any such publication properly presents the financial information and any auditors' report. We request that you advise us of any intended electronic publication before it occurs.

10.2 As auditors, we will review the process by which the financial statements to be published electronically are derived from the financial information contained in the manually signed accounts, check that the proposed electronic version is identical in content with the manually signed accounts and check that the conversion of the manually signed accounts into an electronic format has not distorted the overall presentation of the financial information, for example by highlighting certain information so as to give it greater prominence.

10.3 In accordance with the guidance in Auditing Practices Board Bulletin 2001/1 'The Electronic Publication of Audit Reports' we reserve the right to withhold consent to the electronic publication of our report if the audited financial statements or the auditors' report are to be published in an inappropriate manner or to request amendments to the electronic auditors' report if we are not satisfied with the proposed wording or its presentation in the context of the financial statements.

On recurring audits, the auditor should consider whether circumstances require the terms of the engagement to be revised and whether there is a need to remind the client of the existing terms of the engagement.

When asked to provide special reports on grants where the grant making body requires the report to be addressed to it as well as the grant recipient, auditors should refer to Technical Release 03/03, *'Public Sector Special Reporting Engagements – Grant Claims'* published by the Audit and Assurance Faculty of the ICAEW. This includes examples of tri-partite engagement letters and covers typical examples of when either high level or moderate assurance is sought or whether the approach is one of agreed upon procedures.

47.4   ISA (UK AND IRELAND) 220: QUALITY CONTROL FOR AUDITS OF HISTORICAL FINANCIAL INFORMATION

The engagement partner should be satisfied that the engagement team collectively has the appropriate capabilities, competence and time to perform the audit engagement in accordance with professional standards and regulatory and legal requirements, and to enable an auditor's report that is appropriate in the circumstances to be issued.. The Practice Note states that this will include:

- the scope and nature of the activities of the RSL;
- the most significant parts of the relevant regulator's guidance; and
- the relevant general principles of the RSL SORP.

47.5   ISA (UK AND IRELAND) 240: THE AUDITOR'S RESPONSIBILITY TO CONSIDER FRAUD IN AN AUDIT OF FINANCIAL STATEMENTS

RSLs have been encouraged by their respective regulatory bodies to establish adequate internal controls, especially following the Housing Corporation's Circular R2-25/01. The Circular requires all RSLs to maintain a register of all incidents of actual or attempted fraud and to advise the Corporation of all frauds in excess of £5,000 (£1,000 for smaller RSLs) or equivalent in value immediately on discovery, and any fraud or corrupt act perpetrated or attempted by a board member or senior official of the RSL.

As part of their risk assessment, auditors should review this register and enquire whether the register has been commented upon by the regulatory body during a monitoring visit.

Various external issues could influence an RSL's objectives and strategies. The Practice Note refers to the increase in consolidation within the sector, the increased focus on efficiency and cost control, and the desire to become or remain a Housing Corporation development partner. The strategies being adopted by RSLs to manage these issues may result in an incentive for material misstatement of the financial statements. RSLs often also have significant borrowings with covenants attached (generally interest cover and gearing covenants).This may create pressures on the entity that, in turn, may motivate management to take action to improve the reported business performance or to misstate the financial statements.

The Practice Note comments that where auditors suspect that there may be any matters which they believe should be included in the register they should document their findings and, subject to any requirement to report them directly to a third party, raise them with senior management or a board member as soon as possible. They should also consider reporting the matter to the board and audit committee once they are aware of all the circumstances. When considering the appropriate person to discuss these matters with auditors should bear in mind the management structure of the RSL.

There is no requirement for auditors to report suspected instances of fraud to a regulatory body unless they consider it a matter of public interest or, in the case of an unincorporated, non-exempt charity they believe it would be a matter of material significance in the exercise of the Charity Commission's functions. Section **47.2.7** above on the auditor's relationship with the Regulators sets out the implications of reporting matters to the Regulator.

47.6   ISA (UK AND IRELAND) 250: CONSIDERATION OF LAWS AND REGULATIONS IN AN AUDIT OF FINANCIAL STATEMENTS

While Section A of ISA (UK and Ireland) 250 set out how auditors should plan to obtain sufficient evidence of compliance with relevant law and regulations, the Practice Note only lists those regulations with which auditors should be concerned. It does not provide any guidance on how auditors should set about obtaining evidence of compliance.

The law relating to a specific RSL depends on:

- whether the RSL is constituted as a registered charity, a society registered under the Industrial and Provident Societies Act 1965 or as a non-profit making company; and
- which regulatory body has granted registration to the RSL.

Although, as noted above, the regulations imply that the financial statements of an RSL should be prepared in accordance with the RSL SORP, consideration must also be given to any specific requirements of its governing document.

The auditor should perform further audit procedures to help identify instances of non-compliance with those laws and regulations where non-compliance should be considered when preparing financial statements, specifically:

(a) Inquiring of management as to whether the entity is in compliance with such laws and regulations;

(b) Inspecting correspondence with the relevant licensing or regulatory authorities, e.g. the Housing Corporation; and.

(c) Enquiring of those charged with governance as to whether they are on notice of any such possible instances of non-compliance with law or regulations.

In the UK and Ireland, the auditor's procedures should be designed to help identify possible or actual instances of non-compliance with those laws and regulations which provide a legal framework within which the RSL conducts its business and which are central to its ability to conduct its business and hence to its financial statements.

Laws and regulations which are noted by the Practice Note as likely to be central to a RSL are those where a breach would have any of the following consequences:

- intervention by the regulatory body to direct the affairs of the RSL – for example, non-compliance with the various laws relating to fraud and corruption under which the regulatory body possesses various powers of intervention;
- loss of necessary licences to continue a major element of the RSL's work – primarily laws and regulations applicable to building and planning regulations or contaminated land, or health and safety regulations in relation to homes in multiple occupation; or
- financial effects resulting in liabilities which are likely to exceed the available resources of the RSL – for example, expenditure or activities outside grant conditions imposed by the regulatory body which may lead to disallowance and repayment of grant.

Auditors of RSLs other than unincorporated charities have no statutory duty to report suspected or actual instances of non-compliance with the law or regulations to an appropriate authority, unless they believe it should be reported in the public interest.

In accordance with Practice Note 11, the auditors of unincorporated charities have a statutory duty to report actual or suspected significant instances of non-compliance to the Charities Commission (see **Chapter 43**).

Given the significant cash flows involved in the purchase and development of land, all RSLs should be aware of the risk of money laundering occurring. Regard should be given to the Money Laundering Regulations and Practice Note 12 (revised), see **Chapter 12**.

Instances of non-compliance identified by auditors should be reported to the appropriate level of management. However, if management are involved in the breach, auditors may consider it appropriate to communicate with the Board.

47.7 ISA (UK AND IRELAND) 260: COMMUNICATION OF AUDIT MATTERS WITH THOSE CHARGED WITH GOVERNANCE

As responsibilities in RSLs are delegated by the Board to the management team, auditors need to consider to whom it would be most appropriate to address their reports. Whilst the management team may play a central role in the management of the RSL, their powers come from the Board, and therefore it is to the Board that auditors will normally address their management letters.

ISA (UK and Ireland) 260 sets out examples of areas to consider when communicating to those charged with governance:

- expected modifications to the auditors' report;
- unadjusted misstatements;
- material weaknesses in the accounting and internal control systems;
- views about the qualitative aspects of the RSL's accounting practices and financial reporting;
- matters specifically required by other ISAs (UK and Ireland) to be communicated to those charged with governance, such as fraud and error; and
- any other relevant matters relating to the audit.

All four UK regulators require RSLs to send them copies of auditors' management letters, together with the RSL's response. It is recognised that the management letter addresses only those matters which have come to the attention of the auditors in the course of their audit. This should be filed within six months of the year end.

47.8 ISA (UK AND IRELAND) 300: PLANNING AN AUDIT OF FINANCIAL STATEMENTS

The Practice Note comments that the auditors should obtain an understanding of the accounting principles and their impact on the audit, and that auditors should make use of internal controls, internal audit and reporting arrangements in place at the RSL. At the planning stage auditors should be aware of any additional reporting requirements that they may have and plan their work accordingly.

At the planning stage, auditors should identify any additional procedures or evidence which may be necessary for work on other reports, for example, on service charges.

The auditor should develop an audit plan for the audit in order to reduce audit risk to an acceptably low level and should also document the overall audit strategy and the audit plan, including any significant changes made during the audit engagement.

47.9   ISA (UK AND IRELAND) 315: UNDERSTANDING THE ENTITY AND ITS ENVIRONMENT AND ASSESSING THE RISKS OF MATERIAL MISSTATEMENT

This section of the revised Practice Note which interprets ISA (UK and Ireland) 315 in relation to RSLs, has been subject to major revision and now covers how the auditor should obtain an understanding of relevant industry, regulatory, and other external factors including the applicable financial reporting framework for RSLs including:

- the Constitution of RSLs, regulation and financial reporting requirements;
- obtaining an understanding of the nature of the entity including the overall structure, activities, finances and governance of the RSL;
- complex projects such as schemes developed under the Private Finance Initiative (PFI) and the accounting for such schemes in accordance with Application Note F of FRS 5;
- the development of both social housing and housing for outright sale, sometimes as part of the same overall scheme. Under such arrangements, surpluses generated on the sale of properties may be used to subsidise other social housing which may be developed without recourse to social housing grant or with lower levels of grant than would normally be the case;
- understanding an RSL's selection and application of accounting policies and considering whether they are appropriate for its business and consistent with the applicable financial reporting framework and accounting policies used in the relevant industry, especially in relation to depreciation, capitalisation of works to existing properties and impairment;
- understanding an RSL's objectives and strategies, and the related

business risks that may result in material misstatement of the financial statements;

- measurement and review of an RSL's financial performance given the considerable external benchmarking and performance review including, for example, participation in benchmarking clubs, other comparative information published by the Housing Corporation and various league tables in the housing press;
- understanding of internal control relevant to the audit including the statutory requirement to report if the RSL has not maintained a satisfactory system of control; the expectation (in Wales, the requirement) that the management letter will be passed on to the regulatory body; and any additional procedures that have been agreed with the client;
- requirements of auditors in relation to control systems including reference to Housing Corporation Circular 25/01 'Internal controls assurance';
- the control environment including considering and understanding the entity's process for identifying business risks relevant to financial reporting objectives and deciding about actions to address those risks, and the results thereof;
- control activities where the Practice Note provides many examples of those control activities which are of particular significance to RSLs. The list is not intended to be exhaustive as there may be other control procedures that are relevant to the activities of a particular RSL; and
- assessing the risks of material misstatement where again the Practice Note provides many helpful examples relevant to RSLs.

47.10   ISA (UK AND IRELAND) 320: AUDIT MATERIALITY

The Practice Note states that consideration of materiality for RSLs does not differ fundamentally from that for other entities. However, auditors should be aware that particular disclosures or expenditure categories may be sensitive and warrant extra attention, and the guidance suggests the Chief Executive's remuneration, restricted funds and bad debt provisions as examples.

47.11   ISA (UK AND IRELAND) 330: THE AUDITOR'S PROCEDURES IN RESPONSE TO ASSESSED RISKS

When the auditor has determined that it is not possible to reduce the risks of material misstatement at the assertion level to an acceptably low level with audit evidence obtained only from substantive procedures, the auditor should perform tests of relevant controls to obtain audit evidence about their operating effectiveness. Many RSL activities involve a large number of small transactions, e.g. rental income. Auditors seek evidence to determine the completeness and accuracy of rental income. Where auditors are satisfied, through evaluation and testing, that there are appropriate and effective controls, including, for example, the effective reconciliation of housing management and finance systems, they can use the results of this internal control testing as a source of audit evidence about the completeness and accuracy of recorded transactions.

When the auditor has determined that an assessed risk of material misstatement at the assertion level is a significant risk, the auditor should perform substantive procedures that are specifically responsive to that risk. Possible significant risks in the context of RSLs are listed in the Practice Note covering ISA (UK and Ireland) 315. In respect of a significant risk arising from capitalisation, the auditor considers whether the RSL's policy, for example on the types of works to be capitalised, as well as the approach to the capitalisation of internal development costs and interest, is in compliance with FRS 15 and the detailed interpretation set out in the RSL SORP. The auditor will then carry out detailed checks to ensure compliance with the policy.

Auditors of RSLs also need to consider the risks surrounding significant and complex transactions and other factors such as:

- property development work including:
  - incorrect allocation of costs to schemes,
  - cost overruns due to poor budgeting or unauthorised expenditure leading to costs in excess of the original project appraisal,
  - fraud risks arising from purchasing frauds, such as payment for services not supplied, or
  - collusion;
- lack of experience of RSL staff in carrying out such non-core activities;
- the complexity of the transactions, e.g. legal structures, tax, accounting and funding arrangements;
- involvement of, and reliance on, third parties;
- viability arising from cost overruns; and
- issues relating to the vires of the RSL.

47.12   ISA (UK AND IRELAND) 402: AUDIT CONSIDERATIONS RELATING TO ENTITIES USING SERVICE ORGANISATIONS

Where an RSL makes use of a service organisation it does not alter the ultimate responsibility of the board or the audit committee to meet their legal responsibilities, neither does it diminish auditors' responsibilities when reporting on financial statements.

Examples of activities undertaken by a service organisation may include:

- maintenance of the RSL accounting records;
- processing of the payroll;
- other financial functions which involve establishing the carrying value of items in financial statements;
- management of assets, including outsourcing of repairs, maintenance and development work;
- management of agency schemes;
- internal audit; and
- undertaking or making arrangements for transactions as agents of the user entity, e.g., property management contracts.

47.13   ISA (UK AND IRELAND) 500: AUDIT EVIDENCE

In order for the auditor to obtain reliable audit evidence, the information upon which the audit procedures are based needs to be sufficiently complete and accurate. For example, in auditing rental income and bad debt provisions, the auditor considers the accuracy of the ageing of rental debtors derived from the housing management system. Obtaining audit evidence about the completeness and accuracy of the information produced by the housing management system may be performed concurrently with the actual audit procedure applied to the information when obtaining such audit evidence is an integral part of the audit procedure itself.

In other situations, the auditor may have obtained audit evidence of the accuracy and completeness of such information by testing controls over the production and maintenance of the information. However, in some situations the auditor may determine that additional audit procedures are needed. For example, these additional procedures may include using computer-assisted audit techniques (CAATs) to recalculate the information.

Given the large number of housing properties owned and managed by RSLs, physical inspection is unlikely to be an appropriate means of testing existence. The auditor views or obtains confirmation of documents of title from solicitors or the Land Registry. Such tests do not establish that the valuation of properties is appropriate.

47.14 ISA (UK AND IRELAND) 505: EXTERNAL CONFIRMATIONS

Situations in which external confirmations may be used by RSL auditors may include:

- Bank balances and other information from bankers;
- Loan balances and terms and conditions;
- Balances with local authorities, agencies and other partners;
- Property title deeds held by lawyers.

Confirmations are unlikely to be appropriate as a means of checking balances with tenants and leaseholders given the volume and size of individual balances.

47.15 ISA (UK AND IRELAND) 520: ANALYTICAL PROCEDURES

The income and expenditure of RSLs, and in particular the levels of capital and maintenance expenditure, interest payable and rental income, are predictable. This facilitates comparisons with budgets, with other organisations in the sector and proof in total tests.

In addition, as RSLs are required to submit a number of returns to their Regulator, many publish a comprehensive range of information and data, which may assist auditors by indicating trends and current ratios.

Examples of items to consider and features of data are detailed in **Table 2**.

TABLE 2: Analytical procedures

Capital and repairs and maintenance expenditure

- movements and unexpected or unusual relationships between current and prior year capital programme, allocations, budgeted amounts and cash planning targets for acquisitions and disposals
- comparison of the level of development department activity and professional fees with recorded additions to housing properties
- major repairs grants and repairs costs in comparison to budget and previous years' costs
- the ratio of repairs and maintenance to the cost of housing, land and buildings
- comparison against prior year and expected amounts for construction costs per property
- comparison of actual expenditure against costs in stock condition surveys
- for special need housing, comparison of the ratio of care staff to the number of bed spaces

---

- review of amount of grant as a percentage of development cost
- movements on any suspense or construction in progress accounts
- comparison of interest and overheads capitalised with prior years
- comparison with external benchmark indicators.

Rental income

- the relationship between the number of housing units available for occupation, the incidence of empty units and rents receivable
- movements, and any unexpected or unusual relationships, between current and prior year budgets for rent received or service charges
- movements, and unexpected or unusual relationships, between current year, prior year and budget for voids and bad debts as a percentage of rents
- rents and service charges for each month.

Other income and administrative expenses

- amounts are usually related to comparable information for prior periods
- amounts are usually directly comparable to other RSLs of similar size and nature
- some amounts are closely related to non-financial information such as the number of units, the number of employees and the size of office buildings.

47.16   ISA (UK AND IRELAND) 540: AUDIT OF ACCOUNTING ESTIMATES

The main areas where estimates are likely to be involved in the audit of RSLs are:

- depreciation of housing properties, and especially the estimated useful economic life;
- the level of bad and doubtful debt provisions against tenant arrears; and
- impairment provisions, including situations where existing use valuations are below net cost but the RSL assesses the net realisable value of the property, after deducting any grants that would need to be repaid or recycled, to be higher than net cost. Further judgments may be required in order to determine whether an alternative measure of service potential may be more appropriate where assets are held for social purposes.

47.17   ISA (UK AND IRELAND) 545: AUDITING FAIR VALUE MEASUREMENTS AND DISCLOSURES

Fair value measurements and disclosures are most likely to apply to those RSLs who hold fixed assets at valuation.

Under acquisition accounting, the identifiable assets and liabilities of the RSL acquired should be included in the acquirer's balance sheet at their fair value at the date of acquisition. The auditor ensures that the valuation method and amount adopted is appropriately supported and properly reflected in the financial statements.

In principle the fair value of housing properties is the Existing Use Value Social Housing (EUV-SH) of these properties. The fair value of other assets and liabilities can be assessed in accordance with the requirements of FRS 7. The auditor considers whether the information provided is consistent with the financial records subject to audit. Fixed rate loans should be revalued in the light of interest rates at the time of acquisition.

47.18   ISA (UK AND IRELAND) 550: RELATED PARTIES

The principles and procedures set out in ISA (UK and Ireland) 550 apply to the audit of RSLs as for other entities. In addition, those RSLs that are companies need to comply with relevant sections of the Companies Acts.

Subject to certain exemptions, members of the board and those associated with them, and those associated with senior managers, are not allowed to benefit financially from their connection with the RSL. If there is any evidence of the existence of such related party transactions, then both ISA (UK and Ireland) 550 and ISA (UK and Ireland) 250 *Consideration of law and regulations* applies.

In England, auditors may take account of the results of any examination of related party transactions undertaken by the Housing Corporation's review teams. However, such examinations do not remove the requirement for auditors to obtain sufficient and appropriate audit evidence that material, identified related party transactions are properly recorded and disclosed.

The auditor considers in particular whether appropriate disclosure, as required by Financial Reporting Standard (FRS) 8 – Related Party Disclosures, is made in the financial statements of transactions between the RSL and board members. The provisions of FRS 8 in the context of related parties and RSL management, are applied to all members of 'key management' not just members of the board. Key management may be taken to include those persons having authority and responsibility for planning, directing and controlling the activities of the RSL, directly or indirectly, including any director (whether executive or otherwise) or officer of that RSL.

47.19   ISA (UK AND IRELAND) 560: SUBSEQUENT EVENTS

Requirements for auditors to consider subsequent events do not differ for RSLs compared to other entities. Auditors should be aware, however, that in most RSLs the non-executive board plays a crucial role in approving the financial statements. This may be a significant time after the formal audit clearance meeting has taken place.

47.20   ISA (UK AND IRELAND) 570: GOING CONCERN

RSLs should normally prepare accounts on a going concern basis, and where they are not the Accounting Requirements for Registered Social Landlords General Determination 2000 requires disclosure of that fact.

The Practice Note recommends that auditors consider the circumstances in which RSLs may cease to continue in operational existence. This takes the same form as for other entities. The board has primary responsibility to make an assessment as to whether the going concern concept is applicable.

As RSLs have a relatively long business cycle the board may need to consider a longer period than normal. This is likely to involve an assessment of the extent to which there may be adverse variations or uncertainties, and because of this it may be appropriate for auditors to obtain representations from the board on these. Where there are uncertainties, confirmation of particular sources of funds or revenues of the RSL may need to be obtained by auditors in the same way as confirmation of facilities may be required for a company.

Factors which may indicate a potential going concern problem are listed in **Table 3** below.

TABLE 3:   Factors indicating potential going concern problems

- transfers of the entire housing stock, or a significant proportion of it;
- potential action from the regulatory body;
- for a transferee RSL, transfers of housing stock where the acquisition cost or carrying value is not covered by the long-term projected net rental income;
- onerous contract terms;
- inability to service interest payments;
- a significant amount of variable interest rate borrowings at a time when interest rates are rising or are predicted to rise;
- a significant short-term repair liability that the RSL will have difficulty in meeting from its own resources;

- failure to take account of the withdrawal of tax relief grant;
- loan repayments or refinancing which cannot be met from the RSL's own resources;
- breach of loan covenants; and
- significant loans to subsidiaries involved in activities such as shared ownership or developments for sale.

In assessing going concern, the board considers the extent to which there may be adverse variations from anticipated funding or revenue, or additional unexpected costs, and any uncertainties as to whether or not the RSL can continue in operational existence for the foreseeable future. Typically, RSLs acquire properties with the assistance of grants or long term borrowings. This method of financing leads to predictable cash flows in that loan repayments can be predicted and, accordingly, the RSL should be able to plan to meet its obligations from available resources. RSLs have a relatively long business cycle and, in preparing its medium term financial forecasts, the board may consider a longer period of time than for other entities.

If there are any indications that a particular source of funds or revenue may need to be renewed or renegotiated, the auditor may elect to request the RSL to contact the source of such funds for confirmation that the facility, or grant, will continue to be made available to the RSL. Where there continues to be uncertainty, it may be necessary for the board to disclose the circumstances in the financial statements and for the auditor to draw attention to the matter within their report.

47.21   ISA (UK AND IRELAND) 580: MANAGEMENT REPRESENTATIONS

The Practice Note guidance on the need for written confirmation of management representations does not vary greatly from that in the ISA (UK and Ireland). It does recommend, however, that auditors may include in their representation letters confirmation that all minutes and correspondence with the regulatory body have been made available to them.

47.22   ISA (UK AND IRELAND) 610: CONSIDERING THE WORK OF INTERNAL AUDIT

Auditors should make use of any internal audit function in place at the RSL. Larger RSLs are required to determine what is an appropriate internal audit function. For example, the Housing Corporation's Circular R2-25/01, 'Internal Controls Assurance', for English RSLs with more than 250 units, suggests that it would be difficult to meet the requirements on internal controls assurance without an internal audit function, although it is up to each RSL to decide what is appropriate given its size and activities.

The Practice Note comments that although liaison with internal audit may reduce the extent of the external auditors' procedures, this is a matter for their professional judgement, which should take account of the particular circumstances of the RSL and the auditors' assessment of the internal audit function.

Auditors should also be aware of the ICAEW's Audit and Assurance Faculty guidance *'The Power of Three, Understanding the roles and relationships of internal and external auditors and audit committees'* which was published in May 2003.

47.23   ISA (UK AND IRELAND) 620: USING THE WORK OF AN EXPERT

ISA (UK and Ireland) 620, alongside ISA (UK and Ireland) 545, *Auditing Fair Value Measurements and Disclosures* are likely to be relevant where properties are shown at a valuation. The SORP requires that valuations should be on the 'existing use value social housing' basis, and any departure from this basis should be disclosed in the accounts. Normal auditing considerations apply and these are dealt with in **Chapter 28**.

The other area where auditors may rely on the work of an expert is where information is supplied by an actuary about the surpluses or deficits on defined benefit pension schemes.

47.24   ISA (UK AND IRELAND) 700: THE INDEPENDENT AUDITOR'S REPORT ON A COMPLETE SET OF GENERAL PURPOSE FINANCIAL STATEMENTS

The Practice Note contains guidance on the reports made by auditors of RSLs and provides example reports and responsibility statements. An unqualified report and responsibility statement are shown in **Tables 4** and **5** respectively.

TABLE 4:   Unqualified auditors' report for an RSL

Report of the Independent auditors to the members of [registered social landlord]
We have audited the financial statements of [registered social landlord] for the year ended [date] on pages ... to ... which comprise (state the primary financial statements such as the Income and Expenditure Account, the Balance Sheet) and the related notes. These financial statements have been prepared under the historical cost convention and the accounting policies set out therein.

This report is made solely to the [association/company/agency/society]'s members, as a body, in accordance with the Friendly and Industrial and Provident Societies Act 1968 [applies only to RSLs that are industrial and provident societies] and Schedule 1 paragraph 16 to the Housing Act 1996. Our audit work has been undertaken so that we might state to the [association/company/agency/society]'s members those matters we are required to state to them in an auditors' report and for no other purpose. To the fullest extent permitted by law, we do not accept or assume responsibility to anyone other than the [association/company/agency]and the [association/company/agency/society]'s members as a body, for our audit work, for this report, or for the opinions we have formed.[1]

Respective responsibilities of the board and auditors
As described in the statement of responsibilities on page ..., the board is responsible for the preparation of the financial statements in accordance with applicable law and United Kingdom Accounting Standards (United Kingdom Generally Accepted Accounting Practice).

Our responsibility is to audit the financial statements in accordance with relevant legal and regulatory requirements and International Standards on Auditing (UK and Ireland).

We report to you our opinion as to whether the financial statements give a true and fair view and are properly prepared in accordance with the Industrial and Provident Societies Acts 1965 to 2002 [applies only to RSLs that are industrial and provident societies] the Housing Act 1996 and the Accounting Requirements for Registered Social Landlords General Determination 2006. We also report to you if, in our opinion, a satisfactory system of internal control over transactions has not been maintained, if the RSL has not kept proper accounting records, or if we have not received all the information and explanations we require for our audit.

We read other information contained in the Report of the Board and consider whether it is consistent with the audited financial statements. This other information comprises only ... *[examples could include the Operating and Financial Review, Chairman's Statement]*. We consider the implications for our report if we become aware of any apparent misstatements or material inconsistencies with the financial statements. Our responsibilities do not extend to any other information.

Basis of audit opinion
We conducted our audit in accordance with International Standards on Auditing (UK and Ireland) issued by the Auditing Practices Board. An audit includes examination, on a test basis, of evidence relevant to the amounts and disclosures in the financial statements. It also includes an assessment of the significant estimates and judgements made by the board in the preparation of the financial statements, and of whether the accounting policies are appropriate to [RSL]'s circumstances, consistently applied and adequately disclosed.

We planned and performed our audit so as to obtain all the information and explanations which we considered necessary in order to provide us with sufficient evidence to give reasonable assurance that the financial statements are free from material misstatement, whether caused by fraud or other irregularity or error. In forming our opinion we also evaluated the overall adequacy of the presentation of information in the financial statements.

Opinion
In our opinion:

- the financial statements give a true and fair view, in accordance with United Kingdom Generally Accepted Accounting Practice, of the state of [RSL]'s affairs as at [date] and of its surplus/deficit for the year then ended;
- the financial statements have been properly prepared in accordance with the Industrial and Provident Societies Acts 1965 to 2002 [applies only to RSLs that are industrial and provident societies] Schedule 1 to the Housing Act 1996 and The Accounting Requirements for Registered Social Landlords General Determination 2006; and
- the information given in the Report of the Board is consistent with the financial statements.

Registered Auditors
Address
Date

[1] The guidance in Practice Note 14 (Revised) does not include a Bannerman statement, as the working group felt that its inclusion is a matter for consideration for individual firms. However, in keeping with other reports throughout this publication, an example paragraph has been inserted, see **Chapter 3**.

TABLE 5: Example responsibility statement for RSL board

The Board is responsible for preparing financial statements in accordance with applicable law and United Kingdom Generally Accepted Accounting Practice for each financial year which give a true and fair view of the state of affairs of the Association and of the surplus or deficit for that period. In preparing those financial statements, the Board is required to:

- select suitable accounting policies and then apply them consistently;

- make judgements and estimates that are reasonable and prudent;
- state whether applicable accounting standards have been followed, subject to any material departures disclosed and explained in the financial statements; and
- prepare the financial statements on the going concern basis unless it is inappropriate to presume that the RSL will continue in business.

The board is responsible for keeping proper accounting records which disclose with reasonable accuracy at any time the financial position of the RSL and to enable it to ensure that the financial statements comply with the Industrial and Provident Societies Acts 1965 to 2002, Schedule 1 to the Housing Act 1996 and the Accounting Requirements for Registered Social Landlords Determination 2006. It has general responsibility for taking reasonable steps to safeguard the assets of the RSL and to prevent and detect fraud and other irregularities.

ISA (UK and Ireland) 700 also requires auditors' reports to contain any further matters required by statute or other requirements applicable to the particular engagement. For RSLs, these matters may be set out in a number of areas, depending on the legal form and jurisdiction of the RSL:

- the Housing Act 1996, together with any Statutory Instrument or Accounting Determination or Order issued under the Act;
- the Industrial and Provident Societies Acts 1965 to 2002;
- the Companies Act 1985;
- the Charities Act 2006;
- the trust deed.

Of particular note is the requirement for RSLs to maintain adequate books and records and satisfactory systems of internal control which vary depending on the legislation under which they are formed. Auditors are required to report if this is not the case, and consideration should also be given to a qualification on the grounds of limitation of scope.

47.25   ISA (UK AND IRELAND) 720: OTHER INFORMATION IN DOCUMENTS CONTAINING AUDITED FINANCIAL STATEMENTS

Although there may be no statutory requirement for auditors to review other information in RSL annual reports, it is noted that 'one of the fundamental principles set out in the APB's *The Auditors' Code* is that auditors allow their reports to be included in documents containing other information only if they consider that the additional information is not in conflict with the matters covered by their report and they have no cause to believe it to be misleading'.

Examples of other information that may be included are:

- statements by the patron, president, chair or chief executive;
- an operating and financial review;
- a statement concerning arrangements for corporate governance;
- the board's statement on internal control in accordance with (in England) Housing Corporation Circular R2-25/01, 'Internal Controls Assurance';
- a treasurer's report;
- financial summaries; and
- projections of future expenditure based on planned activity
- Where an inconsistency is identified between other information and corresponding or related amounts or disclosures in audited financial statements and conclude that the other information should be amended, they discuss the matter with management or the board of the RSL with a view to appropriate amendments being made.

47.26 MISCELLANEOUS REPORTS

For many of the returns on which auditors are asked to report the guidance provided by ISA (UK and Ireland) 700 can be adapted to suit the specific circumstances.

There are many returns where auditors are asked to report which will vary from one RSL to another. Due to the variety, it is impracticable to list them in this guidance. Auditors should refer to guidance contained in ISA (UK and Ireland) 700 which can be adapted to such returns and also the ICAEW's Technical Release Audit 03/03 *Public Sector Special Reporting Engagements – Grant Claims*, see **Chapter 48**.

47.27 SERVICE CHARGE AUDITS

Under the Commonhold and Leasehold Reform Act 2002 various amendments were made to the Landlord and Tenant Act 1985, notably relating to the preparation of annual service charge statements, making these mandatory rather than upon request by a tenant. As at the date of issue of the Practice Note in March 2006, the provisions relating to annual service charge statements have yet to come into force.

The auditors' report is addressed to the landlord or managing agent. The Practice Note stresses that auditors must communicate clearly the basis and scope of the audit on which they are reporting. The Practice Note comments that leaseholders and tenants should understand that they are not receiving any assurance regarding whether they are being charged a reasonable amount for services or whether those services have been provided effectively.

The format of the report varies depending upon the contents of the service charge statement. The example in **Table 6** should be amended depending on whether the service charge statement is prepared in accordance with the Landlord and Tenant Act 1985, in accordance with the requirements of a lease, or voluntarily.

TABLE 6:   Example service charge auditors' report

Independent auditors' report on service charge

Report of the auditors to the landlord/managing agent of [property]
In accordance with our engagement letter dated [date], we have examined the service charge statement set out on pages ...to... in respect of [property] for the year ended [date] together with the books and records maintained by [landlord/managing agent] in so far as they relate to [property].

Under the terms of this engagement, we were not required to, and did not, form any opinion as to either the reasonableness of the costs included within the service charge statement or the standard of the services or works provided.

Respective responsibilities of the board and auditors
Under the Landlord and Tenant Act 1985/Under clause [ ] of the tenancy agreement (or lease) dated [date] between the landlord and [the tenant], the landlord is responsible for the preparation of this service charge statement in respect of the costs in respect of [property]. [The managing agent has undertaken responsibility for the preparation of the service charge statement on behalf of the landlord.].

It is our responsibility to form an independent opinion, based on our examination, on the service charge statement and to report our opinion exclusively to the landlord/managing agent.

This report is made solely to the landlord/managing agent of [property]. Our audit work has been undertaken so that we might state to the tenants/leaseholders those matters we are required to state to them in an auditors' report and for no other purpose. To the fullest extent permitted by law, we do not accept or assume responsibility to anyone other than tenants/leaseholders as a body, for our audit work, for this report, or for the opinions we have formed.[1]

Basis of audit opinion
Our work included examination, on a test basis, of evidence relent to the amounts included in the statement and their disclosure. [It also included an assessment of the significant estimates and judgements made by the landlord/managing agent in the preparation of the service charge statement.]

We planned and performed our examination so as to obtain all the information and explanations which we considered necessary in order to provide us with sufficient evidence to give reasonable assurance that the service charge statement is a fair summary of the costs relating to [property] and is sufficiently

---

supported by accounts, receipts and other documents which have been made available to us. In view of the purpose for which this service charge statement has been prepared, however, we did not evaluate the overall adequacy of the presentation of the information which would have been required if we were to express an audit opinion under Auditing Standards issued by the Auditing Practices Board.

Opinion

In our opinion the service charge statement presents a fair summary of the income and expenditure for the year ended [date], is sufficiently supported by accounts, receipts and other documents and has been prepared in accordance with [section 21 (5) of the Landlord and Tenants Act 1985 and] clause [ ] of the tenancy agreement (or lease) dated [ ] between the tenant (leaseholders) and XYZ Registered Social Landlord.

Registered Auditors
Address
Date

[1] The guidance in Practice Note 14 (Revised) does not include a Bannerman statement, as the working group felt that its inclusion is a matter for consideration for individual firm. However, in keeping with other reports throughout this publication, an example paragraph has been inserted, see **Chapter 3**.

48 PUBLIC SECTOR AUDITS

48.1 INTRODUCTION

In recent years the accountability of central government departments and other public bodies has become a topic of increasing public interest. There has been continuing debate concerning their audit arrangements with increasingly more audits being carried out by private sector auditors as opposed to the National Audit Office.

In January 2006, the APB issued a further revision to Practice Note 10, *Audit of Financial Statements of Public Sector Entities in the United Kingdom*. The revised Practice Note replaces the previous revision from April 2001, which in turn superseded the original Practice Note 10, *Audit of Central Government Financial Statements in the United Kingdom* issued in February 1996 and Practice Note 17, *The Audit of Regularity in the Central Government Sector,* issued in September 1998.

The January 2006 revision updated the guidance following the introduction of ISAs (UK and Ireland) and also included legal and regulatory developments since April 2001.

As well as providing guidance on the application of each ISA (UK and Ireland) to public sector audits, the Practice Note also considers the role of the public sector auditor.

At the same time as issuing this further revision to Practice Note 10, the APB issued Bulletin 2006/2, *Illustrative Auditor's Reports on Public Sector Financial Statements in the United Kingdom*, which revised the example audit reports provided in earlier versions of the Practice Note.

In 2002, the APB issued Practice Note 10(1), *Audit of central government financial statements in the Republic of Ireland*. The guidance takes account of the current legislative requirements governing the financial statement audit of Irish central government bodies and is designed to promote a common approach to the application of Auditing Standards. The guidance is also consistent with the equivalent guidance for public sector auditors in the UK, set out in Practice Note 10.

In 2003, three further pieces of guidance were issued for auditors of public sector entities:

- Bulletin 2003/1 *Corporate Governance: Requirements of Public Sector Auditors (Central Government)*;
- Bulletin 2003/2 *Corporate Governance: Requirements of Public Sector Auditors (National Health Service Bodies)*;
- Technical Release Audit 03/03 *Public Sector Special Reporting Engagements – Grant Claims.*

These were joined by Bulletin 2004/2, *Corporate Governance: Requirements of Public Sectors Auditors (Local Government Bodies)* in June 2004. These documents are detailed in **48.10** and **48.11**

48.2 THE ROLE OF THE PUBLIC SECTOR AUDITOR

Those responsible for public finance and for spending public money are accountable for ensuring that public business is conducted in accordance with proper standards and the law and that public money is safeguarded and properly accounted for. External auditors are an essential part of the process of accountability and make an important contribution to the stewardship of public money.

As part of this role, external auditors may be asked to give an independent opinion on the financial statements and may also review and report on aspects of the arrangements in place to ensure that resources are used economically, efficiently and effectively.

48.2.1 Auditor responsibilities

Public sector auditors are given authority to carry out their work by mandates which are embodied in legislation or set out in codes of audit practice. These mandates will vary according to the area of central government being audited and geographical location.

Broadly, these mandates establish responsibilities in relation to:

- the financial statements;
- compliance with legislative and other authorities (also known as 'regularity');
- economy, efficiency and effectiveness ('value for money' or 'use of resources').

48.2.2   Financial statements

The legislative framework governing each public sector body sets out different requirements in relation to the preparation of financial statements. The requirements include:

- format of financial statements;
- period within which financial statements must be prepared;
- who the financial statements are reviewed by.

48.2.3   Regularity

For central government bodies in England, external auditors have to report on whether transactions included in the financial statements conform with the legislation that authorises them. The Comptroller and Auditor General then satisfies himself that expenditure and income have been applied in accordance with Parliament's wishes and reports to Parliament accordingly. Similar requirements exist or are being developed in Scotland and Northern Ireland respectively.

A similar requirement also exists in England and Wales in relation to health authorities and other specified National Health Service entities which are to be consolidated respectively into the financial statements of the Department of Health and National Assembly for Wales. In Northern Ireland this requirement exists for health and social service boards.

In other health entities and in local government there is no requirement for external auditors to report on regularity, but they should be alert to questions of legality and review the procedures in place to ensure the legality of transactions that might have a significant financial consequence. Any transactions or events of questionable legality coming to light as a result of this review should be reported to the appropriate authorities.

Auditors' responsibilities in relation to regularity are discharged at the same time as the audit of the financial statements and are covered in a separate part of the audit report.

Guidance on regularity for auditors is set out in a separate section of the Practice Note. In particular, the section considers:

- understanding the regulatory framework;
- testing for regularity, including auditing compliance with European Union authorities; and
- regularity and reporting.

48.2.4 Other assignments

External auditors may also be asked to review and report on other information prepared by public bodies on aspects of their corporate governance and on their arrangements to secure economy, efficiency and effectiveness in their use of resources. This information may include:

- *performance information* – for central government, where external auditors are invited to report on such information by the Minister responsible;
- *grant claims* – external auditors act as agents of the Audit Commission when reporting on the extent to which a grant claim has been prepared in accordance with the requirements of the government entity and that the figures presented have been properly and fairly presented;
- *corporate governance* – some public sector bodies are required to include corporate governance statements in their financial statements;
- *best value* – auditors of local government in England and Wales are required to report on whether the public bodies' Best Value Performance Plans are prepared and published in accordance with legislation and statutory guidance;
- *economy, efficiency and effectiveness* – auditors' responsibilities vary between different parts of the public sector, and so auditors should review relevant legislation for details; and
- *standards of financial conduct* – public sector auditors are required to review and report on issues relating to standards of financial conduct in public bodies and aspects of the arrangements set in place by the audited body to ensure the proper conduct of its financial affairs.

48.3 STANDARDS GOVERNING PUBLIC SECTOR AUDITS

The standards covering the conduct and reporting of the audit of financial statements in the public sector are determined by the national audit agencies. However, the objectives of the audits are no different to those in other sectors and so public sector auditors apply the basis principles set out in Auditing Standards.

The Practice Note gives auditors guidance on the application of each ISA (UK and Ireland) to the audit of public sector financial statements.

The major differences to the audit of Companies Act financial statements are set out below.

48.4 INTERNATIONAL STANDARD ON QUALITY CONTROL (UK AND IRELAND) 1

International Standard on Quality Control (UK and Ireland) 1 (ISQC 1) is relevant in its entirety to the audit of financial statements of public sector entities. Practice Note 10 (Revised) provides additional guidance in relation to withdrawing from an engagement and threats to auditor independence.

In the public sector, under statute auditors may not be able to withdraw from an engagement, and even if withdrawal is permissible, there may be other alternatives. In most cases there is a duty to publicly report matters that would have otherwise caused withdrawal from the engagement.

If a national audit agency is appointed by statute there is no option to withdraw from an engagement where threats to independence have been identified and other steps should be taken to reduce these threats. Where an audit firm has been appointed as an agent of a national audit agency, that agency will assess the firm's independence when it is appointed. The firm must comply with the requirements of ISQC 1 on independence when carrying out their work.

48.5 ISA (UK AND IRELAND) 200 OBJECTIVE AND GENERAL PRINCIPLES GOVERNING AN AUDIT OF FINANCIAL STATEMENTS

The general principles of auditing are the same in both private and public entities, but auditors of public entities often have wider duties and further responsibilities laid down in legislation, directives and codes of practice.

For public sector auditors:

- for central government, specified health entities and probation boards there is a requirement to obtain evidence on compliance with authorities; and
- in recognition of the importance of regularity to the audit of these entities, the auditors' report includes an explicit opinion on the regularity of transactions.

48.6 ISA (UK AND IRELAND) 210 TERMS OF AUDIT ENGAGEMENTS

For many central government assignments the terms of engagement are set out in legislation and no engagement letter is necessary although auditors may choose to set out their understanding in such a letter, sometimes called a letter of understanding.

Where the legislation does not prescribe the terms, these are covered in a detailed letter of appointment from the relevant national audit agency, rather than in a letter from the auditors. If the auditors choose to send a letter this will not replace the agency's letter. The agency's letter normally covers all the terms contained in a standard audit engagement letter. These terms and the nature of the engagement cannot be changed by auditors.

48.7   ISA (UK AND IRELAND) 220 QUALITY CONTROL FOR AUDITS OF HISTORICAL FINANCIAL INFORMATION

ISA (UK and Ireland) 220 requires an engagement quality control review of the audit of listed clients. In the public sector, audit teams should consider whether such a review is necessary for each client. Reviews are likely to be appropriate for larger, more complex entities or those with a high profile.

48.8   ISA (UK AND IRELAND) 230 DOCUMENTATION

In addition to the requirements of ISA (UK and Ireland) 230 (see **Chapter 19**), auditors of public sector entities may have additional responsibilities with regard to confidentiality or the retention of working papers. These may be imposed by Statute, such as the Official Secrets Act 1989 and auditors should be aware of these.

48.9   ISA (UK AND IRELAND) 240 THE AUDITOR'S RESPONSIBILITY TO CONSIDER FRAUD IN AN AUDIT OF FINANCIAL STATEMENTS

The Practice Note provides additional guidance on:

- responsibilities of the entity and the auditors;
- fraud in the context of the regularity assertion;
- consideration of fraud risk factors;
- auditors' other responsibilities relating to fraud and corruption; and
- reporting to third parties.

48.9.1   *Responsibilities of the entity and auditors*

For central government entities the Accounting Officer is usually the permanent head or senior full-time official of the entity and directs its management. They are personally responsible for ensuring that:

- proper financial procedures are followed;
- assets and public funds are properly managed and safeguarded; and
- funds are applied to the extent and for the purposes authorised by Parliament.

The entity's management are generally responsible for developing and maintaining effective controls to prevent fraud and detecting it when it does occur.

In local government an officer is appointed to have responsibility for the arrangements for the proper administration of financial affairs. For health entities in England and Wales, the Accounting Officer and other directors are responsible for ensuring that:

- systems are in place to produce reliable financial information and proper accounting records;
- there are controls in place over the security of financial systems and data; and
- there is a fraud and corruption policy and response plan in place.

Responsibilities in Scotland and Northern Ireland are broadly similar to England and Wales.

Under ISA (UK and Ireland) 240, auditors should plan, perform and evaluate their work so as to have a reasonable expectation of identifying the risk of material misstatement arising from fraud and error. These requirements apply to audits of public sector entities as well as private entities, but they are extended in the public sector context to ensure a reasonable expectation of detecting material breaches of regularity arising from fraud or error.

48.9.2 Fraud in the context of the regularity assertion

Fraudulent transactions cannot, by definition, be regular and where material fraud is proven a qualification on the regularity assertion is necessary. Where the auditors suspect fraud the matter should be discussed with management to discover whether the transactions are in compliance with the authorities which govern them. If management do not accept the views of the auditors it may be necessary to communicate the matter to higher authorities and to qualify the audit report.

48.9.3 Consideration of fraud risk factors

When gaining an understanding of the public entity and its environment, including its internal controls, auditors should consider whether fraud risk factors are present. The risk of external fraud may be high if the entity is making grants to the public or collecting tax revenues.

Internally, fraudulent financial reporting may occur where bodies are required to meet externally set targets, such as where financial results affect performance ratings by an inspectorate.

48.9.4   *Auditors' other responsibilities*

Public sector auditors are required to have a wider regard to fraud and corruption than just the potential impact on the financial statements as addressed by ISA (UK and Ireland) 240. These additional responsibilities include consideration of the financial aspects of corporate governance arrangements for local government and health entities in England and Wales, and review of Treasury and other appropriate guidance on corporate governance for central government auditors.

If auditors become aware of fraud when addressing these additional responsibilities, they should also ensure that they consider the impact of these findings on the financial statements in accordance with ISA (UK and Ireland) 240.

ISA (UK and Ireland) 240 recommends that where auditors encounter circumstances arising from fraud or a suspected fraud which bring into question their ability to continue with the audit, they should consider resigning. For public sector clients, auditors cannot decline or withdraw from an engagement if they have been appointed by statute. There is usually a statutory requirement to make a public report about any matter which would have caused withdrawal, had such action been permissible.

The ISA (UK and Ireland) requires auditors to presume that a risk of material misstatement due to fraud will exist. For some public sector entities this will not apply, and as with other entities where this presumption can be rebutted, this conclusion must be clearly documented.

48.9.5   *Reporting to third parties*

When considering whether to report a suspected or actual fraud, auditors must have regard to:

- the relevant provisions that set out management's responsibilities for reporting fraud or other irregularity;
- the duties to report to a third party set out in the auditors' terms of engagement.

When management is implicated in the fraud, or refuses to report a fraud themselves, the auditors have a duty to report to third parties depending on the type of public sector entity involved. The different entities are set out in **Table 1**.

TABLE 1: Third parties to whom fraud may be reported	
Public sector type	*Fraud reportable to*
Central government departments in England and Wales	The Treasury
National Assembly for Wales and its sponsored public bodies	The Compliance Officer of the National Assembly for Wales
Central government departments in Scotland	The Auditor General for Scotland
Central government departments in Northern Ireland	The Department of Finance and Personnel
Non-departmental public bodies and executive agencies	The sponsor department
Local government entities	The relevant authority as set out in ISA (UK and Ireland) 240
Health entities	Counter Fraud and Security Management Service.

48.10 ISA (UK AND IRELAND) 250 CONSIDERATION OF LAWS AND REGULATIONS IN AN AUDIT OF FINANCIAL STATEMENTS

ISA (UK and Ireland) 250 is concerned with laws and regulations that, if not complied with, may materially affect the financial statements. These fall into two categories, those which set out the form or contents of the financial statements and those which set the provisions under which an entity is allowed to conduct its business. Auditors are required to obtain an general understanding of both categories of laws and regulations. Where auditors are required to report on compliance with certain provisions of laws or regulations, as with the regularity assertion for public entities, as well as being familiar with the law itself, they must test the entity's compliance with its provisions.

Auditors of local government and health entities have separate statutory responsibilities when matters come to their attention that indicate that unlawful expenditure has been or will be incurred or that a financial loss or deficiency will arise. This is irrespective of the potential for material impact on the financial statements. In addition, auditors must report on the elements of the local government or health entities' corporate governance arrangements that relate to the legality of transactions which might have a financial consequence.

48.11   ISA (UK AND IRELAND) 260 COMMUNICATION OF AUDIT MATTERS WITH THOSE CHARGED WITH GOVERNANCE

In addition to the requirements of ISA (UK and Ireland) 260 the Practice Note stresses the importance of reports to management as a means of reporting non-compliance with:

- regularity;
- propriety; and
- other official guidance to Accounting Officers.

Where matters relating to other duties and responsibilities are reported to management in the same letter as matters arising from the audit of the financial statements, auditors must be sure that the letter still meets the requirements of ISA (UK and Ireland) 260.

The Practice Note sets out the correct addressee of the management report for each type of public sector entity.

Public sector auditors sometimes have a responsibility to submit an annual audit letter to a third party from where it may be made public. Even where this is not the case, reports to management may come into the possession of third parties and auditors may wish to limit their liability should reliance be placed on their audit letter. This can be achieved by including a caveat in their report to management.

48.12   ISA (UK AND IRELAND) 300 PLANNING AN AUDIT OF FINANCIAL STATEMENTS

With regard to the overall audit planning the Practice Note covers the additional matters which should be considered, including:

- auditors' other responsibilities laid down in Statute or in the letter of appointment; and
- planning the audit of regularity.

48.13 ISA (UK AND IRELAND) 315 UNDERSTANDING THE ENTITY AND ITS ENVIRONMENT AND ASSESSING THE RISKS OF MATERIAL MISSTATEMENT AND ISA (UK AND IRELAND) 330 THE AUDITOR'S PROCEDURES IN RESPONSE TO ASSESSED RISKS

Auditors are required to obtain an understanding of the relevant financial reporting framework and regulatory factors and their impact on the audit. These include the financial reporting framework and other regulations set out in:

- the specific legislation that has established the audited entity and determines its activities;
- UK GAAP;
- accounts directions;
- Government Accounting and the Government Financial Reporting Manual;
- other HM Treasury guidance on the application of accounting standards, the Companies Act and the disclosure of information;
- manuals for accounts of NHS entities; and
- relevant SORPs.

An additional consideration for public sector auditors is the additional assertion of regularity. When assessing risk for reporting on the regularity assertion, auditors should consider the following specific factors:

- the complexity of the regulations;
- the introduction of major new legislation or changes in existing regulations;
- services and programmes administered under European Union authorities, where the framework of authorities may be complex;
- services and programmes delivered through third parties; and
- payments and receipts made on the basis of claims or declarations.

ISA (UK and Ireland) 315 requires auditors to obtain an understanding of an entity's business objectives and strategies and assess any resulting business risks. Public sector entities may have a number of additional business risks as a result of their closely regulated regimes, public reporting process and typically high number of transactions processed. The practice note highlights the following as possible significant risks in the public sector:

- financial transactions entered into by the entity in the period do not conform to the authorities that govern them;
- organisations issuing grants have been subject to fraudulent grant claims;

- the financial statements have been manipulated to meet externally set targets; and
- Private Finance Initiative transactions have not been accounted for in accordance with UK GAAP and guidance issued by HM Treasury.

48.14 ISA (UK AND IRELAND) 320 AUDIT MATERIALITY

When assessing the qualitative aspects of materiality auditors should consider the interest of the body to whom the audit report is addressed. Auditors should consider any higher body, into whose financial statements the results of the audited entity is being consolidated, to be the addressee of the audit report. Auditors should also be aware of any special considerations applying to the reporting of certain classes of misstatement when assessing the materiality of uncorrected misstatements.

Where public sector auditors have a responsibility to report on matters that do not affect the opinion on the financial statements, they may adopt an appropriate level of materiality for these items which differs from the materiality level applied to the audit of the financial statements.

The concept of materiality applies to the audit of regularity as to any other assertions in the financial statements. Where required to report on regularity, auditors need only to obtain sufficient evidence to give an opinion on whether expenditure and income has been applied for the intended purposes 'in all material respects'. As with other financial statements assertions, the assessment of materiality will include both qualitative and quantitative judgements.

48.15 ISA (UK AND IRELAND) 402 AUDIT CONSIDERATIONS RELATING TO ENTITIES USING SERVICE ORGANISATIONS

The requirement for public sector auditors to give an opinion on the regularity of transactions may require inspection of records maintained by service organisations beyond that in other audits. ISA (UK and Ireland) 402 does not automatically secure access rights to this information, and so it is important that the contract terms between the public sector entity and its service provider allow sufficient access by the entity's auditor. Guidance on model conditions of contract are available in the Office of Government Commerce's *Successful Delivery Toolkit*.

48.16   ISA (UK AND IRELAND) 500 AUDIT EVIDENCE

When testing the regularity assertion, auditors plan and perform procedures to confirm that the entity's expenditure and income comply with the specific authorities governing them. The principles and procedures applied are the same as those applied in the audit of any other financial statements assertion. However, there may be particular considerations in relation to the design of audit procedures as auditors may encounter difficulties obtaining reliable audit evidence in relation to some aspects of regularity, such as the eligibility for grants. For example, auditors may require access to the records of a third party who has received the grant, to ascertain whether conditions for its grant have been met.

48.17   ISA (UK AND IRELAND) 510 INITIAL ENGAGEMENTS – OPENING BALANCES AND CONTINUING ENGAGEMENTS – OPENING BALANCES

The Practice Note states that the guidance in ISA (UK and Ireland) 510 is relevant for public sector entities, and also sets out additional guidance which is reproduced in **Table 2**.

TABLE 2: Additional guidance on the audit of opening balances	
Nature of opening balances	*Additional guidance*
Opening balance amounts are identifiable from the preceding period's audited financial statements for another entity.	This will require that the balances are clearly identifiable. Additional procedures may also be necessary to confirm that there are no aspects of the change in status of the new entity that result in changes to the basis on which the balances were prepared.
Opening balance amounts are not identifiable from the preceding period's audited financial statements for another entity, but have been derived from balances contained in those statements.	Subject to the arrangements for co-operation, the auditor may discuss with the outgoing auditor whether information is available that would provide substantive evidence for the opening balances. Such evidence would be considered in the context of the requirements of ISA (UK and Ireland) 600.

In the absence of evidence available through such co-operation, the auditor considers carrying out substantive testing of opening balances.	Opening balances have been calculated as part of a separate disaggregation/merger exercise, subject to a separate specific review and report by an auditor. The auditor considers the scope of the specific review and report in the context of the requirements of ISA (UK and Ireland) 600 as if the auditor were the principal auditor. Where the work from the separate specific review cannot be used, the auditor considers carrying out substantive testing of opening balances.
Opening balances have been calculated as part of a separate disaggregation/merger exercise, but not subject to separate specific review and report.	The audit considers carrying out substantive testing of opening balances.

ISA (UK and Ireland) 510 states that outgoing auditors have no legal or ethical obligation to provide information to incoming auditors or allow access to their work papers. In the public sector predecessor auditors are expected by the national audit agencies to adopt a co-operative approach in the interests of efficiency and reducing the audit burden.

48.18   ISA (UK AND IRELAND) 520 ANALYTICAL PROCEDURES

In addition to the relationships set out in ISA (UK and Ireland) 520, public sector auditors also consider relationships in two classes:

- programme expenditure and income; and
- management costs.

Each class has certain features that will influence the type of analytical procedures performed.

Programme expenditure and income
Programme expenditure and income relate to the actual function of the entity, for example grant payments and health care treatments. These are:

- usually closely related to non-financial information such as the number of bodies in receipt of grant or persons receiving hospital treatment;

- not always directly comparable to prior periods because of changes to eligibility rules and Government policy; and
- often comparable to expenditure plans included in published departmental or entity strategy.

Management costs

Management costs relate to the running of the entity and can be distinguished from programme expenditure as they are:

- usually related to comparable information for the prior period and are less subject to change as a result of Government policy changes;
- closely related to information such as number of employees, size of buildings, etc; and
- directly comparable to other entities with similar establishment sizes.

48.19   ISA (UK AND IRELAND) 550 RELATED PARTIES

The Practice Note provides little specific guidance on the audit of related party transactions for public sector entities. It does note, however, that related parties of these entities are subject to specific restrictions on the nature and scope of the transactions that they enter with the entity. Guidance varies for each part of the public sector and auditors should be aware of these restrictions.

48.20   ISA (UK AND IRELAND) 560 SUBSEQUENT EVENTS

For central government entities, auditors must also consider matters arising from relevant parliamentary procedures as part of their subsequent events review. Auditors should consult relevant legislation to determine the dates the financial statements are deemed to be 'issued' and 'laid before members', as this varies for each central government entity.

For auditors of local government and health entities, the concept of subsequent events is limited. The statutory audit opinion is only issued when the audit is concluded and all responsibilities have been met. Thus the auditors' duties are concluded at the date of the issue of the statutory audit certificate and their powers for that audit are at an end. Where, as is common, auditors have given an opinion in advance of concluding the audit, the final statutory opinion will contain references back to earlier opinions and any additional work performed since those opinions were given.

48.21   ISA (UK AND IRELAND) 570 GOING CONCERN

The Practice Note gives guidance on the following areas:

- auditors' other responsibilities relating to going concern;
- entities that prepare their financial statements on the going concern basis;
- circumstances affecting going concern;
- consideration of the foreseeable future;
- auditors' responsibilities in considering going concern;
- written representations on going concern.

48.21.1   *Auditors' other responsibilities relating to going concern*

Auditors of local government and health entities in England and Wales must review and report on aspects of the entity's corporate governance arrangements as they relate to the ongoing financial standing of the entity. Similar requirements exist for local government in Scotland. In Northern Ireland, auditors are expected to assess the financial standing of the audited entity.

These requirements are outside the intended scope of ISA (UK and Ireland) 570, but auditors should ensure that when matters come to their attention through these additional responsibilities, they consider their impact on the financial statements in line with the requirements of the ISA (UK and Ireland).

48.21.2   *Entities that prepare their financial statements on the going concern basis*

The legislation determining the format of the financial statements will normally indicate whether the going concern basis should be adopted.

Where central government entities prepare financial statements on a cash basis the going concern basis does not apply. However, the auditors should still report to Parliament in the rare circumstance that there are matters which may affect the entity's ability to continue as a going concern. They do not, however, qualify their opinion on the proper presentation of the financial statements.

48.21.3   *Circumstances affecting going concern*

It is unlikely that a central government entity will cease to operate as a result of insolvency or inability to finance operations unless they operate in a trading capacity at arm's length from Government.

Cessation is most likely to result from a decision by Government and may involve transferring the operations to another entity. In such cases the individual circumstances should be considered when assessing whether the going concern basis is appropriate.

48.21.4   Consideration of the foreseeable future

Government policy is inherently subject to political uncertainty, but political decisions are no more uncertain than the risks faced by private entities. Therefore the provisions in ISA (UK and Ireland) 570 relating to 'foreseeable future' can be applied by auditors of public sector entities.

48.21.5   Auditors' responsibilities in considering going concern

Public sector auditors should consider two factors:

- the risk associated with changes in policy direction (for example, where there is a change in Government); and
- the operational, or business, risk (for example, the entity has insufficient working capital).

Auditors need to obtain evidence concerning the government's intentions in the particular area of policy that the entity operates in. This would include whether:

- they intend to review policy, for example a manifesto commitment;
- a review has been announced;
- an efficiency review has concluded that rationalisation is necessary; or
- there is a known intention to privatise its activities.

Trading operations may also be subject to risks arising from changes in policy direction as well as operational and business risks.

48.21.6   Written representations on going concern

The Practice Note suggests that the receipt of written representations from the Accounting Officer about going concern may not be sufficient audit evidence as the officer may not be capable of making judgements about future conditions for support.

If the going concern assumption is only substantiated by written confirmation of support from the sponsoring department, auditors should consider whether there is a need to refer to these confirmations in the financial statements.

Other evidence of the intention to continue the entity's activities could come from the most recent:

- Public Expenditure Survey;
- Supply Estimates; and
- financial management and policy review.

The Practice Note contains example audit procedures in relation to going concern.

48.22   ISA (UK AND IRELAND) 580 MANAGEMENT REPRESENTATIONS

Each type of public sector entity has a person or group of people with responsibility for the preparation and signing of the financial statements. Auditors should review relevant regulations to determine to whom this responsibility falls. The responsible person signs letters of representation, including specific representations on the regularity assertion.

48.23   ISA (UK AND IRELAND) 600 USING THE WORK OF ANOTHER AUDITOR

There are five situations where auditors of public sector entities are deemed to be principal auditors:

- if the public sector entity consolidates the results of lower tier bodies into its own financial statements, the principal and other auditor relationship is identical to that within a group of companies;
- where the Comptroller and Auditor General audits the Whole of Government Accounts. This is a situation analogous to the audit of a group of companies;
- if the entity has pooled budgets or shared services audited by another auditor;
- where an entity has contracted out services to another party, a principal/ other auditor relationship exists and auditors apply the guidance in ISA (UK and Ireland) 402 accordingly; and
- where there is a duty to give an opinion on regularity and the auditor of the entity seeks to use the work of the grant recipient's auditor to reduce the extent of their own procedures.

Auditors have a duty under ISA (UK and Ireland) 600 to assess the competence of any auditor on whose work they seek to rely. Where the auditor is appointed by a national audit agency they will have had to demonstrate professional qualifications, experience and resources to the national audit agency. Whilst the principal auditor will still need to perform their own checks, this will provide a clear framework within which to make this assessment.

48.24 ISA (UK AND IRELAND) 610 CONSIDERING THE WORK OF INTERNAL AUDIT

The requirements of ISA (UK and Ireland) 610 are as relevant to the audit of public sector entities as to private companies. Internal audit is normally a mandatory element of a public sector entity's internal control framework, and auditors may have a responsibility to provide negative assurance on a Statement of Internal Control which will necessitate an assessment of the internal control function even if it is not possible to rely on its work in relation to the financial statements.

48.25 ISA (UK AND IRELAND) 700 THE AUDITOR'S REPORT ON FINANCIAL STATEMENTS

When reporting on central government financial statements the requirements of ISA (UK and Ireland) 700 should be followed, bearing in mind any specific reporting requirements of the engagement, such as to whom the audit report is addressed.

The Practice Note gives additional guidance on responsibility statements which should draw attention to the responsibilities of the Accounting Officers or other financial officer with responsibility for the financial statements, separately from those of any other officers. **Table 3** sets out the expected disclosures in a public sector entity's Statement of Responsibilities.

TABLE 3:   Expected disclosures in a public sector entity's Statement of Responsibilities

Responsibility for:
- Proper accounting records that disclose with reasonable accuracy at any time the financial position of the entity and enable the entity to ensure that financial statements are prepared to comply with statutory requirements.
- Safeguarding the assets of the entity and for taking reasonable steps for the prevention and detection of fraud and other irregularities.
- Preparation of financial statements for each financial year that give a true and fair view of/present fairly the state of affairs of the entity and its performance for that period.
- In preparing financial statements:
  - Selecting suitable accounting policies and then applying them consistently;
  - Making judgements and estimates that are reasonable and prudent;
  - Stating whether applicable accounting standards have been followed, subject to any material departures disclosed and explained in the financial statements; and
  - Preparing the financial statements on the going concern basis, unless it is inappropriate to presume that the entity will continue in business.
- The regularity of the public finances for which the Accounting/Accountable Officer is answerable, where a regularity opinion is given.

The wording of the audit opinion depends on the particular auditing framework. Bulletin 2006/2, issued in January 2006 with the revision to Practice Note 10 provides examples of unmodified audit reports and reports modified for regularity issues. The opinion paragraph should clearly indicate the financial reporting framework used to prepare the financial statements and the statute which requires the financial statements to be audited. These vary from body to body and the Practice Note provides a list of alternatives.

Where auditors are reporting on regularity, a separate and explicit opinion is given on the regularity of transactions in the entity's financial statements. In addition, auditors may provide separate reports, other than through their audit opinions, on issues of regularity. Where auditors give a qualified opinion on regularity, this does not in itself lead to a qualification of the truth and fairness, fair presentation or proper presentation part of the opinion.

48.26   ISA (UK AND IRELAND) 720 OTHER INFORMATION IN DOCUMENTS CONTAINING AUDITED FINANCIAL STATEMENTS

Most public sector entities are required to include a foreword in the same document as the financial statements. The foreword usually contains the information which would be included in the directors' report in a set of Companies Act financial statements, and the auditors' opinion does not extend to the contents of the foreword.

Other information required will vary depending on the type of public sector entity.

48.27   CORPORATE GOVERNANCE

In November 2003, the APB issued two Bulletins concerning the requirements of auditors in relation to corporate governance in central government and National Health Service bodies, and in June 2004 a Bulletin covering corporate governance in local government bodies was issued. Separate Bulletins are required as public sector bodies do not operate within a common legislative framework, which means that different models of governance have evolved. The APB anticipates issuing further Bulletins to cover other areas.

48.27.1   *Central government*

Background

The central government sector consists of the following main types of entity:

- government departments;
- executive agencies;
- trading funds;
- bodies not administered as government departments but which are subject to Ministerial and department control, for example non-departmental public bodies; and
- the Scottish Executive, the National Assembly for Wales, the Northern Ireland Executive, their executive agencies and sponsored/related public bodies.

Whilst parts of the Combined Code and the general tenets of the Turnbull recommendations are relevant to central government, the environment is significantly different to that of listed companies. The private sector Board model that contains both non-executive and executive directors is not generally found in central government. Directors of a company have collective responsibility, but the Accounting Officer in central government has full responsibility under the Minister, for the organisation and management of the entity.

Statement on internal control

Following consideration of the Combined Code and Turnbull Report, the Treasury introduced the requirement for central government entities to:

- maintain a system of internal control, with emphasis on risk management;
- review at least annually the effectiveness of the system; and
- include a Statement on Internal Control (SIC) in the accounts.

SICs are required to including the following disclosures:

- acknowledgement of the Accounting Officer's responsibility for ensuring that a sound system of internal control is maintained;
- an explanation that the system of internal control is designed to manage rather than eliminate risk of failure to achieve policies, aims and objectives – it can therefore only provide reasonable and not absolute assurance of effectiveness;
- reference to an ongoing process designed to identify the principle risks to achievement of the entities policies, aims and objectives, evaluate and manage them and confirmation that the process accords with Treasury guidance. A comment is also included on the staff's capacity to manage the risk process;
- confirmation that the above process was in place for the duration of the

financial year and remained so up until the date of the approval of the annual report and accounts;

- acknowledgement of the Accounting Officer's responsibility for reviewing the effectiveness of the system of internal control, and describing the process for review;
- confirmation that the results of the Accounting Officer's review of the effectiveness of internal control has been discussed with the Board, the Audit Committee and, if applicable, the Risk Committee for 2003/04 and subsequently; and
- where appropriate, set out details of actions taken, or proposals to deal with significant internal control issues.

The auditors' review of the SIC is not designed to provide 'positive assurance', therefore, to avoid misunderstanding, the APB recommends that the engagement or understanding letter explains the scope of the review and that the auditors discuss the findings of their review with senior management before releasing their report. Example extracts from an engagement letter are given in **Table 4**.

TABLE 4:   Example extracts from an engagement letter

Review of the Accounting Officer's Statement on Internal Control

Responsibilities

As Accounting Officer of the Authority you are responsible for ensuring that the [name of entity] complies with the guidance issued by HM Treasury entitled 'Corporate Governance: statement on internal control'. This requires you to include alongside the accounts a statement on internal control. The guidance requires the external auditors to review the statement.

Scope of review

Our review of the statement will be conducted in compliance with the relevant recommendations of Bulletins issued by the Auditing Practices Board, which, among other things, set out the scope of our review. For this purpose you will provide us with such information and explanations as we consider necessary. We may request you to provide written confirmation of oral representations which you make to us during the course of our review. We shall request sight of all documents or statements which are due to be issued with the statement on internal control and all documentation prepared in support of the statement. Our work will be restricted to a consideration of whether your statement:

- provides the disclosures required by the Treasury guidance; and
- is not inconsistent with the information of which we have become aware from our audit of the financial statements.

As our work is not designed to consider whether your statement on internal control covers all risks and controls, or form an opinion on the effectiveness of [name of entity]'s risk and control procedures, our work on internal control will

---

not be sufficient to enable us to express any assurance as to whether or not your internal controls are effective. In addition our financial statements audit should not be relied upon to draw to your attention matters that may be relevant to your consideration as to whether or not your system of internal control is effective.

Auditors' review of the SIC

The auditors' review of the SIC will be directed at:

- considering the completeness of the disclosures in meeting Treasury requirements; and
- identifying inconsistencies between the disclosures and the information that the auditor is aware of from their work on the financial statements and other work (including any 'value for money' work carried out in the year).

The auditors' assessment will, therefore, be narrower in scope than the review performed by the Accounting Officer. Auditors are not expected to assess whether all risks and controls have been addressed by the Accounting Officer, or that risks are matched by internal controls. To clarify this, the following wording should be included in the auditors' certificate on the financial statements:

'We are not required to consider, nor have we considered whether the Accounting Officer's statements on internal control cover all risks and controls. We are also not required to form an opinion on the effectiveness of the entity's corporate governance procedures or its risk and control procedures.'

Possible procedures to obtain appropriate evidence about disclosures are detailed in **Table 5**.

TABLE 5: Example procedures to test disclosure in the SIC

- Consider whether the disclosures are consistent with the auditors' review of management board and committee minutes.
- Review supporting documents prepared for the board that are relevant to disclosures made in the SIC. In doing this auditors will pay particular attention to the documentation prepared for Accounting Officers to support their statement made in connection with their effectiveness review and assess whether or not it provides sound support for that statement.
- Gain an understanding of the process defined by the Accounting Officer for his review of the effectiveness of internal control through enquiry of the senior management and comparing their understanding to the statement made by the Accounting Officer in the SIC.
- Attend Audit Committee meetings at which corporate governance, internal control and risk management matters are considered.

- Review the Head of Internal Audit's formal annual report to the Accounting Officer which includes the overall opinion of the adequacy and effectiveness of the organisation's risk management, control and governance processes.
- Relate the statement made by the Accounting Officer to the auditors' knowledge of the entity obtained during the audit of the financial statements.

Significant internal control issues

The Accounting Officer is required to disclose in the SIC details of actions taken or proposed to deal with significant internal control issues. The term 'significant internal control issue' cannot be absolutely defined, but the following characteristics may indicate that the issue is significant enough to be reported:

- it seriously prejudices or prevents achievement of a Public Service Agreement target;
- it has resulted in the need to seek additional funding from Treasury/the sponsoring department to allow resolution, or has required funds to be diverted from another aspect of the business;
- the external auditor would regard it as having a material impact on the accounts;
- the Audit Committee advises that it should be significant;
- the Head of Internal Audit has reported on it as significant in the annual opinion on the whole risk, control and governance; or
- it, or its impact, has attracted significant public interest or has damaged the reputation of the department.

The auditors are not required to assess whether the procedures described in the SIC will remedy any underlying weakness, rather they are required to assess whether the description of the rectification process is appropriate.

Reporting on the SIC

The auditors report by exception in the opinion paragraph of their report on the financial statements, if they conclude:

- that the Accounting Officer's summary of the process applied in reviewing the effectiveness of internal control is either not supported by, or does not reflect the auditors' understanding of that process;
- that the processes disclosed to deal with significant internal control issues do not appropriately reflect the auditors' understanding of the process undertaken;
- that, when the Accounting Officer has failed to conduct a review of the effectiveness of internal control, this has not been disclosed;
- when it is disclosed that no review of the effectiveness of internal control has taken place, the disclosure is not consistent with the auditors' understanding;

- that the Accounting Officer has not disclosed that the review has not covered all the entities within the accounting boundary.

The suggested wording for the opinion paragraph is set out in **Table 6**. This form of report is not a qualified audit opinion, and should be included under the heading 'Other matter'.

TABLE 6: Model opinion paragraph when the auditor reports by exception on the SIC (Central Government)

Opinion

In our opinion:

- the financial statements give a true and fair view of the state of affairs of ... at [date] and of the net resource outturn, resources applied to objectives, recognised gains and losses and cash flows for the year then ended, and have been properly prepared in accordance with the Government Resources and Accounts Act 2000 and directions made thereunder by the Treasury; and
- in all material respects the expenditure and income have been applied to the purposes intended by Parliament and the financial transactions conform to the authorities which govern them.

Other matter

We have reviewed the Accounting Officer's description of his/her processes for reviewing the effectiveness of internal control set out on page [x] of the annual report. In our opinion the Accounting Officer's comments concerning ... do not appropriately reflect our understanding of the process undertaken by the Accounting Officer because ....

Audit committees

The purpose of an Audit Committee in the central government sector is to give advice to the Accounting Officer on the adequacy of audit arrangements, both internal and external, and on the implications of assurances provided in respect of risk and control in an organisation. Audit Committees are not mandatory in the central government section, but are strongly encouraged.

Auditors have no specific reporting responsibilities in relation to the establishment and workings of the Audit Committee.

Auditors' responsibilities

Auditors have different responsibilities for different parts of the annual report and accounts. They are required to audit the financial statements, review the SIC and read all the other information. In addition, in some instances auditors are required to report positively on their findings, in others they have to report by exception.

Therefore, it is important that there is a clear statement of the auditors' responsibilities. Examples are provided in **Table 7**.

TABLE 7:   Example statement of auditors' responsibilities (Central Government)

...Our responsibilities as independent auditors [are established by statute] and we have regard to the standards and guidance issued by the Auditing Practices Board and the ethical guidance applicable to the auditing profession.

We report our opinion as to whether the financial statements give a true and fair view and are properly prepared in accordance with the [Government Resources and Accounts Act 2000] and Treasury directions made thereunder and whether in all material respects the expenditure and income have been applied to the purposes intended by Parliament and the financial transactions conform to the authorities which govern them. We also report if in our opinion the Foreword is not consistent with the financial statements, if the [Department/Agency/entity] has not kept proper accounting records or if we have not received all the information and explanations we require for my audit.

We read the other information contained in the [Accounts/Annual Report] and consider whether it is consistent with the audited financial statements. We consider the implications for our certificate if we become aware of any apparent misstatements or material inconsistencies with the financial statements.

We review whether the statement on page ... reflects the [Department's/ Agency's/entity's] compliance with Treasury's guidance 'Corporate Governance: Statement on Internal Control'. We report if it does not meet the requirements specified by the Treasury or if the statement is misleading or inconsistent with other information we are aware of from our audit of the financial statements. We are not required to consider, nor have we considered whether the Accounting Officer's statements on internal control cover all risks and controls. We are also not required to form an opinion on the effectiveness of the [Department's/Agency's/entity's] corporate governance procedures or its risk and control procedures.

48.27.2   *National Health Service bodies*

Background

Chief Executives of NHS bodies are designated by the Department of Health as Accountable Officers (rather than the Accounting Officers for central government departments). They have personal responsibility for, amongst other things, ensuring that management systems are in place which safeguard public funds, achieving value for money, ensuring that assets are safeguarded and ensuring that expenditure complies with Parliamentary requirements.

NHS bodies operate a Board model similar to that of private sector listed companies, comprising both executive and non-executive members.

Corporate governance developments in the NHS have included:

- designation of Chief Executives as Accountable Officers;
- the establishment of remuneration committees and audit committees (mandatory) and risk management committees (optional);
- adoption of measures recommended by Greenbury relating to disclosure of directors' remuneration; and
- the introduction of a statement on internal control.

The involvement of auditors

Much of the guidance in Bulletin 2003/2 relating to NHS bodies is identical to that in Bulletin 2003/1 on central government, and it is not repeated. However, some terminology differs between sectors, and for that reason a number of the example wordings and reports given in **48.10.1** are provided again below, suitably adapted for use by auditors involved in NHS reporting.

The following tables for use by auditors of NHS bodies detail:

- model opinion paragraph when the auditor reports by exception on the SIC (**Table 8**); and
- example statement of auditors' responsibilities (**Table 9**).

TABLE 8: Model opinion paragraph when the auditor reports by exception on the SIC (NHS bodies)

Opinion

In our opinion:

- the financial statements give a true and fair view of the state of affairs of [xx] NHS Trust at [date] and of its income and expenditure for the year then ended....;

Other matter

We have reviewed the Accountable Officer's description of the processes undertaken for reviewing the effectiveness of the system of internal control as set out on page [x]. In our opinion the Accountable Officer's comments concerning ... do not appropriately reflect our understanding of the processes undertaken because ....

TABLE 9:   Example statement of auditors' responsibilities (NHS bodies)

...Our responsibilities as independent auditors are established by statute, and by the Code of Audit Practice issued by the Audit Commission, which requires adherence to the auditing standards issued by the Auditing Practices Board (APB) and relevant ethical standards. It also requires us to have regard to other guidance and advice issued by the APB.

We report to you our opinion as to whether the financial statements give a true and fair view of the state of affairs of the Trust and its income and expenditure for the year, in accordance with the accounting policies directed by the Secretary of State as being relevant to the National Health Service in England.

We review whether the directors' statement on internal control reflects compliance with the Department of Health's guidance 'The Statement on Internal Control 2003/04'. We report if it does not meet the requirements specified by the Department of Health or if the statement is misleading or inconsistent with other information we are aware of from our audit of the financial statements. We are not required to consider, nor have we considered whether the directors' statements on internal control cover all risks and controls. We are also not required to form an opinion on the effectiveness of the Trust's corporate governance procedures or its risk and control procedures. Our review was not performed for any purpose connected with any specific transaction and should not be relied upon for any such purpose.

We read the information contained in the Annual Report and consider the implications for our report if we become aware of any apparent misstatements or material inconsistencies with the statement of accounts.

48.27.3   *Local government bodies*

Background

Bulletin 2004/2 provides guidance on the corporate governance arrangements for local government bodies subject to the Local Authority SORP. In England, Wales and Scotland this is local authorities, police authorities, fire authorities, joint committees and joint boards of principal authorities, and, in England and Wales, relevant parish, town and community councils. In Northern Ireland the SORP applies to all district councils.

Local government bodies are governed by elected or appointed members who are supported by professional officers. The body itself is responsible for ensuring that a sound system of financial management and internal control are in place, but it will have three designated statutory officers each of whom has a specific role in relation to accountability and control:

- Head of Paid Service – usually the Chief Executive, responsible to the full council for the corporate and overall strategic management of the authority;

- Monitoring Officer – responsible for reporting to the authority any actual or potential breaches of the law or any maladministration, and for ensuring that procedures for recording and reporting key decisions are operating effectively; and
- Chief Financial Officer – local authorities are required to appoint an officer with responsibility for the proper administration of their financial affairs.

The involvement of auditors

As with Bulletin 2003/2, much of the guidance in Bulletin 2004/2 relating to local government bodies is identical to that in Bulletin 2003/1 on central government, and it is not repeated here. Again, some terminology differs between the sectors, and example wordings and reports given in **48.22.1** are provided again below, adapted for use by auditors involved in local government reporting.

The following tables show:

- the model opinion paragraph when the auditor reports by exception on the SIC (**Table 10**); and
- an example statement of auditors' responsibilities (**Table 11**).

TABLE 10: Model opinion paragraph when the auditor reports by exception on the SIC (Local Government)

Opinion

In our opinion the statement of accounts present fairly the financial transactions of XYZ Authority at [date] and its income and expenditure for the year then ended.

Other matter

We have reviewed the authority's description of the processes undertaken for reviewing the effectiveness of the system of internal control as set out on page [x]. In our opinion the authority's comments concerning ... do not appropriately reflect our understanding of the processes undertaken because ....

TABLE 11: Example statement of responsibilities (Local Government)

Respective Responsibilities of Chief Financial Officer and Auditors
As described on page [x], the Chief Financial Officer is responsible for the preparation of the statement of accounts in accordance with the Statement of Recommended Practice on Local Authority Accounting in the United Kingdom. Our responsibilities as independent auditors are established by statute, and by the Code of Audit Practice issued by the Audit Commission, which requires adherence to the auditing standards issued by the Auditing

Practices Board (APB) and relevant ethical standards. It also requires us to have regard to other guidance and advice issued by the APB.

We report to you our opinion as to whether the statement of accounts present fairly the financial position of the Council and its income and expenditure for the year.

We review whether the statement on internal control on page [x] reflects compliance with CIPFA's guidance 'The Statement on Internal Control in Local Government: Meeting the Requirements of the Accounts and Audit Regulations 2003'. We report if it does not comply with proper practices specified by CIPFA or if the statement is misleading or inconsistent with other information we are aware of from our audit of the financial statements. We are not required to consider, nor have we considered, whether the statement on internal control covers all risks and controls. We are also not required to form an opinion on the effectiveness of the authority's corporate governance procedures or its risk and control procedures. Our review was not performed for any purpose connected with any specific transaction and should not be relied upon for any such purpose.

We read the other information published with the statement of accounts and consider the implications for our report if we become aware of any apparent misstatements or material inconsistencies with the statement of accounts.

48.28   GRANT CLAIMS

48.28.1   Background

Grants received from government departments and other funding agencies may be unconditional or may have detailed controls imposed over their expenditure. The guidance in Audit Technical Release 03/03 refers only to situations where a grant paying body has awarded a grant for specific purposes and it has requested that a special accountants' report be provided. A grant recipient may ask an accountant to provide assurance on the eligibility of amounts claimed and/or on the use of grant money and to sign special reports that have been requested by the grant paying body.

The Technical Release builds on the principles outlined in Audit 1/01 *Reporting to Third Parties*, see **Chapter 42**, and applies from September 2003.

There are three categories of people who will require consideration from the accountants when reporting on grant claims. These are detailed below:

Recipients who are entitled to rely on reports and may suffer a direct loss

A grant paying body usually requires assurance that the recipient meets the criteria for receiving the grant and that the grant monies have been spent in accordance with its terms and conditions. Even when accountants are not providing their report directly to the grant paying body, but rather to the grant recipient, the grant provider is also likely to rely on the report.

Therefore, the accountants should enter into an agreement with both the grant provider and the grant receiver, acknowledging the duty of care to both parties.

If the grant provider has a sponsoring body which is ultimately responsible for the monies paid by the grant provider, they may seek to rely on the accountants' report and should be bound into the engagement separately.

Recipients who may use them, are entitled to place reliance on them, but will not suffer a direct loss
These may include audit agencies such as the National Audit Office, Parliament and sponsoring bodies who have not entered into an engagement with the accountants.

The accountants should establish who has statutory rights of access to their report and seek to stipulate that it should not be disclosed to another person without consent from the accountants.

General access to reports where no entitlement for reliance may be placed
These reports are widely available as a result of statute, but it is not reasonable for the accountants to owe a duty of care to anyone who reads their report. Therefore, if a body writes to the accountants in an attempt to indicate reliance on their report, the accountants should issue a disclaimer in writing.

48.28.2   Terms of engagement

The accountants' understanding of the risks involved in the engagement will determine whether they accept the work. Depending on the circumstances, the accountants can either:

- accept that they owe a duty of care to the grant provider and enter into an engagement with both the grant provider and the grant receiver, limiting liability as necessary;
- engage with the grant receiver, but require the grant paying body to acknowledge in writing that no duty of care is owed by the accountants before the report is released to them;
- engage with the grant receiver, but disclaim or limit any liability or duty to the grant provider in the accountants' report; or
- refuse to accept the appointment.

Where other parties such as the sponsoring body also require access to the report, they may require input into the wording of the report. Accountants need to be clear about who is permitted access and to whom a duty of care is owed.

Where the accountants assess the report as low risk, because the grant provider could suffer little or no loss, or where the grant provider is willing to accept in writing that they are owed no duty of care, there may be no formal engagement between the accountant and the grant provider.

The possible courses of action are set out in the flow chart in **Table 12**.

An example tri-partite engagement letter is set out in **Table 13**. As there are likely to be a large number of recipients for a particular grant scheme, the provider may be unwilling to agree individual engagement letters. If this is the case, the grant paying body will issue a standardised terms of engagement, an example of which is in **Table 14**. These terms may need to be tailored in certain circumstances.

If the grant provider will agree to neither the tri-partite engagement letter nor the standardised terms of engagement the accountant may choose not to accept the engagement.

TABLE 12: Reporting accountants' process in accepting a request for a report from a grant provider

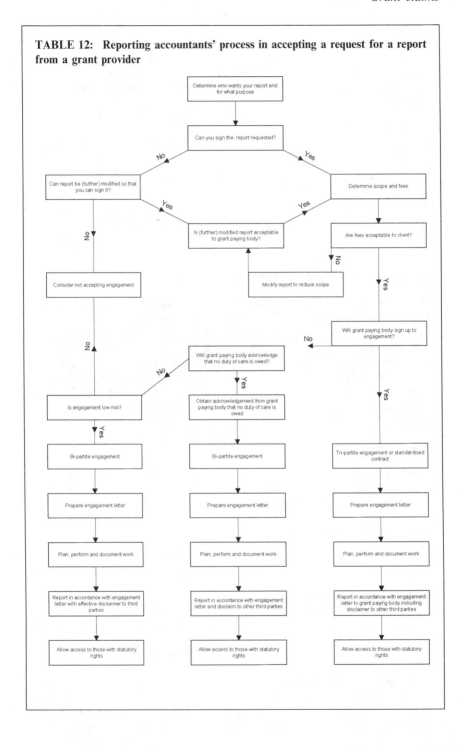

TABLE 13:   Example tri-partite engagement letter

Where a sponsoring body is to be bound into the engagement process, then all references to the grant paying body should also include references to the sponsoring body.

[Grant paying body]

[Address]

[Grant recipient]

[Address]

[Date]

Dear Sirs

Government Grant reports/confirmations

We are writing to confirm the terms and conditions on which you have engaged [name of firm] to provide reports/confirmations in connection with [description or name of grant] paid by [grant paying body] to [grant recipient]. These terms and conditions will apply to the reports/confirmations to be supplied for the period [ended/ending ...] and for subsequent periods unless otherwise agreed in writing. We will write separately to the grant recipient regarding practical matters such as the timing of our work, staffing and our charges. Our invoices will be addressed to [grant recipient], who will be solely responsible for payment in full.

Scope of our work

We will complete the relevant work specified below on the schedule (as defined in the offer letter). The schedule is to be prepared by, and is the sole responsibility of [grant recipient].

Our work will comprise the following:

[Details of planned work relevant to the nature of the claim or grant, level of assurance and form and content of report required]

[**High level assurance**] On the basis of the detailed tests carried out, we will report whether, in our opinion, we have obtained sufficient appropriate evidence that the amounts shown in the schedule are [presented fairly in all material respects in the context of reporting upon this grant claim and in accordance with the terms and conditions set by the grant paying body].

[**Moderate assurance**] We will report whether anything has come to our attention arising from the limited tests carried out (as specified in the schedule) to suggest that the amounts shown in the schedule have not been spent in accordance with the terms and conditions set by the grant paying body.

[**Agreed upon procedures**] We will complete the specified limited scope procedures set out below on the attached schedule. Upon completion of the procedures, we will provide you with a report of our findings. You have both agreed that the scope of our work, as specified below, is sufficient for your purposes.

[Preparation of any document that [grant recipient] may be required to submit to [grant paying body] in connection with our work will be the responsibility of [grant recipient]'s Directors, who will also be responsible for ensuring that [grant recipient] maintains proper accounting records and such other records as may be required by [grant paying body]. [Grant recipient]'s Directors will on request supply us with confirmation of matters affecting our work which are dependent on the Directors' judgement.]

Save as set out above, we will not seek to establish the accuracy, completeness or reliability of any of the information or documentation made available to us. Our work will not amount to an audit of financial statements and will not give the same level of assurance as an audit.

Our audit work on the financial statements of [grant recipient] is carried out in accordance with our statutory obligations and is subject to separate terms and conditions. This engagement will not be treated as having any effect on our separate duties and responsibilities as [grant recipient]'s external auditors. Our audit report on the financial statements is intended for the sole benefit of [grant recipient]'s shareholders as a body, to whom it is addressed, to enable them to exercise their rights as a body in a general meeting. Our audits of [grant recipient]'s financial statements are not planned or conducted to address or reflect matters in which anyone other than such shareholders as a body may be interested in for such purpose.

To the fullest extent permitted by law we do not and will not, by virtue of our reports/confirmations or otherwise, assume or accept any duty of care or liability under this engagement to [grant recipient] or to [grant paying body] or to any other party, whether in contract, negligence or otherwise in relation to our audits of [grant recipient]'s financial statements.

Having set out our work we will issue reports/confirmations addressed to [grant recipient] and [grant paying body] in the form set out in the appendix to this engagement letter, if our findings support this. In determining the form of our report we will take into account, (though without being bound by it) any form of reporting that the [grant paying body] has suggested or agreed with the Institute of Chartered Accountants in England and Wales following consultation with them. We will deliver copies to [grant recipient] at the same time. This letter will be identified in our reports/confirmations as the 'tri-partite agreement' under which our reports/confirmations have been issued. Our reports/confirmations will be released on the basis that they are not to be copied, referred to or disclosed, in whole or in part, to any other party without our prior written consent, which may be conditional. If we need to qualify our opinion, we will issue a qualified report but will continue to use the agreed form of report for all aspects that are not qualified.

Other matters

Our duties and liabilities in connection with this engagement owed to [grant recipient] and to [grant paying body] will differ.

[Detail any exclusions and limitations on the firm's liability to both the grant paying body and the grant recipient and any relevant qualifications required to satisfy statutory reasonableness criteria. See **Table 13**.]

Our duty to [grant paying body] will be limited to delivery of reports/confirmations in the agreed form to enable it to meet its statutory obligations. Delivery of such reports/confirmations (or the supply of confirmation that we are unable to do so in the agreed form) at any time will discharge that obligation in full. We will not owe [grant paying body] any other duty, in contract, negligence or otherwise, in connection with our reports/confirmations or their preparation [(see alternative wording in **Table 13**)].

This agreement shall be subject to and governed by English law and all disputes arising from, or under it, shall be subject to the exclusive jurisdiction of the English Courts.

[Detail or append any other terms and conditions to apply to this work.]

Please confirm, by signing below your agreement to this letter. Once you have done so this letter will form a tri-partite contract between us in respect of the matters covered. If you wish to discuss any aspects of this letter, please contact [name and telephone number].

Yours faithfully

[Name of accountant]

[Grant recipient]

[Grant paying body]

TABLE 14:　Example standardised terms of engagement

Where a sponsoring body is to be bound into the engagement process, then all references to the grant paying body should also include references to the sponsoring body.

The following are the terms of engagement on which the [grant paying body] agrees to engage accountants to perform [a high or medium level of assurance or agreed upon procedures] engagement and report in connection with the [name of grant claim].

An agreement between [grant recipient], its reporting accountants and the [grant paying body] on these terms is formed when [grant recipient] and the accountant signs and submits to the [grant paying body] a report as set out in Clause 3 herein. [NB: The [grant paying body] will not need to sign anything. By publishing this document the [grant paying body] makes an offer to engage on these terms. Once the offer is accepted by the [grant recipient] and the accountants then an agreement is formed. If the terms of the standardised engagement letter are to be revised, the [grant paying body] will need to confirm its acceptance of the new terms before an agreement is formed.]

In these terms of engagement:

'[grant paying body]' refers to the body that is providing the grant funding;

'the [grant recipient]' refers to the organisation that is required to submit the report to the [grant paying body];

'the accountant' refers to the [grant recipient]'s reporting accountants.

1   Introduction

The [grant recipient] is required to submit to the [grant paying body] reports as set out in Clause 3 below that are also signed by an accountant to provide independent assurance. These terms of engagement set out the basis on which the accountant will sign the report.

2   The [grant recipient]'s responsibilities

2.1   The grant recipient is responsible for producing the [information], maintaining proper records complying with the terms of any legislation or regulatory requirements and the [grant paying body]'s terms and conditions of grant ('the grant conditions') and providing relevant information to the [grant paying body] on a basis in accordance with the requirements of the grant conditions. The [grant recipient] is responsible for ensuring that the non-financial records can be reconciled to the financial records.

2.2   The management of the [grant recipient] will make available to the accountant all records, correspondence, information and explanations that the accountant considers necessary to enable the accountant to perform the accountant's work.

2.3   The [grant recipient] and the [grant paying body] accept that the ability of the accountant to perform his work effectively depends upon the grant recipient providing full and free access to the financial and other records and the [grant recipient] shall procure that any such records held by a third party are made available to the accountant.

2.4   The accountant accepts that, whether or not the [grant recipient] meets its obligations, the accountant remains under an obligation to the [grant paying body] to perform his work with reasonable care. The failure by the [grant recipient] to meet its obligations may cause the accountant to qualify his report or be unable to provide a report.

3   Scope of the accountant's work

3.1   The [grant recipient] will provide the accountant with such information, explanations and documentation that the accountant considers necessary to carry out his responsibilities. The accountant will seek written representations from management in relation to matters for which independent corroboration is not available. The accountant will also seek confirmation that any significant matters of which the accountant should be aware have been brought to the accountant's attention.

3.2   The accountant will perform the following work in relation to reports required by the [grant paying body]:

3.2.1 Grant return: The accountant will [carry out a high/medium level of assurance assignment or perform agreed tests] [as set out in the terms and conditions of the grant] and subject to any adverse findings will produce a report in the form set out in the attached Appendix.

3.2.2 Where a [high/medium] level of assurance is required by the [grant paying body], the criteria is identified as per the Appendix to this letter.

3.2.3 For an agreed upon procedures engagement, the tests are as laid out in the Appendix to this letter.

4   Form of the accountant's report

4.1   The accountant's reports are prepared on the following basis:

4.1.1 The accountant's reports are prepared solely for the confidential use of the [grant recipient] and the [grant paying body] and solely for the purpose of submission to the [grant paying body] in connection with the [grant paying body]'s requirements in connection with [name of grant]. They may not be relied upon by the [grant recipient], or the [grant paying body] for any other purpose except as provided in 4.1.2 below;

4.1.2 The [grant paying body] may only disclose the reports to others who may have statutory rights of access to the report. There may be an actual or potential liability to [other bodies] that may arise out of the eligibility and/or use of monies by the [grant recipient], and [the others] who will be entitled to rely on the report;

4.1.3 Neither the [grant recipient], nor the [grant paying body] [nor others] may rely on any oral or draft reports the accountant provides. The accountant accepts responsibility to the [grant recipient], the [grant paying body] for the accountant's final signed reports only;

4.1.4 The accountant's reports must not be recited or referred to in whole or in part in any other document (including, without limitation, any publication issued by the [grant paying body]) without the prior written approval of the accountant;

4.1.5 Except to the extent required by court order, law or regulation or to assist in the resolution of any court proceedings the accountant's reports must not be made available, copied or recited to any other person (including, without limitation, any person who may use or refer to any of the [grant paying body]'s publications);

4.1.6 Except as provided by 4.1.2 herein, the firm of accountants, its partners and staff neither owe nor accept any duty to any other person (including, without limitation, any person who may use or refer to any of the [grant paying body]'s publications) and shall not be liable for any loss, damage or expense whatsoever nature which is caused by their reliance on representations in the accountant's reports.

5   Liability provisions

5.1   The accountant will perform the engagement with reasonable skill and care and acknowledges that it will be liable to the [grant recipient] and the [grant paying body] for losses, damages, costs or expenses ('losses') caused by its breach of contract, negligence or wilful default, subject to the following provisions:

5.1.1 The accountant will not be so liable if such losses are due to the provision of false, misleading or incomplete information or documentation or due to the acts or omissions of any person other than the accountant, except where, on the basis of the enquiries normally undertaken by accountants within the scope set out in these terms of engagement, it would have been reasonable for the accountant to discover such defects;

5.1.2 The accountant accepts liability without limit for the consequences of its own fraud and for any other liability which it is not permitted by law to limit or exclude;

5.1.3 Subject to the previous paragraph (5.1.2), the total aggregate liability of the accountant whether in contact, tort (including negligence) or otherwise, to the [grant paying body] and the sponsoring body, arising from or in connection with the work which is the subject of these terms (including any addition or variation to the work), shall not exceed the amount of [to be discussed and agreed].

5.2 The [grant recipient] and the [grant paying body] agree that they will not bring any claims or proceedings against any individual partners, members, directors or employees of the accountant. This clause is intended to benefit such partners, members, directors and employees who may enforce this clause pursuant to the Contracts (Rights of Third Parties) Act 1999 ('the Act'). Notwithstanding any benefits or rights conferred by this agreement on any third party by virtue of the Act, the parties to this agreement may agree to vary or rescind this agreement without any third party's consent. Other than as expressly provided in these terms, the provisions of the Act are excluded;

5.3 Any claims, whether in contract, negligence or otherwise, must be formally commenced within [years] after the party bringing the claim becomes aware (or ought reasonably become aware) of the facts which give rise to the action and in any event no later than [years] after any alleged breach of contract, negligence or other cause of actions. This expressly overrides any statutory provision which would otherwise apply;

5.4 This engagement is separate from, and unrelated to, the accountant's audit work on the financial statements of the [grant recipient] for the purposes of the Companies Act 1985 (or its successor) or other legislation and nothing herein creates obligations or liabilities regarding the accountant's statutory audit work, which would not otherwise exist. [To be amended where the grant recipient is other than a Companies Act entity.]

6   Fees

The accountant's fees, together with VAT and out of pocket expenses, will be agreed with and billed to the [grant recipient]. The [grant paying body] is not liable to pay the accountant's fees.

7 Quality of service

The accountant will investigate all complaints. The [grant paying body] or the [grant recipient] have the right to take any complaint to the Institute of Chartered Accountants in England and Wales ('the ICAEW'). The [grant paying body] or the [grant recipient] may obtain an explanation of the mechanisms that operate in respect of a complaint to the ICAEW at www.icaew.co.uk/complaints or by writing to the ICAEW. To contact the ICAEW write to the Professional Standards Office, Silbury Court, 412–416 Silbury Boulevard, Central Milton Keynes, MK9 2AF.

8 Providing services to other parties

The accountant will not be prevented or restricted by virtue of the accountant's relationship with the [grant recipient] and the [grant paying body], including anything in these terms of engagement, from providing services to other clients. The accountant's standard internal procedures are designed to ensure that confidential information communicated to the accountant during the course of an assignment will be maintained confidentially.

9 Applicable law and jurisdiction

9.1 This agreement shall be governed by, and interpreted and construed in accordance with, English Law.

9.2 The [grant recipient], the [grant paying body] and the accountant irrevocably agree that the Courts of England shall have exclusive jurisdiction to settle any dispute (including claims for set-off and counterclaims) which may arise in connection with the validity, effect, interpretation or performance of, or the legal relationship established by the agreement or otherwise arising in connection with this agreement.

10 Alteration to terms

All additions and variations to these terms of engagement shall be binding only if in writing and signed by the duly authorised representatives of the parties. These terms supersede any previous agreements and representations between the parties in respect of the scope of the accountant's work and the accountant's report or the obligations of any of the parties relating thereto (whether oral or written) and represents the entire understanding between the parties.

Accountants should consider whether to include a disclaimer or liability limitation in their engagement terms. Examples are given in **Tables 15** and **16**.

TABLE 15: Example disclaimer notice for an accountant's report

Where the grant paying body signs the engagement letter

Our Report is prepared solely for the confidential use of [grant recipient] [and [grant paying body]], and solely for the purpose of [describe the purpose]. It may not be relied upon by [grant recipient] [or [grant paying body]] for any other purpose whatsoever. Our Report must not be recited or referred to in whole or in part in any other published document without the written permission of the accountant. [(Please see comments in **Table 12** item 4.1.4.)]

Our Report must not be made available, copied or recited to any other party without our express written permission in every case except for [grant paying body] may disclose the report where it has a statutory obligation to do so. Other than to [grant recipient] [and [grant paying body]], [accountant] neither owes nor accepts any duty to any other party to whom their Report may be disclosed.

Where the grant paying body does not sign the engagement letter

Our Report is prepared solely for the confidential use of [grant recipient] and solely for the purpose of [describe the purpose]. It may not be relied upon by [grant recipient] for any other purpose whatsoever. Our Report must not be recited or referred to in whole or in part in any other published document without the written permission of the accountant. Our Report must not be made available, copied or recited to any other party without our express written permission in every case to any other party, except for [grant paying body], to whom we owe no duty of care. Accountant neither owes nor accepts any duty to any other party who may receive our Report and specifically disclaims any liability for any loss, damage or expense of whatsoever nature, which is caused by their reliance on our Report.

TABLE 16: Example of a liability cap for an accountant's reporting engagement

The total aggregate liability, whether to [grant recipient] or [grant paying body] or any other party, of whatever nature, whether in contract, tort (including negligence) or otherwise, of [accountant] for any losses whatsoever and howsoever caused arising from or in any way connected with this engagement [and this transaction] shall not exceed [insert amount] (including interest). We limit liability to that proportion of the loss or damage suffered by the [grant paying body] for which the [accountant] has contributed to the overall cause for such loss or damage, as agreed between the parties, or in the absence of an agreement, as finally determined by the courts (subject to an upper limit).

Where there is more than one addressee of the engagement, the limit of the liability specified will have to be allocated between these addressees. Such allocation will be entirely a matter for the addressees, and the addressees will be under no obligation to inform [accountant] of it; if (for whatever reason) no such allocation is agreed, the addressees will not dispute the validity, enforceability or operation of the limit of liability on the grounds that no such allocation was agreed.

48.28.3   *Types of engagement*

There are no UK auditing standards covering this type of engagement, but international guidance does exist. This guidance sets out three types of engagement which could be performed:

- agreed upon procedures;
- assurance engagements (high level assurance); and
- assurance engagements (moderate level assurance).

The level of testing will depend on the type of engagement required, and this should be agreed at the outset of the engagement.

Agreed upon procedures

An 'agreed upon procedures' assignment involves the accountant performing certain procedures which have been specified by the grant provider, and which the provider uses to derive its assurance. Audit 1/01 *Reporting to Third Parties* suggests that this type of procedure will normally best meet the expectations of the third party and the client as the procedures are agreed in advance and set out in the engagement letter. In addition, the accountant will attach a copy of their proposed report format to the engagement letter.

Assurance engagements

For an engagement to provide a specific level assurance it needs to exhibit all of the following elements:

- a three party relationship involving a professional accountant, a responsible party and an intended user;
- a subject matter;
- suitable criteria;
- an engagement process; and
- a conclusion.

Therefore the grant provider is required to determine suitable criteria on which the accountant will conclude.

High level of assurance is usually regarded as providing a conclusion in positive terms, such as 'the grant conditions have been met'. In order to provide this opinion a significant amount of work must be performed by the accountants, up to 100 per cent testing levels.

Moderate level assurance requires the above elements of an assurance engagement to exist, but with a lesser level of testing. This will lead to a negative opinion in the style of 'nothing has come to our attention to suggest that the grant has not been spent for the intended purpose'.

48.28.4   Reporting

Agreeing the form of report to be given at the outset of the engagement helps to narrow any expectation gap that may arise. The grant provider should carefully consider the form of words it will require for its purpose, but good practice suggests that all parties should be involved in agreeing the wording. If possible, standard forms should be avoided, particularly those that cannot be justified by any level of work, and undefined terms such as 'review' or 'reasonable' should not be used without clarification of their meaning. Terms required by statute or legislation should be clearly defined to avoid later misunderstanding.

Typically an accountants' report will contain the following:

- addressee(s);
- identification of the applicable engagement letter and specific information on which the work has been performed and tests have been applied;
- under an agreed upon procedures engagement, a statement that the procedures/tests performed were those agreed with the grant recipient (and grant paying body);
- under a high or moderate assurance engagement, a statement of the procedures necessary to provide the agreed level of assurance;
- identification of the purpose for which the procedures/tests were performed;
- listing of the specific procedures/tests performed;
- description of the accountants' findings, including sufficient details of errors and exceptions found;
- statement that the procedures/tests performed do not constitute either an audit or a review;
- statement that the report is restricted to those parties that are bound by the terms of the engagement letter;
- statement that the engagement is separate from the audit of the annual financial statements and that the report relates only to the matters specified and that it does not extend to the grant recipient's annual financial statements taken as a whole;
- name and signature of reporting accountants; and
- date of the report.

48.28.5   Access to accountants' working papers

Government departments or audit agencies may require access to the accountants' working papers. Most accountants will agree to this as long as an authorisation letter is signed by the grant recipient permitting the accountants to give access to their papers and a release letter is signed by the party requiring access agreeing that no duty of care or liability exists to them. Further details can be found in **Chapter 19**.

Model authorisation and release letters are provided in **Tables 17** and **18.**

TABLE 17: Authorisation letter

We understand that the [body requesting access] believes that it would be helpful if they were to review our working papers and report on [grant claim].

Our policy does not normally allow me to disclose our working papers to any third party. In accordance with the guidance contained within Technical Release Audit 3/03 *Public Sector Special Reporting Engagements – Grant Claims* issued by the ICAEW, this firm is content to allow such access to the working papers and report providing certain conditions are met. We are now writing to confirm your agreement to the terms set out in this letter and to secure the authorisation of the grant recipient for that access.

As a condition of providing access and responding to any request for information or explanations in relation to the working papers in the course of or in connection with the review of the papers, this firm requires the [body requiring access] to agree to the terms of the letter.

Prior to making the working papers and reports on [grant claim] available, we need the consent of [grant recipient]. In addition, we will require from [body requiring access] an agreement (in the form of a release letter) that they will not acquire any rights against [name of firm] as a result of such access, and an acknowledgement from [body requiring access] that they recognise the basis on which such access is provided.

As you will appreciate, our working papers were created for the sole particular purpose of providing assurance on [grant claim] in line with [procedures/ expectations] agreed with yourselves [and [body requiring access]]. They were not created for any other purpose. Furthermore, it is not this firm's function or responsibility to provide to the [body requiring access] any papers that come into existence or information that may come to the firm's attention after the date of this letter. Consequently, the working papers, report and any subsequent information and explanations provided in relation to the working papers and report are subject to the following conditions:

(1) the [grant paying body] or any other parties involved, do not misuse any confidential information obtained from their review of the working papers and reports or from any explanations provided by the firm; and

(2) the [grant paying body] accept that, to the fullest extent permitted by law, [firm] owes them no duty of care or other obligation and will incur no liability whatsoever to them in relation to or in connection with their review as a result of granting them access or providing explanations.

Please, therefore, confirm that you agree to our disclosing the working papers, reports and providing explanations in relation to the working papers and reports on [grant claim] on the terms described above by signing and dating and returning to us the enclosed copy of this letter on behalf of the [grant recipient] and returning it to us.

Yours faithfully

Name of firm

Acknowledged and agreed, for and on behalf of [grant paying body] and its directors

Director   Date

TABLE 18:   Release letter

In connection with [grant claim], the [grant recipient] has requested us to allow [body requiring access] access to our working papers, reports and provision of explanations in relation to the working papers and reports as necessary.

The procedures and working papers were designed and prepared solely for the purpose of forming our opinion, in accordance with the form of report agreed in the engagement letter with the [grant recipient] and the [grant paying body]. Accordingly, we have not expressed any opinion or other form of assurance on other issues related to [grant recipient].

You should note that we have only reported on transactions related to [grant claim] in accordance with the agreed procedures/expectations for the period of [date] and to [date] and significant events may well have occurred since that date.

Neither the working papers, reports and explanations provided, can in any way serve to substitute enquiries that you may need to make for the purpose of satisfying yourself in relation to the review that you are carrying out.

Notwithstanding the purposes for which the working papers and reports were prepared, we are prepared to grant [body requiring access] access to them on the condition that the [body requiring access] acknowledges and accepts the previous paragraphs and agree to the following conditions upon which access will be granted:

[body requiring access] agrees and acknowledges that:

- to the extent that any of the working papers or reports may be construed as relating to the state of affairs of the [grant recipient] the onus will be on the [body requiring access] to verify the information directly with the [grant recipient] before relying upon it for the purpose of their review;
- to the fullest extent permitted by law, the [grant paying body] accept that the [name of firm] owes no duty of care to it whether in contract or tort or under statute or otherwise and will not bring any actions, proceedings or claims against the [name of firm] with respect to or in connection with the working papers [or report] on [grant claim]; and
- to the fullest extent permitted by law, [name of firm] has no liability to it for any loss or damage suffered or costs incurred by it, arising out of or in connection with the provision of access to the working papers [or reports], however such loss or damage is caused, including as a result of negligence.

Please confirm your agreement to the foregoing terms and conditions and your acceptance of the rest of this letter by signing, dating and returning to us a copy of this letter.

Yours faithfully

[Name of firm]

The [body requiring access] acknowledges and agrees to the provisions of this letter.

For and behalf of [body requiring access]   Date

49 REGULATED ENTITIES

49.1 INTRODUCTION

In October 2003 the Audit and Assurance Faculty of the ICAEW issued Technical Release Audit 5/03 *Reporting to Regulators of Regulated Entities* to assist accountants when reporting on regulatory information.

Regulated entities, see **Table 1**, are often required to submit a large volume of financial information to their regulated body as part of the regulatory process and the exact requirements can vary significantly between industries. Regulators use this information in a number of ways, for example, in ensuring that costs and pricing are transparent, and the regulatory body often requires an independent accountant's report on elements of this information.

The guidance in Audit 5/03 is based on Audit 1/01 *Reporting to Third Parties*, see **Chapter 41**, and has been developed after discussion and consultation with a number of regulators. It does not apply to reporting to other regulatory bodies, such as the Financial Services Authority, see **Chapter 8**.

TABLE 1: Regulatory bodies

The Government appointed regulatory bodies that oversee the activities of regulated entities for the purpose of Audit 5/03 are:

- Ofgem (The Office of Gas and Electricity Markets);
- Ofwat (Office of Water Services);
- Oftel (Office of Telecommunications);
- Postcomm (Postal Services Commission);
- ORR (Office of the Rail Regulator);
- Ofreg (Office for the Regulation of Electricity and Gas in Northern Ireland);
- OfCom (Office of Communications).

49.2   DUTY OF CARE AND ENGAGEMENT CONTRACTS

As noted in **Chapter 41**, when an accountant knows that a third party obtains and relies on their report, the accountant will owe that third party a duty of care unless an effective disclaimer is in place.

Regulatory returns and regulatory accounts are required by an individual regulator, who will specify what information they will contain and who uses that information as part of its overall role. The accountant will only accept a duty of care to the regulator if either a tri-partite or bi-partite engagement contract with a written notice is in place. If the regulator will not enter into a suitable engagement contract the accountant will not accept a duty of care to the regulator and will make it clear in their report. However, the report will be addressed to the company and the regulator in order to meet the requirements of the regulatory licence.

The accountant will exclude a duty of care to any other third party by including a suitable disclaimer in their report. A third party may only rely on the report once they have become party to the engagement contract.

49.2.1   Tri-partite engagement contracts

A tri-partite engagement contract is a written engagement contract between the accountant, the regulated entity and the regulator. The contract will contain appropriate terms clarifying and limiting the scope and extent of the accountant's responsibilities and liability.

Table 2 sets out an example tri-partite engagement contract.

TABLE 2:   Example tri-partite engagement contract

Private and Confidential

The Directors

[Name and address of Regulated Entity]

For the attention of [ ]

The Director General

[Name and address of Regulator]

For the attention of [ ]

[Date]

[Name of Regulated Entity] ('the Company')

Audit of the regulatory financial statements for the year ended [date]

Dear Sirs

Introduction

This letter (including the attached Appendices and the Terms and Conditions) sets out our understanding of the basis on which we act as auditors reporting on the regulatory financial statements ('the Regulatory Accounts') as specified in [licence condition or other reference] of the Instrument of Appointment of the Company as a [type of business] under the [applicable legislation] ('the Regulatory Licence') and the Regulatory Accounting Guidelines ('RAGs') [agreed with/] issued by the Director General of [identity of Regulator], [name of Regulator] ('the Regulator'). We also set out the respective areas of responsibility of the directors of the Company ('the Directors'), the Regulator and ourselves, in respect of the audit of the Regulatory Accounts (the 'Services'). This letter (with all its attachments) applies only to the audit report on the Regulatory Accounts and the scope of our work will be limited accordingly. If any additional work or report is required, separate engagement terms and conditions will need to be agreed.

This letter and the attached terms and conditions together comprise the entire contract ('the Contract') for the provision of the Services [to the exclusion of any other express or implied terms, whether expressed orally or in writing including any conditions, warranties and representations unless made fraudulently] and shall supersede all previous contracts, letters of engagement, undertakings, agreements and correspondence regarding the Services.

Responsibilities of the Directors and the Auditors
The Directors are required to ensure that the Company complies with all of the terms of its Regulatory Licence [or other reference].

The Directors are required to prepare Regulatory Accounts in accordance with the Company's Regulatory Licence [or other reference] and the RAGs [agreed with/] issued by the Regulator, a copy of which are attached as Appendix [ ]. The Directors are also required to:

- [other licence conditions on which the Directors are required to give a finance-based report per the Regulatory Licence, for example];
- [confirm that, in their opinion, the Company has sufficient financial and management resources for the next twelve months];
- [confirm that, in their opinion, the Company has sufficient rights and assets which would enable a special administrator to manage the affairs, business and property of the Company];
- [Report to the Director General of [name of Regulator] changes in the Company's activities which may be material in relation to the Company's ability to finance its regulated activities];
- [Undertake the transactions entered into by the business consisting of the carrying out of the regulated activity ('the appointed business'), with or for the benefit of any group companies or related companies ('associated companies') or activities of the appointed business, at arm's length]; and
- [Keep proper accounting records which comply with [licence condition or other reference].

We refer to the above as 'the Specific Obligations'.

Other than reporting on whether or not proper accounting records have been kept by the Company as required by Condition [ ] of the Regulatory Licence [or other reference], it is not our responsibility in providing the Services to report on the Specific Obligations or on any other obligations of the Company or the Directors under the Regulatory Licence [or other reference].

The Directors are also responsible for ensuring that the Company maintains accounting records which disclose with reasonable accuracy, at any time, the financial position of the company, and for preparing Regulatory Accounts which present the results of the Company fairly in accordance with the Regulatory Licence. They are also responsible for making available to us, as and when required, all of the Company's accounting records, all other relevant records, including minutes of all directors', management and shareholders' meetings, and such information and explanations which we consider necessary for the performance of our duties as auditors.

It is our responsibility to form an independent opinion, based on our audit, on the Regulatory Accounts and to report our opinion to the Company and the Regulator.

Our report will be addressed to the Company and the Regulator and will state whether, in our opinion the Regulatory Accounts present fairly in accordance with conditions [ ], [ ] and [ ] of the Regulatory Licence [or other reference] the state of the Company's affairs at [date] and of its profit (or loss) for the year then ended, and have been properly prepared in accordance with conditions [ ], [ ] and [ ] of that Licence [or other reference].

Our report will be made in accordance with the Contract, solely to the Company and the Regulator in order to meet the requirements of the Regulatory Licence [or other reference]. Our audit work will be undertaken so that we might state to the Company and the Regulator those matters we have agreed in the Contract to state to them in our report in order to (a) assist the Company to [meet its obligations under the Regulatory Licence to procure such a report] and (b) to facilitate the carrying out by the Regulator of its regulatory functions, and for no other purpose. To the fullest extent permitted by law, we will not accept or assume responsibility to anyone other than the Company and the Regulator for our audit work, for our report, or for the opinions we will form. Our report will contain a disclaimer of liability to other parties to this effect.

The Contract does not confer benefits on any parties who are not parties to it and the application of the Contracts (Rights of Third Parties) Act 1999 is excluded.

In arriving at our opinion, and in accordance with the Regulatory Licence (condition [reference]) [or other reference], we will consider the following matters, and report on any in respect of which we are not satisfied:

- whether appropriate accounting records have been kept by the Company and proper returns adequate for our audit have been received from operating locations not visited by us;
- whether the Regulatory Accounts are in agreement with the accounting

records and returns retained for the purpose of preparing the Regulatory Accounts; and
- whether we have obtained all the information and explanations which we consider necessary for the purpose of our audit.

Our responsibilities also include:

- providing in our report a description of the Directors' responsibilities for the Regulatory Accounts where the Regulatory Accounts or accompanying information do not include such a description; and
- considering whether other information in documents containing the Regulatory Accounts is consistent with those Regulatory Accounts.

The Regulator and the Company acknowledge and agree that:

- wherever the Regulatory Accounts or other Regulatory Information covered by the Independent Accountants' report are published or otherwise made available in full, our audit report will also be published or otherwise made available in full as part of that communication;
- wherever substantial extracts from the Regulatory Accounts or other Regulatory Information covered by the Independent Accountants' report are published or otherwise made available, and reference is made to the fact that they are audited or otherwise examined by an Independent Accountant, there will be explicit statements by the Regulator: (a) that the information published is only an extract; and (b) about the limitation of scope of the Independent Accountants' report and the duty of care owed by the Independent Accountants; and (c) referring to where the full set of Regulatory Accounts can be found or otherwise obtained; and
- wherever any other information is referenced from the Regulatory Accounts or other Regulatory Information covered by the Independent Accountants' report, there will be an explicit reference by the Regulator to the source of that information and the limitation of scope of the Independent Accounts' report and the duty of care owed by the Independent Accountant.

Relationship between the Regulator and the Company
For the avoidance of doubt, nothing in this Contract is intended to nor does it affect or in any way alter the relationship or the rights and obligations between the Company and the Regulator as set out in the Regulatory Licence [and all relevant legislation].

Scope of our audit
Our audit will be performed with regard to the guidance contained in Audit 05/ 03 *Reporting to Regulators of Regulated Entities* issued by the Institute of Chartered Accountants in England and Wales.

Our audit will be conducted in accordance with International Standards on Auditing (UK and Ireland) issued by the Auditing Practices Board except that, as the nature, form and content of Regulatory Accounts are determined by the Regulator, we will not evaluate the overall adequacy of the presentation of the information, which would have been required if we were to express an audit opinion under International Standards on Auditing (UK and Ireland). Our audit will include such tests of transactions and of the existence, ownership and valuation of assets and liabilities as we consider necessary. We shall obtain an understanding of the accounting and internal financial control systems to the extent necessary in order to assess their adequacy as a basis for the preparation of the Regulatory Accounts and to establish whether appropriate accounting records have been maintained by the Company.

We shall expect to obtain such appropriate evidence as we consider sufficient to enable us to draw reasonable conclusions therefrom. The nature and extent of our procedures will vary according to our assessment of the Company's accounting system and, where we wish to place reliance on it, the internal financial control system and may cover any aspect of the business operations.

[The Regulatory Accounts are prepared by disaggregating balances recorded in the general ledgers and other accounting records of the [name of statutory entity] maintained in accordance with the Companies Act 1985 and used, in accordance with that Act, for the preparation of [name of statutory entity]'s statutory financial statements.]

[No additional tests will be performed of the transactions and balances which are recorded in the general ledgers of [name of statutory entity] other than those carried out in performing the audit of the statutory financial statements that include the Company.]

Our audit includes assessing the significant estimates and judgements made by the Directors in the preparation of the Regulatory Accounts and whether the accounting policies are appropriate to the Company's circumstances, consistently applied and adequately disclosed.

[We will read the [specify information] ('Other Information') contained within the Regulatory Accounts, including any supplementary schedules on which we do not express an audit opinion, and consider the implications for our report if we become aware of any apparent misstatements or material inconsistencies with the Regulatory Accounts. We will not perform any audit procedures nor provide any other assurance on the Other Information.]

We will plan our work to gain reasonable assurance that the Regulatory Accounts are free from material error, whether caused by fraud or other misstatement.

The concept of materiality affects our audit planning and our consideration of matters arising from our audit. We take into account both qualitative and quantitative factors when assessing materiality. We will only express an opinion on the Regulatory Accounts as a whole and not on individual factors/ components within Regulatory Accounts.

Where the Regulator requires specific factors to be reported upon by us, this should be addressed through the powers vested in the Regulator through the Regulatory Licence [or other reference]. For such reporting, we will agree a list of procedures ('Agreed Upon Procedures') that we will perform for the Regulator. These procedures will be specified in a separate engagement contract between us and the Regulator [and will be shown to the Company]. We will report the findings of the Agreed Upon Procedures separately from the Regulatory Accounts opinion, by way of a factual report to the Regulator, in which we will not express an opinion on the results of the Agreed Upon Procedures, nor the appropriateness of those procedures for the purposes of the Regulator. As with the form and content of Regulatory Accounts, the Regulator will need to make its own assessment of the appropriateness of the Agreed Upon Procedures and the reported findings.

Where Agreed Upon Procedures are required in addition to an opinion on the Regulatory Accounts, we may choose not to complete our work nor express an opinion on the Regulatory Accounts until:

- the Agreed Upon Procedures that have been specified by the Regulator have been completed and reported upon; and
- the Regulator has provided a written notice to us confirming that nothing has come to the attention of the Regulator from that report (or otherwise) that indicates that there are any matters which the Regulator believes that we should take into account in arriving at our opinion on the Regulatory Accounts. If such matters do exist we will consider, in arriving at our opinion on the Regulatory Accounts, the matters noted by the Regulator and/or agree additional Agreed Upon Procedures with the Regulator.

The Services are separate from our audit work on the statutory financial statements of the Company which is carried out in accordance with our statutory obligations under the Companies Act 1985. Our audit report on those statutory financial statements is intended for the sole benefit of the Company's shareholders as a group, to whom it is addressed, and not for any other purpose. Our audit of the Company's statutory financial statements are not planned or conducted in contemplation of the requirements of anyone other than such shareholders and, consequently, our audit work is not intended to address or reflect matters in which anyone other than such shareholders may be interested.

We do not and will not, by virtue of this report or otherwise in connection with this engagement, assume any responsibility whether in contract, negligence or otherwise in relation to our audits of the Company's statutory financial statements required by the Companies Act 1985; we and our employees shall have no liability whether in contract, tort (including negligence) or otherwise to any parties other than the Company and its members in relation to our audit of the Company's statutory financial statements.

The nature and format of the Regulatory Accounts are determined by the requirements of the Regulator. It is not appropriate for us to assess, and accordingly we will not make any assessment on, whether the nature of the information being reported upon is suitable or appropriate for the Regulator's purpose. It is a matter for the Regulator to consider whether the information being reported upon is appropriate for its own purposes and we will not give any implicit or explicit affirmation that the information being reported upon is suitable for the Regulator's purpose.

The Regulator and the Company accept that there [may be/are] differences between United Kingdom Generally Accepted Accounting Principles ('UK

GAAP') and the basis of information provided in the Regulatory Accounts. Financial information, other than that prepared on the basis of UK GAAP, does not necessarily represent a true and fair view of the financial performance or financial position of a Company.

Internal audit

In developing our audit plan, we will liaise with the Company's internal auditors to ensure that our work is properly co-ordinated with theirs. It is our policy to rely upon internal audit work whenever possible, whilst ensuring that adequate audit coverage is achieved of all significant areas.

Meetings with the Regulator

We are willing to attend meetings with the Regulator to discuss the Services, if requested to do so, provided that we can agree appropriate terms on which such meetings are held. For the avoidance of doubt appropriate terms will include meeting only on a tri-partite basis in the absence of specific consent of the Company allowing us to meet with the Regulator [and its advisors].

Management representations

The information used by the Directors in preparing the Regulatory Accounts will invariably include facts or judgements which are not themselves recorded in the accounting records. As part of our normal audit procedures, we shall request appropriate Directors or senior officials/management of the company to provide written confirmation each year of such facts or judgements and any other oral representation which we have received during the course of the audit on matters having a material effect on the Regulatory Accounts. We will also ask the Directors to confirm in that letter that all important and relevant information has been brought to our attention. In connection with representations and the supply of information to us generally, we draw your attention to section 389A of the Companies Act 1985 under which it is an offence for an officer of the company to mislead the auditors.

Detection of fraud, error and non-compliance with laws and regulations

The responsibility for safeguarding the assets of the Company and for the prevention and detection of fraud, error and non-compliance with law or regulations rests with the Directors. However, we shall endeavour to plan our audit so that we have a reasonable expectation of detecting material misstatement in the Regulatory Accounts or accounting records (including any material misstatements resulting from fraud, error or non-compliance with law or regulations), but our examination should not be relied upon to disclose all such material misstatements or frauds, errors or instances of non-compliance as may exist.

Timetable

We expect to commence our work on [date] and would normally expect to issue our report by [date].

Completion of our work will depend on receiving, without undue delay, full co-operation from all relevant officials of the Company and their disclosure to us of all the accounting records of the Company and all other records and related information (including certain representations) that we may need for the purpose of our work.

Other requirements
In order to assist us with the examination of the Regulatory Accounts, we shall request early sight of all documents or statements which are due to be issued with those Regulatory Accounts.

Once we have issued our report we have no further direct responsibility in relation to the Regulatory Accounts for that financial year.

Preparation of Regulatory Accounts
Assistance with the preparation of Regulatory Accounts does not form a part of the audit function, but we shall discuss the Company's accounting principles with the management and/or the Directors and we may propose adjusting entries for their consideration.

Other services
We shall not be treated as having notice, for the purposes of our regulatory audit responsibilities, of information provided to members of our firm other than those engaged on the audit (for example information provided in connection with accounting, taxation and other services).

Fiduciary responsibilities
Because our audit work under the terms of this engagement is directed at forming an opinion on the Company's Regulatory Accounts our audit procedures will not formally extend to assets or documents of title in respect of assets that are in the Company's possession but owned by others.

Terms and Conditions
The attached Terms and Conditions set out the duties of all parties in respect of the Services. The Terms and Conditions amongst other things:

- limit our liability to a maximum aggregate amount of £[X]. This limitation shall be allocated between the Company and the Regulator. [It is agreed that such allocation will be entirely a matter for the addressees of this letter, who shall be under no obligation to inform [name of auditor] of it, provided always that if (for whatever reason) no such allocation is agreed, neither the Company nor the Regulator shall dispute the validity, enforceability or operation of the limit of liability on the grounds that no such allocation was agreed]; and
- limit the period within which a claim may be brought.

[Name of auditor] alone will be responsible for the performance of the engagement contract formed by this letter. You therefore agree that you will not bring any claim in respect of or in connection with this engagement whether in contact, tort (including negligence), breach of statutory duty or otherwise against any partner or employee of [name of auditors]. The foregoing exclusion does not apply to any liability that cannot be excluded under the laws of England and Wales.

Fees
[Details]

The fee for the work covered by this engagement letter will be agreed with, and paid by, the Company.

Safeguarding service

It is our desire to provide you at all times with a high quality service to meet your needs. If at any time you would like to discuss with us how our service to you could be improved or if you are dissatisfied with any aspect of our services, please raise the matter immediately with the partner responsible for that aspect of our services to you. If, for any reason, you would prefer to discuss these matters with someone other than that partner, please contact [ ] at [ ]. In this way we are able to ensure that your concerns are dealt with carefully and promptly. We undertake to look into any complaint carefully and promptly and to do all we can to explain the position. This will not affect your right to complain to the Institute of Chartered Accountants in England and Wales.

Acknowledgement and acceptance

Please acknowledge your acceptance of the terms of our engagement under the Contract by signing the confirmation below and returning a copy of this letter and the attached Terms and Conditions to us at the above address, whereupon the Contract will take effect from the date of the commencement by us of the Services.

Once it has been agreed, this letter will remain effective, from one audit appointment to another, until it is replaced.

If you have any questions regarding this Contract, please do not hesitate to contact us.

Yours faithfully

[Name of auditor]

I have read the above letter and accept the terms and conditions set out therein.

Signed

_____ (Name and position)   [date]

for an on behalf of [name of Company]

_____ (Name and position)   [date]

for an on behalf of [name of Regulator]

49.2.2   *Bi-partite engagement contracts*

A bi-partite engagement contract is a written engagement contract between the accountant and the regulated entity only. In order for the accountant to owe a duty of care to the regulator when a bi-partite engagement contract exists, there must be provision in that contract for the accountant to accept a responsibility to the regulator separately in a written notice. The contract will cap any financial liability to the regulator and regulated entity in aggregate to that which would have been paid to the regulated entity if no separate agreement had been made with the regulator.

A copy of the bi-partite engagement contract between the accountant and the regulated entity will be attached to the written notice.

Tables 3 and **4** set out an example bi-partite engagement contract and written notice respectively.

TABLE 3: Example bi-partite engagement contract

Private and Confidential

The Directors

[Name and address of Regulated Entity]

For the attention of [ ]

[Date]

[Name of Regulated Entity] ('the Company')

Audit of the regulatory financial statements for the year ended [date]

Dear Sirs

Introduction

This letter (including the attached Appendices and the Terms and Conditions) sets out our understanding of the basis on which we act as auditors reporting on the regulatory financial statements ('the Regulatory Accounts') as specified in [licence condition or other reference] of the Instrument of Appointment of the Company as a [type of business] under the [applicable legislation] ('the Regulatory Licence') and the Regulatory Accounting Guidelines ('RAGs') [agreed with/] issued by the Director General of [identity of Regulator], [name of Regulator] ('the Regulator'). We also set out the respective areas of responsibility of the directors of the Company ('the Directors') and ourselves, in respect of the audit of the Regulatory Accounts (the 'Services'). This letter (with all its attachments) applies only to the audit report on the Regulatory Accounts and the scope of our work will be limited accordingly. If any additional work or report is required, separate engagement terms and conditions will need to be agreed.

This letter and the attached terms and conditions together comprise the entire contract ('the Contract') for the provision of the Services [to the exclusion of any other express or implied terms, whether expressed orally or in writing including any conditions, warranties and representations unless made fraudulently] and shall supersede all previous contracts, letters of engagement, undertakings, agreements and correspondence regarding the Services.

The Regulator is not a party to the Contract. On condition that the Regulator accepts in writing a notice in the form appended ('the Regulator's Contract'), we will accept duties and responsibilities to the Regulator in respect of our audit work, our audit report and our audit opinion on the Regulatory Accounts. Any such agreement will be on the basis that, amongst other things,

---

the Company and the Regulator agree that our aggregate liability to the Company and the Regulator is limited to the maximum amount which would have been payable to the Company alone in respect of any breach of our obligations to the Company. References to rights and obligations between the Regulator and the auditors in relation to the Services and the Agreed upon Procedures are included in the Contract for the purpose only of the Regulator's Contract and are not intended to create rights or obligations between the Regulator and the Company.

Responsibilities of the Directors and the Auditors
The Directors are required to ensure that the Company complies with all of the terms of its Regulatory Licence [or other reference].

The Directors are required to prepare Regulatory Accounts in accordance with the Company's Regulatory Licence [or other reference] and the RAGs [agreed with/] issued by the Regulator, a copy of which are attached as Appendix [ ]. The Directors are also required to:

- [other licence conditions on which the Directors are required to give a finance-based report per the Regulatory Licence, for example]:
- [confirm that, in their opinion, the Company has sufficient financial and management resources for the next twelve months];
- [confirm that, in their opinion, the Company has sufficient rights and assets which would enable a special administrator to manage the affairs, business and property of the Company];
- [Report to the Director General of [name of Regulator] changes in the Company's activities which may be material in relation to the Company's ability to finance its regulated activities];
- [Undertake the transactions entered into by the business consisting of the carrying out of the regulated activity ('the appointed business'), with or for the benefit of any group companies or related companies ('associated companies') or activities of the appointed business, at arm's length]; and
- [Keep proper accounting records which comply with [licence condition or other reference].

We refer to the above as 'the Specific Obligations'.

Other than reporting on whether or not proper accounting records have been kept by the Company as required by Condition [ ] of the Regulatory Licence [or other reference], it is not our responsibility in providing the Services to report on the Specific Obligations or on any other obligations of the Company or the Directors under the Regulatory Licence [or other reference].

The Directors are also responsible for ensuring that the Company maintains accounting records which disclose with reasonable accuracy, at any time, the financial position of the company, and for preparing Regulatory Accounts which present the results of the Company fairly in accordance with the Regulatory Licence. They are also responsible for making available to us, as and when required, all of the Company's accounting records, all other relevant records, including minutes of all directors', management and shareholders' meetings, and such information and explanations which we consider necessary for the performance of our duties as auditors.

It is our responsibility to form an independent opinion, based on our audit, on the Regulatory Accounts and to report our opinion to the Company and the Regulator.

Our report will be made in accordance with the Contract, solely to the Company and the Regulator in accordance with the Regulatory Licence [or other reference]. Our audit work will be undertaken so that we might state to the Company and the Regulator those matters we have agreed in the Contract to state to them in our report in order to (a) assist the Company to [meet its obligations under the Regulatory Licence to procure such a report] and (b) to facilitate the carrying out by the Regulator of its regulatory functions, and for no other purpose. To the fullest extent permitted by law, we will not accept or assume responsibility to anyone other than the Company for our audit work, for our report, or for the opinions we will form. Our report will contain a disclaimer of liability to all other parties but we will confirm acceptance in our report of responsibility in respect of our audit work to the Regulator also if the Regulator has agreed to the Regulator's Contract by signing the written notice appended.

Our report will be addressed to the Company and the Regulator to meet the requirements of the Regulatory Licence and will state whether, in our opinion the Regulatory Accounts present fairly in accordance with conditions [ ], [ ] and [ ] of the Company's Regulatory Licence [or other reference] the state of the Company's affairs at [date] and of its profit (or loss) for the year then ended, and have been properly prepared in accordance with conditions [ ], [ ] and [ ] of that licence [or other reference].

The Contract does not confer benefits on any parties who are not parties to it and the application of the Contracts (Rights of Third Parties) Act 1999 is excluded.

In arriving at our opinion, and in accordance with the Regulatory Licence (condition [reference]) [or other reference], we will consider the following matters, and report on any in respect of which we are not satisfied:

- whether appropriate accounting records have been kept by the Company and proper returns adequate for our audit have been received from operating locations not visited by us;
- whether the Regulatory Accounts are in agreement with the accounting records and returns retained for the purpose of preparing the Regulatory Accounts; and
- whether we have obtained all the information and explanations which we consider necessary for the purpose of our audit.

Our responsibilities also include:

- providing in our report a description of the Directors' responsibilities for the Regulatory Accounts where the Regulatory Accounts or accompanying information do not include such a description; and
- considering whether other information in documents containing the Regulatory Accounts is consistent with those Regulatory Accounts.

The Company and (where the Regulator signs the written notice appended) the Regulator acknowledge and agree that:

- wherever the Regulatory Accounts or other Regulatory Information covered by the Independent Accountants' report are published or otherwise made available in full, our audit report will also be published or otherwise made available in full as part of that communication;
- wherever substantial extracts from the Regulatory Accounts or other Regulatory Information covered by the Independent Accountants' report are published or otherwise made available, and reference is made to the fact that they are audited or otherwise examined by an Independent Accountant, there will be explicit statements by the Regulator: (a) that the information published is only an extract; and (b) about the limitation of scope of the Independent Accountants' report and the duty of care owed by the Independent Accountants; and (c) referring to where the full set of Regulatory Accounts can be found or otherwise obtained; and
- wherever any other information is referenced from the Regulatory Accounts or other Regulatory Information covered by the Independent Accountants' report, there will be an explicit reference by the Regulator to the source of that information and the limitation of scope of the Independent Accounts' report and the duty of care owed by the Independent Accountant.

Where the Regulator does not sign a written notice in the form appended, the Company will procure that these events take place in the circumstances identified.

Relationship between the Regulator and the Company

For the avoidance of doubt, nothing in this Contract is intended to nor does it affect or in any way alter the relationship or the rights and obligations between the Company and the Regulator as set out in the Regulatory Licence [and all relevant legislation].

Scope of our audit

Our audit will be performed with regard to the guidance contained in Audit 05/ 03 *Reporting to Regulators of Regulated Entities* issued by the Institute of Chartered Accountants in England and Wales.

Our audit will be conducted in accordance with International Standards on Auditing (UK and Ireland) issued by the Auditing Practices Board except that, as the nature, form and content of Regulatory Accounts are determined by the Regulator, we will not evaluate the overall adequacy of the presentation of the information, which would have been required if we were to express an audit opinion under International Standards on Auditing (UK and Ireland). Our audit will include such tests of transactions and of the existence, ownership and valuation of assets and liabilities as we consider necessary. We shall obtain an understanding of the accounting and internal financial control systems to the extent necessary in order to assess their adequacy as a basis for the preparation of the Regulatory Accounts and to establish whether appropriate accounting records have been maintained by the Company.

We shall expect to obtain such appropriate evidence as we consider sufficient to enable us to draw reasonable conclusions therefrom. The nature and extent of our procedures will vary according to our assessment of the Company's accounting system and, where we wish to place reliance on it, the internal financial control system and may cover any aspect of the business operations.

[The Regulatory Accounts are prepared by disaggregating balances recorded in the general ledgers and other accounting records of the [name of statutory entity] maintained in accordance with the Companies Act 1985 and used, in accordance with that Act, for the preparation of [name of statutory entity]'s statutory financial statements.]

[No additional tests will be performed of the transactions and balances which are recorded in the general ledgers of [name of statutory entity] other than those carried out in performing the audit of the statutory financial statements that include the Company.]

Our audit includes assessing the significant estimates and judgements made by the Directors in the preparation of the Regulatory Accounts and whether the accounting policies are appropriate to the Company's circumstances, consistently applied and adequately disclosed.

[We will read the [specify information] ('Other Information') contained within the Regulatory Accounts, including any supplementary schedules on which we do not express an audit opinion, and consider the implications for our report if we become aware of any apparent misstatements or material inconsistencies with the Regulatory Accounts. We will not perform any audit procedures nor provide any other assurance on the Other Information.]

We will plan our work to gain reasonable assurance that the Regulatory Accounts are free from material error, whether caused by fraud or other misstatement.

The concept of materiality affects our audit planning and our consideration of matters arising from our audit. We take into account both qualitative and quantitative factors when assessing materiality. We will only express an opinion on the Regulatory Accounts as a whole and not on individual factors/ components within Regulatory Accounts.

Where the Regulator requires specific factors to be reported upon by us, this should be addressed through the powers vested in the Regulator through the Regulatory Licence [or other reference]. For such reporting, we will agree a list of procedures ('Agreed Upon Procedures') that we will perform for the Regulator. These procedures will be specified in a separate engagement contract between us and the Regulator [and will be shown to the Company]. We will report the findings of the Agreed Upon Procedures separately from the Regulatory Accounts opinion, by way of a factual report to the Regulator, in which we will not express an opinion on the results of the Agreed Upon Procedures, nor the appropriateness of those procedures for the purposes of the Regulator. As with the form and content of Regulatory Accounts, the Regulator will need to make its own assessment of the appropriateness of the Agreed Upon Procedures and the reported findings.

Where Agreed Upon Procedures are required in addition to an opinion on the Regulatory Accounts, we may choose not to complete our work nor express an opinion on the Regulatory Accounts until:

- the Agreed Upon Procedures that have been specified by the Regulatory have been completed and reported upon; and
- the Regulator has provided a written notice to us confirming that nothing has come to the attention of the Regulator from that report (or otherwise) that indicates that there are any matters which the Regulator believes that we should take into account in arriving at our opinion on the Regulatory Accounts. If such matters do exist we will consider, in arriving at our opinion on the Regulatory Accounts, the matters noted by the Regulator and/or agree additional Agreed Upon Procedures with the Regulator.

The Services are separate from our audit work on the statutory financial statements of the Company which is carried out in accordance with our statutory obligations under the Companies Act 1985. Our audit report on those statutory financial statements is intended for the sole benefit of the Company's shareholders as a group, to whom it is addressed, and not for any other purpose. Our audit of the Company's statutory financial statements are not planned or conducted in contemplation of the requirements of anyone other than such shareholders and, consequently, our audit work is not intended to address or reflect matters in which anyone other than such shareholders may be interested.

We do not and will not, by virtue of this report or otherwise in connection with this engagement, assume any responsibility whether in contract, negligence or otherwise in relation to our audits of the Company's statutory financial statements required by the Companies Act 1985; we and our employees shall have no liability whether in contract, tort (including negligence) or otherwise to any parties other than the Company and its members in relation to our audit of the Company's statutory financial statements.

The nature and format of the Regulatory Accounts are determined by the requirements of the Regulator. It is not appropriate for us to assess, and accordingly we will not make any assessment on, whether the nature of the information being reported upon is suitable or appropriate for the Regulator's purpose. It is a matter for the Regulator to consider whether the information being reported upon is appropriate for its own purposes and we will not give any implicit or explicit affirmation that the information being reported upon is suitable for the Regulator's purpose.

There [may be/are] differences between United Kingdom Generally Accepted Accounting Principles ('UK GAAP') and the basis of information provided in the Regulatory Accounts. Financial information, other than that prepared on the basis of UK GAAP, does not necessarily represent a true and fair view of the financial performance or financial position of a Company.

Internal audit
In developing our audit plan, we will liaise with the Company's internal auditors to ensure that our work is properly co-ordinated with theirs. It is our

policy to rely upon internal audit work whenever possible, whilst ensuring that adequate audit coverage is achieved of all significant areas.

Meetings with the Regulator
We are willing to attend meetings with the Regulator to discuss the Services, if requested to do so, provided that we can agree appropriate terms on which such meetings are held. For the avoidance of doubt appropriate terms will include meeting only on a tri-partite basis in the absence of specific consent of the Company allowing us to meet with the Regulator [and its advisors].

Management representations
The information used by the Directors in preparing the Regulatory Accounts will invariably include facts or judgements which are not themselves recorded in the accounting records. As part of our normal audit procedures, we shall request appropriate Directors or senior officials/management of the company to provide written confirmation each year of such facts or judgements and any other oral representation which we have received during the course of the audit on matters having a material effect on the Regulatory Accounts. We will also ask the Directors to confirm in that letter that all important and relevant information has been brought to our attention. In connection with representations and the supply of information to us generally, we draw your attention to section 389A of the Companies Act 1985 under which it is an offence for an officer of the company to mislead the auditors.

Detection of fraud, error and non-compliance with laws and regulations
The responsibility for safeguarding the assets of the Company and for the prevention and detection of fraud, error and non-compliance with law or regulations rests with the Directors. However, we shall endeavour to plan our audit so that we have a reasonable expectation of detecting material misstatement in the Regulatory Accounts or accounting records (including any material misstatements resulting from fraud, error or non-compliance with law or regulations), but our examination should not be relied upon to disclose all such material misstatements or frauds, errors or instances of non-compliance as may exist.

Timetable
We expect to commence our work on [date] and would normally expect to issue our report by [date].
Completion of our work will depend on receiving, without undue delay, full co-operation from all relevant officials of the Company and their disclosure to us of all the accounting records of the Company and all other records and related information (including certain representations) that we may need for the purpose of our work.

Other requirements
In order to assist us with the examination of the Regulatory Accounts, we shall request early sight of all documents or statements which are due to be issued with those Regulatory Accounts.

Once we have issued our report we have no further direct responsibility in relation to the Regulatory Accounts for that financial year.

Preparation of Regulatory Accounts

Assistance with the preparation of Regulatory Accounts does not form a part of the audit function, but we shall discuss the Company's accounting principles with the management and/or the Directors and we may propose adjusting entries for their consideration.

Other services

We shall not be treated as having notice, for the purposes of our regulatory audit responsibilities, of information provided to members of our firm other than those engaged on the audit (for example information provided in connection with accounting, taxation and other services).

Fiduciary responsibilities

Because our audit work under the terms of this engagement is directed at forming an opinion on the Company's Regulatory Accounts our audit procedures will not formally extend to assets or documents of title in respect of assets that are in the Company's possession but owned by others.

Terms and Conditions

The attached Terms and Conditions set out the duties of all parties in respect of the Services. The Terms and Conditions amongst other things:

- limit our liability to a maximum aggregate amount of £[X]. Where the Regulator accepts in writing a notice in the form appended (and on that basis we accept duties and responsibilities to the Regulator), this limitation shall be allocated between the Company and the Regulator. [It is agreed that such allocation will be entirely a matter for the addressees of this letter, who shall be under no obligation to inform [name of auditor] of it, provided always that if (for whatever reason) no such allocation is agreed, neither the Company nor the Regulator shall dispute the validity, enforceability or operation of the limit of liability on the grounds that no such allocation was agreed]; and
- limit the period within which a claim may be brought.

[Name of auditor] alone will be responsible for the performance of the engagement contract formed by this letter. You therefore agree that you will not bring any claim in respect of or in connection with this engagement whether in contact, tort (including negligence), breach of statutory duty or otherwise against any partner or employee of [name of auditors]. The foregoing exclusion does not apply to any liability that cannot be excluded under the laws of England and Wales.

Fees

[Details]

The fee for the work covered by this engagement letter will be agreed with, and paid by, the Company.

Safeguarding service

It is our desire to provide you at all times with a high quality service to meet your needs. If at any time you would like to discuss with us how our service to you could be improved or if you are dissatisfied with any aspect of our services, please raise the matter immediately with the partner responsible for that aspect of our services to you. If, for any reason, you would prefer to discuss these matters with someone other than that partner, please contact [ ] at [ ]. In this way we are able to ensure that your concerns are dealt with carefully and promptly. We undertake to look into any complaint carefully and promptly and to do all we can to explain the position. This will not affect your right to complain to the Institute of Chartered Accountants in England and Wales.

Acknowledgement and acceptance

Please acknowledge your acceptance of the terms of our engagement under the Contract by signing the confirmation below and returning a copy of this letter and the attached Terms and Conditions to us at the above address, whereupon the Contract will take effect from the date of the commencement by us of the Services.

Once it has been agreed, this letter will remain effective, from one audit appointment to another, until it is replaced.

If you have any questions regarding this Contract, please do not hesitate to contact us.

Yours faithfully

[Name of auditor]

I have read the above letter and accept the terms and conditions set out therein.

Signed

_____ (Name and position)   [date]

for an on behalf of [name of Company]

TABLE 4: Example written notice

Private and Confidential

The Director General

[Name and address of Regulator]

For the attention of [ ]

[Date]

[Name of Regulated Entity] ('the Company')

Audit of the regulatory financial statements for the year ended [date]

Dear Sirs

We refer to our engagement letter with the Company dated [date] ('the Contract') relating to our audit of the Company's regulatory financial statements for the year ended [date] ('the Regulatory Accounts'). A copy of the Contract is attached as Appendix 1 to this letter.

In the Contract we set out the basis on which we will act as auditors reporting on the Regulatory Accounts of the Company, together with the respective areas of responsibility of the directors of the Company and ourselves in respect of that audit and the scope of our audit. We also set out in the Contract the agreed extent of our liability to the Company in respect of our work. We confirm in the Contract that we will address our report on the Regulatory Accounts to the Company and, in order to meet the requirements of the Regulatory Licence, to you as well but we clarify that in our report we will deny liability in respect of our audit work and our report to any party other than the Company.

You have confirmed your interest in our audit of the Regulatory Accounts in your capacity as the Company's Regulator and your interest in the scope of our engagement agreed with the Company. You have asked us to accept responsibility for our audit work and our report to you as well as to the Company so that there is no denial of responsibility to you in our report. This letter ('the Regulator's Contract') sets out the basis on which we are willing to accept such a responsibility, in return for your agreement to the terms of this letter including the following:

- Our duties and responsibilities to you and your obligations to us will be those set out in the Contract as incorporated into this letter. This sets out, amongst other things, terms relating to the disclosure of the Regulatory Accounts and other Regulatory Information covered by the Independent Accountants' Report.
- Our aggregate liability to you will be strictly limited to £[ ] in the event of any breach of our obligations to you under the Regulator's Contract.
- You do not wish to acquire rights against us in respect of use of the audit report for any purposes other than as the Company's Regulator and accept the disclaimer of liability to any Third Party (being a person other than the Company or the Regulator) as set out in the Contract.
- You accept that the nature and format of the Regulatory Accounts are determined by your requirements and that it will be for you to consider whether the information on which we report as auditors is suitable or appropriate for your needs and purposes.
- You will not be bound by any amendment to the Contract, whether written, oral or arising from the Contract, which is not formally accepted by you in writing.

Please acknowledge your acceptance of the terms and conditions of this by signing the confirmation below and returning a copy of it and the Contract to us at the above address.

Yours faithfully

[Independent Accountants]

I have read the above letter and accept the terms and conditions on behalf of [name of Regulator].

Signed

_____ (Name and position)   [date]

[cc: The Directors, [name of Company]

Enclosure: Copy of the Contract

49.3   REPORTING

Each regulator will stipulate in its regulatory licence the information to be included in reports it receives and state that the report should be accompanied by an independent accountants' report.

The report should follow the guidelines set out in ISA (UK and Ireland) 700 *The Auditor's Report on Financial Statements* (see **Chapter 3**). An example is given in **Table 5**, which should be modified for the particular circumstances of the engagement.

Accountants should make clear in their report the regulatory information on which they are providing assurance, and that on which they are not. Where the regulatory information is part of a wider report or return, the material covered by the accountants' report should be clearly identified.

TABLE 5:   Example unqualified independent accountants' report

Independent Accountants' Report to the Director General, [Regulator] ('the Regulator') and ABC Limited

We have audited the Regulatory Accounts of ABC Limited ('the Company') on pages [x to x] which comprise the profit and loss account, the statement of total recognised gains and losses, the balance sheet, [the cashflow statement] and the related notes to the Regulatory Accounts.

This report is made, on terms that have been agreed, solely to the Company and the Regulator in order to meet [the requirements of the Regulatory Licence]. Our audit work has been undertaken so that we might state to the Company and the Regulator those matters that we have agreed to state to them in our report, in order (a) to assist the Company to [meet its obligation under the Regulatory Licence to procure such a report] and (b) to facilitate the carrying out by the Regulator of its regulatory functions, and for no other purpose. To the fullest extent permitted by law, we do not accept or assume responsibility to anyone other than the Company and the Regulator, for our audit work, for this report or for the opinions we have formed.

Basis of preparation
The Regulatory Accounts have been prepared under the historical cost convention (as modified by the revaluation of certain fixed assets) and in accordance with conditions [ ], [ ] and [ ] of the Company's Regulatory Licence, Regulatory Accounting Guidelines [ ], [ ] and [ ] ('the RAGs') issued by the Regulator and the accounting policies set out in the statement of accounting policies.

The Regulatory Accounts are separate from the statutory financial statements of the Company and have not been prepared under the basis of Generally Accepted Accounting Principles in the United Kingdom ('UK GAAP'). Financial information other than that prepared on the basis of UK GAAP does not necessarily represent a true and fair view of the financial performance or

---

financial position of a company as shown in financial statements prepared in accordance with the Companies Act 1985.

Respective responsibilities of the Regulator, the Directors and Auditors
The nature, form and content of Regulatory Accounts are determined to the Regulator. It is not appropriate for us to assess whether the nature of the information being reported upon is suitable or appropriate for the Regulator's purposes. Accordingly we make no such assessment.

The directors' responsibilities for preparing the Regulatory Accounts in accordance with conditions [ ], [ ] and [ ] of the Regulatory Licence are set out in the statement of directors' responsibilities on page [x].

Our responsibility is to audit the Regulatory Accounts in accordance with International Standards on Auditing (UK and Ireland), issued by the Auditing Practices Board, except as stated in the 'Basis of audit opinion', below and having regard to the guidance contained in Audit 05/03 *Reporting to Regulators of Regulated Entities.*

We report our opinion as to whether the Regulatory Accounts present fairly, in accordance with conditions [ ], [ ] and [ ] of the Company's Regulatory Licence, the RAGs [ ], [ ] and [ ], and the accounting policies set out on page [x], the results and financial position of the company. We also report to you if, in our opinion, the Company has not kept proper accounting records or if we have not received all the information and explanations we require for our audit.

[We read the other information contained within the Regulatory Accounts, including any supplementary schedules on which we do not express an audit opinion, and consider the implications for our report if we become aware of any apparent misstatements or material inconsistencies with the Regulatory Accounts.]

Basis of audit opinion
We conducted our audit in accordance with International Standards on Auditing (UK and Ireland) issued by the Auditing Practices Board except as noted below. An audit includes examination, on a test basis, of evidence relevant to the amounts and disclosures in the Regulatory Accounts. It also includes an assessment of the significant estimates and judgements made by the Directors in the preparation of the Regulatory Accounts, and of whether the accounting policies are consistently applied and adequately disclosed.

We planned and performed our audit so as to obtain all the information and explanations which we considered necessary in order to provide us with sufficient evidence to give reasonable assurance that the Regulatory Accounts are free from material misstatement, whether caused by fraud or other irregularity or error. However, as the nature, form and content of Regulatory Accounts are determined by the Regulator, we did not evaluate the overall adequacy of the presentation of the information, which would have been required if we were to express an audit opinion under International Standards on Auditing (UK and Ireland).

Our opinion on the Regulatory Accounts is separate from our opinion on the statutory accounts of the Company on which we reported on [date], which are prepared for a different purpose. Our audit report in relation to the statutory accounts of the Company (our 'Statutory' audit) was made solely to the Company's members, as a body, in accordance with section 235 of the Companies Act 1985. Our Statutory audit work was undertaken so that we might state to the Company's members those matters we are required to state to them in a Statutory auditor's report and for no other purpose. In these circumstances, to the fullest extent permitted by law, we do not accept or assume any responsibility to anyone other than the Company and the Company's members as a body, for our Statutory audit work, for our Statutory audit report, or for the opinions we have formed in respect of that Statutory audit.

Opinion
In our opinion the Regulatory Accounts:

- fairly present in accordance with conditions [ ], [ ] and [ ] of the Company's Regulatory Licence, Regulatory Accounting Guidelines [ ], [ ] and [ ], and the accounting policies set out on page [x], the state of the Company's affairs at [date] and of its profit (or loss) [and cashflow] for the year then ended; and
- have been properly prepared in accordance with those conditions, guidelines and accounting policies.

[Name of auditor]

[Chartered Accountants and Registered Auditors]

[Address]

[Date]

49.4 MATERIALITY

Increasingly regulators are requiring entities to include a number of different analyses of their business segments or operations and for accountants to report on them. In order to do this accountants must use their professional judgement to assess materiality in the context of the regulatory accounts as a whole and in line with the principles outlined in ISA (UK and Ireland) 320 *Audit Materiality*, see **Chapter 18**. Their opinion should be on the regulatory accounts as a whole, not on the individual analyses.

If the regulator requires specific items to be reported on in detail, this should form the basis of a separate, 'agreed upon procedures' engagement, which is reported on separately to the opinion on the accounts.

49.5   WORKING WITH INDEPENDENT EXPERTS

Accountants may need to rely on the work of independent experts when reporting on regulatory accounts and other regulatory information, such as technical or engineering experts to determine whether the cost of projects should be capitalised or expensed.

Where this is the case, the accountants would follow the guidance in ISA (UK and Ireland) 620 *Using the Work of an Expert* (see **Chapter 39**), and would not refer to the expert's work in their audit report. If an 'agreed upon procedures' engagement is undertaken and no opinion is given in the accountants' report, reference to the expert's work is likely. Consent should be obtained from the expert prior to issuing any report which refers to them or includes extracts of their work.

50 INVESTMENT CIRCULAR REPORTING

50.1 LEGAL BACKGROUND

Generally when shares are offered to the public for the first time, or when a company whose shares are listed on the Stock Exchange or traded on AIM enters into a major transaction, an investment circular is required which contains relevant financial information.

This information is accompanied by an accountants' report from a reporting accountant engaged specifically for the purpose. The term 'reporting accountant' may include the company's auditors where they are carrying out a role in connection with an investment circular, rather than their role as auditors reporting on the financial statements.

50.2 GUIDANCE

Until the issue of the Standards for Investment Reporting (SIRs) (previously named Statements of Investment Circular Reporting Standards) the only guidance came from Auditing Guideline *Prospectuses and the Reporting Accountant*. The current SIRs are:

- SIR 1000 – *Investment Reporting Standards Applicable to all Engagements Involving an Investment Circular*;
- SIR 2000 – *Investment Reporting Standards Applicable to Public Reporting Engagements on Historical Financial Information*;
- SIR 3000 – *Investment Reporting Standards Applicable to Public Reporting Engagements on Profit Forecasts*; and
- SIR 4000 – *Investment Reporting Standards Applicable to Public Reporting Engagements on Pro Forma Financial Information*.

SIRs 1000 and 2000 are effective for reports signed after 31 August 2005 and SIRs 3000 and 4000 for reports signed after 31 March 2006.

SIR 4000 updates guidance issued in Bulletin 1998/8 *Reporting on Pro*

Forma Information Pursuant to the Listing Rules. Whilst the Bulletin has not yet been officially withdrawn, we comment on SIR 4000 rather than the Bulletin as it contains the most up to date guidance.

- SIRs 1000 and 2000 were revised in 2005 following the implementation of the Prospective Directive and FSA's review of the Listing Regime. The revised FSA rules came into force on 1 July 2005 and had a significant effect on the work undertaken by reporting accountants. This is particularly so in relation to historical financial information.

Under the revised rules the issuers, rather than the reporting accountants, are responsible for preparing and presenting historical financial information and the reporting accountant's role will be to express an opinion on whether the information presents a true and fair view.

In October 2006, the APB issued the *Ethical Standard for Reporting Accountants* (ESRA). This document follows the format used for the Ethical Standards discussed in **Chapter 2**, and is applicable for all engagements where SIRs are used. It is detailed in **50.8** below. The ESRA replaces Bulletin 2005/7, *Integrity, Objectivity and Independence – guidance for Reporting Accountants undertaking engagements in connection with an investment circular* which was issued in July 2005 as an interim measure to provide limited ethical guidance so that reporting accountants could meet the requirement of SIR 1000 to consider ethical standards when deciding whether to accept or continue with an engagement.

In November 1998, Bulletin 1998/8 *Reporting on Pro Forma Information Pursuant to the Listing Rules* was issued. This provides guidance on the requirement under the Listing Rules for an issuer's reporting accountant to provide an opinion on the pro forma information to be included in an investment circular and is discussed in **50.7** below.

In April 2006, the Audit and Assurance Faculty of the ICAEW issued a technical release AAF 02/06, *Identifying and managing certain risks arising from the inclusion of reports from auditors and accountants in prospectuses (and certain other investments circulars)* to provide guidance for reporting accountants. It develops the principles set out in Audit 1/03 *The audit report and auditors' duty of care to third parties*, which was issued following the Bannerman case (see **3.18**). It is detailed in **50.9** below.

50.3   STRUCTURE OF THE SIRS

The format of the SIRs is similar to that of the ISAs (UK and Ireland) with standards in bold type and further explanatory material in normal type. However, they are a separate series because the work of reporting accountants encompasses more than auditing and is not within the audit regulation regime.

Reporting accountants undertake a wide range of engagements, split into 'public reporting engagements', where a reporting accountant expresses a conclusion that is published in an investments circular and 'other reporting engagements' which typically involve reporting privately to an issue, sponsor or regulator.

Public reporting engagements are themselves of two types:

- those analogous to audits, where the reporting accountant's opinion is in terms of a 'true and fair' view on historical financial information (covered by ED SIR 2000); and
- those where the reporting accountant's conclusion is expressed as to whether financial information has been properly compiled.

50.4 SIR 1000

50.4.1 General

SIR 1000, *Investment Reporting Standards Applicable to all Engagements Involving an Investment Circular* is an overarching SIR setting out basic principles and essential procedures that apply to all engagements involving an investment circular.

50.4.2 Acceptance and continuance

SIR 1000 states that auditors can only accept or continue an engagement if nothing has come to their attention to indicate that the requirements of relevant ethical standards will not be satisfied. The *Ethical Standard for Reporting Accountants* (ESRA) was issued by the APB in October 2006. This is detailed in **50.8** below.

Reporting accountants should only accept or continue with an engagement if the scope of the engagement is sufficient to support the required report, they will be able to carry out the procedures required by the SIRs and they have personnel with the necessary professional experience and expertise to carry out that work.

50.4.3 Terms of the engagement

SIR 1000.4 states that specific terms of engagement should be agreed in writing with the instructing party. This may be either in the form of a letter of instruction from that party which is confirmed by the reporting accountants or a letter prepared by the reporting accountants and accepted by the other party.

The engagement letter should summarise:

- the obligations and responsibilities of the respective parties;
- the scope of the engagement; and
- the form of the report(s) to be given.

The engagement letter should encompass the whole of the reporting accountants' contractual responsibilities to those instructing them. The guidance to the SIR notes that it is important to clarify the requirements of the directors and the sponsors, together with the scope and content of the reports and letters at the earliest possible stage.

SIR 1000.4 states that the engagement letter should specify:

- those reports intended for publication;
- other reports that are required; and
- to whom all the reports should be addressed.

This restricts the use of the reports to those mentioned in the engagement letter.

The guidance notes that it is important that the scope of the reporting accountants' work is defined realistically. The engagement letter sets out the contractual responsibilities and reporting accountants should not accept responsibility for matters or entities in respect of which they are not specifically instructed, nor report on matters which fall into other advisers' areas of expertise.

In preparing their report, reporting accountants will need to rely on evidence supplied by, and representations from, the entity's directors, its employees or its agents. The engagement letter should limit the extent of the reporting accountants' responsibility where information which is material to their task is withheld or concealed from them or misrepresented to them. Where reporting accountants are aware of any such concealment they should inform the directors and sponsors as soon as is practicable.

Any subsequent changes to the terms of the engagement should be agreed in writing.

50.4.4 Independence and ethical standards

When conducting any engagement in connection with an investment circular, SIR 1000.5 requires reporting accountants to comply with the ethical standards issued by the APB and their professional body. These are contained in the *Ethical Standard for Reporting Accountants*, see **50.8**, and reporting accountants should be mindful of their requirements when performing their work.

50.4.5 Legal and regulatory requirements

As with an audit, the reporting accountant should be familiar with the applicable laws and regulations governing the report to be given.

50.4.6 Quality control

There are two SIRs on quality control which require:

- the reporting accountant to comply with the requirements of ISQC (UK and Ireland) 1 and ISA (UK and Ireland) 220 (see **Chapter 20**); and
- a partner with appropriate experience be involved in any work concerning an investment circular.

This would mean *inter alia* that some form of hot review would be necessary, see **20.3.7**.

50.4.7 Planning and execution

Reporting accountants should 'develop and document a plan for their work so as to perform the engagement in an effective manner' (SIR 1000.9). The objective of planning is to:

- assess whether the timescale is realistic;
- ensure that appropriate attention is directed to the various aspects of the engagement;
- ensure that potential problems are identified and procedures are designed to deal with them;
- consider the need for the involvement of specialists; and
- facilitate review.

The plan should be amended as necessary as work progresses, and these changes should be documented.

An initial plan should be prepared to document the chosen approach. At this stage a preliminary review of the information available, together with previous audit opinions may indicate issues which could lead to a qualification or modification of the report. Such issues should be reported to the entity and the sponsors immediately.

An appropriate level of materiality should be set, except in agreed-upon procedures engagements, where materiality may be determined for the reporting accountant.

Reporting accountants should obtain sufficient appropriate evidence under SIR 1000.11 on which to base their opinions, reports or letters. Evidence will be obtained from a variety of techniques including:

- inspection;
- observation;
- enquiry;
- computation; and
- analytical procedures.

The choice of procedures will depend on the circumstances of the engagement and the report being given in the context of the overall investment circular. The reporting accountant will obtain written confirmation of representations made by the entity's directors.

If evidence is withheld, concealed or otherwise misrepresented, the reporting accountant should consider whether this fact should be reported, and seek legal advice as necessary.

50.4.8   Documentation

The working papers should document:

- evidence that supports the report given and that the engagement was performed in accordance with SIRs; and
- reasoning on all significant matters that require the exercise of judgement, and the conclusions thereon.

The form of working papers will depend on:

- the nature of the engagement;
- the form of the report and the opinion, if any, to be given;
- the nature and complexity of the entity's business;
- the nature and condition of the entity's accounting and internal control system;
- the needs, in the particular circumstances, for direction, supervision and review of the work of members of the reporting accountants' team; and
- the specific methodology and technology that the reporting accountants use.

The guidance notes that working papers should be designed and organised to meet the circumstances and the reporting accountants' needs for each part of the engagement.

50.4.9   Professional scepticism

SIR 1000.16 requires the reporting accountant to plan and perform the engagement with an 'attitude of professional scepticism' to ensure that they make a critical assessment of the evidence obtained. They should remain alert to contradictory evidence and consider explanations received in the context of findings from other areas of their work.

50.4.10   Reporting

SIR 1000.17 covers the content of the reporting accountants' report, which should:

- be addressed only to those identified in the engagement letter or to the relevant regulatory body;
- identify the information to which the report relates;
- address all matters that are required by the engagement letter;
- explain the basis of the report or opinion;
- give a clear expression of opinion;
- include the reporting accountants' signature;
- include the reporting accountant's address; and
- state the date of the report or letter.

The engagement letter usually sets out the form of the report to be issued, and the report is normally signed and dated on the same date as the directors authorise the issue of the investment circular.

In all public reporting engagements the reporting accountant's report will include:

- a statement of compliance with SIRs; and
- a summary description of the work performed by the reporting accountant.

The level of assurance provided by a reporting accountant's report will vary from engagement to engagement. Therefore, the report should clarify the scope of the opinion or the level of assurance provided.

50.4.11   Modified opinions

The reporting accountant must give a modified opinion if there is a limitation on the scope of their work or where the outcome is materially misstated. In some situations, regulations will not allow the giving of a qualified opinion. Where this is the case, the reporting accountant will be unable to report, and should discuss with the party to whom the report is to be given, whether information in the investment circular can be amended to remove the obstacle to issuing an unmodified report, or whether the information itself can be omitted from the circular.

50.4.12 Pre-existing financial information

Where the issuer already has audited financial statements or audited or reviewed financial information which meets the needs of the investment circular, the audit firm is not required to consent to the inclusion of its earlier reports in the circular.

50.4.13 Consent

In certain cases, reporting accountants are required to give consent for the inclusion of their report or their name in the investment circular. SIR 1000.21 states that in these circumstances, before giving their consent, reporting accountants should consider their report in the form and context in which it appears. This involves:

- comparing their report with other information in the document to ensure that there is no inconsistency; and
- assessing whether they have any cause to believe any information in the investment circular to be misleading.

The SIR continues by requiring reporting accountants, where there is inconsistency or misleading information, to withhold their consent until the investment circular has been appropriately amended.

The reporting accountant should not give their consent for any of their reports to be included in the investment circular until all of their reports in that circular have been finalised.

The requirement for reporting accountants to give consent for the inclusion of their report comes from the relevant regulations governing the engagement. These are:

- the Prospectus Rules – which require that where a statement from an expert, including reporting accountants, is given in a document their consent is obtained and that this is stated in the document;
- the Listing Rules and the AIM rules– these have the same requirements as the Prospectus Rules for listings not subject to those Rules;
- Listing Rule 13.4.1(6) – which requires an expert to consent to the inclusion in any Class 1 circular of any report, letter or statement provided or made by that expert; and
- the City Code – which requires that where a takeover document includes an accountants' report on a profit forecast included in that document, it should be accompanied by a statement that the reporting accountants have given, and not withdrawn, their consent to publication. Any subsequent documents containing the report must include a statement that they have no objection to their report continuing to apply.

An example consent letter is given in **Table 1**.

TABLE 1: Example consent letter

The Directors

Issuer plc

Dear Sirs

We hereby give our consent to the inclusion in the Prospectus/Listing Particulars dated [...] issued by ABC plc of [our accountant's report]/[our letter relating to the profit estimate for the year ended 200X]/[our letter relating to the pro forma financial information for the year ended 200X] dated [...] [and the reference to our name] in the form and context in which [it]/[they] are included, as shown in the enclosed proof of the Prospectus/Listing Particulars which we have signed for identification.

Our consent is required by [provision requiring consent] and is given for the purpose of complying with that provision and for no other purpose.

[We also hereby authorise the contents of the [report]/[and]/[letters] referred to above included in the Prospectus for the purposes of Prospectus Rule [5.5.3R (2) (f)] [5.5.4R (2) (f)] *or* [We also hereby authorise the contents of the [report[s]] referred to above which [is/are] included in the Listing Particulars for the purposes of Regulation 6(1)(e) of the Financial Services and Markets Act 2000 (Official Listing of Securities) Regulations 2001.] *or* [We also hereby authorise the contents of the reports[s] referred to above which [is/are] included in the Admission Document for the purposes of Schedule Two to the AIM Rules]

Yours faithfully

Reporting Accountant

Consent is not required for documents already in the public domain unless it is with regard to an earlier report or opinion which is being repeated or referred to again. Where this is the case, the reporting accountants should ensure that there have been no events in the intervening period which mean that their report might require modification.

Although consent letters do not extend their responsibilities beyond their report, reporting accountants should be aware of the other parts of the document and consider whether there are any inconsistencies with their report.

Consent letters should be dated the same day as the relevant document.

50.4.14   *Events after the reporting accountant's report*

There may be situations where the reporting accountant becomes aware of events that occur after the date of their report, but before the completion date of the transaction, which may have caused them to issue a different report or withhold consent. If this occurs, the reporting accountant should discuss the matter with those responsible for the investment circular and take legal advice as necessary.

50.5   SIR 2000

50.5.1   *General*

SIR 2000, *Investment Reporting Standards Applicable to Public Reporting Engagements on Historical Financial Information* sets out basic principles and essential procedures that apply to all engagements involving the examination of historical financial information that is intended to give a true and fair view for the purposes of the engagement circular. The reporting accountant is required to obtain sufficient evidence to express a true and fair opinion of the financial information.

The guidance in the SIR applies only to situations where new opinions are provided by the reporting accountant, not where pre-existing audit reports are available and are used in the investment circular.

The reporting accountant's exercise will not differ greatly from that of an auditor and reporting accountants will perform or rely on work that meets the requirements of ISAs (UK and Ireland). Their work does vary in that:

- they are likely to have the evidence collected by the original auditors of the historical information available to them;
- they may have the benefit of being able to see the outcome of issues that were difficult or contentious at the time of the original audit; and
- they do not have the statutory reporting responsibilities of an auditor, for example, there is no requirement to report if proper accounting records have been kept by the entity.

In addition some of the requirements of ISAs (UK and Ireland) do not apply to the work of reporting accountants. An example would be where the ISA (UK and Ireland) requirement is based on the existence of an ongoing or continuous relationship between auditor and client, which does not exist in the same way for reporting accountants. SIR 2000 provides a list of requirements that do not apply.

50.5.2   True and fair view

SIR 2000.2 requires reporting accountants to ensure that when reporting in true and fair terms, the investment circular complies with relevant financial reporting standards to the extent that they are applicable.

For historical financial information presented in a prospectus, the relevant financial reporting standards are set out in the Prospectus Rules and the most recent years' financial information should be presented in a form consistent with that which will be adopted in the issuer's financial statements. Reporting accountants should ensure that the directors have selected appropriate accounting policies to reflect the situation of the issuer once the transaction has been completed.

For information presented in a Class 1 circular, the reporting criteria are set out in the Listing Rules and financial information should be presented in a form consistent with the accounting policies adopted in the issuer's latest annual consolidated accounts.

Directors should consider accepted conventions when establishing and disclosing the accounting principles to be used. An annexure to SIR 2000 sets out conventions that address:

- making adjustments to previously published financial statements and dealing with entities which have not previously prepared consolidated accounts;
- carve outs;
- acquisitions; and
- newly formed issuers.

The aim of presenting this information in an annexure, rather than in the body of, or as an appendix to, the SIR, is that it can be easily updated without having to re-expose the whole SIR.

50.5.3   Professional considerations

The applicable ethical standards and guidance relating to engagement letters is set out in SIR 1000 and the draft Ethical Standards for Reporting Accountants, see **50.8**.

Where reporting accountants rely on historical evidence obtained by auditors they should ensure that their documentation identifies the work papers used and states how the auditor addressed the risks identified by the reporting accountant's risk assessment procedures.

Reporting accountants should consider who those charged with governance are for the purpose of reporting. Where an audit committee has already been set up, the reporting accountant should report to that committee, otherwise reports should be made to the directors.

50.5.4   Planning

The reporting accountant is required to perform and document their risk assessment. The reporting accountant may consider the following areas as part of their planning:

- any previous modifications to the audit report on relevant financial statements;
- the nature of adjustments to previously published historical financial information and evidence to support these adjustments;
- the interaction with other roles taken by the reporting accountant, such as preparation of the long-form report;
- staffing, including relevant experience and skills;
- liaison with the auditor and terms of access to their working papers;
- the nature and timing of procedures to support their reliance on the auditor's evidence;
- whether the financial reporting framework used for the audited financial statements is the same as that applied to the financial information contained in the investment circular, e.g., UK FRS compared to IFRS;
- whether there are any special circumstances surrounding the appointment, resignation or reporting responsibilities of the auditor;
- whether there is evidence of any limitation having been placed on the work of the auditor; and
- whether corrections or adjustments to subsequent financial statements indicate possible inadequacies in the audits of earlier periods.

Where the reporting accountant intends to rely on the auditor's evidence, the reporting accountant should first consider the qualifications, independence and competence of the auditor and the quality control systems of the audit firm.

50.5.5   Understanding the entity and risk assessment

Reporting accountants are required to obtain an understanding of the entity and its environment, including internal control, sufficient to allow them to assess the risks of material misstatement of the historical financial information and to plan procedures. Many of the methods used will be identical to those employed by auditors, but reporting accountants will have regard to the fact that misstatements in earlier periods may have been detected in subsequent periods or that uncertainties may have been resolved over time. They should also have regard to any other relevant work performed in relation to the investment circular.

50.5.6 Materiality

Reporting accountants determine planning materiality for their own work and in the context of the report they will be giving. Therefore the reporting accountant's materiality may differ from that used by the auditors of the historical information.

50.5.7 Reporting accountant's procedures

Reporting accountants should perform procedures to obtain sufficient evidence that the work of the auditor can be relied upon or, where it cannot be relied upon or access is not possible, procedures to compensate for this. The procedures of the auditor and the reporting accountant together should comply with ISAs (UK and Ireland) except where a requirement of an ISA (UK and Ireland) is not relevant or where it is not possible for the reporting accountant to perform such procedures. Where the reporting accountant chooses not to meet a requirement of an ISA (UK and Ireland) they should document the reason for not meeting the requirement and why there is no impact on their opinion. This is unless the requirement is listed as not applicable Appendix A to SIR 2000.

The reporting accountant should assess whether the procedures undertaken by the auditor are sufficient to address the assessment of risk performed by the reporting accountant or are conducted to an appropriate materiality level. Where they are not, the reporting accountant would be required to perform further procedures themselves.

SIR 2000.9 requires the reporting accountant's substantive procedures to include:

- examining material adjustments made to the previously published historical financial information and considering the reasons for the adjustments;
- evaluating whether all such necessary adjustments have been made; and
- checking the extraction of the historical information in the investment circular from the previously published information.

50.5.8 Access to audit work papers

When a firm other than the company's auditor or former auditor is appointed as reporting accountant, they will require access to the audit work papers related to the historical information to be included in the investment circular. Access will usually be granted, with the auditors accepting no responsibility or liability to the reporting accountant in connection with the use of the audit work papers.

Where access is denied or is impossible, the reporting accountant has to reperform the audit procedures themselves.

Whether or not access is granted, reporting accountants should obtain from the auditors or directors a copy of any communications with those charged with governance, together with responses to those communications, for the relevant periods.

50.5.9 Post balance sheet events

Unless a post balance sheet event indicates that there has been an error in the preparation of the historical financial information in an earlier period, the reporting accountant will only consider the impact of post balance sheet events occurring up to the date of their report. After the date of their report the reporting accountant has no obligation to perform procedures or make enquiries about such events.

However, if, in the period between the date of their report and the completion date of the transaction, the reporting accountant becomes aware of matters which might have caused them to issue a different report or withhold consent if they had occurred before the date of their report, the reporting accountant should discuss these matters with those responsible for the investment circular.

If there is a significant change affecting any matter in the document or a material mistake or inaccuracy is noted once the prospectus has been approved by the FSA and before the closing date of the offering, a supplementary prospectus must be prepared.

50.5.10 Going concern

The reporting accountant will include in their report an emphasis of matter paragraph on any material uncertainty related to going concern. If the uncertainty will be resolved as a result of the offering, the reporting accountant should consider whether this is adequately disclosed in the basis of preparation note to the historical financial information.

50.5.11 Representations

Where auditors have already obtained written representations, it may not be necessary for reporting accountants to repeat the request for written confirmation. However, reporting accountants will usually require confirmation that:

- the directors or management of the entity are responsible for the preparation of the historical financial information; and
- any adjustments made to historical financial statements are necessary,

have been correctly determined and that no further adjustments are required.

50.5.12   *Joint reporting accountants*

Where joint reporting accountants are appointed, the division of work will be agreed between the parties and may be set out in their engagement letter. The joint reporting accountants are jointly and severally liable for the report.

Each reporting accountant will participate in the planning of the engagement, will review the work of the other, and records the result of that review. A common set of working papers is normally maintained.

50.5.13   *Reporting*

SIR 2000 requires reporting accountants to include in their report:

- a statement that the work was conducted in accordance with SIRs; and
- reference to the basis of preparation and the applicable financial reporting framework.

The opinion is usually expressed in terms of whether the financial information gives a true and fair view of the state of affairs and profits, cash flow and statement of changes in equity.

If a limitation of scope exists, perhaps because no audit of the underlying financial information was performed and there is an absence of contemporary evidence, reporting accountants should consider whether they are able to form an opinion. Because of the reliance to be placed on the financial information by its readers, reporting accountants would not normally agree to be associated with financial information where a disclaimer of opinion needs to be given on the information for the entire period.

The reporting accountant does not refer to any audit opinions previously given on the financial statements on which the historical financial information is based. However, if the issuer has referred to details of earlier disclaimers or qualifications, the reporting accountant considers the disclosures made by the issuer and whether they may give rise to queries about the reporting accountant's opinion. If the reporting accountant is not satisfied with the disclosures they should discuss the matter with those responsible for the investment circular and ensure that further appropriate information is included either by the issuer or in their report.

An example reporting accountant's report on historical financial information is shown in **Table 2**.

TABLE 2:   Example reporting accountant's report on historical financial information

The Directors

ABC plc

Dear Sirs

We report on the financial information set out [in paragraphs ... to ...]. This financial information has been prepared for inclusion in the [prospectus]/[listing particulars]/[Class 1 Circular relating to the acquisition of XYZ Limited] dated ... of ABC plc on the basis of the accounting policies set out in paragraph [...]. This report is required by [relevant regulation] and is given for the purpose of complying with that [relevant regulation] and for no other purpose.

Responsibilities

[As described in paragraph [...]] [T/t]he Directors of ABC plc are responsible for preparing the financial information [on the basis of preparation set out in [note x to the financial information]] [and in accordance with [the applicable financial reporting framework]].

It is our responsibility to form an opinion [on the financial information] [as to whether the financial information gives a true and fair view, for the purposes of the [prospectus]/[listing particulars]/[Class 1 Circular]], and to report our opinion to you.

Basis of opinion

We conducted our work in accordance with the Standards of Investment Reporting Standards issued by the Auditing Practices Board in the United Kingdom. Our work included an assessment of evidence relevant to the amounts and disclosures in the financial information. It also included an assessment of significant estimates and judgements made by those responsible for the preparation of the financial statements underlying the financial information and whether the accounting policies are appropriate to the entity's circumstances, consistently applied and adequately disclosed.

We planned and performed our work so as to obtain all the information and explanations which we considered necessary in order to provide us with sufficient evidence to give reasonable assurance that the financial information is free from material misstatement whether caused by fraud or other irregularity or error.

Opinion

In our opinion, the financial information gives, for the purposes of the [prospectus]/[listing particulars]/[Class 1 Circular] dated ..., a true and fair view of the state of affairs of [ABC plc]/[XYZ Limited] as at the dates stated and of its profits, cash flows and recognised gains and losses for the periods then ended in accordance with the basis of preparation set out in note x and in accordance with [the applicable financial reporting framework] as described in note y] [and has been prepared in a form that is consistent when the accounting policies adopted in [ABC plc's latest annual accounts*].

Yours faithfully

Reporting Accountant

* The wording in these square brackets is appropriate for inclusion where the report relates to historical financial information include in a Class 1 circular.

50.6 SIR 3000

50.6.1 General

SIR 3000, *Investment Reporting Standards Applicable to Public Reporting Engagements on Profit Forecasts*, sets out standards to be applied when reporting accountants are engaged to report publicly on profit forecasts which are to be included in an investment circular under:

- the PD Regulation or other regulations with similar requirements;
- the City Code;
- requirements of the London Stock Exchange in respect of an AIM admission document.

Profit forecasts are inherently uncertain because they are based on assumptions and events and circumstances may not occur as expected, or may not be predicted at all. However, profit forecasts should be:

- reliable;
- understandable;
- comparable; and
- relevant.

It is the directors' responsibility to determine whether a profit forecast is relevant to, and should be included in, the investment circular. Reporting accountants are required to consider whether the profit forecast has been properly compiled, not whether it is correct to include it in the circular. In order to assess whether the forecast has been properly compiled, reporting accountants considers its reliability, understandability and comparability.

Reliability
ICAEW guidance for directors published in 2003, explains that in order for a profit forecast to be reliable it must be:

- able to be depended on by the intended user as a faithful representation of what it either purports to represent or could reasonably be expected to represent;
- neutral and free from bias;
- free from material error;
- materially complete; and
- prudent, ie a degree of caution is applied in making judgements.

If a profit forecast does not correctly predict the actual outcomes it does not mean that it was not reliable when it was made.

Forecasts will be most reliable when they are based on good quality business analysis performed by the directors.

Understandability
A profit forecast can only be understandable if it contains sufficient information to allow the reader to appreciate the degree of uncertainty it contains and the assumptions made. Reasonable disclosure will include details of the basis of preparation, the factors that will affect whether the assumptions will be borne out in practice and the likely outcomes if the assumptions do not prove to be correct.

Comparability
In order for profit forecasts to be of greatest use they must be comparable to actual results and to equivalent information for other reporting periods. This means that profit forecasts should be prepared using the same accounting policies as the historical information contained in the investment circular.

50.6.2   Compilation process

Directors are responsible for compiling the profit forecast and would typically complete the steps set out in **Table 3**. When assessing the reliability, understandability and comparability of the profit forecast, reporting accountants would consider whether these steps have been followed.

TABLE 3:   Steps in the compilation of a profit forecast

The process followed by the preparer would be expected to include:

- an appropriate analysis of the business (what is appropriate will depend on a number of factors including the complexity and predictability of the business and the length of the period being forecast and accordingly the content, degree of detail and presentation of such analyses may vary significantly);
- identification of material uncertainties;
- selection of appropriate assumptions;

- where relevant, identification of, and reference to, appropriate third party information (eg market research reports);
- arithmetic computation of the profit forecast;
- appropriate sensitivity analysis;
- appropriate disclosure to enable the intended users to understand the profit forecast; and
- appropriate consideration of the profit forecast and approval of it by the directors of the entity.

50.6.3 Agreeing the terms of the engagement

Before accepting an engagement, reporting accountants should complete the procedures set out in SIR 1000 and ascertain whether the directors intend to comply with all relevant regulatory requirements. They should also consider the ethical requirements set out in SIR 1000.

Example of engagement letter clauses for profit forecast engagements are set out in **Table 4**.

TABLE 4: Example engagement letter extracts

Financial information on which the report is to be given

The [investment circular] will contain a profit forecast for the company for the period ending [date] (the "PFI") prepared and presented in accordance with [item 13 of Annex I of the PD Regulation] [the requirements of the City Code] [other applicable regulation]. We will prepare a report on the profit forecast addressed to [...] expressing our opinion on the profit forecast, in the form described below to be included in the [investment circular].

We will ask the Directors to make certain representations to us regarding the PFI. If the PFI is intended only to be a hypothetical illustration, or the Directors are unable to make such representations to us, we will not wish to be associated with the PFI and accordingly, will be unable to report publicly on it.

Responsibilities

The preparation and presentation of the profit forecast will be the responsibility solely of the Directors. [This responsibility includes the identification and disclosure of the assumptions underlying the profit forecast.(omit if no assumptions)]. The Directors are also responsible for ensuring that the PFI is prepared and presented in accordance with [item 13 of Annex I of the PD Regulation] [the requirements of the City Code] [other applicable regulation].

We will require the Directors to formally adopt the PFI before we report on it. We understand that the Directors will have regard to the guidance issued by The Institute of Chartered Accountants in England & Wales entitles "Prospective Financial Information – Guidance for UK directors" in preparing the PFI.

It is our responsibility to form an opinion as to whether the profit forecast has been properly compiled on the basis stated and whether such basis is consistent with the accounting policies normally adopted by ABC plc.

If the results of our work are satisfactory, and having regard to the requirements of [item 13.2 of Annex I of the PD Regulation] [the City Code] [other applicable regulation], we shall prepare a report on the profit forecast for inclusion in the [investment circular]. An illustration of the form of our report is attached.

Scope of work

Our work will be undertaken in accordance with Standard for Investments Reporting (SIR) 3000 "Investment Reporting Standards Applicable to Public Reporting Engagements on Profit Forecasts" issued by the Auditing Practices Board and will be subject to the limitations described therein.

We draw your attention in particular to paragraph 75 of SIR 3000 which would preclude us from expressing any opinion if the Directors have not complied with the regulatory requirements set out in Appendix 2 of that SIR.

As the purpose of our engagement is restricted as described above and since the PFI and the assumptions on which it is based relate to the future and may be affected by unforeseen events, we will not provide any opinion as to how closely the actual result achieved will correspond to the profit forecast. Accordingly we neither confirm nor otherwise accept responsibility for the ultimate accuracy and achievability of the PFI.

Assumptions

We will discuss the assumptions with the persons responsible for preparing the PFI together with the evidence they have to support the assumptions, but we will not seek to independently verify or audit those assumptions. We are not responsible for identifying the assumptions.

In the event that anything comes to our attention to indicate that any of the assumptions adopted by the Directors which in our opinion, are necessary for a proper understanding of the PFI have not been disclosed or if any material assumption made by the Directors appears to us to be unrealistic we will inform the Directors so that steps can be taken to resolve the matter. However, we are required to comment in our report if an assumption is published which appears to us to be unrealistic or an assumption is omitted which appears to us to be important to an understanding of the PFI.

50.6.4   *Planning and performing the engagement*

SIR 1000 sets out the basic principles in respect of the planning of all reporting engagements. SIR 3000 requires the reporting accountant to obtain an understanding of the subject matter sufficient to assess the risk of the profit forecast not being properly compiled. Reporting accountants should consider:

- the background to, and nature of, the circumstances in which the profit forecast was made, including whether the forecast is being made for the first time or whether it is being updated for this purpose;
- the entity's business and the business analysis performed by the directors; and
- the procedures used to prepare the profit forecast, see **Table 3** above.

Reporting accountants discuss the plans, strategies and risk analysis of the preparer of the forecast and consider whether they are in keeping with the findings of the business analysis and review the assumptions made. It may be the case that not all the assumptions used are disclosed in the profit forecast, as only those necessary to aid understanding of the forecast are required. Reporting accountants will also consider whether there are cash flow statements and balance sheets to act as checks of omissions and inaccuracies in the forecast.

If profit forecasts are regularly prepared by the entity, reporting accountants should consider whether these regular forecasts prove close to actual outcomes and look at the directors' analysis of variances.

50.6.5 Materiality

For a profit forecast to be reliable it must be free from material error. In this context an error will include:

- assumptions that are not consistent with the analysis of the business;
- mathematical or clerical mistakes in the compilation of the profit forecast;
- misapplication of accounting policies;
- misapplication of stated assumptions;
- known misstatement in historical financial information embodied in the forecast without adjustment;
- failure to disclose an assumption or other explanation which is necessary for an understanding of the forecast; and
- presenting the forecast in a way that it is not capable of being compared with subsequent published results.

Materiality should be determined in relation to how users who have a reasonable knowledge of business, economic activities and accounting would be influenced by an error in making economic decisions.

50.6.6 Historical financial information

Where historical financial information has been included in the profit forecast, SIR 3000 requires reporting accountants to:

- consider the results of any audit or review of that information;

- evaluate the suitability of unaudited historical financial information in the forecast;
- assess whether historical financial information has been appropriately included in the forecast; and
- where any adjustments have been made to previously published historical financial information, consider whether these are appropriate.

If historical financial information has been audited, the reporting accountant would ordinarily gain access to the relevant audit work papers.

Where historical information has not been audited, the reporting accountant should perform the procedures set out in **Table 5**.

TABLE 5: Procedures in relation to unaudited historical information contained in profit forecasts

The reporting accountant should:

- understand the internal control environment of the entity relevant to the historical financial information;
- discuss with management the accounting polices applied and any differences from the method of preparing the entity's published financial statements;
- enquire of management, including internal audit, whether there have been any changes in the financial reporting systems or internal controls, or any breakdowns in systems and controls, which might affect the reliability of the financial information;
- enquire about changes in the entity's procedures for recording, classifying and summarising transactions, accumulating information for disclosure and preparing the financial statements;
- consider the accuracy of unaudited historical financial information by comparing it to audited financial statements for the same period;
- compare the historical financial information to previous budgets or forecasts prepared by the entity in respect of the period covered by the historical financial information and gain an understanding of the reason for any significant differences; and
- check the historical financial information used in the profit forecast agrees to, or reconciles with, the underlying accounting records of the entity.

50.6.7   *Consistent accounting policies*

Where the profit forecast relates to the expansion of the existing business the reporting accountant's primary consideration is the consistency of the accounting policies used in the forecast with those used for the most recent historical financial information in the investment circular. However, they should also consider whether these continue to be appropriate on an ongoing basis.

Where the profit forecast relates to a start up situation, reporting accountants consider only the appropriateness of the policies chosen.

50.6.8 Presentation of the profit forecast

Reporting accountants should consider whether:

- the forecast is presented in an understandable way;
- assumptions are clearly disclosed, ensuring that the significance of each assumption is apparent;
- the degree of inherent uncertainty is clearly disclosed;
- the choice of captions and subtotals are such that they allow easy comparison with subsequent historical financial information;
- additional disclosure is included with any sensitivity analysis to ensure that it is understood; and
- useful information is obscured by the inclusion of immaterial items or meaningless headings.

50.6.9 Representation letter

Many of the assumptions used in the compilation of a profit forecast will depend on the intent of directors, and so written representation of such intent is a particularly important source of evidence.

50.6.10 Reporting

SIR 3000 requires reporting accountants to include in their reports:

- a statement that the reporting accountants' responsibility is to form an opinion on the compilation of the profit forecast and to report their opinion to the addressees of the report;
- a statement that the profit forecast and the assumptions on which it is based are the responsibility of the directors; and
- in the basis of preparation section of their report, cross references to disclosures that explain the basis of preparation of the profit forecast including:
  - assumptions made;
  - accounting policies applied; and
  - where appropriate, the source of historical financial information embodied in the profit forecast.

Where the profit forecast relates to the expansion of an existing business, it is normal for the reporting accountants' report to include reference to the fact that the basis of accounting is consistent with existing accounting policies. Where this is not the case a more detailed explanation of the accounting policies used will be appropriate.

In the basis of opinion section of the report, the reporting accountant should include a statement that where the profit forecast and any assumption on which it is based relate to the future, the reporting accountant does not express any opinion as to whether the actual results achieved will correspond to those shown in the profit forecast.

Reporting accountants cannot give an unmodified opinion when the directors have not applied the criteria set out in Appendix 2 of SIR 3000, which sets out the reporting accountant's criteria as listed in relevant regulations, and the effect of this omission is material.

An example report is given in **Table 6**.

TABLE 6:   Example unmodified report on profit forecasts

[Addressees]

Dear Sirs

[ABC plc]

We report on the profit forecast comprising [*insert description of items comprising the prospective financial information*] of ABC plc ("the Company") and its subsidiaries (together "the ABC Group") for the [period] ending [date] (the "Profit Forecast"). The Profit Forecast, and the material assumptions upon which it is based, are set out on pages [x] to [y] of the [describe document] ("the [Document]") issued by the Company dated [date]. This report is required by [relevant regulation] and is given for the purpose of complying with that [relevant regulation] and for no other purpose.

[*Substitute the following text of the last sentence of the immediately preceding paragraph, where a profit forecast is made by an Offeree in the context of a takeover*. This report is required by Rule 28.3(b) of the City Code and is given for the purpose of complying with that rule and for no other purpose. Accordingly, we assume no responsibility in respect of this report to the Offeror or any person connected to, or acting in concert with, the Offeror or to any other person who is seeking or may in future seek to acquire control of the Company (an "Alternative Offeror") or to any other person connected to, or acting in concert with, an Alternative Offeror.]

Responsibilities

It is the responsibility of the Directors of ABC plc to prepare the Profit Forecast in accordance with the requirements of the [PD Regulation]/[Listing Rules]/[City Code]/ [guidance issued by the London Stock Exchange].

It is our responsibility to form an opinion as required by the [PD Regulation]/ [Listing Rules]/[City Code]/ [guidance issued by the London Stock Exchange] as to the proper compilation of the Profit Forecast and to report that opinion to you.

Basis of preparation of the Profit Forecast

The Profit Forecast has been prepared on the basis stated on page [x] of the [Document] and is based on the [audited/unaudited] interim financial results for the [six] months ended [date], the unaudited management accounts for the [x] months ended [date] and a forecast to [date]. The Profit Forecast is required to be presented on a basis consistent with the accounting policies of the ABC Group.

Basis of opinion

We conducted our work in accordance with the Standards for Investment Reporting issued by the Auditing Practices Board in the United Kingdom. Our work included [evaluating the basis on which the historical financial information included in the Profit Forecast has been prepared and] considering whether the Profit Forecast has been accurately computed based upon the disclosed assumptions and the accounting policies of the ABC Group. Whilst the assumptions upon which the Profit Forecast are based are solely the responsibility of the Directors, we considered whether anything came to our attention to indicate that any of the assumptions adopted by the Directors, which, in our opinion, are necessary for a proper understanding of the Profit Forecast have not been disclosed and whether any material assumption made by the Directors appears to us to be unrealistic.

We planned and performed our work so as to obtain the information and explanations we considered necessary in order to provide us with reasonable assurance that the Profit Forecast has been properly compiled on the basis stated.

Since the Profit Forecast and the assumptions on which it is based relate to the future and may therefore be affected by unforeseen events, we can express no opinion as to whether the actual results reported will correspond to those shown in the Profit Forecast and differences may be material.

[*This paragraph may be omitted if the document is not be distributed outside the UK* – Our work has not been carried out in accordance with auditing or other standards and practices generally accepted in the United States of America [or other jurisdictions] and accordingly should not be relied upon as if it had been carried out in accordance with those standards and practices.]

Opinion

In our opinion, the Profit Forecast has been properly compiled on the basis [stated]/[of the assumption made by the directors] and the basis of accounting used is consistent with the accounting policies used by ABC Group [*or refer to the actual policies used if different*].

Declaration [*to be given if report is included in a Prospectus*]

For the purpose of [Prospectus Rule [5.53R(2)(f)] [guidance issued by the London Stock Exchange] we are responsible for [this report as part] [the following parts(s)] of the [prospectus] [registration document] [AIM admission document] and declare that we have taken all reasonable care to ensure that the information contained [in this report] [those parts] is, to the best of our knowledge, in accordance with the facts and contains no omission likely to affect its import. This declaration is included in the [prospectus] [registration document] [AIM admission document] in compliance with [item 1.2 of Annex I of the PD Regulation] [item 1.2 of Annex III of the PD Regulation] [guidance issued by the London Stock Exchange].

Yours faithfully

Reporting Accountant

50.6.11   Consent

SIR 1000 sets out the basic requirements in respect of reporting accountants giving consent for their reports to be included in investment circulars. In addition, for profit forecasts, reporting accountants consider whether other disclosures in the circular are consistent with the assumptions and other disclosures relating to the profit forecast before giving their consent.

50.7   SIR 4000

50.7.1   General

The APB issued SIR 4000, *Investment Reporting Standards Applicable to Public Reporting Engagements on Pro Forma Financial Information* in January 2006. Pro forma financial information is defined as net assets, profit or cash flow statements that demonstrate the impact of a transaction on previously published financial information together with the explanatory notes thereto. The compilation of pro forma financial information would usually include:

* the accurate extraction of information from permitted sources;
* the making of adjustments that are arithmetically correct, appropriate and complete;
* arithmetic computation of the pro forma financial information;
* consideration of accounting policies;
* appropriate disclosure to allow the user to understand the financial information; and
* consideration and approval of the pro forma financial information by the directors of the entity.

50.7.2   Agreeing the terms of the engagement

Before accepting an engagement, reporting accountants should complete the procedures set out in SIR 1000 and ascertain whether the directors intend to comply with all relevant regulatory requirements. They should also consider the ethical requirements set out in SIR 1000.

Example of engagement letter clauses for pro forma financial information engagements are set out in **Table 7**.

TABLE 7: Example engagement letter clauses for a pro forma financial information engagement

Financial information on which the report is to be given

The [investment circular] will include a pro forma [balance sheet/profit and loss account] together with a description of the basis of preparation (including the accounting policies used) and supporting notes to illustrate how the transaction might have affected the financial information of the company had the transaction been undertaken at the beginning of the period[s] concerned or as at the date[s] stated (the "pro forma financial information").

Responsibilities

The pro forma financial information, which will be the responsibility solely of the Directors, will be prepared for illustrative purposes only. This is required to be prepared in accordance with items 1 to 6 of Annex II of the PD Regulation. It is our responsibility to form an opinion as to whether the pro forma financial information has been properly compiled on the basis stated and that such basis is consistent with the accounting policies of ABC plc.

If the results of our work are satisfactory, and having regard to the requirements of item 7 of Annex II of the PD Regulation, we shall prepare a report on the pro forma financial information for inclusion in the [describe document]. An illustration of the form of our report is attached.

Scope of work

Our work will be undertaken in accordance with Standard for Investments Reporting (SIR) 4000 "Investment Reporting Standards Applicable to Public Reporting Engagements on Pro Forma Financial Information" issued by the Auditing Practices Board and will be subject to the limitations described therein.

We draw your attention in particular to paragraph 62 of SIR 4000 which would preclude us from expressing any opinion if the Directors have not complied with the regulatory requirements set out in Appendix 1 of that SIR.

50.7.3 Planning and performing the engagement

In addition to the procedures set out in SIR 1000, the reporting accountant should gain an understanding of:

- the nature of the transaction being undertaken;
- the entity's business; and
- the procedures adopted, or planned to be adopted by the directors to prepare the pro forma financial information.

By understanding these areas, reporting accountants will be able to identify the risk of the pro forma financial information not being properly compiled.

Reporting accountants should obtain sufficient evidence that the unadjusted financial information has been correctly extracted from a suitable source and that the adjustments applied to it are in accordance with the criteria set out in legislation, and included in Appendix 1 to SIR 4000. The PD Regulation requires adjustments to be:

- clearly shown and explained;
- directly attributable to the transaction; and
- factually supportable.

In addition, in respect of a pro form profit and loss account or cash flow statement, those adjustments which are expected to have a continuing impact on the issuer must be clearly identified.

The requirements of the PD Regulation that adjustments must be directly attributable to the transaction and factually supported may mean that directors are not able to make all the adjustments they wish to. For any adjustment which is omitted in this way, reporting accountants should consider whether the omission renders the pro forma financial information misleading. Any concerns may be removed by providing details of the omitted adjustment in the notes to the pro forma financial information. However, where the omitted adjustment is so fundamental that disclosure is not sufficient to remove the uncertainty, the reporting accountant should discuss the matter with the directors and the issuer's advisors, and may not be able to issue their report.

Reporting accountants should also evaluate whether the adjustments made are consistent with the accounting policies adopted in the last, or to be adopted in the next, financial statements of the entity.

Reporting accountants are also required to ensure that the calculations within the pro forma financial information are mathematically correct.

50.7.4   Materiality

For pro forma financial information to be reliable it must be free from material error. In this context an error will include:

- use of an inappropriate source for the unadjusted financial information;

- incorrect extraction of the unadjusted financial information from an appropriate source;
- the misapplication, or failure to use, the accounting policies used in the last (or to be adopted in the next) financial statements;
- failure to make an adjustment required by the PD Regulation;
- making an adjustment that does not comply with the PD Regulation;
- a mathematical or clerical mistake; and
- inadequate or incorrect disclosures.

Materiality should be determined in relation to how users who have a reasonable knowledge of business, economic activities and accounting would be influenced by an error in making economic decisions.

50.7.5 *Presentation of the pro forma financial information*

Reporting accountants are required by SIR 4000 to consider whether they are aware of anything that would suggest that the presentation of the pro forma financial information is misleading or difficult to understand. Where there are concerns they should be discussed with the directors and the reporting accountant should consider whether to issue their report.

50.7.6 *Reporting*

SIR 4000 requires reporting accountants to include in their reports:

- a statement that the reporting accountants' responsibility is to form an opinion on the compilation of the pro forma financial information and to report their opinion to the addressees of the report;
- a statement that the pro forma financial information is the responsibility of the directors; and
- in the basis of preparation section of their report, cross references to disclosures that explain the basis of preparation of the pro forma financial information.

Reporting accountants cannot give an unmodified opinion when the directors have not applied the criteria set out in Appendix 1 of SIR 4000 and the effect of this omission is material. The appendix sets out the reporting criteria as listed in relevant regulations.

An example report is given in **Table 8**.

TABLE 8:   Example unmodified report on pro forma financial information

[Addressees]

Dear Sirs

[ABC plc]

We report on the pro forma [financial information] (the "Pro forma financial information") set out in Part [...] of the [investment circular] dated ..., which has been prepared on the basis described [in note x], for illustrative purposes only, to provide information about how the [transaction] might have affected the financial information presented on the basis of the accounting policies [adopted/to be adopted] by ABC plc in preparing the financial statements for the period [ended/ending] [date]. This report is required by [relevant regulation] and is given for the purpose of complying with that [relevant regulation] and for no other purpose.

Responsibilities

It is the responsibility of the Directors of ABC plc to prepare the Pro forma financial information in accordance with [item 20.2 of Annex I of the PD Regulation]/[guidance issued by the London Stock Exchange].

It is our responsibility to form an opinion as required by [item 7 of Annex II of the PD Regulation]/ [the guidance issued by the London Stock Exchange] as to the proper compilation of the Profit Forecast and to report that opinion to you.

In providing this opinion we are not updating or refreshing any reports or opinions previously made by us on any financial information used in the compilation of the Pro forma financial information, nor do we accept responsibility for such reports or opinions beyond that owed to those to whom those reports or opinions were addressed by us at the dates of their issue.

Basis of opinion

We conducted our work in accordance with the Standards for Investment Reporting issued by the Auditing Practices Board in the United Kingdom. The work that we performed for the purpose of making this report, which involved no independent examination of any of the underlying financial information, consisted primarily of comparing the unadjusted financial information with the source documents, considering the evidence supporting the adjustments and discussing the Pro forma financial information with the directors of ABC plc.

We planned and performed our work so as to obtain the information and explanations we considered necessary in order to provide us with reasonable assurance that the Pro forma financial information has been properly prepared on the basis stated and that such basis is consistent with the accounting policies of ABC plc.

> [*This paragraph may be omitted if the document is not be distributed outside the UK* – Our work has not been carried out in accordance with auditing or other standards and practices generally accepted in the United States of America [or other jurisdictions] and accordingly should not be relied upon as if it had been carried out in accordance with those standards and practices.]
>
> **Opinion**
>
> In our opinion:
>
> - the Pro forma financial information has been properly compiled on the basis stated; and
> - such basis is consistent with the accounting policies used by ABC plc.
>
> **Declaration** [*to be given if report is included in a Prospectus*]
>
> For the purpose of [Prospectus Rule [5.53R(2)(f)] [5.5.4R(2)(f)]] [guidance issued by the London Stock Exchange] we are responsible for [this report as part] [the following parts(s)] of the [prospectus] [registration document] [AIM admission document] and declare that we have taken all reasonable care to ensure that the information contained [in this report] [those parts] is, to the best of our knowledge, in accordance with the facts and contains no omission likely to affect its import. This declaration is included in the [prospectus] [registration document] [AIM admission document] in compliance with [item 1.2 of Annex I of the PD Regulation] [item 1.2 of Annex III of the PD Regulation] [guidance issued by the London Stock Exchange].
>
> Yours faithfully
>
> Reporting Accountant

50.8 ETHICAL STANDARDS FOR REPORTING ACCOUNTANTS

Given the high level of public interested in investment circulars and the degree of similarity between the work of reporting accountants and auditors of financial statements, it is reasonable for users to expect similar ethical requirements to apply to reporting accountants as for auditors. Therefore, in October 2006, the APB issued the *Ethical Standard for Reporting Accountants* (ESRA) based on the principles contained in the *Ethical Standards for Auditors* (ESs), which are detailed in **Chapter 2**.

The ESRA replaces Bulletin 2005/7, *Integrity, Objectivity and Independence – guidance for Reporting Accountants undertaking engagements in connection with an investment circular* which was issued in July 2005. The Bulletin was issued at the same time as SIR 1000 to provide limited ethical guidance so that reporting accountants could meet the requirement of that SIR to consider ethical standards when deciding whether to accept or continue with an engagement.

The ESRA applies to all public reporting engagements to which SIRs apply, and also to private reporting engagements which are undertaken in connection with an investment circular on which the reporting accountant is intending to issue a public report.

Many of the requirements of the ESRA mirror those in the ESs, focusing on potential threats to integrity, objectivity and independence and it should be read in conjunction with the ESs. It requires reporting accountants to consider not only their relationship with the client, but also with the sponsor, other parties to the engagement letter and other entities involved in the transaction. The independence requirement will relate not only to the engagement team, but also to others who can directly influence the conduct and outcome of the engagement. As investment circulars relate to transactions that are price sensitive and therefore confidential, there is likely to be only a limited number of people within a firm who are aware of the investment circular reporting engagement. For this reason the requirements of the ESRA only apply to those within the engagement team or with a direct supervisory or management responsibility for the team and those who have actual knowledge of the engagement, unless certain requirements of the ESRA specifically state that they apply to the whole firm.

The ESRA does not prohibit audit engagement partner and senior audit staff from being members of an investment circular reporting engagement team. Rather than lose the accumulated knowledge held by the audit team, the ESRA prefers to require such involvement of audit team members to be disclosed to those charged with governance and any other persons from whom the engagement letter states the reporting accountant should take instructions.

Contingent fees for investment circular reporting are prohibited by the ESRA, as are contingent fees in respect of other work performed by the firm during the relevant period where the:

- contingent fees are material to the firm; or
- the outcome of the service is dependent on a judgment made by the reporting accountant in relation to the investment circular.

The ESRA is effective for investment circular reporting engagements commencing on or after 1 April 2007. There are transitional arrangements for business relationships, loan staff arrangements and the supply of other services which were in place at 31 October 2006 but which are now prohibited by the ESRA.

50.9 LIMITING RISKS FOR REPORTING ACCOUNTANTS

50.9.1 Background

Technical Release AAF 02/06, Identifying and managing certain risks arising from the inclusion of reports from auditors and accountants in prospectuses (and certain other investments circulars) was issued in April 2006 to expand the guidance in Audit 1/03 issued following the Bannerman case, for reporting accountants.

Audit 1/03 *The audit report and auditors' duty of care to third parties*, suggested that auditors might be able to manage the risk of taking on duties to their parties by inserting appropriate paragraphs in their audit reports. Audit 01/03 and the relevant paragraphs to be inserted are detailed in section **3.17**.

The risk that a third party may seek to prove that reporting accountants had a duty of care to them is not limited to reports made on financial statements under section 235 of the Companies Act 1985 and many other types of report now contain similar paragraphs to that outlined in Audit 01/03.

There has been no court ruling on the extent of an reporting accountant's liability to third parties when their audit report or a separate reporting accountant's report is included or referred to in a prospectus or certain other investment circular. The Prospectus Rules set out the parts of a prospectus for which a reporting accountant is responsible. The reporting accountant should take care that these responsibilities are stated in the prospectus and not left open to third parties.

50.9.2 Inclusion of a statutory audit report in an investment circular

It could be argued that by giving consent for their audit report to be included in an investment circular, reporting accountant's are accepting responsibility for their report beyond that intended when the report was first issued. AAF 2/6 states that there will be no widening of responsibility as long as auditors:

- consent to the inclusion of the audit report only;
- clarity when consenting the specific purpose for which the consent is given; and
- consider and follow SIR 1000 in connection with the form and context in which the audit report appears in the investment circular.

There is no need to insert additional clarification over and above that in the section 235 audit report itself, and auditors should not consent to the inclusion of anything other than their original section 235 report. An example consent letter is given in **Table 1** above.

In some situations, for example where an audit report has previously been issued) auditors are not required to given consent for the republication of their report. In such a situation, auditors should not send a consent letter where it is not needed, as this may be construed as providing additional assurance about their audit report.

50.9.3   *Special purpose reports*

Even when reports are prepared specifically for inclusion in a investment circular, the entity responsible for the circular must obtain the reporting accountant's consent for the inclusion of their report. Their report should include a Bannerman type statement, see **Table 9**. Care should be taken that the wording of their consent letter does is consistent with this statement and does not undermine its meaning.

TABLE 9:   Example wording for inclusion in a reporting accountant's special purpose report

This report is required by [applicable rule or regulation] and is given for the purpose of complying with that regulation and for no other purpose.

Save for any responsibility arising under [applicable rule or regulation] to any person as and to the extent there provided [, and save for any responsibility we have expressly agreed in writing to assume], to the fullest extent permitted by law we do not assume any responsibility and will not accept any liability to any other person for any loss suffered by any such other person as a result of, arising out of, or in connection with this report [or our statements, required by and given solely for the purposes of complying with [applicable rule or regulation], consenting to its inclusion in [document].

50.9.4   *Other financial information*

In some situations there may be a requirement for certain historical financial information other than audited financial statements to be included in an investment circular. In such situations, the acceptance of responsibility or the granting of consent by the auditor is not an issue as it not permissible for the audit report which relates to any statutory accounts from which the non-statutory financial information was extracted to accompany the non-statutory information.

50.9.5   *Addressing the report*

Any person who is to be an addressee of the reporting accountant's report should be party to the engagement letter. Where a reporting accountant is asked to include a party as an addressee to their report, they should consider:

- why the person has asked to be included as an addressee;
- the role the person will undertake in relation to the transaction or investment circular; and
- whether, how and to what extent the person has assumed responsibility in relation to the transaction or investment circular.

APPENDIX

EXISTING GUIDANCE AT 30 APRIL 2007

Table A sets out the Ethical Standards. Table B lists the ISAs (UK and Ireland) and Statements of Auditing Standards (SASs) international ISAs issued for comment by the APB and documents issued by the APB as part of the IAASB's clarity project. Table C sets out Standards for Investment Reporting (SIRS), Practice Notes and Bulletins. These are all issued by the APB and are extant as at 30 April 2007.

Table D lists the ICAEW Statements extant on 30 April 2007.

TABLE A	
APB Guidance	*Status*
The scope and authority of APB pronouncements (revised)	ISSUED
ES1 Integrity, objectivity and independence	ISSUED
ES2 Financial, business, employment and personal relationships	ISSUED
ES3 Long association with the audit engagement	ISSUED
ES4 Fees, remuneration and evaluation policies, litigation, gifts and hospitality	ISSUED
ES5 Non-audit services provided to audit clients	ISSUED
ES Provisions available for smaller entities	ISSUED
Ethical Standard for Reporting Accountants	ISSUED

TABLE B		
ISA (UK and Ireland)	*Status*	*SAS*
200 Objective and General Principles Governing an Audit of Financial Statements	ISSUED	100 Objective and general principles governing an audit of financial statements
210 Terms of Audit Engagements	ISSUED	140 Engagement letters
220 Quality Control for Audits of Historical Financial Information	ISSUED	240 Quality control for audit work (Revised)
230 (revised) Audit Documentation	ISSUED	230 Working papers

TABLE B (continued)		
ISA (UK and Ireland)	*Status*	*SAS*
240 The Auditor's Responsibility to Consider Fraud in an Audit of Financial Statements	ISSUED	110 Fraud and error
250 Part A Consideration of Laws and Regulations in an Audit of Financial Statements	ISSUED	120 Consideration of law and regulations (revised)
250 Part B The Auditor's Right and Duty to Report to Regulators in the Financial Sector	ISSUED	620 The auditors' right and duty to report to regulators in the financial sector (revised)
260 Communication of Audit Matters with those Charged with Governance 260 (revised) The Auditor's Communication with those Charged with Governance	ISSUED DRAFT	610 Communication of audit matters to those charged with governance (Revised)
300 Planning an Audit of Financial Statements	ISSUED	200 Planning
315 Understanding the Entity and its Environment and Assessing the Risks of Material Misstatement	ISSUED	210 Knowledge of the business
320 Audit Materiality 320 (revised) Materiality in the identification and evaluation of misstatements	ISSUED DRAFT	220 Materiality and the audit
330 The Auditor's Procedures in Response to Assessed Risks	ISSUED	300 Accounting and internal control systems and audit risk assessment
402 Audit Considerations Relating to Entities Using Service Organisations	ISSUED	480 Service organisations
500 Audit Evidence	ISSUED	400 Audit evidence
501 Audit Evidence – Additional Considerations for Specific Items	ISSUED	
505 External Confirmations	ISSUED	

TABLE B (continued)		
ISA (UK and Ireland)	*Status*	*SAS*
510 Initial Engagements – Opening Balances and Continuing Engagements – Opening Balances	ISSUED	450 Opening balances and comparatives
520 Analytical Procedures	ISSUED	410 Analytical procedures
530 Audit Sampling and other Means of Testing	ISSUED	430 Audit sampling
540 Audit of Accounting Estimates 540 (revised) Auditing accounting estimates and related disclosures (other than those involving fair value measurements and disclosures)	ISSUED DRAFT	420 Audit of accounting estimates
545 Auditing Fair Value Measurements and Disclosures	ISSUED	
550 Related Parties	ISSUED	460 Related parties
560 Subsequent Events	ISSUED	150 Subsequent events
570 Going Concern	ISSUED	130 Going concern
580 Management Representations	ISSUED	440 Management representations
	ISSUED	470 Overall review of financial statements
600 Using the Work of Another Auditor 600 (revised) The Audit of Group Financial Statements	ISSUED DRAFT	510 The relationship between principal auditors and other auditors
610 Considering the Work of Internal Audit	ISSUED	500 Considering the work of internal audit
620 Using the Work of an Expert	ISSUED	520 Using the work of an expert
700 The Auditor's Report on Financial Statements 700 (revised) The Independent Auditor's Report on a Complete Set of General Purpose Financial Statements	ISSUED DRAFT	600 Auditor's reports on financial statements 601 Imposed limitation audit scope
701 The Independent Auditor's Report on other Historical Financial Information	DRAFT	

TABLE B (continued)		
ISA (UK and Ireland)	*Status*	*SAS*
705 Modifications to the Opinion in the Independent Auditor's Report	DRAFT	
706 Emphasis of Matter Paragraphs and Other Matters Paragraphs in the Independent Auditor's Report	DRAFT	
710 Comparatives	ISSUED	
720 Other Information in Documents Containing Audited Financial Statements (Revised)	ISSUED	160 Other information in documents containing audited financial statements (Revised)
ISQC 1 Quality Control for Firms that Perform Audits and Reviews of Historical Financial Information, and Other Assurance and Related Service Engagements	ISSUED	
ISA 800 The Independent Auditor's Report on Summary Financial Statements	DRAFT	
Statement of Standards for Reporting Accountants ISRE (UK and Ireland) 2410 Review of Interim Financial Information Performed by the Independent Auditor of the Entity	DRAFT	
IAASB Clarity Document: Background and current status		
IAASB Clarity Document: The APB's Approach to IAASB 'clarified' EDs		
IAASB Clarity Document: The APB's Response to the October 2005 ED		
IAASB Clarity Document: ISA 230 Audit documentation		

TABLE B (continued)		
ISA (UK and Ireland)	*Status*	*SAS*
IAASB Clarity Document: ISA 240 The auditor's responsibility to consider fraud in an audit of financial instruments		
IAASB Clarity Document: ISA 260 Communication with those charged with governance		
IAASB Clarity Document: ISA 300 Planning an audit of financial statements		
IAASB Clarity Document: ISA 315 Obtaining an understanding of the entity and its environment and assessing the risks of material misstatement		
IAASB Clarity Document: ISA 320 and ISA 450 Materiality and Evaluation of Misstatements		
IAASB Clarity Document: ISA 330 The auditor's procedures in response to assessed risks		
IAASB Clarity Document: Auditing accounting estimates, including fair value accounting estimates and related disclosures		
IAASB Clarity Document: ISA 550 Related parties		
IAASB Clarity Document: ISA 560 Subsequent events		
IAASB Clarity Document: ISA 570 Going concern		
IAASB Clarity Document: ISA 580 Written representations		
IAASB Clarity Document: ISA 600 The audit of group financial statements		

Appendix

TABLE B (continued)		
ISA (UK and Ireland)	*Status*	*SAS*
IAASB Clarity Document: ISA 610 The auditor's consideration of the internal audit function		
IAASB Clarity Document: ISA 720 The auditor's responsibility in relation to other information in documents containing financial statements		

TABLE C	
	Status
SIR 1000 Investment reporting standards applicable to all engagements involving an investment circular	ISSUED
SIR 2000 Investment reporting standards applicable to public reporting engagements on historical financial information	ISSUED
SIR 3000 Investment reporting standards applicable to public reporting engagements on profit forecasts	ISSUED
SIR 4000 Investment reporting standards applicable to public reporting engagements on pro forma financial information	ISSUED
PN9 Reports by auditors under company legislation in the Republic of Ireland	ISSUED
PN10 Audit of financial statements of public sector entities in the United Kingdom (Revised)	ISSUED
PN10(I) (Revised) Audit of central government financial statements in the Republic of Ireland	ISSUED
PN11 The audit of charities in the United Kingdom (Revised)	ISSUED
PN12 (Revised) Money laundering – Interim guidance for auditors in the United Kingdom	ISSUED
PN13 The audit of small businesses	ISSUED
Consultation Papers: Guidance for Smaller Entity Auditors	DRAFT
PN14 The audit of registered social landlords in the United Kingdom (revised)	ISSUED

TABLE C (continued)	
	Status
PN15 The audit of occupational pension schemes in the United Kingdom (revised)	ISSUED
PN15(I) Interim guidance for the auditors of occupational pension schemes in the Republic of Ireland	ISSUED
PN16 Bank reports for audit purposes	ISSUED
PN 16 Bank reports for audit purposes (Revised): Interim Guidance	ISSUED
PN16 Bank reports for audit purposes (Revised)	DRAFT
PN18 The audit of building societies in the United Kingdom	ISSUED
PN19 The Audit of Banks and Building Societies in the United Kingdom	ISSUED
PN19(I) Banks in the Republic of Ireland	ISSUED
PN20 The audits of insurers in the United Kingdom (Revised)	ISSUED
PN20(I) The audits of insurers in the Republic of Ireland	ISSUED
PN21 The audit of investment business in the United Kingdom	ISSUED
PN21 The audit of investment business in the United Kingdom (Revised)	DRAFT
PN22 The auditors' consideration of FRS17 "Retirement Benefits" – defined benefit schemes	ISSUED
PN23 Auditing derivative financial instruments	ISSUED
PN24 The audit of friendly societies in the United Kingdom (Revised)	ISSUED
PN25 Attendance at stocktaking	ISSUED
Bulletin 1997/3 The FRSSE: Guidance for auditors	ISSUED
Bulletin 1999/4 Review of interim financial information	ISSUED
Bulletin 1999/6 The auditors' statement on the summary financial statement	ISSUED
Bulletin 2000/3 Departure from Statements of Recommended Practice for the Preparation of Financial Statements: Guidance for Auditors	ISSUED
Bulletin 2001/1 The Electronic Publication of Auditors' Reports	ISSUED

TABLE C (continued)	
	Status
Bulletin 2001/2 Revisions to the Wording of Auditors' Reports on Financial Statements and the Interim Review Report	ISSUED
Bulletin 2001/3 E-Business: identifying financial statement risks	ISSUED
Bulletin 2001/7 Supplementary guidance for auditors of investment businesses in the United Kingdom following 'N2'	ISSUED
Bulletin 2002/2 The United Kingdom Directors' Remuneration Report Regulations 2002	ISSUED
Bulletin 2002/3 Guidance for reporting accountants of stakeholder pension schemes in the United Kingdom	ISSUED
Bulletin 2003/1 Corporate Governance: Requirements of public sector auditors (central government)	ISSUED
Bulletin 2003/2 Corporate Governance: Requirements of public sector auditors (NHS bodies)	ISSUED
Bulletin 2004/1 The auditors' association with preliminary announcements	ISSUED
Bulletin 2004/2 Corporate Governance: Requirements of public sector auditors (local government bodies)	ISSUED
Bulletin 2005/1 Audit risk and fraud – Supplementary guidance for auditors of charities	ISSUED
Bulletin 2005/2 Audit Risk and Fraud – Supplementary guidance for auditors of investment businesses	ISSUED
Bulletin 2005/3 Guidance for auditors on first time application of IFRSs in the United Kingdom and the Republic of Ireland	ISSUED
Bulletin 2006/1 Auditor's reports on financial statements in the Republic of Ireland	ISSUED
Bulletin 2006/2 Illustrative auditors' reports on public sector financial statements in the United Kingdom	ISSUED
Bulletin 2006/3 The special auditor's report on abbreviated accounts in the United Kingdom	ISSUED
Bulletin 2006/4 Regulatory and legislative background to the application of Standards for Investment Reporting in the Republic of Ireland	ISSUED
Bulletin 2006/5 The Combined Code on Corporate Governance: Requirements of auditors under the Listing Rules of the Financial Services Authority and the Irish Stock Exchange	ISSUED

TABLE C (continued)	
	Status
Bulletin 2006/6 Auditor's reports on financial statements in the United Kingdom	ISSUED
Bulletin 2007/1 Example reports by auditors under company legislation in Great Britain	ISSUED
Bulletin 2007/2 The duty of auditors in the Republic of Ireland to report to the Director of Corporate Enforcement	ISSUED
Directors' compliance statements: Reports by auditors under company law in the Republic of Ireland	DRAFT
Guidance for auditors on first-time application of IFRSs in the United Kingdom	DRAFT
Effective communication between audit committees and external auditors	
Briefing Paper: Providing assurance on internal control	
Consultation Paper: Aggressive earnings management	
Communication between auditors and audit committees	
Improving the auditing of entities subject to common control	
Fraud and audit: Choices for society	

TABLE D
ICAEW Statements on Auditing
FRAG 27/93: Paid cheques
FRAG 1/94: Reading of auditors' reports at annual general meetings
AUDIT 1/97 Derivatives in a corporate environment: a guide for auditors
AUDIT 2/99: The receipt of information in confidence by auditors
AUDIT 1/00: Guidance for reporting in accordance with Global Investment Performance Standards
AUDIT 4/00: Firm's reports and duties to lenders in connection with loans and other facilities to clients and related covenants
AUDIT 1/01: Reporting to third parties
AUDIT 2/01: Requests for references on clients' financial status and their ability to service loans

TABLE D (continued)
AUDIT 1/02: Practical points for auditors in connection with the implementation of FRS 17 'Retirement Benefits' – defined benefit schemes
AUDIT 2/02: New arrangements for reporting to the ABTA
AUDIT 3/02: Bank reports for audit purposes – explanatory note
AUDIT 4/02: Management representation letters
AUDIT 1/03: The audit report and auditors' duty of care to third parties
AUDIT 2/03: New arrangements for reporting to the Civil Aviation Authority (CAA) in connection with the Civil Aviation (Air Travel Organisers' Licensing) Regulations 1995
AUDIT 3/03: Public sector special reporting engagements – grant claims
AUDIT 4/03: Access to working papers by investigating accountants
AUDIT 5/03: Reporting to regulators of regulated entities
AUDIT 1/04: Reporting to the Audit Bureau of Circulations Limited (ABC)
AUDIT 2/04: Chartered accountants' reports on the compilation of financial statements of incorporated entities
AUDIT 3/04: Audit implications of IFRS transition
AUDIT 1/05: Chartered accountants' reports on the compilation of historical financial information of unincorporated entities
AUDIT 2/05: Guidance on the implications of the Freedom of Information Act 2000
AAF 1/06 Assurance Reports on internal controls of service organisations made available to third parties
AAF 2/06 Identifying and managing certain risks arising from the inclusion of reports from auditors and accountants in prospectuses (and certain other investment circulars)
AAF 3/06 The ICAEW Assurance Service on Unaudited financial statements
AAF 4/06 Assurance engagements: management of risk and liability
AAF 1/07 Independent accountants report on packaging waste

INDEX

All indexing is to section number

audit clients *see* clients
audit committees
discussions with, and interim reports 16.13
external auditors, communication with
audit findings 15.9.5
Communication between external auditors and audit committees (APB Briefing Paper) 15.11.1
expectation of both parties, establishing 15.11.2
guidance booklets, ICAEW *see* **ICAEW (Institute of Chartered Accountants for England and Wales)**: guidance booklets
independence of auditors 15.11.5
plans for conducting audit 15.9.3
Power of Three (ICAEW Audit and Assurance Faculty) 15.12
private 15.9.4
role of audit committee 15.9.1, 15.9.2
SAS 610 (*Communication of audit matters to those charged with governance*) 15.11.1
scope of audit 15.11.3
Hempel Code, changes from 15.6.3
International Financial Reporting Standards 39.5
Registered Social Landlords, responsibilities relating to 47.2.3
role
designing communication to complement 15.9.2
understanding 15.9.1
Terms of Reference 15.6.3
audit engagement, long association with
Ethical Standard 3 2.5.3
audit evidence *see* **evidence**
audit exemption limit, increase in
requirements 7.5
audit findings
accounting and internal control system, material weaknesses 15.11.4
audit committees, communication with external auditors 15.9.5, 15.11.4

audit report, expected modifications to 15.11.4
external auditors, audit committees, communication with 15.9.5, 15.11.4
going concern
entity not considered to be 13.6.1
inadequate disclosures 13.6.2
inadequate steps, taking 13.6.3
material uncertainty 13.6.4
report extracts, example 13.6.5
management, reports to 9.8.5
misstatements, unadjusted 15.11.4
quality of accounting practices/ financial reporting 15.1
audit firms
control of 2.3
Audit Inspection Unit *see* **AIU (Audit Inspection Unit)**
Audit News (ICAEW) 2.15.1
Audit of Central Government Financial Statements in the Republic of Ireland (Practice Note 10(1)) 48.1
Audit of Charities (Practice Note 11) 43.2
Audit of Financial Statements of Public Sector Entities in the United Kingdom (Practice Note 10) 48.1
Audit of Investment Businesses in the United Kingdom (Practice Note 21)
accounting records 8.11.7
annual reports to FSA, general principles 8.11.4
auditing standards 8.7.3
auditor's report 8.11.6
client assets 8.11.8
closely linked entities 8.11.1
consultation draft 8.2
international standards
ISA 210 46.5.1
ISA 250, Section A 46.5.2
ISA 250, Section B 46.5.3
ISA 260 46.5.4
ISA 315 46.5.5
ISA 402 46.5.6
ISA 540 46.5.7
items reportable on ad hoc basis 8.11.2
minor breaches, cumulative 8.11.3
periodic financial statements, reconciliation with annual 8.11.5

external auditors—*cont.*
audit committees, communication
with—*cont.*
audit findings 15.11.4
*Communication between external
auditors and audit committees*
(APB Briefing Paper) 15.11.1
expectations of both parties,
establishing 15.11.2
ICAEW guidance booklets *see*
**ICAEW (Institute of Chartered
Accountants for England and
Wales)**: guidance booklets
independence of auditors 15.11.5
plans for conducting audit 15.9.3
Power of Three (ICAEW Audit and
Assurance Faculty) 15.12
private 15.9.4
SAS 610 (*Communication of audit
matters to those charged with
governance*) 15.11.1 scope of
audit 15.11.3
and grant claims, public sector audits
48.2.4

fair presentation
and role of accounting standards
3.12.1
fair value
auditing standards *see* **ISA (UK and
Ireland) 545** (*Auditing fair value
measurements and disclosures*)
disclosures 28.7
entity's approach, evaluating 28.4
entity's process, understanding 28.3
expert, using work of 28.5
governance, communication with
those charged with 28.8
guidance 28.2
IFRS 39.6.11
independent estimates 28.6.2
measurement 28.1
procedures
assumptions, testing 28.6.1
data 28.6.1
independent estimates 28.6.2
model 28.6.1
subsequent events 28.6.3
family/personal relationships
Ethical Standard 2 (APB) 2.5.2

fees
Ethical Standard 4 (APB) 2.5.4
financial assistance
guidance 6.4.2
legal background 6.4.1
*Financial Assistance for Acquisition of a
Company's Own Shares* (No 26/94)
6.4.2
financial conduct
public sector audits 48.2.4
financial relationships
Ethical Standard 2 (APB) 2.5.2
**Financial Reporting and Auditing Group
statements** *see* **FRAGs (Financial
Reporting and Auditing Group
statements)**
Financial Reporting Council *see* **FRC
(Financial Reporting Council)**
**Financial Reporting Review Panel
(FRRP)** 2.12
**Financial Reporting Standard for Smaller
Entities** *see* **FRSSE (Financial
Reporting Standard for Smaller
Entities)**
Financial Reporting Standards (FRSs)
and primary statements 3.12.2
see also particular FRSs, e.g. **FRS
18 (Accounting Policies)**
Financial Services and Markets Act *see*
**FSMA (Financial Services and
Markets Act) 2000**
Financial Services Authority *see* **FSA
(Financial Services Authority)**
financial statements
abbreviated accounts
audit procedures 5.4.3
guidance 5.4.2
legal background 5.4.1
annual, reconciliation with periodic
investment businesses 8.11.5
approval of
accountants' reports 7.3.5
auditing standards *see* **ISA (UK and
Ireland) 700** (*Auditor's report on
financial statements*); **SAS 600**
(*Auditor's reports on financial
statements*)
investment businesses, reporting on
8.7.2
laws with direct effect on 11.6.1
misleading, incorporated entities 7.3.4